ILLINOIS JURISPRUDENCE

4

CRIMINAL LAW AND PROCEDURE

§§ 30:01 — 54:05

By the Editorial Staff of the Publisher

LEXIS
LAW PUBLISHING

CHARLOTTESVILLE, VA

Cite by title and section, e.g.
Illinois Jur, Criminal Law and Procedure § 30:01

This replacement volume includes material derived from the following sources:
Illinois Reporter, through 2nd Series, Volume 177, p. 1.
Illinois Appellate Reporter, through 3rd Series, Volume 291, p. 512.
Northeastern Reporter, through 2nd Series, Volume 702, p. 524.
Illinois Decisions, through Volume 226, p. 591.
Supreme Court Reporter, through Volume 118, p. 1351.
Federal Reporter, through 3rd Series, Volume 136, p. 1333.
Federal Supplement, through Volume 989, p. 264.
Federal Rules Decisions, through Volume 176, p. 589.
Bankruptcy Reports, through Volume 217, p. 357.
Opinions of the Attorney General.
Chicago Kent Law Review, through Volume 72, p. 947.
Depaul Business Law Journal, through Volume 10, p. 168.
Depaul Law Review, through Volume 46, p. 1057.
Illinois Bar Journal, through Volume 86, p. 232.
John Marshall Law Review, through Volume 31, p. 298.
Loyola University of Chicago Law Journal, through Volume 29, p. 271.
Northern Illinois University Law Review, through Volume 17, p. 376.
Northwestern University Law Review, through Volume 92, p. 139.
Southern Illinois University Law Journal, through Volume 21, Summer, p. 960.
University Chicago Law Review, through Volume 65, p. 385.
University Illinois Law Review, through Volume 1997, p. 957.
American Law Reports, 4th and 5th Series.

COPYRIGHT© 1999
By
Matthew Bender & Company, Inc.
All Rights Reserved.

COPYRIGHT© 1998
By
LEXIS® Law Publishing,
A Division of Reed Elsevier Inc.
All Rights Reserved.

COPYRIGHT© 1997
By
LEXIS®-NEXIS®,
a division of Reed Elsevier Inc.

COPYRIGHT© 1992-1997
by LAWYERS COOPERATIVE PUBLISHING,
A DIVISION OF THOMSON INFORMATION SERVICES INC.

ISBN 0-327-01768-6

6343411

All rights reserved
LEXIS and NEXIS are registered trademarks of Reed Elsevier Properties Inc., used here under license.

Managing Editor
EDWIN J. TISDALE

Editorial Line Manager
MARY JANE DIVINE

Publication Manager
STEVEN M. RIESENMAN

Contributing Writers

MARY R. COLLINA	THOMAS CURRY
DIANE C. BUSCH	LISA K. FOX
EVAN M. BUTTERFIELD	KAREN L. STAFFORD
RUSSELL W. SAVORY	ROBERT L. MARGOLIS

Composition Specialist
LINDA R. CORNICK

ILLINOIS JURISPRUDENCE
PREFACE

Illinois Jurisprudence is a concise textual presentation of Illinois civil and criminal substantive law, based on modern authority. The stress is on emerging concepts and on cases decided within the past 50 years, although earlier cases may be cited for fundamental points. Federal cases applying Illinois law are covered, as well as United States Supreme Court cases that affect the validity of Illinois statutes or doctrines.

All relevant statutes and rules are discussed, and administrative regulations are cited. Special effort has been made to treat statutes of current interest in depth. Illinois Jurisprudence consists only of the "bread and butter" areas of the law. Topical areas covered are:

Criminal Law and Procedure
Probate, Estates and Trusts
Family Law
Business Relationships
Property

Personal Injury and Torts
Labor and Employment
Municipal Law
Commercial Law
Insurance Law

Special features of Illinois Jurisprudence include:

Scope statements at the beginning of each chapter within a topic to describe its coverage

Federal Aspects statements showing the application of federal law.

Treated Elsewhere statements indicating what is covered in other chapters or topics

Research References at the beginning of each chapter within a topic and in each major subdivision of a chapters including citations to standard reference works.

National Background statements comparing Illinois law to the law of other jurisdictions, or showing the law's development

Comments, Cautions, Illustrations, Practice Guides, Recommendations, and Reminders, which point out strategies to follow and pitfalls to avoid, show the application of the law to factual situations arising in Illinois, and otherwise call attention to matters of practical significance to the Illinois lawyer.

PREFACE

The basic upkeep will consist of pocket supplements and an interim supplement, published annually.

This fourth volume of the **Criminal Law and Procedure** topic begins with a continuation of the discussion begun in volume three regarding posttrial matters and appeals. Appellate review is first covered at length, followed by discussions of original actions in the Supreme Court, pardon and parole, expungement, and costs and fees. Next begins a lengthy discussion on juvenile offenders. The volume then focuses on particular crimes and offenses, with chapters covering abandonment, abduction and kidnapping, abortion, abuse of process, animals, arson, assault and battery, automobiles and other vehicles, blackmail, breach of peace, bribery, burglary, civil rights, computer crimes, conspiracy, contributing to the criminal delinquency of a juvenile, deceptive practices and false personation, disorderly conduct and disseminating conviction information. Other subjects related to **Criminal Law and Procedure** can be found in subsequent volumes of the **Illinois Jurisprudence**.

THE PUBLISHERS

ILLINOIS JURISPRUDENCE
CRIMINAL LAW AND PROCEDURE

TABLE OF CONTENTS

Page

Table of Abbreviations ix
Outline of Chapters xi

CHAPTERS IN THIS VOLUME

PART FOUR
CRIMINAL PROSECUTION (Continued)

D. POSTTRIAL MATTERS; APPEALS (Continued)

Chapter	*Page*
30. APPELLATE REVIEW	1
31. ORIGINAL ACTIONS IN THE SUPREME COURT	149
32. PARDON AND PAROLE	175
33. EXPUNGEMENT	209
34. COSTS AND FEES	217

PART FIVE
JUVENILE OFFENDERS

Chapter	*Page*
35. DELINQUENT MINORS	229

PART SIX
PARTICULAR CRIMES AND OFFENSES

Chapter	*Page*
36. ABANDONMENT.	323
37. ABDUCTION, KIDNAPING AND RELATED OFFENSES	327
38. ABORTION.	347

39. ABUSE OF PROCESS	363
40. ANIMALS	365
41. ARSON	373
42. ASSAULT AND BATTERY	383
43. AUTOMOBILES AND OTHER VEHICLES	407
44. BLACKMAIL	445
45. BREACH OF PEACE	447
46. BRIBERY	455
47. BURGLARY	463
48. CIVIL RIGHTS	479
49. COMPUTER CRIMES	489
50. CONSPIRACY	499
51. CONTRIBUTING TO THE CRIMINAL DELINQUENCY OF A JUVENILE	507
52. DECEPTIVE PRACTICES AND FALSE PERSONATION	511
53. DISORDERLY CONDUCT	533
54. DISSEMINATING CONVICTION INFORMATION	541

Table Of Abbreviations

Abbreviation	Report, Periodical, Etc.
ABA J	American Bar Association Journal
ALR	American Law Reports
ALR Fed	American Law Reports, Federal
ALR2d	American Law Reports, Second Series
ALR3d	American Law Reports, Third Series
ALR4th	American Law Reports, Fourth Series
ALR5th	American Law Reports, Fifth Series
Am J Fam L	American Journal of Family Law
Am Jur 2d	American Jurisprudence, Second Edition
Am Jur Legal Forms 2d	American Jurisprudence Legal Forms, Second Edition
Am Jur Pl & Pr Forms (Rev)	American Jurisprudence Pleading and Practice Forms, Revised Edition
Am Jur POF	American Jurisprudence Proof of Facts
Am Jur POF2d	American Jurisprudence Proof of Facts, Second Series
Am Jur POF3d	American Jurisprudence Proof of Facts, Third Series
Am Jur Trials	American Jurisprudence Trials
Am Law Prod Liab 3d	American Law of Products Liability 3d
Bus Rel	Business Relationships
Chicago B Rec	Chicago Bar Record
Chicago-Kent L Rev	Chicago Kent Law Review
Com Law	Commercial Law
Crim L	Criminal Law and Procedure
De Paul L Rev	De Paul Law Review
Fam L	Family Law
Fam L Q	Family Law Quarterly
F	Federal Reporter
F2d	Federal Reporter, Second Series
F3d	Federal Reporter, Third Series
FR Serv 2d	Federal Rules Service, Second Series
F Supp	Federal Supplement
Fed Proc	Federal Procedure, Lawyer's Edition
Fed Proc Forms	Federal Procedural Forms, Lawyer's Edition
FRCP	Federal Rule of Civil Procedure
FRCrP	Federal Rules of Criminal Procedure
FRD	Federal Rules Decisions
Ill B J	Illinois Bar Journal
ILCS	Illinois Compiled Statutes
Ill Const	Illinois Constitution

Table of Abbreviations (Continued)

Illinois Digest 2d	Illinois Digest, Second Series (West Publishing Co.)
Illinois Jur	Illinois Jurisprudence
Ins.	Insurance
J Mar L Rev	John Marshall Law Review
J Fam L	Journal of Family Law
Labor	Labor and Employment
L Ed	Lawyers' Edition, United States Supreme Court Reports
L Ed 2d	Lawyers' Edition, United States Supreme Court Reports, Second Series
Loy U Chi L J	Loyola University of Chicago Law Journal
Municip L	Municipal Law
NE	North Eastern Reporter
NE2d	North Eastern Reporter, Second Series
N Ill U L Rev	Northern Illinois University Law Review
NW U L Rev	Northwestern University Law Review
Pers Inj & Torts	Personal Injury and Torts
Prac Law	Practical Lawyer
Prob Est & Trusts	Probate, Estates and Trusts
Prop	Property
Restatement	Restatement of the Law (American Law Institute)
S Ill U L J	Southern Illinois University Law Journal
S Ct	Supreme Court Reporter
UCC	Uniform Commercial Code
UCCRS	Uniform Commercial Code Reporting Service
U Chi L Rev	University of Chicago Law Review
USCS	United States Code Service
US Const	United States Constitution
US	United States Supreme Court Reports
U Ill L Rev	University of Illinois Law Review.

CRIMINAL LAW AND PROCEDURE

Outline of Chapters

PART FOUR
CRIMINAL PROSECUTION (Continued)

D. POSTTRIAL MATTERS; APPEALS (Continued)

CHAPTER
- 30. APPELLATE REVIEW
- 31. ORIGINAL ACTIONS IN THE SUPREME COURT
- 32. PARDON AND PAROLE
- 33. EXPUNGEMENT
- 34. COSTS AND FEES

PART FIVE
JUVENILE OFFENDERS

CHAPTER
- 35. DELINQUENT MINORS

PART SIX
PARTICULAR CRIMES AND OFFENSES

CHAPTER
- 36. ABANDONMENT
- 37. ABDUCTION, KIDNAPING AND RELATED OFFENSES
- 38. ABORTION
- 39. ABUSE OF PROCESS
- 40. ANIMALS
- 41. ARSON
- 42. ASSAULT AND BATTERY
- 43. AUTOMOBILES AND OTHER VEHICLES
- 44. BLACKMAIL

Outline of Chapters (Continued)

45. BREACH OF PEACE
46. BRIBERY
47. BURGLARY
48. CIVIL RIGHTS
49. COMPUTER CRIMES
50. CONSPIRACY
51. CONTRIBUTING TO THE CRIMINAL DELINQUENCY OF A JUVENILE
52. DECEPTIVE PRACTICES AND FALSE PERSONATION
53. DISORDERLY CONDUCT
54. DISSEMINATING CONVICTION INFORMATION

For detailed outlines, see each chapter

PART FOUR

CRIMINAL PROSECUTION (Continued)

SUBPART D

Posttrial Matters; Appeals (Continued)

CHAPTER 30

APPELLATE REVIEW

by

Evan M. Butterfield, J.D.

Mary R. Collina, J.D.

Thomas Curry, J.D.

Lisa K. Fox, J.D.

and

Karen L. Stafford, J.D.

Scope of Chapter:
This chapter covers the general principles and procedures applicable to appellate review in criminal prosecutions. It includes discussions of the nature and scope of appellate review and appellate jurisdiction, taking and perfecting the appeal, preparing the record and briefs, presumptions on review, questions of fact, the weight and sufficiency of the evidence, the distinction between harmless and prejudicial error and appeals in postconviction proceedings.

Federal Aspects:
> To the extent that various provisions of the federal Constitution and statutes apply to appeals in criminal prosecutions, those provisions and the United States Supreme Court decisions construing them are included in the discussion.

Treated Elsewhere:
> Appeal and trial court jurisdiction, see Chapter 12.
>
> Arraignment and pleas, see Chapter 14.
>
> Bail pending appeal, see Chapter 6.
>
> Delinquent minors, see Chapter 35.
>
> Saving questions for review, see Chapter 29.

Research References:
> **Text References:**
>> Ruebner, Illinois Criminal Procedure 2d ed
>>
>> Illinois Lawyers Manual
>
> **Annotation References:**
>> Index and Annotations: Appeal and Error; Appeal and Supersedeas Bond; Habeas Corpus; Harmless and Prejudicial Error
>>
>> ALR Digest to 3d, 4th, 5th, and Federal: Appeal and Error
>
> **Practice References:**
>> Lane's Goldstein Tr Tech (3d ed)
>>
>> Nichols Drinking/Driving Lit
>>
>> 7 POF2d 477, Prejudice Resulting From Unreasonable Delay in Trial
>>
>> 6 Am Jur Trials 605, Making and Preserving the Record—Objections; 20 Am Jur Trials 441, Motion in Limine Practice
>>
>> Am Jur 2d, Appeal and Error; Habeas Corpus
>
> **Forms:**
>> Lane's Goldstein Lit Forms
>>
>> 2 Am Jur Pl & Pr Forms (Rev), Appeal and Error; 8 Am Jur Pl & Pr Forms (Rev), Criminal Procedure

Auto-Cite®: Cases and annotations referred to in this chapter can be further researched through the Auto-Cite® computer-assisted research service. Use Auto-Cite® to check citations for form, parallel references,

APPELLATE REVIEW

prior and later history, and annotation references.

I. GENERALLY

§ 30:01. Nature and scope of remedy
§ 30:02. Constitutional and statutory provisions
§ 30:03. Proper mode of review
§ 30:04. Joinder of proceedings
§ 30:05. Appellate jurisdiction

II. DECISIONS REVIEWABLE

§ 30:06. Final judgments
§ 30:07. Interlocutory appeals

III. RIGHT TO REVIEW

§ 30:08. Generally
§ 30:09. Right of state
§ 30:10. Right of defendant

IV. TAKING AND PERFECTING

§ 30:11. Generally
§ 30:12. Notice of appeal
§ 30:13. Docketing
§ 30:14. Bonds and stays
§ 30:15. Appeal by defendant from judgment entered on guilty plea
§ 30:16. Appeals by poor persons
§ 30:17. Direct appeals to supreme court
§ 30:18. Appeal from appellate court to supreme court
§ 30:19. —Time, contents and service of petition
§ 30:20. —Records and abstracts
§ 30:21. —Answer
§ 30:22. —Transmittal of record
§ 30:23. —Briefs
§ 30:24. Appeals to supreme court on certificate
§ 30:25. Appeal as of right

V. RECORD

§ 30:26. Contents—Generally
§ 30:27. —Preserving errors for review
§ 30:28. Affidavits and motions
§ 30:29. Matters improperly included
§ 30:30. —Plea
§ 30:31. —Jury trial
§ 30:32. —Presence of accused
§ 30:33. —Waiver of counsel
§ 30:34. —Trial proceedings

§ 30:35.	—Sentence
§ 30:36.	—Additional and supplemental material
§ 30:37.	Preparation and certification of record
§ 30:38.	Filing of record
§ 30:39.	—Extensions of time
§ 30:40.	—Notice of filing
§ 30:41.	Abstract of record
§ 30:42.	Procedure if no transcript available
§ 30:43.	Transmission of record or certificate in lieu of record
§ 30:44.	Amendment
§ 30:45.	Return
§ 30:46.	Conclusiveness and effect of record
§ 30:47.	Issues and matters not apparent—Generally
§ 30:48.	—Jury selection
§ 30:49.	—Conduct of counsel
§ 30:50.	—Evidence and evidentiary rulings
§ 30:51.	—Jury instructions
§ 30:52.	—Sentence

VI. MOTIONS, BRIEFS, ARGUMENT AND REHEARING

§ 30:53.	Motions
§ 30:54.	Briefs—Generally
§ 30:55.	—Form and contents
§ 30:56.	—Filing and serving
§ 30:57.	—Amicus curiae
§ 30:58.	Oral argument
§ 30:59.	Rehearings

VII. DISMISSAL AND ABATEMENT

| § 30:60. | Dismissal |
| § 30:61. | Abatement |

VIII. SCOPE AND MODE OF REVIEW

§ 30:62.	Generally
§ 30:63.	Power of reviewing court
§ 30:64.	Rulings by lower court
§ 30:65.	Trial de novo

IX. LOWER COURT DISCRETION AND PRESUMPTIONS ON REVIEW

§ 30:66.	Generally
§ 30:67.	Matters of record
§ 30:68.	Matters not shown by record
§ 30:69.	Pretrial matters
§ 30:70.	Trial and related proceedings
§ 30:71.	—Effective assistance of counsel

§ 30:72. —Evidentiary matters
§ 30:73. ——Witnesses
§ 30:74. —Verdict, judgment, and sentence

X. QUESTIONS OF FACT, WEIGHT AND SUFFICIENCY
§ 30:75. Generally
§ 30:76. —Quantum of evidence
§ 30:77. —Reasonable doubt test
§ 30:78. —Province of jury or trial court

XI. HARMLESS AND REVERSIBLE ERROR
§ 30:79. Types of error generally
§ 30:80. Errors affecting constitutional rights
§ 30:81. Cumulative error
§ 30:82. Establishing prejudice
§ 30:83. Intended and invited errors
§ 30:84. Cured errors
§ 30:85. Plain and waived errors

XII. DETERMINATION AND DISPOSITION OF CAUSE
§ 30:86. Decision and mandates
§ 30:87. Issuance, stay and recall of reviewing court mandates
§ 30:88. Affirmance
§ 30:89. Reduction or mitigation of sentence
§ 30:90. Modification or correction of judgment
§ 30:91. Reversal
§ 30:92. Entry of judgment
§ 30:93. Mandate and proceedings in lower court
§ 30:94. Jurisdiction and proceedings of appellate court after remand

XIII. APPEALS IN POSTCONVICTION PROCEEDINGS
§ 30:95. Right of appeal
§ 30:96. Notice to petitioner of adverse judgment
§ 30:97. Indigents
§ 30:98. Procedure

I. GENERALLY

Research References:
Text References:
Ruebner, Illinois Criminal Procedure 2d ed §§ 7.01, 7.02, 7.06
Annotation References:
Index and Annotations: Appeal and Error
ALR Digest to 3d, 4th, 5th, and Federal: Appeal and Error §§ 1–3, 40–42, 100, 101

Practice References:
4 Am Jur 2d, Appeal and Error § 1 et seq.

State Legislation:
Ill Const Art VI §§ 4, 6
Supreme Court Rule 341, 602, 603, 606

Miscellaneous References:
West's Illinois Digest 2d, Criminal Law §§ 1004–1020½

National Background:
A procedure providing for appellate review of trial court decisions is not a necessary part of a legal system and is not required by due process. The right of appeal is not an inherent or inalienable right. However, some provision for review is traditional in the Anglo-American legal system as well as in the jurisprudence of most nations. The court system of each of the United States, as well as that of the federal government, makes provision, either by statute or by constitution, for some type of review procedure. 4 Am Jur 2d, Appeal and Error § 1.

§ 30:01. Nature and scope of remedy

An appeal is a statutory procedure whereby errors made at the trial level can be corrected.[1] An appeal is a privilege and not an inherent or inalienable right.[2] The right to have any judgment reviewed by appeal did not exist at common law.[3]

Appellate review of a criminal case is not intended to decide whether the record is perfect, but to determine whether the defendant received a fair trial free from substantial and prejudicial errors and whether the conviction is based on evidence establishing the defendant's guilt beyond a reasonable doubt.[4] Appeals are

1. People v Johnston, 96 Ill App 3d 364, 51 Ill Dec 904, 421 NE2d 412 (3d Dist 1981).

2. People v Ross, 344 Ill App 407, 101 NE2d 112 (1951); People v Cornelius, 332 Ill App 271, 74 NE2d 900 (1947).

3. People v Cornelius, 332 Ill App 271, 74 NE2d 900 (1947).

4. People v Yarbrough, 97 Ill App 2d 457, 240 NE2d 200 (1st Dist 1968); People v Conrad, 81 Ill App 2d 34, 225 NE2d 713 (1st Dist 1967), affd 41 Ill 2d 13, 241 NE2d 423.

Annotation References: When criminal case becomes moot so as to

not designed to interpret what a judgment means, as opposed to whether it is erroneous.[5]

Like other constitutional rights, the right to appeal may be waived, whether by neglect or by conscious choice.[6]

The right to appeal does not exist in a vacuum.[7] Because it is statutory, there must be compliance with the conditions prescribed by statute.[8]

§ 30:02. Constitutional and statutory provisions

It is well settled that there is no federal constitutional right to an appeal.[9] Unless granted under a state constitution, the right of appeal, as it is presently known in criminal cases, is purely a creature of statute.[10] In order to exercise the statutory right of appeal, one must come within the terms of the applicable statute.[11]

The Illinois Constitution does contain provisions on the right to appeal a criminal conviction.[12] Under the Illinois Constitution,

---

preclude review of or attack on conviction or sentence, 9 ALR3d 462.

5. People v Hollingsworth, 89 Ill 2d 466, 60 Ill Dec 640, 433 NE2d 682 (1982).

6. People v Fearing, 101 Ill App 3d 643, 442 NE2d 939 (1982).

7. People v Tyler, 49 Ill App 3d 982, 8 Ill Dec 536, 365 NE2d 922 (5th Dist 1977).

8. People v Tyler, 49 Ill App 3d 982, 8 Ill Dec 536, 365 NE2d 922 (5th Dist 1977); People v Anders, 20 Ill App 3d 984, 313 NE2d 520 (2d Dist 1974).

See § 30:02 et seq.

9. People ex rel. Mosley v Carey, 74 Ill 2d 527, 25 Ill Dec 669, 387 NE2d 325 (1979), cert den 444 US 940, 62 L Ed 2d 306, 100 S Ct 292; Abney v United States, 431 US 651, 52 L Ed 2d 651, 97 S Ct 2034 (1977); Estelle v Dorrough, 420 US 534, 43 L Ed 2d 377, 95 S Ct 1173 (1975), on remand 512 F2d 1061 (CA5 Tex).

10. People ex rel. Mosley v Carey, 74 Ill 2d 527, 25 Ill Dec 669, 387 NE2d 325 (1979), cert den 444 US 940, 62 L Ed 2d 306, 100 S Ct 292; Abney v United States, 431 US 651, 52 L Ed 2d 651, 97 S Ct 2034 (1977).

11. Abney v United States, 431 US 651, 52 L Ed 2d 651, 97 S Ct 2034 (1977).

§ 30:02   ILLINOIS JURISPRUDENCE: CRIMINAL LAW

appeals from the appellate court to the supreme court are a matter of right if a question under the United States Constitution or the Illinois Constitution arises for the first time in and as a result of the action of the appellate court, or if a division of the appellate court certifies that a case decided by it involves a question of such importance that the case should be decided by the supreme court.[13] The supreme court also has the authority under the Illinois Constitution to provide by rule for appeals from the appellate court in other cases.[14]

The Illinois Supreme Court Rules provide that appeals in criminal cases in which a statute of the United States or of Illinois has been held invalid and appeals by defendants from judgments of the circuit court imposing the death penalty are to be taken directly to the Illinois Supreme Court as a matter of right.[15] All other appeals in criminal cases are taken to the appellate court.[16]

Illinois Supreme Court Rule 604(a)(1) is the sole source of authority for interlocutory appeals by the state in criminal cases.[17]

12. See Ill Const Art VI, § 6.

13. Ill Const Art VI, § 4(c).

14. Ill Const Art VI, § 4(c).

Text References: Ruebner, Illinois Criminal Procedure 2d ed § 7.01.

15. Supreme Court Rule 603.

16. Supreme Court Rule 603.

17. People v Riley, 209 Ill App 3d 212, 154 Ill Dec 74, 568 NE2d 74 (1st Dist 1991).

Under Illinois Supreme Court Rule 604(d), a motion to withdraw a guilty plea and vacate judgment is not jurisdictional in the same sense as a notice of appeal is essential to vest the appellate court with jurisdiction over a civil appeal; thus, although a defendant generally waives his or her right to appeal by failing to file a motion to withdraw a guilty plea and vacate judgment, an appellate court still has jurisdiction over such a defendant's appeal. People v McKay, 282 Ill App 3d 108, 218 Ill Dec 96, 668 NE2d 580 (2d Dist 1996).

See § 30:07.

Text References: Ruebner, Illinois Criminal Procedure 2d ed § 7.06.

§ 30:03. Proper mode of review

Under prior law, review of criminal convictions could be obtained through a writ of error.[18] The Illinois Supreme Court Rules now provide that the only method of review in criminal cases in which judgment was entered on or after January 1, 1964, is by appeal.[19] The party appealing is known as the appellant and the adverse party is the appellee.[20] The name of the case, however, does not change.[21]

§ 30:04. Joinder of proceedings

A direct appeal and a postconviction appeal may be combined and heard in the same proceedings on review.[22] In a consolidated appeal involving a judgment of conviction and the dismissal of a postconviction petition, trial and postconviction issues cannot be indiscriminately commingled.[23] Issues that were not either preserved at trial or raised in a postconviction petition cannot be intertwined with those that were.[24]

The appellate court will not consolidate or adjust the schedule of cases on appeal when the two appeals arise out of distinct and separate occurrences and present different issues for review.[25]

---

18. See People v Johnson, 15 Ill 2d 244, 154 NE2d 274 (1958), cert den 359 US 930, 3 L Ed 2d 632, 79 S Ct 614.

19. Supreme Court Rule 602.

20. Supreme Court Rule 602.

21. Supreme Court Rule 602.

22. People v Brown, 7 Ill App 3d 748, 289 NE2d 452 (4th Dist 1972).

23. People v McCarroll, 10 Ill App 3d 249, 294 NE2d 52 (1st Dist 1973).

24. People v McCarroll, 10 Ill App 3d 249, 294 NE2d 52 (1st Dist 1973).

25. People v Fenner, 191 Ill App 3d 801, 138 Ill Dec 917, 548 NE2d 147 (2d Dist 1989), later proceeding 193 Ill App 3d 695, 140 Ill Dec 498, 549 NE2d 1370 (2d Dist), app gr 132 Ill 2d 550, 144 Ill Dec 262, 555 NE2d 381 and affd in part and revd in part, cause remanded 143 Ill 2d 11, 155 Ill Dec 807, 570 NE2d 320, appeal after remand 251 Ill App 3d 580, 191 Ill Dec 134, 623 NE2d 379 (2d Dist).

§ 30:05. Appellate jurisdiction

Appellate jurisdiction is the authority of a superior tribunal to review, reverse, correct or affirm the decisions of an inferior court, or of a tribunal having the attributes of a court, in cases where those decisions are brought before the superior tribunal pursuant to law.[26] Appellate jurisdiction is derived from the constitutional or statutory provisions by which it is created and it can be acquired and exercised only in the manner prescribed.[27]

Before the merits of an appeal are addressed, the appellate court first has the duty to determine whether it has jurisdiction.[28] The appellate court must consider the issue of jurisdiction whether or not the issue is raised by the parties.[29]

Under the Illinois Constitution, the supreme court may exercise original jurisdiction in cases relating to revenue, mandamus, prohibition or habeas corpus and as may be necessary to the complete determination of any case on review.[30] Judgments of the circuit court imposing a sentence of death are appealed directly to the supreme court as a matter of right.[31] The supreme court may provide by rule for direct appeal in other cases.[32]

Appeals from the appellate court to the supreme court are a matter of right if a question under the Constitution of the United States or of Illinois arises for the first time in and as a result of the action of the appellate court, or if a division of the appellate court

---

26. 4 Am Jur 2d, Appeal and Error, § 1.

27. 4 Am Jur 2d, Appeal and Error, § 4.

28. People v Biederman, 100 Ill App 3d 558, 55 Ill Dec 851, 426 NE2d 1225 (2d Dist 1981); People v Williams, 53 Ill App 3d 335, 11 Ill Dec 155, 368 NE2d 706 (1st Dist 1977).

29. People v Blanchette, 182 Ill App 3d 396, 131 Ill Dec 49, 538 NE2d 237 (2d Dist 1989); People v Scruggs, 161 Ill App 3d 468, 113 Ill Dec 25, 514 NE2d 807 (2d Dist 1987).

30. Ill Const Art VI, § 4(a).

31. Ill Const Art VI, § 4(b).

32. Ill Const Art VI, § 4(b).

APPELLATE REVIEW § 30:05

certifies that a case decided by it involves a question of such importance that the case should be decided by the supreme court.[33] The supreme court may provide by rule for appeals from the appellate court in other cases.[34]

Appeals from final judgments of a circuit court are a matter of right to the appellate court in the judicial district in which the circuit court is located except in cases appealable directly to the supreme court and except that, after a trial on the merits in a criminal case, there may be no appeal from a judgment of acquittal.[35] The supreme court is authorized to provide by rule for appeals to the appellate court from other than final judgments of the circuit courts.[36] The appellate court may exercise original jurisdiction when necessary to the complete determination of any case on review.[37]

The timely filing of a notice of appeal is necessary to the appellate court's jurisdiction in a criminal case.[38] No step in the perfection of an appeal other than the filing of the notice of appeal is jurisdictional.[39]

A statement of fact unsupported by the record cannot confer jurisdiction on the appellate court.[40] The existence of an actual

---

33. Ill Const Art VI, § 4(c).

34. Ill Const Art VI, § 4(c).

35. Ill Const Art VI, § 6.

36. Ill Const Art VI, § 6.

37. Ill Const Art VI, § 6.

38. People v Blanchette, 182 Ill App 3d 396, 131 Ill Dec 49, 538 NE2d 237 (2d Dist 1989); People v Delgado, 126 Ill App 3d 239, 81 Ill Dec 475, 466 NE2d 1277 (1st Dist 1984).

See § 30:12.

Text References: Ruebner, Illinois Criminal Procedure 2d ed § 7.02.

39. Supreme Court Rule 606(a).

People v Anders, 20 Ill App 3d 984, 313 NE2d 520 (2d Dist 1974).

40. People v Blanchette, 182 Ill App 3d 396, 131 Ill Dec 49, 538 NE2d 237 (2d Dist 1989).

controversy is an essential requisite to appellate jurisdiction.[41] Reviewing courts will decline to consider abstract questions.[42] An appeal must be dismissed if there is no actual controversy.[43]

Appellate courts, subject to statutory exceptions, are without jurisdiction to review judgments, orders or decrees which are not final.[44] In a criminal case, a final judgment is one which terminates the litigation on its merits and usually that consists of a judgment of guilt and the imposition of a sentence.[45]

The rule that points not argued are waived on appeal[46] is only a warning to the parties and is not a limitation upon the jurisdiction of the reviewing court.[47]

II. DECISIONS REVIEWABLE

Research References:
  Text References:
    Ruebner, Illinois Criminal Procedure 2d ed §§ 7.03, 7.06

---

41. People v Turner, 74 Ill App 3d 840, 30 Ill Dec 400, 393 NE2d 55 (1st Dist 1979).

42. People v McCullum, 66 Ill 2d 306, 5 Ill Dec 836, 362 NE2d 307 (1977); People v Turner, 74 Ill App 3d 840, 30 Ill Dec 400, 393 NE2d 55 (1st Dist 1979).

43. People v Turner, 74 Ill App 3d 840, 30 Ill Dec 400, 393 NE2d 55 (1st Dist 1979).

44. People v Biederman, 100 Ill App 3d 558, 55 Ill Dec 851, 426 NE2d 1225 (2d Dist 1981); People v Culhane, 34 Ill App 3d 158, 340 NE2d 63 (1st Dist 1975).

45. People v Biederman, 100 Ill App 3d 558, 55 Ill Dec 851, 426 NE2d 1225 (2d Dist 1981); In Interest of M., 94 Ill App 3d 86, 49 Ill Dec 630, 418 NE2d 484 (2d Dist 1981).

See § 30:06.

46. Supreme Court Rule 341(e)(7).

See § 30:27.

47. People v Torres, 47 Ill App 3d 101, 5 Ill Dec 480, 361 NE2d 803 (1st Dist 1977).

Annotation References:

Index and Annotations: Appeal and Error

ALR Digest to 3d, 4th, 5th, and Federal: Appeal and Error §§ 5–7, 38, 39

Practice References:

4 Am Jur 2d, Appeal and Error §§ 159–161

State Legislation:

725 ILCS 5/103-5; Supreme Court Rule 315, 318, 612

Miscellaneous References:

West's Illinois Digest 2d, Criminal Law §§ 1021–1023

§ 30:06. Final judgments

Absent authorization by statute or court rule, one may not appeal from a nonfinal order in a criminal case because the reviewing court generally has jurisdiction only over final judgments.[48] In Illinois, it is established law that the appealability of an order is to be determined by its substance as opposed to its form.[49]

A judgment of guilty in a criminal case becomes final when sentence is imposed.[50] Until a sentence is imposed, the judgment cannot be appealed.[51] There is, however, an exception to this rule. When a case is properly on appeal from a final judgment on

---

48. People v Whigam, 202 Ill App 3d 252, 147 Ill Dec 556, 559 NE2d 896 (1st Dist 1990); People v Biederman, 100 Ill App 3d 558, 55 Ill Dec 851, 426 NE2d 1225 (2d Dist 1981).

Text References: Ruebner, Illinois Criminal Procedure 2d ed § 7.03.

Annotation References: Appealability of order suspending imposition or execution of sentence, 51 ALR4th 939.

Appealability of state criminal court order requiring witness other than accused to undergo psychiatric examination, 17 ALR4th 867.

Appealability of orders or rulings, prior to final judgment in criminal case, as to accused's mental competency, 16 ALR3d 714.

Practice References: Lane's Goldstein Tr Tech § 24:10 et seq. (3d ed).

49. People v Lang, 127 Ill App 3d 313, 82 Ill Dec 523, 468 NE2d 1303 (1st Dist 1984), affd in part and revd in part 113 Ill 2d 407, 101 Ill Dec 597, 498 NE2d 1105.

§ 30:06   ILLINOIS JURISPRUDENCE: CRIMINAL LAW

another offense, the reviewing court may also review the appealed conviction of an offense for which no sentence was imposed.[52] If the reviewing court acts to affirm the incomplete judgment of conviction, the reviewing court must remand the cause for imposition of sentence.[53]

A final order decides the controversy on the merits.[54] For a judgment to be appealable, it need not dispose of all the issues presented by the pleadings.[55] However, it must be final in the sense that it disposes of the rights of the parties, either upon the entire controversy or some definite part thereof.[56]

Generally, orders entered pursuant to discovery rules are interlocutory and not immediately appealable.[57] As preliminary orders in a pending case, discovery orders are reviewable on

50. People v Frantz, 150 Ill App 3d 296, 103 Ill Dec 649, 501 NE2d 966 (5th Dist 1986); People v Dean, 61 Ill App 3d 612, 18 Ill Dec 784, 378 NE2d 248 (5th Dist 1978).

51. People ex rel Filkin v Flessner, 48 Ill 2d 54, 268 NE2d 376 (1971); People v Frantz, 150 Ill App 3d 296, 103 Ill Dec 649, 501 NE2d 966 (5th Dist 1986).

52. People v Burrage, 269 Ill App 3d 67, 206 Ill Dec 450, 645 NE2d 455 (1st Dist 1994); People v Frantz, 150 Ill App 3d 296, 103 Ill Dec 649, 501 NE2d 966 (5th Dist 1986).

53. People v Frantz, 150 Ill App 3d 296, 103 Ill Dec 649, 501 NE2d 966 (5th Dist 1986); People v Dean, 61 Ill App 3d 612, 18 Ill Dec 784, 378 NE2d 248 (5th Dist 1978).

54. People v Kuhn, 126 Ill 2d 202, 127 Ill Dec 827, 533 NE2d 909 (1988); People v Whigam, 202 Ill App 3d 252, 147 Ill Dec 556, 559 NE2d 896 (1st Dist 1990).

55. People v Lang, 127 Ill App 3d 313, 82 Ill Dec 523, 468 NE2d 1303 (1st Dist 1984), affd in part and revd in part 113 Ill 2d 407, 101 Ill Dec 597, 498 NE2d 1105; People v Nordstrom, 73 Ill App 2d 168, 219 NE2d 151 (2d Dist 1966), app dismd 37 Ill 2d 270, 226 NE2d 19.

56. People v Lang, 127 Ill App 3d 313, 82 Ill Dec 523, 468 NE2d 1303 (1st Dist 1984), affd in part and revd in part 113 Ill 2d 407, 101 Ill Dec 597, 498 NE2d 1105; People v Nordstrom, 73 Ill App 2d 168, 219 NE2d 151 (2d Dist 1966), app dismd 37 Ill 2d 270, 226 NE2d 19.

57. In re October 1985 Grand Jury No. 746, 154 Ill App 3d 288, 107 Ill Dec 342, 507 NE2d 6 (1st Dist 1987), app gr 116 Ill 2d 558, 113 Ill Dec 304, 515

APPELLATE REVIEW § 30:07

appeal from the final order in that case.[58] Where, however, a discovery order concludes a proceeding begun against a witness, the order is final even though entered in the context of another proceeding, due to the separate and independent nature of the proceeding involved.[59]

§ 30:07. Interlocutory appeals

An interlocutory order has been defined as one that does not have the character of finality or a decision which is intermediate.[60] It is well established that an interlocutory order may not be appealed unless a statute or court rule specifically authorizes that review.[61] However, the Illinois Supreme Court Rules contemplate

---

NE2d 113 and vacated on other grounds 124 Ill 2d 466, 125 Ill Dec 295, 530 NE2d 453.

58. In re October 1985 Grand Jury No. 746, 154 Ill App 3d 288, 107 Ill Dec 342, 507 NE2d 6 (1st Dist 1987), app gr 116 Ill 2d 558, 113 Ill Dec 304, 515 NE2d 113 and vacated on other grounds 124 Ill 2d 466, 125 Ill Dec 295, 530 NE2d 453.

59. In re October 1985 Grand Jury No. 746, 154 Ill App 3d 288, 107 Ill Dec 342, 507 NE2d 6 (1st Dist 1987), app gr 116 Ill 2d 558, 113 Ill Dec 304, 515 NE2d 113 and vacated on other grounds 124 Ill 2d 466, 125 Ill Dec 295, 530 NE2d 453.

60. 4 Am Jur 2d, Appeal and Error, § 50.

61. People v Miller, 35 Ill 2d 62, 219 NE2d 475 (1966); People v Zach, 77 Ill App 3d 17, 32 Ill Dec 528, 395 NE2d 758 (3d Dist 1979).

Trial court's denial of defendant's motion to dismiss counts of indictment after state moved to amend the counts to substitute defendant's name for the name of another, where defendant alleged misnomer was a substantial defect that resulted in substantial prejudice to him, constituted neither a final judgment nor an appealable interlocutory order; thus, appellate court lacked jurisdiction to entertain the matter. People v Baptist, 284 Ill App 3d 382, 219 Ill Dec 890, 672 NE2d 398 (4th Dist 1996).

There is no basis for a defendant to appeal interlocutorily the order of a trial court denying in whole or in part a motion to suppress. People v Bielawski, 255 Ill App 3d 635, 194 Ill Dec 373, 627 NE2d 710 (2d Dist 1994).

Text References: Ruebner, Illinois Criminal Procedure 2d ed § 7.06.

Practice References: Appeal, 20 Am Jur Trials 441, Motion in Limine

review of interlocutory judgments even though such review is not favored.[62]

The denial of a defendant's pretrial motion to suppress evidence is not appealable by the defendant since an interlocutory appeal of a pretrial order regarding the suppression of evidence is available only to the state.[63]

The issue of whether the trial court properly denied a defendant's motion for a discharge pursuant to the requirements of the speedy trial statute[64] ordinarily is deemed to be a nonappealable interlocutory order.[65] However, where the speedy trial issue is coupled with an appeal on double jeopardy grounds over which the appellate court has clear jurisdiction, the appellate court may elect to exercise jurisdiction over the speedy trial issue in pursuance of efficient judicial administration.[66]

III. RIGHT TO REVIEW

Research References:

  Text References:

    Ruebner, Illinois Criminal Procedure 2d ed §§ 7.03, 7.05, 7.11–7.13.

  Annotation References:

    Index and Annotations: Appeal and Error

    Practice §§ 67–69.

62. See Supreme Court Rule 315(a), Supreme Court Rule 318(b), Supreme Court Rule 612(b).

63. People v Zach, 77 Ill App 3d 17, 32 Ill Dec 528, 395 NE2d 758 (3d Dist 1979).

64. 725 ILCS 5/103-5.

See ch 20.

Practice References: 7 POF2d 477, Prejudice Resulting from Unreasonable Delay in Trial § 1 et seq.

65. People v Miller, 35 Ill 2d 62, 219 NE2d 475 (1966); People v Gathings, 128 Ill App 3d 475, 83 Ill Dec 840, 470 NE2d 1260 (1st Dist 1984).

66. People v Gathings, 128 Ill App 3d 475, 83 Ill Dec 840, 470 NE2d 1260 (1st Dist 1984).

ALR Digest to 3d, 4th, 5th, and Federal: Appeal and Error §§ 64, 67, 74–77

Practice References:
4 Am Jur 2d, Appeal and Error §§ 267, 268

State Legislation:
Ill Const Art VI § 6
725 ILCS 5/114-1, 730 ILCS 5/5-5-1—5/5-7-8, 5/5-6-1—5/5-6-4, 5/5-7-7—5/5-7-8,; Supreme Court Rule 315, 604

Miscellaneous References:
West's Illinois Digest 2d, Criminal Law §§ 1023½ to 1027

§ 30:08. Generally

The legislature may not impose substantive conditions which qualify or restrict the right to appeal conferred by the Illinois Constitution.[67] Because the Illinois Constitution establishes that appeals from final judgments are a matter of right,[68] establishing substantive conditions precedent to a defendant's right to appeal from specific final judgments which are otherwise appealable by right would result in the legislature overstepping its constitutional bounds.[69]

The Illinois Constitution does place a limit on the right to appeal final judgments by providing that, after a trial on the merits in a criminal case, there may be no appeal from a judgment of acquittal.[70] It is also clear that a defendant may not seek review of a conviction where his or her appeal has not been properly

---

67. People v Stark, 121 Ill App 3d 787, 77 Ill Dec 188, 460 NE2d 47 (5th Dist 1984).

> **Periodicals:** Stith, The Risk of Legal Error in Criminal Cases: Some Consequences of the Asymmetry in the Right to Appeal, U Chi L Rev, Vol 57, No. 1 (Winter, 1990).

68. Ill Const Art VI, § 6.

> See § 30:02.

69. People v Stark, 121 Ill App 3d 787, 77 Ill Dec 188, 460 NE2d 47 (5th Dist 1984).

70. Ill Const Art VI, § 6.

§ 30:08 ILLINOIS JURISPRUDENCE: CRIMINAL LAW

perfected.[71] The Illinois Constitution authorizes the Illinois Supreme Court to provide by rule for appeals to the appellate court from other than final judgments of the circuit courts.[72]

The defendant or the state may appeal to the appellate court from an order holding the defendant unfit to stand trial or to be sentenced.[73]

§ 30:09. Right of state

In criminal cases, the state may appeal only as permitted by Supreme Court Rule.[74] If the Supreme Court Rules do not provide for an appeal, the state may not appeal.[75]

The right of the state to appellate review in criminal prosecutions is limited to those rulings which substantially impair the prosecution of the case.[76] In criminal cases, the state may appeal only from an order or judgment the substantive effect of which results in:

---

71. People v Scruggs, 161 Ill App 3d 468, 113 Ill Dec 25, 514 NE2d 807 (2d Dist 1987); People v Nogas, 18 Ill App 3d 279, 309 NE2d 651 (1974).

See § 30:11 et seq.

72. Ill Const Art VI, § 6.

See §§ 30:09, 30:10.

73. Supreme Court Rule 604(e).

74. People v Johnson, 113 Ill App 3d 367, 69 Ill Dec 285, 447 NE2d 502 (2d Dist 1983).

Text References: Ruebner, Illinois Criminal Procedure 2d ed §§ 7.11 – 7.13.
Ill Law Man § L1.4.

Annotation References: Appeal by state of order granting new trial in criminal case, 95 ALR3d 596.

75. People v Montaigne, 86 Ill App 3d 220, 41 Ill Dec 609, 407 NE2d 1107 (2d Dist 1980).

76. People v Lentini, 106 Ill App 3d 695, 62 Ill Dec 308, 435 NE2d 1280 (2d Dist 1982) (superseded by statute on other grounds as stated in Algonquin v Ford, 145 Ill App 3d 19, 99 Ill Dec 148, 495 NE2d 595 (2d Dist)).

APPELLATE REVIEW § 30:09

- dismissal of the charge for any of the grounds enumerated for a pretrial motion to dismiss;[77]
- arresting judgment because of a defective indictment, information or complaint;
- quashing an arrest or search warrant; or
- suppressing evidence.[78]

This rule allows the state to bring an interlocutory appeal of a pretrial suppression order if the prosecution certifies to the trial court that suppression of the evidence substantially impairs the state's ability to prosecute the case.[79] The state may petition for leave to appeal under Supreme Court Rule 315(a).[80]

> ☞ *Illustration:* The State was allowed to appeal the suppression of the defendant's statement, which was suppressed on the grounds it was privileged, despite the defendant's argument that a motion in limine excluding evidence on the ground of privilege does not have the same substantive effect as a motion to suppress evidence obtained as a result of police misconduct, because if the trial court grants a defendant's motion in limine and suppresses evidence and the State's Attorney certifies that the suppression substantially impairs the State's ability to prosecute the case, the State's right to appeal is established.[81]

---

77. See 725 ILCS 5/114-1.

78. Supreme Court Rule 604(a)(1).

79. People v Young, 82 Ill 2d 234, 45 Ill Dec 150, 412 NE2d 501 (1980) (ovrld on other grounds as stated in People v Tomasello, 98 Ill App 3d 588, 54 Ill Dec 35, 424 NE2d 785 (2d Dist)) and on remand 98 Ill App 3d 585, 54 Ill Dec 56, 424 NE2d 806 (2d Dist), affd 92 Ill 2d 236, 65 Ill Dec 506, 441 NE2d 641, 36 ALR4th 900.

80. Supreme Court Rule 604(a)(2).

See Supreme Court Rule 315(a).

See also § 30:18.

81. People v Krause, 273 Ill App 3d 59, 209 Ill Dec 566, 651 NE2d 744 (3d Dist 1995).

☞ *Illustration:* State could bring appeal pursuant to Supreme Court Rule 604(a)(1) where the trial court's sustaining defendant's objection to the State's attempt to call him to the witness stand in probation revocation hearing was based on defendant's claimed exercise of a constitutional right as opposed to a mere evidentiary ruling.[82]

☞ *Practice Tip:* The State's failure to appeal an order granting defendant's motion in limine in the first trial which ended in mistrial, does not estop the court from reconsidering the motion at the second trial.[83]

§ 30:10. Right of defendant

A defendant who has been placed under supervision or found guilty and sentenced to probation or conditional discharge[84] or to periodic imprisonment[85] may appeal from the judgment and may seek review of the conditions of supervision, or of the finding of guilt or the conditions of the sentence, or both.[86] The defendant

---

82. People v Martin, 226 Ill App 3d 753, 168 Ill Dec 415, 589 NE2d 815 (4th Dist 1992).

83. People v McGee, 245 Ill App 3d 703, 185 Ill Dec 635, 614 NE2d 1320 (5th Dist 1993).

84. See 730 ILCS 5/5-6-1—5/5-6-4.

85. See 730 ILCS 5/5-5-1—5/5-7-8.

The 1995 amendment of 730 ILCS 5/5-5-6 by P.A. 89-203, effective July 21, 1995, in subsection (b) added the second and third sentences regarding restitution to domestic violence shelters.

The 1994 amendment of 730 ILCS 5/5-5-3.2 by P.A. 88-678, effective July 1, 1995, added subdivision (a)(16) and the paragraph following, concerning criminal acts committed on or near school property; the 1994 amendment of 730 ILCS 5/5-5-3.2 by P.A. 88-680, effective January 1, 1995, added subdivision (b)(8); and added subsection (b-1) both of which address organized gangs.

86. Supreme Court Rule 604(b).

Text References: Ruebner, Illinois Criminal Procedure 2d ed § 7.03.
Ill Law Man § L1.40.

APPELLATE REVIEW § 30:11

may also appeal from an order modifying the conditions or revoking such an order or sentence.[87]

Before conviction, a defendant may appeal to the appellate court from an order setting, modifying, revoking, denying, or refusing to modify bail or the conditions of bail.[88]

The defendant may appeal to the appellate court the denial of a motion to dismiss a criminal proceeding on grounds of former jeopardy.[89]

IV. TAKING AND PERFECTING

Research References:
  Text References:
    Ruebner, Illinois Criminal Procedure 2d ed §§ 7.02, 7.04, 7.07–7.10, 7.15–7.17.
  Annotation References:
    Index and Annotations: Appeal and Error; Appeal and Supersedeas Bond
    ALR Digest to 3d, 4th, 5th, and Federal: Appeal and Error §§ 100–110, 117.5–130, 236–238
  Practice References:
    4 Am Jur 2d, Appeal and Error § 292 et seq.
  State Legislation:
    Supreme Court Rule 21, 302, 303, 315, 316, 317, 341–344, 352, 402, 604, 606, 607, 609
  Miscellaneous References:
    West's Illinois Digest 2d, Criminal Law §§ 1068½ to 1084

§ 30:11. Generally

Because the procedures for effecting one's right of appeal and

---

87. Supreme Court Rule 604(b).

Text References: Ruebner, Illinois Criminal Procedure 2d ed § 7.05.

88. Supreme Court Rule 604(c).

See ch 6.

89. Supreme Court Rule 604(f).

§ 30:11 ILLINOIS JURISPRUDENCE: CRIMINAL LAW

invoking the appellate court's jurisdiction are provided by the supreme court through its rule-making power, the conditions of the rules must be complied with.[90] These procedural rules are binding upon defendants in criminal cases.[91]

In cases in which a death sentence is imposed, an appeal is automatically perfected without any action by the defendant or the defendant's counsel.[92] In other cases, appeals must be perfected by filing a notice of appeal with the clerk of the trial court.[93] The notice may be signed by the appellant or his or her attorney.[94] If the defendant makes a request in open court at the time he or she is advised of the right to appeal, or if a subsequent written request is made, the clerk of the trial court must prepare, sign and promptly file a notice of appeal for the defendant.[95]

> *Practice Tip:* There is no requirement for the State to file any type of post-trial motion to perfect an appeal.[96]

No step in the perfection of an appeal other than the filing of the notice of appeal is jurisdictional.[97]

---

90. People v Carter, 91 Ill App 3d 635, 47 Ill Dec 292, 415 NE2d 17 (1st Dist 1980).

91. People v Stacey, 68 Ill 2d 261, 12 Ill Dec 240, 369 NE2d 1254 (1977) and (ovrld in part on other grounds as stated in People v Evans, 174 Ill 2d 320, 220 Ill Dec 332, 673 NE2d 244); People v Scruggs, 161 Ill App 3d 468, 113 Ill Dec 25, 514 NE2d 807 (2d Dist 1987).

92. Supreme Court Rule 606(a).

93. Supreme Court Rule 606(a).

See § 30:12.

Text References: Ruebner, Illinois Criminal Procedure 2d ed §§ 7.15–7.17.

94. Supreme Court Rule 606(a).

95. Supreme Court Rule 606(a).

96. People v Marty, 241 Ill App 3d 266, 181 Ill Dec 852, 608 NE2d 1326 (4th Dist 1993)

97. Supreme Court Rule 606(a).

§ 30:12. Notice of appeal

Except in the case of an appeal by a defendant from a judgment entered upon a plea of guilty,[98] the notice of appeal must be filed with the clerk of the circuit court within 30 days after the entry of the final judgment appealed from or, if a motion directed against the judgment is timely filed, within 30 days after entry of the order disposing of the motion.[99]

> ☛ *Illustration:* Defendant's notice of appeal was considered timely filed even though it was filed more than 30 days after final judgment where the trial judge mistakenly informed defendant that he had 30 days to appeal from the day the mittimus would issue.[1]

> ☛ *Practice Guide:* Notices of appeal mailed within the 30-day period and received thereafter are timely filed. Proof of mailing may be made by filing with the clerk a certificate of the attorney, or affidavit of a person other than the attorney, who deposited the notice of appeal in the mail, properly addressed, stating the date and place of mailing and the fact that proper postage was prepaid. Proof of mailing may also be made by a United States Postal Service certificate of mailing. Merely attaching a copy of a letter to the clerk to a reply brief cannot stand as a supplement to the record.[2]

Within five days of its filing, a copy of the notice of appeal or

---

98. See § 30:15.

99. Supreme Court Rule 606(b).

Text References: Ruebner, Illinois Criminal Procedure 2d ed §§ 7.02, 7.04.

Practice References: Lane's Goldstein Tr Tech §§ 24:24–24:29.

Forms: Petition for Appeal. 2 Am Jur Pl & Pr Forms (Rev), Appeal and Error, Forms 1 et seq.
Notice of Appeal. 8 Am Jur Pl & Pr Forms (Rev), Criminal Procedure, Forms 421, 422.
Lane's Goldstein Lit Forms §§ 64:17–64:21.

1. People v Robinson, 229 Ill App 3d 627, 170 Ill Dec 606, 593 NE2d 148 (3d Dist 1992), app den 146 Ill 2d 646, 176 Ill Dec 816, 602 NE2d 470.

§ 30:12 ILLINOIS JURISPRUDENCE: CRIMINAL LAW

an amendment of the notice of appeal must be transmitted by the clerk of the circuit court to the clerk of the court to which the appeal is taken.[3]

No appeal may be taken from a trial court to a reviewing court after the expiration of 30 days from the entry of the order or judgment from which the appeal is taken except in cases involving an appeal by a defendant from a judgment entered on a guilty plea[4] or upon the granting of an extension.[5] When the notice of appeal is not timely filed, the reviewing court may grant leave to appeal and order the clerk to transmit the notice of appeal to the trial court for filing.[6] An extension may be requested:

- by a motion, supported by a showing of a reasonable excuse for failing to file a notice of appeal on time, which must be filed in the reviewing court within 30 days of the expiration of the time for filing the notice of appeal; or

- by motion supported by an affidavit showing that there is merit to the appeal and that the failure to file a notice of appeal on time was not due to the appellant's culpable negligence which must be filed in the reviewing court within six months of the expiration of the time for filing the notice of appeal.[7]

In either case, the motion must be accompanied by the proposed notice of appeal.[8]

The notice of appeal should be substantially in the form provided by statute.[9] The notice should state:

2. People v Blanchette, 182 Ill App 3d 396, 131 Ill Dec 49, 538 NE2d 237 (2d Dist 1989).

3. Supreme Court Rule 606(b).

4. See § 30:15.

5. Supreme Court Rule 606(b).

6. Supreme Court Rule 606(c).

7. Supreme Court Rule 606(c).

8. Supreme Court Rule 606(c).

9. Supreme Court Rule 606(d).

- the court to which the appeal is taken;
- the name and address to which notices must be sent;
- the name and address of the appellant's attorney on appeal;
- if the appellant is indigent, and has no attorney, an indication of whether the appellant wants one appointed;
- the date of the judgment or order;
- the offense of which the appellant was convicted;
- the sentence imposed; and
- if the appeal is not from a conviction, the nature of the order appealed from.[10]

The notice of appeal may be signed by the appellant, the attorney for the appellant or the clerk of the court.[11]

When the defendant is the appellant and the action was prosecuted by the State, the clerk shall send a copy of the notice of appeal to the State's Attorney of the county in which the judgment was entered and a copy to the Attorney General at his Springfield, Illinois, office.[12] If the defendant is the appellant and the action was prosecuted by a governmental entity other than the State for the violation of an ordinance, the copy of the notice of appeal shall be sent to the chief legal officer of the entity (e.g., corporation counsel, city attorney), or if his name and address does not appear of record, then to the chief administrative officer of the entity at his official address.[13] When the State or other prosecuting entity is the appellant a copy of the notice of appeal shall be sent to the defendant and a copy to his counsel.[14]

When the notice of appeal is filed, the appellate court's jurisdiction attaches immediately and the cause is beyond the jurisdiction of the trial court.[15]

10. Supreme Court Rule 606(d).
11. Supreme Court Rule 606(d).
12. Supreme Court Rule 606(e)(1).
13. Supreme Court Rule 606(e)(2).
14. Supreme Court Rule 606(e)(3).

§ 30:12 ILLINOIS JURISPRUDENCE: CRIMINAL LAW

A notice of appeal is to be liberally construed.[16] The appellate court will have jurisdiction if the notice, when considered as a whole, fairly and adequately sets out the judgment complained of and the relief sought.[17] The appellate court will not be deprived of jurisdiction where the state alleges no prejudice and the alleged defect is one of form over substance.[18]

> *Illustration:* The incorrect numerical designation on a notice of appeal of the decision sought to be reviewed may be considered to be a clerical error and will not affect the reviewing court's jurisdiction if the body of the notice of appeal clearly refers to the correct decision and all of the defendant's arguments pertain only to that case.[19]

A consultation between the defendant and his or her attorney or an affirmative showing of a desire on the defendant's part prior to the filing of a notice that he or she desires to appeal from an adverse criminal judgment is not a condition precedent to the filing of the notice of appeal.[20] Because of the attorney's representative role, the filing of a notice of appeal predicated on perceived trial error is seen as a necessary extension of the attorney's role.[21] If the defendant does not wish to appeal, the

---

15. Daley v Laurie, 106 Ill 2d 33, 86 Ill Dec 918, 476 NE2d 419 (1985); People v Carter, 91 Ill App 3d 635, 47 Ill Dec 292, 415 NE2d 17 (1st Dist 1980).

16. People v Hansen, 198 Ill App 3d 160, 144 Ill Dec 438, 555 NE2d 797 (4th Dist 1990); People v Gallinger, 191 Ill App 3d 488, 138 Ill Dec 848, 548 NE2d 78 (4th Dist 1989).

17. People v Hansen, 198 Ill App 3d 160, 144 Ill Dec 438, 555 NE2d 797 (4th Dist 1990).

18. People v Hansen, 198 Ill App 3d 160, 144 Ill Dec 438, 555 NE2d 797 (4th Dist 1990).

19. People v Bennett, 144 Ill App 3d 184, 98 Ill Dec 725, 494 NE2d 847 (4th Dist 1986).

20. People v Stark, 121 Ill App 3d 787, 77 Ill Dec 188, 460 NE2d 47 (5th Dist 1984).

21. People v Stark, 121 Ill App 3d 787, 77 Ill Dec 188, 460 NE2d 47 (5th Dist 1984).

defendant's remedy is to withdraw the otherwise valid appeal.[22]

Procedural rules are binding upon defendants in criminal cases and, therefore, notices of appeal from adverse judgments must be timely filed.[23] The filing of a notice of appeal is jurisdictional and the appellate court has no discretion to extend its jurisdiction.[24] Failure to file a timely notice of appeal cannot be waived by the parties.[25]

§ 30:13. Docketing

When the clerk of the reviewing court receives the copy of the notice of appeal[26] or upon the entry of an order granting a motion for leave to appeal,[27] the clerk must enter the appeal upon the docket.[28] Within 14 days after the filing of the notice of appeal and pursuant to notice to the appellee's attorney, the party filing the notice of appeal must file with the clerk of the reviewing court a docketing statement, together with proof of service and a $25 filing fee.[29]

---

22. People v Stark, 121 Ill App 3d 787, 77 Ill Dec 188, 460 NE2d 47 (5th Dist 1984).

23. People v Stacey, 68 Ill 2d 261, 12 Ill Dec 240, 369 NE2d 1254 (1977) and (ovrld in part on other grounds as stated in People v Evans, 174 Ill 2d 320, 220 Ill Dec 332, 673 NE2d 244); People v Scruggs, 161 Ill App 3d 468, 113 Ill Dec 25, 514 NE2d 807 (2d Dist 1987).

24. People v Blanchette, 182 Ill App 3d 396, 131 Ill Dec 49, 538 NE2d 237 (2d Dist 1989); People v Scruggs, 161 Ill App 3d 468, 113 Ill Dec 25, 514 NE2d 807 (2d Dist 1987); People v Williams, 82 Ill App 3d 681, 37 Ill Dec 550, 402 NE2d 440 (3d Dist 1980).

Technical mistakes in the heading of a notice of appeal did not deprive the reviewing court of jurisdiction. People v Chaney, 257 Ill App 3d 247, 195 Ill Dec 480, 628 NE2d 944 (1st Dist 1993).

25. People v Blanchette, 182 Ill App 3d 396, 131 Ill Dec 49, 538 NE2d 237 (2d Dist 1989).

26. Supreme Court Rule 606(b).

See § 30:12.

27. Supreme Court Rule 606(c).

28. Supreme Court Rule 606(f).

§ 30:13   ILLINOIS JURISPRUDENCE: CRIMINAL LAW

The form and contents of the docketing statement, as set out by statute, must include:

- the docket number in the reviewing court;
- the complete case title;
- the name, address and telephone number of the appellant's counsel on appeal;
- the name, address and telephone number of trial counsel, if different from counsel on appeal;
- the name, address and telephone number of the appellee's counsel on appeal;
- the name, address and telephone number of the court reporter;
- the approximate duration of the trial proceedings to be transcribed;
- the nature of the case;
- a general statement of the issues proposed to be raised;
- certification of the attorney for the appellant that the clerk of the circuit court has been requested to prepare the record and that the court reporter has been requested in writing to prepare the transcript; and
- acknowledgment of the court reporter or supervisor of receipt of an order for the preparation of a report of proceedings.[30]

Within seven days after the filing of the docketing statement, the appellee's attorney may file a short responsive statement with the clerk of the reviewing court.[31]

§ 30:14. Bonds and stays

A death sentence may not be carried out until entry of a final

---

29. Supreme Court Rule 606(g).

Practice References: Lane's Goldstein Tr Tech §§ 24:30, 24:31.

30. Supreme Court Rule 606(g).
31. Supreme Court Rule 606(g).

order by the supreme court.[32]

A defendant may be admitted to bail and the sentence or condition of imprisonment or periodic imprisonment may be stayed, with or without bond, by a judge of the trial or reviewing court if the appeal is taken from:

- a judgment following which the defendant is sentenced to imprisonment or periodic imprisonment, or to probation or conditional discharge conditioned upon periodic imprisonment; or
- an order revoking or modifying the conditions of imprisonment or periodic imprisonment.[33]

Upon motion showing good cause, the reviewing court or a judge of that court may revoke the order of the trial court that the amount of bail be increased or decreased.[34]

On appeals in other cases, the judgment or order may be stayed by a judge of the trial or reviewing court, with or without bond.[35] Upon motion showing good cause, the reviewing court or a judge thereof may revoke the order of the trial court or order that the amount of bail be increased or decreased.[36]

§ 30:15. Appeal by defendant from judgment entered on guilty plea

In order to appeal from a judgment entered on a plea of guilty, the defendant must, within 30 days of the date on which sentence is imposed, file in the trial court a motion to reconsider the sentence, if only the sentence is being challenged, or, if the plea is being challenged, a motion to withdraw the plea of guilty and vacate the judgment.[37] The motion must be in writing and must

---

32. Supreme Court Rule 609(a).
33. Supreme Court Rule 609(b).
34. Supreme Court Rule 609(b).
35. Supreme Court Rule 609(c).
36. Supreme Court Rule 609(c).
37. Supreme Court Rule 604(d).

Text References: Ruebner, Illinois Criminal Procedure 2d ed §§ 7.04.

state the grounds for the motion.[38] If the motion is based on facts which do not appear in the record, it must be supported by affidavit.[39]

The motion must be promptly presented to the judge who sentenced the defendant.[40] If the judge is not then sitting in the court, the motion must be presented to the chief judge of the circuit court or to such other judge as the chief judge designates.[41]

The trial court must determine whether the defendant is represented by counsel.[42] If the defendant is indigent and wants to be represented by counsel, the trial court must appoint counsel.[43] If the defendant is indigent, the trial court must order that a copy of the transcript be furnished to the defendant at no cost.[44]

The defendant's attorney must file with the trial court a certificate stating that the attorney has:

- consulted with the defendant either by mail or in person to ascertain the defendant's contentions of error in the entry of the plea of guilty;
- examined the trial court file and report of proceedings of the plea of guilty; and
- made any amendments to the motion necessary for adequate presentation of any defects in those proceedings.[45]

Annotation References: Validity and effect of criminal defendant's express waiver of right to appeal as part of negotiated plea agreement, 89 ALR3d 864.

38. Supreme Court Rule 604(d).
39. Supreme Court Rule 604(d).
40. Supreme Court Rule 604(d).
41. Supreme Court Rule 604(d).
42. Supreme Court Rule 604(d).
43. Supreme Court Rule 604(d).
44. Supreme Court Rule 604(d).
   See Supreme Court Rule 402(e).

The motion must be heard promptly.[46] If the motion is allowed, the trial court must vacate the judgment and permit the defendant to withdraw the plea of guilty and plead anew.[47] If the motion is denied, a notice of appeal from the judgment and sentence must be filed within the time provided under the perfection of appeal rule[48] as measured from the date of entry of the order denying the motion.[49]

> *Practice Guide:* In drafting the motion to withdraw the plea of guilty, it should be remembered that any issue not raised in the motion to withdraw the plea and vacate the judgment will be deemed waived on appeal.[50]

§ 30:16. Appeals by poor persons

The trial court must determine whether the defendant is represented by counsel on appeal upon the imposition of a death sentence, or upon the filing of a notice of appeal in any case in which:

- the defendant has been found guilty of a felony or a Class A misdemeanor;
- the defendant has been found guilty of a lesser offense and sentenced to imprisonment or periodic imprisonment, or to probation or conditional discharge conditioned upon periodic imprisonment;
- a sentence of probation or conditional discharge has been revoked or the conditions attached to such a sentence modified and a sentence of imprisonment or periodic imprisonment imposed; and

---

45. Supreme Court Rule 604(d).
46. Supreme Court Rule 604(d).
47. Supreme Court Rule 604(d).
48. See Supreme Court Rule 606.
    See § 30:12.
49. Supreme Court Rule 604(d).
50. Supreme Court Rule 604(d).

§ 30:16 ILLINOIS JURISPRUDENCE: CRIMINAL LAW

- the state appeals.[51]

If the defendant is not represented and the court determines that the defendant is indigent and desires counsel on appeal, the court is to appoint counsel on appeal.[52] When a death sentence has been imposed, the court may appoint two attorneys.[53] One of the attorneys is designated as the "responsible attorney" and the other as the assistant attorney for the appeal.[54] Compensation and reimbursement for expenses of appointed attorneys must be provided according to statute.[55]

The defendant may petition the court in which he or she was convicted for a report of the proceedings at the trial or hearing in any case in which the defendant was found guilty and sentenced:

- to imprisonment, probation or conditional discharge;
- to periodic imprisonment;
- to pay a fine;
- or in which a hearing has been held resulting in the revocation of, or modification of the conditions of, probation or conditional discharge.[56]

If the conduct on which the case was based was also the basis of a juvenile proceeding which was dismissed so that the case could proceed, the defendant may include in his or her petition a request for a report of proceedings in the juvenile proceeding period.[57]

---

51. Supreme Court Rule 607(a).
52. Supreme Court Rule 607(a).

   Text References: Ruebner, Illinois Criminal Procedure 2d ed §§ 7.07–7.10.
   Forms: Petition to appeal in forma pauperis. 8 Am Jur Pl & Pr Forms (Rev), Criminal Procedure, Forms 423–426.
   Lane's Goldstein Lit Forms § 64:22.

53. Supreme Court Rule 607(a).
54. Supreme Court Rule 607(a).
55. Supreme Court Rule 607(a).
56. Supreme Court Rule 607(b).
57. Supreme Court Rule 607(b).

§ 30:16 APPELLATE REVIEW

The petition must be verified by the petitioner and must state facts showing that he or she was, at the time of conviction, or at the time probation or conditional discharge was revoked or its conditions modified, and is at the time of filing the petition, without financial means with which to obtain the report of proceedings.[58]

If the judge who imposed sentence or entered the order revoking probation or conditional discharge or modifying the conditions, or in that judge's absence, any other judge of the court, finds that the defendant is without financial means with which to obtain the report of proceedings at the trial or hearing, the judge must order the court reporter to transcribe an original and copy of his or her notes.[59] Upon written request of the defendant, the clerk of the court must then release a copy of the report of proceedings to the defendant's attorney of record on appeal.[60] If no attorney appears of record, the clerk must, upon written request of the defendant, release the report of proceedings to the defendant or to the defendant's guardian or custodian.[61] The reporter who prepares this report of proceedings must be paid the same fee for preparing the transcript as is provided by law for the compensation of reporters for preparing transcripts in other cases.[62]

> ☞ *Practice Tip:* The state must furnish an indigent defendant a record of sufficient completeness to permit proper consideration of his claims on appeal, but this does not necessarily mean that a complete verbatim transcript is required, and alternate means such as a bystander's report or

---

58. Supreme Court Rule 607(b).

Annotation References: Determination of indigency of accused entitling him to transcript or similar record for purposes of appeal, 66 ALR3d 954.

59. Supreme Court Rule 607(b).

60. Supreme Court Rule 607(b).

61. Supreme Court Rule 607(b).

62. Supreme Court Rule 607(b).

an agreed statement of facts may be sufficient unless there is a colorable need for a complete transcript.[63]

If the defendant is represented by court-appointed counsel, the clerk of the reviewing court must docket the appeal and accept papers for filing without the payment of fees.[64]

If the defendant is represented by court-appointed counsel, the clerk of the supreme court must accept for filing at least 15 legible copies of briefs or petitions for leave to appeal or answers thereto.[65] The clerk of the appellate court must accept for filing not less than 6 legible copies of briefs.[66]

§ 30:17. Direct appeals to supreme court

Final judgments of the circuit courts may be directly appealed to the Illinois Supreme Court:

- in cases in which a statute of the United States or of Illinois has been held invalid; and
- in proceedings commenced to compel compliance with certain orders entered by a chief circuit judge.[67]

After the filing of the notice of appeal to the appellate court in a case in which the public interest requires prompt adjudication by the supreme court, the supreme court or a justice of that court may order that the appeal be takenly directly to it.[68] Upon the entry of such an order, any documents already filed in the appellate court must be transmitted by the clerk of the appellate court to the clerk of the supreme court.[69] From that point on, the

---

63. People v Luke, 253 Ill App 3d 136, 192 Ill Dec 392, 625 NE2d 352 (1st Dist 1993), mod and reh den (Nov 18, 1993).

64. Supreme Court Rule 607(c).

65. Supreme Court Rule 607(d).

66. Supreme Court Rule 607(d).

67. Supreme Court Rule 302(a).

See Supreme Court Rule 21(c).

Text References: Ruebner, Illinois Criminal Procedure 2d ed §§ 7.15–7.16.

68. Supreme Court Rule 302(b).

case proceeds in all respects as though the appeal had been taken directly to the supreme court.[70]

After the briefs have been filed, the supreme court may dispose of any case without oral argument or opinion if no substantial question is presented or if jurisdiction is lacking.[71]

§ 30:18. Appeal from appellate court to supreme court

Except as provided below for appeals from the Industrial Commission division of the appellate court, a petition for leave to appeal to the supreme court from the appellate court may be filed by any party, including the state, in any case not appealable from the appellate court as a matter of right.[72] Whether the petition will be granted is a matter of sound judicial discretion.[73] Among the factors the court may consider in determining whether to grant the petition are:

- the general importance of the question presented:
- the existence of a conflict between the decision sought to be reviewed and a decision of the supreme court or of another division of the appellate court;
- the need for the exercise of the supreme court's supervisory authority; and
- the final or interlocutory character of the judgment sought to be reviewed.[74]

Oral argument may be requested as provided in the rules of the supreme court.[75]

---

69. Supreme Court Rule 302(b).
70. Supreme Court Rule 302(b).
71. Supreme Court Rule 302(c).
72. Supreme Court Rule 315(a).
73. Supreme Court Rule 315(a).
74. Supreme Court Rule 315(a).

Text References: Ruebner, Illinois Criminal Procedure 2d ed § 7.17.

75. Supreme Court Rule 315(h).

§ 30:19. —Time, contents and service of petition

Unless a timely petition for rehearing is filed in the appellate court, a party seeking leave to appeal must file the petition for leave in the Supreme Court within 21 days after entry of the judgment of the appellate court, or within the same 21 days file with the appellate court an affidavit of intent to file a petition for leave, and file the petition within 35 days after the entry of such judgment.[76] If a timely petition for rehearing is filed, the party seeking review must file the petition for leave to appeal within 21 days after the entry of the order denying the petition for rehearing, or within the same 21 days must file with the appellate court an affidavit of intent to file a petition, and file the petition within 35 days after entry of such order.[77] If a petition is granted, the petition for leave to appeal must be filed within 21 days of the entry of the judgment on rehearing, or if within the same 21 days an affidavit of intent is filed with the appellate court, then within 35 days after the entry of such judgment.[78] The supreme court or a supreme court justice may, on motion, extend the time for petitioning for leave to appeal.[79] However, these motions are not favored and will be allowed only in the most extreme and compelling circumstances.[80]

The petition for leave to appeal must contain, in the following order:

- a prayer for leave to appeal;
- a statement of the date upon which the judgment was entered;
- whether an affidavit of intent to seek review was filed and, if so, the date it was filed;

See Supreme Court Rule 352(a).

76. Supreme Court Rule 315(b).
77. Supreme Court Rule 315(b).
78. Supreme Court Rule 315(b).
79. Supreme Court Rule 315(b).
80. Supreme Court Rule 315(b).

- whether a petition for rehearing was filed and, if so, the date of the denial of the petition or the date of the judgment on rehearing;
- a statement of the points relied upon for reversal of the judgment of the appellate court;
- a fair and accurate statement of the facts which must contain the facts necessary to an understanding of the case, without argument or comment, with appropriate references to the pages of the record on appeal or to the pages of the abstract, if one has been filed;
- a short argument, including appropriate authorities, stating why review by the supreme court is warranted and why the decision of the appellate court should be reversed or modified; and
- an appendix, which shall include a copy of the opinion or order of the Appellate Court and any documents from the record which are deemed necessary to the consideration of the petition[81]

The petition must be duplicated, served, and filed in accordance with the requirements for briefs.[82]

§ 30:20. —Records and abstracts

If an abstract has been filed in the appellate court, the petitioner must file two or, if available, eight copies of the abstract in the supreme court.[83] For that purpose, the clerk of the appellate court must, when requested, release to the petitioner any available copies of the abstract.[84] The clerk of the supreme court must send

---

81. Supreme Court Rule 315(b).

82. Supreme Court Rule 315(c).

Supreme Court Rule 315(c) was amended in 1993 by the addition of the requirement that a petition for leave to appeal must also be prepared in accordance with the requirements for briefs except that it shall be limited to 20 pages excluding only the appendix.

83. Supreme Court Rule 315(d).

84. Supreme Court Rule 315(d).

§ 30:20   ILLINOIS JURISPRUDENCE: CRIMINAL LAW

notice of the filing of the petition to the clerk of the appellate court.[85]

Upon request of the clerk of the supreme court, the clerk of the appellate court must, at the expense of the petitioner, transmit to the clerk of the supreme court the record on appeal that was filed in the appellate court and a certified copy of the appellate court record.[86] If leave to appeal is not granted, any certified papers and, to the extent available, copies of abstracts must be returned promptly to the clerk of the appellate court.[87]

§ 30:21. —Answer

While it is not required, the respondent may file an answer, with proof of service, within 14 days after the expiration of the time for filing of the petition, or within such further time as the supreme court or a justice of that court may grant within that 14-day period.[88] The answer must set forth reasons why the petition should not be granted and must conform, to the extent appropriate, to the form specified for the petition,[89] omitting the first four and sixth items in the list except to the extent that correction of the petition is considered necessary.[90]

The answer must be duplicated, served, and filed in accordance with the requirements for briefs, except that it shall be limited to 20 pages excluding only the appendix[91] No reply to the answer may be filed.[92]

> ☛ *Practice Guide:* If the respondent does not file an answer or otherwise appear but wants notice of the disposition of the

---

85. Supreme Court Rule 315(d).
86. Supreme Court Rule 315(d).
87. Supreme Court Rule 315(d).
88. Supreme Court Rule 315(e).
89. Supreme Court Rule 315(b).
90. Supreme Court Rule 315(e).
91. Supreme Court Rule 315(e).
92. Supreme Court Rule 315(e).

APPELLATE REVIEW § 30:23

petition for leave to appeal, a letter requesting that notice should be directed to the clerk of the Illinois Supreme Court in Springfield.[93]

§ 30:22. —Transmittal of record

If the petition for leave to appeal is granted, and to the extent that copies have not already been filed, the appellant must file 20 copies of the abstract, as filed in the appellate court, within the time for filing his or her brief.[94] If no abstract was filed in the appellate court, the supreme court may order that an abstract be prepared and filed in accordance with its rules.[95]

Upon direction of the supreme court, or upon the request of any party made at any time before oral argument, the clerk of the appellate court, at the expense of the petitioner, must transmit to the supreme court the record on appeal that was filed in the appellate court and the appellate court record if not already filed in the supreme court.[96]

§ 30:23. —Briefs

If leave to appeal is allowed, the appellant may allow his or her petition for leave to appeal to stand as his or her brief or a brief may be filed in place of, or as a supplement to, the petition.[97] Within 14 days after the date on which leave to appeal was allowed, the appellant must serve on all counsel of record notice of his or her election to allow the petition for leave to appeal to stand as his or her brief, or to file an additional brief.[98] Within that same time period, the appellant must file a copy of the notice

---

93. Supreme Court Rule 315(e).
94. Supreme Court Rule 315(f).
95. Supreme Court Rule 315(f).

   See Supreme Court Rule 342.

96. Supreme Court Rule 315(f).

   Forms: 2 Am Jur Pl & Pr Forms (Rev), Appeal and Error, Forms 531 et seq.

97. Supreme Court Rule 315(g).

   Practice References: Lane's Goldstein Tr Tech §§ 24:50–24:52.

§ 30:23 ILLINOIS JURISPRUDENCE: CRIMINAL LAW

with the clerk of the supreme court.[99]

If the appellant elects to allow the petition for leave to appeal to stand as his or her brief, the appellant must file with the notice a complete table of contents, with page references, of the record on appeal and a statement of the applicable standard of review for each issue, with citation to authority, in accordance with Supreme Court Rule 341(e)(3).[1] If the appellant elects to file an additional brief, it must be filed within 35 days from the date on which leave to appeal was allowed.[2] Motions to extend the time for filing an additional brief are not favored and will be allowed only in the most extreme and compelling circumstances.[3]

The appellee may allow his or her answer to the petition for leave to appeal to stand as his or her brief or the appellee may file a brief in place of, or as a supplement to, the petition.[4] If the appellant has elected to allow the petition for leave to appeal to stand as his or her brief, the appellee must, within 14 days after the due date of the appellant's notice, serve on all counsel of record notice of this election to let the answer stand as his or her brief, or to file an additional brief.[5] Within the same time period, the appellee must file a copy of the notice with the clerk of the supreme court.[6] If the appellee elects to file an additional brief, that brief must be filed within 35 days of the due date of the appellant's notice of election to let his or her petition for leave to appeal stand as his or her brief.[7]

---

98. Supreme Court Rule 315(g).

99. Supreme Court Rule 315(g).

1. Supreme Court Rule 315(g).

See also Supreme Court Rule 341(e)(3).

2. Supreme Court Rule 315(g).

3. Supreme Court Rule 315(g).

4. Supreme Court Rule 315(g).

5. Supreme Court Rule 315(g).

6. Supreme Court Rule 315(g).

7. Supreme Court Rule 315(g).

If the appellant has elected to file an additional brief, the appellee must, within 14 days after the due date of the appellant's brief, serve on all counsel of record notice of his or her election to let his or her answer stand as his or her brief or to file an additional brief.[8] Within the same time, the appellee must file a copy of the notice with the clerk of the supreme court.[9] If the appellee elects to file an additional brief, it must be filed within 35 days of the due date of the appellant's brief.[10]

If an appellee files a brief, the appellant may file a reply brief within 14 days of the due date of the appellee's brief.[11] If the appellee's brief includes arguments in support of cross-relief, the appellant's arguments in opposition must be included in his or her reply brief and the appellee may file a reply brief confined strictly to those arguments within 14 days of the due date of the appellant's reply brief.[12] If the appellee's brief contains arguments in support of cross-relief, the cover of the brief must be captioned: "Brief of Appellee. Cross-Relief Requested."[13]

In cases involving multiple parties, including cases consolidated for purposes of the appeal, any number of appellants or appellees may join in a single brief.[14] Similarly, any appellant or appellee may adopt by reference any part of the brief of another.[15] Parties may also join in reply briefs.[16]

§ 30:24. Appeals to supreme court on certificate

Appeals from the appellate court may be taken to the supreme

---

8. Supreme Court Rule 315(g).
9. Supreme Court Rule 315(g).
10. Supreme Court Rule 315(g).
11. Supreme Court Rule 315(g).
12. Supreme Court Rule 315(g).
13. Supreme Court Rule 315(g).
14. Supreme Court Rule 315(g).
15. Supreme Court Rule 315(g).
16. Supreme Court Rule 315(g).

§ 30:24 ILLINOIS JURISPRUDENCE: CRIMINAL LAW

court upon the certification by the appellate court that a case decided by it involves a question of such importance that it should be decided by the supreme court.[17] Application for a certificate of importance may be included in a petition for rehearing or may be made by filing four copies of a petition, clearly setting forth the grounds relied upon, with the clerk of the appellate court within 21 days after the entry of the judgment appealed from if no petition for rehearing is filed, or, or within 35 days if an affidavit of intent if filed.[18] If a petition for rehearing is filed, the application must be filed within 14 days after the denial of the petition or the entry of the judgment on rehearing.[19]

An application for a certificate of importance does not extend the time for filing a petition for leave to appeal to the supreme court.[20]

When the appellate court has granted a certificate of importance, the clerk of that court must transmit to the clerk of the supreme court:

- the record on appeal that was filed in the appellate court;
- a certified copy of the appellate court record and opinions; and
- the certificate of importance of the appellate court.[21]

The appellate court may require a bond as a condition of granting a certificate of importance.[22] The record must be transmitted to the office of the clerk of the supreme court not later than 14 days from the date the certificate of importance is granted.[23]

---

17. Supreme Court Rule 316.

    Text References: Ruebner, Illinois Criminal Procedure 2d ed § 7.16.

18. Supreme Court Rule 316.
19. Supreme Court Rule 316.
20. Supreme Court Rule 316.
21. Supreme Court Rule 316.
22. Supreme Court Rule 316.

Briefs must be filed as provided by supreme court rule.[24] The appellant's brief must contain a copy of the appellate court opinion.[25] If an abstract was filed in the appellate court, 20 copies of the abstract must be filed with the briefs.[26] However, if the supreme court so orders, an abstract must be prepared and filed in accordance with supreme court rule.[27]

§ 30:25. Appeal as of right

Appeals may be taken from the appellate court to the supreme court as a matter of right in cases in which a question under the Constitution of the United States or of Illinois arises for the first time in, and as a result of, the action of the appellate court.[28] The appeal may be initiated by filing a petition for leave to appeal[29] except that the petition must be entitled "Petition for Appeal as a Matter of Right."[30] The petition must state that the appeal is being taken as a matter of right and must contain argument as to why appeal to the supreme court is a matter of right.[31] In other respects, the procedure is governed by the rule on leave to appeal from the appellate court to the supreme court.[32]

---

23. Supreme Court Rule 316.
24. Supreme Court Rule 316.
   See Supreme Court Rule 341 through 344.
25. Supreme Court Rule 316.
26. Supreme Court Rule 316.
27. Supreme Court Rule 316.
   See Supreme Court Rule 342.
28. Supreme Court Rule 317.
   Text References: Ruebner, Illinois Criminal Procedure 2d ed § 7.16.
29. Supreme Court Rule 317.
   See Supreme Court Rule 315.
30. Supreme Court Rule 317.
31. Supreme Court Rule 317.
32. Supreme Court Rule 317.

§ 30:25   ILLINOIS JURISPRUDENCE: CRIMINAL LAW

If leave to appeal is to be sought in the alternative, the request must be included in the petition along with an alternative prayer for leave to appeal and the argument as to why in the alternative leave to appeal should be allowed as a matter of sound judicial discretion.[33] When both appeal as a matter of right and leave to appeal are sought, both requests will be disposed of by a single order.[34]

If the court allows the petition, briefs and abstracts in cases in which they are required must be filed as provided in the case of appeal by leave.[35]

V. RECORD

Research References:
  Text References:
    Ruebner, Illinois Criminal Procedure 2d ed §§ 5.42, 7.04, 7.08, 7.09, 7.19, 7.20, 7.22.
  Annotation References:
    Index and Annotations: Appeal and Error
    ALR Digest to 3d, 4th, 5th, and Federal: Appeal and Error §§ 130–156, 188–192, 198–216, 241–263, 295
  Practice References:
    4 Am Jur 2d, Appeal and Error § 397 et seq.
  State Legislation:
    730 ILCS 5/5-5-6; Supreme Court Rule 323, 324, 325, 327, 329, 331, 342, 373, 401, 608, 612, 615
  Miscellaneous References:
    West's Illinois Digest 2d, Criminal Law §§ 1028–1068, 1086.1–1128

See Supreme Court Rule 315.
33. Supreme Court Rule 317.
34. Supreme Court Rule 317.
35. Supreme Court Rule 317.
    See Supreme Court Rule 315.

National Background:
The "record" or "record on appeal" consists of those papers which the trial court is required to transmit or certify to the appellate court and on which the appellate court decides the cause. At common law, the record consisted of little more than the required papers, such as the pleadings, any rulings on those papers, the process, the verdict and the judgment in the case. Neither the testimony nor the court's oral rulings were included. Often, the papers which are to be included in the record on appeal are specified by statute. In some jurisdictions, however, the traditional requirements as to the formal record to be submitted to the reviewing court have been replaced by a simplified system under which the lower court sends up all the papers on the case and this inclusive, unprinted record is always before the court. 4 Am Jur 2d, Appeal and Error § 397.

§ 30:26. Contents—Generally

Upon the filing of a notice of appeal, and in all cases in which a death sentence is imposed, the clerk of the circuit court must prepare the record on appeal.[36] In a death sentence case, the clerk also shall prepare in the same manner as the original, in accordance with the rules, a duplicate of the record which shall be so designated and used by the parties in any collateral proceedings.[37]

Among the things which must be included in the record on appeal are:

- a cover sheet showing the title of the case;[38]
- a certificate of the clerk showing the impaneling of the grand jury if the prosecution was commenced by indictment;[39]
- the indictment, information or complaint;[40]

---

36. Supreme Court Rule 608(a)

Practice References: Lane's Goldstein Tr Tech §§ 24:32–24:37, 24:53–24:73.
Nichols Drinking/Driving Lit § 19:02.
Forms: 2 Am Jur Pl & Pr Forms (Rev), Appeal and Error, Forms 531–612.

37. Supreme Court Rule 608(a).

38. Supreme Court Rule 608(a)(1).

39. Supreme Court Rule 608(a)(2).

§ 30:26   ILLINOIS JURISPRUDENCE: CRIMINAL LAW

- a transcript of the proceedings at the defendant's arraignment and plea;[41]
- all motions, transcript of motion proceedings and orders entered on those motions;[42]
- all arrest warrants, search warrants, consent to search forms, eavesdropping orders, and any similar documents;[43]
- a transcript of proceedings regarding waiver of counsel and waiver of jury trial, if any;[44]
- the verdict of the jury or finding of the court;[45]
- posttrial motions, including motions for a new trial, motions in arrest of judgment, motions for judgment notwithstanding the verdict and the testimony, arguments and rulings on those motions;[46]
- a transcript of proceedings at sentencing, including the presentence investigation report, testimony offered and objections made, offers of proof, argument, and rulings made by the court, arguments of counsel, and statements by the defendant and the court;[47]
- the judgment and sentence;[48] and
- the notice of appeal, if any.[49]

The record on appeal must also include the report of proceedings.[50]

---

40. Supreme Court Rule 608(a)(3).
41. Supreme Court Rule 608(a)(4).
42. Supreme Court Rule 608(a)(5).
43. Supreme Court Rule 608(a)(6).
44. Supreme Court Rule 608(a)(7).
45. Supreme Court Rule 608(a)(11).
46. Supreme Court Rule 608(a)(12).
47. Supreme Court Rule 608(a)(13).
48. Supreme Court Rule 608(a)(14).
49. Supreme Court Rule 608(a)(15).

In cases in which a sentence of death is imposed, the record on appeal must contain a transcript of all proceedings regarding the selection of the jury.[51] In other cases, the court reporter must take full stenographic notes of the proceedings regarding the selection of the jury, but the notes need not be transcribed unless a party designates that the proceedings be included in the record on appeal.[52]

The record on appeal must also contain the exhibits offered at trial and sentencing, along with objections, offers of proof, arguments and the applicable rulings.[53] However, physical and demonstrative evidence, other than photographs, which do not fit on a standard-size record page are not to be included in the record on appeal unless ordered by a court upon motion of a party or upon the court's own motion.[54]

The party bringing an appeal must present a record which fully and fairly presents all matters necessary and material to the resolution of the issues presented.[55] Where the defendant is the party bringing the appeal, the responsibility for proper preservation of the record of the proceedings before the trial court rests upon the defendant.[56] Similarly, where the state brings the appeal, such as an appeal from an order dismissing an indictment, the

---

50. Supreme Court Rule 608(a)(8).

See § 30:34.

51. Supreme Court Rule 608(a)(9).

52. Supreme Court Rule 608(a)(9).

53. Supreme Court Rule 608(a)(10).

54. Supreme Court Rule 608(a)(10).

55. People v Bonner, 68 Ill App 3d 424, 25 Ill Dec 95, 386 NE2d 366 (1st Dist 1979).

56. People v Donatelli, 176 Ill App 3d 1086, 126 Ill Dec 436, 531 NE2d 1063 (3d Dist 1988); People v Majer, 131 Ill App 3d 80, 86 Ill Dec 272, 475 NE2d 269 (2d Dist 1985); People v Stevens, 125 Ill App 3d 854, 81 Ill Dec 519, 466 NE2d 1321 (3d Dist 1984); People v Malley, 103 Ill App 3d 534, 59 Ill Dec 207, 431 NE2d 708 (3d Dist 1982); People v Brown, 90 Ill App 3d 742, 46 Ill Dec 591, 414 NE2d 475 (3d Dist 1980); People v Gregorich, 71 Ill App 3d 251, 27 Ill Dec

§ 30:26   ILLINOIS JURISPRUDENCE: CRIMINAL LAW

state has the burden of presenting the record to the appellate court.[57]

> ☛ *Practice Tip:* No reason exists why any defendant should be provided with copies of transcripts before filing an appeal. Supreme court rule clearly contemplates that transcripts will normally be prepared only after defendant files a notice of appeal.[58]

The record on appeal must be of sufficient completeness to permit proper consideration of the specific claims made on appeal.[59] When properly authenticated, the trial record is the sole conclusive and unimpeachable evidence of the proceedings in the trial court.[60] Where the record is incomplete or silent, the reviewing court will apply the presumption that the trial court ruled or acted correctly.[61] The reviewing court will presume any state of facts embraced by the pleadings and not inconsistent with the record which supports the decision appealed from.[62]

> ☛ *Illustration:* There was no colorable need for a complete transcript, and denial of such did not violate defendant's due process where the missing portion of the transcript contained

555, 389 NE2d 619 (5th Dist 1979); People v Spellman, 58 Ill App 3d 648, 16 Ill Dec 259, 374 NE2d 1034 (1st Dist 1978).

57. People v Buffalo Confectionery Co., 63 Ill App 3d 1007, 20 Ill Dec 764, 380 NE2d 973 (1st Dist 1978), withdrawn by publisher, mod, reh den 67 Ill App 3d 112, 24 Ill Dec 495, 385 NE2d 407 (1st Dist), affd in part and revd in part on other grounds, 78 Ill 2d 447, 36 Ill Dec 705, 401 NE2d 546.

58. People v Lemons, 242 Ill App 3d 941, 184 Ill Dec 642, 613 NE2d 1234 (4th Dist 1993).

59. People v Adams, 28 Ill App 3d 717, 329 NE2d 294 (1975).

60. People v Henderson, 36 Ill App 3d 355, 344 NE2d 239 (1st Dist 1976).

61. People v Odumuyiwa, 188 Ill App 3d 40, 135 Ill Dec 909, 544 NE2d 405 (2d Dist 1989); People v Green, 179 Ill App 3d 1, 128 Ill Dec 902, 535 NE2d 413 (1st Dist 1988).

62. People v Bonner, 68 Ill App 3d 424, 25 Ill Dec 95, 386 NE2d 366 (1st Dist 1979).

the testimony of the two complaining witnesses, the parties entered an agreed statement of facts regarding the missing testimony, defendant did not complain that the agreed statement was inadequate nor did he attempt to secure a more detailed record, and it was defendant's duty, as appellant, to preserve the record on appeal.[63]

§ 30:27. —Preserving errors for review

Objections must be recorded to be properly preserved for review.[64] If a party does not properly preserve objections, they may be considered waived.[65] By failing to raise an issue in the trial court, by failing to preserve it in a posttrial motion and by failing to brief the issue in the appellate court, the appellant waives the issue.[66]

The plain error rule is an exception to the waiver rule which is invoked upon a party's failure to conform to a primary rule of appellate procedure.[67] Under the Supreme Court Rules, plain errors or defects affecting substantial rights may be noticed although they were not brought to the attention of the trial court.[68] To avoid the waiver rule, the record must clearly show the

---

63. People v Luke, 253 Ill App 3d 136, 192 Ill Dec 392, 625 NE2d 352 (1st Dist 1993), mod and reh den (Nov 18, 1993).

64. People v Baynes, 88 Ill 2d 225, 58 Ill Dec 819, 430 NE2d 1070 (1981); People v Coles, 74 Ill 2d 393, 24 Ill Dec 553, 385 NE2d 694 (1979).

See ch 29.

Text References: Ruebner, Illinois Criminal Procedure 2d ed §§ 7.19, 7.20.

Periodicals: Seidenfeld, Levenstam, and Gallopoulos, Preserving Error for Appeal in Illinois. 78 Ill BJ 494 (October, 1990).

Practice References: Lane's Goldstein Tr Tech §§ 24:02–24:04 (3d ed).
6 Am Jur Trials 605, Making and Preserving the Record—Objections § 1 et seq.

65. People v Baynes, 88 Ill 2d 225, 58 Ill Dec 819, 430 NE2d 1070 (1981).

66. People v Coles, 74 Ill 2d 393, 24 Ill Dec 553, 385 NE2d 694 (1979).

67. People v Baynes, 88 Ill 2d 225, 58 Ill Dec 819, 430 NE2d 1070 (1981).

68. Supreme Court Rule 615(a).

§ 30:27 ILLINOIS JURISPRUDENCE: CRIMINAL LAW

commission of an error that substantially affected the defendant's rights.[69] The reviewing court may exercise its discretion in taking notice of those errors which deprive the accused of a fair and impartial trial.[70] The court must consider if, even in the absence of objection at trial, the defendant was prejudiced to the extent that he or she was prevented from receiving a fair trial.[71] To determine whether the defendant was prevented from receiving a fair trial, the reviewing court evaluates the evidence to determine if it was sufficiently close so that the alleged error could have affected the outcome of the trial.[72]

> ☞ *Illustration:* Despite the State's contentions that the defendant waived the issue of an illegal arrest when he failed to file a pretrial motion to quash arrest and raised it for the first time on appeal, waiving the issue, the court considered the issue because the court may in a case involving the deprivation of life or liberty take notice of errors appearing upon the record which deprived the accused of substantial means of enjoying a fair and impartial trial, though no exceptions were preserved or the question was improperly presented; thus because the record in the present case contained ample evidence for the appellate court to address

---

69. People v Baynes, 88 Ill 2d 225, 58 Ill Dec 819, 430 NE2d 1070 (1981); People v Jackson, 84 Ill 2d 350, 49 Ill Dec 719, 418 NE2d 739 (1981), on remand 97 Ill App 3d 928, 53 Ill Dec 670, 424 NE2d 83 (3d Dist); People v Foster, 76 Ill 2d 365, 29 Ill Dec 449, 392 NE2d 6 (1979), cert den 469 US 1193, 83 L Ed 2d 975, 105 S Ct 972, (superseded by statute on other grounds as stated in People v Snowden, 147 Ill App 3d 763, 101 Ill Dec 288, 498 NE2d 612 (5th Dist)); People v Coles, 74 Ill 2d 393, 24 Ill Dec 553, 385 NE2d 694 (1979).

70. People v Baynes, 88 Ill 2d 225, 58 Ill Dec 819, 430 NE2d 1070 (1981); People v Pickett, 54 Ill 2d 280, 296 NE2d 856 (1973).

71. People v Baynes, 88 Ill 2d 225, 58 Ill Dec 819, 430 NE2d 1070 (1981); People v Jackson, 84 Ill 2d 350, 49 Ill Dec 719, 418 NE2d 739 (1981), on remand 97 Ill App 3d 928, 53 Ill Dec 670, 424 NE2d 83 (3d Dist).

72. People v Baynes, 88 Ill 2d 225, 58 Ill Dec 819, 430 NE2d 1070 (1981); People v Carlson, 79 Ill 2d 564, 38 Ill Dec 809, 404 NE2d 233 (1980); People v Pickett, 54 Ill 2d 280, 296 NE2d 856 (1973); People v Bradley, 30 Ill 2d 597, 198 NE2d 809 (1964).

the issue of whether the defendant's statements were the product of an illegal arrest, the court considered the issue despite the alleged waiver.[73]

§ 30:28. Affidavits and motions

The report of proceedings,[74] together with the clerk's mandatory record on appeal, constitute the complete record on appeal.[75] That record may not be supplemented by affidavits.[76] Similarly, motions are not part of the record.[77] Motions and affidavits cannot become part of the record merely because the clerk of the court copies them into the record and certifies them.[78]

§ 30:29. Matters improperly included

Just as the reviewing court is not required to and may not pass on questions not presented by the record,[79] matters which are not properly a part of the record may not be considered on appeal even though they are included in the record.[80] Matters which are simply included in or attached to the record without authority of law do not become part of the record and cannot be considered by the reviewing court.[81]

---

73. People v Hill, 272 Ill App 3d 597, 208 Ill Dec 864, 650 NE2d 558 (1st Dist 1995).

74. See § 30:34.

75. People v Husar, 22 Ill App 3d 758, 318 NE2d 24 (1st Dist 1974).

76. People v Husar, 22 Ill App 3d 758, 318 NE2d 24 (1st Dist 1974).

77. People v Connors, 413 Ill 386, 108 NE2d 774 (1952), cert den 344 US 931, 97 L Ed 716, 73 S Ct 502 and cert den 347 US 993, 98 L Ed 1126, 74 S Ct 858; People v Pignatelli, 405 Ill 302, 90 NE2d 761 (1950).

78. People v Barnes, 405 Ill 30, 89 NE2d 791 (1950), cert den 339 US 944, 94 L Ed 1360, 70 S Ct 792.

79. See § 30:27.

80. People v Sheridan, 51 Ill App 3d 963, 10 Ill Dec 34, 367 NE2d 422 (4th Dist 1977), cert den 435 US 975, 56 L Ed 2d 68, 98 S Ct 1622.

81. 4 Am Jur 2, Appeal and Error § 491.

§ 30:30. —Plea

The issue of a defendant's entry of a plea of guilty is a question of constitutional dimension.[82] For a guilty plea to withstand appellate review, the record must affirmatively disclose that the defendant entered the plea understandingly and voluntarily.[83] The record must demonstrate that the defendant's plea was intelligently made.[84]

Where the trial court accepts a guilty plea, the record must show that the defendant was fully informed of the punishment which could be imposed upon a plea of guilty.[85]

A common-law record of a defendant's plea proceeding containing no mention that the defendant either had been advised of, or had waived the right to, counsel at that proceeding would be insufficient, in the absence of an additional record or report of proceedings, to show a valid waiver of counsel.[86]

§ 30:31. —Jury trial

It is the responsibility of the trial judge to secure from the defendant, in open court, an express waiver of the right to trial by jury.[87] Where no waiver appears in the record, a new trial is in order.[88] Lack of an express waiver is ground for reversal,[89] and it

---

82. People v Turner, 111 Ill App 3d 358, 67 Ill Dec 43, 443 NE2d 1167 (2d Dist 1982).

See ch 14.

83. Brady v United States, 397 US 742, 25 L Ed 2d 747, 90 S Ct 1463 (1970).

84. People v Daubman, 190 Ill App 3d 684, 138 Ill Dec 24, 546 NE2d 1079 (5th Dist 1989); People v Akers, 137 Ill App 3d 922, 92 Ill Dec 305, 484 NE2d 1160 (4th Dist 1985).

Text References: Ruebner, Illinois Criminal Procedure 2d ed §§ 7.04, 7.22.

85. People v Mackey, 33 Ill 2d 436, 211 NE2d 706 (1965).

86. People v Nikonowicz, 127 Ill App 3d 738, 83 Ill Dec 18, 469 NE2d 625 (5th Dist 1984).

See § 30:33.

87. People v Clark, 30 Ill 2d 216, 195 NE2d 631 (1964); People v Jones, 93 Ill App 3d 475, 48 Ill Dec 915, 417 NE2d 647 (1st Dist 1981).

APPELLATE REVIEW § 30:31

is not necessary that the issue be raised at trial in order to preserve it.[90]

When an entry in the common-law record indicates that a jury waiver has been made, a defendant seeking review of that question should include in the record on appeal a transcript, or suitable substitute for one, of the corresponding proceeding.[91] A defendant claiming error in the jury waiver must cite the specific error that occurred and substantiate that claim by the presentation of a sufficient record.[92] If the state believes that the jury waiver was made on an occasion other than that suggested in the record, then the state may request that the record be supplemented with the corresponding report.[93]

Review of the validity of the defendant's waiver of the right to a jury trial depends on the existence of an adequate record of the event, if it occurred at all.[94] Given the statutory requirement that a

88. People v Villareal, 114 Ill App 3d 389, 70 Ill Dec 324, 449 NE2d 198 (2d Dist 1983).

89. People v Villareal, 114 Ill App 3d 389, 70 Ill Dec 324, 449 NE2d 198 (2d Dist 1983); People v Rettig, 88 Ill App 3d 888, 44 Ill Dec 7, 410 NE2d 1099 (3d Dist 1980).

90. People v Smith, 10 Ill App 3d 61, 293 NE2d 465 (3d Dist 1973) (superseded by statute on other grounds as stated in People v Shanklin, 26 Ill App 3d 167, 324 NE2d 711 (5th Dist)).

91. People v Smith, 106 Ill 2d 327, 88 Ill Dec 42, 478 NE2d 357 (1985) (superseded by statute on other grounds as stated in People v Tucker, 183 Ill App 3d 333, 131 Ill Dec 890, 539 NE2d 243 (2d Dist)).

Despite the existence of a signed jury waiver, the defendant was entitled to an evidentiary hearing on his post-conviction claim that his constitutional right to a jury trial was violated. People v Dockery, 296 Ill App 3d 271, 230 Ill Dec 630, 694 NE2d 599 (1st Dist 1998).

92. People v Oatis, 47 Ill App 3d 229, 5 Ill Dec 618, 361 NE2d 1146 (4th Dist 1977).

93. People v Smith, 106 Ill 2d 327, 88 Ill Dec 42, 478 NE2d 357 (1985) (superseded by statute on other grounds as stated in People v Tucker, 183 Ill App 3d 333, 131 Ill Dec 890, 539 NE2d 243 (2d Dist)).

See § 30:36.

§ 30:31   ILLINOIS JURISPRUDENCE: CRIMINAL LAW

jury waiver be made in open court,[95] a suitable report of the proceeding in which the waiver is supposed to have occurred will be an essential part of the record in an appeal that raises the question.[96] The necessary report may take the form of:

- a verbatim transcript of the proceeding;
- a proposed report of proceedings; or
- an agreed statement of facts.[97]

The trial judge should take a few moments of trial time to directly elicit from the defendant a response indicating that the defendant understands that he or she is entitled to a jury trial and whether or not the defendant wishes to be tried by a jury or by the court without a jury.[98] From the point of both the prosecution and the defense, as well as in the interest of justice and expeditious judicial administration, it is plain that the parties and the trial judge should take steps to insure that a waiver of a jury trial is incorporated in the report of proceedings.[99] A defendant who

94. People v Chitwood, 67 Ill 2d 443, 10 Ill Dec 565, 367 NE2d 1331 (1977).

95. 725 ILCS 5/103-6.

96. People v Smith, 106 Ill 2d 327, 88 Ill Dec 42, 478 NE2d 357 (1985) (superseded by statute on other grounds as stated in People v Tucker, 183 Ill App 3d 333, 131 Ill Dec 890, 539 NE2d 243 (2d Dist)).

97. People v Smith, 106 Ill 2d 327, 88 Ill Dec 42, 478 NE2d 357 (1985) (superseded by statute on other grounds as stated in People v Tucker, 183 Ill App 3d 333, 131 Ill Dec 890, 539 NE2d 243 (2d Dist)).

See Supreme Court Rule 323(c); Supreme Court Rule 323(d); Supreme Court Rule 612(c).

98. People v Chitwood, 67 Ill 2d 443, 10 Ill Dec 565, 367 NE2d 1331 (1977); People v Bell, 104 Ill App 2d 479, 244 NE2d 321 (1st Dist 1968).

99. People v Chitwood, 67 Ill 2d 443, 10 Ill Dec 565, 367 NE2d 1331 (1977).

Judgment reversed and remanded because defendant did not waive his right to a jury trial in open court when the only purported waiver was a document submitted to the court outside defendant's presence and neither defendant or his attorney was addressed upon the right of a trial by jury or the waiver of that right in defendant's presence. People v Scott, 293 Ill App 3d 241, 227 Ill Dec 669, 687 NE2d 1151 (5th Dist 1997), app gr 177 Ill 2d 582, 232 Ill Dec 456, 698 NE2d 547 and affd 1999 Ill LEXIS 664 (Ill).

waives a court reporter during voir dire will not have an adequate record to challenge jury selection on appeal.[1]

> *Illustration:* Record failed to demonstrate that defendant made a knowing and understanding oral waiver of his right to a jury trial in open court where there was only one occasion where the issue of a jury waiver was discussed in defendant's presence and that was following sentencing when trial court noted the absence of a written jury waiver, inquired as to whether defendant would be willing to sign a waiver and was told by defendant's attorney he had not waived his right.[2]

> *Illustration:* Though the trial court's admonitions regarding defendant's right to a jury trial were somewhat cursory, they were nevertheless sufficient to insure that he understandingly waived the right; the court ascertained that defendant understood he had a constitutional right to a jury trial, that waiver of this right was irrevocable, and that waiving the right would result in a judge deciding the case, and defendant's criminal record consisted of four previous convictions through which he was presumably familiar with this constitutional right and the ramifications attendant to its waiving.[3]

In order to make a claim of a denial of equal protection based on the state's purposeful discrimination in its exercise of peremptory challenges,[4] the trial record must disclose the race of the challenged prospective jurors.[5]

---

1. People v Torres, 198 Ill App 3d 1066, 145 Ill Dec 123, 556 NE2d 741 (1st Dist 1990); People v McCoy, 156 Ill App 3d 194, 108 Ill Dec 871, 509 NE2d 567 (1st Dist 1987).

See § 30:48.

2. People v Eyen, 291 Ill App 3d 38, 225 Ill Dec 249, 683 NE2d 193 (2d Dist 1997).

3. People v Tooles, 177 Ill 2d 462, 227 Ill Dec 125, 687 NE2d 48 (1997).

4. See Batson v Kentucky, 476 US 79, 90 L Ed 2d 69, 106 S Ct 1712 (1986).

§ 30:32. —Presence of accused

The accused has a well-established right to appear and defend in person as well as by counsel.[6] The defendant is entitled to be present and to participate at every stage of the trial.[7] The fact the defendant was present during trial and at the imposition of sentence must be affirmatively shown by the record.[8] The failure of the record to show that the defendant was present is not cured by the presumption that favors judgments of trial courts.[9]

§ 30:33. —Waiver of counsel

The proceeding on a defendant's waiver of counsel[10] are to be taken verbatim.[11] Upon order of the trial court, the report of the proceedings is to be transcribed, filed and made a part of the common-law record.[12] This rule is intended to insure the preparation of a transcript of the proceedings in which counsel was purportedly waived so that, should the accused later contend that his or her purported waiver was ineffective, the record will be sufficient for the appellate court to dispose of that contention on the merits.[13]

---

5. People v Rosa, 206 Ill App 3d 1074, 151 Ill Dec 950, 565 NE2d 221 (1st Dist 1990), cert den 502 US 911, 116 L Ed 2d 251, 112 S Ct 309, habeas corpus granted 1992 US Dist LEXIS 12971 (ND Ill), vacated, remanded 36 F3d 625 (CA7 Ill).

See § 30:48.

6. People v Smith, 6 Ill 2d 414, 129 NE2d 164 (1955); People v Brindley, 369 Ill 486, 17 NE2d 218 (1938).

Text References: Ruebner, Illinois Criminal Procedure 2d ed §§ 5.42, 7.08.

7. People v Smith, 6 Ill 2d 414, 129 NE2d 164 (1955); People v Brindley, 369 Ill 486, 17 NE2d 218 (1938).

8. People v Smith, 6 Ill 2d 414, 129 NE2d 164 (1955).

9. People v Smith, 6 Ill 2d 414, 129 NE2d 164 (1955).

See § 30:26.

10. Supreme Court Rule 401(a).

11. Supreme Court Rule 401(b).

12. Supreme Court Rule 401(b).

§ 30:34. —Trial proceedings

One part of the record on appeal is the report of proceedings.[14] The report of proceedings contains the testimony and exhibits, the rulings of the trial judge and all other proceedings before the trial judge unless the parties designate or stipulate for less.[15] As specifically listed by statute, the report of proceedings is to include:

- opening statements by counsel;
- testimony offered at trial and objections to that testimony;
- offers of proof and the arguments and rulings on those offers;
- instructions offered and given, and the objections and rulings on those instructions;
- communications from the jury during deliberations; and
- responses and supplement instructions to the jury and objections, arguments and rulings thereon.[16]

The report of proceedings must be certified by the reporter or the trial judge and must be filed in the trial court within 49 days after the filing of the notice of appeal.[17] However, if a death sentence was imposed, the report of proceedings must be filed within 49 days from the date of the sentence.[18]

The report of proceedings must be taken as true and correct unless it is shown to be otherwise.[19] It may be corrected in accordance with the rule on amending the record on appeal.[20]

---

13. People v Harpole, 135 Ill App 3d 79, 90 Ill Dec 17, 481 NE2d 817 (5th Dist 1985).

14. See Supreme Court Rule 608.

Text References: Ruebner, Illinois Criminal Procedure 2d ed § 7.09.

15. Supreme Court Rule 608(b).

16. Supreme Court Rule 608(a)(8).

17. Supreme Court Rule 608(b).

18. Supreme Court Rule 608(b).

19. Supreme Court Rule 608(b).

§ 30:34   ILLINOIS JURISPRUDENCE: CRIMINAL LAW

For the purpose of determining what is properly before the reviewing court, there is no distinction between the common law record and the report of proceedings.[21]

§ 30:35. —Sentence

It is well established that a trial court is not required to detail for the record the process it uses in reaching its determination of a proper sentence.[22] However, it is an abuse of discretion for a court to fail to adequately indicate on the record that it considered the proper sentencing criteria.[23]

All information appearing in a presentence report may be relied upon by the sentencing judge to the extent that the judge finds the information probative and reliable.[24] The sentencing judge is not required to specify for the record those portions of the presentence report upon which he or she is relying.[25]

Where the defendant is entitled to be sentenced under one of two sentencing acts, the trial court is not required to explain the differences between the acts prior to the defendant's election.[26] It is the duty of the defendant's attorney to explain the sentencing acts and suggest what appears to be the better choice.[27] However, there is no requirement that the advice regarding sentencing

20. Supreme Court Rule 608(b).

See Supreme Court Rule 329.

21. Supreme Court Rule 608(a).

22. People v La Pointe, 88 Ill 2d 482, 59 Ill Dec 59, 431 NE2d 344 (1981); People v Burba, 134 Ill App 3d 228, 88 Ill Dec 916, 479 NE2d 936 (1st Dist 1985); People v Bergman, 121 Ill App 3d 100, 76 Ill Dec 570, 458 NE2d 1370 (2d Dist 1984).

23. People v Faysom, 131 Ill App 3d 517, 86 Ill Dec 566, 475 NE2d 945 (1st Dist 1985).

24. People v Powell, 199 Ill App 3d 291, 145 Ill Dec 278, 556 NE2d 896 (4th Dist 1990).

25. People v Powell, 199 Ill App 3d 291, 145 Ill Dec 278, 556 NE2d 896 (4th Dist 1990).

26. People v Williams, 90 Ill App 3d 524, 45 Ill Dec 727, 413 NE2d 60 (1st Dist 1980), cert den 452 US 943, 69 L Ed 2d 958, 101 S Ct 3090.

statutes given to the defendant by either the trial court or by defense counsel be specifically detailed and made a part of the record in the trial court.[28] Therefore, in the absence of a claim of ineffective assistance of counsel, the fact the record does not reflect what the defendant was advised is not an error warranting remandment for resentencing.[29]

In all convictions for offenses in violation of the Criminal Code in which the person received any injury to their person or damage to their real or personal property as a result of the criminal act of the defendant, the court shall order restitution as statutorily provided at the sentence hearing.[30]

§ 30:36. —Additional and supplemental material

Within 14 days after the notice of appeal is filed or after a sentence of death is imposed, the appellant and the appellee may file a designation of additional portions of the circuit court record to be included in the record on appeal.[31] The clerk of the circuit court must then include those portions in the record on appeal.[32] Additionally, upon motion of a party, the court may allow photographs of exhibits to be filed as a supplemental record on appeal, in lieu of the exhibits themselves, when those photographs accurately depict the exhibits themselves.[33]

---

27. People v Williams, 90 Ill App 3d 524, 45 Ill Dec 727, 413 NE2d 60 (1st Dist 1980), cert den 452 US 943, 69 L Ed 2d 958, 101 S Ct 3090.

28. People v Edwards, 76 Ill App 3d 228, 32 Ill Dec 52, 394 NE2d 1391 (3d Dist 1979).

29. People v Williams, 90 Ill App 3d 524, 45 Ill Dec 727, 413 NE2d 60 (1st Dist 1980), cert den 452 US 943, 69 L Ed 2d 958, 10i S Ct 3090; People v Crooks, 78 Ill App 3d 711, 34 Ill Dec 105, 397 NE2d 561 (3d Dist 1979).

30. 730 ILCS 5/5-5-6.

The 1995 amendment of 730 ILCS 5/5-5-6 by P.A. 89-203, effective July 21, 1995, in subsection (b) added the second and third sentences regarding restitution to domestic violence shelters.

31. Supreme Court Rule 608(a).

32. Supreme Court Rule 608(a).

33. Supreme Court Rule 608(a).

Where the record is incomplete, the proper course is to provide a bystander's report[34] or an agreed statement of facts.[35] No other method or device is permitted or acceptable.[36]

Attachments to briefs on appeal of material not otherwise before the reviewing court cannot be used to supplement the record.[37] The proper place to present and analyze such material is in the trial court.[38]

§ 30:37. Preparation and certification of record

The clerk of the trial court must prepare, bind, and certify the record on appeal.[39] The record shall be arranged in three sections: the common law record, the report of proceedings, and the trial exhibits.[40] The common law record and report of proceedings shall be in chronological order.[41] All pages of the common law record shall be numbered consecutively with the letter "C" preceding the number of each page,[42] and all pages of the report of proceedings shall be numbered consecutively by volume.[43] However, in lieu of renumbering the pages of exhibits, a list of exhibit numbers shall be provided.[44]

---

34. Supreme Court Rule 323(c).

35. Supreme Court Rule 323(d).

36. People v Turner, 110 Ill App 3d 519, 66 Ill Dec 211, 442 NE2d 637 (1st Dist 1982); People v Bruhn, 51 Ill App 3d 269, 9 Ill Dec 421, 366 NE2d 932 (1st Dist 1977).

37. People v Blanchette, 182 Ill App 3d 396, 131 Ill Dec 49, 538 NE2d 237 (2d Dist 1989); People v Lutz, 103 Ill App 3d 976, 59 Ill Dec 252, 431 NE2d 753 (2d Dist 1982).

38. People v Lutz, 103 Ill App 3d 976, 59 Ill Dec 252, 431 NE2d 753 (2d Dist 1982).

39. Supreme Court Rule 324.

40. See Supreme Court Rule 324.

41. Supreme Court Rule 324.

42. Supreme Court Rule 324.

43. Supreme Court Rule 324.

44. Supreme Court Rule 324.

There is to be only one record on appeal even if more than one appeal is taken.[45]

§ 30:38. Filing of record

The record, and, in a case in which a death sentence is imposed, a duplicate, shall be filed in the reviewing court within 63 days from the date the notice of appeal is filed in the trial court or from the date of the imposition of the sentence of death.[46] If more than one appellant appeals from the same judgment or from different judgments in the same cause to the same reviewing court, the trial court may prescribe the time for filing the record in the reviewing court, which shall not be more than 63 days from the date the last notice of appeal is filed.[47] If the time for filing the report of the proceedings has been extended,[48] the record on appeal must be filed within 14 days after the expiration of the extended time.[49]

Unless received after the due date, the time of filing records, as well as briefs or other papers required to be filed within a specified time, will be the date on which they are actually received by the clerk of the reviewing court.[50] If received after the due date, the time of mailing will be deemed the time of filing.[51] Proof of mailing may be made by filing with the clerk a certificate of the attorney, or affidavit of a person other than the attorney, who deposited the paper in the mail.[52] This certificate or affidavit should state the date and place of mailing and the fact that proper postage was prepaid.[53] Service by mail is complete four days after mailing.[54]

45. Supreme Court Rule 324.

46. Supreme Court Rule 608(c).

47. Supreme Court Rule 608(c).

48. See § 30:39.

49. Supreme Court Rule 608(c).

50. Supreme Court Rule 373.

51. Supreme Court Rule 373.

52. Supreme Court Rule 373.

See Supreme Court Rule 12.

§ 30:39. —Extensions of time

The reviewing court or any judge of the reviewing court may extend the time for filing, in the trial court, the report of proceedings or agreed statement of facts or for serving a proposed report of proceedings.[55] To obtain an extension, a notice of motion and motion must be filed in the reviewing court before the expiration of the original or extended time, or on notice and motion filed within 35 days thereafter.[56] Motions for extensions of time must be supported by an affidavit showing the necessity for the extension.[57] Motions which are made after the expiration of the original or extended time must also be supported by a showing of reasonable excuse for failure to file the motion earlier.[58]

§ 30:40. —Notice of filing

Upon the filing of the record on appeal or the certificate in lieu of record, whichever occurs first, the clerk of the reviewing court shall provide notice of filing to all parties to the appeal.[59]

§ 30:41. Abstract of record

The abstract of the trial record is the pleading of the appellant.[60] It is the means by which the cause of action established in the transcript of record is presented for review.[61] The abstract of record serves as an aid to the appellate court in accurately and precisely dealing with those portions of the record which relate to the questions which all the parties involved desire

---

53. Supreme Court Rule 12.

54. Supreme Court Rule 12.

55. Supreme Court Rule 608(d).

56. Supreme Court Rule 608(d).

57. Supreme Court Rule 608(d).

58. Supreme Court Rule 608(d).

59. Supreme Court Rule 327.

60. People v Jordan, 61 Ill App 3d 117, 18 Ill Dec 487, 377 NE2d 1123 (1st Dist 1978); People v Garner, 91 Ill App 2d 7, 234 NE2d 39 (2d Dist 1968).

61. People v Garner, 91 Ill App 2d 7, 234 NE2d 39 (2d Dist 1968).

the court to consider.[62]

The appellant must prepare a fair abstract[63] which presents the matters contained in the record in a fair manner.[64] An abstract which omits important evidence against the appellant is not a fair abstract.[65]

The abstract must be sufficient to apprise the court of the errors relied upon for reversal without examination of the record itself.[66] The court will not examine the record to reverse judgment where an insufficient abstract is filed.[67] A pragmatic reason for this rule is that reviewing courts are multiple judge courts and only one transcript of the record is filed.[68]

No abstract of the record on appeal is to be filed unless the reviewing court orders that one must be filed.[69] In that event, the appellant must file the abstract with his or her brief.[70]

The abstract must refer to the pages of the record by numerals on the margin.[71] It must be preceded by a table of contents conforming with the requirements established for the appendix to a brief.[72] However, the page references to items included in the abstract must be to abstract pages, and page references to the record pages of omitted items must bear the prefix "R."[73]

---

62. 4 Am Jur 2, Appeal and Error, § 407.

63. People v Thomas, 80 Ill App 2d 88, 225 NE2d 103 (1st Dist 1967).

64. People v Jordan, 61 Ill App 3d 117, 18 Ill Dec 487, 377 NE2d 1123 (1st Dist 1978); People v Thomas, 80 Ill App 2d 88, 225 NE2d 103 (1st Dist 1967).

65. People v Thomas, 80 Ill App 2d 88, 225 NE2d 103 (1st Dist 1967).

66. People v Garner, 91 Ill App 2d 7, 234 NE2d 39 (2d Dist 1968).

67. People v Garner, 91 Ill App 2d 7, 234 NE2d 39 (2d Dist 1968).

68. People v Garner, 91 Ill App 2d 7, 234 NE2d 39 (2d Dist 1968).

69. Supreme Court Rule 342(b).

70. Supreme Court Rule 342(b).

71. Supreme Court Rule 342(b)(1).

72. Supreme Court Rule 342(b)(2).

See Supreme Court Rule 342(a).

§ 30:41   ILLINOIS JURISPRUDENCE: CRIMINAL LAW

If the record contains the evidence, it must be condensed in narrative form so as to present clearly and concisely its substance.[74] Actual quotations may be used in place of a narrative for any portion of the evidence.[75]

Matters in the record on appeal not necessary for a full understanding of the question presented for decision are not to be abstracted.[76] The abstract will be taken as sufficient unless the appellee files an additional abstract with his or her brief.[77]

In cases brought to the supreme court from the appellate court, copies of any abstract filed in the appellate court must be filed in the supreme court without change.[78] Upon request and to the extent practicable, the clerk of the appellate court must provide the appellant with the copies of any abstract filed in that court for transmission to the supreme court as a part of the 20 copies required to be filed with the brief in the supreme court.[79]

Regardless of whether or not an abstract is filed, the entire record on appeal is available to the reviewing court for examination or reference.[80] Omission of any relevant portion of the record from the abstract will not prejudice a party unless the reviewing court finds that there has been no good-faith effort to comply with the rules.[81]

The actual and reasonable cost of producing an abstract required to be filed by the reviewing court, or of an additional abstract proved by affidavit satisfactory to the clerk of the

---

73. Supreme Court Rule 342(b)(2).
74. Supreme Court Rule 342(b)(3).
75. Supreme Court Rule 342(b)(3).
76. Supreme Court Rule 342(b)(4).
77. Supreme Court Rule 342(b)(5).
78. Supreme Court Rule 342(c).
79. Supreme Court Rule 342(c).
80. Supreme Court Rule 342(d).
81. Supreme Court Rule 342(d).

reviewing court, is to be taxed as costs in the case.[82] However, the cost of including unnecessary matter in the abstract or additional abstract may be disallowed as costs.[83]

§ 30:42. Procedure if no transcript available

If no verbatim transcript of the evidence of proceedings is available, the appellant may prepare a proposed report of proceedings from the best available sources.[84] This may include recollection.[85] In any trial court, a party may request from the court official any audiotape, videotape or other recording of the proceedings.[86] he court official or any person who prepared and kept, in accordance with these rules, any audiotape, videotape, or other report of the proceedings must produce a copy of such materials to be provided at the party's expense.[87] Such material may be transcribed for use in preparation of a bystander's report.[88]

The proposed report shall be served on all parties within 28 days after the notice of appeal is filed.[89] Within 14 days after service of the proposed report of proceedings, any other party may serve proposed amendments or an alternative proposed report of proceedings.[90] Within 7 days after that, the appellant must, upon notice, present the proposed report or reports and any proposed amendments to the trial court for settlement and approval.[91]

82. Supreme Court Rule 342(e).
83. Supreme Court Rule 342(e).
84. Supreme Court Rule 323(c).
85. Supreme Court Rule 323(c).
86. Supreme Court Rule 323(c).
87. Supreme Court Rule 323(c).
88. Supreme Court Rule 323(c).
89. Supreme Court Rule 323(c).
90. Supreme Court Rule 323(c).
91. Supreme Court Rule 323(c).

After holding any necessary hearings, the court must promptly settle, certify, and order filed an accurate report of proceedings.[92] In the absence of a stipulation by the parties, only this certified report of proceedings will be included in the record on appeal.[93]

By written stipulation, the parties may agree upon a statement of facts material to the controversy.[94] The agreed statement of facts may be filed without certificate in place of and within the time for filing a report of proceedings.[95]

§ 30:43. Transmission of record or certificate in lieu of record

Upon payment of the estimated prescribed fee, and estimated transportation costs, the clerk of the trial court must transmit the record to the reviewing court or, upon request, deliver it to the appellant for transmission.[96] If the defendant is represented by court-appointed counsel, no fees need to be paid to the clerk of the court.[97]

To facilitate work on the appeal, the clerk of the trial court must, at the request of any party, deliver to the appellant a certificate that the record has been prepared and certified in the form required for transmission to the reviewing court.[98] The timely filing of the certificate in the reviewing court will be considered the filing of the record on appeal.[99] The certificate in lieu of record is to follow the form set out in the rule.[1]

---

92. Supreme Court Rule 323(c).
93. Supreme Court Rule 323(c).
94. Supreme Court Rule 323(d).
95. Supreme Court Rule 323(c).
96. Supreme Court Rule 325.
97. Supreme Court Rule 612(e).
98. Supreme Court Rule 325.
99. Supreme Court Rule 325.
1. Supreme Court Rule 325.

§ 30:44. Amendment

The record on appeal is to be taken as true and correct unless it is shown to be otherwise.[2] If the record is shown to be other than true and correct, it may be corrected in accordance with the applicable rule of the supreme court.[3] Material omissions or inaccuracies or improper authentication may be corrected by stipulation of the parties or by the trial court.[4] The correction by stipulation may be entered into either before or after the record is transmitted to the reviewing court.[5] The reviewing court or a judge of that court may also correct material omissions or inaccuracies or improper authentication.[6]

Any controversy as to whether the record accurately discloses what occurred in the trial court must be submitted to, and settled by, that court and the record made to conform to the truth.[7] If the record is insufficient to fully and fairly present the questions involved, the requisite portions may be supplied at the cost of the appellant.[8] If necessary, a supplemental record may be certified and transmitted.[9]

§ 30:45. Return

After the reviewing court has made its final decision, the record on appeal must be returned by the clerk of the reviewing court to the clerk of the trial court.[10]

---

2. Supreme Court Rule 329.
3. See Supreme Court Rule 329.
4. Supreme Court Rule 329.
5. Supreme Court Rule 329.
6. Supreme Court Rule 329.
7. Supreme Court Rule 329.
8. Supreme Court Rule 329.
9. Supreme Court Rule 329.
   See § 30:36.
10. Supreme Court Rule 331.

§ 30:46. Conclusiveness and effect of record

The reviewing court is bound by the record on appeal in a criminal case.[11] The record of the trial court imports veracity, and it is the unimpeachable evidence of the proceedings there.[12] The record is presumed to be correct unless it is contradicted by other facts in the record.[13]

The purpose of a review on appeal is to evaluate the record of the trial court proceeding, and the review will generally be limited to what appears in the record.[14] When the appellant is responsible for the incompleteness of the record in the appellate court, the reviewing court will indulge in every reasonable presumption favorable to the conclusion reached by the trial court.[15] Any doubt arising from an incomplete record will be resolved against the appellant.[16]

§ 30:47. Issues and matters not apparent—Generally

A court of review must determine the issues before it solely on the basis of the record made in the trial court.[17] The reviewing court evaluates the record, as it is, for error.[18] Where the record is insufficient or does not demonstrate the alleged error, the

---

11. People v Martin, 35 Ill 2d 289, 220 NE2d 170 (1966).

12. People v Gates, 29 Ill 2d 586, 195 NE2d 161 (1963), cert den 377 US 934, 12 L Ed 2d 298, 84 S Ct 1338; People v Henderson, 36 Ill App 3d 355, 344 NE2d 239 (1st Dist 1976).

13. People v Kelly, 25 Ill App 3d 64, 322 NE2d 545 (1975); People v Lyons, 19 Ill App 3d 294, 311 NE2d 370 (2d Dist 1974); People v Irvin, 6 Ill App 3d 550, 286 NE2d 105 (2d Dist 1972).

14. People v Wilson, 92 Ill App 3d 370, 48 Ill Dec 31, 415 NE2d 1315 (1st Dist 1981).

15. People v Blake, 130 Ill App 3d 948, 85 Ill Dec 932, 474 NE2d 892 (2d Dist 1985); People v Wilson, 92 Ill App 3d 370, 48 Ill Dec 31, 415 NE2d 1315 (1st Dist 1981).

16. People v Blake, 130 Ill App 3d 948, 85 Ill Dec 932, 474 NE2d 892 (2d Dist 1985); People v Hefley, 109 Ill App 3d 74, 64 Ill Dec 621, 440 NE2d 173 (5th Dist 1982); People v Wilson, 92 Ill App 3d 370, 48 Ill Dec 31, 415 NE2d 1315 (1st Dist 1981).

APPELLATE REVIEW § 30:47

reviewing court must refrain from supposition and decide accordingly.[19]

Only evidence which appears in the trial record will be considered on appeal.[20] Regardless of the degree to which matters may be of "common knowledge," those matters cannot be relied upon by the appellate court if they are not part of the record.[21] The appellate court cannot speculate on facts which do not appear in the record.[22] Evidence that is not made part of the record will not be considered by the reviewing court and portions of the brief which relate to newly raised evidence may be stricken.[23] Neither statements in the appellant's brief nor assertions in a posttrial motion can substitute for a proper report of proceedings.[24]

If the record of an appeal is incomplete, the reviewing court will indulge in every reasonable presumption favorable to the judgment, order or ruling appealed from, including that the trial court ruled or acted correctly.[25] Any doubt arising from any

17. People v Reimolds, 92 Ill 2d 101, 65 Ill Dec 17, 440 NE2d 872 (1982); People v Jackson, 28 Ill 2d 37, 190 NE2d 823 (1963); People v Miller, 27 Ill App 3d 788, 327 NE2d 253 (4th Dist 1975).

18. People v Edwards, 74 Ill 2d 1, 23 Ill Dec 73, 383 NE2d 944 (1978), cert den 442 US 931, 61 L Ed 2d 299, 99 S Ct 2862.

19. People v Edwards, 74 Ill 2d 1, 23 Ill Dec 73, 383 NE2d 944 (1978), cert den 442 US 931, 61 L Ed 2d 299, 99 S Ct 2862.

20. People v Gacho, 122 Ill 2d 221, 119 Ill Dec 287, 522 NE2d 1146 (1988), cert den 488 US 910, 102 L Ed 2d 252, 109 S Ct 264.

21. People v Brannon, 45 Ill App 3d 616, 4 Ill Dec 338, 360 NE2d 85 (5th Dist 1976).

22. People v Colon, 20 Ill App 3d 858, 314 NE2d 664 (1st Dist 1974).

23. People v Phillips, 159 Ill App 3d 483, 110 Ill Dec 873, 511 NE2d 1193 (3d Dist 1987); People v Gossage, 80 Ill App 3d 36, 35 Ill Dec 500, 399 NE2d 334 (3d Dist 1980).

24. People v Turner, 110 Ill App 3d 519, 66 Ill Dec 211, 442 NE2d 637 (1st Dist 1982).

25. People v Turner, 110 Ill App 3d 519, 66 Ill Dec 211, 442 NE2d 637 (1st Dist 1982); People v Benford, 31 Ill App 3d 892, 335 NE2d 106 (1st Dist 1975).

§ 30:47   ILLINOIS JURISPRUDENCE: CRIMINAL LAW

incompleteness of the record will be resolved against the appellant.[26]

§ 30:48. —Jury selection

Appeals involving the propriety of voir dire are factual in nature.[27] Therefore, it is impossible to review issues involving jury selection without an adequate record.[28] The responsibility for preserving this record rests on the appellant.[29] Where a record of the voir dire has not been preserved, the reviewing court cannot assume merely on the representations of the defendant that the trial court's voir dire examination failed to adequately inquire as to the possible prejudices the prospective jurors might have had against the defendant's theory of defense.[30] If the defendant fails to preserve the record of the voir dire examination, the reviewing court will not consider the accused's contention that the prospective jurors should have been excused for cause.[31]

By waiving a court reporter during voir dire, the defendant will fail to preserve the record necessary to challenge jury selection on appeal.[32] Therefore, a stipulation by the parties that the voir dire examination not be recorded would generally preclude any

26. People v Turner, 110 Ill App 3d 519, 66 Ill Dec 211, 442 NE2d 637 (1st Dist 1982); People v Benford, 31 Ill App 3d 892, 335 NE2d 106 (1st Dist 1975).

27. People v Torres, 198 Ill App 3d 1066, 145 Ill Dec 123, 556 NE2d 741 (1st Dist 1990).

28. People v Torres, 198 Ill App 3d 1066, 145 Ill Dec 123, 556 NE2d 741 (1st Dist 1990).

29. People v Edwards, 74 Ill 2d 1, 23 Ill Dec 73, 383 NE2d 944 (1978), cert den 442 US 931, 61 L Ed 2d 299, 99 S Ct 2862; People v Torres, 198 Ill App 3d 1066, 145 Ill Dec 123, 556 NE2d 741 (1st Dist 1990).

30. People v Robinson, 102 Ill App 3d 884, 58 Ill Dec 23, 429 NE2d 1356 (1st Dist 1981).

31. People v McCoy, 156 Ill App 3d 194, 108 Ill Dec 871, 509 NE2d 567 (1st Dist 1987); People v Johnson, 43 Ill App 3d 649, 2 Ill Dec 174, 357 NE2d 151 (1st Dist 1976).

32. People v Torres, 198 Ill App 3d 1066, 145 Ill Dec 123, 556 NE2d 741 (1st Dist 1990).

APPELLATE REVIEW § 30:48

subsequent raising of voir dire issues on appeal.[33]

The propriety of the trial court's refusal to ask a proposed voir dire question will not be considered by the appellate court where the question was not made part of the record.[34] The failure to include the precise question requested would require that appellate court to guess or conjecture as to both the phraseology and the content of the question.[35]

Where the defendant argues on appeal that the prosecution acted in a purposefully discriminatory manner in excluding prospective jurors on the basis of race,[36] the defendant should have properly preserved a record showing that prospective jurors were being excluded from the jury for no apparent reason other than race.[37] Without a record of the race of the excluded jurors and a record of the race of the rest of the venire, the defendant will have failed to make a prima facie case of purposeful discrimination,[38] and the issue may be deemed by the appellate court to have been waived.[39] However, because the right to an unbiased jury is so intimately related to justice and the integrity of the judicial system, the failure of the defendant to preserve all relevant details for review might not necessarily result in a waiver of the issue of purposeful discrimination in jury selection.[40]

33. People v Jenkins, 88 Ill App 3d 719, 44 Ill Dec 53, 410 NE2d 1145 (1st Dist 1980).

34. People v Chamness, 129 Ill App 3d 871, 85 Ill Dec 108, 473 NE2d 476 (1st Dist 1984); People v Aldaco, 107 Ill App 3d 672, 63 Ill Dec 256, 437 NE2d 905 (1st Dist 1982).

35. People v Chamness, 129 Ill App 3d 871, 85 Ill Dec 108, 473 NE2d 476 (1st Dist 1984); People v Aldaco, 107 Ill App 3d 672, 63 Ill Dec 256, 437 NE2d 905 (1st Dist 1982).

36. See Batson v Kentucky, 476 US 79, 90 L Ed 2d 69, 106 S Ct 1712 (1986).

37. People v Mitchell, 163 Ill App 3d 58, 114 Ill Dec 345, 516 NE2d 500 (1st Dist 1987).

38. See People v Brown, 152 Ill App 3d 996, 106 Ill Dec 91, 505 NE2d 397 (4th Dist 1987).

39. People v Mitchell, 163 Ill App 3d 58, 114 Ill Dec 345, 516 NE2d 500 (1st Dist 1987).

§ 30:48   ILLINOIS JURISPRUDENCE: CRIMINAL LAW

☞ *Illustration:* In a habeas corpus proceeding reviewing a claim of racial discrimination in jury selection where a magistrate conducted the Batson hearing more than eight years subsequent to the voir dire proceeding, and neither the magistrate nor the district court judge who reviewed the magistrate's decision were present at the voir dire, the appellate court conducted a de novo review of the record.[41]

§ 30:49. —Conduct of counsel

Arguments relating to the misconduct of counsel will not be considered on review where the matter was not included in the record and where no objection was made at trial.[42] The alleged misconduct of opposing counsel must be apparent in the record.[43] Where the error alleged on appeal is based on the misconduct of counsel such as an improper approach to the jury, exhibiting items not in evidence to the jury, or an assertedly improper argument to the jury, the record must show that the conduct complained of occurred.[44]

Conjectural or speculative conflicts of interest between an attorney and client raised for the first time on appeal will not justify the reversal of a criminal conviction.[45] The existence of a possibility of prejudice from joint representation at the time counsel was appointed must be shown in the record.[46]

The appellate court cannot speculate about the possible harm done to the appellant or hypothesize about the context in which

---

40. See People v Batchelor, 202 Ill App 3d 316, 147 Ill Dec 608, 559 NE2d 948 (1st Dist 1990).

41. Holder v Welborn, 60 F3d 383 (CA7 Ill 1995).

42. People v Sanders, 168 Ill App 3d 295, 119 Ill Dec 53, 522 NE2d 715 (1st Dist 1988), app den 122 Ill 2d 589, 125 Ill Dec 231, 530 NE2d 259.

43. People v Parson, 33 Ill App 3d 827, 341 NE2d 744 (5th Dist 1975).

44. 2 Am Jur 2, Appeal and Error, § 541.

45. People v Husar, 22 Ill App 3d 758, 318 NE2d 24 (1st Dist 1974).

46. People v Husar, 22 Ill App 3d 758, 318 NE2d 24 (1st Dist 1974).

allegedly prejudicial remarks were made if the record is not complete.[47] The appellate court cannot consider whether the prosecution's final argument was improper if the final arguments do not appear in the record.[48]

§ 30:50. —Evidence and evidentiary rulings

A trial court's determination of the relevancy of evidence is given great deference on review and it will be reversed on appeal only when an abuse of discretion is found to have resulted in prejudice to the defendant.[49] Therefore, the record must sufficiently reflect those factors which caused the ruling so that, upon review, the appellate court can discern whether or not there was an abuse of discretion resulting in prejudice to the defendant.[50]

Where a party fails to bring the entire report of proceedings to the reviewing court it will be presumed that the trial court heard sufficient evidence to support its judgment.[51] The reviewing court cannot consider a question concerning the sufficiency of the evidence in the absence of a complete record.[52] The appellate court will not consider a mere general assertion that incompetent evidence was admitted where the testimony complained of is not specified.[53]

47. People v Edwards, 74 Ill 2d 1, 23 Ill Dec 73, 383 NE2d 944 (1978), cert den 442 US 931, 61 L Ed 2d 299, 99 S Ct 2862.

48. People v Stombaugh, 132 Ill App 2d 859, 271 NE2d 69 (2d Dist 1971), revd 52 Ill 2d 130, 284 NE2d 640; People v Brown, 89 Ill App 2d 231, 231 NE2d 262 (2d Dist 1967).

49. People v Gardner, 47 Ill App 3d 529, 5 Ill Dec 701, 362 NE2d 14 (5th Dist 1977).

50. People v Gardner, 47 Ill App 3d 529, 5 Ill Dec 701, 362 NE2d 14 (5th Dist 1977); People v Therriault, 42 Ill App 3d 876, 1 Ill Dec 717, 356 NE2d 999 (1st Dist 1976).

51. People v Glass, 41 Ill App 3d 43, 353 NE2d 214 (1st Dist 1976).

52. People v Johnson, 15 Ill 2d 244, 154 NE2d 274 (1958), cert den 359 US 930, 3 L Ed 2d 632, 79 S Ct 614; People v Glass, 41 Ill App 3d 43, 353 NE2d 214 (1st Dist 1976).

§ 30:51. —Jury instructions

In order to raise on appeal the trial court's refusal of jury instructions, an appellant must present a record containing the instructions offered and given.[54] The appellant cannot allege error in the giving, refusal or modification of instructions, unless the record contains all the instructions which were given and tendered and indicates who offered the instruction argued to have been improperly given.[55]

Supreme Court Rule 608[56] provides that the instructions offered and given are to be included in the record on appeal.[57] The record should reflect which of the given instructions were submitted by the defendant and which were submitted by the prosecution.[58] The record should also reflect any objections to the instructions that were raised at trial.[59] The appellant's failure to provide a record containing the instructions tendered will result in a waiver of any issue regarding the trial court's refusal to give those instructions.[60]

§ 30:52. —Sentence

The imposition of sentence is a matter of judicial discretion and, unless there is a showing in the record of substantial and justifiable reason for doing so, the appellate court will not disturb

---

53. People v Brendeland, 10 Ill 2d 469, 140 NE2d 708 (1957).

54. People v Daily, 41 Ill 2d 116, 242 NE2d 170 (1968), cert den 395 US 966, 23 L Ed 2d 752, 89 S Ct 2112; People v Mack, 107 Ill App 3d 164, 62 Ill Dec 869, 437 NE2d 396 (4th Dist 1982).

55. People v Denniss, 19 Ill App 2d 579, 154 NE2d 801 (1959).

56. Supreme Court Rule 608.

57. Supreme Court Rule 608(a)(8).

See § 30:34.

58. People v Davis, 27 Ill 2d 33, 188 NE2d 43 (1963).

59. People v Lenker, 6 Ill App 3d 335, 285 NE2d 807 (1st Dist 1972).

60. People v Bell, 53 Ill 2d 122, 290 NE2d 214 (1972); People v Leonard, 171 Ill App 3d 380, 122 Ill Dec 138, 526 NE2d 397 (2d Dist 1988), cert den 490 US 1008, 104 L Ed 2d 162, 109 S Ct 1647; People v Owens, 151 Ill App 3d 1043, 105 Ill Dec 317, 504 NE2d 186 (3d Dist 1987).

the sentence of the trial court.[61] To modify a sentence which is within the statutory limits, it must appear to the appellate court that the sentence imposed is a clear departure from the spirit and purpose of the fundamental law and the requirement of the constitution that the sentence be proportionate to the nature of the offense and measure possibilities for rehabilitation.[62]

The propriety of the trial court's judgment must be based on the record before the appellate court.[63] The appellant in a criminal case is responsible for providing a complete appellate record for review.[64] The report of proceedings of the sentencing hearing is necessary for a review of the trial court's sentencing decision.[65] In the absence of the report of proceedings, the reviewing court will indulge every reasonable presumption favorable to the conclusion reached by the trial court.[66] An appellant who challenges his or her sentence but who fails to provide the relevant report of proceedings is not entitled to relief.[67]

> ☞ *Illustration:* A sentence cannot be affirmed if the reviewing court is unable to ascertain from the record the

---

61. People v Lewton, 2 Ill App 3d 882, 277 NE2d 781 (4th Dist 1972).

62. People v Plantinga, 132 Ill App 3d 512, 87 Ill Dec 771, 477 NE2d 1299 (1st Dist 1985); People v Henderson, 45 Ill App 3d 798, 4 Ill Dec 76, 359 NE2d 909 (5th Dist 1977), cert den 446 US 986, 64 L Ed 2d 844, 100 S Ct 2971; People v Grau, 29 Ill App 3d 327, 330 NE2d 530 (5th Dist 1975); People v Smith, 28 Ill App 3d 908, 329 NE2d 896 (5th Dist 1975).

63. People v Nelson, 41 Ill 2d 364, 243 NE2d 225 (1968); People v Lewton, 2 Ill App 3d 882, 277 NE2d 781 (4th Dist 1972).

64. People v Blake, 130 Ill App 3d 948, 85 Ill Dec 932, 474 NE2d 892 (2d Dist 1985); People v Hefley, 109 Ill App 3d 74, 64 Ill Dec 621, 440 NE2d 173 (5th Dist 1982).

65. People v Blake, 130 Ill App 3d 948, 85 Ill Dec 932, 474 NE2d 892 (2d Dist 1985).

66. People v Blake, 130 Ill App 3d 948, 85 Ill Dec 932, 474 NE2d 892 (2d Dist 1985).

67. People v Blake, 130 Ill App 3d 948, 85 Ill Dec 932, 474 NE2d 892 (2d Dist 1985); People v Holman, 43 Ill App 3d 56, 1 Ill Dec 833, 356 NE2d 1115 (2d Dist 1976).

§ 30:52   ILLINOIS JURISPRUDENCE: CRIMINAL LAW

weight given an improper factor in passing sentence.[68]

A sentence appealed from is presumed to be proper.[69] Only where this presumption has been rebutted by an affirmative showing of error will a reviewing court find a sentencing decision to be an abuse of discretion.[70] Because the appellate court's power to reduce a sentence should be exercised with considerable caution and only in those cases where the penalty constitutes a substantial departure from the spirit and purposes of fundamental law,[71] the burden is on the defendant to provide an adequate record to preserve the contention in the reviewing court that the penalty was excessive.[72]

While similarly situated defendants should not receive grossly disparate sentences,[73] a defendant who contends that fundamental fairness requires reduction of a disparate sentence has the burden to produce a record from which a rational comparison between the two sentences can be made.[74]

In order for a defendant to argue that his or her sentence was substantially disparate with the sentences received by the codefendants, the defendant must produce records of the codefendants' circumstances upon which a rational comparison

68. People v Jordan, 247 Ill App 3d 75, 186 Ill Dec 633, 616 NE2d 1265 (1st Dist 1993).

69. People v Plantinga, 132 Ill App 3d 512, 87 Ill Dec 771, 477 NE2d 1299 (1st Dist 1985); People v Spinks, 80 Ill App 3d 1096, 36 Ill Dec 214, 400 NE2d 634 (3d Dist 1980); People v Choate, 71 Ill App 3d 267, 27 Ill Dec 606, 389 NE2d 670 (5th Dist 1979).

70. People v Plantinga, 132 Ill App 3d 512, 87 Ill Dec 771, 477 NE2d 1299 (1st Dist 1985); People v Spinks, 80 Ill App 3d 1096, 36 Ill Dec 214, 400 NE2d 634 (3d Dist 1980); People v Choate, 71 Ill App 3d 267, 27 Ill Dec 606, 389 NE2d 670 (5th Dist 1979).

71. People v Caldwell, 39 Ill 2d 346, 236 NE2d 706, 37 ALR3d 226 (1968).

72. People v Winters, 1 Ill App 3d 533, 275 NE2d 220 (1st Dist 1971).

73. People v Jaffe, 64 Ill App 3d 831, 21 Ill Dec 571, 381 NE2d 1018 (2d Dist 1978).

74. People v Jaffe, 64 Ill App 3d 831, 21 Ill Dec 571, 381 NE2d 1018 (2d Dist 1978); People v Hansen, 132 Ill App 2d 911, 270 NE2d 137 (2d Dist 1971).

can be made.[75] The appellate court will not merely take judicial notice of the record on appeal and briefs filed in a codefendant's separate appeal.[76]

The burden of presenting mitigating circumstances in a record falls on the defendant.[77] Where evidence is offered in mitigation, the sentencing judge will be presumed to have considered that evidence unless there is some statement in the record, aside from the sentence imposed, that would tend to indicate otherwise.[78]

A trial judge is not required to state every factor he or she considered in determining a defendant's sentence.[79] Although the requirement of an explanation or designation by the sentencing court of certain reasons necessary for imposition of the death penalty has been noted with approval in decisions upholding the validity of death penalty statutes,[80] the Illinois Supreme Court has consistently held that a statement of findings is not constitutionally required.[81] The trial judge's failure to state whether he or

---

75. People v Kline, 92 Ill 2d 490, 65 Ill Dec 843, 442 NE2d 154 (1982), habeas corpus proceeding, summary judgment gr 707 F Supp 368 (ND Ill); People v Wooton, 198 Ill App 3d 591, 144 Ill Dec 695, 555 NE2d 1214 (3d Dist 1990); People v Treece, 159 Ill App 3d 397, 111 Ill Dec 66, 511 NE2d 1361 (3d Dist 1987).

76. People v Treece, 159 Ill App 3d 397, 111 Ill Dec 66, 511 NE2d 1361 (3d Dist 1987).

77. People v Nelson, 41 Ill 2d 364, 243 NE2d 225 (1968).

78. People v Plantinga, 132 Ill App 3d 512, 87 Ill Dec 771, 477 NE2d 1299 (1st Dist 1985); People v Goodman, 116 Ill App 3d 125, 71 Ill Dec 639, 451 NE2d 607 (2d Dist 1983).

79. People v Plantinga, 132 Ill App 3d 512, 87 Ill Dec 771, 477 NE2d 1299 (1st Dist 1985); People v Gornick, 107 Ill App 3d 505, 63 Ill Dec 243, 437 NE2d 892 (1st Dist 1982).

80. See Gregg v Georgia, 428 US 153, 49 L Ed 2d 859, 96 S Ct 2909 (1976).

81. People v Stewart, 104 Ill 2d 463, 85 Ill Dec 422, 473 NE2d 1227 (1984), cert den 471 US 1120, 86 L Ed 2d 267, 105 S Ct 2368, cert den 488 US 900, 102 L Ed 2d 234, 109 S Ct 246, cert den 502 US 853, 116 L Ed 2d 126, 112 S Ct 162, habeas corpus den 1993 US Dist LEXIS 7962 (ND Ill), affd 60 F3d 296 (CA7 Ill), mod, reh den 70 F3d 955 (CA7 Ill), cert den 518 US 1033, 135 L Ed 2d 1095, 116 S Ct 2580; People v Kubat, 94 Ill 2d 437, 69 Ill Dec 30, 447 NE2d 247

she found the defendant's criminal record to be significant or insignificant is not an impediment to appellate review of the sentence.[82]

When one sentence is vacated, the appellate court is normally required to examine the transcripts of the sentencing hearing to determine if the trial court was influenced by the vacated conviction in imposing the other sentence.[83]

VI. MOTIONS, BRIEFS, ARGUMENT AND REHEARING

Research References:
  Annotation References:
    Index and Annotations: Appeal and Error
    ALR Digest to 3d, 4th, 5th, and Federal: Appeal and Error §§ 105–117, 236, 237, 678–701, 1011–1020

  Practice References:
    5 Am Jur 2d, Appeal and Error §§ 678–701

  State Legislation:
    Supreme Court Rule 341, 345, 352, 361, 367, 372, 610—612; Uniform Administrative and Procedural Rules, Rule 8

  Miscellaneous References:
    West's Illinois Digest 2d, Appeal and Error §§ 337–368, 755–774, 824

§ 30:53. Motions

The criminal appeals rules specify that the Civil Appeals Rules should be followed in matters regarding motions.[84] Under those

---

(1983), cert den 464 US 865, 78 L Ed 2d 174, 104 S Ct 199, cert den 481 US 1007, 95 L Ed 2d 207, 107 S Ct 1634, later proceeding 690 F Supp 725 (ND Ill) and affd 867 F2d 351 (CA7 Ill), cert den 493 US 874, 107 L Ed 2d 159, 110 S Ct 206; People v Brownell, 79 Ill 2d 508, 38 Ill Dec 757, 404 NE2d 181 (1980), appeal after remand 123 Ill App 3d 307, 78 Ill Dec 817, 462 NE2d 936 (2d Dist) and cert dismd 449 US 811, 66 L Ed 2d 14, 101 S Ct 59.

82. People v King, 109 Ill 2d 514, 94 Ill Dec 702, 488 NE2d 949 (1986), cert den 479 US 872, 93 L Ed 2d 173, 107 S Ct 249.

83. People v Blake, 130 Ill App 3d 948, 85 Ill Dec 932, 474 NE2d 892 (2d Dist 1985).

APPELLATE REVIEW § 30:53

rules, to apply for relief, in all cases a motion must be filed to apply for relief, unless the rules specify otherwise.[85] The motion must be in written form and must specify the relief sought and the grounds therefor.[86] If the record has not been filed the movant shall file with the motion an appropriate supporting record.[87] When the motion is based on facts that do not appear of record, it shall be supported by affidavit.[88] Argument not contained in the motion may be made in a supporting memorandum.[89]

☛ *Caution:* The filing of the notice of appeal does not begin the process of transcribing and preparing the record and each clerk's office has a different procedure. Consequently, it is advisable to inquire of the clerk of the appropriate court what the procedures for that court are. In general, a letter requesting the court reporter transcribe the record is required. Once transcribed, the record must be accumulated. To set the wheels in motion for accumulation, another letter may be required, or an oral request may be sufficient, depending on the court's procedures.

☛ *Caution:* Check the record carefully to determine if all essential documents have been included. If something is

---

84. Supreme Court Rule 610, Supreme Court Rule 361.

85. Supreme Court Rule 361(a).

86. Supreme Court Rule 361(a).

87. Supreme Court Rule 361(a).

See Supreme Court Rule 328.

The Supreme Court Rules were amended in 1993 by the addition of rule 328 which sets out the requirements to be used for a supporting record. Any party seeking relief from the reviewing court before the record on appeal is filed must file with his or her application an appropriate supporting record containing enough of the trial court record to show an appealable order or judgment, a timely filed and served notice of appeal (if required for appellate jurisdiction) and any other matter necessary to the application made.

88. Supreme Court Rule 361(a).

89. Supreme Court Rule 361(a).

§ 30:53 ILLINOIS JURISPRUDENCE: CRIMINAL LAW

missing, follow the procedures for supplementing the record.

The motion must be filed on the opposing party and filed with either the appellate court or the Supreme Court, if it is in session.[90] The rules specify the procedure to be followed for filing with the Supreme Court when it is not in session.[91] Whether the motion is filed in the appellate court or the Supreme Court, the motion must be filed with the clerk of that court and must be accompanied by proof of service.[92] Only in the case of necessity will filing and service be excused.[93]

Responses to a motion must be in writing and be filed, with proof of service, within 5 days after personal service of the motion, or 10 days after mailing of the motion if service is by mail, or within such further time as the court or a judge thereof may allow.[94] Except by order of court, replies to responses will not be allowed and oral arguments on motions will not be heard.[95]

In an effort to promote prompt disposition of criminal cases, motions for extensions of time must be supported by an affidavit of counsel or the party showing:[96]

- how many extensions have been granted previously;[97]
- the grounds for each of those extensions;[98]
- the grounds for the present request;[99]

---

90. Supreme Court Rule 361(b).
91. Supreme Court Rule 361(c).
92. Supreme Court Rule 361(b)(1).
93. Supreme Court Rule 361(b)(1).
94. Supreme Court Rule 361(b)(2).
95. Supreme Court Rule 361(b)(2).
96. Supreme Court Rule 361(f).
97. Supreme Court Rule 361(f).
98. Supreme Court Rule 361(f).
99. Supreme Court Rule 610(3).

- the date on which counsel was engaged or appointed to prosecute the appeal;[1] and
- the date on which the complete record was filed in the reviewing court.[2]

The clerk is authorized to make corrections in any document of a party to any pending case upon receipt of written request from that party together with proof that a copy of the request has been transmitted to all other parties.[3]

§ 30:54. Briefs—Generally

Briefs for criminal appeals are governed by the Civil Appeals Rules.[4] Under those rules, the appellant's and the appellee's briefs each are limited to 50 printed pages or 75 unprinted pages, excluding appendices, except for the appellant's reply brief which is limited to 20 printed pages or 27 unprinted pages.[5]

> ☞ *Practice Guide:* The court will not accept any device, such as narrowing of margins, used in an attempt to sidestep the page requirements.[6]

In either brief, footnotes should only be used sparingly.[7]

While not favored, a motion may be filed at least 10 days before the brief is due or 5 days before the reply brief is due to request a page extension.[8] The motion must specify the maximum number of pages needed and be accompanied by an affidavit explaining the necessity of those additional pages.[9]

---

1. Supreme Court Rule 610(1).
2. Supreme Court Rule 610(2).
3. Supreme Court Rule 361(e).
4. Supreme Court Rule 612.
5. Supreme Court Rule 341(a).
6. Supreme Court Rule 341(a).
7. Supreme Court Rule 341(a).
8. Supreme Court Rule 341(a).
9. Supreme Court Rule 341(a).

§ 30:54   ILLINOIS JURISPRUDENCE: CRIMINAL LAW

The cover of the brief must contain:

- which trial court heard the case;
- the name of the case at the trial level, indicating which party is appealing;
- the number the case was given on appeal;
- the name of the reviewing court;
- the name of the trial judge; and
- the names and addresses of the attorneys or the defendant, if he or she has no attorney.[10]

In the text of the brief, the parties must be referred to as they were at the trial level and not as appellant or appellee.[11] The citation format is also specified.[12] The official cite for Illinois cases must be given, listing the first page of the case and the page on which the support appears.[13]

§ 30:55. —Form and contents

The required structure for the appellant's brief is outlined in detail in the rules, with illustrations.[14] Basically, the brief must include:

- a summary statement of the argument presented with authorities cited;
- a description of the nature of the action and whether there is any question on the pleadings;
- the issues presented, without authorities;
- a statement of jurisdiction;
- pertinent statutory or constitutional provisions;
- a statement of facts;

---

10. Supreme Court Rule 341(b).
11. Supreme Court Rule 341(c).
12. Supreme Court Rule 341(d).
13. Supreme Court Rule 341(d).
14. Supreme Court Rule 341(e).

APPELLATE REVIEW § 30:55

- the argument; and
- a conclusion.[15]

The appellant's brief must also include an appendix, which has its own specific requirements.[16] The appendix must contain:

- a copy of the judgment appealed from;
- opinions, memorandums or findings of fact filed or entered by the trial judge;
- pertinent pleadings;
- the notice of appeal; and
- a table of contents, the form of which is also specified in the rules.[17]

The appellant need not file an abstract of the record unless specifically ordered by the court to do so.[18] If the court orders an abstract, its form is governed by the rules.[19]

☞ *Practice Guide:* Whether the record is abstracted or it is submitted in its entirety, the entire record is available to the

---

15. Supreme Court Rule 341(e).
16. Supreme Court Rule 341(e).
17. Supreme Court Rule 342.

Supreme Court Rule 342(a) was amended in 1993 by the addition of the language stating that the appellee's brief may include in a supplementary appendix other materials from the record which also are the basis of the appeal or are essential to any understanding of the issues raised in the appeal.

Supreme Court Rule 342(a) was amended in 1993 by the addition of the requirements that the appellant's brief must include a table of contents to the appendix, any opinion, memorandum, or findings of fact filed or entered by any administrative agency or its officers, and any other materials from the record which are the basis of the appeal or pertinent to it. Further, the pages of the appendix must be numbered consecutively with the letter "A" preceding the number of each page. If an appendix is voluminous, it may be bound separately from the brief and labeled "Separate Appendix."

18. Supreme Court Rule 342(b).
19. Supreme Court Rule 342(b).

§ 30:55 ILLINOIS JURISPRUDENCE: CRIMINAL LAW

reviewing court on appeal.[20] If the record has been abstracted and a pertinent portion has been omitted, the appellant will not be prejudiced by the omission, unless the court determines that the omission was in bad faith.[21]

The appellee's brief is subject to the same rules, but it need not include all of the same information.[22] The appellee only needs to include the summary of the argument, the argument and the conclusion.[23] The other material required of the appellant's brief only needs to be included if the appellee feels that the appellant's statements are unsatisfactory.[24]

The appellant's reply brief, on the other hand, should be limited to argument in response to the appellee's brief.[25]

Where the petition for leave to appeal or appeal as a matter of right, or answer to either is used as a party's main brief, that party may file a supplemental brief.[26]

Prior to the due date of the reply brief, any party to the appeal may, for the purpose of work on the appeal, request, in writing, the clerk of the reviewing court to transmit the record on appeal to the clerk of the trial court or to the party's attorney.[27] The clerk shall comply with the request, without the necessity of obtaining an order of court, by sending the record to the clerk of the trial court or the attorney, charges collect. Upon receiving the record on appeal, the clerk of the trial court or the attorney is responsible for its safekeeping and shall return the record to the clerk of the reviewing court by prepaid mail or express not later than the day upon which the reply brief is due.[28] The parties may unbind the

20. Supreme Court Rule 342(d).
21. Supreme Court Rule 342(d).
22. Supreme Court Rule 341(f).
23. Supreme Court Rule 341(f).
24. Supreme Court Rule 341(f).
25. Supreme Court Rule 341(g).
26. Supreme Court Rule 341(h).
27. Supreme Court Rule 372(a).

record for the purpose of photocopying, but the party responsible for unbinding the record must restore it to its original condition.[29]

☞ *Caution:* Except as otherwise provided in this rule, no record shall be taken from the files of the reviewing court except on leave granted by the court, or judge thereof. The clerk shall report promptly to the court every violation of this rule.[30]

§ 30:56. —Filing and serving

The civil appeals rules govern the filing and serving of criminal appeal briefs.[31] The rules state that the appellant must file his or her brief within 35 days of the record on appeal being filed.[32] Within 35 days from the due date of the appellant's brief, or in the case of multiple appellants, the latest due date of any appellant's brief, the appellee shall file his or her brief in the reviewing court.[33] Within 14 days from the due date of the appellee's brief, or in the case of multiple appellees, the latest due date of any appellee's brief, the appellant may file a reply brief.[34] The reviewing court or a judge thereof, sua sponte or upon the motion of a party supported by an affidavit showing good cause, may extend or shorten the time of any party to file a brief.[35]

When it is time to file, nine copies of each brief and the abstract, if there is one, must be filed, except if the appeal is of an Industrial Commission order, in which case, 15 copies must be filed, along

---

28. Supreme Court Rule 372(a).
29. Supreme Court Rule 372(a).
30. Supreme Court Rule 372(b).
31. Supreme Court Rule 612(k).
32. Supreme Court Rule 343(a).
33. Supreme Court Rule 343(a).
34. Supreme Court Rule 343(a).
35. Supreme Court Rule 343(c).

Annotation References: Consequences of prosecution's failure to file timely brief in appeal by accused, 27 ALR4th 213.

§ 30:56   ILLINOIS JURISPRUDENCE: CRIMINAL LAW

with proof of service.[36] In appeals to the Supreme Court, 20 copies of the abstract, if any, and of each brief shall be filed.[37] Each party represented by a separate attorney, including both the Attorney General and the State's Attorney, where both are involved, must be served with three copies of the brief.[38]

The form of the briefs and abstract, in any, must meet specific requirements.[39] For example, the briefs and abstracts, if any, must be produced on white paper of a specified size and carbon copies are not acceptable.[40] The size of the print is regulated and footnotes are discouraged.[41] The required cover colors of the briefs are:

- abstract = gray
- appellant's brief or petition = white
- appellee's brief or answer = light blue
- appellant's reply brief = light yellow
- appellee's reply brief = light red
- petition for rehearing = light green
- answer to petition for rehearing = tan, and a
- reply on rehearing = orange.[42] If a separate appendix is filed, the cover shall be the same color as that of the brief which it accompanies.[43]

§ 30:57. —Amicus curiae

An amicus curiae brief is a brief which is filed to give the court information on a point of law or to bring a point of law to the

---

36. Supreme Court Rule 344(a).
37. Supreme Court Rule 344(a).
38. Supreme Court Rule 344(a).
39. Supreme Court Rule 344(b).
40. Supreme Court Rule 344(b).
41. Supreme Court Rule 344(b).
42. Supreme Court Rule 344(c).
43. Supreme Court Rule 344(c).

court's attention which might have otherwise escaped the court's notice.[44] The rules followed for filing amicus curiae briefs are the civil appeals rules.[45]

Prior to filing an amicus curiae brief, the party seeking to file must have received a request from the court to file or be given leave of court.[46] The brief must be filed on or before the due date of the initial brief of the party whose position it supports, unless the court allows otherwise.[47] When filed, the brief must conform to the requirements for the appellee's brief,[48] but unlike the appellee's brief, it may not be argued orally.[49]

§ 30:58. Oral argument

The sequence and manner of calling criminal cases and other matters regarding oral arguments are determined by the civil appeals rules, except for death penalty cases.[50] Cases in which the death sentence has been imposed have priority over other cases, as criminal appeals, in general, have priority over civil appeals.[51]

A party must request oral argument by stating on the bottom of

---

44. The latin term "amicus curiae" translated literally means "friend of the court." The term means one who gives information to the court on some matter of law with respect to which the court is doubtful. The term implies the friendly intervention of counsel to call the court's attention to a legal matter which has escaped or might escape the court's consideration.

45. Supreme Court Rule 612(m).

46. Supreme Court Rule 345(a).

47. Supreme Court Rule 345(b).

48. Supreme Court Rule 345(b).

Supreme Court Rule 345(b) was amended in 1993 by the addition of the requirement that an amicus curiae brief must identify the amicus as such on the cover of the brief. Further, the color of the cover must be the same as that of the party's brief whose position it supports.

See also § 30:54.

49. Supreme Court Rule 345(c).

50. Supreme Court Rule 611.

51. Supreme Court Rule 611.

§ 30:58   ILLINOIS JURISPRUDENCE: CRIMINAL LAW

the cover page of his or her brief that oral argument is requested.[52] If the party did not file a brief, but instead allowed a petition for leave to appeal or answer stand in place of the brief, the request must be mailed to the clerk and opposing parties within the time allotted for filing a supplemental brief.[53] Once one party has made the request for oral argument, all of the other parties may argue orally, as well, without an additional request.[54]

Despite a request, a party will not be allowed to present an oral argument if he or she has not filed a brief or paid the required fees.[55] If a party, after having requested oral argument, then waives oral argument, the clerk and the opposing parties must be notified promptly.[56] At that time, a party who had not requested oral argument previously may do so.[57] This party also must notify the clerk and the opposing parties of his or her request.[58]

☛ *Practice Guide:* Counsel should check with the clerk of the reviewing court to determine what the procedure is for the day of argument. Some courts require that counsel register the day of the argument, and some do not.

If no oral argument is requested, the case will be decided on the briefs, unless oral argument is ordered by the court.[59] The court also has the option to dispose of cases without oral argument where no substantial questions are presented, but must do so only sparingly.[60]

In a capital case, each side has up to 30 minutes to present their

---

52. Supreme Court Rule 352(a).
53. Supreme Court Rule 352(a).
54. Supreme Court Rule 352(a).
55. Supreme Court Rule 352(a).
56. Supreme Court Rule 352(a).
57. Supreme Court Rule 352(a).
58. Supreme Court Rule 352(a).
59. Supreme Court Rule 352(g).
60. Supreme Court Rule 352(a).

main argument, but in a noncapital case each side has only 20 minutes to present their main argument.[61] The appellant is limited to 10 minutes for rebuttal and if only one side argues, then the argument may not exceed 15 minutes.[62] The court has the option to limit the allotted time prior to the hearing.[63]

The parties are not required to use the entire time allotted to them, if it is not necessary.[64] In fact, if the court determines that further argument is not needed, it may terminate the argument itself.[65] If, however, a party anticipates needing more time than allotted for thorough presentation, that party may file a motion prior to the date set for the hearing requesting more time.[66]

At the hearing, the court will not allow lengthy excerpts from the record, briefs or authorities cited to be read.[67]

In general, only two attorneys from each side may argue a case.[68] Divided arguments are not favored, but the court may allow more than two attorneys to argue for a side where there are multiple parties on the same side with diverse interests.[69] The order of argument in cases where there are several parties is as the parties agree or as the court directs.[70]

Briefs may not be filed after oral argument, unless the court gives leave for the filing.[71]

---

61. Supreme Court Rule 352(b).
62. Supreme Court Rule 352(b).
63. Supreme Court Rule 352(b).
64. Supreme Court Rule 352(b).
65. Supreme Court Rule 352(b).
66. Supreme Court Rule 352(b).
67. Supreme Court Rule 352(c).
68. Supreme Court Rule 352(d).
69. Supreme Court Rule 352(d).
70. Supreme Court Rule 352(e).
71. Supreme Court Rule 352(f).

§ 30:58 ILLINOIS JURISPRUDENCE: CRIMINAL LAW

☞ *Caution:* Counsel should be aware of Rule 8 of the Uniform Administrative and Procedural Rules which requires that the opinions of the Illinois Appellate Court which have been published in abstract form only, shall not be cited in the briefs of litigants unless the entire text of said abstract opinion is appended to the brief. Additionally, when on oral argument counsel cites authorities from other jurisdictions, he shall provide this court with four copies of the full text of such authorities.[72]

§ 30:59. Rehearings

Rehearings of criminal appeals are governed by the civil appeals rules.[73] Under those rules, a petition for a rehearing may be filed up to 21 days after the filing of the judgment disposing of the case.[74] The 21-day time frame may be altered by the court on motion, but an extension of time is not favored.[75] More than 21 days will only be allowed in extreme circumstances.[76]

The petition is limited to 20 printed pages or 27 unprinted pages, unless the court authorizes a different length.[77] In the pages allowed, the petitioner must point out what he or she alleges the court to have overlooked or misapprehended.[78] Each point made by the petitioner needs to indicate where the portion of the record and brief which is being referred to may be found.[79] Authorities and argument may be presented in support of the petitioner's claims, but reargument of the case may not be.[80]

---

72. Uniform Administrative and Procedural Rules, Rule 8.
73. Supreme Court Rule 612(p).
74. Supreme Court Rule 367(a).
75. Supreme Court Rule 367(a).
76. Supreme Court Rule 367(a).
77. Supreme Court Rule 367(a).
78. Supreme Court Rule 367(b).
79. Supreme Court Rule 367(b).
80. Supreme Court Rule 367(b).

The rules governing briefs regarding number of copies, reproduction and service apply to petitions for rehearing, as well, except that petitions for rehearing or petitions for extension of time to file petitions for rehearing that are directed to the Supreme Court must be delivered or mailed first class to the Court and the Reporter of Decisions.[81] The Supreme Court also must be provided with a certificate of mailing.[82]

An answer to a petition for a rehearing may not be filed unless and until the petition is granted or the court requests an answer.[83] In either case, the answer must be filed within 21 days or being requested of the petition being granted.[84] The petitioner then will have 14 days after the due date of the answer to reply to it.[85]

The opposing counsel must be served with three copies and the proof of service filed with the clerk.[86]

The petition, answer and reply may not be briefed.[87] Rather, the original briefs of the parties, accompanied by the petition, answer and reply stand in the place of briefs.[88]

Oral argument will not be had unless the court orders it on its own motion.[89]

Once the court has granted a petition for rehearing and the order is entered, further petitions for rehearing may not be filed.[90]

---

81. Supreme Court Rule 367(c).
82. Supreme Court Rule 367(c).
83. Supreme Court Rule 367(d).
84. Supreme Court Rule 367(d).
85. Supreme Court Rule 367(d).
86. Supreme Court Rule 367(d).
87. Supreme Court Rule 367(d).
88. Supreme Court Rule 367(d).
89. Supreme Court Rule 367(d).
90. Supreme Court Rule 367(e).

VII. DISMISSAL AND ABATEMENT

Research References:

Annotation References:

Index and Annotations: Appeal and Error

ALR Digest to 3d, 4th, 5th, and Federal: Appeal and Error §§ 388–410

Practice References:

4 Am Jur 2d, Appeal and Error § 285; 5 Am Jur 2d, Appeal and Error §§ 905–930

State Legislation:

Supreme Court Rule 309, 341

Miscellaneous References:

West's Illinois Digest 2d, Criminal Law §§ 1131–1133

§ 30:60. Dismissal

The rules of the supreme court provide that, before the record on appeal is filed in the reviewing court, the trial court may dismiss the appeal of any party on the motion of that party or on stipulation of the parties.[91] A copy of the order of dismissal filed in the trial court must be forwarded by the clerk to the reviewing court within 5 days after the entry of the order.[92]

A reviewing court may dismiss an appeal where the appellant's brief fails to comply with the supreme court rules applicable to briefs.[93] However, if the rule violated by the appellant is only an admonishment to the parties and not a limitation upon the reviewing court's jurisdiction, the reviewing court may nevertheless consider the merits of the party's appeal.[94] The failure to file essential pleadings with the reviewing court warrants dismissal

---

91. Supreme Court Rule 309.

92. Supreme Court Rule 309.

93. In re A.H., 215 Ill App 3d 522, 159 Ill Dec 32, 575 NE2d 261 (4th Dist 1991).

See Supreme Court Rule 341.

94. In re A.H., 215 Ill App 3d 522, 159 Ill Dec 32, 575 NE2d 261 (4th Dist 1991).

of an appeal.[95]

A defendant has no basis to appeal from a count upon which no conviction and no judgment has been entered.[96] Where no final judgment has been entered, an appeal will be dismissed.[97] Thus, an appeal from a nonappealable interlocutory order must be dismissed based on the reviewing court's lack of jurisdiction.[98] A trial court's express statement that an order is final for purposes of appeal does not necessarily make the order appealable.[99]

The failure to file any posttrial motion, written or oral, may be considered a waiver of the errors raised on appeal warranting a dismissal of an appeal.[1] In the absence of a posttrial motion, nothing would be properly before the reviewing court for it to consider.[2]

An appeal may be dismissed where the defendant has waived the right to appeal as part of a negotiated plea agreement.[3] The use of appeal waivers in the context of plea bargaining, although

---

95. People v Stewart, 66 Ill App 3d 342, 23 Ill Dec 152, 383 NE2d 1179 (1st Dist 1978), cert den 441 US 907, 60 L Ed 2d 376, 99 S Ct 1998.

Forms: 2 Am Jur Pl & Pr Forms (Rev), Appeal and Error, Forms 1061–1085.

96. People v Matzke, 102 Ill App 3d 905, 58 Ill Dec 411, 430 NE2d 353 (1st Dist 1981).

97. People v Koonce, 65 Ill App 3d 86, 22 Ill Dec 127, 382 NE2d 447 (1st Dist 1978); People v De Groot, 108 Ill App 2d 1, 247 NE2d 177 (1st Dist 1969).

98. People v Martinez, 54 Ill App 3d 607, 12 Ill Dec 417, 370 NE2d 40 (1st Dist 1977).

99. People v Martinez, 54 Ill App 3d 607, 12 Ill Dec 417, 370 NE2d 40 (1st Dist 1977); People v McGary, 120 Ill App 2d 170, 256 NE2d 374 (2d Dist 1970).

1. People v Lamparter, 56 Ill App 3d 823, 13 Ill Dec 905, 371 NE2d 997 (5th Dist 1977); People v Hammond, 48 Ill App 3d 707, 6 Ill Dec 441, 362 NE2d 1361 (5th Dist 1977).

2. People v Lamparter, 56 Ill App 3d 823, 13 Ill Dec 905, 371 NE2d 997 (5th Dist 1977).

3. People v Nichols, 143 Ill App 3d 673, 97 Ill Dec 870, 493 NE2d 677 (2d Dist 1986).

§ 30:60　　　ILLINOIS JURISPRUDENCE: CRIMINAL LAW

not a common practice, has been found to be valid in a majority of jurisdictions.[4] Because an appeal waiver operates much like a guilty plea in that it insulates a conviction from review, the defendant should be admonished regarding the rights being waived by an appeal waiver.[5]

§ 30:61. Abatement

"Abatement" is a term used to mean the complete extinguishment of a cause of action.[6] In this sense, a cause of action is said to "abate" when the right of action is extinguished by the death of the person in whose favor or against whom the cause of action existed.[7] At common law, every pending action abated as a matter of procedure upon the death of a sole plaintiff or defendant.[8]

A defendant's death during the pendency of his or her appeal abates the appeal.[9] The death of the defendant frustrates the purpose of the appeal.[10] Once the defendant has ceased to exist, an appeal cannot effectively confer vindication or impose punishment.[11]

---

4. People v Nichols, 143 Ill App 3d 673, 97 Ill Dec 870, 493 NE2d 677 (2d Dist 1986).

  Annotation References: Validity and Effect of Criminal Defendant's Express Waiver of Right To Appeal as Part of Negotiated Plea Agreement, 89 ALR3d 864.

5. People v Nichols, 143 Ill App 3d 673, 97 Ill Dec 870, 493 NE2d 677 (2d Dist 1986).

6. 1 Am Jur 2d, Abatement, Survival and Revival, § 1.

7. 1 Am Jur 2d, Abatement, Survival and Revival, § 1.

8. 1 Am Jur 2d, Abatement, Survival and Revival, § 47.

9. People v Crosby, 61 Ill App 3d 115, 18 Ill Dec 482, 377 NE2d 1118 (1st Dist 1978); People v Cook, 18 Ill App 3d 190, 309 NE2d 623 (1st Dist 1974).

  Annotation References: Abatement of state criminal case by accused's death pending appeal of conviction—modern cases, 80 ALR4th 189.

10. People v Mazzone, 74 Ill 2d 44, 23 Ill Dec 76, 383 NE2d 947 (1978).

11. People v Mazzone, 74 Ill 2d 44, 23 Ill Dec 76, 383 NE2d 947 (1978).

VIII. SCOPE AND MODE OF REVIEW

Research References:
  Annotation References:
    Index and Annotations: Appeal and Error
    ALR Digest to 3d, 4th, 5th, and Federal: Appeal and Error §§ 432, 478, 660

  Practice References:
    5 Am Jur 2d, Appeal and Error §§ 702–705
  State Legislation:
    Supreme Court Rule 615
  Miscellaneous References:
    West's Illinois Digest 2d, Criminal Law §§ 1134–1139

§ 30:62. Generally

To justify the attention of the appellate court, an error, defect, irregularity or variance must affect a substantial right, or it will be disregarded.[12] Those errors which affect substantial rights may be noticed by the reviewing court whether they were brought to the trial court's attention or not.[13] In other words, an error which was not properly preserved at the trial level may still be considered on appeal if it rises to the level of plain error.[14]

§ 30:63. Power of reviewing court

The reviewing court has the power to:

- reverse, affirm, or modify the judgment or order from which the appeal is taken;
- set aside, affirm, or modify any or all of the proceedings subsequent to or dependent upon the judgment or order from which the appeal is taken;

---

12. Supreme Court Rule 615(a).
13. Supreme Court Rule 615(a).
14. Supreme Court Rule 615(a).
    See also § 29:18.

§ 30:63   ILLINOIS JURISPRUDENCE: CRIMINAL LAW

- reduce the degree of the offense of which the appellant was convicted;
- reduce the punishment imposed by the trial court; or
- order a new trial.[15]

§ 30:64. Rulings by lower court

On appeal, the reviewing court will affirm the lower court's ruling if the judgment is justified, even if the trial court's reasoning was faulty.[16] In fact, the appellate court does not have to rely on the lower court's reasoning, but may affirm on any ground that was properly preserved.[17] In other words, the trial court's conclusion is more important than its rationale.[18] It is the propriety of a judgment itself which is before a reviewing court on appeal, and not the lower court's reasoning.[19]

§ 30:65. Trial de novo

The reviewing court accepts the trial court's factual determinations and evaluations of witness credibility.[20] Legal determinations made by the trial court, however, are subject to de novo review.[21] In other words, the reviewing court will consider those issues not dealing with facts or witness credibility as though they have never been heard before.[22] For example, even though a

---

15. Supreme Court Rule 615(b).

16. People v Church, 102 Ill App 3d 155, 57 Ill Dec 679, 429 NE2d 577 (4th Dist 1981); People v Sylvester, 86 Ill App 3d 186, 41 Ill Dec 504, 407 NE2d 1002 (1st Dist 1980).

17. People v Everette, 141 Ill 2d 147, 152 Ill Dec 377, 565 NE2d 1295 (1990), mod and reh den 1991 Ill LEXIS 7 (Ill) and on remand 220 Ill App 3d 453, 163 Ill Dec 158, 581 NE2d 109 (1st Dist), habeas corpus granted 808 F Supp 1332 (ND Ill), revd 37 F3d 257 (CA7 Ill), cert den 515 US 1163, 132 L Ed 2d 862, 115 S Ct 2620.

18. People v Tobe, 49 Ill 2d 538, 276 NE2d 294 (1971).

19. People ex rel. Waller v 1990 Ford Bronco, 158 Ill 2d 460, 199 Ill Dec 694, 634 NE2d 747 (1994).

20. People v Foskey, 136 Ill 2d 66, 143 Ill Dec 257, 554 NE2d 192 (1990).

21. People v Foskey, 136 Ill 2d 66, 143 Ill Dec 257, 554 NE2d 192 (1990).

ruling on a motion to suppress will not be set aside unless the trial court's determination was clearly erroneous, whether to grant a motion to suppress is a legal issue subject to de novo review on appeal.[23]

☛ *Illustration:* Although the courts have declined to engage in a de novo review when there is an underlying claim that a defendant's confession was involuntary, where the testimony is uncontested and the credibility of the witnesses is not questioned, a question of law is presented and a reviewing court may consider the case de novo.[24]

☛ *Illustration:* Where neither the facts nor the credibility of the witnesses is disputed, the existence of probable cause is a legal issue that may be reviewed de novo.[25]

IX. LOWER COURT DISCRETION AND PRESUMPTIONS ON REVIEW

Research References:

Annotation References:

Index and Annotations: Appeal and Error

ALR Digest to 3d, 4th, 5th, and Federal: Appeal and Error §§ 433, 440–449, 455, 469, 545–562

Practice References:

Nichols Drinking/Driving Lit § 19:05.

5 Am Jur 2d, Appeal and Error §§ 723–729, 736–738, 772–775, 781, 797–809, 815, 818, 819, 838, 867, 888–890, 895, 896

---

22. The term "de novo" means anew; again; or a second time.

23. People v Mourecek, 208 Ill App 3d 87, 152 Ill Dec 964, 566 NE2d 841 (2d Dist 1991); People v Froio, 198 Ill App 3d 116, 144 Ill Dec 411, 555 NE2d 770 (2d Dist 1990).

24. People v Ravellette, 263 Ill App 3d 906, 200 Ill Dec 914, 636 NE2d 105 (4th Dist 1994).

25. People v Woods, 241 Ill App 3d 285, 181 Ill Dec 818, 608 NE2d 1292 (2d Dist 1993).

Federal Legislation:
US Const Amend VI

State Legislation:
725 ILCS 5/103-5, 5/104-11, 5/114-8; Supreme Court Rule 415

Miscellaneous References:
West's Illinois Digest 2d, Criminal Law §§ 1141–1156

§ 30:66. Generally

A reviewing court may not simply substitute its own judgment for the trial court's lawful discretion.[26] On review, all presumptions are in favor of the trial court's decisions, and the burden is on the appellant to affirmatively prove the errors charged in order to overcome that presumption.[27] Thus, absent evidence to the contrary, the reviewing court assumes that a trial court's actions are in conformity with the law, and will neither presume that an alleged error occurred nor that the trial court misunderstood the law.[28]

☛ *Practice Tip:* A reviewing court is not required to divine a court's lack of awareness of its discretion from the wording

---

26. People v Illgen, 145 Ill 2d 353, 164 Ill Dec 599, 583 NE2d 515, 24 ALR5th 864 (1991); People v Streit, 142 Ill 2d 13, 153 Ill Dec 245, 566 NE2d 1351 (1991); People v Jenkins, 209 Ill App 3d 249, 154 Ill Dec 122, 568 NE2d 122 (1st Dist 1991); People v Ward, 194 Ill App 3d 229, 141 Ill Dec 162, 550 NE2d 1208 (1st Dist 1990).

27. People v Stewart, 186 Ill App 3d 833, 134 Ill Dec 569, 542 NE2d 915 (1st Dist 1989); People v Henderson, 136 Ill App 3d 1041, 91 Ill Dec 582, 483 NE2d 1068 (4th Dist 1985).

Practice References: Nichols Drinking/Driving Lit § 19:05.

28. People v Christy, 206 Ill App 3d 361, 151 Ill Dec 261, 564 NE2d 238 (4th Dist 1990); People v Lagle, 200 Ill App 3d 948, 146 Ill Dec 551, 558 NE2d 514 (5th Dist 1990); People v Alexander, 127 Ill App 3d 1007, 83 Ill Dec 651, 470 NE2d 1071 (1st Dist 1984), cert den 471 US 1019, 85 L Ed 2d 308, 105 S Ct 2027; People v Jones, 109 Ill App 3d 120, 64 Ill Dec 709, 440 NE2d 261 (1st Dist 1982).

United States v Daniels, 902 F2d 1238 (CA7 Ill 1990), cert den 498 US 981, 112 L Ed 2d 522, 111 S Ct 510;

of its ruling. The burden is on defendant to establish that the judge did not exercise discretion, not on the State to demonstrate that the judge did.[29]

The constitutionality of legislative enactments is presumed, and the party alleging unconstitutionality or the violation of a constitutional right bears the burden of proving the violation.[30]

§ 30:67. Matters of record

Absent a showing to the contrary, the reviewing court presumes that the record is accurate,[31] and indulges in all reasonable presumptions necessary to support the trial court's conclusion.[32] The burden is on the appellant to overcome this presumption of validity, and to provide the reviewing court with a complete record of the proceedings below sufficient to support his or her claim of error.[33]

§ 30:68. Matters not shown by record

Where the record on appeal is silent, insufficient, or fails to demonstrate the alleged error, the reviewing court may not engage in supposition, but rather must decide the issues in question as they are or are not reflected in the record at hand.[34] The reviewing

---

29. People v Washington, 243 Ill App 3d 138, 183 Ill Dec 395, 611 NE2d 1043 (1st Dist 1993).

30. People v Blackorby, 146 Ill 2d 307, 166 Ill Dec 902, 586 NE2d 1231 (1992); People v Bales, 108 Ill 2d 182, 91 Ill Dec 171, 483 NE2d 517 (1985); People v Goodey, 227 Ill App 3d 232, 169 Ill Dec 222, 591 NE2d 102 (4th Dist 1992).

31. People v Zipprich, 141 Ill App 3d 123, 95 Ill Dec 535, 490 NE2d 8 (1st Dist 1986).

32. People v Henderson, 136 Ill App 3d 1041, 91 Ill Dec 582, 483 NE2d 1068 (4th Dist 1985); People v Blake, 130 Ill App 3d 948, 85 Ill Dec 932, 474 NE2d 892 (2d Dist 1985).

33. People v Harp, 193 Ill App 3d 838, 141 Ill Dec 117, 550 NE2d 1163 (4th Dist 1990); People v Odumuyiwa, 188 Ill App 3d 40, 135 Ill Dec 909, 544 NE2d 405 (2d Dist 1989).

34. People v Odumuyiwa, 188 Ill App 3d 40, 135 Ill Dec 909, 544 NE2d 405 (2d Dist 1989); People v Perry, 183 Ill App 3d 534, 132 Ill Dec 639, 540 NE2d

§ 30:68   ILLINOIS JURISPRUDENCE: CRIMINAL LAW

court's presumption is against a waiver of the right to counsel, and the record must be closely scrutinized to find evidence of a waiver in the words and actions of the defendant.[35] Similarly, the reviewing court may not presume that a waiver of the right to a jury trial was knowingly and intelligently made simply on the basis of a silent record.[36] Nor may a waiver of the right to remain silent be presumed from the absence of its express or implied exercise.[37]

Where the record is silent, a delay will not be presumed to have been due to the defendant's dilatory conduct.[38] Generally, however, all presumptions are in favor of the judgment entered where the record on appeal is incomplete.[39]

Because it is the appellant's responsibility to provide a complete record, any questions arising from an insufficient record are

379 (1st Dist 1989); In Interest of S.K., 137 Ill App 3d 1065, 92 Ill Dec 767, 485 NE2d 578 (2d Dist 1985).

35. People v Holmes, 141 Ill 2d 204, 152 Ill Dec 268, 565 NE2d 950 (1990); People v Cooper, 204 Ill App 3d 1035, 150 Ill Dec 368, 562 NE2d 1171 (5th Dist 1990); People v Phillips, 195 Ill App 3d 560, 142 Ill Dec 678, 553 NE2d 28 (1st Dist 1990); People v Kosyla, 143 Ill App 3d 937, 98 Ill Dec 823, 494 NE2d 945 (2d Dist 1986); People v Graves, 134 Ill App 3d 473, 89 Ill Dec 399, 480 NE2d 1142 (1st Dist 1984).

United States v Martin-Trigona, 684 F2d 485 (CA7 Ill 1982).

36. People v Purnell, 126 Ill App 3d 608, 82 Ill Dec 87, 467 NE2d 1160 (1st Dist 1984); United States ex rel. Williams v De Robertis, 715 F2d 1174 (CA7 Ill 1983), cert den 464 US 1072, 79 L Ed 2d 219, 104 S Ct 982.

37. People v Brown, 146 Ill App 3d 101, 99 Ill Dec 928, 496 NE2d 1020 (1st Dist 1986).

38. 725 ILCS 5/103-5.

People v Reimolds, 92 Ill 2d 101, 65 Ill Dec 17, 440 NE2d 872 (1982); People v Grudzien, 131 Ill App 3d 385, 86 Ill Dec 702, 475 NE2d 1081 (3d Dist 1985); People v Jump, 127 Ill App 3d 440, 82 Ill Dec 498, 468 NE2d 1278 (3d Dist 1984).

39. People v Hall, 186 Ill App 3d 123, 133 Ill Dec 931, 541 NE2d 1369 (1st Dist 1989); People v Majer, 131 Ill App 3d 80, 86 Ill Dec 272, 475 NE2d 269 (2d Dist 1985); People v Maquet, 113 Ill App 3d 109, 68 Ill Dec 758, 446 NE2d 929 (3d Dist 1983).

APPELLATE REVIEW § 30:69

resolved against the appellant, the presumption being that the missing record would have supported the trial court's decision.[40]

☛ *Practice Guide:* Generally, an appellant's failure to supply a portion of the trial court record creates a presumption that the missing material would support the trial court.[41] This rule applies equally to deficiencies in the common law record as well as the report of proceedings.[42]

§ 30:69. Pretrial matters

The statements contained in an affidavit offered in support of a search warrant are presumptively true and accurate for purposes of appeal unless the defendant specifically attacks their veracity.[43]

A trial court's ruling on a motion to suppress evidence will not

---

40. Foutch v O'Bryant, 99 Ill 2d 389, 76 Ill Dec 823, 459 NE2d 958 (1984); People v Harp, 193 Ill App 3d 838, 141 Ill Dec 117, 550 NE2d 1163 (4th Dist 1990); People v Atwood, 193 Ill App 3d 580, 140 Ill Dec 490, 549 NE2d 1362 (4th Dist 1990); People v Hall, 186 Ill App 3d 123, 133 Ill Dec 931, 541 NE2d 1369 (1st Dist 1989); People v Perry, 183 Ill App 3d 534, 132 Ill Dec 639, 540 NE2d 379 (1st Dist 1989); People v Green, 179 Ill App 3d 1, 128 Ill Dec 902, 535 NE2d 413 (1st Dist 1988); People v Peters, 144 Ill App 3d 310, 98 Ill Dec 731, 494 NE2d 853 (2d Dist 1986); People v Dowdy, 140 Ill App 3d 631, 94 Ill Dec 933, 488 NE2d 1326 (2d Dist 1986); People v Hartfield, 137 Ill App 3d 679, 92 Ill Dec 281, 484 NE2d 1136 (1st Dist 1985); People v Davenport, 133 Ill App 3d 553, 88 Ill Dec 680, 479 NE2d 15 (2d Dist 1985).

Because the court requested explanations from the prosecution to determine whether or not the defendant's prima facie Batson case had been overcome, presumption on appeal was that a prima facie case had been made, despite the record's silence. People v Baisten, 203 Ill App 3d 64, 148 Ill Dec 463, 560 NE2d 1060 (1st Dist 1990).

41. People v Atwood, 193 Ill App 3d 580, 140 Ill Dec 490, 549 NE2d 1362 (4th Dist 1990); Fischer v Mann, 161 Ill App 3d 424, 112 Ill Dec 903, 514 NE2d 566 (2d Dist 1987).

42. People v Atwood, 193 Ill App 3d 580, 140 Ill Dec 490, 549 NE2d 1362 (4th Dist 1990); Fischer v Mann, 161 Ill App 3d 424, 112 Ill Dec 903, 514 NE2d 566 (2d Dist 1987).

43. People v McCoy, 135 Ill App 3d 1059, 90 Ill Dec 493, 482 NE2d 200 (2d Dist 1985).

be disturbed on appeal unless it was manifestly erroneous.[44] A trial court's decision regarding a defendant's competency to enter a guilty plea, will also not be disturbed absent manifest error, since it is presumed that the trial court had the greater opportunity to accurately evaluate the defendant.[45] Unless the appellant can demonstrate that a guilty plea was entered under a misapprehension of law or fact, or that he or she has a legitimate defense, or that there is sufficient doubt of his or her guilt that the case should be tried, a trial court's refusal to allow a defendant to withdraw a guilty plea will not be disturbed.[46]

Unless there is a clear showing by the appellant of prejudicial error, a trial court's exercise of its discretion with regard to severance,[47] motions in limine,[48] the granting or denial of a continuance,[49] the imposition of sanctions for discovery violations or dilatory conduct,[50] or the determination of a defendant's fitness

44. People v Williams, 147 Ill 2d 173, 167 Ill Dec 853, 588 NE2d 983 (1991), cert den 506 US 876, 121 L Ed 2d 156, 113 S Ct 218; People v Tisler, 103 Ill 2d 226, 82 Ill Dec 613, 469 NE2d 147 (1984); People v Thomas, 199 Ill App 3d 79, 145 Ill Dec 344, 556 NE2d 1246 (2d Dist 1990).

45. People v Kraus, 122 Ill App 3d 882, 78 Ill Dec 202, 461 NE2d 1036 (2d Dist 1984).

46. People v Roesler, 195 Ill App 3d 1007, 142 Ill Dec 501, 552 NE2d 1242 (5th Dist 1990); People v Turley, 174 Ill App 3d 621, 124 Ill Dec 200, 528 NE2d 1091 (2d Dist 1988); People v Gasper, 167 Ill App 3d 218, 118 Ill Dec 102, 521 NE2d 170 (3d Dist 1988); People v Hillenbrand, 121 Ill App 3d 537, 521 NE2d 900 (1988).

See ch 14.

47. 725 ILCS 5/114-8.

People v Weaver, 92 Ill 2d 545, 65 Ill Dec 944, 442 NE2d 255 (1982) (superseded by statute on other grounds as stated in People v Modrowski, 296 Ill App 3d 735, 231 Ill Dec 299, 696 NE2d 28 (1st Dist)); People v Harris, 198 Ill App 3d 1002, 145 Ill Dec 91, 556 NE2d 709 (1st Dist 1990); People v Harmon, 194 Ill App 3d 135, 141 Ill Dec 94, 550 NE2d 1140 (1st Dist 1990), affd 95 F3d 620 (CA7 Ill); People v Hall, 164 Ill App 3d 770, 115 Ill Dec 750, 518 NE2d 275 (1st Dist 1987), cert den 488 US 867, 102 L Ed 2d 143, 109 S Ct 174; People v Wilson, 161 Ill App 3d 995, 113 Ill Dec 827, 515 NE2d 812 (1st Dist 1987), appeal after remand 257 Ill App 3d 670, 195 Ill Dec 8, 628 NE2d 472 (1st Dist).

to stand trial,[51] will not be reviewed on appeal.

The trial court is afforded broad discretion in the conduct of voir dire,[52] and its determination as to whether or not a prospective juror will be fair and impartial will not be set aside

---

48. People v Williams, 205 Ill App 3d 715, 146 Ill Dec 914, 558 NE2d 1248 (1st Dist 1990); People v Jordan, 205 Ill App 3d 116, 150 Ill Dec 415, 562 NE2d 1218 (2d Dist 1990); People v Batchelor, 202 Ill App 3d 316, 147 Ill Dec 608, 559 NE2d 948 (1st Dist 1990); People v McCoy, 156 Ill App 3d 194, 108 Ill Dec 871, 509 NE2d 567 (1st Dist 1987).

See ch 21.

49. People v Little, 207 Ill App 3d 720, 152 Ill Dec 678, 566 NE2d 365 (1st Dist 1990); People v Amos, 204 Ill App 3d 75, 149 Ill Dec 411, 561 NE2d 1107 (1st Dist 1990); People v Camp, 201 Ill App 3d 330, 147 Ill Dec 26, 559 NE2d 26 (1st Dist 1990; People v Phelps, 197 Ill App 3d 954, 145 Ill Dec 465, 557 NE2d 235 (1st Dist 1990); People v Watts, 195 Ill App 3d 899, 142 Ill Dec 307, 552 NE2d 1048 (5th Dist 1990); People v Waddell, 190 Ill App 3d 914, 138 Ill Dec 13, 546 NE2d 1068 (4th Dist 1989).

50. Supreme Court Rule 415; 725 ILCS 5/103-5.

People v Bowman, 138 Ill 2d 131, 149 Ill Dec 263, 561 NE2d 633 (1990); People v Howard, 205 Ill App 3d 702, 151 Ill Dec 113, 563 NE2d 1219 (5th Dist 1990); People v Montenegro, 203 Ill App 3d 314, 148 Ill Dec 337, 560 NE2d 934 (2d Dist 1990); People v King, 190 Ill App 3d 1, 137 Ill Dec 209, 545 NE2d 970 (1st Dist 1989); People v Capers, 186 Ill App 3d 367, 134 Ill Dec 349, 542 NE2d 528 (4th Dist 1989); People v Tinoco, 185 Ill App 3d 816, 133 Ill Dec 760, 541 NE2d 1198 (1st Dist 1989); People v Landgham, 182 Ill App 3d 148, 130 Ill Dec 652, 537 NE2d 981 (1st Dist 1989; People v Norks, 137 Ill App 3d 1078, 92 Ill Dec 406, 484 NE2d 1261 (2d Dist 1985).

51. 725 ILCS 5/104-11

People v Williams, 205 Ill App 3d 715, 146 Ill Dec 914, 558 NE2d 1248 (1st Dist 1990); People v Newell, 196 Ill App 3d 373, 143 Ill Dec 15, 553 NE2d 722 (3d Dist 1990); People v Brown, 131 Ill App 3d 859, 87 Ill Dec 8, 476 NE2d 469 (2d Dist 1985).

See ch 15.

52. People v Gleash, 209 Ill App 3d 598, 154 Ill Dec 348, 568 NE2d 348 (1st Dist 1991); People v Seaman, 203 Ill App 3d 871, 148 Ill Dec 882, 561 NE2d 188 (5th Dist 1990); People v Edwards, 167 Ill App 3d 324, 118 Ill Dec 117, 521 NE2d 185 (2d Dist 1988); People v Johnson, 162 Ill App 3d 952, 114 Ill Dec 188, 516 NE2d 343 (1st Dist 1987).

on appeal unless the decision was contrary to the manifest weight of the evidence.[53]

§ 30:70. Trial and related proceedings

The trial court has broad discretion over the orderly conduct of a trial.[54] This discretion includes such matters as interpreters,[55] courtroom demonstrations,[56] limitations on the scope of counsels' arguments,[57] and requests for change of counsel,[58] as well as the probative value and admissibility of evidence.[59] The court also has

---

53. People v Gleash, 209 Ill App 3d 598, 154 Ill Dec 348, 568 NE2d 348 (1st Dist 1991); People v Britz, 185 Ill App 3d 191, 133 Ill Dec 423, 541 NE2d 505 (4th Dist 1989); People v Pecina, 132 Ill App 3d 948, 87 Ill Dec 685, 477 NE2d 811 (3d Dist 1985).

54. People v Schuld, 175 Ill App 3d 272, 124 Ill Dec 819, 529 NE2d 800 (2d Dist 1988).

55. People v Lopez, 114 Ill App 3d 1018, 70 Ill Dec 580, 449 NE2d 927 (1st Dist 1983).

56. People v Summers, 202 Ill App 3d 1, 147 Ill Dec 793, 559 NE2d 1133 (4th Dist 1990); People v Rose, 77 Ill App 3d 330, 32 Ill Dec 700, 395 NE2d 1081 (1st Dist 1979).

57. People v Boland, 205 Ill App 3d 1009, 150 Ill Dec 836, 563 NE2d 963 (1st Dist 1990); People v Williams, 205 Ill App 3d 715, 146 Ill Dec 914, 558 NE2d 1248 (1st Dist 1990); People v Siefke, 195 Ill App 3d 135, 141 Ill Dec 833, 551 NE2d 1361 (2d Dist 1990); People v Holloway, 119 Ill App 3d 1014, 75 Ill Dec 472, 457 NE2d 466 (1st Dist 1983).

58. People v Adams, 195 Ill App 3d 870, 142 Ill Dec 653, 553 NE2d 3 (5th Dist 1990).

59. People v Illgen, 145 Ill 2d 353, 164 Ill Dec 599, 583 NE2d 515, 24 ALR5th 864 (1991), habeas corpus dismissed 1994 US Dist LEXIS 4499 (ND Ill);

People v Shum, 117 Ill 2d 317, 111 Ill Dec 546, 512 NE2d 1183 (1987), cert den 484 US 1079, 98 L Ed 2d 1022, 108 S Ct 1060; People v Stewart, 105 Ill 2d 22, 85 Ill Dec 241, 473 NE2d 840 (1984), cert den 471 US 1131, 86 L Ed 2d 283, 105 S Ct 2666, cert den 488 US 900, 102 L Ed 2d 234, 109 S Ct 246, affd 60 F3d 296 (CA7 Ill), mod, reh den 70 F3d 955 (CA7 Ill), cert den 518 US 1033, 135 L Ed 2d 1095, 116 S Ct 2580; People v Schutz, 201 Ill App 3d 154, 147 Ill Dec 289, 559 NE2d 289 (4th Dist 1990); People v Zarebski, 186 Ill App 3d 285, 134 Ill Dec 266, 542 NE2d 445 (2d Dist 1989).

See § 30:71.

APPELLATE REVIEW § 30:70

the discretion to limit the scope of cross-examination and rebuttal.[60] In all cases, there must be a clear showing that the trial court abused its discretion and that the abuse was manifestly prejudicial to the appellant for the decision to be reviewed.[61]

☛ *Practice Guide:* Although the Sixth Amendment[62] guarantees a defendant's right to cross-examine the witnesses testifying against him or her, that right has been held not to deprive a trial court of its discretionary authority to impose reasonable limitations on the permissible scope of cross-examination.[63]

---

60. People v Franklin, 135 Ill 2d 78, 142 Ill Dec 152, 552 NE2d 743 (1990), cert den 498 US 881, 112 L Ed 2d 182, 111 S Ct 228, cert den 517 US 1122, 134 L Ed 2d 524, 116 S Ct 1357, habeas corpus den, dismd 993 F Supp 1162 (ND Ill); People v Williams, 209 Ill App 3d 709, 154 Ill Dec 388, 568 NE2d 388 (1st Dist 1991); People v Sprawls, 205 Ill App 3d 337, 150 Ill Dec 262, 562 NE2d 1065 (1st Dist 1990), appeal after remand, remanded 240 Ill App 3d 165, 181 Ill Dec 56, 608 NE2d 129 (1st Dist); People v Torres, 200 Ill App 3d 253, 146 Ill Dec 682, 558 NE2d 645 (2d Dist 1990); People v Thomas, 199 Ill App 3d 79, 145 Ill Dec 344, 556 NE2d 1246 (2d Dist 1990); People v Lewis, 198 Ill App 3d 976, 145 Ill Dec 79, 556 NE2d 697 (1st Dist 1990); People v Sanders, 191 Ill App 3d 483, 138 Ill Dec 873, 548 NE2d 103 (4th Dist 1989); People v Dale, 189 Ill App 3d 704, 136 Ill Dec 997, 545 NE2d 521 (1st Dist 1989); People v Williams, 180 Ill App 3d 294, 129 Ill Dec 228, 535 NE2d 993 (1st Dist 1989).

61. See, e.g., People v Summers, 202 Ill App 3d 1, 147 Ill Dec 793, 559 NE2d 1133 (4th Dist 1990); People v Thomas, 199 Ill App 3d 79, 145 Ill Dec 344, 556 NE2d 1246 (2d Dist 1990); People v Adams, 195 Ill App 3d 870, 142 Ill Dec 653, 553 NE2d 3 (5th Dist 1990); People v Schuld, 175 Ill App 3d 272, 124 Ill Dec 819, 529 NE2d 800 (2d Dist 1988); People v Smith, 172 Ill App 3d 94, 122 Ill Dec 456, 526 NE2d 849 (1st Dist 1988).

The trial judge is in a superior position to gauge the meaning of a prospective juror's responses during voir dire, and the judge's determination must therefore be granted deference. People v Childress, 158 Ill 2d 275, 198 Ill Dec 794, 633 NE2d 635 (1994), cert den 513 US 881, 130 L Ed 2d 143, 115 S Ct 215.

62. US Const Amend VI.

63. People v Harris, 123 Ill 2d 113, 122 Ill Dec 76, 526 NE2d 335 (1988), cert den 488 US 902, 102 L Ed 2d 240, 109 S Ct 251, post-conviction proceeding, remanded 249 Ill App 3d 924, 189 Ill Dec 170, 619 NE2d 871 (3d Dist), post-

§ 30:70   ILLINOIS JURISPRUDENCE: CRIMINAL LAW

There is a strong presumption that judges rely solely on proper evidence in reaching determinations on the merits.[64] This presumption may only be rebutted by an affirmative showing to the contrary in the record.[65]

The trial court is presumptively in the best position to decide whether a defendant's motion for a mistrial should or should not be granted, and its ruling will not be reversed unless the decision was manifestly erroneous or contrary to the interests of justice, and the defendant was prejudiced by the denial.[66] Similarly, a decision on a motion seeking a new trial is reversible on appeal only upon a showing that the trial court abused its discretion.[67]

§ 30:71. —Effective assistance of counsel

It is the strong presumption of a reviewing court that a defendant was provided with reasonably professional and

---

conviction proceeding, cause remanded 273 Ill App 3d 71, 209 Ill Dec 865, 652 NE2d 405 (3d Dist); Delaware v Van Arsdall, 475 US 673, 89 L Ed 2d 674, 106 S Ct 1431 (1986), on remand 524 A2d 3 (Del); United States v Spivey, 841 F2d 799 (CA7 1988).

64. People v Ticey, 214 Ill App 3d 1043, 158 Ill Dec 697, 574 NE2d 810 (1st Dist 1991), habeas corpus granted 1992 US Dist LEXIS 18211 (ND Ill), revd 8 F3d 498 (CA7 Ill).

65. People v Ticey, 214 Ill App 3d 1043, 158 Ill Dec 697, 574 NE2d 810 (1st Dist 1991), habeas corpus granted 1992 US Dist LEXIS 18211 (ND Ill), revd 8 F3d 498 (CA7 Ill); People v Bradford, 187 Ill App 3d 903, 135 Ill Dec 350, 543 NE2d 918 (1st Dist 1989).

66. People v Logston, 196 Ill App 3d 30, 142 Ill Dec 525, 552 NE2d 1266 (4th Dist 1990); People v McKinney, 193 Ill App 3d 1012, 140 Ill Dec 719, 550 NE2d 604 (4th Dist 1990); People v Alvarez, 186 Ill App 3d 541, 134 Ill Dec 391, 542 NE2d 737 (1st Dist 1989); United States v McAnderson, 914 F2d 934, 31 Fed Rules Evid Serv 341 (CA7 Ill 1990).

67. People v Molstad, 101 Ill 2d 128, 77 Ill Dec 775, 461 NE2d 398 (1984); People v Villareal, 201 Ill App 3d 223, 147 Ill Dec 77, 559 NE2d 77 (1st Dist 1990); People v Green, 198 Ill App 3d 525, 144 Ill Dec 689, 555 NE2d 1208 (3d Dist 1990), affd without op 48 F3d 1222 (CA7 Ill), reported in full 1995 US App LEXIS 4644 (CA7 Ill); People v Peters, 144 Ill App 3d 310, 98 Ill Dec 731, 494 NE2d 853 (2d Dist 1986); United States v Goodwin, 770 F2d 631 (CA7 Ill 1985), cert den 474 US 1084, 88 L Ed 2d 897, 106 S Ct 858.

effective representation by counsel.[68] The presumed range of reasonable representation is wide, and any challenged action is initially considered a question of trial tactics or strategy.[69] Only a showing by clear and convincing proof of prejudicial incompetency may overcome the presumption of reasonable professional assistance of counsel.[70] However, there is a presumption of prejudice where counsel fails to perfect the defendant's appeal.[71]

> ☞*Illustration:* In any ineffectiveness case, a particular decision not to investigate must be directly assessed for reasonableness in all the circumstances, applying a heavy measure of deference to counsel's judgments, and when a defendant has given counsel reason to believe that pursuing certain investigations would be fruitless or even harmful, counsel's failure to pursue those investigations may not later be challenged as unreasonable.[72]

---

68. People v Watkins, 206 Ill App 3d 228, 150 Ill Dec 679, 563 NE2d 806 (1st Dist 1990); People v Powell, 180 Ill App 3d 315, 129 Ill Dec 243, 535 NE2d 1008 (1st Dist 1989).

Annotation References: Adequacy of defense counsel's representation of criminal client regarding prior convictions, 14 ALR4th 227.

69. People v Furby, 228 Ill App 3d 1, 169 Ill Dec 360, 591 NE2d 533 (Cal App 2nd Dist 1992); People v Watkins, 206 Ill App 3d 228, 150 Ill Dec 679, 563 NE2d 806 (1st Dist 1990); People v Powell, 180 Ill App 3d 315, 129 Ill Dec 243, 535 NE2d 1008 (1st Dist 1989); People v Thurman, 169 Ill App 3d 996, 120 Ill Dec 273, 523 NE2d 1184 (1st Dist 1988); United States v Zylstra, 713 F2d 1332 (CA7 Ill 1983), cert den 464 US 965, 78 L Ed 2d 344, 104 S Ct 403.

70. People v Williams, 139 Ill 2d 1, 150 Ill Dec 544, 563 NE2d 431 (1990), cert den 499 US 979, 113 L Ed 2d 726, 111 S Ct 1630, habeas corpus granted 863 F Supp 697 (ND Ill), affd 59 F3d 673 (CA7 Ill); People v Moore, 133 Ill 2d 331, 140 Ill Dec 385, 549 NE2d 1257 (1990), cert den 510 US 1118, 127 L Ed 2d 387, 114 S Ct 1068; People v Montague, 149 Ill App 3d 332, 102 Ill Dec 699, 500 NE2d 592 (4th Dist 1986); People v Purnell, 126 Ill App 3d 608, 82 Ill Dec 87, 467 NE2d 1160 (1st Dist 1984); United States ex rel. Kowal v Attorney Gen. of Illinois, 550 F Supp 447 (ND Ill 1982).

71. People v Moore, 133 Ill 2d 331, 140 Ill Dec 385, 549 NE2d 1257 (1990), cert den 510 US 1118, 127 L Ed 2d 387, 114 S Ct 1068.

§ 30:72. —Evidentiary matters

The question of whether or not evidence is admissible at trial is within the sound discretion of the trial court; a decision on an evidentiary issue will not generally be overturned on appeal unless there is a showing of a clear abuse of discretion.[73] Such abuse is shown where the trial court's decision is arbitrary, fanciful or unreasonable.[74] But where a court finds evidence to be relevant and material, its decision will be reversed only upon a clear showing that the court abused its discretion.[75]

☛ *Illustration:* In a criminal sexual assault and home invasion case, the trial court's decision to exclude the defendant's evidence offered to show that someone other

---

72. Jones v Page, 76 F3d 831 (CA7 Ill 1996), cert den 519 US 951, 136 L Ed 2d 254, 117 S Ct 363.

73. People v Cruz, 162 Ill 2d 314, 205 Ill Dec 345, 643 NE2d 636 (1994); People v Illgen, 145 Ill 2d 353, 164 Ill Dec 599, 583 NE2d 515, 24 ALR5th 864 (1991); People v Hayes, 139 Ill 2d 89, 151 Ill Dec 348, 564 NE2d 803 (1990), cert den 499 US 967, 113 L Ed 2d 664, 111 S Ct 1601; People v Franklin, 135 Ill 2d 78, 142 Ill Dec 152, 552 NE2d 743 (1990), cert den 498 US 881, 112 L Ed 2d 182, 111 S Ct 228; People v Tisler, 103 Ill 2d 226, 82 Ill Dec 613, 469 NE2d 147 (1984); People v Austin, 207 Ill App 3d 896, 152 Ill Dec 805, 566 NE2d 492 (1st Dist 1990); People v Summers, 202 Ill App 3d 1, 147 Ill Dec 793, 559 NE2d 1133 (4th Dist 1990); People v Bryant, 202 Ill App 3d 290, 147 Ill Dec 590, 559 NE2d 930 (1st Dist 1990), cert den 502 US 824, 116 L Ed 2d 61, 112 S Ct 89; People v Murray, 201 Ill App 3d 573, 147 Ill Dec 174, 559 NE2d 174 (1st Dist 1990); People v James, 200 Ill App 3d 380, 146 Ill Dec 769, 558 NE2d 732 (4th Dist 1990); People v Brown, 199 Ill App 3d 860, 145 Ill Dec 841, 557 NE2d 611 (1st Dist 1990); People v Williams, 196 Ill App 3d 851, 144 Ill Dec 1, 554 NE2d 1040 (1st Dist 1990); People v Pettis, 184 Ill App 3d 743, 133 Ill Dec 231, 540 NE2d 1097 (2d Dist 1989); People v Turner, 179 Ill App 3d 510, 128 Ill Dec 159, 534 NE2d 179 (2d Dist 1989).

74. People v Illgen, 145 Ill 2d 353, 164 Ill Dec 599, 583 NE2d 515, 24 ALR5th 864 (1991).

75. People v Debeck, 204 Ill App 3d 15, 149 Ill Dec 385, 561 NE2d 1081 (3d Dist 1990); People v Castro, 190 Ill App 3d 227, 137 Ill Dec 717, 546 NE2d 662 (1st Dist 1989); People v Ware, 180 Ill App 3d 921, 129 Ill Dec 663, 536 NE2d 713 (1st Dist 1988); People v Bullock, 154 Ill App 3d 266, 107 Ill Dec 380, 507 NE2d 44 (1st Dist 1987).

than the defendant committed the offense did not constitute an abuse of discretion, because the defendant failed to establish the necessary showing of a close connection between the third person and the commission of the offense.[76]

The mere fact that reasonable minds might differ, or that a different conclusion might rationally be drawn from the same facts, is insufficient to overcome the deference afforded the trial court's evidentiary ruling.[77]

For instance, the issue of whether the probative value of proffered evidence is outweighed by any prejudicial effect it might have on the defendant is within the trial court's discretion.[78] When the record clearly reflects that the trial court was advised of potential prejudice but nonetheless admitted the evidence, the presumption on appeal, absent evidence to the contrary, is that the court weighed the prejudicial and probative effects and exercised its discretion appropriately.[79] Thus, a trial court's

76. People v Ward, 101 Ill 2d 443, 79 Ill Dec 142, 463 NE2d 696 (1984); People v Maberry, 193 Ill App 3d 250, 140 Ill Dec 323, 549 NE2d 974 (4th Dist 1990).

77. People v Illgen, 145 Ill 2d 353, 164 Ill Dec 599, 583 NE2d 515, 24 ALR5th 864 (1991), habeas corpus dismissed 1994 US Dist LEXIS 4499 (ND Ill).

78. People v Illgen, 145 Ill 2d 353, 164 Ill Dec 599, 583 NE2d 515, 24 ALR5th 864 (1991); People v Stewart, 105 Ill 2d 22, 85 Ill Dec 241, 473 NE2d 840 (1984), cert den 471 US 1131, 86 L Ed 2d 283, 105 S Ct 2666, cert den 488 US 900, 102 L Ed 2d 234, 109 S Ct 246, cert den 502 US 853, 116 L Ed 2d 126, 112 S Ct 162, habeas corpus den 1993 US Dist LEXIS 7962 (ND Ill), affd 60 F3d 296 (CA7 Ill), mod, reh den 70 F3d 955 (CA7 Ill), cert den 518 US 1033, 135 L Ed 2d 1095, 116 S Ct 2580; United States v Field, 875 F2d 130, 28 Fed Rules Evid Serv 149 (CA7 Ind 1989).

79. People v Winters, 97 Ill 2d 151, 73 Ill Dec 439, 454 NE2d 299 (1983); People v Watkins, 206 Ill App 3d 228, 150 Ill Dec 679, 563 NE2d 806 (1st Dist 1990); People v Elzey, 203 Ill App 3d 153, 148 Ill Dec 510, 560 NE2d 1107 (1st Dist 1990); People v Brooks, 175 Ill App 3d 136, 124 Ill Dec 751, 529 NE2d 732 (1st Dist 1988); People v Graves, 142 Ill App 3d 885, 97 Ill Dec 81, 492 NE2d 517 (1st Dist 1986); People v Purnell, 129 Ill App 3d 253, 84 Ill Dec 433, 472 NE2d 183 (1st Dist 1984); People v Johnson, 110 Ill App 3d 965, 66 Ill Dec 552, 443 NE2d 235 (1st Dist 1982); People v Jones, 109 Ill App 3d 120, 64 Ill Dec 709, 440 NE2d 261 (1st Dist 1982).

§ 30:72   ILLINOIS JURISPRUDENCE: CRIMINAL LAW

decision to admit evidence of prior crimes will be overturned on appeal only if there is a clear showing of an abuse of discretion.[80] Similarly, the admission of photographic evidence will not be reversed unless the appellant can demonstrate a prejudicial abuse of discretion.[81]

The party challenging the admission of evidence bears the burden of proving that the alleged error was substantial, and not merely harmless.[82] In the absence of a clear showing to the contrary, it is presumed that the jury complied with the court's instructions to disregard inadmissible testimony, and that any potential prejudice arising from such evidence was cured.[83]

The decision whether or not to grant a postconviction petition seeking an evidentiary hearing is within the sound discretion of the trial court, and will not be reversed on appeal absent a showing of abuse of that discretion.[84]

---

80. People v Jenkins, 209 Ill App 3d 249, 154 Ill Dec 122, 568 NE2d 122 (1st Dist 1991); People v Stevenson, 204 Ill App 3d 342, 149 Ill Dec 866, 562 NE2d 330 (1st Dist 1990); People v Smith, 199 Ill App 3d 839, 145 Ill Dec 826, 557 NE2d 596 (1st Dist 1990); People v Brown, 199 Ill App 3d 860, 145 Ill Dec 841, 557 NE2d 611 (1st Dist 1990); People v McManus, 197 Ill App 3d 1085, 144 Ill Dec 272, 555 NE2d 391 (2d Dist 1990); People v Clark, 173 Ill App 3d 443, 122 Ill Dec 97, 526 NE2d 356 (2d Dist 1988); People v Brozan, 163 Ill App 3d 73, 115 Ill Dec 83, 517 NE2d 285 (1st Dist 1987).

81. People v Redd, 135 Ill 2d 252, 142 Ill Dec 802, 553 NE2d 316 (1990), appeal after remand 173 Ill 2d 1, 218 Ill Dec 861, 670 NE2d 583, cert den 519 US 1063, 136 L Ed 2d 621, 117 S Ct 699; People v Young, 206 Ill App 3d 789, 151 Ill Dec 592, 564 NE2d 1254 (1st Dist 1990); People v Gibson, 205 Ill App 3d 361, 150 Ill Dec 339, 562 NE2d 1142 (1st Dist 1990).

82. People v Sanchez, 191 Ill App 3d 1099, 139 Ill Dec 128, 548 NE2d 513 (1st Dist 1989); People v Foster, 190 Ill App 3d 1018, 138 Ill Dec 311, 547 NE2d 478 (1st Dist 1989), cert den 498 US 837, 112 L Ed 2d 78, 111 S Ct 108; People v Smith, 139 Ill App 3d 21, 93 Ill Dec 512, 486 NE2d 1347 (1st Dist 1985).

United States v Barnes, 907 F2d 693 (CA7 Ill 1990), appeal after remand 948 F2d 325 (CA7 Ill); United States v Montoya, 827 F2d 143 (CA7 Ill 1987).

83. People v Lasley, 158 Ill App 3d 614, 110 Ill Dec 484, 511 NE2d 661 (1st Dist 1987); United States v McAnderson, 914 F2d 934 (CA7 Ill 1990), affd 1994 US App LEXIS 10651 (CA7 Ill).

§ 30:73. ——Witnesses

The determination of a witness' competency to testify[85] or an expert's qualification[86] are within the discretion of the trial court, and will be disturbed only if the appellant can demonstrate an abuse of that discretion.[87]

Exclusion of a witness for violating a court order barring witnesses from the courtroom is within the trial court's sound discretion, and the exclusion will not be reversed on appeal unless there is a clear showing that a party has been deprived of the opportunity to present material testimony as a result.[88] The admission of the testimony of unlisted witnesses is also within the discretion of the trial court, and will be reviewed only if the appellant can show surprise or prejudice.[89]

---

84. People v Saunders, 187 Ill App 3d 734, 135 Ill Dec 510, 543 NE2d 1078 (2d Dist 1989).

85. People v Barfield, 187 Ill App 3d 257, 134 Ill Dec 874, 543 NE2d 157 (1st Dist 1989); People v Wolfe, 176 Ill App 3d 299, 126 Ill Dec 19, 531 NE2d 152 (3d Dist 1988); People v Spencer, 119 Ill App 3d 971, 75 Ill Dec 479, 457 NE2d 473 (1st Dist 1983).

86. People v Coleman, 205 Ill App 3d 567, 150 Ill Dec 883, 563 NE2d 1010 (4th Dist 1990); People v Moody, 199 Ill App 3d 455, 145 Ill Dec 565, 557 NE2d 335 (1st Dist 1990); People v Bradley, 172 Ill App 3d 545, 122 Ill Dec 523, 526 NE2d 916 (4th Dist 1988) (superseded by statute on other grounds as stated in People v Rushing, 192 Ill App 3d 444, 139 Ill Dec 403, 548 NE2d 788 (4th Dist); People v Sequoia Books, Inc., 172 Ill App 3d 627, 122 Ill Dec 678, 527 NE2d 50 (2d Dist 1988), cert den 490 US 1097, 104 L Ed 2d 1002, 109 S Ct 2447; People v Cole, 170 Ill App 3d 912, 120 Ill Dec 744, 524 NE2d 926 (1st Dist 1988); People v Server, 148 Ill App 3d 888, 102 Ill Dec 239, 499 NE2d 1019 (4th Dist 1986), cert den 484 US 842, 98 L Ed 2d 88, 108 S Ct 131; People v Knox, 121 Ill App 3d 579, 76 Ill Dec 942, 459 NE2d 1077 (3d Dist 1984).

87. See, e.g., People v Coleman, 205 Ill App 3d 567, 150 Ill Dec 883, 563 NE2d 1010 (4th Dist 1990); People v Cole, 170 Ill App 3d 912, 120 Ill Dec 744, 524 NE2d 926 (1st Dist 1988).

88. People v Bridgeforth, 51 Ill 2d 52, 281 NE2d 617, 54 ALR3d 757 (1972); People v Young, 187 Ill App 3d 977, 135 Ill Dec 418, 543 NE2d 986 (1st Dist 1989), app den 128 Ill 2d 671, 139 Ill Dec 521, 548 NE2d 1077, habeas corpus den, motion gr 1998 US Dist LEXIS 19139 (ND Ill); People v Bodeman, 105 Ill App 3d 39, 60 Ill Dec 902, 433 NE2d 1140 (1st Dist 1982).

§ 30:74. —Verdict, judgment, and sentence

Following a jury trial, all reasonable presumptions must be made on appeal in favor of the verdict reached.[90] In reviewing a conviction, the appellate court considers the evidence, and draws all reasonable inferences from it, in the light most favorable to the prosecution.[91] In this context, the sole question is whether any rational trier of fact could have found the essential elements of the crime charged beyond a reasonable doubt.[92] It is not the function

89. People v Schutz, 201 Ill App 3d 154, 147 Ill Dec 289, 559 NE2d 289 (4th Dist 1990); People v Zarebski, 186 Ill App 3d 285, 134 Ill Dec 266, 542 NE2d 445 (2d Dist 1989).

90. United States v O'Connor, 910 F2d 1466 (CA7 Ill 1990), cert den 498 US 1082, 112 L Ed 2d 1041, 111 S Ct 953.

91. See, e.g., People v Young, 128 Ill 2d 1, 131 Ill Dec 78, 538 NE2d 453 (1989), cert den 497 US 1031, 111 L Ed 2d 798, 110 S Ct 3290; People v Waldron, 208 Ill App 3d 234, 153 Ill Dec 126, 566 NE2d 976 (4th Dist 1991); People v Patrick, 205 Ill App 3d 222, 150 Ill Dec 224, 562 NE2d 1027 (1st Dist 1990); People v Moody, 199 Ill App 3d 455, 145 Ill Dec 565, 557 NE2d 335 (1st Dist 1990); United States v Atterson, 926 F2d 649, 32 Fed Rules Evid Serv 379 (CA7 Ill 1991), cert den 501 US 1259, 115 L Ed 2d 1072, 111 S Ct 2909; United States v Medley, 913 F2d 1248 (CA7 Ill 1990), affd without op 1 F3d 1244 (CA7 Ill), cert den 510 US 1013, 126 L Ed 2d 569, 114 S Ct 604; United States v Bennett, 908 F2d 189 (CA7 Ill 1990), cert den 498 US 991, 112 L Ed 2d 544, 111 S Ct 534, post-conviction proceeding 1992 US Dist LEXIS 11629 (ND Ill), affd 19 F3d 21 (CA7 Ill), cert den 513 US 850, 130 L Ed 2d 87, 115 S Ct 148; United States v Garrett, 903 F2d 1105 (CA7 Ill 1990), cert den 498 US 905, 112 L Ed 2d 227, 111 S Ct 272; United States v De Soto, 885 F2d 354, 28 Fed Rules Evid Serv 623 (CA7 Ill 1989), supp op 1989 US Dist LEXIS 13279 (ND Ill).

92. See, e.g., People v Hurtado, 208 Ill App 3d 110, 153 Ill Dec 8, 566 NE2d 858 (2d Dist 1991); People v Waldron, 208 Ill App 3d 234, 153 Ill Dec 126, 566 NE2d 976 (4th Dist 1991); People v Jamison, 207 Ill App 3d 565, 152 Ill Dec 530, 566 NE2d 58 (3d Dist 1991); People v Snulligan, 204 Ill App 3d 110, 149 Ill Dec 429, 561 NE2d 1125 (1st Dist 1990); People v Maloney, 201 Ill App 3d 599, 146 Ill Dec 943, 558 NE2d 1277 (1st Dist 1990); People v Brown, 199 Ill App 3d 860, 145 Ill Dec 841, 557 NE2d 611 (1st Dist 1990); People v Geneva, 196 Ill App 3d 1017, 143 Ill Dec 621, 554 NE2d 556 (1st Dist 1990); People v Batinich, 196 Ill App 3d 1078, 143 Ill Dec 678, 554 NE2d 613 (1st Dist 1990); People v Murray, 194 Ill App 3d 653, 141 Ill Dec 290, 551 NE2d 283 (1st Dist 1990).

of the reviewing court, however, to retry the defendant.[93] Thus, a conviction will only be set aside when the evidence on which it was based is so unsatisfactory or improbable as to create a reasonable doubt of the defendant's guilt.[94]

Matters of sentencing are within the trial court's discretion, and so a trial court's judgment as to the appropriate punishment is afforded great deference by the reviewing court, and will not be overturned absent a showing that the sentence imposed constitutes an abuse of the trial court's discretion.[95] This is

---

United States v Bennett, 908 F2d 189 (CA7 Ill 1990), cert den 498 US 991, 112 L Ed 2d 544, 111 S Ct 534, post-conviction proceeding 1992 US Dist LEXIS 11629 (ND Ill), affd 19 F3d 21 (CA7 Ill), reported in full 1994 US App LEXIS 4383 (CA7 Ill) and cert den 513 US 850, 130 L Ed 2d 87, 115 S Ct 148, affd 1999 US App LEXIS 2721 (CA7 Ill); United States v Medley, 913 F2d 1248 (CA7 Ill 1990), affd without op 1 F3d 1244 (CA7 Ill), reported in full 1993 US App LEXIS 20050 (CA7 Ill) and cert den 510 US 1013, 126 L Ed 2d 569, 114 S Ct 604.

93. People v Urioste, 203 Ill App 3d 1062, 149 Ill Dec 193, 561 NE2d 471 (5th Dist 1990); People v Lindbeck, 202 Ill App 3d 831, 148 Ill Dec 175, 560 NE2d 477 (3d Dist 1990); People v Colclasure, 200 Ill App 3d 1038, 146 Ill Dec 742, 558 NE2d 705 (5th Dist 1990); People v Broderick, 191 Ill App 3d 933, 139 Ill Dec 43, 548 NE2d 428 (1st Dist 1989); People v Barnett, 173 Ill App 3d 477, 123 Ill Dec 433, 527 NE2d 1071 (2d Dist 1988).

94. People v Summers, 202 Ill App 3d 1, 147 Ill Dec 793, 559 NE2d 1133 (4th Dist 1990); People v Turner, 193 Ill App 3d 152, 140 Ill Dec 437, 549 NE2d 1309 (2d Dist 1990); People v Campbell, 146 Ill App 3d 363, 586 NE2d 1261 (1992).

95. People v Johnson, 146 Ill 2d 109, 165 Ill Dec 682, 585 NE2d 78 (1991), cert den 506 US 834, 121 L Ed 2d 65, 113 S Ct 106; People v Illgen, 145 Ill 2d 353, 164 Ill Dec 599, 583 NE2d 515, 24 ALR5th 864 (1991); People v Steidl, 142 Ill 2d 204, 154 Ill Dec 616, 568 NE2d 837 (1991), cert den 502 US 853, 116 L Ed 2d 125, 112 S Ct 161 and post-conviction proceeding, cause remanded 177 Ill 2d 239, 226 Ill Dec 592, 685 NE2d 1335; People v Andrews, 132 Ill 2d 451, 139 Ill Dec 469, 548 NE2d 1025 (1989), appeal after remand 146 Ill 2d 413, 167 Ill Dec 996, 588 NE2d 1126, appeal after remand 155 Ill 2d 286, 185 Ill Dec 499, 614 NE2d 1184; People v Felella, 131 Ill 2d 525, 137 Ill Dec 547, 546 NE2d 492 (1989); People v Ward, 113 Ill 2d 516, 101 Ill Dec 834, 499 NE2d 422 (1986), cert den 479 US 1096, 94 L Ed 2d 168, 107 S Ct 1314; People v Lopez, 223 Ill App 3d 520, 165 Ill Dec 891, 585 NE2d 622 (3d Dist 1992); People v

§ 30:74 ILLINOIS JURISPRUDENCE: CRIMINAL LAW

because the presumption on review is that the trial court is in a superior position to evaluate the relevant factors and determine the appropriate punishment.[96] Mere disagreement with a properly imposed sentence, without a clear showing of an abuse of the court's discretion, does not establish the basis for substituting a new sentence on appeal.[97] Thus, the scope of review on an appeal of a sentence is limited to an examination of the record solely to

---

Jenkins, 209 Ill App 3d 249, 154 Ill Dec 122, 568 NE2d 122 (1st Dist 1991); People v Bell, 209 Ill App 3d 438, 154 Ill Dec 238, 568 NE2d 238 (1st Dist 1991); People v Gleash, 209 Ill App 3d 598, 154 Ill Dec 348, 568 NE2d 348 (1st Dist 1991); People v Williams, 209 Ill App 3d 709, 154 Ill Dec 388, 568 NE2d 388 (1st Dist 1991); People v Coleman, 201 Ill App 3d 803, 147 Ill Dec 243, 559 NE2d 243 (1st Dist 1990); People v Smith, 199 Ill App 3d 839, 145 Ill Dec 826, 557 NE2d 596 (1st Dist 1990); People v Williams, 196 Ill App 3d 851, 144 Ill Dec 1, 554 NE2d 1040 (1st Dist 1990), app den 133 Ill 2d 570, 149 Ill Dec 335, 561 NE2d 705; People v Schuld, 191 Ill App 3d 809, 138 Ill Dec 923, 548 NE2d 336 (1st Dist 1989); People v Whitehead, 171 Ill App 3d 900, 121 Ill Dec 777, 525 NE2d 1084 (1st Dist 1988); People v Escobar, 168 Ill App 3d 30, 118 Ill Dec 736, 522 NE2d 191 (1st Dist 1988); People v Jackiewicz, 163 Ill App 3d 1062, 115 Ill Dec 114, 517 NE2d 316 (4th Dist 1987); United States v McKenzie, 922 F2d 1323 (CA7 Ill 1991), cert den 502 US 854, 116 L Ed 2d 127, 112 S Ct 163.

96. People v Holmes, 198 Ill App 3d 766, 144 Ill Dec 861, 556 NE2d 539 (1st Dist 1989); People v Center, 198 Ill App 3d 1025, 145 Ill Dec 106, 556 NE2d 724 (1st Dist 1990); People v Geneva, 196 Ill App 3d 1017, 143 Ill Dec 621, 554 NE2d 556 (1st Dist 1990); People v Wyatt, 186 Ill App 3d 772, 134 Ill Dec 526, 542 NE2d 872 (1st Dist 1989); People v Jones, 172 Ill App 3d 1048, 123 Ill Dec 58, 527 NE2d 521 (4th Dist 1988); People v Branham, 137 Ill App 3d 896, 92 Ill Dec 371, 484 NE2d 1226 (2d Dist 1985).

97. People v Griffis, 200 Ill App 3d 752, 146 Ill Dec 501, 558 NE2d 464 (1st Dist 1990); People v Ward, 194 Ill App 3d 229, 141 Ill Dec 162, 550 NE2d 1208 (1st Dist 1990); People v Haepp, 194 Ill App 3d 207, 141 Ill Dec 148, 550 NE2d 1194 (1st Dist 1990); People v Agnew, 192 Ill App 3d 620, 139 Ill Dec 583, 548 NE2d 1139 (2d Dist 1989), app den 131 Ill 2d 561, 142 Ill Dec 883, 553 NE2d 397, subsequent app 206 Ill Dec 905, 646 NE2d 37 (App 2d Dist), subsequent app 263 Ill App 3d 1121, 225 Ill Dec 380, 683 NE2d 548 (2d Dist); People v Wyatt, 186 Ill App 3d 772, 134 Ill Dec 526, 542 NE2d 872 (1st Dist 1989); People v Rogers, 141 Ill App 3d 374, 95 Ill Dec 660, 490 NE2d 133 (2d Dist 1986); People v Williams, 128 Ill App 3d 384, 83 Ill Dec 720, 470 NE2d 1140 (4th Dist 1984).

determine whether or not an abuse of the trial court's discretion occurred.[98]

The trial court is presumed to have considered the evidence in mitigation and aggravation prior to pronouncing the sentence,[99] and not to have relied on any improper factors,[1] which the court is presumed to have recognized and disregarded.[2]

---

98. People v Andrews, 132 Ill 2d 451, 139 Ill Dec 469, 548 NE2d 1025 (1989), appeal after remand 146 Ill 2d 413, 167 Ill Dec 996, 588 NE2d 1126, appeal after remand 155 Ill 2d 286, 185 Ill Dec 499, 614 NE2d 1184; People v O'Neal, 125 Ill 2d 241, 531 NE2d 366 (1988); People v Pirrello, 207 Ill App 3d 208, 152 Ill Dec 82, 565 NE2d 324 (2d Dist 1991); People v Camp, 201 Ill App 3d 330, 147 Ill Dec 26, 559 NE2d 26 (1st Dist 1990); People v Noble, 201 Ill App 3d 1056, 147 Ill Dec 887, 560 NE2d 35 (4th Dist 1990); People v Stephenson, 198 Ill App 3d 189, 144 Ill Dec 443, 555 NE2d 802 (4th Dist 1990); People v Logston, 196 Ill App 3d 30, 142 Ill Dec 525, 552 NE2d 1266 (4th Dist 1990); People v Helton, 195 Ill App 3d 410, 142 Ill Dec 48, 552 NE2d 398 (4th Dist 1990); People v Compton, 193 Ill App 3d 896, 140 Ill Dec 755, 550 NE2d 640 (4th Dist 1990); People v Migliore, 170 Ill App 3d 581, 121 Ill Dec 376, 525 NE2d 182 (2d Dist 1988).

99. People v Lopez, 223 Ill App 3d 520, 165 Ill Dec 891, 585 NE2d 622 (3d Dist 1992); People v Moskowitz, 209 Ill App 3d 812, 154 Ill Dec 427, 568 NE2d 427 (3d Dist 1991); People v Goodwin, 208 Ill App 3d 829, 153 Ill Dec 708, 567 NE2d 666 (3d Dist 1991); People v Clark, 207 Ill App 3d 439, 152 Ill Dec 455, 565 NE2d 1373 (4th Dist 1991); People v Watkins, 206 Ill App 3d 228, 150 Ill Dec 679, 563 NE2d 806 (1st Dist 1990), app den 137 Ill 2d 671, 156 Ill Dec 568, 571 NE2d 155; People v Hernandez, 204 Ill App 3d 732, 149 Ill Dec 755, 562 NE2d 219 (2d Dist 1990); People v Fields, 198 Ill App 3d 438, 144 Ill Dec 617, 555 NE2d 1136 (5th Dist 1990); People v Roesler, 195 Ill App 3d 1007, 142 Ill Dec 501, 552 NE2d 1242 (5th Dist 1990); People v Compton, 193 Ill App 3d 896, 140 Ill Dec 755, 550 NE2d 640 (4th Dist 1990); People v Berry, 175 Ill App 3d 420, 124 Ill Dec 884, 529 NE2d 1001 (1st Dist 1988).

See ch 28.

1. People v Evans, 125 Ill 2d 50, 125 Ill Dec 790, 530 NE2d 1360 (1988), cert den 490 US 1113, 104 L Ed 2d 1036, 109 S Ct 3175; People v Alvelo, 201 Ill App 3d 496, 147 Ill Dec 131, 559 NE2d 131 (1st Dist 1990); United States v Farmer, 924 F2d 647 (CA7 Ill 1991), post-conviction proceeding 1992 US App LEXIS 27555 (CA7).

2. People v Peterson, 202 Ill App 3d 33, 147 Ill Dec 422, 559 NE2d 762 (1st Dist 1990); People v Walker, 113 Ill App 3d 1074, 69 Ill Dec 748, 448 NE2d 208 (5th Dist 1983), cert den 465 US 1031, 79 L Ed 2d 697, 104 S Ct 1297.

Where a defendant is sentenced to death, the Illinois Supreme Court's duty is to determine whether the sentence was imposed arbitrarily or capriciously, or is unduly harsh in light of the circumstances of the offense and the character and rehabilitative potential of the defendant.[3]

X. QUESTIONS OF FACT, WEIGHT AND SUFFICIENCY

Research References:
  Annotation References:
    Index and Annotations: Appeal and Error
    ALR Digest to 3d, 4th, 5th, and Federal: Appeal and Error §§ 660, 681–686, 715
  Practice References:
    Nichols Drinking/Driving Lit § 19:04.
    5 Am Jur 2d, Appeal and Error §§ 815, 821, 882, 883
  Miscellaneous References:
    West's Illinois Digest 2d, Criminal Law §§ 1158–1160

§ 30:75. Generally

On appeal, the reviewing court is highly deferential to the original trier of fact, because the original trier of fact is in the best position to evaluate the credibility of the witnesses and their testimony and to weigh the evidence, having been present for the original trial.[4] Consequently, the reviewing court will only disturb the findings of the original fact-finder, be it the trial court or a jury, if the record does not support the fact-finder's findings.[5] If

---

3. People v Bean, 137 Ill 2d 65, 147 Ill Dec 891, 560 NE2d 258 (1990), cert den 499 US 932, 113 L Ed 2d 270, 111 S Ct 1338.

See ch 28.

4. People v Steidl, 142 Ill 2d 204, 154 Ill Dec 616, 568 NE2d 837 (1991), cert den 502 US 853, 116 L Ed 2d 125, 112 S Ct 161 and post-conviction proceeding, cause remanded 177 Ill 2d 239, 226 Ill Dec 592, 685 NE2d 1335; People v Sanchez, 131 Ill 2d 417, 137 Ill Dec 629, 546 NE2d 574 (1989), cert den 519 US 967, 136 L Ed 2d 308, 117 S Ct 392; People v Newell, 103 Ill 2d 465, 83 Ill Dec 229, 469 NE2d 1375 (1984).

5. People v Bowman, 138 Ill 2d 131, 149 Ill Dec 263, 561 NE2d 633 (1990).

there is evidence in support of the verdict, but it is conflicting, the reviewing court would not be justified in substituting its judgment for that of the trial court or the jury.[6] Rather, to justify the overturning of a trial verdict, the evidence supporting the trial verdict would have to be found by the reviewing court to be so improbable and unconvincing as to raise a reasonable doubt as to the defendant's guilt.[7] In other words, the trial verdict would have to be manifestly erroneous.[8] The reasonable doubt test is applied to evaluate whether a reviewing court is justified in interfering with a trial verdict.[9]

As with the credibility of witnesses and what weight to give their testimony, inferences drawn from the evidence presented are to be drawn by the original trier of fact.[10] If the inferences drawn are reasonable, then a judgment made by an original fact-finder will not be disturbed.[11]

---

6. People v Mehmedoski, 207 Ill App 3d 275, 152 Ill Dec 202, 565 NE2d 735 (2d Dist 1990).

7. People v Steidl, 142 Ill 2d 204, 154 Ill Dec 616, 568 NE2d 837 (1991), cert den 502 US 853, 116 L Ed 2d 125, 112 S Ct 161 and post-conviction proceeding, cause remanded 177 Ill 2d 239, 226 Ill Dec 592, 685 NE2d 1335.

People v Gordon, 204 Ill App 3d 123, 149 Ill Dec 468, 561 NE2d 1164 (1st Dist 1990); People v Pintos, 172 Ill App 3d 1096, 122 Ill Dec 814, 527 NE2d 312 (1st Dist 1988), app gr 123 Ill 2d 564, 128 Ill Dec 897, 535 NE2d 408 and affd 133 Ill 2d 286, 139 Ill Dec 832, 549 NE2d 344.

8. People v House, 141 Ill 2d 323, 152 Ill Dec 572, 566 NE2d 259 (1990); People v Murray, 137 Ill 2d 382, 148 Ill Dec 7, 560 NE2d 309 (1990); People v Thomas, 137 Ill 2d 500, 148 Ill Dec 751, 561 NE2d 57 (1990), cert den 498 US 1127, 112 L Ed 2d 1196, 111 S Ct 1092, cert den 142 L Ed 2d 905, 119 S Ct 907 (US); People v Foskey, 136 Ill 2d 66, 143 Ill Dec 257, 554 NE2d 192 (1990).

9. People v Herrett, 137 Ill 2d 195, 148 Ill Dec 695, 561 NE2d 1 (1990).

See also § 30:77.

10. People v Steidl, 142 Ill 2d 204, 154 Ill Dec 616, 568 NE2d 837 (1991), cert den 502 US 853, 116 L Ed 2d 125, 112 S Ct 161 and post-conviction proceeding, cause remanded 177 Ill 2d 239, 226 Ill Dec 592, 685 NE2d 1335.

11. People v Steidl, 142 Ill 2d 204, 154 Ill Dec 616, 568 NE2d 837 (1991), cert den 502 US 853, 116 L Ed 2d 125, 112 S Ct 161 and post-conviction proceeding, cause remanded 177 Ill 2d 239, 226 Ill Dec 592, 685 NE2d 1335.

§ 30:76. —Quantum of evidence

In the event that the quantum of evidence is challenged, the reviewing court has the duty to evaluate the evidence presented at trial, while keeping in mind the fact that the trial court or the jury as fact-finder was present for the testimony.[12] If the reviewing court, after making such an evaluation, finds that the evidence does not remove all reasonable doubt and consequently, does not support a finding of guilty, then the conviction must be reversed.[13] On the other hand, where there is substantial and credible evidence substantiating the trial court's verdict, the verdict will not be overturned.[14]

§ 30:77. —Reasonable doubt test

The reasonable doubt test is the standard used by the reviewing court to evaluate sufficiency of evidence.[15] Under the test, a conviction will not be set aside unless there is a reasonable doubt as to the defendant's guilt resulting from evidence which the reviewing court finds to be too improbable and unconvincing,[16] despite being considered in the light most favorable to the State.[17]

12. People v Holmes, 141 Ill 2d 204, 152 Ill Dec 268, 565 NE2d 950 (1990); People v Sanchez, 131 Ill 2d 417, 137 Ill Dec 629, 546 NE2d 574 (1989), cert den 519 US 967, 136 L Ed 2d 308, 117 S Ct 392; People v Newell, 103 Ill 2d 465, 83 Ill Dec 229, 469 NE2d 1375 (1984).

   Practice References: Nichols Drinking/Driving Lit § 19:04.

13. People v Holmes, 141 Ill 2d 204, 152 Ill Dec 268, 565 NE2d 950 (1990).

14. People v Laughlin, 163 Ill App 3d 115, 114 Ill Dec 380, 516 NE2d 535 (1st Dist 1987).

15. People v Herrett, 137 Ill 2d 195, 148 Ill Dec 695, 561 NE2d 1 (1990); People v Pintos, 133 Ill 2d 286, 139 Ill Dec 832, 549 NE2d 344 (1989).

16. People v Jimerson, 127 Ill 2d 12, 129 Ill Dec 124, 535 NE2d 889 (1989), cert den 497 US 1031, 111 L Ed 2d 796, 110 S Ct 3288, reh den 497 US 1050, 111 L Ed 2d 828, 111 S Ct 14, post-conviction proceeding, cause remanded 166 Ill 2d 211, 209 Ill Dec 738, 652 NE2d 278.

17. People v Patrick, 205 Ill App 3d 222, 150 Ill Dec 224, 562 NE2d 1027 (1st Dist 1990).

☞ *Caution:* The hypothesis of innocence standard, which required the reviewing court to disregard the inferences of the prosecution, and instead look only to the inferences of the defense to see if it could be concluded reasonably that the evidence was consistent with the defendant's hypothesis of innocence justifying reversal of a conviction, is no longer used.[18] The reasonable doubt test has replaced the hypothesis of innocence test.[19]

§ 30:78. —Province of jury or trial court

It is the province of the fact-finder to assess the credibility of the witnesses, weigh the evidence and draw reasonable inferences.[20] Either the jury or the court, in a bench trial, may act as fact-finder.[21] Because the fact-finder, be it jury or court, hears the presentation of the evidence first-hand, the trier of fact's judgment is deferred to by the reviewing court.[22]

XI. HARMLESS AND REVERSIBLE ERROR

Research References:

  Annotation References:

    Index and Annotations: Appeal and Error; Harmless and Prejudicial Error

---

18. United States v Moya, 721 F2d 606 (CA7 Ill 1983), cert den 465 US 1037, 79 L Ed 2d 709, 104 S Ct 1312.

19. People v Pintos, 133 Ill 2d 286, 139 Ill Dec 832, 549 NE2d 344 (1989).

20. People v Roy, 201 Ill App 3d 166, 146 Ill Dec 874, 558 NE2d 1208 (4th Dist 1990), cert den 502 US 1082, 117 L Ed 2d 154, 112 S Ct 993, cert den 502 US 1071, 117 L Ed 2d 131, 112 S Ct 965.

21. People v Claver, 162 Ill App 3d 62, 113 Ill Dec 515, 515 NE2d 324 (3d Dist 1987); People v Martinez, 129 Ill App 3d 145, 84 Ill Dec 504, 472 NE2d 464 (1st Dist 1984).

22. People v Boclair, 129 Ill 2d 458, 136 Ill Dec 29, 544 NE2d 715 (1989), cert den 503 US 962, 118 L Ed 2d 213, 112 S Ct 1567; People v Davenport, 176 Ill App 3d 142, 125 Ill Dec 709, 530 NE2d 1118 (1st Dist 1988).

ALR Digest to 3d, 4th, 5th, and Federal: Appeal and Error §§ 597 et seq., 739, 740, 742, 761, 809, 854–864, 873–878.5, 880–928, 939, 950

Practice References:

Nichols Drinking/Driving Lit § 19:03.

5 Am Jur 2d, Appeal and Error §§ 776–819

State Legislation:

Supreme Court Rule 451, 615

Miscellaneous References:

West's Illinois Digest 2d, Criminal Law §§ 1162–1180

§ 30:79. Types of error generally

In terms of their impact upon the disposition of the criminal case under review, errors may be categorized as either harmless or reversible. "Reversible error" is also sometimes referred to as "prejudicial error." An error is harmless if it was not a material factor in influencing the defendant's conviction,[23] or, in other words, if it was not prejudicial,[24] so that reversal because of the

---

23. See People v Brown, 51 Ill 2d 271, 281 NE2d 682 (1972); People v Bracey, 51 Ill 2d 514, 283 NE2d 685 (1972); People v Lawler, 194 Ill App 3d 547, 141 Ill Dec 612, 551 NE2d 799 (5th Dist 1990), app gr 132 Ill 2d 551, 144 Ill Dec 263, 555 NE2d 382 and affd 142 Ill 2d 548, 154 Ill Dec 674, 568 NE2d 895; People v Spence, 188 Ill App 3d 761, 136 Ill Dec 145, 544 NE2d 831 (2d Dist 1989); People v Johnson, 150 Ill App 3d 1075, 104 Ill Dec 41, 502 NE2d 304 (1st Dist 1986); People v Bovio, 118 Ill App 3d 836, 74 Ill Dec 400, 455 NE2d 829 (2d Dist 1983); People v Chianakas, 114 Ill App 3d 496, 69 Ill Dec 902, 448 NE2d 620 (2d Dist 1983); People v Kennedy, 88 Ill App 3d 365, 43 Ill Dec 520, 410 NE2d 520 (3d Dist 1980); People v Beacham, 87 Ill App 3d 457, 43 Ill Dec 87, 410 NE2d 87 (1st Dist 1980).

Harmless error under federal constitutional law, see ch 2.

24. People v Emerson, 97 Ill 2d 487, 74 Ill Dec 11, 455 NE2d 41 (1983), appeal after remand 122 Ill 2d 411, 119 Ill Dec 250, 522 NE2d 1109, cert den 488 US 900, 102 L Ed 2d 235, 109 S Ct 246, post-conviction proceeding 153 Ill 2d 100, 180 Ill Dec 46, 606 NE2d 1123, cert den 507 US 1037, 123 L Ed 2d 485, 113 S Ct 1865, habeas corpus proceeding 1994 US Dist LEXIS 3745 (ND Ill), habeas corpus granted, in part, habeas corpus den, in part, request den 883 F Supp 225 (ND Ill), motion to modify den 902 F Supp 143 (ND Ill) and affd 91 F3d 898 (CA7 Ill), reh, en banc, den 1996 US App LEXIS 24806 (CA7 Ill) and cert den

error is not required.[25] On the other hand, where an error has prejudiced the defendant by affecting the outcome of the prosecution, it is generally reversible error, in that it calls for reversal of the defendant's conviction.[26]

A defendant in a criminal case is guaranteed a fair and impartial trial,[27] not one totally free from error.[28] Accordingly, a

---

520 US 1122, 137 L Ed 2d 339, 117 S Ct 1260 and motion gr, cert den 520 US 1139, 137 L Ed 2d 364, 117 S Ct 1289 and (criticized in People v Coleman, 183 Ill 2d 366, 233 Ill Dec 789, 701 NE2d 1063); People v Lawler, 194 Ill App 3d 547, 141 Ill Dec 612, 551 NE2d 799 (5th Dist 1990), app gr 132 Ill 2d 551, 144 Ill Dec 263, 555 NE2d 382 and affd 142 Ill 2d 548, 154 Ill Dec 674, 568 NE2d 895.

See People v Manzella, 56 Ill 2d 187, 306 NE2d 16 (1973), cert den 417 US 933, 41 L Ed 2d 236, 94 S Ct 2644 and (ovrld in part by People v Huckstead, 91 Ill 2d 536, 65 Ill Dec 232, 440 NE2d 1248); People v Spence, 188 Ill App 3d 761, 136 Ill Dec 145, 544 NE2d 831 (2d Dist 1989); People v Johnson, 150 Ill App 3d 1075, 104 Ill Dec 41, 502 NE2d 304 (1st Dist 1986), app den 106 Ill Dec 52, 505 NE2d 358 and app den 114 Ill 2d 552, 108 Ill Dec 421, 508 NE2d 732 and (criticized by People v McEwen, 157 Ill App 3d 222, 109 Ill Dec 453, 510 NE2d 74 (1st Dist)); People v Chianakas, 114 Ill App 3d 496, 69 Ill Dec 902, 448 NE2d 620 (2d Dist 1983).

25. People v Lawler, 194 Ill App 3d 547, 141 Ill Dec 612, 551 NE2d 799 (5th Dist 1990), app gr 132 Ill 2d 551, 144 Ill Dec 263, 555 NE2d 382 and affd 142 Ill 2d 548, 154 Ill Dec 674, 568 NE2d 895; People v Spence, 188 Ill App 3d 761, 136 Ill Dec 145, 544 NE2d 831 (2d Dist 1989); People v Poliszczuk, 151 Ill App 3d 578, 104 Ill Dec 937, 503 NE2d 799 (1st Dist 1987); People v Johnson, 150 Ill App 3d 1075, 104 Ill Dec 41, 502 NE2d 304 (1st Dist 1986); People v Rios, 145 Ill App 3d 571, 99 Ill Dec 368, 495 NE2d 1103 (1st Dist 1986); People v Chianakas, 114 Ill App 3d 496, 69 Ill Dec 902, 448 NE2d 620 (2d Dist 1983).

26. See People v Stadtman, 59 Ill 2d 229, 319 NE2d 813 (1974); People v Lawler, 194 Ill App 3d 547, 141 Ill Dec 612, 551 NE2d 799 (5th Dist 1990), app gr 132 Ill 2d 551, 144 Ill Dec 263, 555 NE2d 382 and affd 142 Ill 2d 548, 154 Ill Dec 674, 568 NE2d 895; People v Spence, 188 Ill App 3d 761, 136 Ill Dec 145, 544 NE2d 831 (2d Dist 1989); People v Johnson, 150 Ill App 3d 1075, 104 Ill Dec 41, 502 NE2d 304 (1st Dist 1986); People v Grant, 69 Ill App 3d 940, 26 Ill Dec 257, 387 NE2d 1087 (1st Dist 1979).

Practice References: Nichols Drinking/Driving Lit § 19:03.

27. People v Boyd, 87 Ill App 3d 978, 42 Ill Dec 777, 409 NE2d 392 (2d Dist 1980).

§ 30:79 ILLINOIS JURISPRUDENCE: CRIMINAL LAW

reviewing court is not concerned with whether the record is perfect, but with whether the defendant had a fair trial[29] and whether the evidence proves the defendant's guilt beyond a reasonable doubt.[30] Errors which do not affect substantial rights are disregarded on review.[31] The determination of whether a particular error is harmless or constitutes reversible error usually must be analyzed on the particular facts of each case, considering the trial record as a whole.[32] Where the record is incomplete, the reviewing court may focus only on the error itself, to see if it might have reasonably contributed to the conviction.[33]

Where error is shown to exist, presumptions as to whether it was prejudicial can depend on the nature of the error as well as the sufficiency of the evidence not affected by the error.[34] As to some types of error, a court of review will not presume that any prejudice exists.[35] On the other hand, some errors affecting constitutional rights can never be harmless.[36]

Federal constitutional right to fair and impartial trial, see ch 2.

28. People v Boyd, 87 Ill App 3d 978, 42 Ill Dec 777, 409 NE2d 392 (2d Dist 1980).

29. People v Gamboa, 30 Ill App 3d 242, 332 NE2d 543 (1st Dist 1975); People v Gaines, 21 Ill App 3d 839, 316 NE2d 14 (1st Dist 1974).

30. People v Gamboa, 30 Ill App 3d 242, 332 NE2d 543 (1st Dist 1975).

31. Supreme Court Rule 615(a).

32. People v Spence, 188 Ill App 3d 761, 136 Ill Dec 145, 544 NE2d 831 (2d Dist 1989); People v Myles, 131 Ill App 3d 1034, 87 Ill Dec 341, 476 NE2d 1333 (1st Dist 1985).

33. See, e.g., People v Spence, 188 Ill App 3d 761, 136 Ill Dec 145, 544 NE2d 831 (2d Dist 1989).

34. People v Lawler, 194 Ill App 3d 547, 141 Ill Dec 612, 551 NE2d 799 (5th Dist 1990), app gr 132 Ill 2d 551, 144 Ill Dec 263, 555 NE2d 382 and affd 142 Ill 2d 548, 154 Ill Dec 674, 568 NE2d 895; People v Spence, 188 Ill App 3d 761, 136 Ill Dec 145, 544 NE2d 831 (2d Dist 1989).

35. People v Spence, 188 Ill App 3d 761, 136 Ill Dec 145, 544 NE2d 831 (2d Dist 1989).

36. See § 30:80.

§ 30:80. Errors affecting constitutional rights

There are some errors affecting constitutional rights which, in the setting of a particular case, are so unimportant and insignificant that they may be deemed harmless,[37] so that automatic reversal of a conviction because of the error is not required.[38] However, before a constitutional error can be considered harmless, it must be harmless beyond a reasonable doubt.[39] Accordingly, reversal of a conviction on certain constitutional grounds is not warranted where it can be determined beyond a reasonable doubt that the error was harmless.[40]

Periodicals: Meltzer, Harmless error and constitutional remedies. 61 Chi L Rev 1 (1994).

37. People v Knippenberg, 66 Ill 2d 276, 6 Ill Dec 46, 362 NE2d 681 (1977); People v Poliszczuk, 151 Ill App 3d 578, 104 Ill Dec 937, 503 NE2d 799 (1st Dist 1987); People v Bracey, 51 Ill 2d 514, 283 NE2d 685 (1972); People v Hansen, 90 Ill App 3d 407, 45 Ill Dec 770, 413 NE2d 103 (1st Dist 1980), cert den 454 US 848, 70 L Ed 2d 136, 102 S Ct 167; People v Earl, 89 Ill App 3d 980, 45 Ill Dec 294, 412 NE2d 645 (3d Dist 1980); People v Morris, 79 Ill App 3d 318, 34 Ill Dec 363, 398 NE2d 38 (1st Dist 1979); People v Bundy, 79 Ill App 3d 127, 34 Ill Dec 670, 398 NE2d 345 (1st Dist 1979); People v Evans, 78 Ill App 3d 996, 34 Ill Dec 651, 398 NE2d 326 (3d Dist 1979).

Harmless error under federal constitution, see ch 2.

38. People v Poliszczuk, 151 Ill App 3d 578, 104 Ill Dec 937, 503 NE2d 799 (1st Dist 1987); People v Hansen, 90 Ill App 3d 407, 45 Ill Dec 770, 413 NE2d 103 (1st Dist 1980), cert den 454 US 848, 70 L Ed 2d 136, 102 S Ct 167.

39. People v Fierer, 124 Ill 2d 176, 124 Ill Dec 855, 529 NE2d 972 (1988), appeal after remand 196 Ill App 3d 404, 143 Ill Dec 100, 553 NE2d 807 (3d Dist), cert den 501 US 1219, 115 L Ed 2d 999, 111 S Ct 2830, appeal after remand 260 Ill App 3d 136, 197 Ill Dec 755, 631 NE2d 1214 (3d Dist); People v Titone, 115 Ill 2d 413, 105 Ill Dec 923, 505 NE2d 300 (1986), cert den 484 US 873, 98 L Ed 2d 162, 108 S Ct 210; People v Green, 74 Ill 2d 444, 25 Ill Dec 1, 386 NE2d 272 (1979); People v Knippenberg, 66 Ill 2d 276, 6 Ill Dec 46, 362 NE2d 681 (1977); People v Bracey, 51 Ill 2d 514, 283 NE2d 685 (1972); People v Poliszczuk, 151 Ill App 3d 578, 104 Ill Dec 937, 503 NE2d 799 (1st Dist 1987); People v Earl, 89 Ill App 3d 980, 45 Ill Dec 294, 412 NE2d 645 (3d Dist 1980); Chapman v California, 386 US 18, 17 L Ed 2d 705, 87 S Ct 824, 24 ALR3d 1065 (1967).

§ 30:80 ILLINOIS JURISPRUDENCE: CRIMINAL LAW

☞ *Practice Tip:* Where it is established that an error of constitutional magnitude has occurred, the burden is on the one gaining advantage from the error, rather than on the one claiming prejudice, to prove that the error did not contribute to the verdict and was harmless beyond a reasonable doubt.[41]

Nonetheless, there are some constitutional rights so basic to a fair trial that under no circumstances can their infraction be treated as harmless error in a criminal prosecution.[42] The United States Supreme Court ultimately determines which federal constitutional rights are this fundamental.[43]

---

40. People v Bracey, 51 Ill 2d 514, 283 NE2d 685 (1972).

41. People v Childs, 159 Ill 2d 217, 201 Ill Dec 102, 636 NE2d 534 (1994).

42. Chapman v California, 386 US 18, 17 L Ed 2d 705, 87 S Ct 824, 24 ALR3d 1065 (1967); Gideon v Wainwright, 372 US 335, 9 L Ed 2d 799, 83 S Ct 792, (1963), on remand 153 So 2d 299 (Fla); Tumey v Ohio, 273 US 510, 71 L Ed 749, 47 S Ct 437, (1927).

   Annotation References: Circumstances giving rise to prejudicial conflict of interests between criminal defendant and defense counsel—state cases, 18 ALR4th 360.
   Violation of federal constitutional rule (Mapp v Ohio) excluding evidence obtained through unreasonable search or seizure, as constituting reversible or harmless error, 30 ALR3d 128.
   Violation of federal constitutional rule (Griffin v California) prohibiting adverse comment by prosecutor or court upon accused's failure to testify, as constituting reversible or harmless error, 24 ALR3d 1093.

43. See, e.g., Arizona v Fulminante, 499 US 279, 113 L Ed 2d 302, 111 S Ct 1246, 91 CDOS 2209, 91 Daily Journal DAR 3530 (1991); Chapman v California, 386 US 18, 17 L Ed 2d 705, 87 S Ct 824, 24 ALR3d 1065 (1967); Gideon v Wainwright, 372 US 335, 9 L Ed 2d 799, 83 S Ct 792 (1963), on remand 153 So 2d 299 (Fla); Tumey v Ohio, 273 US 510, 71 L Ed 749, 47 S Ct 437 (1927).

   Annotation References: Harmless error, error in evidentiary ruling in federal civil case as harmless or prejudicial under Rule 103(a), Federal Rules of Evidence, 84 ALRFed 28.
   Supreme Court's application of rule of Bruton v United States (1968) 391 US 123, 20 L Ed 2d 476, 88 S Ct 1620, holding that accused's rights under confrontation clause of Federal Constitution's Sixth Amendment are violated where codefendant's statement inculpating accused is admitted at joint trial, 95 L Ed 2d 892.

☞ *Illustration:* A constitutionally deficient reasonable-doubt instruction cannot be harmless error.[44]

☞ *Illustration:* For many years, the right of a defendant not to have the defendant's coerced confession used against him or her was among the rights which the United States Supreme Court considered so basic to a fair trial that their infraction could never be treated as harmless error.[45] However, in 1991, the Supreme Court's view was changed, and the Court determined that the harmless error analysis does apply to coerced confessions.[46]

§ 30:81. Cumulative error

Sometimes the errors committed in the course of a trial, while individually not so prejudicial that relief is called for, are collectively so prejudicial that reversal is required.[47] Under the

---

Supreme Court's views as to what constitute harmless errors or plain errors, under Rule 52 of Federal Rules of Criminal Procedure, 84 L Ed 2d 876.

Supreme Court cases determining whether admission of evidence at criminal trial in violation of federal constitutional rule is prejudicial error or harmless error, 31 L Ed 2d 921.

44. Sullivan v Louisiana, 508 US 275, 124 L Ed 2d 182, 113 S Ct 2078 (1993), on remand, remanded 623 So 2d 1315 (La), appeal after remand 688 So 2d 1245 (La App 4th Cir), cert den 700 So 2d 504 (La) and cert den 140 L Ed 2d 649, 118 S Ct 1390 (US).

45. See Arizona v Fulminante, 499 US 279, 113 L Ed 2d 302, 111 S Ct 1246, 91 CDOS 2209, 91 Daily Journal DAR 3530 (1991); Rose v Clark, 478 US 570, 92 L Ed 2d 460, 106 S Ct 3101 (1986).

46. See Arizona v Fulminante, 499 US 279, 113 L Ed 2d 302, 111 S Ct 1246, 91 CDOS 2209, 91 Daily Journal DAR 3530 (1991).

47. People v Albanese, 102 Ill 2d 54, 79 Ill Dec 608, 464 NE2d 206 (1984), cert den 469 US 892, 83 L Ed 2d 205, 105 S Ct 268, cert den 490 US 1075, 104 L Ed 2d 652, 109 S Ct 2088, affd sub nom, without op Albanese v Peters, 19 F3d 21 (CA7 Ill), reported in full 1994 US App LEXIS 4962 (CA7 Ill), cert den 513 US 1156, 130 L Ed 2d 1078, 115 S Ct 1114; People v Hunter, 124 Ill App 3d 516, 79 Ill Dec 755, 464 NE2d 659 (1st Dist 1984) (superseded by statute on other grounds as stated in People v Clemons, 275 Ill App 3d 1117, 212 Ill Dec 408,

doctrine of cumulative error, reversal is required where the cumulative effect of numerous errors deprives the defendant of a fair trial.[48] The standard to be applied is whether the cumulative error was so prejudicial that the defendant did not receive a fair and impartial trial.[49] Alternatively, the standard is sometimes stated as whether it can be said that the jury's verdict might have been different had the improprieties not occurred.[50]

The doctrine of cumulative error cannot be applied where there is only one error.[51] Also, the number of errors alone does not invoke the doctrine if it is not established that their cumulative effect was to deprive the defendant of a fair trial.[52] The

---

657 NE2d 388 (1st Dist)); People v Brown, 113 Ill App 3d 625, 69 Ill Dec 576, 447 NE2d 1011 (1st Dist 1983); People v Medley, 111 Ill App 3d 444, 67 Ill Dec 230, 444 NE2d 269 (4th Dist 1983); People v Radford, 65 Ill App 3d 107, 22 Ill Dec 166, 382 NE2d 486 (1st Dist 1978); People v Whitley, 49 Ill App 3d 493, 7 Ill Dec 350, 364 NE2d 511 (1st Dist 1977); People v Patterson, 44 Ill App 3d 894, 3 Ill Dec 479, 358 NE2d 1164 (1st Dist 1976); People v Killian, 42 Ill App 3d 596, 1 Ill Dec 297, 356 NE2d 423 (4th Dist 1976).

48. People v Medley, 111 Ill App 3d 444, 67 Ill Dec 230, 444 NE2d 269 (4th Dist 1983).

49. People v Hunter, 124 Ill App 3d 516, 79 Ill Dec 755, 464 NE2d 659 (1st Dist 1984) (superseded by statute on other grounds as stated in People v Clemons, 275 Ill App 3d 1117, 212 Ill Dec 408, 657 NE2d 388 (1st Dist)); People v Brown, 113 Ill App 3d 625, 69 Ill Dec 576, 447 NE2d 1011 (1st Dist 1983).

50. People v Hunter, 124 Ill App 3d 516, 79 Ill Dec 755, 464 NE2d 659 (1st Dist 1984) (superseded by statute on other grounds as stated in People v Clemons, 275 Ill App 3d 1117, 212 Ill Dec 408, 657 NE2d 388 (1st Dist)); People v Panczko, 86 Ill App 3d 409, 41 Ill Dec 490, 407 NE2d 988 (1st Dist 1980).

51. People v Medley, 111 Ill App 3d 444, 67 Ill Dec 230, 444 NE2d 269 (4th Dist 1983).

The cumulative error doctrine is inapplicable where all but one of numerous errors complained of are without merit, and the one recognized error does not warrant reversal. People v Wills, 153 Ill App 3d 328, 106 Ill Dec 207, 505 NE2d 754 (2d Dist 1987), app den 116 Ill 2d 574, 113 Ill Dec 315, 515 NE2d 124.

52. See People v Albanese, 102 Ill 2d 54, 79 Ill Dec 608, 464 NE2d 206 (1984), cert den 469 US 892, 83 L Ed 2d 205, 105 S Ct 268, cert den 490 US 1075, 104 L

cumulation alone does not enhance the prejudicial effect of each individual error if the defendant still had a fair trial,[53] or, in other words, the whole can be no greater than the sum of its parts.[54]

§ 30:82. Establishing prejudice

In order to require reversal of a conviction, an error must have had a prejudicial effect upon the defendant.[55] A defendant's attempt to raise a claim of prejudice must be founded on more than mere conjecture.[56] The effect of the error must be so

---

Ed 2d 652, 109 S Ct 2088, affd sub nom, without op Albanese v Peters, 19 F3d 21 (CA7 Ill), reported in full 1994 US App LEXIS 4962 (CA7 Ill), cert den 513 US 1156, 130 L Ed 2d 1078, 115 S Ct 1114.

53. See People v Albanese, 102 Ill 2d 54, 79 Ill Dec 608, 464 NE2d 206 (1984), cert den 469 US 892, 83 L Ed 2d 205, 105 S Ct 268, cert den 490 US 1075, 104 L Ed 2d 652, 109 S Ct 2088, affd sub nom, without op Albanese v Peters, 19 F3d 21 (CA7 Ill), reported in full 1994 US App LEXIS 4962 (CA7 Ill), cert den 513 US 1156, 130 L Ed 2d 1078, 115 S Ct 1114.

54. People v Albanese, 102 Ill 2d 54, 79 Ill Dec 608, 464 NE2d 206 (1984), cert den 469 US 892, 83 L Ed 2d 205, 105 S Ct 268, cert den 490 US 1075, 104 L Ed 2d 652, 109 S Ct 2088, affd sub nom, without op Albanese v Peters, 19 F3d 21 (CA7 Ill), reported in full 1994 US App LEXIS 4962 (CA7 Ill), cert den 513 US 1156, 130 L Ed 2d 1078, 115 S Ct 1114.

55. See § 30:79.

> **Annotation References:** Counsel's reference in criminal case to wealth, poverty, or financial status of defendant or victim as ground for mistrial, new trial, or reversal, 36 ALR3d 839.
> Statement by counsel relating to race, nationality, or religion in civil action as prejudicial, 99 ALR2d 1249.
> Prejudicial effect of prosecuting attorney's argument or disclosure during trial that another defendant has been convicted or has pleaded guilty, 48 ALR2d 1016.

56. People v Williams, 59 Ill 2d 402, 320 NE2d 849 (1974); People v Gonzales, 40 Ill 2d 233, 239 NE2d 783 (1968); People v Kelley, 23 Ill 2d 193, 177 NE2d 830 (1961), cert den 370 US 928, 8 L Ed 2d 507, 82 S Ct 1570; People v Spence, 188 Ill App 3d 761, 136 Ill Dec 145, 544 NE2d 831 (2d Dist 1989); People v Velez, 123 Ill App 3d 210, 78 Ill Dec 627, 462 NE2d 746 (1st Dist 1984); People v Anderson, 46 Ill App 3d 607, 4 Ill Dec 938, 360 NE2d 1371 (1st Dist 1977); People v Smith, 42 Ill App 3d 109, 355 NE2d 601 (1st Dist 1976).

Mere apprehension of a particular result will not sustain an allegation of

§ 30:82 ILLINOIS JURISPRUDENCE: CRIMINAL LAW

significant that the error cannot be considered harmless.[57]

There are some constitutional rights so basic to a fair trial that their infraction is always considered prejudicial.[58] The evidentiary context in which an error has occurred can also cause it to be automatically deemed prejudicial, unless the record affirmatively shows otherwise.[59] For example, where guilt or innocence depends entirely on the credibility of an accuser and the defendant, no error should be permitted to intervene.[60] Under these circumstances, where error is shown to exist, a reversal of the defendant's conviction is mandatory, unless the record affirmatively shows

---

prejudice to the defendant. People v Ruiz, 94 Ill 2d 245, 68 Ill Dec 890, 447 NE2d 148 (1982), cert den 462 US 1112, 77 L Ed 2d 1341, 103 S Ct 2465, appeal after remand 132 Ill 2d 1, 138 Ill Dec 201, 547 NE2d 170, cert den 496 US 931, 110 L Ed 2d 652, 110 S Ct 2632; People v Gendron, 41 Ill 2d 351, 243 NE2d 208 (1968), cert den 396 US 889, 24 L Ed 2d 164, 90 S Ct 179.

57. See § 30:79.

58. See § 30:80.

59. See People v Emerson, 97 Ill 2d 487, 74 Ill Dec 11, 455 NE2d 41 (1983), appeal after remand 122 Ill 2d 411, 119 Ill Dec 250, 522 NE2d 1109, cert den 488 US 900, 102 L Ed 2d 235, 109 S Ct 246, cert den 507 US 1037, 123 L Ed 2d 485, 113 S Ct 1865, habeas corpus granted, in part, habeas corpus den, in part, request den 883 F Supp 225 (ND Ill), motion to modify den 902 F Supp 143 (ND Ill) and affd 91 F3d 898 (CA7 Ill), cert den 520 US 1122, 137 L Ed 2d 339, 117 S Ct 1260 and motion gr, cert den 520 US 1139, 137 L Ed 2d 364, 117 S Ct 1289; People v Lawler, 194 Ill App 3d 547, 141 Ill Dec 612, 551 NE2d 799 (5th Dist 1990), app gr 132 Ill 2d 551, 144 Ill Dec 263, 555 NE2d 382 and affd 142 Ill 2d 548, 154 Ill Dec 674, 568 NE2d 895.

See also § 30:79.

60. People v Emerson, 97 Ill 2d 487, 74 Ill Dec 11, 455 NE2d 41 (1983), appeal after remand 122 Ill 2d 411, 119 Ill Dec 250, 522 NE2d 1109, cert den 488 US 900, 102 L Ed 2d 235, 109 S Ct 246, cert den 507 US 1037, 123 L Ed 2d 485, 113 S Ct 1865, habeas corpus granted, in part, habeas corpus den, in part, request den 883 F Supp 225 (ND Ill), motion to modify den 902 F Supp 143 (ND Ill) and affd 91 F3d 898 (CA7 Ill), cert den 520 US 1122, 137 L Ed 2d 339, 117 S Ct 1260 and motion gr, cert den 520 US 1139, 137 L Ed 2d 364, 117 S Ct 1289; People v Lawler, 194 Ill App 3d 547, 141 Ill Dec 612, 551 NE2d 799 (5th Dist 1990), app gr 132 Ill 2d 551, 144 Ill Dec 263, 555 NE2d 382 and affd 142 Ill 2d 548, 154 Ill Dec 674, 568 NE2d 895.

that the error was not prejudicial.[61]

Depending on the nature of the error, it may be possible to render it harmless by nullifying or minimizing the error's prejudicial effect.[62] The curing of error is usually accomplished by means of corrective action taken by the trial court.[63]

Sometimes the question of an error's prejudicial effect is not reached, or at least is less compelling, because the error was invited by the party complaining of it on review.[64] Similarly, a party generally cannot complain about an error and its prejudicial effect if that party or that party's counsel caused the problem.[65] Also, the question of prejudicial effect may not be reached where the party complaining of the error has failed to properly preserve the question for review.[66] However, plain errors or defects affecting substantial rights may be considered by the reviewing court even if they were not brought to the attention of the trial court.[67]

---

61. People v Emerson, 97 Ill 2d 487, 74 Ill Dec 11, 455 NE2d 41 (1983), appeal after remand 122 Ill 2d 411, 119 Ill Dec 250, 522 NE2d 1109, cert den 488 US 900, 102 L Ed 2d 235, 109 S Ct 246, cert den 507 US 1037, 123 L Ed 2d 485, 113 S Ct 1865, habeas corpus granted, in part, habeas corpus den, in part, request den 883 F Supp 225 (ND Ill), motion to modify den 902 F Supp 143 (ND Ill) and affd 91 F3d 898 (CA7 Ill), cert den 520 US 1122, 137 L Ed 2d 339, 117 S Ct 1260 and motion gr, cert den 520 US 1139, 137 L Ed 2d 364, 117 S Ct 1289; People v Lawler, 194 Ill App 3d 547, 141 Ill Dec 612, 551 NE2d 799 (5th Dist 1990), app gr 132 Ill 2d 551, 144 Ill Dec 263, 555 NE2d 382 and affd 142 Ill 2d 548, 154 Ill Dec 674, 568 NE2d 895.

62. See § 30:84.

63. See § 30:84.

64. See § 30:83.

65. See § 30:83.

66. See § 30:85.

Saving questions for review, generally, see ch 29.

67. Supreme Court Rule 615(a).

See § 30:85.

§ 30:83. Intended and invited errors

A convicted defendant cannot complain on review of an error which he or she secured and sought to profit by.[68] A defendant may not interject an issue into his or her case and then contend that bringing it to the attention of the jury was erroneous.[69]

> 👉 *Illustration:* On review of a conviction for driving while his or her license was revoked, the introduction of the defendant's driving record into evidence at trial does not constitute reversible error where the defendant is the party who introduced the driving record.[70] A defendant cannot complain that evidence which he or she put into the record is prejudicial to the defendant.[71]

A defendant cannot contend on appeal that the giving of a particular instruction to the jury and providing the jury with a particular verdict form constituted error where the instruction and verdict form were tendered by the defendant.[72]

---

68. People v Payne, 98 Ill 2d 45, 74 Ill Dec 542, 456 NE2d 44 (1983), cert den 465 US 1036, 79 L Ed 2d 708, 104 S Ct 1310; People v Scott, 194 Ill App 3d 634, 141 Ill Dec 295, 551 NE2d 288 (1st Dist 1990); People v Graves, 134 Ill App 3d 473, 89 Ill Dec 399, 480 NE2d 1142 (1st Dist 1984); People v Craig, 79 Ill App 3d 584, 35 Ill Dec 334, 399 NE2d 168 (5th Dist 1979); People v Hamelin, 75 Ill App 3d 445, 31 Ill Dec 364, 394 NE2d 566 (1st Dist 1979); People v O'Neal, 62 Ill App 3d 146, 19 Ill Dec 497, 379 NE2d 12 (1st Dist 1978); People v Davis, 53 Ill App 3d 424, 11 Ill Dec 170, 368 NE2d 721 (1st Dist 1977); People v Lewis, 52 Ill App 3d 477, 10 Ill Dec 257, 367 NE2d 710 (3d Dist 1977); People v Curwick, 33 Ill App 3d 757, 338 NE2d 468 (3d Dist 1975); People v Dillon, 28 Ill App 3d 11, 327 NE2d 225 (1st Dist 1975).

69. People v George, 49 Ill 2d 372, 274 NE2d 26 (1971); People v Jenkins, 209 Ill App 3d 249, 154 Ill Dec 122, 568 NE2d 122 (1st Dist 1991); People v Lewis, 52 Ill App 3d 477, 10 Ill Dec 257, 367 NE2d 710 (3d Dist 1977).

70. People v Morrison, 149 Ill App 3d 282, 102 Ill Dec 549, 500 NE2d 442 (3d Dist 1986), cert den 482 US 915, 96 L Ed 2d 675, 107 S Ct 3187.

71. People v Jenkins, 209 Ill App 3d 249, 154 Ill Dec 122, 568 NE2d 122 (1st Dist 1991).

72. See, e.g., People v Hamelin, 75 Ill App 3d 445, 31 Ill Dec 364, 394 NE2d 566 (1st Dist 1979).

Similarly, a defendant is not permitted to complain of an alleged error which was acquiesced in,[73] or invited by, the defendant's behavior and that of the defendant's attorney.[74]

☛ *Illustration:* A defendant may not claim prejudice from comments made by the prosecutor during the prosecutor's rebuttal of the defense counsel's closing argument where the prosecutor's comments were in response to, and invited by, the arguments of defense counsel.[75]

§ 30:84. Cured errors

Sometimes the otherwise prejudicial effect of an error may be nullified or reduced, rendering the error harmless, as a result of other events in the case or corrective action taken by the trial judge.[76] This is often referred to as "curing" the error.[77] Whether

---

73. People v Payne, 98 Ill 2d 45, 74 Ill Dec 542, 456 NE2d 44 (1983), cert den 465 US 1036, 79 L Ed 2d 708, 104 S Ct 1310; People v Jenkins, 209 Ill App 3d 249, 154 Ill Dec 122, 568 NE2d 122 (1st Dist 1991); People v Edsall, 73 Ill App 3d 1020, 30 Ill Dec 117, 392 NE2d 772 (5th Dist 1979); People v Owens, 46 Ill App 3d 978, 5 Ill Dec 321, 361 NE2d 644 (1st Dist 1977); People v Durham, 23 Ill App 3d 737, 320 NE2d 144 (1st Dist 1974).

74. People v Payne, 98 Ill 2d 45, 74 Ill Dec 542, 456 NE2d 44 (1983), cert den 465 US 1036, 79 L Ed 2d 708, 104 S Ct 1310; People v Jenkins, 209 Ill App 3d 249, 154 Ill Dec 122, 568 NE2d 122 (1st Dist 1991); People v Chitwood, 148 Ill App 3d 730, 102 Ill Dec 212, 499 NE2d 992 (4th Dist 1986); People v Friedman, 144 Ill App 3d 895, 98 Ill Dec 638, 494 NE2d 760 (1st Dist 1986); People v Morgan, 112 Ill App 3d 111, 492 NE2d 1303 (1986).

75. People v Richardson, 123 Ill 2d 322, 123 Ill Dec 908, 528 NE2d 612 (1988), cert den 489 US 1100, 103 L Ed 2d 943, 109 S Ct 1577; People v Mitchell, 200 Ill App 3d 969, 146 Ill Dec 596, 558 NE2d 559 (5th Dist 1990); People v Piscotti, 136 Ill App 3d 420, 91 Ill Dec 81, 483 NE2d 363 (1st Dist 1985); People v Jackson, 100 Ill App 3d 318, 55 Ill Dec 807, 426 NE2d 1132 (1st Dist 1981); People v Stokes, 75 Ill App 3d 813, 31 Ill Dec 479, 394 NE2d 681 (1st Dist 1979); People v Collins, 71 Ill App 3d 815, 28 Ill Dec 296, 390 NE2d 463 (1st Dist 1979); People v Fochs, 40 Ill App 3d 966, 353 NE2d 326 (1st Dist 1976).

A defendant cannot provoke an irresponsible reply to his or her own outrageous argument and then claim error. People v Rock, 34 Ill App 3d 1007, 341 NE2d 190 (3d Dist 1976).

§ 30:84   ILLINOIS JURISPRUDENCE: CRIMINAL LAW

an error has in fact been cured can depend upon the nature of the error, the curative steps taken, and the circumstances of the particular case.[78]

☞ *Illustration:* Where a timely objection is made at trial, either to an improper interrogation, or to an improper remark by counsel to the jury, the trial court can, by sustaining the objection and instructing the jury to disregard the answer or remark, usually correct the error and render it harmless.[79]

The trial court may cure the error in the failure to disclose the defendant's statement to defense counsel by ordering disclosure, granting a continuance, excluding the evidence, or entering an order as the court sees fit under the circumstances.[80]

Generally, errors corrected by the trial court with instructions

76. See People v Gleash, 209 Ill App 3d 598, 154 Ill Dec 348, 568 NE2d 348 (1st Dist 1991); People v Helton, 195 Ill App 3d 410, 142 Ill Dec 48, 552 NE2d 398 (4th Dist 1990); People v Moody, 199 Ill App 3d 455, 145 Ill Dec 565, 557 NE2d 335 (1st Dist 1990); People v McKinney, 193 Ill App 3d 1012, 140 Ill Dec 719, 550 NE2d 604 (4th Dist 1990); People v Chrisos, 151 Ill App 3d 142, 104 Ill Dec 498, 502 NE2d 1158 (1st Dist 1986); People v Taylor, 146 Ill App 3d 45, 99 Ill Dec 688, 496 NE2d 263 (3d Dist 1986); People v Thornton, 145 Ill App 3d 669, 99 Ill Dec 660, 496 NE2d 6 (1st Dist 1986).

77. See, e.g., People v McKinney, 193 Ill App 3d 1012, 140 Ill Dec 719, 550 NE2d 604 (4th Dist 1990).

78. See, e.g., People v McKinney, 193 Ill App 3d 1012, 140 Ill Dec 719, 550 NE2d 604 (4th Dist 1990).

79. People v Moody, 199 Ill App 3d 455, 145 Ill Dec 565, 557 NE2d 335 (1st Dist 1990); People v Cisewski, 144 Ill App 3d 597, 98 Ill Dec 454, 494 NE2d 576 (1st Dist 1986), affd 118 Ill 2d 163, 113 Ill Dec 58, 514 NE2d 970; People v Whitfield, 140 Ill App 3d 433, 94 Ill Dec 840, 488 NE2d 1087 (5th Dist 1986) (superseded by statute on other grounds as stated in People v Clemons, 275 Ill App 3d 1117, 212 Ill Dec 408, 657 NE2d 388 (1st Dist)).

80. Supreme Court Rule 415(g)(i).

People v Eliason, 117 Ill App 3d 683, 73 Ill Dec 83, 453 NE2d 908 (2d Dist 1983).

Discovery and sanctions for discovery violations, generally, see ch 16.

APPELLATE REVIEW § 30:84

to the jury do not require a reversal.[81] This is based upon the premise that juries follow instructions.[82] Where the error concerns improperly admitted evidence, curing the error usually also involves striking that evidence.[83] A further indication that the error was cured would be a polling of the jury by the trial judge, to determine if every jury member was able to disregard the evidence, with affirmative answers from the jurors.[84] However, it may be impossible for the appellate court to conclude that the error was cured in extreme cases, where it is manifest that the prejudicial effect of the erroneously admitted evidence remained with the jurors despite its exclusion, and that this evidence influenced the verdict.[85]

> *Illustration:* In a prosecution for aggravated criminal sexual assault, the prosecutor erred in commenting in closing on the defendant's failure to present two potential alibi witnesses where the witnesses were not more accessible to the defense and were interjected into the case through the testimony of a State's witness and the prosecutor's examination characterizing the witnesses as alibi witnesses. The error rose to the level of reversible error depriving the defendant of a fair trial, where the case was close and hinged on the credibility of the complainant and the defendant, and the court's action in sustaining a defense objection and

---

81. People v Helton, 195 Ill App 3d 410, 142 Ill Dec 48, 552 NE2d 398 (4th Dist 1990).

Jury instructions, generally, see ch 24.

82. People v Helton, 195 Ill App 3d 410, 142 Ill Dec 48, 552 NE2d 398 (4th Dist 1990).

83. People v McKinney, 193 Ill App 3d 1012, 140 Ill Dec 719, 550 NE2d 604 (4th Dist 1990); People v Endress, 5 Ill App 3d 821, 284 NE2d 725 (4th Dist 1972).

84. People v McKinney, 193 Ill App 3d 1012, 140 Ill Dec 719, 550 NE2d 604 (4th Dist 1990).

85. People v McKinney, 193 Ill App 3d 1012, 140 Ill Dec 719, 550 NE2d 604 (4th Dist 1990); People v Endress, 5 Ill App 3d 821, 284 NE2d 725 (4th Dist 1972).

§ 30:84   ILLINOIS JURISPRUDENCE: CRIMINAL LAW

instructing the jury was insufficient to cure the error.[86]

Where erroneously admitted State's evidence seriously damaged and undermined the defense, and the trial court never instructed the jury to disregard the evidence, there is a greater likelihood that the reviewing court will determine that the error requires reversal of a conviction.[87]

The curing of an error in a charging instrument, sometimes accomplished by a verdict, is discussed in another chapter.[88]

§ 30:85. Plain and waived errors

As a general rule, the failure to properly raise and preserve an issue in the trial court results in waiver of the issue for appellate review.[89] For matters within this general rule, the question of whether the error is harmless or reversible need not be reached by the reviewing court. The error is not within the reviewing court's scope of review.[90]

The waiver rule is not absolute.[91] Plain error or defects affecting

---

86. People v Lawrence, 259 Ill App 3d 617, 197 Ill Dec 630, 631 NE2d 852 (2d Dist 1994).

87. People v Moody, 199 Ill App 3d 455, 145 Ill Dec 565, 557 NE2d 335 (1st Dist 1990); People v Nolan, 152 Ill App 3d 260, 105 Ill Dec 336, 504 NE2d 205 (2d Dist 1987).

88. See ch 9.

89. See People v Davis, 145 Ill 2d 240, 164 Ill Dec 151, 582 NE2d 714 (1991); People v Pickett, 54 Ill 2d 280, 296 NE2d 856 (1973); People v Edwards, 218 Ill App 3d 184, 160 Ill Dec 679, 577 NE2d 1250 (1st Dist 1991); People v Hood, 210 Ill App 3d 743, 155 Ill Dec 228, 569 NE2d 228 (4th Dist 1991).

Saving questions for review, generally, see ch 29.

90. Scope of review, see § 30:62 et seq.

91. See Supreme Court Rule 615(a).

People v Davis, 145 Ill 2d 240, 164 Ill Dec 151, 582 NE2d 714 (1991); People v Enoch, 122 Ill 2d 176, 119 Ill Dec 265, 522 NE2d 1124 (1988), cert den 488 US 917, 102 L Ed 2d 263, 109 S Ct 274, cert den 506 US 816, 121 L Ed 2d 26, 113 S Ct 57, cert den 519 US 829, 136 L Ed 2d 50, 117 S Ct 95 and stay gr, cause remanded 233 Ill Dec 832, 701 NE2d 1106; People v Lucas, 88 Ill 2d 245, 58 Ill Dec 840, 430 NE2d 1091 (1981); People v Jackson, 84 Ill 2d 350, 49 Ill

APPELLATE REVIEW § 30:85

substantial rights may be noticed by the reviewing court even though they were not brought to the attention of the trial court.[92] The doctrine of plain error is applied to remedy errors so plain and prejudicial that failure to object to them is not a waiver for purposes of appeal.[93]

> *Illustration:* Under the plain error doctrine, the defendant's conviction was overturned and the cause remanded for a new trial where a police detective testified that the defendant was voluntarily taken to the polygraph unit and arrested following the exam, giving rise to an inference that

---

Dec 719, 418 NE2d 739 (1981), on remand 97 Ill App 3d 928, 53 Ill Dec 670, 424 NE2d 83 (3d Dist); People v Carlson, 79 Ill 2d 564, 38 Ill Dec 809, 404 NE2d 233 (1980); People v Pickett, 54 Ill 2d 280, 296 NE2d 856 (1973); People v Edwards, 218 Ill App 3d 184, 160 Ill Dec 679, 577 NE2d 1250 (1st Dist 1991); People v Hood, 210 Ill App 3d 743, 155 Ill Dec 228, 569 NE2d 228 (4th Dist 1991); People v Burns, 144 Ill App 3d 345, 98 Ill Dec 750, 494 NE2d 872 (4th Dist 1986).

92. Supreme Court Rule 615(a).

If the admission of evidence constitutes plain error that causes a miscarriage of justice on a defendant or a tainting of the integrity and reputation of the judicial process, the error is considered although it was not brought to the attention of the trial court. People v Gard, 158 Ill 2d 191, 198 Ill Dec 415, 632 NE2d 1026 (1994).

93. People v Davis, 145 Ill 2d 240, 164 Ill Dec 151, 582 NE2d 714 (1991); People v Lucas, 88 Ill 2d 245, 58 Ill Dec 840, 430 NE2d 1091 (1981); People v Jackson, 84 Ill 2d 350, 49 Ill Dec 719, 418 NE2d 739 (1981), on remand 97 Ill App 3d 928, 53 Ill Dec 670, 424 NE2d 83 (3d Dist); People v Carlson, 79 Ill 2d 564, 38 Ill Dec 809, 404 NE2d 233 (1980); People v Edwards, 218 Ill App 3d 184, 160 Ill Dec 679, 577 NE2d 1250 (1st Dist 1991); People v Hood, 210 Ill App 3d 743, 155 Ill Dec 228, 569 NE2d 228 (4th Dist 1991); People v Young, 33 Ill App 3d 443, 337 NE2d 40 (3d Dist 1975).

While it was error for the trial court to admit a witness's prior consistent statements where no suggestion was made as to recent fabrication, the admission of the prior consistent statement did not constitute plain error, because although the witness's testimony was crucial to the prosecution, it was not the only evidence connecting the defendant to the crime. People v Beard, 273 Ill App 3d 135, 209 Ill Dec 925, 652 NE2d 465 (4th Dist 1995), remanded 301 Ill App 3d 279, 234 Ill Dec 691, 703 NE2d 552 (4th Dist).

§ 30:85   ILLINOIS JURISPRUDENCE: CRIMINAL LAW

the defendant failed a polygraph examination to which no limiting instruction was provided so that nothing prevented the jury from considering that failure as evidence of guilt; thus, the cause was reversed and remanded for a new trial even though the case against the defendant was strong because the admission of polygraph evidence constitutes reversible error regardless of whether the defendant was prejudiced by the introduction of the polygraph evidence.[94]

☛ *Practice Guide:* A waived issue may be considered on appeal if it amounts to plain error but the plain error rule is not a general savings clause; therefore, a waived issue should be considered under the plain error rule in exceptional circumstances when evidence at trial was closely balanced or the alleged error was so prejudicial that it denied the defendant a fair trial.[95]

Another exception to the waiver rule applies to substantial defects in jury instructions, if the interest of justice so requires.[96] This exception applies only to correct serious or grave errors, to cases that are factually close, and to cases in which the error threatens the fundamental fairness of the defendant's trial.[97]

The fact that a reviewing court considers a particular error to be reviewable because it is within an exception to the waiver rule may not necessarily preclude a determination that the error nonetheless was harmless.[98]

---

94. People v Daniels, 272 Ill App 3d 325, 208 Ill Dec 767, 650 NE2d 224 (1st Dist 1994).

95. People v Garrett, 276 Ill App 3d 702, 213 Ill Dec 195, 658 NE2d 1216 (1st Dist 1995).

96. Supreme Court Rule 451(c).

Jury instructions, generally, see ch 24.

97. People v Hood, 210 Ill App 3d 743, 155 Ill Dec 228, 569 NE2d 228 (4th Dist 1991); People v Burns, 144 Ill App 3d 345, 98 Ill Dec 750, 494 NE2d 872 (4th Dist 1986).

98. People v Davis, 145 Ill 2d 240, 164 Ill Dec 151, 582 NE2d 714 (1991).

XII. DETERMINATION AND DISPOSITION OF CAUSE

Research References:

Annotation References:

Index and Annotations: Appeal and Error

ALR Digest to 3d, 4th, 5th, and Federal: Appeal and Error §§ 955, 971, 973–984

Practice References:

5 Am Jur 2d, Appeal and Error §§ 897–1008

State Legislation:

Supreme Court Rule 368, 612—615

Miscellaneous References:

West's Illinois Digest 2d, Criminal Law §§ 1181–1193

§ 30:86. Decision and mandates

When a death sentence is affirmed, the Supreme Court must set a time for the execution of the sentence.[99] A certified copy of the order of execution is the authority to the warden of the penitentiary for execution of the sentence at the time therein specified.[1] If the judgment is reversed or modified, the Supreme Court must direct the trial court to proceed in accordance with the mandate.[2] In all other cases, the reviewing court directs the appellate or trial court to proceed in accordance with the mandate.[3]

Should a judgment be reversed while an appellant is serving the sentence imposed by the trial court, it is the duty of the imprisoning officer to release the appellant promptly upon receipt of a certified copy of the Supreme Court mandate.[4] As with reversal, if the judgment is reversed and remanded for further proceedings, the clerk of the court will send a certified copy of the

---

99. Supreme Court Rule 613(a).

1. Supreme Court Rule 613(a).

2. Supreme Court Rule 613(a).

3. Supreme Court Rule 613(b).

4. Supreme Court Rule 613(c).

mandate to the imprisoning officer.[5] It is then the duty of the imprisoning officer, upon recipt of the mandate to return the appellant to the trial court to which the cause was remanded.[6]

In the situation where the appellant is serving the sentence imposed by the trial court and the judgment is reversed and a new trial is ordered, the appellant will receive credit for time served pending appeal should another sentence subsequently be imposed.[7]

§ 30:87. Issuance, stay and recall of reviewing court mandates

The rules indicate that the civil appeals rules should be followed for issuance, stay and recall of mandates.[8] Under the those rules, at least 21 days after a judgment is entered, the clerk of the reviewing court will transmit the mandate of the reviewing court to the circuit court, unless the court orders otherwise.[9] At the same time, the clerk will also notify the parties.[10] A mandate may be stayed, however, by a petition for rehearing, if the petition is filed in a timely manner, unless the court orders otherwise.[11] If the petition for rehearing is denied, the mandate may be issued seven days after the order is entered denying the petition.[12] The court does have the option to alter the seven day time frame.[13]

In cases in which an injunction has been modified or set aside by the Appellate Court, that court's mandate may be stayed only upon order of that court, the Supreme Court or a judge of either court.[14] In all other cases, a mandate is stayed automatically when

5. Supreme Court Rule 613(c).
6. Supreme Court Rule 613(c).
7. Supreme Court Rule 613(d).
8. Supreme Court Rule 612(q).
9. Supreme Court Rule 368(a).
10. Supreme Court Rule 368(a).
11. Supreme Court Rule 368(a).
12. Supreme Court Rule 368(a).
13. Supreme Court Rule 368(a).

review by the Supreme Court is sought by a person entitled to Supreme Court review.[15] For the mandate to be stayed automatically, prior to seeking review, the party seeking review must file either a petition for review with the Supreme Court or an affidavit indicating his or her good faith intention to seek Supreme Court review.[16] The stay remains effective until the time for seeking review has expired or if review is sought in a timely manner, until the case reaches disposition.[17]

☛ *Practice Guide:* Either the party seeking the stay or his or her attorney may execute the affidavit. It is not necessary that both execute the affidavit.[18]

The Supreme Court, the Appellate Court and judges of both have the power to alter the terms of a stay.[19] This power extends to allow the Supreme Court, the Appellate Court or judges of either not only to stay a mandate but also to stay the issuance or recall of a mandate of the Appellate Court until the time for seeking Supreme Court review has expired, or if review is pursued in a timely manner until review is either granted or denied, or if review is granted until the Supreme Court hands down the disposition of the case.[20] If review is sought from the United States Supreme Court, a judge of the court whose decision is to be reviewed, that court itself, or the Supreme Court of Illinois may stay or recall the subject mandate, as may be appropriate.[21]

§ 30:88. Affirmance

In order to alleviate the problem of defendants not being

---

14. Supreme Court Rule 368(b).
15. Supreme Court Rule 368(b).
16. Supreme Court Rule 368(b).
17. Supreme Court Rule 368(b).
18. Supreme Court Rule 368(b).
19. Supreme Court Rule 368(b).
20. Supreme Court Rule 368(c).
21. Supreme Court Rule 368(c).

informed of the affirmance of their case until after the date for filing a petition to the Supreme Court for leave to appeal, when a judgment imposing a prison sentence is affirmed for a person incarcerated in a penal institution, the clerk of the court must mail a copy of the court opinion to the prisoner by certified mail, return receipt requested in an envelope labelled in bold: "OFFICIAL LEGAL MAIL-ADDRESSEE MUST ACKNOWLEDGE RECEIPT IN WRITING."[22] The date the opinion is mailed must be noted by the clerk in the court records.[23]

§ 30:89. Reduction or mitigation of sentence

On appeal, the reviewing court has the power to reduce the sentence imposed by the trial court.[24] However, the sentencing decisions of the trial court are accorded great deference and in general, those decisions will not be overturned if the sentence is within the statutory guidelines and there is no evidence that that the trial court abused its discretion.[25] That a trial could have imposed a lesser sentence is not sufficient for a finding of abuse justifying the reviewing court imposing a lesser sentence.[26] On the other hand, if the sentence imposed is clearly excessive[27] or exceeds the statutory guidelines,[28] the reviewing court may exercise its discretionary power to rectify the situation.

22. Supreme Court Rule 614.

23. Supreme Court Rule 614.

24. Supreme Court Rule 615(b)(4).

25. People v Almo, 108 Ill 2d 54, 90 Ill Dec 885, 483 NE2d 203 (1985).

People v Gutirrez, 205 Ill App 3d 231, 151 Ill Dec 395, 564 NE2d 850 (1st Dist 1990); People v Batchelor, 202 Ill App 3d 316, 147 Ill Dec 608, 559 NE2d 948 (1st Dist 1990).

26. People v McCartney, 206 Ill App 3d 50, 150 Ill Dec 934, 563 NE2d 1061 (1st Dist 1990).

27. People v Franklin, 159 Ill App 3d 923, 111 Ill Dec 681, 512 NE2d 1318 (1st Dist 1987).

28. People v Rodarte, 190 Ill App 3d 992, 138 Ill Dec 635, 547 NE2d 1256 (1st Dist 1989).

☛ *Illustration:* A court of review has the power to reduce a defendant's sentence on appeal once it has been determined that the trial court's sentencing decision was unlawful or an abuse of discretion. Although the power to reduce a sentence should be exercised cautiously and sparingly, the authority to reduce a criminal sentence remains an important and valuable tool in the appellate court's choice of remedies when reviewing sentences imposed by the circuit court.[29]

☛ *Practice Tip:* On remand for resentencing, the trial court should simply reconsider the matter without relying on the factor found to be improper. If the trial court states that it did not place any weight on the improper factor, then it is free to reimpose the same sentence.[30]

§ 30:90. Modification or correction of judgment

The reviewing court has the power to reduce the degree of the offense of which the defendant was convicted.[31] This power may only be exercised, however, where a lesser included offense is involved.[32] A reviewing court may not reduce a charge out of benevolence, but may reduce to a lesser included offense where the reviewing court determines that the evidence presented by the State is too weak to support the greater offense.[33] But since the

---

29. People v Jones, 168 Ill 2d 367, 213 Ill Dec 659, 659 NE2d 1306.

30. People v Flanery, 243 Ill App 3d 759, 184 Ill Dec 27, 612 NE2d 903 (3d Dist 1993).

31. Supreme Court Rule 615(b)(3).

32. People v Jackson, 181 Ill App 3d 1048, 130 Ill Dec 725, 537 NE2d 1054 (3d Dist 1989).

A reviewing court has the authority to reduce the degree of the offense of which defendant was convicted when the evidence fails to prove beyond a reasonable doubt an element of the greater offense. This authority is only available where a lesser-included offense is involved. People v Sims, 245 Ill App 3d 221, 185 Ill Dec 452, 614 NE2d 893 (3d Dist 1993).

33. People v Munday, 134 Ill App 3d 971, 89 Ill Dec 787, 481 NE2d 338 (2d Dist 1985).

§ 30:90   ILLINOIS JURISPRUDENCE: CRIMINAL LAW

evaluation of the evidence is the purview of the trier of fact, who heard the evidence on initial presentation, the court must be careful to exercise the power to reduce a charge with caution.[34]

☞ *Illustration:* Conviction of attempted murder could be reduced to aggravated battery where there was no evidence that defendant had specific intent to kill the victim, but there was evidence that he intended great bodily harm to the victim when he shot him.[35]

§ 30:91. Reversal

The cumulative effect of alleged errors must be evaluated by the court to determine if the effect was prejudicial enough to have deprived the defendant of a fair trial.[36] If, indeed, the defendant was deprived of a fair trial, reversal is in order.[37]

☞ *Practice Tip:* In deciding whether to reverse a sentence imposed by the trial court, the reviewing court should not focus on a few words or statements of the trial court. Rather, the determination of whether a sentence was rendered properly must be made by considering the entire record as a whole.[38]

A conviction also may be reversed where the statute the defendant was convicted under is determined to be unconstitutional.[39]

---

34. People v McVay, 170 Ill App 3d 443, 120 Ill Dec 605, 524 NE2d 635 (4th Dist 1988).

35. People v Wagner, 189 Ill App 3d 1041, 137 Ill Dec 529, 546 NE2d 283 (4th Dist 1989).

36. People v Smith, 141 Ill 2d 40, 152 Ill Dec 218, 565 NE2d 900 (1990), subsequent app 1999 Ill LEXIS 18 (Ill); People v Johnson, 202 Ill App 3d 417, 147 Ill Dec 701, 559 NE2d 1041 (1st Dist 1990), app den 135 Ill 2d 562, 151 Ill Dec 388, 564 NE2d 843.

37. People v Smith, 141 Ill 2d 40, 152 Ill Dec 218, 565 NE2d 900 (1990), subsequent app 1999 Ill LEXIS 18 (Ill).

38. People v Draheim, 242 Ill App 3d 80, 182 Ill Dec 510, 609 NE2d 1044 (2d Dist 1993).

§ 30:92. Entry of judgment

Judgment is entered on the day the reviewing court files its opinion.[40] This date is not changed by the filing of a petition for rehearing.[41] However, if a rehearing is granted, the effective date of judgment is postponed until such time as the judgment on the rehearing is entered.[42] At that time, the previous opinion is superceded by the modified opinion.[43]

§ 30:93. Mandate and proceedings in lower court

By mandate, the reviewing court revests the lower court with the jurisdiction to carry out whatever action the mandate directs.[44] The circuit court must conform to the direction of the mandate or risk proceeding without authority.[45] If a lower court does act outside the direction of the mandate, its action will be deemed void and its order will be reversed and vacated. This is known as the law of the case doctrine.[46] Under the law of the case doctrine, once an issue has been decided, it is error for the lower court to rehear that issue and rule on it, without having been

---

39. People v Orange, 121 Ill 2d 364, 118 Ill Dec 1, 521 NE2d 69 (1988), cert den 488 US 900, 102 L Ed 2d 235, 109 S Ct 247, post-conviction proceeding, remanded 168 Ill 2d 138, 213 Ill Dec 589, 659 NE2d 935; People v Clark, 114 Ill 2d 450, 103 Ill Dec 102, 501 NE2d 123 (1986).

40. People v Brooks, 173 Ill App 3d 153, 122 Ill Dec 938, 527 NE2d 436 (1st Dist 1988).

41. People v Brooks, 173 Ill App 3d 153, 122 Ill Dec 938, 527 NE2d 436 (1st Dist 1988).

42. People v Brooks, 173 Ill App 3d 153, 122 Ill Dec 938, 527 NE2d 436 (1st Dist 1988).

43. People v Brooks, 173 Ill App 3d 153, 122 Ill Dec 938, 527 NE2d 436 (1st Dist 1988).

44. People ex rel. Daley v Schreier, 92 Ill 2d 271, 65 Ill Dec 874, 442 NE2d 185 (1982).

45. People ex rel. Daley v Schreier, 92 Ill 2d 271, 65 Ill Dec 874, 442 NE2d 185 (1982).

46. People v Abata, 165 Ill App 3d 184, 116 Ill Dec 244, 518 NE2d 1065 (2d Dist 1988).

§ 30:93   ILLINOIS JURISPRUDENCE: CRIMINAL LAW

given jurisdiction to do so.[47] Thus, the lower court must act in accordance with any specific directions given by the reviewing court and if no directions are given, the trial court has the duty to determine what action should be taken that would be consistent with the opinion issued by the superior court.[48]

☞ *Practice Guide:* When a mandate issues which remands a cause to the trial court for proceedings consistent with the opinion issued by the reviewing court, the trial court must look to the opinion for directions and will of necessity construe the language of the opinion when needed. In such an instance, the trial court is allowed to embrace matters not expressly stated in the remanding order which are the clear and necessary implication from the language employed in the remanding order of the reviewing court. When a mandate issues which fails to remand a cause to the trial court, and which simply states that writs and motion for supervisory order are denied, it cannot reasonably be said that it embraces the revesting of jurisdiction in the trial court by clear and necessary implication. Unless and until further action is taken by the reviewing court, jurisdiction does not revest in the trial court, but remains in the reviewing court.[49]

☞ *Illustration:* When a sentence is vacated on appeal and the cause remanded for a new sentencing hearing, the trial court should not construe the action of the reviewing court as a mandate to impose a lesser sentence. Further, when the appellate court directs the lower court to consider a particular factor as weighing in favor of mitigation on remand, the lower court cannot simply disagree and ignore that mandate.[50]

---

47. People v Abata, 165 Ill App 3d 184, 116 Ill Dec 244, 518 NE2d 1065 (2d Dist 1988).

48. People v Webb, 109 Ill App 3d 328, 64 Ill Dec 854, 440 NE2d 406 (4th Dist 1982).

49. People v Palmer, 148 Ill 2d 70, 170 Ill Dec 260, 592 NE2d 940 (1992).

§ 30:94. Jurisdiction and proceedings of appellate court after remand

Under the law of the case doctrine, once an issue in a case has been decided by the appellate court, it is binding not only on the trial court, but also on the appellate court on subsequent appeal of the same case.[51] This is true even if the appellate court which originally heard the appeal applied an erroneous rule.[52]

XIII. APPEALS IN POSTCONVICTION PROCEEDINGS

Research References:
  Annotation References:
   Index and Annotations: Appeal and Error; Habeas Corpus
   ALR Digest to 3d, 4th, 5th, and Federal: Appeal and Error § 38

  Practice References:
   5 Am Jur 2d, Appeal and Error § 871; 39 Am Jur 2d, Habeas Corpus §§ 169, 170

  State Legislation:
   725 ILCS 5/122-2.1; Supreme Court Rule 651

  Miscellaneous References:
   West's Illinois Digest 2d, Habeas Corpus § 113

§ 30:95. Right of appeal

An appeal as a matter of right may be taken from final judgments imposed by a circuit court in a postconviction proceeding.[53] If the final judgment resulted in a death sentence, the appeal is to the Supreme Court, but in noncapital cases the appeal is to the Appellate Court in the district court where the circuit court is located.[54]

---

50. People v Colter, 237 Ill App 3d 486, 178 Ill Dec 457, 604 NE2d 980 (3d Dist 1992).

51. People v Lyles, 208 Ill App 3d 370, 153 Ill Dec 438, 567 NE2d 396 (1st Dist 1990).

52. People v Lynch, 151 Ill App 3d 987, 105 Ill Dec 17, 503 NE2d 857 (2d Dist 1987).

53. Supreme Court Rule 651(a).

§ 30:96. Notice to petitioner of adverse judgment

Should an adverse judgment be entered against the petitioner in a postconviction proceeding, the clerk or the trial court must mail or deliver promptly a notice of the order entered to the petitioner.[55] The notice must take a form similar to:

You are hereby notified that on _____ — 19— the court entered an order, a copy of which is enclosed herewith. You have a right to appeal. In the case of an appeal from a postconviction proceeding involving a judgment imposing a sentence of death, the appeal is to the Illinois Supreme Court. In all other cases, the appeal is to the Illinois Appellate Court in the district in which the circuit is located. If you are indigent, you have a right to a transcript of the record of the postconviction proceedings and to the appointment of counsel on appeal, both without cost to you. To preserve your right to appeal you must file a notice of appeal in the trial court within 30 days from the date the order was entered.[56]

§ 30:97. Indigents

The court will order preparation of the transcript of the record of the postconviction hearing, including a transcript of the evidence, if necessary, to be filed with the clerk of the reviewing court and an attorney will be appointed by the court, all at no cost to the petitioner, if the petitioner filed the notice of appeal of the postconviction judgment in a timely manner and is found to be indigent.[57] A showing must be made in the record when filed that the attorney appointed:

- has conferred with the petitioner regarding the petitioner's allegations that his or her constitutional rights were infringed upon;
- examined the record of the trial proceedings; and

---

54. Supreme Court Rule 651(a).
55. Supreme Court Rule 651(b).
56. Supreme Court Rule 651(b).
57. Supreme Court Rule 651(c).

- has amended the petitioner's pro se petitions to the extent necessary to ensure adequate presentation of the petitioner's allegations.[58]

☛ *Caution:* The courts have been unable to agree as to the relationship between this section and 725 ILCS 5/122-2.1 of the Post-Conviction Hearing Act which allows the court to dismiss a petition for a postconviction hearing if it finds the petition to be frivolous or patently without merit.[59] The issue on which the courts seem to diverge is whether or not courts should be allowed to dismiss petitions for the foregoing reasons prior to the appointment of counsel.

§ 30:98. Procedure

To the extent possible, the rules for criminal appeals govern appeals for postconvictions proceedings.[60]

---

58. Supreme Court Rule 651(c).
59. Supreme Court Rule 651.
   See also 725 ILCS 5/122-2.1.
60. Supreme Court Rule 651(d).

CHAPTER 31

ORIGINAL ACTIONS IN THE SUPREME COURT

by

Evan M. Butterfield, J.D.

and

Robert L. Margolis, Esq.

Scope of Chapter:

This chapter discusses the bringing of actions in the Illinois Supreme Court under its constitutionally established original jurisdiction. Writs of prohibition and mandamus, and habeas corpus actions are defined and analyzed. In addition, this chapter examines the federal requirement of exhaustion of state remedies as it applies to the original jurisdiction of the state supreme court.

Federal Aspects:

To the extent they are relevant, federal decisions are cited that discuss or analyze Illinois law. Mandamus, prohibition, or habeas corpus actions arising under federal law are not discussed, except with regard to the requirement that all state remedies have been exhausted. See 21 Am Jur 2d Criminal Law § 418; 21A Am Jur 2d Criminal Law §§ 870, 971, 975; 39 Am Jur 2d Habeas Corpus.

Treated Elsewhere:

Arrest and detention, see Chapter 5.

Jurisdiction generally, see Chapter 12.

Research References:
  Text References:
    Ruebner, Illinois Criminal Procedure 2d ed §§ 7.01, 7.11–7.12, 7.18, 7.30–7.34
    Ill Law Man
  Annotation References:
    ALR Digest: Habeas Corpus; Mandamus; Prohibition

ILLINOIS JURISPRUDENCE: CRIMINAL LAW

Index and Annotations: Exhaustion of Remedies; Habeas Corpus; Mandamus; Original Jurisdiction; Prohibition Writ

Practice References:

20 Am Jur 2d, Courts; 39 Am Jur 2d, Habeas Corpus; 52 Am Jur 2d, Mandamus; 63A Am Jur 2d, Prohibition

5 Am Jur POF2d 267, Ineffective Assistance of Counsel

20 Am Jur Trials 1, Federal Habeas Corpus Practice; 22 Am Jur Trials 1, Prisoners' Rights Litigation; 39 Am Jur Trials 157, Historical Aspects and Procedural Limitations of Federal Habeas Corpus

Forms:

13 Am Jur Pl & Pr Forms (Rev), Habeas Corpus; 17 Am Jur Pl & Pr Forms (Rev), Mandamus; 20A Am Jur Pl & Pr Forms (Rev), Prohibition

Auto-Cite®: Cases and annotations referred to in this chapter can be further researched through the Auto-Cite® computer-assisted research service. Use Auto-Cite® to check citations for form, parallel references, prior and later history, and annotation references.

I. ORIGINAL ACTIONS GENERALLY

§ 31:01. Constitutional and statutory considerations
§ 31:02. —Petition
§ 31:03. —Service of process
§ 31:04. —Objections
§ 31:05. —Briefs and oral argument

II. PROHIBITION, MANDAMUS, AND HABEAS CORPUS

§ 31:06. Prohibition
§ 31:07. Mandamus
§ 31:08. —Availability
§ 31:09. —Procedure
§ 31:10. —Judgment
§ 31:11. Habeas corpus
§ 31:12. —Petition
§ 31:13. —Return
§ 31:14. —Reply and hearing
§ 31:15. —Remand and discharge
§ 31:16. —Statutory penalties and civil action
§ 31:17. —Federal actions

ORIGINAL ACTIONS IN THE SUPREME COURT § 31:01

I. ORIGINAL ACTIONS GENERALLY

Research References:

Text References:

Ruebner, Illinois Criminal Procedure 2d ed §§ 7.18, 7.30–7.34

Ill Law Man § K8.03

Annotation References:

ALR Digest: Habeas Corpus § 1 et seq.; Mandamus § 1 et seq.; Prohibition § 1 et seq.

Index and Annotations: Habeas Corpus; Mandamus; Original Jurisdiction; Prohibition Writ

Practice References:

20 Am Jur 2d, Courts §§ 107, 108; 39 Am Jur 2d, Habeas Corpus § 1 et seq.; 52 Am Jur 2d, Mandamus § 1 et seq.; 63A Am Jur 2d, Prohibition § 1 et seq.

State Legislation:

Ill Const Art VI §§ 4, 4(a)

Supreme Court Rules 341–344, 381

Miscellaneous References:

West's Illinois Digest 2d, Habeas Corpus § 1 et seq.; Mandamus § 1 et seq.; Prohibition § 1 et seq.

§ 31:01. Constitutional and statutory considerations

Under the Iliniois Constitution,[1] the state supreme court may exercise original jurisdiction in those cases involving revenue,[2] prohibition, mandamus, and habeas corpus.[3] The Illinois Supreme Court's original jurisdiction is limited to matters of law, and it will not assume jurisdiction of an original action if the pleadings present issues of fact.[4]

1. Ill Const art VI, § 4.

2. Ill Const art VI, § 4(a).

See, e.g., People ex rel. No. 3 J. & E. Discount, Inc. v Whitler, 81 Ill 2d 473, 43 Ill Dec 721, 410 NE2d 854 (1980).

3. Ill Const art VI, § 4(a).

Text References: Ruebner, Illinois Criminal Procedure 2d ed § 7.18.
Ill Law Man § K8.03.

§ 31:02. —Petition

Original actions in the Illinois Supreme Court seeking writs of mandamus, prohibition, and habeas corpus are instituted by filing a motion, supported by explanatory suggestions, for leave to file a sworn complaint seeking appropriate relief.[5] The court considers only issues of law,[6] and the proposed complaint must be sworn to and include the lower court records or other pertinent material that fully presents the issues of law.[7]

> ☞ *Practice Guide:* If the motion seeking mandamus, prohibition, or habeas corpus is filed when the supreme court is not in session, a movant whose case arises in the first judicial district files the original motion and five copies with the clerk in the Chicago satellite office, and sends a copy to the chambers of the other district courts.[8] A movant whose case arises in the second, third, fourth, or fifth judicial district files the original and one copy with the clerk in Springfield, and sends a copy to each district judge in his or her chambers.[9]

If leave to file the motion is denied, the decision is not an adjudication on the merits and the petitioner is not barred from seeking relief in the circuit courts or from later perfecting an appeal to the supreme court.[10]

---

4. People ex rel. Burris v Ryan, 147 Ill 2d 270 (1992), cert den 504 US 973, 119 L Ed 2d 565, 112 S Ct 2940.

See Supreme Court Rule 381(a).

5. Supreme Court Rule 381(a).

Text References: Ruebner, Illinois Criminal Procedure 2d ed §§ 7.01, 7.18.

6. Supreme Court Rule 381(a).

7. Supreme Court Rule 381(a).

8. Supreme Court Rule 381(a).

9. Supreme Court Rule 381(a).

10. See, e.g., Monroe v Collins, 393 Ill 553, 66 NE2d 670 (1946); Torjesen v Smith, 114 Ill App 3d 147, 69 Ill Dec 813, 448 NE2d 273 (5th Dist 1983).

§ 31:03. —Service of process

A copy of the motion, together with the proposed complaint, is served on the other party or parties, including nominal ones.[11] Proof of service is to be filed at the time the motion is filed with the court.[12]

In an original action to review a judge's judicial act, the judge is only a nominal party in the proceeding, and need not respond to the motion or complaint unless instructed to do so by the court.[13] A judge's failure to respond is not construed as an admission of any allegation contained in the motion.[14] A prevailing party's counsel may file appropriate papers on behalf of that party, but not in the name of the judge who is a nominal party.[15]

§ 31:04. —Objections

The respondent has seven days to file any objections to the motion.[16] The movant must be served with the objections, and the respondent must file proof of service with the clerk of the court.[17]

§ 31:05. —Briefs and oral argument

The court may permit oral argument on the motion.[18] In any event, if the motion is allowed, briefs[19] are to be filed in support of the pleadings within the time fixed by the court.[20] A party may, by

---

11. Supreme Court Rule 381(b).
12. Supreme Court Rule 381(b).
13. Supreme Court Rule 381(c).
14. Supreme Court Rule 381(c).
15. Supreme Court Rule 381(c).
16. Supreme Court Rule 381(d).
17. Supreme Court Rule 381(d).
18. Supreme Court Rule 381(d).

19. See Supreme Court Rules 341 and, 342 for the formal requirements of briefs and appendices, and Supreme Court Rules 343 and 344 for service and filing requirements.

20. Supreme Court Rule 381(e).

§ 31:05 ILLINOIS JURISPRUDENCE: CRIMINAL LAW

providing notice to the court and other parties, allow his or her original papers to stand as his or her brief without a court order.[21]

☛ *Practice Guide:* The Illinois Supreme Court Rules set forth specific formal requirements for briefs, including page limitations, cover specifications, the proper way to reference parties, citation forms, and an outline of the required sections of each brief.[22] In addition, the Rules require an appendix which includes a copy of the judgment appealed from, any opinion, memorandum, or findings of fact filed or entered by the trial judge, or by any administrative agency or its officers, any pleadings or other materials from the record which are the basis of the appeal or pertinent to it, the notice of appeal, and a complete table of contents, with page references, of the record on appeal.[23] Counsel should consult the Rules before undertaking to draft a brief and compile an appendix. Where an appellant's brief fails to comply with the Supreme Court rules, an appellate court has the inherent authority to dismiss the appeal due to noncompliance with the rules.[24]

II. PROHIBITION, MANDAMUS, AND HABEAS CORPUS

Research References:
 Text References:
  Ruebner, Illinois Criminal Procedure 2d ed §§ 7.30–7.34.
  Ill Law Man §§ K8.11, K8.13, K8.16, K8.18–K8.21, K8.23, K8.26, L1.20, L1.42.

---

21. Supreme Court Rule 381(e).

22. Supreme Court Rule 341.

23. Supreme Court Rule 342.

24. People v Kraft, 277 Ill App 3d 221, 213 Ill Dec 857, 660 NE2d 1233 (1st Dist 1995).

Annotation References:
> ALR Digest: Habeas Corpus § 1 et seq; Mandamus § 1 et seq.; Prohibition § 1 et seq.
>
> Index and Annotations: Exhaustion of Remedies; Habeas Corpus; Mandamus; Original Jurisdiction; Prohibition Writ

Practice References:
> 39 Am Jur 2d, Habeas Corpus § 1 et seq.; 52 Am Jur 2d, Mandamus § 1 et seq.; 63A Am Jur 2d, Prohibition § 1 et seq.
>
> 5 Am Jur POF2d 267, Ineffective Assistance of Counsel § 12.
>
> 20 Am Jur Trials 1, Federal Habeas Corpus Practice §§ 19–21; 22 Am Jur Trials 1, Prisoners' Rights Litigation § 76; 39 Am Jur Trials 157, Historical Aspects and Procedural Limitations of Federal Habeas Corpus § 27.

Federal Legislation:
> 28 USC § 2254.

State Legislation:
> Ill Const Art I § 9, Art VI § 6.
>
> 735 ILCS 5/10–101 et seq.; 735 ILCS 5/14–101; Supreme Court Rule 381(a).

Forms:
> 13 Am Jur Pl & Pr Forms (Rev), Habeas Corpus, Forms 41 et seq., 209–218, 233–263; 17 Am Jur Pl & Pr Forms (Rev), Mandamus, Form 1 et seq.; 20A Am Jur Pl & Pr Forms (Rev), Prohibition, Form 1 et seq.

§ 31:06. Prohibition

The purpose of a writ of prohibition is to allow a court of superior jurisdiction to prevent a lower court from exceeding its legal jurisdictional authority, and to restrain it from further action in order to avoid any damage or injustice.[25] A writ of

---

25. Maloney v Bower, 113 Ill 2d 473, 101 Ill Dec 594, 498 NE2d 1102 (1986); Hughes v Kiley, 67 Ill 2d 261, 10 Ill Dec 247, 367 NE2d 700 (1977).

Text References: Ill Law Man § K8.26.

Annotation References: Availability of writ of prohibition or similar remedy against acts of public prosecutor, 16 ALR4th 112.
> Availability of mandamus or prohibition to compel or to prevent discovery proceedings, 95 ALR2d 1229.
> Former jeopardy as ground for prohibition, 94 ALR2d 1048.

§ 31:06   ILLINOIS JURISPRUDENCE: CRIMINAL LAW

prohibition is an extraordinary remedy,[26] and four conditions must be satisfied for one to issue:

- the action sought to be prohibited must be judicial in nature;
- the court against which the writ is sought must be inferior to the issuing court;
- the action sought to be prohibited must be beyond the lower court's jurisdiction or authority; and
- there must be no other adequate remedy available.[27]

The absence of a remedy will be found where the petitioner will suffer some injury due to the unauthorized exercise of jurisdiction of which he or she complains.[28] Further, although only arguments relating to jurisdiction will be heard, an administrative act that is essentially judicial in nature nonetheless is subject to the issuance of a writ of prohibition.[29]

However, the fact that a petitioner could have sought relief through another extraordinary remedy, such as a writ of mandamus or supervisory order, is not necessarily a bar to the issuance of a writ of prohibition.[30]

Availability of writ of prohibition to prevent illegal or unauthorized taking of depositions, 73 ALR2d 1169.
Mandamus or prohibition as remedy to enforce right to jury trial, 41 ALR2d 780.

Forms: Prohibition—In general. 20A Am Jur Pl & Pr Forms (Rev), Prohibition, Form 1 et seq.

26. See, e.g., Hughes v Kiley, 67 Ill 2d 261, 10 Ill Dec 247, 367 NE2d 700 (1977).

27. Maloney v Bower, 113 Ill 2d 473, 101 Ill Dec 594, 498 NE2d 1102 (1986); People ex rel. No. 3 J. & E. Discount, Inc. v Whitler, 81 Ill 2d 473, 43 Ill Dec 721, 410 NE2d 854 (1980); Hughes v Kiley, 67 Ill 2d 261, 10 Ill Dec 247, 367 NE2d 700 (1977).

28. People ex rel. No. 3 J. & E. Discount, Inc. v Whitler, 81 Ill 2d 473, 43 Ill Dec 721, 410 NE2d 854 (1980).

29. People ex rel. No. 3 J. & E. Discount, Inc. v Whitler, 81 Ill 2d 473, 43 Ill Dec 721, 410 NE2d 854 (1980).

30. Maloney v Bower, 113 Ill 2d 473, 101 Ill Dec 594, 498 NE2d 1102 (1986).

§ 31:07. Mandamus

The purpose of a writ of mandamus is to provide affirmative relief, rather than prohibitive relief, to an injured petitioner.[31]

A writ of mandamus is a summary writ issued from a court of competent jurisdiction that commands the officer to whom it is issued to perform a duty to which the petitioner is entitled as a matter of right; the only purpose of a mandamus proceeding is to enforce rights already lawfully vested.[32]

A writ of mandamus is an extraordinary remedy and discretionary in nature.[33] To be entitled to the issuance of a writ of mandamus, the petitioner normally must show that:

- he or she has a clear right to the relief sought;
- the respondent has a clear duty to act;
- the respondent has clear authority to comply with the terms of relief;[34]
- the petitioner has exhausted all ordinary remedies, and has no other adequate remedy available;[35] and

---

31. People ex rel. Roberts v Orenic, 88 Ill 2d 502, 59 Ill Dec 68, 431 NE2d 353 (1981); Rock v Thompson, 85 Ill 2d 410, 55 Ill Dec 566, 426 NE2d 891 (1981).

32. See Doe v Carlson, 250 Ill App 3d 570, 189 Ill Dec 205, 619 NE2d 906 (2d Dist 1993); Crump v Illinois Prisoner Review Bd., 181 Ill App 3d 58, 129 Ill Dec 825, 536 NE2d 875 (1st Dist 1989); Rexroat v Abatte, 163 Ill App 3d 796, 114 Ill Dec 895, 516 NE2d 1050 (3d Dist 1987); Field v Rollins, 156 Ill App 3d 786, 109 Ill Dec 484, 510 NE2d 105 (1st Dist 1987).

See generally 735 ILCS 5/14-101 et seq.

Text References: Ill Law Man § K8.11.

Annotation References: Private citizen's right to institute mandamus to compel a magistrate or other appropriate official to issue a warrant, or the like, for an arrest, 49 ALR2d 1285.
Mandamus to compel judge or other officer to grant accused bail or to accept proffered sureties, 23 ALR2d 803.

33. People v Latona, 184 Ill 2d 260, 234 Ill Dec 801, 703 NE2d 901 (1998).

34. See, e.g., People v Latona, 184 Ill 2d 260, 234 Ill Dec 801, 703 NE2d 901 (1998); Orenic v Illinois State Labor Relations Bd., 127 Ill 2d 453, 130 Ill Dec 455, 537 NE2d 784 (1989).

- the remedy sought is not one involving a matter wholly in the discretion or judgment of the respondent,[36] although mandamus may issue to compel the performance of an action that requires the exercise of discretion.[37]

👉 *Practice Guide:* A mandamus action is not necessarily barred by the existence of other remedies; rather, the existence of other remedies may be grounds for denying the writ.[38]

Thus, mandamus will not ordinarily lie to correct an abuse of discretion,[39] or to regulate such matters as discovery.[40] Where there are issues of fact to be decided, mandamus is improper.[41] A mandamus petition will be dismissed as moot if no actual rights or interests of the parties remain or if events occur that make it impossible for the court to grant effectual relief to either party.[42] However, the Supreme Court has held that even in circumstances in which the issuance of a writ is unwarranted, the court may nonetheless grant the relief sought through the exercise of its supervisory authority where the issues raised are of vital importance to the administration of justice, even if all of the normal requirements for the writ's award are not met initially.[43]

---

35. Weiner v Forest Preserve Dist., 126 Ill App 3d 206, 81 Ill Dec 484, 466 NE2d 1286 (1st Dist 1984).

36. Doherty v Caisley, 104 Ill 2d 72, 83 Ill Dec 361, 470 NE2d 319 (1984).

37. Rock v Thompson, 85 Ill 2d 410, 55 Ill Dec 566, 426 NE2d 891 (1981).

38. 735 ILCS 5/14-108.

39. Owen v Mann, 105 Ill 2d 525, 86 Ill Dec 507, 475 NE2d 886 (1985); Brown v Scotillo, 104 Ill 2d 54, 83 Ill Dec 378, 470 NE2d 504 (1984); People ex rel. Daley v Schreir, 92 Ill 2d 275, 442 NE2d 185 (1982).

40. Owen v Mann, 105 Ill 2d 525, 86 Ill Dec 507, 475 NE2d 886 (1985); People ex rel. Daley v Moran, 94 Ill 2d 41, 67 Ill Dec 790, 445 NE2d 270 (1983); Balciunas v Duff, 94 Ill 2d 176, 68 Ill Dec 508, 446 NE2d 242 (1983).

41. Kerr v Cicero, 235 Ill App 3d 528, 176 Ill Dec 535, 601 NE2d 1233 (1st Dist 1992).

42. Jackson v Peters, 251 Ill App 3d 865, 191 Ill Dec 249, 623 NE2d 839 (3d Dist 1993).

§ 31:07

> ☛ *Illustration:* A writ of mandamus was issued in a homicide case to compel the trial court to comply with mandatory sentencing guidelines imposed by statute.[44] On the other hand, mandamus was not available in a case in which the trial court exercised its discretion and precluded the state from questioning prospective jurors on the subject of the death penalty.[45]

Mandamus is an extraordinary remedy,[46] civil in nature,[47] to which the doctrine of laches may apply.[48] The limitations period for seeking a writ of mandamus is generally six months, although a longer period may be allowed where the petitioner has a reasonable excuse for the delay.[49]

> ☛ *Practice Guide:* Because a complaint seeking a writ of mandamus is essentially civil in nature, indigent petitioners do not have a constitutional right to the appointment of counsel.[50]

---

43. People v Latona, 184 Ill 2d 260, 234 Ill Dec 801, 703 NE2d 901 (1998); Baker v Department of Corrections, 106 Ill 2d 100, 87 Ill Dec 560, 477 NE2d 686 (1985).

See People ex rel. Yarrow v Lueders, 287 Ill 107, 122 NE 374 (1919).

44. People ex rel. Daley v Strayhorn, 119 Ill 2d 331, 116 Ill Dec 226, 518 NE2d 1047 (1988).

See also United States v Spilotro, 884 F2d 1003 (CA7 Ill 1989) (superseded by statute as stated in United States v McDowell, 117 F3d 974 (CA7 Ill)).

45. Daley v Hett, 113 Ill 2d 75, 99 Ill Dec 132, 495 NE2d 513 (1986).

46. People v Latona, 184 Ill 2d 260, 234 Ill Dec 801, 703 NE2d 901 (1998); Doherty v Caisley, 104 Ill 2d 72, 83 Ill Dec 361, 470 NE2d 319 (1984); Hughes v Kiley, 67 Ill 2d 261, 10 Ill Dec 247, 367 NE2d 700 (1977).

47. Doherty v Caisley, 104 Ill 2d 72, 83 Ill Dec 361, 470 NE2d 319 (1984).

48. People ex rel. Daley v Strayhorn, 121 Ill 2d 470, 118 Ill Dec 387, 521 NE2d 864 (1988).

49. Rexroat v Abatte, 163 Ill App 3d 796, 114 Ill Dec 895, 516 NE2d 1050 (3d Dist 1987).

§ 31:08. —Availability

The Illinois Constitution prohibits the state from appealing judgments of acquittal in criminal cases.[51] The state may not circumvent this constitutional bar by means of substituting mandamus for direct appeal.[52] However, a defendant in a criminal case who has a meritorious double jeopardy defense may properly file a pretrial motion for leave to file an original petition for mandamus seeking correction of a trial court's erroneous denial of his or her motion to dismiss.[53] Where the alleged error is a matter of judicial discretion, rather than simply ministerial, however, mandamus will not lie to correct the alleged abuse.[54] It is not necessary that the petitioner have made a demand upon the lower court to vacate an allegedly erroneous order where the order involves the public interest or the issue is of considerable importance to the administration of justice rather than a purely private right.[55]

> *Illustration:* Cases in which issues of sufficiently compelling importance to the administration of justice were found include writs granted to compel sentencing by the lower court in accordance with a prior order issued on appeal;[56] to

---

50. Marrero v Peters, 229 Ill App 3d 752, 171 Ill Dec 346, 593 NE2d 1166 (4th Dist 1992); Doherty v Caisley, 104 Ill 2d 72, 83 Ill Dec 361, 470 NE2d 319 (1984); Tedder v Fairman, 92 Ill 2d 216, 65 Ill Dec 398, 441 NE2d 311 (1982).

51. Ill Const art VI, § 6.

Text References: Ruebner, Illinois Criminal Procedure 2d ed §§ 7.11–7.12.

52. People ex rel. Daley v Limperis, 86 Ill 2d 459, 56 Ill Dec 666, 427 NE2d 1212 (1981).

53. People ex rel. Roberts v Orenic, 88 Ill 2d 502, 59 Ill Dec 68, 431 NE2d 353 (1981); People ex rel. Mosley v Carey, 74 Ill 2d 527, 25 Ill Dec 669, 387 NE2d 325 (1979), cert den 444 US 940, 62 L Ed 2d 306, 100 S Ct 292.

See Eisenberg v United States Dist. Court, 910 F2d 374 (CA7 1990).

54. People ex rel. Daley v Schreier, 92 Ill 2d 271, 65 Ill Dec 874, 442 NE2d 185 (1982).

55. Owen v Mann, 105 Ill 2d 525, 86 Ill Dec 507, 475 NE2d 886 (1985); People ex rel. Daley v Schreier, 92 Ill 2d 271, 65 Ill Dec 874, 442 NE2d 185 (1982).

compel the trial court to expunge its order directing the return of property ordered seized under a warrant issued by another judge;[57] to compel the trial court to grant the state's discovery motion for notice of a defendant's possible alibi defense and the identity of potential alibi witnesses;[58] and to compel a three judge panel to convene for the purpose of conducting a death penalty hearing.[59]

§ 31:09. —Procedure

When an action seeking the issuance of a writ of mandamus is commenced,[60] the plaintiff files a complaint with the clerk of the court, who issues a summons as similar in form as possible to that issued in other civil cases.[61] The summons is returnable at a designated date between 5 and 30 days after service.[62] A defendant who is served with summons in a mandamus action must answer or otherwise plead prior to the return date, and may not introduce, by way of joinder, counterclaim, or otherwise, issues extraneous to the distinctive purpose of the mandamus proceeding.[63] Within five days of receiving the defendant's answer, the plaintiff may reply or otherwise plead to the answer; the court may grant an extension of time.[64]

The fact that a plaintiff is found to have sought the wrong

---

56. People ex rel. Daley v Schreier, 92 Ill 2d 271, 65 Ill Dec 874, 442 NE2d 185 (1982).

57. People ex rel. Carey v Covelli, 61 Ill 2d 394, 336 NE2d 759 (1975).

58. People ex rel. Carey v Strayhorn, 61 Ill 2d 85, 329 NE2d 194 (1975).

59. People ex rel. Rice v Cunningham, 61 Ill 2d 353, 336 NE2d 1 (1975).

60. 735 ILCS 5/14-101.

61. 735 ILCS 5/14-102.

   Text References: Ill Law Man § K8.13.

   Forms: Application or petition for writ of mandamus. 17 Am Jur Pl & Pr Forms (Rev), Mandamus, Form 1 et seq.

62. 735 ILCS 5/14-102 (court may grant extension of time).

63. 735 ILCS 5/14-103.

64. 735 ILCS 5/14-104.

§ 31:09   ILLINOIS JURISPRUDENCE: CRIMINAL LAW

remedy is not fatal to the mandamus action, and the mistake may be corrected by amendment if the court finds that allowing amendment would be just and reasonable in light of the defendant's rights.[65]

The death, resignation, or removal from office of a defendant, whether by lapse of time or otherwise, will not abate the proceeding.[66] Rather, the officer's successor may be named as a party to the mandamus action, and any relief granted may be directed against him or her.[67]

§ 31:10. —Judgment

If judgment is entered in favor of the plaintiff, he or she recovers damages and costs.[68] On the other hand, if the defendant prevails, he or she recovers any costs incurred in the action.[69] The recovery of damages against a defendant shelters him or her from liability in any subsequent action or proceeding for having made a false return.[70]

§ 31:11. Habeas corpus

Any person who is imprisoned or deprived of his or her liberty may petition for habeas corpus.[71] While the Illinois Constitution guarantees that the privilege of habeas corpus will not be

---

65. 735 ILCS 5/14-109.

People ex rel. Foreman v Nash, 118 Ill 2d 90, 112 Ill Dec 714, 514 NE2d 180 (1987).

66. 735 ILCS 5/14-107.

67. 735 ILCS 5/14-107.

68. 735 ILCS 5/14-105.

Text References: Ill Law Man § K8.16.

Annotation References: Allowance of attorneys' fees in mandamus proceedings, 34 ALR4th 457.

69. 735 ILCS 5/14-105.

70. 735 ILCS 5/14-106.

71. 735 ILCS 5/10-102.

Text References: Ruebner, Illinois Criminal Procedure 2d ed §§ 7.30–7.34.

suspended except for public safety purposes in cases of rebellion or invasion,[72] the remedy is available only in a limited number of specific circumstances, defined by statute.[73] These are:

- the lower court has exceeded its jurisdiction with regard to subject matter, place, sum, or person;

- a subsequent act, omission, or event has rendered the petitioner entitled to discharge from an originally lawful imprisonment;

- the process is defective in a substantial form required by law;

- the process in proper form has been issued in an extra-legal case or circumstance;

- process was obtained by false pretense or bribery; or

---

72. Ill Const art I, § 9.

73. 735 ILCS 5/10-101 et seq.

People v Neal, 179 Ill 2d 541, 228 Ill Dec 619, 689 NE2d 1040 (1997); Faheem-El v Klincar, 123 Ill 2d 291, 122 Ill Dec 809, 527 NE2d 307 (1988); Hughes v Kiley, 67 Ill 2d 261, 10 Ill Dec 247, 367 NE2d 700 (1977).

Text References: Ruebner, Illinois Criminal Procedure 2d ed § 7.30. Ill Law Man §§ K8.18, K8.19.

Annotation References: When is a person in custody of governmental authorities for purpose of exercise of state remedy of habeas corpus—modern cases, 26 ALR4th 455.

Insanity of accused at time of commission of offense, not raised at trial, as ground for habeas corpus or coram nobis after conviction, 29 ALR2d 703.

Habeas corpus on ground of deprivation of right to appeal, 19 ALR2d 789.

Former jeopardy as ground for habeas corpus, 8 ALR2d 285.

Periodicals: Meyer, "Nothing we say matters": Teague and new rules, 61 U Chi L Rev 423 (1994).

Jochner, 'Til habeas do us part: recent Supreme Court habeas corpus rulings, 81 Ill BJ 250 (1993).

Schwartz, The Preiser Puzzle: Continued Frustrating Conflict Between the Civil Rights and Habeas Corpus Remedies for State Prisoners, 37 DePaul L Rev 85, Winter 1988.

Practice References: Habeas Corpus. 5 Am Jur POF2d 267, Ineffective Assistance of Counsel § 12.

§ 31:11 ILLINOIS JURISPRUDENCE: CRIMINAL LAW

- in a criminal case, the petitioner is imprisoned without a conviction.[74] Where none of these grounds apply, habeas must be denied.[75]

☞ *Illustration:* The Illinois Supreme Court has held that habeas corpus relief is not available to a prisoner serving time of mandatory supervised release who is seeking to review revocation proceedings, because such a prisoner does not fall within one of the limited categories of relief provided by statute.[76]

Nonjurisdictional claims may not be reviewed by means of habeas corpus, even when they involve a denial of constitutional rights.[77]

A person imprisoned for contempt of court for the nonperformance of an order or judgment for the payment of money is entitled to relief by habeas corpus, and to discharge from confinement, but not from any lien, if the nonpayment is due to inability to comply or to endure confinement.[78]

§ 31:12. —Petition

A person who has been imprisoned or deprived of his or her liberty may apply directly to the supreme court for a writ of habeas corpus.[79] Application is made by complaint, signed either by the complainant or by some other person in his or her behalf,

---

74. 735 ILCS 5/10-124.

See, e.g., People v Neal, 179 Ill 2d 541, 228 Ill Dec 619, 689 NE2d 1040 (1997); Faheem-El v Klincar, 123 Ill 2d 291, 122 Ill Dec 809, 527 NE2d 307 (1988); Walker v Hardiman, 116 Ill 2d 413, 107 Ill Dec 696, 507 NE2d 849 (1987), cert den 484 US 866, 98 L Ed 2d 141, 108 S Ct 189; Hughes v Kiley, 67 Ill 2d 261, 10 Ill Dec 247, 367 NE2d 700 (1977).

Text References: Ruebner, Illinois Criminal Procedure 2d ed §§ 7.32–7.33.

75. People v Neal, 179 Ill 2d 541, 228 Ill Dec 619, 689 NE2d 1040 (1997).

76. Barney v Prisoner Review Board, 184 Ill 2d 428, 235 Ill Dec 1, 704 NE2d 350 (1998).

77. Hughes v Kiley, 67 Ill 2d 261, 10 Ill Dec 247, 367 NE2d 700 (1977).

78. 735 ILCS 5/10-137.

ORIGINAL ACTIONS IN THE SUPREME COURT § 31:12

and verified by affidavit.[80]

> *Practice Guide:* An application for relief may not be commenced on behalf of a person who has been sentenced to death without the written consent of that person, unless the person, because of a mental or physical condition, is incapable of asserting his or her own claims.[81]

The complaint must state:[82]

- that the petitioner is imprisoned or restrained of his or her liberty;
- the place of imprisonment or restraint;
- the names of the parties, or their descriptions if their names are not known;
- the petitioner's best knowledge and belief of the cause or pretense of the restraint; and
- that the petitioner is not committed or detained by virtue of any process of any court of the United States having exclusive jurisdiction in the case; or by any final judgment of any circuit court or proceeding for the enforcement of such a judgment; or for any treason, felony or other crime committed in any other state or territory of the United States for which the person is legally subject to extradition.[83]

---

79. 735 ILCS 5/10-102.

    Text References: Ill Law Man §§ L1.20, L1.42.

80. 735 ILCS 5/10-103.

    Text References: Ill Law Man §§ K8.20, K8.21.

    Forms: Petition or applications—Habeas Corpus. 13 Am Jur Pl & Pr Forms (Rev), Habeas Corpus, Form 41 et seq.

81. 735 ILCS 5/10–103.

82. See generally 735 ILCS 5/10-104.

83. 735 ILCS 5/10-123.

    See ch 7.

    Text References: Ruebner, Illinois Criminal Procedure 2d ed § 7.34.

§ 31:12 ILLINOIS JURISPRUDENCE: CRIMINAL LAW

When petitioning for a writ of habeas corpus, it is the petitioner's responsibility to attach all lower court records and pertinent materials, in order to fully present the issues of law as required by supreme court rule.[84] If the commitment or restraint is by virtue of a warrant or process, a copy of the warrant or process must be attached.[85] If, however, a copy cannot be obtained due to the prisoner's detention or removal, or due to the refusal of the custodian to produce a copy, the petition must so state.[86] With the exception of the Department of Corrections, anyone having custody of any prisoner who fails to provide a copy of the process or commitment order within 6 hours of the prisoner's demand is subject to forfeit a sum not to exceed $500 to the prisoner.[87]

Unless it appears from the complaint and its accompanying documents that the petitioner cannot be discharged, admitted to bail, or otherwise obtain relief, the court must grant an order of habeas corpus.[88]

While the court may deny a petition for habeas corpus relief if the prisoner no longer is in custody on the grounds that the petition is moot,[89] the court, in its discretion may choose to hear

84. Hughes v Kiley, 67 Ill 2d 261, 10 Ill Dec 247, 367 NE2d 700 (1977).

See Supreme Court Rule 381(a).

85. 735 ILCS 5/10-104(3).

86. 735 ILCS 5/10-104(3).

87. 735 ILCS 5/10-105.

Stone v Chrans, 142 Ill App 3d 235, 96 Ill Dec 551, 491 NE2d 830 (4th Dist 1986).

88. 735 ILCS 5/10-106.

Annotation References: Right of Extraditee to bail after issuance of governor's warrant and pending final disposition of habeas corpus claim, 13 ALR5th 118.

Periodicals: Survey of Illinois Law: Criminal Law and Procedure, 21 S. Ill. U.L.J. 759 (1997).

89. See, e.g., Barney v Prisoner Review Board, 184 Ill 2d 428, 235 Ill Dec 1, 704 NE2d 350 (1998); People v D.T., 287 Ill App 3d 408, 222 Ill Dec 714, 678 NE2d 326 (1st Dist 1997).

an otherwise moot petition if it determines there is a substantial public interest under three criteria:

- whether the question is public in nature;
- whether it is desirable to make an authoritative determination of a question for the guidance of public officials; and
- whether the question is likely to recur.[90]

☛ *Practice Guide:* Where a habeas corpus order is granted by a court or judge, it is to be indorsed with the words "By the habeas corpus law,"[91] certified by the clerk under the seal of the court or by a judge under his or her signature, and directed to the person having custody of the prisoner.[92] The order is to be in substantially this form:

The People of the State of Illinois, to [AB or the Sheriff of X county]: You are hereby commanded to have the body of CD, imprisoned and detained by you, together with the time and cause of such imprisonment and detention by whatsoever name CD is called or charged, before [the name and location of the issuing court or judge] immediately after being served with a certified copy of this order, to be dealt with according to law; and you are to deliver a certified copy of this order with a return thereon of your performance in carrying out this order.[93]

The habeas corpus order may be served by the sheriff, coroner or any person the court which entered the order appoints.[94] The person serving the order must leave a copy with the person to

---

90. Barney v Prisoner Review Board, 184 Ill 2d 428, 235 Ill Dec 1, 704 NE2d 350 (1998); People v D.T., 287 Ill App 3d 408, 222 Ill Dec 714, 678 NE2d 326 (1st Dist 1997).

91. 735 ILCS 5/10-108.

92. 735 ILCS 5/10-107.

93. 735 ILCS 5/10-107.

  Forms: Writ of Habeas Corpus. 13 Am Jur Pl & Pr Forms (Rev), Habeas Corpus, Forms 209–218.

94. 735 ILCS 5/10–110.

§ 31:12   ILLINOIS JURISPRUDENCE: CRIMINAL LAW

whom it is directed, i.e., the defendant, or with any of his or her subordinates at the place where the prisoner is detained. If the person to whom the order is directed cannot be found, or does not have the person imprisoned or restrained in custody, service may be made on any person having the person in custody and the service will have the same effect as if the recipient had been made a defendant in the order.[95]

When the party seeking an order of habeas corpus has been committed on a criminal charge, a subpoena may be issued to summon the witnesses whose names were endorsed on the warrant of commitment to appear at the time the order is returnable.[96]

§ 31:13. —Return

The person having custody of the prisoner makes the return and produces the body of the prisoner simultaneously, unless the prisoner is too sick or infirm to be produced in court without danger.[97] In that case, the judge may either adjourn the proceeding to another time, or proceed with the examination at the prisoner's place of confinement.[98]

The return must state:

- whether the person has custody or control over the prisoner, and if not, whether he or she has had custody or control over the prisoner at any time;
- if the person has custody or control over the prisoner, the authority and true cause of the imprisonment; and
- if the person transferred the prisoner to someone else, the identity of the transferee, the time and reason for the transfer,

---

95. 735 ILCS 5/10–111.

96. 735 ILCS 5/10-109.

97. 735 ILCS 5/10-114.

Text References: Ill Law Man § K8.23.

Forms: Return. 13 Am Jur Pl & Pr Forms (Rev), Habeas Corpus, Forms 233–263.

98. 735 ILCS 5/10-115, 5/10-119.

and the authority for the transfer.[99]

The person making the return must sign it and, except in the case of a sworn public officer making the return in his or her official capacity, must verify the return by oath.[1]

The return, as well as any denials or allegations, may be amended at any time by leave of court.[2]

If the custodian refuses or neglects to obey the order, he or she will be required to forfeit a sum of up to $500 to the prisoner.[3] In addition, the court may issue an order of attachment and cause the sheriff to obtain custody of the prisoner.[4] A similar order may be issued in case of an emergency, such as the imminent departure of the prisoner or person in whose custody he or she is held from the jurisdiction, or the threat of irreparable injury to the prisoner.[5]

§ 31:14. —Reply and hearing

Upon the return of the order and the production of the prisoner, the court must proceed without delay to examine the cause of the imprisonment or restraint.[6] The imprisoned or restrained party may file a reply to the return and, under oath, deny any material facts set forth in the return and allege other material facts.[7] At the examination, the court considers the cause of the imprisonment or restraint, hears evidence produced by any interested persons, and ultimately determines the matter according to law.[8] Should the plaintiff establish that he or she is entitled to relief, but has sought the wrong remedy, the mistake is not

---

99. 735 ILCS 5/10-113.

1. 735 ILCS 5/10-113(4).

2. 735 ILCS 5/10-122.

3. 735 ILCS 5/10-116.

4. 735 ILCS 5/10-117.

5. 735 ILCS 5/10-118.

6. 735 ILCS 5/10-119.

7. 735 ILCS 5/10-120.

8. 735 ILCS 5/10-120.

§ 31:14 ILLINOIS JURISPRUDENCE: CRIMINAL LAW

fatal, and the pleadings may be amended and proper relief granted.[9]

If it appears to the court that there is in fact sufficient legal cause for the commitment of the prisoner, even if the prisoner has been held informally, without authority, or under improperly executed process, the court will correct the commitment or admit the party to bail if the offense is a bailable one.[10]

A judge who fails to bind the prisoner or a material witness against the prisoner by recognizance, or to return a recognizance once taken, is guilty of a Class A misdemeanor in office.[11]

An order of habeas corpus may be entered to bring a prisoner before the court to testify, to be surrendered in discharge of bail, or to stand trial on any criminal charge pending in the court issuing the order.[12] An order may also issue to secure the attendance or testimony of prisoners or witnesses in a criminal proceeding in another state.[13] After the person's testimony has been given, or he or she has been surrendered, has discharged his or her bail, or has been tried, he or she is returned to confinement, and no subsequently imposed imprisonment commences to run until the expiration of the term of any former sentence.[14]

§ 31:15. —Remand and discharge

When a prisoner brought up on habeas corpus is remanded to

---

9. 735 ILCS 5/10-121.

But see Graham v Klincar, 163 Ill App 3d 1091, 115 Ill Dec 195, 517 NE2d 606 (3d Dist 1987).

10. 735 ILCS 5/10-125.

Text References: Ruebner, Illinois Criminal Procedure 2d ed § 7.30.

11. 735 ILCS 5/10-125.

See chs 6 (bail) and 28 (Class A misdemeanors).

12. 735 ILCS 5/10-135.

See ch 7.

13. 735 ILCS 5/10-135.

14. 735 ILCS 5/10-136.

prison, it is the court's duty to deliver an order stating the cause of the remand to the person into whose custody the prisoner is remanded.[15] If the prisoner obtains a second order of habeas corpus, it is the duty of the person into whose custody he or she was remanded to return with the second order the remanding court's statement of cause.[16] If it appears that the prisoner was remanded for a nonbailable offense, the remanding court's order is taken as conclusive, and the prisoner is remanded again without further proceedings.[17] No court may discharge a prisoner on a second order of habeas corpus when the prisoner is clearly and specifically charged with a criminal offense; rather, the court may only admit the prisoner to bail if the offense is bailable, or remand him or her to prison if the offense is not bailable or if the prisoner has failed to provide the required bail.[18]

Once discharged on a habeas corpus order, no person may be reimprisoned or otherwise retained in custody for the same offense unless he or she is afterwards indicted or ordered held by the court to which he or she is bound by recognizance to appear.[19] A person who improperly arrests or restrains a person who has been discharged on a habeas corpus order is required to forfeit $500 for a first offense and $1000 for each subsequent offense.[20] However, in a criminal case, a person is not considered to have been imprisoned, restrained, or kept in custody for the same cause where, after a discharge for a defect of proof or material defect in the commitment the person is rearrested on sufficient proof or proper commitment.[21]

No person discharged on an order of habeas corpus may be removed from the county in which he or she was confined within

---

15. 735 ILCS 5/10-126.
16. 735 ILCS 5/10-126.
17. 735 ILCS 5/10-126.
18. 735 ILCS 5/10-127.
19. 735 ILCS 5/10-128.
20. 735 ILCS 5/10-129.
21. 735 ILCS 5/10-128(1), 5/10-128(3).

§ 31:15   ILLINOIS JURISPRUDENCE: CRIMINAL LAW

15 days next preceding the first day of the calendar month in which his or her trial ought to be held, except to return the prisoner to the county in which the offense is properly cognizable.[22] Nor may a person who is in custody or otherwise committed to prison be removed to another place of custody except by habeas corpus or other legal process expressly allowed by law.[23] A person who violates this provision by removing a prisoner without legal authority or habeas corpus order is required to forfeit to the person held a sum not to exceed $300.[24] Similarly, a person who moves a prisoner in an attempt to avoid the effect of a habeas corpus order is guilty of a Class 4 felony, and only the intent to avoid such an order need be proven, not the fact of the order's entry.[25]

§ 31:16. —Statutory penalties and civil action

Where monetary penalties are imposed for failure to provide a prisoner with a copy of the process or commitment order, for nonperformance of or refusal to obey an order of habeas corpus, or for the improper restraint or removal of a prisoner, the forfeit is sued for, with costs, by the attorney general or the state's attorney.[26] The amount recovered is paid over without deduction to the party for whose benefit the habeas corpus order was entered.[27] The statutory imposition and recovery of monetary penalties do not bar a subsequent civil action for damages.[28]

§ 31:17. —Federal actions

Federal courts have jurisdiction to hear habeas corpus petitions

---

22. 735 ILCS 5/10-130.
23. 735 ILCS 5/10-131.
24. 735 ILCS 5/10-131.
25. 735 ILCS 5/10-132.
    See ch 28 (Class 4 felonies).
26. 735 ILCS 5/10-133.
27. 735 ILCS 5/10-133.
28. 735 ILCS 5/10-134.

ORIGINAL ACTIONS IN THE SUPREME COURT § 31:17

from persons who have exhausted state court procedures and who are in custody in violation of the Constitution or laws or treaties of the United States.[29] The claim for federal habeas relief must be dismissed if it contains any claim that has not been exhausted at the state level,[30] unless there is either no corrective process available at the state level, or circumstances render the process ineffective.[31] A federal habeas petitioner who fails to present his or her claims to the state's highest court will be held to have procedurally defaulted on those claims, if there is no showing of cause for the default and prejudice from the alleged constitutional infirmities.[32]

> ☞ *Illustration:* Thus, if a federal habeas petitioner wishes to claim an evidentiary ruling at a state court trial denied him or her due process of law, the petitioner must say so, not only in federal court but in state court as well.[33]

Habeas corpus is an equitable remedy, and a district court should hear a successive writ if failing to do so would be a

---

29. 28 USC § 2254.

30. Williams v Washington, 59 F3d 673 (CA7 Ill 1995); United States ex rel. Johnson v McGinnis, 734 F2d 1193 (CA7 Ill 1984).

Annotation References: Propriety of federal court's considering state prisoner's petition under 28 USCS sec. 2254 where prisoner has exhausted state remedies as to some, but not all, claims in petition, 43 ALR Fed 631.
Exhaustion of state remedies as condition of issuance by federal court of writ of habeas corpus for release of state prisoner—Supreme Court cases, 54 L Ed 2d 873.

Practice References: Requirement of exhaustion of state remedies. 20 Am Jur Trials 1, Federal Habeas Corpus Practice §§ 19–21.
Habeas Corpus. 22 Am Jur Trials 1, Prisoners' Rights Litigation § 76.
Exhaustion of state remedies. 39 Am Jur Trials 157, Historical Aspects and Procedural Limitations of federal Habeas Corpus § 27.

31. United States ex rel. Johnson v McGinnis, 734 F2d 1193 (CA7 Ill 1984).
28 USC § 2254.

32. Lostutter v Peters, 50 F3d 292 (CA7 Ill 1995).

33. Thompson v Keohane, 516 US 99, 133 L Ed 2d 383, 116 S Ct 457 (1995).

fundamental miscarriage of justice, which is limited to the rare situation in which a constitutional violation has probably resulted in the conviction of one who is actually innocent.[34]

If a federal habeas corpus petitioner challenges a state court conviction on the ground that the state courts committed constitutional error, then the petitioner, in order to be entitled to an evidentiary hearing on a claim that material facts were not adequately developed in the earlier state court proceedings, must show either (a) cause for the petitioner's failure to develop the facts, and actual prejudice resulting from the failure, or (b) that a fundamental miscarriage of justice would result from failure to hold a federal evidentiary hearing.[35]

Where the rights asserted in the federal habeas corpus action are the same as those asserted in the state supreme court, a petition for a writ of mandamus must have been exhausted at the state level.[36]

Claims that state courts have incorrectly decided issues related to Miranda v. Arizona,[37] which requires certain warnings to be given to a suspect interrogated while in police custody in order to safeguard the uncounseled individual's privilege against self-incrimination under the federal constitution's Fifth Amendment, are appropriately considered on federal habeas corpus review.[38]

---

34. Whitlock v Godinez, 51 F3d 59 (CA7 Ill 1995), cert den 516 US 852, 133 L Ed 2d 95, 116 S Ct 150.

35. Keeney v Tamayo-Reyes, 504 US 1, 118 L Ed 2d 318, 112 S Ct 1715 (1992).

36. United States ex rel. Johnson v McGinnis, 734 F2d 1193 (CA7 Ill 1984); Toney v Franzen, 687 F2d 1016 (CA7 Ill 1982).

37. 384 US 436, 16 L Ed 2d 694, 86 S Ct 1602 (1966).

38. Thompson v Keohane, 516 US 99, 133 L Ed 2d 383, 116 S Ct 457 (1995).

CHAPTER 32

PARDON AND PAROLE

by

Lisa K. Fox, J.D.

and

Robert L. Margolis, Esq.

Scope of Chapter:
    The first half of this chapter discusses the procedures that must be followed to obtain executive clemency, while the second half of the chapter covers the establishment of the Prisoner Review Board and its role and the procedures followed for parole and mandatory supervised release. The discussion of parole and mandatory supervised release takes into consideration the promulgation of the Amendatory Act of 1977 and its effect on the statutory provisions governing the subject of parole.

Treated Elsewhere:
    Juveniles, see Chapter 35.
    Punishment, see Chapter 4.
    Sentencing, see Chapters 4, 28.

Research References:
  Text References:
    Bailey & Rothblatt, Handling Narcotic and Drug Cases (1972)
    Ruebner, Illinois Criminal Procedure 2d ed §§ 6.21–6.23
  Annotation References:
    ALR Digest: Criminal Law
    Index and Annotations: Parole, Probation, and Pardon
  Forms:
    18A Am Jur Pl & Pr Forms (Rev), Pardon and Parole

Auto-Cite®: Cases and annotations referred to in this chapter can be further researched through the Auto-Cite® computer-assisted research service. Use Auto-Cite® to check citations for form, parallel references, prior and later history, and annotation references.

I. PARDONS

§ 32:01. Generally

II. PAROLE

§ 32:02. Generally
§ 32:03. Prisoner Review Board
§ 32:04. —Powers and duties
§ 32:05. Eligibility
§ 32:06. Hearings
§ 32:07. Furloughs and authorized absences
§ 32:08. Release to warrant or detainer
§ 32:09. Conditions
§ 32:10. Release and supervision
§ 32:11. Parole services and half-way houses
§ 32:12. Violations and revocation
§ 32:13. —Revocation proceedings
§ 32:14. —Eligibility after revocation
§ 32:15. Discharge from parole
§ 32:16. Interstate parole reciprocal agreements

I. PARDONS

Research References:
  Text References:
    59 Am Jur 2d, Pardon and Parole §§ 1–72
  Annotation References:
    ALR Digest: Criminal Law § 203, 207, 216.4
    Index and Annotations: Parole, Probation, and Pardon
  State Legislation:
    730 ILCS 5/3–3–13
  Forms:
    18A Am Jur Pl & Pr Forms (Rev), Pardon and Parole, Forms 1–4
  Miscellaneous References:
    West's Illinois Digest 2d, Pardon and Parole §§ 21–28

§ 32:01. Generally

In seeking a commutation, pardon or reprieve, a convicted person must send a signed, written petition to the Governor and the Prisoner Review Board ("Board").[1] The petition may be signed either by the convicted person or by someone on that person's behalf.[2] However, an application for executive clemency may not be filed on behalf of a person sentenced to death without that person's written consent, unless he or she is incapable of asserting his or her own claim due to a mental or physical condition.[3] When it is filed, the petition must include a brief history of the case and the reasons allegedly justifying executive clemency.[4]

Upon receipt of the application, the Board will notify the committing court and the State's Attorney for the county in which the person was convicted of that person's application for clemency.[5]

If a request for a hearing on the application is made with due notice, the Board will grant a hearing,[6] allowing representation by counsel.[7] Following the hearing, the Board will make a confidential recommendation to the Governor based on the vote of the majority of the Board.[8] The Board is required to meet to

---

1. 730 ILCS 5/3-3-13(a).

For definitions of "commutation," "pardon" and "reprieve," see Glossary, Vol 5.

> **Periodicals:** For article, "Survey of Illinois Law: Criminal Law and Procedure," see 21 S. Ill. U.L.J. 759 (1997).
>
> **Forms:** Petition, order for pardon. 18A Am Jur Pl & Pr Forms (Rev), Pardon and Parole, Forms 1–4.

2. 730 ILCS 5/3-3-13(a).
3. 730 ILCS 5/3–13(c).
4. 730 ILCS 5/3-3-13(a).
5. 730 ILCS 5/3-3-13(b).
6. 730 ILCS 5/3-3-13(c).
7. 730 ILCS 5/3-3-13(c).

consider applications for clemency at least 4 times a year.[9]

After having received and considered the Board's recommendation on an application, the Governor will make a decision on the matter and notify the Board as to that decision.[10] Nothing in the statute governing executive clemency is to be construed to limit the governor's power under the constitution to grant a repreive, commutation of sentence, or pardon.[11] It is then the Board's responsibility to notify the applicant of the Governor's decision.[12]

Sheriffs may request that the Board send them written notification on a continuing basis of petitioners who had been convicted of a Class X felony in their county who have been granted clemency.[13] In addition, law enforcement agencies serving municipalities with a population of 10,000 or more may request written notification from the Board of clemency being granted to any person who was arrested in that municipality.[14] It is the Board's duty to act on those requests for notification.[15]

II. PAROLE

Research References:
  Text References:
    Ruebner, Illinois Criminal Procedure 2d ed §§ 6.21–6.23
  Annotation References:
    ALR Digest: Criminal Law § 203–223
    Index and Annotations: Parole, Probation, and Pardon

---

8. 730 ILCS 5/3-3-13(c).
9. 730 ILCS 5/3-3-13(c).
10. 730 ILCS 5/3-3-13(d).
11. 730 ILCS 5/3-3-13(e).
12. 730 ILCS 5/3-3-13(d).
13. 730 ILCS 5/3-3-13(d).
14. 730 ILCS 5/3-3-13(d).
15. 730 ILCS 5/3-3-13(d).

Practice References:
> Bailey & Rothblatt, Handling Narcotic and Drug Cases § 406 (1972)
>
> 59 Am Jur 2d, Pardon and Parole §§ 9, 73–113

State Legislation:
> 20 ILCS 2605/55a; 705 ILCS 405/1–1 et seq., 705 ILCS 405/5–33; 725 ILCS 5/102–16, 720 ILCS 120/4.5(d)(4); 730 ILCS 5/3-3-1 through 5/3-14-4, 730 ILCS 5/5-8-6, 730 ILCS 105/10(b), 730 ILCS 105/35

Forms:
> 18A Am Jur Pl & Pr Forms (Rev), Pardon and Parole, Forms 21, 31–36

Miscellaneous References:
> West's Illinois Digest 2d, Pardon and Parole § 41 et seq.

§ 32:02. Generally

"Parole" means the conditional and revocable release of a committed person under the supervision of a paroling authority.[16] Offenders who are sentenced under the Amendatory Act of 1977, effective February 1, 1978, and those prisoners who accepted the fixed release date are not eligible for parole.[17] In fact, with the exception of those prisoners sentenced to natural life, all offenders sentenced after February 1, 1978 and all prisoners opting for a fixed release date must serve their entire sentence, less the time credit they are given for good behavior.[18] Persons subject to natural life terms may not be paroled or released except by executive clemency.[19]

For prisoners sentenced prior to February 1, 1978, release dates were fixed no later than 7 days after the prisoner's first parole hearing following that date, except where the prisoner received an indeterminate sentence of 20 years or more.[20] Prisoners sentenced

---

16. 725 ILCS 5/102–16.
17. 730 ILCS 5/3-3-3(b).
18. 730 ILCS 5/3-3-3(c).
19. 730 ILCS 5/3-3-3(d).
20. 730 ILCS 5/3-3-2.1.

under the law in effect prior to February 2, 1978 and who received indeterminate sentences of less than 20 years were notified of the change in the law effected by the Amendatory Act of 1977.[21] Under the new provisions, those prisoners were given the choice to keep their indeterminate sentence and continue to be eligible for parole or waive the right to parole and accept the release date set for them by the Prisoner Review Board ("Board").[22] The notice sent to the prisoners explained that by accepting the release date they were giving up their eligibility for parole, but that they would be released on a specific date, subject to mandatory supervised release.[23] The notice also explained the criteria used to set the release date indicated and stated that the prisoner had 60 days to opt for the specified release date or stay subject to parole.[24]

In the event a prisoner felt the release date set was not fair, he or she could request reconsideration of the date.[25] The Board had 60 days from the date of receipt of the request to decide whether or not to reconsider the release date previously set.[26] Whether the Board decided to reconsider the date or not, its decision was final.[27]

At a reconsideration hearing, neither the prisoner petitioning nor that prisoner's attorney had the right to be present, but the Board could request the appearance of either or both.[28]

---

21. 730 ILCS 5/3-3-2.1.

   Bailey & Rothblatt, Handling Narcotic and Drug Cases § 406 (1972).

   Annotation References: Validity of statutes prohibiting or restricting parole, probation, or suspension of sentence in cases of violent crimes, 100 ALR3d 431.

22. 730 ILCS 5/3-3-2.1.
23. 730 ILCS 5/3-3-2.1.
24. 730 ILCS 5/3-3-2.1.
25. 730 ILCS 5/3-3-2.1.
26. 730 ILCS 5/3-3-2.1.
27. 730 ILCS 5/3-3-2.1.

§ 32:03. Prisoner Review Board

The legislature set up the Prisoner Review Board ("Board") to be separate from and independent of the Department of Corrections ("Department").[29] In this capacity, the Board is responsible for acting as the reviewing authority for:

- persons sentenced under the law in effect prior to February 1, 1978;
- cases involving the revocation of good conduct credit or suspension or reduction in the rate set for accumulating good conduct credit;
- recommendations for use of executive clemency by the Governor;
- establishing release dates for prisoners sentenced under the law in effect prior to February 1, 1978; and
- setting conditions of parole and release dates for prisoners charged with felonies and for determining whether a violation of the conditions set should result in revocation of parole, mandatory supervised release or imposition of other sanctions.[30]

The 12 member Board is appointed by the Governor and is approved by the Illinois Senate, who may also provide advice as to appointments.[31] The members serve six-year terms, staggered from the date of appointment.[32] The Governor may, however, remove any member for incompetence, neglect of duty, malfeasance or inability to serve.[33]

---

28. 730 ILCS 5/3-3-2.1.
29. 730 ILCS 5/3-3-1(a).
30. 730 ILCS 5/3-3-1(a).
31. 730 ILCS 5/3-3-1(b).
32. 730 ILCS 5/3-3-1(c).
33. 730 ILCS 5/3-3-1(c).

§ 32:04. —Powers and duties

The legislature intended the Prisoner Review Board to have complete discretion in determining whether to grant parole when the denial of parole is not mandated by statute.[34] A panel consisting of three of the twelve members of the Prisoner Review Board ("Board") is responsible for parole issues involving:

- prisoners sentenced under the law in effect prior to February 1, 1978, who are eligible for parole;
- determination of parole conditions, setting the date of discharge, imposition of sanctions for violations of parole and revocation of parole for those prisoners sentenced under the law in effect prior to February 1, 1978; and
- determination of the conditions of mandatory supervised release, the date of discharge from mandatory supervised release, imposition of sanctions for violations and revocation of mandatory supervised release for those prisoners sentenced after February 1, 1978.[35]

A majority of the Board is required to parole and set the conditions of parole for a prisoner sentenced prior to February 1, 1978, for first degree murder or who received an indeterminate sentence of 20 or more years.[36]

While it is within the Department of Correction's ("Department") purview to revoke good conduct credit from a prisoner in their custody, if the time sought to be revoked exceeds 30 days by itself or 30 cumulative days over a 12-month period, the Department must request approval from a three-member panel of the Board for the revocation of good time credit.[37] The panel's duties include hearing the case and deciding whether to grant the revocation, but it may not revoke any more time than the

---

34. Hanrahan v Williams, 174 Ill 2d 268, 220 Ill Dec 339, 673 NE2d 251 (1996), cert den 139 L Ed 2d 20, 118 S Ct 56.

35. 730 ILCS 5/3-3-2(a)(2).

36. 730 ILCS 5/3-3-2(a).

37. 730 ILCS 5/3-3-2(a)(4).

Department requested and it may not participate in the revocation decision if the time sought to be revoked does not exceed 30 days independently or cumulatively or if the revocation is within 60 days of the prisoner's release.[38] At the recommendation of the Department, the Board also may restore good time credit which had been revoked previously.[39]

In addition, a panel of at least three members will hear requests for pardons, reprieves, and commutation of sentences and make recommendations regarding these hearings to the Governor.[40]

Should witness testimony or documentary evidence be necessary for a complete investigation, the Chairperson of the Board has the power to issue subpoenas for witnesses to appear or evidence to be produced.[41] Fees and mileage are paid to the witnesses under the same guidelines used by the circuit courts.[42] If a subpoena is disobeyed, the Board may request that the circuit court issue a petition requiring the attendance of the witness or the production of evidence.[43] The subject of the petition will be mailed or personally served with a copy of the petition and notice of a hearing which is set at least 10, but not more than 15 days from the mailing or the personal service of the notice and copy of the petition.[44] If, on the filing of the petition, the court subsequently orders the subject of the petition to appear or to produce evidence, failure to do so constitutes contempt of court and may be punished accordingly.[45]

§ 32:05. Eligibility

The legislature intended the Prisoner Review Board to have

---

38. 730 ILCS 5/3-3-2(a)(4).

39. 730 ILCS 5/3-3-2(b).

40. 730 ILCS 5/3-3-2(a)(6).

41. 730 ILCS 5/3-3-2(f).

42. 730 ILCS 5/3-3-2(f).

43. 730 ILCS 5/3-3-2(f).

44. 730 ILCS 5/3-3-2(f).

45. 730 ILCS 5/3-3-2(f).

§ 32:05   ILLINOIS JURISPRUDENCE: CRIMINAL LAW

complete discretion in determining whether to grant parole when the denial of parole is not mandated by statute.[46] With the exception of those prisoners who accepted the release date fixed by the Prisoner Review Board ("Board") in 1978, offenders serving a sentence imposed under the law in effect prior to February 1, 1978 are eligible for parole after having served:

- the minimum term of an indeterminate sentence, less credit given for good behavior, or 20 years, minus time for good behavior, whichever is less;
- 20 years of a life sentence, minus time for good behavior; or
- 20 years or $\frac{1}{3}$ of an indeterminate sentence, minus time for good behavior, whichever is less.[47]

Offenders who are sentenced under the Amendatory Act of 1977, effective February 1, 1978, and those prisoners who accepted the fixed release date are not eligible for parole.[48] In fact, with the exception of those prisoners sentenced to natural life, all offenders sentenced after February 1, 1978 and all prisoners opting for a fixed release date must serve their entire sentence, less the time credit they are given for good behavior.[49] After having served the full term of their sentence, these offenders are released under the mandatory supervised release program.[50] Persons subject to natural life terms may not be paroled or released except by executive clemency.[51]

> ☞ *Caution:* Juvenile offenders are dealt with differently than adult offenders with regard to parole if the offender is tried as a juvenile, but if the offender is tried as an adult, the above provisions apply.[52]

---

46. Hanrahan v Williams, 174 Ill 2d 268, 220 Ill Dec 339, 673 NE2d 251 (1996), cert den 139 L Ed 2d 20, 118 S Ct 56.

47. 730 ILCS 5/3-3-3(a).

48. 730 ILCS 5/3-3-3(b).

49. 730 ILCS 5/3-3-3(c).

50. 730 ILCS 5/3-3-3(c).

51. 730 ILCS 5/3-3-3(d).

If the offender is tried as a juvenile and is sentenced to confinement in the State correctional institution, he or she is eligible for parole without regard to how the juvenile was confined or whether a minimum sentence was specified.[53]

§ 32:06. Hearings

Parole decisions are made by the Prisoner Review Board ("Board").[54] The Board has discretion in matters relating to the grant or denial of parole, but has promulgated rules to govern the exercise of that discretion.[55]

Parole is considered by the Board for eligible adult offenders no later than 30 days prior to the date the prisoner becomes eligible for parole, and for eligible juvenile offenders no later than 30 days prior to the expiration of the juvenile's first year of confinement.[56]

Prior to their parole hearing, eligible offenders must prepare a parole plan that complies with the rules of the Board.[57] The offender may obtain assistance in the preparation of the plan from the Department of Corrections ("Department") in the form of information and records.[58] In addition, an offender may be released on furlough or authorized absence to work on the plan.[59]

To aid in the execution of their job, the Board has access to

---

52. 730 ILCS 5/3-3-3(e).

See 705 ILCS 405/5-33; 730 ILCS 5/5-8-6.

53. 730 ILCS 5/3-3-3(e).

See 705 ILCS 405/5-33; 730 ILCS 5/5-8-6.

54. 730 ILCS 5/3-3-4.

55. 730 ILCS 5/3-3-4(h).

Hanrahan v Williams, 174 Ill 2d 268, 220 Ill Dec 339, 673 NE2d 251 (1996), cert den 139 L Ed 2d 20, 118 S Ct 56.

56. 730 ILCS 5/3-3-4(a).

57. 730 ILCS 5/3-3-4(b).

58. 730 ILCS 5/3-3-4(b).

59. 730 ILCS 5/3-3-4(b).

See § 32:07.

§ 32:06   ILLINOIS JURISPRUDENCE: CRIMINAL LAW

prisoners at all reasonable times and to those prisoners' master files.[60] The Department assists the Board by providing them with reports, as necessary, regarding the conduct and character of the subject prisoner.[61]

When the Board is ready to make its evaluation regarding paroling a prisoner, it may consider:

- material submitted by the clerk of the committing court;
- a social evaluation made by the Department, which may include medical, psychological, educational and vocational conditions and history, and the circumstances of the offense;
- reports by the Department and the chief administrative officer of the institution or facility;
- a progress report;
- a medical and psychological report, if deemed necessary by the Board;
- material submitted by the subject offender;
- material submitted by the State's Attorney; and
- material submitted by the victim.[62]

The State's Attorney and victims of violent crimes each will be notified of the parole hearing at least 15 days in advance of the hearing to give them an opportunity to prepare material for submission.[63] The victim may enter a statement either oral, written, on video tape, or by other electronic means in the form and manner required by the Prison Review Board to be considered at the time of the hearing.[64] The State's Attorney, however, may waive written notice.[65]

---

60. 730 ILCS 5/3-3-4(c).

61. 730 ILCS 5/3-3-4(c).

62. 730 ILCS 5/3-3-4(d).

See also 730 ILCS 5/3-8-2, 5/3-10-2.

63. 730 ILCS 5/3-3-4(e), 5/3-3-4(f).

See 725 ILCS 120/4.5(d)(4) (victim notified within seven days of prisoner being granted parole).

The Board shall receive and consider victim impact statements.[66] The inmate or the inmate's attorney must be informed of the existence of a victim impact statement and its contents.[67] The inmate is to be given the opportunity to answer a victim impact statement, either orally or in writing.[68]

Material submitted by the offender, the State's Attorney and/or the victim, may take the form of writing, film, video tape or other electronic recording, as designated by the Board, but in any case, must be both aural and visual.[69] Also, the recording must include an identification of everyone present when it was made, with a statement from the person submitting the recording, the date the recording was made and the name of the subject offender.[70] The Board may retain the recordings for use at later hearings, if at the time of the later hearing, the person who originally submitted the recording submits a written declaration indicating that the recording still represents their position regarding the issues to be considered.[71]

In preparation for the hearing, at least one member of the Board must interview the offender if the subject offender is in the custody of the Department, unless a psychiatric exam has already determined that the offender could not make a meaningful contribution to the interview.[72] A report of the interview is prepared and made available to the Board for consideration.[73]

Hearings may be held as often as is necessary to consider parole

---

64. 730 ILCS 105/10(b).
65. 730 ILCS 5/3-3-4(e).
66. 730 ILCS 105/35.
67. 730 ILCS 105/35.
68. 730 ILCS 105/35.
69. 730 ILCS 5/3-3-4(g).
70. 730 ILCS 5/3-3-4(g).
71. 730 ILCS 5/3-3-4(g).
72. 730 ILCS 5/3-3-5(b).
73. 730 ILCS 5/3-3-5(b).

§ 32:06   ILLINOIS JURISPRUDENCE: CRIMINAL LAW

of eligible prisoners.[74] Generally, the actions of the Board are conducted by a panel comprised of three members and the actions of the majority of the panel are considered to be the actions of the Board.[75] When a juvenile matter is being heard, a majority of the members experienced in juvenile matters must be present.[76]

If a juvenile has not already been released on or before his or her 20th birthday, the juvenile must be paroled at that time for a period to last until the juvenile's 21st birthday.[77] Since parole is mandatory for a 20-year-old juvenile, neither an interview, nor a hearing need be held.[78] However, a hearing and interview need not be held for a person who has served a maximum sentence, minus time for good behavior.[79]

Parole of an adult will not be granted if the Board determines that:

- there is a substantial possibility that the offender will not comply with the conditions of parole;
- release of the offender would undermine the serious treatment of the offense;
- release of the offender would promote disrespect for the law; or
- release of the prisoner would have a substantially negative impact on institutional discipline.[80]

After the hearing, the Board will hand down a decision within a reasonable time.[81] Notice of the decision and its basis will be put

74. 730 ILCS 5/3-3-5(a).

75. 730 ILCS 5/3-3-5(a).

   See § 32.04.

76. 730 ILCS 5/3-3-5(a).

   See § 32.04.

77. 730 ILCS 5/3-3-5(b), 5/3-3-5(d).

78. 730 ILCS 5/3-3-5(b), 5/3-3-5(d).

79. 730 ILCS 5/3-3-5(b), 5/3-3-5(e).

80. 730 ILCS 5/3-3-5(c).

PARDON AND PAROLE § 32:06

in the record and sent to the subject offender.[82] If parole is granted, the decision will note the date set for parole, and if it is not granted, when the rehearing will be held.[83] For persons originally sentenced or up for parole between January 1, 1973 and September 30, 1977 for whom parole is denied, the Board may schedule a rehearing for three years from the date of denial if there is no reasonable expectation that parole would be granted in the interim.[84]

> ☛ *Practice Guide:* The amendment to the statute governing parole hearings which increasee to three years the maximum time between hearings is not an ex post facto law as it has no constitutionally significant effect on any prisoner's actual term of confinement; the amended provision does not have the prohibited effect of increasing punishment and it is tailored to the determination of the likelihood that a prisoner would be released sooner than an extended parole hearing date[85]

If parole is granted, but the offender is not released in response to the release order within 90 days of its effective date, the matter returns to the Board for review.[86]

A registry of the Board's decisions to grant parole is kept and made available to the public for inspection and copying during business hours. The registry lists each decision in favor of parole, with:

- the name and case number of the offender;
- the highest charge for which the prisoner was sentenced;

---

81. 730 ILCS 5/3-3-5(f).

82. 730 ILCS 5/3-3-5(f).

83. 730 ILCS 5/3-3-5(f).

84. 730 ILCS 5/3-3-5(f).

85. Fletcher v Williams, 179 Ill 2d 225, 227 Ill Dec 942, 688 NE2d 635 (1997), cert den 140 L Ed 2d 654, 118 S Ct 1396.

86. 730 ILCS 5/3-3-5(f).

- the date the prisoner was sentenced;
- the date parole was granted;
- the Board's reasons for granting parole; and
- the vote of the Board.[87]

A Board decision concerning parole or parole revocation shall be final at the time the decision is delivered to the inmate, subject to any rehearing granted under Board rules.[88] A common law writ of certiorari may not be issued to review the merits of the Prisoner Review Board's decision to deny a petitioner's parole.[89]

The Board may restrict the number of individuals allowed to attend parole hearings in accordance with physical limitations, security requirements of the hearing facilities or those giving repetitive or cumulative testimony.[90] The Board may deny admission or continued attendance at parole hearings to individuals who threaten or present danger to the security of the building where the hearing is being held; threaten or present a danger to other attendees or participants; or disrupt the hearing.[91] Also, the Board may close parole hearings to consider the oral testimony and any other relevant information received from applicants, parolees, victims, or others; or provide applicants and parolees the opportunity to challenge information other than that which, if the person's identity were to be exposed, would possibly subject them to bodily harm or death, which they believe detrimental to their parole determination hearing.[92]

§ 32:07. Furloughs and authorized absences

Furloughs and authorized absences are the means by which the

---

87. 730 ILCS 5/3-3-5(f).

88. 730 ILCS 105/20.

89. Hanrahan v Williams, 174 Ill 2d 268, 220 Ill Dec 339, 673 NE2d 251 (1996) cert den 139 L Ed 2d 20, 118 S Ct 56.

90. 730 ILCS 105/15(a).

91. 730 ILCS 105/15(b).

92. 730 ILCS 105/15(c).

PARDON AND PAROLE § 32:07

Department of Corrections ("Department") may extend the limits of a person's confinement.[93] An authorized absence may be approved by the Department for any reason and is used for juvenile offenders to allow the offender to leave his or her place of confinement.[94] The length of the absence also is determined by the Department, but the decision as to whether the juvenile is to be accompanied during the absence is made by the chief administrative officer of the institution or facility to which the juvenile is confined.[95]

As with authorized absences for juveniles, furloughs may be granted to adults for the purpose of extending the limit of the adult's confinement.[96] Also like authorized absences for juveniles, whether an adult offender is to be accompanied on furlough is determined by the chief administrative officer of the institution or facility to which the adult is confined.[97] If the decision is made that the offender need not be accompanied on furlough, in lieu of supervision, the Department must give prior written notice of the furlough to the State's Attorney in the county in which the offender was originally sentenced and to the State's Attorney and Sheriff of the county in which the furlough is to occur.[98] If, however, the reason for the furlough is an emergency, such that prior written notice is not feasible under the circumstances, oral notice will suffice, but must be given.[99]

The reason for furlough determines the amount of time to be granted.[1] For example, furloughs with a maximum duration of 14 days may be granted for the following reasons:

---

[93]. 730 ILCS 5/3-9-4 (juveniles), 730 ILCS 5/3-11-1 (adult offenders).

[94]. 730 ILCS 5/3-9-4.

[95]. 730 ILCS 5/3-9-4.

[96]. 730 ILCS 5/3-11-1(a).

[97]. 730 ILCS 5/3-11-1(a).

[98]. 730 ILCS 5/3-11-1(c).

[99]. 730 ILCS 5/3-11-1(c).

[1]. 730 ILCS 5/3-11-1(a).

- to visit a relative, including a spouse, child, parent, grandparent or sibling who is seriously ill or to attend the funeral of one of these relatives;
- to obtain medical, psychiatric, or psychological services where the services of the facility of confinement are not adequate;
- to make contacts for employment;
- to find a place to live after release;
- to visit the offender's family; or
- to make an appearance on television or radio or at gatherings meeting for the purpose of studying the prevention of crime.[2]

Furloughs granted under the Civil Adminstrative Code of Illinois may be for any period of time.[3]

§ 32:08. Release to warrant or detainer

If there is an outstanding warrant or detainer against a person, prior to that person becoming eligible for parole or release, the Prisoner Review Board ("Board") will contact the issuing authority and ascertain whether the authority intends to execute or withdraw the warrant or detainer.[4] If the authority indicates its intention to execute the process, the Board will inform the authority regarding:

- the offender's sentence;
- when the offender will be eligible for parole or release;
- decisions made by the Board relating to the offender;
- the nature of the offender's adjustment during confinement; and
- the date of the offender's impending release or parole, a reasonable period of time prior to the release or parole.[5]

---

2. 730 ILCS 5/3-11-1(a).
3. 730 ILCS 5/3-11-1(b).
   See 20 ILCS 2605/55a.
4. 730 ILCS 5/3-3-6(a).

An offender may be released to another authority holding a warrant or detainer against him or her.[6] It is within the Board's discretion, however, to stipulate as a condition of parole or release, that if the charges which are the basis for the warrant or detainer are dismissed or satisfied, the offender will be returned to the authority which originally held him or her, pending the satisfaction of the remainder of the parole term or part of it.[7] Further, should an offender receive probation or be released in another jurisdiction prior to the fulfillment of his or her term in Illinois, the Board will decide in which jurisdiction the offender may serve the remainder of his or her term.[8]

§ 32:09. Conditions

The Prisoner Review Board ("Board") has the discretion to set the conditions of parole and mandatory supervised release.[9] Some of the conditions set are mandatory for each prisoner and some are tailored to the needs of the individual in terms of what the Board deems necessary to ensure the offender will abide by the law once released or paroled.[10] The conditions that must be met by every offender on parole or mandatory supervised release are:

- the offender must not violate the statutes of any jurisdiction while on parole or release; and

---

5. 730 ILCS 5/3-3-6(b).
6. 730 ILCS 5/3-3-6(c).
7. 730 ILCS 5/3-3-6(c).
8. 730 ILCS 5/3-3-6(d).
9. 730 ILCS 5/3-3-7(a).

Annotation References: The propriety of conditioning parole on defendant's not entering specified geographical area. 54 ALR5th 743.
Propriety of requirement, as condition of probation, that defendant refrain from use of intoxicants, 19 ALR4th 1251.
Validity of requirement that, as condition of probation, defendant submit to warrantless searches, 79 ALR3d 1083.

Forms: Certificate of release. 18A Am Jur Pl & Pr Forms (Rev), Pardon and Parole, Form 21.

10. 730 ILCS 5/3-3-7.

- the offender must not possess a firearm or other dangerous weapon.[11]

In addition, the Board may require that the offender:

- get a job or go to school;
- obtain medical or psychiatric treatment for drug or alcohol addiction;
- live in or attend a facility established for persons on parole or probation;
- support dependents;
- report to a Department of Corrections ("Department") agent;
- allow a Department agent to visit the offender at home or elsewhere in the discharge of his or her duties; and/or
- comply with a domestic violence protection order.[12]

Further, if the offender is a juvenile, the Board may require as a condition that the juvenile offender:

- live with his or her parents or in a foster home;
- go to school;
- attend a nonresidential program; and/or
- contribute to his or her own support.[13]

These conditions may be modified or enlarged after a hearing on the matter.[14]

The offender is to be given notice in writing of the conditions set prior to release.[15] Before being released, the offender must sign the conditions, a copy of which is given to the offender, along with a copy of a protective order, where one applies.[16] Also,

---

11. 730 ILCS 5/3-3-7(a).
12. 730 ILCS 5/3-3-7(b).
13. 730 ILCS 5/3-3-7(b).
14. 730 ILCS 5/3-3-7(d).
15. 730 ILCS 5/3-3-7(c).

copies of each document are transmitted to the officer in charge of the offender's supervision.[17]

The Department provides services to assist inmates and they are notified of these services and their option to avail themselves voluntarily of them.[18]

§ 32:10. Release and supervision

When an inmate is released on parole, mandatory release, final discharge or pardon, the Department of Corrections ("Department") will:

- return the offender's property which was being held pending release;
- provide clothing;
- arrange transportation to a designated place; and
- provide information relating to programs and services to assist the offender in ascertaining whether or not that person has been exposed to human immunodeficiency virus (HIV) or Acquired Immunodeficiency Syndrome (AIDS).[19]

The Department may also provide the offender with money for travel and expenses.[20] The amount and manner of payment is determined by the Department.[21] In addition, a plan is in place to expedite the processing of applications for public aid benefits for qualified individuals scheduled for release.[22]

Written notification of release of any person convicted of a

---

16. 730 ILCS 5/3-3-7(c).

Wilson v Kelkhoff, 86 F3d 1438, 35 FR Serv 3d 1062 (CA7 Ill 1996).

17. 730 ILCS 5/3-3-7(c).
18. 730 ILCS 5/3-3-7(e).
19. 730 ILCS 5/3-14-1.

Text References: Ruebner, Illinois Criminal Procedure 2d ed § 6.22.

20. 730 ILCS 5/3-14-1(a).
21. 730 ILCS 5/3-14-1(a).
22. 730 ILCS 5/3-14-1(b).

felony will be sent by the Department to the State's Attorney and the sheriff of the county in which the offender was convicted and the State's Attorney and sheriff of the county in which the offender is to be paroled or released.[23] The Department must provide written noticiation to the proper law enforcement agency for any municipality of any release of any convicted felon if his or her felony was committed in that municipality, he or she is to be paroled or released there, or the offender resided there at the time of his or her conviction.[24]

The Department retains custody over all offenders who are paroled, subject to mandatory supervised release or release subject to supervision.[25] During the period of supervision, the Department supervises the offender according to the conditions set by the Board.[26] The conditions imposed may include referral to a substance abuse program, where necessary, or an electronic monitoring device.[27]

Prior to the time of release, the Department will assist the offender in preparing a parole plan.[28] The offender is required to sign the conditions, a copy of which is then given to the offender and his or her supervising officer.[29] During the period of supervision, the supervising officer will assist and advise the offender in adjusting to life outside the facility or institution and report to the Board on the offender's progress in assimilating.[30] In fact, the officer is responsible for keeping records and entering those records in the offender's file for the Board's use.[31] The

23. 730 ILCS 5/3-14-1(c).
24. 730 ILCS 5/3-14-1(c).
25. 730 ILCS 5/3-14-2(a).
26. 730 ILCS 5/3-14-2(a).
27. 730 ILCS 5/3-14-2(a).
28. 730 ILCS 5/3-14-2(b).
29. 730 ILCS 5/3-14-2(c).
30. 730 ILCS 5/3-14-2(d).

See § 32:11.

officers receive specialized training on the subjects of female parolees or releasees and the reunification of families.[32]

If a parolee or releasee violates any of the agreed to conditions, the officer has full power to arrest or request a warrant be issued for the violator's arrest.[33] Should a warrant be needed, the officer may detain the parolee or releasee while one is being obtained, during which time the offender may be taken to any secure place pending transfer to the Department.[34] If the parolee or releasee commits a felony using a firearm or knife, the officer must request the department to issue a warrant. The department must issue the warrant and the officer or the department must file a violation report with notice of charges with the Prisoner Review Board.[35]

§ 32:11. Parole services and half-way houses

The Department of Corrections ("Department") is charged with providing services to parolees and releasees to assist them in assimilating smoothly into the community.[36] Some of the services the Department provides are:

- help in finding a place to live;
- assistance in finding counseling and treatment, as necessary;
- financial counseling;
- vocational and educational guidance and placement; and
- referrals for other services.[37]

If the parolee or releasee is unable to pay for needed services, the Department may provide the means to obtain the services to

---

31. 730 ILCS 5/3-14-2(f).

32. 730 ILCS 5/3-14-2(e).

See § 32:11.

33. 730 ILCS 5/3-14-2(c).

34. 730 ILCS 5/3-14-2(c).

35. 730 ILCS 5/4-14-2(c).

36. 730 ILCS 5/3-14-3.

37. 730 ILCS 5/3-14-3.

§ 32:11   ILLINOIS JURISPRUDENCE: CRIMINAL LAW

the extent the parolee or releasee is unable to pay.[38]

Another service the Department may provide is half-way house placement.[39] Such facilities are established and maintained by the Department separately from security institutions, although the Director of the Department has the discretion to designate a work or day release facility be used as a half-way house.[40]

Written notification must be provided by the Department at least 15 days prior to the placement of a parolee or releasee just released or paroled to the State's Attorney and the sheriff of the county in which the half-way house is located as well as the proper law enforcement agency in the municipality in which the half-way house is located.[41] In the case of an emergency, however, oral notice is sufficient if provided within 24 hours and followed by written notice within 5 days.[42] The notification must include information regarding the offender such as:

- the name of the parolee or releasee;
- age;
- physical description;
- photograph; and
- the crime for which the offender was sentenced.[43]

Notification will be provided in the same manner for persons on parole or mandatory supervised release who have been previously released, but are not currently residing in a half-way house.[44]

---

38. 730 ILCS 5/3-14-3.
39. 730 ILCS 5/3-14-4(a).
40. 730 ILCS 5/3-14-4(a).
41. 730 ILCS 5/3-14-4(b).
42. 730 ILCS 5/3-14-4(b).
43. 730 ILCS 5/3-14-4(b).
44. 730 ILCS 5/3-14-4(c).

§ 32:12. Violations and revocation

In the event an offender violates a condition of parole or mandatory supervised release prior to the expiration of his or her term, the Prisoner Review Board ("Board") has the option to:

- continue the term without alteration;
- parole or release the offender to a half-way house; or
- revoke the offender's parole or supervised release and reconfine the offender for a time calculated according to the terms listed in the statute.[45]

The Board has the discretion to decide whether to revoke parole or mandatory supervised release for the remainder of the term or for any other period deemed necessary to adjudicate issues arising prior to the expiration of the term.[46] If parole or mandatory supervised release is revoked, the term is tolled by the issuance of an arrest warrant until such time as the issues involving the alleged violations are resolved.[47] However, if the term is not revoked, the period between the issuance of the arrest warrant and the determination of the charge in the parolee's or releasee's favor is credited to the term.[48]

In the event parole or mandatory supervised release is to be revoked, written notice of the condition violated which constitutes

---

45. 730 ILCS 5/3-3-9(a).

Annotation References: Who may institute proceedings to revoke probation, 21 ALR5th 275.
Propriety of increased sentence following revocation of probation, 23 ALR4th 883.

Periodicals: Bamonte, Peters, The parole revocation process in Illinois. 24 Loy U Chi LJ 211 (1993).

46. 730 ILCS 5/3-3-9(b).

Text References: Ruebner, Illinois Criminal Procedure 2d ed § 6.21–6.23.

47. 730 ILCS 5/3-3-9(b).

48. 730 ILCS 5/3-3-9(b).

Annotation References: Acquittal in criminal proceeding as precluding revocation of parole on same charge, 76 ALR3d 578.

§ 32:12   ILLINOIS JURISPRUDENCE: CRIMINAL LAW

the basis for the revocation must be given to the offender.[49] Revocation of parole does not violate the double jeopardy clause of the constitution because parole and probation are part of the original sentence.[50]

§ 32:13. —Revocation proceedings

Anyone who allegedly violates a parole or mandatory supervised release condition, is entitled to a preliminary hearing to ascertain whether there is sufficient cause to hold that person until a revocation hearing, with two exceptions.[51] A person is not entitled to a preliminary hearing where the revocation is based on new charges and a court finds probable cause on the new charges, or where the revocation is based on a new conviction, a certified copy of which is available.[52] In the event a hearing is held, however, it is presided over by a hearing officer designated by the Prisoner Review Board.[53] The revocation hearing itself, on the other hand, is presided over by one or more members of the Board.[54]

At the hearing, the offender may appear, answer the charge levied against him or her and present witnesses.[55] A record will be made of the hearing.[56] If the decision of the panel is not in the

49. 730 ILCS 5/3-3-9(d).

50. People v Baptist, 284 Ill App 3d 382, 672 NE2d 398, 219 Ill Dec 890 (4th Dist 1996).

51. 730 ILCS 5/3-3-9(c).

> **Periodicals:** Bamonte, Peters, The parole revocation process in Illinois. 24 Loy U Chi LJ 211 (1993).
>
> **Forms:** Revocation of parole. 18A Am Jur Pl & Pr Forms (Rev), Pardon and Parole, Forms 31–36.

52. 730 ILCS 5/3-3-9(c).

53. 730 ILCS 5/3-3-9(c).

54. 730 ILCS 5/3-3-9(e).

55. 730 ILCS 5/3-3-9(e).

> **Annotation References:** Admissibility of hearsay evidence in probation revocation hearings, 11 ALR4th 999.

offender's favor, the panel may choose to revoke parole or supervised mandatory release or continue the term without alteration.[57]

☛ *Practice Guide:* Revocation of parole or mandatory supervised release may not used for failure to make payments as required by the conditions agreed to for parole or mandatory supervised release, unless the Board determines that the failure to pay is the result of a wilfull refusal.[58]

§ 32:14. —Eligibility after revocation

If a person has his or her parole or mandatory supervised release revoked, that person may be rereleased or reparoled by the Board at any time to the full parole or mandatory supervised release term.[59] However, the time for which the parolee or releasee may remain subject to the Board must not exceed the maximum sentence under the law in effect prior to February 2, 1978 for those sentenced prior to that date or the maximum according to the law in effect after that date for those sentenced after February 2, 1978.[60]

While the Board may set an earlier release date,[61] if it does not, those offenders which were sentenced prior to January 1, 1973 must be released to supervision six months prior to the expiration of the maximum sentence under the law, less time credited for good behavior.[62] For those offenders who violated parole, with

56. 730 ILCS 5/3-3-9(e).

57. 730 ILCS 5/3-3-9(f).

58. 730 ILCS 5/3-3-9(g).

59. 730 ILCS 5/3-3-10(a).

   See also 730 ILCS 5/3-3-8.

   Text References: Ruebner, Illinois Criminal Procedure 2d ed §§ 6.21–6.23.

   Periodicals: For article, "Survey of Illinois Law: Criminal Law and Procedure," see 21 S. Ill. U.L.J. 759 (1997).

60. 730 ILCS 5/3-3-10(a).

61. See § 32:10.

§ 32:14   ILLINOIS JURISPRUDENCE: CRIMINAL LAW

the exception of persons sentenced to mandatory supervised release, release to supervision must be six months prior to the expiration of the reconfinement term as set at the adjudication of the parole violation, less good time credit.[63] However, if the offender violated parole within six months of the release date, release as described is not mandatory.[64]

> ☞ *Practice Guide:* Prisoners, except those convicted of first degree murder, serving life terms, or sentenced to death, are entitled to good time credit based on formulas that vary depending on the severity of the crime committed.[65] Most prisoners receive one day of good time credit for each day served.[66] Sanctions reducing a prisoner's good time credit constitute part of the defendant's punishment for his or her original convictin and do not amount to double jeopardy.[67]

> ☞ *Caution:* Offenders released pursuant to these provisions are subject to the rules governing parole or release to warrant or detainer,[68] conditions of parole and mandatory supervised release,[69] violations of those conditions,[70] release from an institution,[71] supervision of parole and mandatory supervised

62. 730 ILCS 5/3-3-10(b)(1), 5/3-6-3.

63. 730 ILCS 5/3-3-10(b)(2), 5/3-3-9, 5/3-6-3.

64. 730 ILCS 5/3-3-10(b)(3).

65. 730 ILCS 5/3-6-3.

66. 730 ILCS 5/3-6-3(a)(2.1).

67. People v Baptist, 284 Ill App 3d 382, 219 Ill Swc 890, 672 NE2d 398 (4th Dist 1996).

68. 730 ILCS 5/3-3-6.

See § 32:08.

69. 730 ILCS 5/3-3-7.

See § 32:09.

70. 730 ILCS 5/3-3-9.

See §§ 32:12, 32:13.

release,[72] parole services[73] and half-way houses.[74]

§ 32:15. Discharge from parole

The length of parole for inmates sentenced prior to February 1, 1978 and the length of mandatory supervised release for those inmates sentenced on or after that date is set out in the statute and will be followed unless the Board enters an order releasing or discharging the inmate from his or her commitment.[75] The Board may enter such an order when it determines that the inmate may be at liberty without a concern that he or she will commit another offense.[76] Juveniles, likewise, may be released or discharged from

---

71. 730 ILCS 5/3-14-1.

See § 32:10.

72. 730 ILCS 5/3-14-2.

See § 32:10.

Text References: Ruebner, Illinois Criminal Procedure 2d ed § 6.22.

73. 730 ILCS 5/3-14-3.

See § 32:11.

74. 730 ILCS 5/3-14-4.

See § 32:11.

75. 730 ILCS 5/3-3-8(a).

See 730 ILCS 5/5-8-1.

Periodicals: For article, "1997 Illinois Supreme Court Criminal Survey: Fitness Hearings, Proportionate Punishment, and More," see 86 Ill. B.J. 202 (1998).

For comment, "The Sixth Amendment: Protecting Defendants' Rights at the Expense of Child Victims," see 30 J. Marshall L. Rev. 767 (1997).

For note, "The Void Left in Illinois Homicide Law after People v. Lopez: The Elimination of Attempted Second Degree Murder," see 46 De Paul L. Rev. 227 (1997).

For comment, "The Buck Stops Here: Illinois Criminalizes Support for International Terrorism," see 30 J. Marshall L. Rev. 871 (1997).

For article, "Lesser-Included Offenses in Illinois: A Look at Recent Developments," see 85 Ill. B.J. 480 (1997).

For article, "Survey of Illinois Law: Criminal Law and Procedure," see 21 S. Ill. U.L.J. 759 (1997).

76. 730 ILCS 5/3-3-8(b).

their commitment prior to its expiration. In any event, a juvenile's parole period ends when the juvenile reaches the age of 21.[77]

An order of discharge becomes effective upon its entry.[78] At that time, the Board will notify the clerk of the committing court of the inmate's discharge or release.[79] When the clerk receives the notification, it is entered in the record that the inmate's commitment has been satisfied pursuant to the order.[80]

Once discharged or released, the rights of the offender are restored to the extent set out in the statute.[81] In particular, the right to hold a constitutional office is restored at the completion of the prisoner's sentence, the right to vote is restored upon release from imprisonment, and all license rights and privileges (excluding driver's license) which had been revoked are restored unless the State determines restoration is not in the public interest.[82] Although a convicted felon does regain some civil rights upon release from prison, the right to possess a firearm is not one of them.[83]

§ 32:16. Interstate parole reciprocal agreements

Illinois is among the states — any of the 50 United States, in addition to Puerto Rico, the Virgin Islands and the District of Columbia — that have entered into an agreement with the consent of the United State's Congress for the purpose of facilitating cooperation between the states with regards to crime prevention.[84] Pursuant to this compact, the participating states

---

77. 730 ILCS 5/3-3-8(a).

See 705 ILCS 405/1-1 et seq.

78. 730 ILCS 5/3-3-8(c).

79. 730 ILCS 5/3-3-8(c).

80. 730 ILCS 5/3-3-8(c).

81. 730 ILCS 5/3-3-8(a).

See 705 ILCS 405/5-33; 730 ILCS 5/5-5-5.

82. 730 ILCS 5/5-5(a)–(d).

83. Melvin v United States, 78 F3d 327 (CA7 Ill 1996), cert den 519 US 963, 136 L Ed 2d 301, 117 S Ct 384.

have agreed that if a convicted offender is placed on probation or released on parole by one state ("sending state") that person may carry out his or her assigned term in another state ("receiving state") if:

- that person actually resides in the receiving state or has family residing there and can find work in the receiving state; or
- the receiving state consents to the presence of the offender.[85]

Prior to giving consent, the receiving state is entitled to investigate the home and potential job of the offender.[86]

> *Practice Guide:* For the purposes of this provision, a person is a resident of the receiving state if he or she was an actual resident of that state for at least one continuous year prior to arriving in the sending state and was not in the sending state for more than six continuous months just prior to the commission of the offense for which the offender is charged.[87]

Once a receiving state grants consent to the presence of the offender, it assumes the responsibility for the supervision and visitation of that probationer or parolee.[88] The standards the supervision or visitation must meet are those which the receiving state would abide by for its own probationers or parolees.[89]

Under the compact, the states also have agreed that officers of the sending state may enter the receiving state for the purpose of

---

84. 730 ILCS 5/3-3-11, 5/3-3-11.1.

Annotation References: Determination that state failed to prove charges relied upon for revocation of probation as barring subsequent criminal action based on same underlying charges. 2 ALR5th 262.

85. 730 ILCS 5/3-3-11(a).

86. 730 ILCS 5/3-3-11(a).

87. 730 ILCS 5/3-3-11(a).

88. 730 ILCS 5/3-3-11(2).

89. 730 ILCS 5/3-3-11(2).

§ 32:16   ILLINOIS JURISPRUDENCE: CRIMINAL LAW

apprehending any person on probation or parole.[90] In the exercise of their duty, these officers do not need to follow any formal guidelines, however they need to be able to establish their authority and the identity of the person they seek.[91] In addition, the agreement expressly waives all legal requirements for the extradition of fugitives from justice.[92]

The decision to retake an offender made by the sending state is not subject to review by the receiving state, unless a criminal charge is pending against that person or that person is suspected of criminal activity, but has not yet been charged.[93] If, indeed, the offender has a charge pending against him or her or is suspected of committing a criminal offense, then the sending state must obtain consent from the receiving state prior to retaking the offender, unless the offender has been discharged from prosecution or imprisonment for that offense.[94] The compact provides that officers of the sending state may transport offenders through states which are parties to the compact without difficulty or interference.[95]

If the authorities in the receiving state determine that a parolee or probationer under their supervision has violated a condition of parole or probation justifying retaking or reincarceration of that offender, the sending state must be notified.[96] Prior to the notification, however, the receiving state will hold a hearing to assess probable cause to believe that a violation has actually occurred, except where the offender waives the hearing.[97] As soon as possible after the resolution of the hearing, the receiving state

90. 730 ILCS 5/3-3-11(3).
91. 730 ILCS 5/3-3-11(3).
92. 730 ILCS 5/3-3-11(3).
93. 730 ILCS 5/3-3-11(3).
94. 730 ILCS 5/3-3-11(3).
95. 730 ILCS 5/3-3-11(4).
96. 730 ILCS 5/3-3-11.4.
97. 730 ILCS 5/3-3-11.4.

will report to the sending state, furnish a copy of the hearing record, and make recommendations as to the action to take along with the notification.[98]

No person convicted of a sexual offense or attempt to commit a sexual offense and sentenced for that offense, given a disposition of court supervision, or otherwise adjudged to be a sexually dangerous person, may be accepted for supervised or conditioned residency in Illinois unless the following conditions are met:

- he or she complies with the registration requirements imposed by the Sex Offender Registration Act;[99]
- he or she submits required blood specimens for genetic marker grouping; and
- he or she signs a form acknowledging an agreement to abide by the conditions set forth in the document and above..[1]

A parolee or probationer who is a nonresident of Illinois or who has family or a job outside of Illinois and who is, consequently, allowed to serve his or her term outside of this state, will be assigned to a person, firm or company in the receiving state by the Illinois Prisoner Review Board.[2] Despite being out of state, the offender is still responsible for making regular monthly written reports to the Department of Corrections, obeying the laws of the receiving state and abiding by the conditions of his or her parole or probation until such time as that person is discharged.[3]

---

98. 730 ILCS 5/3-3-11.4.
99. 730 ILCS 150/1 et seq.
1. 730 ILCS 5/3-3-11.5.
2. 730 ILCS 5/3-3-12.
3. 730 ILCS 5/3-3-12.

CHAPTER 33

EXPUNGEMENT

by

Diane C. Busch, J.D.

and

Robert L. Margolis, Esq.

Scope of Chapter:

This chapter discusses the statutory provisions governing the expungement of arrest records and aliases. The procedural guidelines for obtaining an order of expungement are also set forth briefly. The chapter does not discuss any limitations or procedures which may govern the expungement of records with regard to particular offenses.

Treated Elsewhere:

Arrest, see Chapter 5.

Charging instruments, see Chapter 9.

Research References:

Text References:

Decker, Illinois Criminal Law 2d ed §§ 2.12, 9.01, 9.29, 11.02–11.03, 11.34, 16.02

Ruebner, Illinois Criminal Procedure 2d ed §§ 6.21–6.23

Annotation References:

ALR Digest: Criminal Law § 224

Index and Annotations: Expungement; Parole, Probation, and Pardon

Practice References:

21A Am Jur 2d, Criminal Law § 1021

State Legislation:

20 ILCS 2630/5; 625 ILCS 5/3–707, 5/3–708, 5/3–710, 5/5–401.3, 5/11–501, 5/11–503; 720 ILCS 5/12–4.3, 5/12–15, 5/16A–3, 301/

40–10, 550/10, 570/410; 730 ILCS 5/5–6–3.1

Forms:

8 Am Jur Pl & Pr Forms (Rev), Criminal Procedure, Forms 441–446; 18A Am Jur Pl & Pr Forms (Rev), Pardon and Parole, Form 13

Miscellaneous References:

West's Illinois Digest 2d, Criminal Law § 1226

Auto-Cite®: Cases and annotations referred to in this chapter can be further researched through the Auto-Cite® computer-assisted research service. Use Auto-Cite® to check citations for form, parallel references, prior and later history, and annotation references.

§ 33:01. Arrest records
§ 33:02. Alias
§ 33:03. Procedure for expungement

§ 33:01. Arrest records

An adult, or a minor prosecuted as an adult, charged with a felony, misdemeanor, or municipal ordinance violation, may have his or her arrest record expunged if:

- he or she has never been previously convicted of any criminal offense or municipal ordinance violation; and

- he or she is acquitted or released without being convicted of the crime charged.[1]

Expungement may be ordered by: (1) the chief judge of the circuit in which the charge was brought; (2) any judge of that circuit designated by the chief judge; or (3) in counties with populations less than 3,000,000, the judge who presided at the defendant's trial.[2] The defendant must file a verified petition and

1. 20 ILCS 2630/5(a).

2. 20 ILCS 2630/5(a).

Annotation References: Judicial expunction of criminal record of convicted adult, 11 ALR4th 956.

Periodicals: For article, "Survey of Illinois Law: Criminal Law and Procedure," see 21 S. Ill. U.L.J. 759 (1997).

EXPUNGEMENT § 33:01

may be required to pay a fee equivalent to the cost processing any order to expunge or seal the records.[3] The court may order that the record of arrest be expunged from the official records of the arresting authority and the Department of State Police and that the records of the clerk of the circuit court be sealed until further order of the court upon good cause shown.[4]

The court's determination as to whether records should be expunged is discretionary.[5] The court must weigh the State's interest in maintaining the records with the defendant's interest in having them expunged, and consideration of the public safety is appropriate.[6]

If the arrest results in a disposition of supervision, the record of that arrest may not be expunged until two years after discharge and dismissal of supervision.[7] However, arrest records may not be expunged until five years after the termination of probation or supervision if the defendant has been sentenced under the statutes governing any of the following offenses or sentencing schemes:[8]

---

3. 20 ILCS 2630/5(a).

   Forms: Expungement of record. 8 Am Jur Pl & Pr Forms (Rev), Criminal Procedure, Forms 441–446.
   Petition for expungement of criminal record. 18A Am Jur Pl & Pr Forms (Rev), Pardon and Parole, Form 13.

4. 20 ILCS 2630/5(a).

   Annotation References: Right of exonerated arrestee to have fingerprints, photographs, or other criminal identification or arrest records expunged or restricted, 46 ALR3d 900.

5. People v Wells, 294 Ill App 3d 405, 228 Ill Dec 886, 690 NE2d 645 (1st Dist 1998).

6. People v Wells, 294 Ill App 3d 405, 228 Ill Dec 886, 690 NE2d 645 (1st Dist 1998).

7. 20 ILCS 2630/5(a).

   See also 730 ILCS 5/5-6-3.1(f).

   Text References: Ruebner, Illinois Criminal Procedure 2d ed § 6.21–6.22.

8. 20 ILCS 2630/5(a).

   Text References: Ruebner, Illinois Criminal Procedure 2d ed § 6.21–6.23.

§ 33:01   ILLINOIS JURISPRUDENCE: CRIMINAL LAW

- supervision for operation of an uninsured vehicle;[9]
- supervision for operation of a vehicle when registration has been suspended for noninsurance;[10]
- supervision for the display of a false insurance card;[11]
- supervision for failure of a scrap processor to keep required records;[12]
- supervision for driving under the influence of alcohol or drugs;[13]
- supervision for reckless driving;[14]
- probation for criminal sexual assault;[15]
- probation for retail theft;[16]
- probation for first offense under the Cannabis Control Act;[17]
- probation for first offense under the Controlled Substances Act;[18]
- probation for aggravated battery of a child;[19] and

9. 625 ILCS 5/3-707.
10. 625 ILCS 5/3-708.
11. 625 ILCS 5/3-710.
12. 625 ILCS 5/5-401.3.
13. 625 ILCS 5/11-501.

   Text References: Decker, Illinois Criminal Law 2d ed § 2.12.

14. 625 ILCS 5/11-503.

   Text References: Decker, Illinois Criminal Law 2d ed § 2.12.

15. 720 ILCS 5/12-15.

   Text References: Decker, Illinois Criminal Law 2d ed § 11.03.

16. 720 ILCS 5/16A-3.

   Text References: Decker, Illinois Criminal Law 2d ed §§ 11.02, 11.34.

17. 720 ILCS 550/10.

   Text References: Decker, Illinois Criminal Law 2d ed § 16.02.

18. 720 ILCS 570/410.

- submitting to treatment for a drug or alcohol addiction as a condition of probation.[20]

The court may order all records to be expunged from the records of the arresting authority and be impounded by the court after five years.[21] However, those records may not be expunged by the Department of State Police.[22] Instead, the records must, on court order, be sealed by the Department of State Police and may be disseminated only as required by law or to the arresting authority, State's Attorney, and the court upon a subsequent arrest for the same or a similar offense or for the purpose of sentencing for any subsequent felony.[23] Once an individual has been convicted for any offense, the Department of Corrections must be given access to all sealed records of the Department of State Police.[24]

Whenever a person who has been convicted of an offense is granted a pardon by the governor[25] which specifically authorizes expungement, he or she may, upon verified petition have a court order entered expunging the record of arrest from the official records of the arresting authority and order that the records of the clerk of the circuit court and the department be sealed until further order of the court upon good cause shown, and the name of the defendant obliterated from the circuit court's official index.[26] The order does not affect any index issued by the circuit court clerk before the entry of the order.[27]

---

19. 720 ILCS 5/12-4.3.

   Text References: Decker, Illinois Criminal Law 2d ed §§ 9.01, 9.29.

20. 20 ILCS 301/40-10.

21. 20 ILCS 2630/5(a).

22. 20 ILCS 2630/5(a).

23. 20 ILCS 2630/5(a).

   See also 20 ILCS 2630/5(d).

24. 20 ILCS 2630/5(a).

25. See § 32:01 (pardons).

26. 20 ILCS 2630/5(c).

An order of expungement does not become final for purposes of appeal until thirty days after notice is received by the Department of State Police.[28]

Defendants found not guilty by reason of insanity are eligible for relief under the statutory section concerning expungement of records; upon completion of treatment defendant may be characterized as having been released without a conviction and indeed is relieved of criminal responsibility due to a mental disease or defect.[29] When addressing petitions for expungement by defendants found not guilty by reason of insanity, the following factors should be considered: the strength of the state's case against the petitioner, the State's reasons for wishing to retain the records, the petitioner's age, criminal record, and employment history, the length of time elapsed between the arrest and the petition to expunge, and the specific adverse consequences the petitioner may endure should expungement be denied; the list is not exhaustive, though, and each petition should be considered on an individual basis.[30]

Effective January 1, 2000, records maintained by the Department of State Police for persons arrested prior to their 17th birthday will be expunged in the following circumstances upon a petition by the minor:[31]

- the minor was arrested and no petition for delinquency was filed with the clerk of the circuit court;
- the minor was charged with an offense and was found not delinquent with respect to that offense;

---

27. 20 ILCS 2630/5(c).

28. 20 ILCS 2630/5(f).

29. People v Wells, 294 Ill App 3d 405, 228 Ill Dec 886, 690 NE2d 645 (1st Dist 1998).

30. People v Wells, 294 Ill App 3d 405, 228 Ill Dec 886, 690 NE2d 645 (1st Dist 1998).

31. 20 ILCS 2630/5(a-5); 705 ILCS 405/5-915.

See § 35:04.

- the minor was placed under supervision pursuant and the order of supervision has since been successfully terminated;[32]
- the minor was adjudicated for an offense which would be a Class B misdemeanor if committed by an adult[33]

The court must not order the sealing or expungment of the arrest records and records of the circuit court clerk of any person granted supervision for or convicted of any sexual offense committed against a minor under 18 years of age.[34]

§ 33:02. Alias

If a person has been convicted of a crime or a violation of an ordinance in the name of a person whose identity he or she has stolen or appropriated, the person whose identity was misappropriated may seek to have his or her name removed from all records.[35] Upon learning of the arrest of a person using his or her identity, the aggrieved person must file a verified petition to the chief judge of the circuit in which the arrest was made.[36] The chief judge may enter an order nunc pro tunc to remove the aggrieved's name and substitute the offender's name, if known or ascertainable, to correct the arrest record, conviction record, and all official records of:

- the arresting authority;
- the Department of State Police;
- other criminal justice agencies;
- the prosecutor; and
- the trial court.[37]

However, the Department of State Police and other criminal

---

32. 705 ILCS 405/5–615.
33. 705 ILCS 405/5-915.
34. 20 ILCS 2630/5(g).
35. 20 ILCS 2630/5(b).
36. 20 ILCS 2630/5(b).
37. 20 ILCS 2630/5(b).

justice agencies or prosecutors are not prohibited from listing under an offender's name any false names he or she has used.[38]

§ 33:03. Procedure for expungement

An individual seeking expungement of an arrest record or alias must file a verified petition and notice of that petition must be served on the State's Attorney or prosecutor prosecuting the offense, the Department of State Police, the arresting agency, and the chief legal officer of the local government affecting the arrest.[39] Those entities served with notice then have 30 days to object to the petition.[40] In the absence of any objection, the court must enter an order granting or denying the petition.[41] A copy of that order must then be promptly mailed, by the clerk of the court, to any persons or agencies ordered by the judge.[42]

> *Practice Guide:* In some counties it is common practice to attach to the petition for expungement a file stamped copy of the order of acquittal or other record of disposition.

---

38. 20 ILCS 2630/5(b).

39. 20 ILCS 2630/5(d).

40. 20 ILCS 2630/5(d).

41. 20 ILCS 2630/5(d).

42. 20 ILCS 2630/5(d).

CHAPTER 34

COSTS AND FEES

by

Diane C. Busch, J.D.

and

Robert L. Margolis, Esq.

Scope of Chapter:

This chapter discusses the common law and statutory provisions governing the award and recovery of costs and fees. The discussion sets forth the circumstances and conditions which must be present to justify the appointment of counsel, as well as the manner in which that counsel's fee is paid. The chapter also covers the guidelines for application of the defendant's bail bond toward the payment of certain costs and fees.

Treated Elsewhere:

Appeal, see Chapter 30.

Arraignment and right to counsel, see Chapter 14.

Bail bond provisions, see Chapter 6.

Constitutional right to counsel, see Chapter 2.

Incompetence of counsel, see Chapter 27.

Pretrial motions, see Chapter 16.

Trial, see Chapter 20.

Research References:

  Text References:

   Ruebner, Illinois Criminal Procedure 2d ed §§ 2.27, 2.32, 4.02–4.10, 5.31, 7.07–7.10

  Annotation References:

   ALR Digest: Appeal and Error §§ 985–992; Attorneys' Fees § 4; Costs and Fees §§ 15, 16, 25.5, 27

§ 34:01   ILLINOIS JURISPRUDENCE: CRIMINAL LAW

Index and Annotations: Attorney or Assistance of Attorney; Attorneys' Fees; Costs of Action

Practice References:

7 Am Jur 2d, Attorneys at Law §§ 243, 244; 20 Am Jur 2d, Costs §§ 100–104, 108; 21A Am Jur 2d, Criminal Law §§ 1044–1049

State Legislation:

725 ILCS 5/110-7, 5/124A-5, 240/10; 730 ILCS 5/5-9-1

Miscellaneous References:

West's Illinois Digest 2d, Costs § 284 et seq.

Auto-Cite®: Cases and annotations referred to in this chapter can be further researched through the Auto-Cite® computer-assisted research service. Use Auto-Cite® to check citations for form, parallel references, prior and later history, and annotation references.

§ 34:01.   Costs and fees generally
§ 34:02.   Defense counsel's fees
§ 34:03.   Expert witness fees
§ 34:04.   Costs of appeal

§ 34:01. Costs and fees generally

The allowance and recovery of costs, unknown at common law, rests entirely upon statutory provisions, which must be strictly construed.[1] When a person is convicted of a statutory or common-law offense, the court must enter judgment that the defendant pay the costs of prosecution.[2] Those costs must include the reasonable costs incurred by the sheriff's office for serving any

---

1. People v Nicholls, 71 Ill 2d 166, 15 Ill Dec 759, 374 NE2d 194 (1978); People v Bratcher, 149 Ill App 3d 425, 102 Ill Dec 853, 500 NE2d 954 (5th Dist 1986) (superseded by statute as stated in People v Johnson, 175 Ill App 3d 908, 125 Ill Dec 469, 530 NE2d 627 (4th Dist)); People v Hodges, 120 Ill App 3d 14, 75 Ill Dec 523, 457 NE2d 517 (3d Dist 1983).

Text References: Ruebner, Illinois Criminal Procedure 2d ed § 4.08.

2. 725 ILCS 5/124A-5.

Annotation References: Validity, construction, and application of state statute requiring inmate to reimburse government for expense of incarceration, 13 ALR5th 872.

Periodicals: For article, "Survey of Illinois Law: Criminal Law and Procedure," see 21 S. Ill. U. L.J. 759 (1997).

arrest warrants, for transporting the defendant from another county to that in which he or she was convicted, and for transporting the defendant from any location outside of the state pursuant to extradition or a waiver of extradition.[3] There are also statutory provisions requiring the defendant to pay, if possible, the statutory fees of the State's Attorney at the time of the defendant's conviction.[4]

Imposing costs does not punish defendant in addition to the sentence he or she receives, but is instead a collateral consequence.[5]

By statute, the clerk of the court may retain ten percent of the amount of the bail bond deposited as bail bond costs, when the conditions of the bond have been performed and the defendant has been discharged.[6] The court may, however, exercise its discretion in determining the amount to be retained by the clerk, except that the amount may not be less than five dollars.[7] That discretion also extends to ordering that a bail bond be used to satisfy the financial obligations of that defendant incurred in a different case due to a fine, court costs, restitution or fees of the defendant's attorney.[8] However, the court may not order that the bail bond be used to satisfy those obligations in a different case until it is first used to satisfy court costs in the case in which the bail bond was deposited.[9] In addition, at the defendant's request, the court may require that the amount of the defendant's bail deposit to be returned to him or her be paid directly to his or her

3. 725 ILCS 5/124A–5.

4. 55 ILCS 5/4–2002.

5. People v Terneus, 239 Ill App 3d 669, 180 Ill Dec 499, 607 NE2d 568 (4th Dist 1992).

6. 725 ILCS 5/110-7(f).

Text References: Ruebner, Illinois Criminal Procedure 2d ed § 4.10.

7. 725 ILCS 5/110-7(f).

8. 725 ILCS 5/110-7(f).

9. 725 ILCS 5/110-7(f).

§ 34:01   ILLINOIS JURISPRUDENCE: CRIMINAL LAW

attorney of record.[10]

It should also be noted that there are statutes which authorize that other penalties and charges be added to the judgment for costs entered against the defendant. For example, depending on the offense, certain charges may be imposed for the benefit of the Violent Crime Victims Assistant Fund.[11] There is also a schedule of authorized fines, based on the offense, which are to be collected by the clerk in addition to the fine and costs in the case and are to be deposited into the Traffic and Criminal Conviction Surcharge Fund,[12] the Truama Center Fund,[13] and the Domestic Violence Abuser Services Fund.[14]

A cost order must be vacated when there is no underlying conviction on which the assessment can rest.[15]

§ 34:02. Defense counsel's fees

In all cases, except those in which the only available penalty is a fine, if the defendant is indigent and desires an attorney, the court must appoint the Public Defender as counsel.[16] Further, if the county has a population of 1,000,000 or more, the court must appoint the Public Defender as counsel in all misdemeanor cases involving an indigent defendant, unless the case involves multiple defendants, in which case the court may appoint counsel other than the Public Defender for the other defendants.[17] Further, the court must appoint a licensed attorney other than the Public

---

10. 725 ILCS 5/110-7(f).

11. 725 ILCS 240/10.

12. 730 ILCS 5/5-9-1.

13. 730 ILCS 5/5-9.1, 5/5-9-1.1.

14. 730 ILCS 5/5-9-1.11.

15. People v Fales, 247 Ill App 3d 681, 187 Ill Dec 213, 617 NE2d 421 (3d Dist 1993).

16. 725 ILCS 5/113-3(b).

Text References: Ruebner, Illinois Criminal Procedure 2d ed §§ 2.27–2.32, 4.06–4.09, 5.31.

17. 725 ILCS 5/113-3(b).

Defender as counsel if:

- there is no Public Defender in the county; or
- the defendant requests counsel other than the Public Defender and the court finds that the defendant's rights will be prejudiced by the appointment of the Public Defender.[18]

While an indigent defendant has the right to competent counsel, he or she does not have the right to select the court-appointed attorney.[19]

Any defendant who requests that counsel be appointed must complete and sign an affidavit providing sufficient information for the court to ascertain the assets and liabilities of that defendant.[20] If a defendant knowingly files an affidavit containing false information he or she will be liable to the county for the reasonable value of the services rendered by the Public Defender or other court-appointed counsel to the extent that those services were unjustly or falsely procured.[21]

Once appointed counsel, other than the Public Defender, files a verified statement of services rendered, the court must order the county treasurer to pay counsel a reasonable fee.[22] In determining that amount, the court must consider all relevant circumstances,

---

18. 725 ILCS 5/113-3(b).

19. People v Cook 274 Ill App 3d 718, 216 Ill Dec 234, 665 NE2d 299 (1st Dist 1995).

Text References: Ruebner, Illinois Criminal Procedure 2d ed §§ 4.06–4.07.

20. 725 ILCS 5/113-3(b).

Annotation References: Determination of indigency of accused entitling him to appointment of counsel, 51 ALR3d 1108.

21. 725 ILCS 5/113-3(b).

22. 725 ILCS 5/113-3(c).

Text References: Ruebner, Illinois Criminal Procedure 2d ed § 4.08.

Annotation References: Construction of state statutes providing for compensation of attorney for services under appointment by court in defending indigent accused, 18 ALR3d 1074.

§ 34:02   ILLINOIS JURISPRUDENCE: CRIMINAL LAW

such as the time spent while court was in session, other time spent representing the defendant, and other expenses reasonably incurred by counsel.[23] In arriving at a reasonable fee for the appointed counsel's services, the trial court should consider, in conjunction with other appropriate factors, (1) the time spent and services rendered, (2) the attorney's skill and experience, (3) the complexity of the case, (4) overhead costs, (5) the expenses of trial, and (6) the number of attorneys in the local area who could be called upon to perform pro bono criminal trial work.[24]

In counties with a population greater than 2,000,000, there is a statutory cap on the amount which may be paid to counsel.[25] The statute caps fees at $40 per hour of time spent while court is in session and $30 per hour for all other hours spent representing the defendant; the total compensation may not exceed $150 in misdemeanor cases and $1,250 in felony cases.[26] However, a payment in excess of those limits may be authorized if the court certifies that the amount is necessary to provide fair compensation for protracted representation.[27] Counsel may file the verified statement of services prior to the termination of the cause and the court may order a provisional payment of sums while the case is pending.[28]

Whenever a defendant is represented by court-appointed counsel, the court may order the defendant to pay a reasonable amount to the county or the State as reimbursement for that representation.[29] A hearing must be held to determine whether

23. 725 ILCS 5/113-3(c).
24. People v. Fowler, 700 N.E.2d 216 (1998).
25. 725 ILCS 5/113-3(c).

   Annotation References: Validity and construction of state statute or court rule fixing maximum fees for attorney appointed to represent indigent, 3 ALR4th 576.

26. 725 ILCS 5/113-3(c).
27. 725 ILCS 5/113-3(c).
28. 725 ILCS 5/113-3(c).
29. 725 ILCS 5/113-3.1(a).

reimbursement is required and if so, what the amount of reimbursement should be.[30] In that hearing, the court must consider the defendant's affidavit as to his or her assets and liabilities, as well as any other information pertaining to his or her financial circumstances which may be submitted by the parties.[31] The hearing held to determine that amount may be conducted on the court's own motion or on the motion of the State's Attorney any time after the appointment of counsel, but in no event later than 90 days after the entry of a final order disposing of the case at the trial level.[32] Further, there are statutory limits to the amount that the court may require the defendant to pay; $500 for a defendant charged with a misdemeanor, $5,000 for a defendant charged with a felony, and $2,500 for a defendant who is appealing a conviction of any class offense.[33]

The court may specify the method of any payment required of a defendant to reimburse the county or state for representation.[34] The court may order that payments be made on a monthly basis during the term of representation; however, the sum deposited as money bond may not be used to satisfy this court order.[35] In determining that method of payment, the court may give special consideration to the interests of the defendant's relatives or other third parties who may have posted a money bond on behalf of the defendant to secure his or her release.[36] However, where the

Text References: Ruebner, Illinois Criminal Procedure 2d ed § 4.07.

Annotation References: Validity, construction, and application of state recoupment statutes permitting state to recover counsel fees expended for benefit of indigent criminal defendants, 39 ALR4th 597.

30. People v Love, 177 Ill2d 550, 227 Ill Dec 109, 687 NE2d 32 (1997); People v Webb, 276 Ill App 3d 570, 213 Ill Dec 103, 658 NE2d 852 (3d Dist 1995).

31. 725 ILCS 5/113-3.1(a).

32. 725 ILCS 5/113-3.1(a).

33. 725 ILCS 5/113-3.1(b).

34. 725 ILCS 5/113-3.1(c).

35. 725 ILCS 5/113-3.1(c).

36. 725 ILCS 5/113-3.1(c).

evidence establishes that the defendant has no ability, present or foreseeable, to pay for counsel, there is no basis for inquiring into a third party's financial circumstances.[37] In addition, on its own motion, or that of any party, the court may reduce, increase, or suspend the ordered payment, or modify the method of payment, as required by the interests of fairness.[38] However, the court may not order an increase, suspension, or reduction of payment without a hearing and notice to all parties.[39]

A defendant who fails to obey any order of reimbursement may be punished for contempt of court.[40] Any arrearage in payments may be reduced to judgment and collected by any means authorized by law for the collection of money judgments.[41]

The Clerk of the Circuit Court is responsible for collecting and paying to the county all amounts due pursuant to an order requiring reimbursement and to keep records and make reports to the court in whatever manner the court directs or as required by statute.[42]

> ☞ *Practice Guide:* There does not appear to be any established rule as to whether, or the extent to which the statute governing the payment of court-appointed counsel other than the Public Defender, may apply to the payment for services rendered by investigators.[43]

People v Webb, 276 Ill App 3d 570, 213 Ill Dec 103, 658 NE2d 852 (3d Dist 1995).

37. People v Webb, 276 Ill App 3d 570, 213 Ill Dec 103, 658 NE2d 852 (3d Dist 1995).

38. 725 ILCS 5/113-3.1(c).

39. 725 ILCS 5/113-3.1(c).

40. 725 ILCS 5/113-3.1(g).

41. 725 ILCS 5/113-3.1(g).

42. 725 ILCS 5/113-3.1(d)–(f).

43. People v Gacy, 103 Ill 2d 1, 82 Ill Dec 391, 468 NE2d 1171 (1984), cert den 470 US 1037, 84 L Ed 2d 799, 105 S Ct 1410, and (superseded by statute as stated in People v Wilhoite, 228 Ill App 3d 12, 169 Ill Dec 561, 592 NE2d 48

§ 34:03. Expert witness fees

Pursuant to statute, in a capital case, if the court determines that the defendant is indigent, the court may order the county treasurer to pay reasonable compensation to the necessary expert witnesses for the defendant.[44] However, the Illinois Supreme Court has construed this statute to extend to indigent defendants charged with non-capital felonies.[45] Such persons can call expert witnesses where opinions "go to the heart of the defense."[46] As in the case of court-appointed counsel there is a statutory cap on the amount which may be paid to the witnesses, though the Illinois Supreme Court has held the cap, $1,250, is not a rigid boundary and the county may be required to pay a "reasonable fee" that may exceed $1,250.[47] In order to obtain payment, the witnesses must file with the court a verified statement of services rendered.[48]

For a defendant to receive funds to pay for expert witnesses, there must be some showing on the defendant's part that the requested expert assistance is necessary in proving a crucial issue in the case and that the lack of funds for the expert will therefore prejudice the defendant.[49]

(Cal App 1st Dist)); People v Wilson, 117 Ill App 3d 744, 73 Ill Dec 124, 453 NE2d 949 (4th Dist 1983); People v Veal, 110 Ill App 3d 919, 66 Ill Dec 679, 443 NE2d 605 (1st Dist 1982).

44. 725 ILCS 5/113-3(d).

Text References: Ruebner, Illinois Criminal Procedure 2d ed § 4.09.

Annotation References: Right of indigent defendant in criminal case to aid of state by appointment of investigator or expert, 34 ALR3d 1256.

45. People v Watson, 36 Ill 2d 228, 221 NE2d 645 (1966); People v Evans, 271 Ill App 3d 495, 208 Ill Dec 42, 648 NE2d 964 (5th Dist 1995).

46. People v Watson, 36 Ill 2d 228, 221 NE2d 645 (1966).

47. 725 ILCS 5/113-3(d).

People v Kinion, 97 Ill 2d 322, 78 Ill Dec 528, 454 NE2d 625 (1983).

48. 725 ILCS 5/113-3(d).

49. People v Lawson, 163 Ill 2d 187, 206 Ill Dec 119, 644 NE2d 1172 (1994).

☞ *Illustration:* In one case, where the prosecution's expert's opinion on shoeprint evidence was the strongest evidence presented by the state and where the trial court rejected an indigent defendant's motion for funds to hire his own expert, the conviction was reversed and the case remanded for a new trial.[50] In another, an indigent, left-handed defendant was not entitled to the appointment of an expert in pathology to counter evidence that a left-handed person slit the throat of the victim, as the state's case did not turn on proof that the perpetrator was left-handed, the state's evidence did not exclude the possibility that a right-handed person could have slit the victim's throat, and the primary evidence against the defendant was a coconspirator's testimony that the defendant had admitted complicity and that coconspirator had seen defendant behind the store counter with the victim.[51]

§ 34:04. Costs of appeal

If the State prevails on appeal, it may request a statutorily specified amount in costs, with an additional amount if oral argument is conducted. In counties with population under three million, a $50 fee must be paid to the State's attorney in each case of appeal taken from the state's attorney's county, when the case is prosecuted or defended by that state's attorney.[52] In counties with population of more than three million, a $100 fee must be paid to the State's attorney in each case of appeal taken from the state's attorney's county, when the case is prosecuted or defended by that state's attorney.[53] If the State does not prevail, it must retain the permitted fees from the fines and forfeitures collected in other cases.[54] There is no statutory authority for a defendant in a

---

50. People v Lawson, 163 Ill 2d 187, 206 Ill Dec 119, 644 NE2d 1172 (1994).
51. People v Keene, 169 Ill 2d 1, 214 Ill Dec 194, 660 NE2d 901 (1995).
52. 55 ILCS 5/4-2002(a).
53. 55 ILCS 5/4-2002.1(a).
54. 55 ILCS 5/4-2002.1(a).

criminal appeal to recover his or her costs regardless of the outcome.

PART FIVE

JUVENILE OFFENDERS

CHAPTER 35

DELINQUENT MINORS

by

Evan M. Butterfield, J.D.

and

Robert L. Margolis, Esq.

Scope of Chapter:

This chapter analyzes those aspects of the Illinois Juvenile Court Act relevant to delinquent minors. The rights of parties, transfer of minors to the criminal courts, adjudicatory proceedings, procedural issues, guardianship, commitment, and habitual juvenile offenders are among the topics discussed. Although also covered by the Juvenile Court Act, those issues related to minor witnesses and minor victims of adult offenders, and their consequent custody questions are not the focus of this chapter.

Federal Aspects:

Decisions arising under federal law, the United States Constitution, and United States Supreme Court cases are cited to the extent they are relevant to Illinois law.

Treated Elsewhere:

Capacity, see Chapter 15.

Evidence, see Chapters 17, 18 and 19.

Fitness, see Chapter 15.

Sentencing, see Chapter 28.

Research References:
  Annotation References:
    ALR Digest: Juvenile Delinquents and Dependents
    Index and Annotations: Juvenile Courts and Delinquent Children
  Practice References:
    14 Am Jur Trials 619, Juvenile Court Proceedings
  Forms:
    15 Am Jur Pl & Pr Forms (Rev), Juvenile Courts and Delinquent and Dependent Children

Auto-Cite®: Cases and annotations referred to in this chapter can be further researched through the Auto-Cite® computer-assisted research service. Use Auto-Cite® to check citations for form, parallel references, prior and later history, and annotation references.

I. JUVENILE COURTS

§ 35:01. Generally
§ 35:02. Rights of parties
§ 35:03. Confidentiality of records
§ 35:04. Expungement of records

II. PRELIMINARY MATTERS

§ 35:05. Jurisdiction and venue
§ 35:06. Limitations on criminal prosecutions; transfer from Juvenile Courts
§ 35:07. —Minors prosecuted under criminal law
§ 35:08. —Evidence
§ 35:09. —Weapons
§ 35:10. Arresting or taking minor into custody
§ 35:11. Officers' duties
§ 35:12. —Station adjustment
§ 35:13. —Probation adjustment
§ 35:14. —Duty of officer upon arrest of juvenile
§ 35:15. —Shelter care
§ 35:16. —Detention
§ 35:17. —Confinement
§ 35:18. —Nonsecure custody
§ 35:19. —Home confinement
§ 35:20. Detention hearing

DELINQUENT MINORS

§ 35:21. Preliminary conferences; probation adjustment

III. ADJUDICATORY PROCEEDINGS

§ 35:22. Petition
§ 35:23. —Date for trial
§ 35:24. —Summons and Notice
§ 35:25. —Guardian ad litem
§ 35:26. Pleas and waivers
§ 35:27. Evidence
§ 35:28. Continuance under supervision
§ 35:29. Findings and determination

IV. DISPOSITION

§ 35:30. Social investigation report
§ 35:31. Hearing
§ 35:32. Orders
§ 35:33. Probation
§ 35:34. —Revocation
§ 35:35. Protective supervision
§ 35:36. —Enforcement
§ 35:37. Placement with legal custodian
§ 35:38. —Court review
§ 35:39. Commitment of minor
§ 35:40. —Transfer to Department of Mental Health and Developmental Disabilities
§ 35:41. Wardship of court—Duration
§ 35:42. Habitual juvenile offenders
§ 35:42.50. Violent juvenile offenders
§ 35:43. Appeals

I. JUVENILE COURTS

Research References:

Annotation References:

ALR Digest: Juvenile Delinquents and Dependents § 1–5

Index and Annotations: Juvenile Courts and Delinquent Children

Practice References:

47 Am Jur 2d, Juvenile Courts and Delinquent and Dependent Children §§ 1–15, 59, 59.5

14 Am Jur Trials 619, Juvenile Court Proceedings §§ 14–40

§ 35:01 ILLINOIS JURISPRUDENCE: CRIMINAL LAW

State Legislation:
> 705 ILCS 405/1-1 et seq., 405/5-901 et seq.; 720 ILCS 5/24-1, 5/24-3, 5/24-3.1, 5/24-5, 550/1 et seq., 570/100 et seq.

Forms:
> 15 Am Jur Pl & Pr Forms (Rev), Juvenile Courts and Delinquent and Dependent Children Forms 71, 72, 81

Miscellaneous References:
> West's Illinois Digest 2d, Infants §§ 68, 69, 131–134

§ 35:01. Generally

The Juvenile Court Act provides avenues of relief, intervention, or punishment in the juvenile courts for abused and neglected minors;[1] minors who are truant, runaway, or beyond the control of their parents, guardian or custodian;[2] addicted or alcoholic minors;[3] and the subject of this chapter, minors who are delinquent.[4] The Act does not give any court jurisdiction over a minor solely on the basis of the minor's misbehavior if that misbehavior is not in violation of federal or state law or a municipal ordinance.[5]

> ☛ *Practice Guide:* Delinquency proceedings are governed by the Juvenile Justice Reform Provisions of 1998.[6]

The Act is generally intended to serve the best interests of a minor, rather than to be necessarily punitive.[7] Although a juvenile

1. 705 ILCS 405/2-1 et seq.

2. 705 ILCS 405/3-1 et seq.

   Annotation References: Truancy as indicative of delinquency or incorrigibility, justifying commitment of infant or juvenile, 5 ALR4th 1211.

3. 705 ILCS 405/4-1 et seq.

4. 705 ILCS 405/5-101 et seq.

5. 705 ILCS 405/1-4.

6. 705 ILCS 405/5-101 et seq.

7. People v W.C. (In re W.C.), 167 Ill 2d 307, 212 Ill Dec 563, 657 NE2d 908 (1995); People v Thompson, 229 Ill App 3d 606, 170 Ill Dec 612, 593 NE2d 154 (3d Dist 1992).

proceeding retains certain adversary characteristics, it is not an adversary proceeding in the usual sense but is one to be administered in a spirit of humane concern for the minor, to promote his or her welfare, and to serve the best interests of the community.[8] In fact, the Act's language carefully avoids the terms "criminal convictions" or "sentence," and instead uses "adjudication" and "disposition."[9] An adjudication or disposition under the Juvenile Court Act is not, then, equivalent to a criminal conviction and sentence.[10]

☛ *Practice Guide:* Because an adjudication and disposition under the Juvenile Court Act is not equivalent to a criminal conviction and sentence, a felony sentence may not run consecutively to a noncriminal, nonfelony juvenile disposition.[11]

§ 35:02. Rights of parties

A minor who is the subject of proceedings under the Juvenile Court Act[12] is guaranteed the rights of adults, unless any law

Practice References: Purpose of juvenile court. 14 Am Jur Trials 619, Juvenile Court Proceedings §§ 14–19.

8. In re C.R.H., 251 Ill App 3d 102, 190 Ill Dec 389, 621 NE2d 258 (2d Dist 1993), affd 163 Ill 2d 263, 206 Ill Dec 100, 644 NE2d 1153 (1994).

Annotation References: Availability of discovery at probation revcation hearings, 52 ALR5th 559;
Family court jurisdiction to hear contract claims, 46 ALR5th 735;
Applicability of rules of evidence to juvenile transfer, waiver, or certification hearings,37 ALR5th 703.

9. People v Thompson, 229 Ill App 3d 606, 170 Ill Dec 612, 593 NE2d 154 (3d Dist 1992).

10. People v Thompson, 229 Ill App 3d 606, 170 Ill Dec 612, 593 NE2d 154 (3d Dist 1992).

11. People v Thompson, 229 Ill App 3d 606, 170 Ill Dec 612, 593 NE2d 154 (3d Dist 1992).

See Part IV.

12. 705 ILCS 405/1-1 et seq.

Periodicals: For comment, "The Sixth Amendment: Protecting Defen-

which enhances the protection of minors specifically precludes those procedural rights.[13] The Act presumes that every child has a right to those services that are necessary to his or her proper development, including health, education, and social services, and that the parents' right of custody will not prevail over the best interests of the child.[14] The court is required to liberally interpret the Act to carry out its policies.[15]

Thus, a minor has the right, along with parties respondent who are his or her parents, guardian, legal custodian, or responsible relative, to be present, to be heard, to present material evidence, to cross-examine witnesses, to examine pertinent court files and records,[16] and, even in nonadversarial proceedings, to be represented by counsel.[17] The court will appoint the Public Defender or other counsel to represent any party who is financially unable to employ counsel and who requests that counsel be appointed, with the exceptionof a foster parent who has been permitted to intervene pursuant to statute.[18] Appointed counsel must appear at all stages of the proceedings, including any petition or motion.[19] No hearing may be commenced unless the minor who is its subject is represented by counsel,[20] and each adult respondent is provided with a written notice of his or her

---

dants' Rights at the Expense of Child Victims," see 30 J. Marshall L. Rev. 767 (1997).

13. 705 ILCS 405/1-2(3)(a).

   Practice References: Rights and privilege of juveniles and parents. 14 Am Jur Trials 619, Juvenile Court Proceedings §§ 20–40.

14. 705 ILCS 405/1-2(3)(b), 405/1-2(3)(c).

15. 705 ILCS 405/1-2(4).

16. 705 ILCS 405/1-5(1).

   See, e.g., 705 ILCS 405/2-22, 405/3-28, 405/4-20, 405/5-22.

17. 705 ILCS 405/1-5(1).

18. 705 ILCS 405/1-5(1).

   Forms: Appointment of attorney. 15 Am Jur Pl & Pr Forms (Rev), Juvenile Courts and Delinquent and Dependent Children, Forms 71, 72.

19. 705 ILCS 405/1-5(1).

rights at the time he or she appears at a hearing.[21]

☛ *Practice Guide:* This statute does not undermine the court's power to exclude a legal guardian as a witness from an adjudicatory hearing for the purpose of securing uninfluenced testimony.[22]

Any current or former foster parent or representative of any interested agency has the right to be heard by the court, even if he or she has not been appointed guardian, custodian, or otherwise been made a party to the proceeding.[23] Such a person does not, however, become a party to the proceeding by virtue of their testimony.[24] Further, any current foster parent, and the agency designated by the court or the Department of Children and Family Services (DCFS) as custodian of a dependent[25] or an abused or neglected minor,[26] has the right to adequate notice at all stages of any proceeding that may affect the minor's custody or status.[27] The notice, mailed by the clerk by certified mail marked for delivery to the addressee alone, includes a statement regarding the nature and denomination of the hearing or proceeding, the date, time, and place at which it is to be held, and the change in custody sought.[28] The regular return receipt for certified mail is considered sufficient proof of service.[29]

20. 705 ILCS 405/1-5(1).

21. 705 ILCS 405/1-5(1).

22. People v J.E. (In re J.E.), 285 Ill App 3d 965, 221 Ill Dec 249, 675 NE2d 156 (1st Dist 1996).

23. 705 ILCS 405/1-5(2)(a).

Annotation References: Right of juvenile court defendant to be represented during court proceedings by parent, 11 ALR4th 719.

24. 705 ILCS 405/1-5(2)(a).

25. 705 ILCS 405/2-4.

26. 705 ILCS 405/2-3.

27. 705 ILCS 405/1-5(2)(a).

28. 705 ILCS 405/1-5(2)(a).

§ 35:02   ILLINOIS JURISPRUDENCE: CRIMINAL LAW

The Department of Children and Family Services or the licensed child welfare agency that has placed the minor with the foster parent must notify the clerk of the court of the name and address of the current foster parent.[30] Further, any foster parent who is denied his or her right to be heard may bring a mandamus action against the court or any public agency to enforce that right.[31] The mandamus action may be brought immediately upon the denial of those rights but in no event later than 30 days after the foster parent has been denied the right to be heard.[32]

> ☞ *Practice Guide:* Due process of law requires that notice in juvenile proceedings be equivalent to that constitutionally required in criminal or civil cases, and adequate notice to a minor and his or her parents is a requirement of due process; thus, inadequate notice to a parent whose address is known violates the rights of parent and child to due process.[33]

A foster parent has the right to petition the court to intervene in a proceeding to restore the minor to any parent, guardian or legal custodian for the sole purpose of requesting that the minor be placed with the foster parent under certain circumstances.[34]

At their first appearance, the minor and his or her parents, guardian, custodian, or responsible relative is informed of the nature of the proceedings and their rights, including the right to appeal from an adjudication of wardship.[35]

A minor who is the subject of a juvenile proceeding has the

---

29. 705 ILCS 405/1-5(2).

30. 705 ILCS 405/1-5(2).

31. 705 ILCS 405/1-5(2).

    See§§ 31.07 et seq.

32. 705 ILCS 405/1-5(2).

33. People v C.R.H. (In re C.R.H.), 163 Ill 2d 263, 206 Ill Dec 100, 644 NE2d 1153 (1994).

34. 705 ILCS 405/1–5(2)(b).

35. 705 ILCS 405/1-5(3).

right to refuse to testify, and no sanction may be applied against him or her for refusing or failing to testify in the course of any hearing held prior to final adjudication.[36]

Only persons who, in the court's opinion, have a direct interest in the case or the work of the court may be admitted to the proceedings.[37] The general public, except for the victim and the news media, are thus excluded from any hearing, and the court may, for the minor's protection and for good cause shown, prohibit any person or agency present from disclosing the minor's identity.[38] Further, the minor may be excluded from any part of a dispositional hearing, and, with the consent of his or her parent, guardian, counsel, or guardian ad litem, may be excluded from any adjudicatory hearing.[39]

§ 35:03. Confidentiality of records

The records of law enforcement officers concerning a minor under the age of seventeen must be maintained separately from general arrest records, and must be restricted to the following and when necessary for the discharge of their official duties:[40]

---

36. 705 ILCS 405/1-5(4).

   Periodicals: Freitas, Extending the privilege against self-incrimination to the juvenile waiver hearing. 62 U Chi L Rev 301 (1995).

37. 705 ILCS 405/1-5(6).

38. 705 ILCS 405/1-5(6).

39. 705 ILCS 405/1-5(5).

40. 705 ILCS 405/5-905(1), 5-905(5).

   Periodicals: For comment, "The Sixth Amendment: Protecting Defendants' Rights at the Expense of Child Victims," see 30 J. Marshall L. Rev. 767 (1997).
   For article, "The Supreme Court Turns Back the Clock on Civil Forfeiture in Bennis," see 85 Ill. B.J. 314 (1997).
   For article, "Survey of Illinois Law: Criminal Law and Procedure," see 21 S. Ill. U.L.J. 759 (1997).
   Disclosing the identities of juvenile felons: Introducing accountability to juvenile justice, 27 Loy U Chi LJ 349 (1996).
   O'Reilly, Illinois lifts the veil on juvenile conviction records in some cases, 83 Ill BJ 431.

- a judge of the circuit court and members of the staff of the court designated by the judge;
- law enforcement officers, probation officers or prosecutors or their staff;
- the minor, the minor's parents or legal guardian and their attorneys, but only when the juvenile has been charged with an offense;
- Adult and Juvenile Prisoner Review Boards;
- authorized military personnel;
- persons engaged in bona fide research, with the permission of the judge of juvenile court and the chief executive of the agency that prepared the particular recording: provided that publication of the research results in no disclosure of a minor's identity and protects the confidentiality of the record;
- individuals responsible for supervising or providing temporary or permanent care and custody of minors pursuant to orders of the juvenile court or directives from officials of the Department of Children and Family Services or the Department of Human Services who certify in writing that the information will not be disclosed to any other party except as provided under law or order of court;
- the appropriate school official.

Information identifying victims and alleged victims of sex offenses, may not be disclosed or open to public inspection under any circumstances.[41]

Relevant information, reports and records must be made available to the Department of Corrections when a juvenile offender has been placed in the custody of the Department of Corrections, Juvenile Division.[42]

Cintron, Rehabilitating the juvenile court system: Limiting juvenile transfers to adult criminal court, 90 NW UL Rev 1254 (1996).

41. 705 ILCS 405/5-905(2).

§ 35:03

Photographs contained in the records of law enforcement officers relating to a minor may, however, be disclosed to and inspected by victims or witnesses in the presence of a law enforcement officer for the purpose of identifying or apprehending an offender.[43]

The records of law enforcement officers concerning all minors under 17 years of age may not be open to public inspection or their contents disclosed to the public except by order of the court or when the institution of criminal proceedings has been permitted or required or the minor has been convicted of a crime and is the subject of pre-sentence investigation or when provided by law.[44]

Court files with respect to juvenile delinquency proceedings consist of the petitions, pleadings, victim impact statements, process, service of process, orders, writs and docket entries reflecting hearings held and judgments and decrees entered by the court and are kept separate from other records of the court[45] The file, including information identifying the victim or alleged victim of any sex offense, may be disclosed only to the following parties when necessary for discharge of their official duties:[46]

- a judge of the circuit court and members of the staff of the court designated by the judge;
- parties to the proceedings and their attorneys;
- victims and their attorneys, except in cases of multiple victims of sex offenses in which case the information identifying the nonrequesting victims must be redacted;
- probation officers, law enforcement officers or prosecutors or their staff; or
- the Adult and Juvenile Prisoner Review Board.

---

42. 705 ILCS 405/5-905(3).
43. 705 ILCS 405/5-905(4).
44. 705 ILCS 405/5-905(5).
45. 705 ILCS 405/5-901(1).
46. See generally 705 ILCS 405/5-901(1)(a)(i)–(v).

§ 35:03   ILLINOIS JURISPRUDENCE: CRIMINAL LAW

The court file redacted to remove all information identifying the victim or alleged victim of any sex offense, it may be disclosed only to the following parties when necessary for discharge of their official duties:[47]

- authorized military personnel;
- persons engaged in bona fide research, with the permission of the judge of the juvenile court and the chief executive of the agency that prepared the particular recording: provided that publication of the research results in no disclosure of a minor's identity and protects the confidentiality of the record;
- the Secretary of State;
- the administrator of a bonafide substance abuse student assistance program with the permission of the presiding judge of the juvenile court; or
- any individual, or any public or private agency or institution, having custody of the juvenile under court order or providing educational, medical or mental health services to the juvenile or a court-approved advocate for the juvenile or any placement provider or potential placement provider as determined by the court.

A minor who is the victim or alleged victim in a juvenile proceeding is provided the same confidentiality regarding disclosure of identity as the minor who is the subject of the record.[48] Information identifying victims and alleged victims of sex offenses, may not be disclosed or open to public inspection under any circumstances.[49]

Juvenile court records may not be made available to the general public but may be inspected by representatives of agencies, associations and news media or other properly interested persons by general or special order of the court.[50] The State's Attorney,

47. See generally 705 ILCS 405/5-901(1)(b)(i)–(v).
48. 705 ILCS 405/5-901(3).
49. 705 ILCS 405/5-901(3).

the minor, his or her parents, guardian and counsel must at all times have the right to examine court files and records.[51]

The court must allow the general public to have access to the name, address, and offense of a minor adjudicated a delinquent under either of the following circumstances:[52]

- the minor was convicted of first degree murder, attempt to commit first degree murder, aggravated criminal sexual assault, or criminal sexual assault; or
- the court has made a finding that the minor was at least 13 years of age at the time the act was committed and the adjudication of delinquency was based on the minor's commission of an act in furtherance of the commission of a felony as a member of or on behalf of a criminal street gang, an act involving the use of a firearm in the commission of a felony, an act that would be a Class X felony offense or is the minor's second or subsequent Class 2 or greater felony offense under the Cannabis Control Act[53] if committed by an adult, an act that would be a second or subsequent offense under Section 402 of the Illinois Controlled Substances Act[54] if committed by an adult, or an act that would be an offense under Section 401 of the Illinois Controlled Substances Act[55] if committed by an adult.

The court must allow the general public to have access to the name, address, and offense of a minor who is at least 13 years of age at the time the offense is committed and who is convicted in criminal proceedings permitted or required under Section 5-805,[56]

---

50. 705 ILCS 405/5-901(5).

51. 705 ILCS 405/5-901(5).

52. 705 ILCS 405/5-901(5)(a).

53. 720 ILCS 550/1 et seq.

See § 56:01 et seq.

54. 720 ILCS 570/402 et seq.

See § 56:08 et seq.

55. 720 ILCS 570/401 et seq.

under either of the following circumstances:[57]

- the minor was convicted of first degree murder, attempt to commit first degree murder, aggravated criminal sexual assault, or criminal sexual assault; or
- the court has made a finding that the minor was at least 13 years of age at the time the act was committed and the conviction was based on the minor's commission of an act in furtherance of the commission of a felony as a member of or on behalf of a criminal street gang, an act involving the use of a firearm in the commission of a felony, an act that would be a Class X felony offense or is the minor's second or subsequent Class 2 or greater felony offense under the Cannabis Control Act[58] if committed by an adult, an act that would be a second or subsequent offense under Section 402 of the Illinois Controlled Substances Act[59] if committed by an adult, or an act that would be an offense under Section 401 of the Illinois Controlled Substances Act[60] if committed by an adult.

☞ *Practice Guide:* A state agency seeking the records must show the need for them. In one case, the court denied a request by Alcohol, Tobacco and Firearms because the agency could not show that the information was "essential" to the investigation it was conducting; in fact, the state admitted the information would not be used for a single investigation and did not identify a crime.[61]

---

56. 705 ILCS 405/5-805.

See § 35:42.50.

57. 705 ILCS 405/5-901(5)(a).

58. 720 ILCS 550/1 et seq.

See § 56:01 et seq.

59. 720 ILCS 570/402 et seq.

See § 56:08 et seq.

60. 720 ILCS 570/401 et seq.

Also, a Civil Service Commission or appointing authority examining the character and fitness of an applicant for a position as a law enforcement officer may have access to the records of disposition or evidence made in the course of a juvenile proceeding involving the applicant.[61]

Following any adjudication of delinquency for a crime which would be a felony if committed by an adult, or following any adjudication of delinquency for certain felonies,[63] the State's Attorney must ascertain whether the minor is enrolled in school and, if so, provide a copy of the sentencing order to the principal or chief administrative officer of the school and access to the juvenile records must be limited to the principal or chief administrative officer of the school and any guidance counselor designated by him or her.[64]

An adjudication of delinquency may be used as evidence in any juvenile or criminal proceeding, where it would otherwise be admissible under the rules of evidence, including but not limited to, use as impeachment evidence against any witness, including the minor if he or she testifies.[65]

Information or records may be disclosed to the general public when the court is conducting transfer hearings to criminal court.[66]

§ 35:04. Expungement of records

If a minor was arrested, but no delinquency petition was filed, or the minor was found not delinquent of a charged offense, was

---

61. People v W.L. (In re W.L.), 293 Ill App 3d 818, 228 Ill Dec 403, 689 NE2d 275 (2d Dist 1997).

62. 705 ILCS 405/5-901(7).

63. See 720 ILCS 5/24-1, 5/24-3, 5/24-3.1, or 5/24-5.

64. 705 ILCS 405/5-901(8).

65. 705 ILCS 405/5-901(6).

66. 705 ILCS 405/5-901(12).

   See 705 ILCS 405/5-805 (transfer hearings).

   See 35:06.

§ 35:04   ILLINOIS JURISPRUDENCE: CRIMINAL LAW

placed under supervision, or was found guilty of an offense that would be a Class B misdemeanor if committed by an adult, he or she may petition the court, upon the later of either (1) attaining the age of seventeen or (2) the successful termination of all juvenile court proceedings, to expunge law enforcement and juvenile court records relating to incidents which occurred prior to his or her seventeenth birthday.[67] Further, any person may petition the court to expunge all law enforcement or juvenile court records relating to incidents or crimes, which did not result in proceedings in criminal court and which are not based on first degree murder and sex offenses which would be felonies if committed by an adult, that occurred prior to his or her seventeenth birthday if the person for whom expungement is sought has had no convictions for any crime since his or her 17th birthday and the latter of the following has occurred:

- he or she has reached 21 years of age; or
- five years have elapsed since all juvenile court proceedings relating to him or her have been terminated or his or her commitment to the Department of Corrections, Juvenile Division has been terminated.[68]

Notice of the petition to expunge the law enforcement and juvenile court records is served upon the State's Attorney and the subject arresting authority.[69] The chief judge of the circuit in which the arrest was made, or his or her designee, may order the expungement of the relevant records based on a verified petition.[70]

67. 705 ILCS 405/5-915(1).
Expungement of records. 14 Am Jur Trials 619, Juvenile Court Proceedings § 81.

Annotation References: Admissibility of evidence of other offense where record has been expunged or erased, 82 ALR4th 913.
Expungement of juvenile court records, 71 ALR3d 753.
Consideration of accused's juvenile court record in sentencing for offense committed as adult, 64 ALR3d 1291.

68. 705 ILCS 405/5-915(2).

69. 705 ILCS 405/5-915(3).

70. 705 ILCS 405/5-915(3).

When an order expunging records or files is entered, the offense which the records or files concern is treated as if it never occurred.[71]

II. PRELIMINARY MATTERS

Research References:

  Annotation References:

    ALR Digest: Juvenile Delinquents and Dependents § 6–9

    Index and Annotations: Juvenile Courts and Delinquent Children

  Practice References:

    47 Am Jur 2d, Juvenile Courts and Delinquent and Dependent Children §§ 16–26, 34–43

    14 Am Jur Trials 619, Juvenile Court Proceedings §§ 47–55

  State Legislation:

    20 ILCS 301/1-10; 705 ILCS 405/1-3(15); 705 ILCS 405/5-101 et seq.; 720 ILCS 5/9-3, 5/24-1, 24-6, 31-6, 32-10; 720 ILCS 550/1 et seq.; 720 ILCS 570/100 et seq., 570/401 et seq.; 730 ILCS 5/1-1-1; 740 ILCS 147/10

  Forms:

    15 Am Jur Pl & Pr Forms (Rev), Juvenile Courts and Delinquent and Dependent Children, Forms 1, 3–11, 32

  Miscellaneous References:

    West's Illinois Digest 2d, Infants §§ 131–134, 151–153, 192

§ 35:05. Jurisdiction and venue

Proceedings are properly instituted under the provisions of the Juvenile Justice Reform Act of 1998 concerning any minor who prior to the minor's 17th birthday has violated or attempted to violate, regardless of where the act occurred, any federal or State law or municipal or county ordinance.[72]

---

71. 705 ILCS 405/5-915(4).

72. 705 ILCS 405/5-120.

  Annotation References: Applicability of rules of evidence to juvenile transfer, waiver, or certification hearings, 37 ALR5th 703.

§ 35:05 ILLINOIS JURISPRUDENCE: CRIMINAL LAW

☞ *Practice Guide:* A pleading in a juvenile proceeding that does not name and notify respondents, which includes parents or a legal guardian, fails to invoke the jurisdiction of the court and thereby renders its orders void.[73]

Venue properly lies in the county in which the minor resides or is found, in which the alleged act occurred or was attempted, or in the county where the order of the court, alleged to have been violated by the minor, was made unless subsequent to the order the proceedings have been transferred to another county.[74] If proceedings are commenced in a county other than that in which the minor resides, the court may transfer the case to the county of residence at any time prior to or following an adjudication of wardship.[75] Transfer is accomplished by the transmittal of an authenticated copy of the court record, including all documents, petitions, orders, minute orders, docket entries, and all reports prepared by the agency providing services to the minor to the court sitting in the minor's county of residence.[76] If the minor who is the subject of the proceedings changes his or her residence during the pendency of the proceedings, the case may similarly be transferred to the new county of residence.[77]

§ 35:06. Limitations on criminal prosecutions; transfer from Juvenile Courts

Any minor alleged to have committed a traffic, boating, or fish and game law violation, whether punishable by imprisonment or fine, may be prosecuted for the violation and punished under any statute or ordinance without reference to juvenile proceedings, except that any detention must generally be in compliance with the Juvenile Court Act.[78]

---

73. People v C.R.H. (In re C.R.H.), 163 Ill 2d 263, 206 Ill Dec 100, 644 NE2d 1153 (1994).

74. 705 ILCS 405/5-135(1).

75. 705 ILCS 405/5-135(2).

76. 705 ILCS 405/5-135(2).

77. 705 ILCS 405/5-135(2).

☛ *Definition:* "Traffic violation" includes reckless homicide.[79]

If a petition alleges a minor 15 years of age or older committed a forcible felony under Illinois law, the States Attorney may move to prosecute the minor under the criminal laws of Illinois.[80] If the petition alleges that (i) the minor has previously been adjudicated delinquent or found guilty of a felony and (ii) the offense was committed in furtherance of criminal activity by an organized gang, the Juvenile Court Judge must, upon determining that there is probable cause that both allegations are true, enter an order permitting prosecution under the criminal laws of Illinois.[81]

Similarly, if a petition allages a minor 15 years of age or older committed a felony and the States Attorney alleges in a petition that the minor previously had been convicted of a forcible felony and the instant felony was committed in furtherance of criminal activity by a gang, the Juvenile Court Judge must, upon determining that there is probable cause that both allegations are true, enter an order permitting prosecution under the criminal laws of Illinois.[82]

☛ *Practice Guide:* The "gang transfer" provision has been found constitutional, because it is part of a nonadjudicatory hearing, and does not infringe on the inherent powers of the judiciary, or violate the double-jeopardy, equal protection, or substantive or procedural due process guarantees of the United States and Illinois constitutions.[83]

---

78. 705 ILCS 405/5-125.

Glen Ellyn v Fujinaga, 190 Ill App 3d 584, 137 Ill Dec 871, 546 NE2d 816 (2d Dist 1989).

79. 705 ILCS 405/5-125.

See 720 ILCS 5/9-3.

80. 720 ILCS 405/5-805(1)(a).

81. 720 ILCS 405/5-805(1)(a).

82. 720 ILCS 405/5-805(1)(b).

☞ *Definition:* "Organized gang" is defined as any combination, confederation, alliance, network, conspiracy, understanding, or other similar conjoining in law or in fact, of three or more persons with an established hierarchy that, through its membership or through the agency of any member, engages in a course or pattern of criminal activity.[84]

If a petition alleges that a minor 15 years of age or older committed an act constituting any of the following crimes, the States's attorney may move to permit prosecution of the minor as an adult under the criminal laws:[85]

- a Class X felony other than armed violence;
- aggravated discharge of a firearm;
- armed violence with a firearm when the predicate offense is a Class 1 or Class 2 felony and the State's Attorney's motion to transfer the case alleges that the offense committed is in furtherance of the criminal activities of an organized gang;
- armed violence with a firearm when the predicate offense is a violation of the Illinois Controlled Substances Act[86] or a violation of the Cannabis Control Act;[87]
- armed violence when the weapon involved was a machine gun, sawed-off shotgun, bomb, grenade, molotov cocktail or other artillery projectile.[88]

If the juvenile court judge determines there is probable cause to believe that the allegations in the petition and motion are true,

---

83. People v Schott, 145 Ill 2d 188, 164 Ill Dec 127, 582 NE2d 690 (1991).

84. 740 ILCS 147/10.

85. 720 ILCS 405/5-805(2)(a).

86. 720 ILCS 570/100 et seq.

   See § 56:08 et seq.

87. 720 ILCS 550/1 et seq.

   See § 56:01 et seq.

88. See 720 ILCS 5/24-1(a)(7).

DELINQUENT MINORS § 35:06

there is a rebuttable presumption that the minor is not a fit and proper subject to be dealt with in juvenile court and that the case should be transferred to the criminal court.[89] The presumption may be rebutted if the court finds the minor would be amenable to the care, treatment, and training programs, based on the following criteria:[90]

- the seriousness of the alleged offense;
- whether there is evidence that the alleged offense was committed in an aggressive and premeditated manner;
- the minor's age;
- the minor's history of delinquency;
- the culpability of the minor in committing the alleged offense;
- the minor's history of services, including the minor's willingness to participate meaningfully in available services;
- whether there are facilities particularly available to the Juvenile Court for the minor's treatment and rehabilitation;
- whether there is a reasonable likelihood that the minor can be rehabilitated before the expiration of the juvenile court's jurisdiction;
- whether the minor used or possessed a deadly weapon when he or she allegedly committed the offense.
- the adequacy of the punishment or services available in the juvenile justice system.whether the minor committed a drug offense.

In considering the above factors, the court must give greater weight to the seriousness of the alleged offense and the minor's prior record of delinquency than to the other factors.[91]

89. 720 ILCS 405/5-805(2)(b).

90. 720 ILCS 405/5-805(2)(b).

Annotation References: Possibility of rehabilitation as affecting whether juvenile offender should be tried as adult, 22 ALR4th 1162.

Forms: Petition to transfer from juvenile court. 15 Am Jur Pl & Pr Forms (Rev), Juvenile Courts and Delinquent and Dependent Children, Form 32.

If the minor committed any of the crimes for which the presumption of transfer to a criminal court applies and the State's attorney alleges in a petition that the minor has previously been adjudicated delinquent or found guilty of a forcible felony, transfer becomes mandatory.[92]

If a petition alleges commission by a minor 13 years of age or over of a crime under Illinois law and, on motion of the State's Attorney to permit prosecution of the minor under the criminal laws, a Juvenile Court Judge, after hearing but before commencement of the trial, finds that there is probable cause to believe that the allegations in the motion are true and that it is not in the best interests of the public to proceed under the Juvenile Justice Reform Act, the court may enter an order permitting prosecution under the criminal laws.[93] In making its determination on the motion to permit prosecution under the criminal laws, the court must consider the same factors as described above with respect to presumptive transfers and give greater weight to the seriousness of the alleged offense and the minor's prior record of delinquency than to the other factors.[94]

The rules of evidence relevant to the court's determination are the same as those applicable to a juvenile dispositional hearing,[95] and no hearing on a motion to permit prosecution under the criminal laws may commence unless the minor is represented in court by counsel.[96] If criminal proceedings are instituted, the petition is dismissed with regard to the acts involved in the criminal action.[97] The taking of evidence in an adjudicatory hearing in such a case bars subsequent criminal proceedings based on the conduct alleged in the petition.[98]

---

91. 720 ILCS 405/5-805(2)(b).
92. 720 ILCS 405/5-805(1)(c).
93. 720 ILCS 405/5-805(3)(a).
94. 720 ILCS 405/5-805(3)(b).
95. 705 ILCS 405/5-805(4).
96. 705 ILCS 405/5-805(4).
97. 705 ILCS 405/5-805(5).

§ 35:06

The purpose of any transfer hearing is to balance the best interests of the alleged juvenile offender, particularly as these interests relate to his or her potential for rehabilitation, against society's legitimate interest in being protected from criminal victimization perpetrated by minors.[99]

Where the minor's liberty is at issue, the juvenile adjudication proceeding is more closely analogous to a criminal proceeding.[1] The transfer hearing is not adjudicatory in nature; the state need only present sufficient evidence to persuade the court that a transfer is warranted.[2] States are not barred from requiring substantial evidence that a minor committed an offense as a prerequisite to transfer to the criminal courts as long as the showing is in a nonadjudicatory proceeding.[3] The court's decision is within its sound discretion, and will not be disturbed so long as each of the requisite factors have been considered.[4] The decision will be reversed only for abuse of discretion.[5]

A minor does not lose the protection of the Act until such time as he is charged with one of the offenses subjecting him or her to transfer.[6]

---

98. 705 ILCS 405/5-805(5).

99. People v Fuller, 292 Ill App 3d 651, 226 Ill Dec 657, 686 NE2d 6 (1st Dist 1997).

1. People v R.G. (In re R.G.), 283 Ill App 3d 183, 218 Ill Dec 699, 669 NE2d 1225 (2d Dist 1996).

2. People v R.T. (In the Interest of R.T.), 271 Ill App 3d 673, 208 Ill Dec 121, 648 NE2d 1043 (1st Dist 1995).

3. Breed v Jones, 421 US 519, 44 L Ed 2d 346, 95 S Ct 1779 (1975), on remand 519 F2d 1314 (CA9 Cal).

4. People v Cooks, 271 Ill App 3d 25, 207 Ill Dec 734, 648 NE2d 190 (1st Dist 1995); People v D.B., 202 Ill App 3d 194, 147 Ill Dec 533, 559 NE2d 873 (1st Dist 1990).

See People v Taylor, 76 Ill 2d 289, 29 Ill Dec 103, 391 NE2d 366 (1979).

5. People v Fuller, 292 Ill App 3d 651, 226 Ill Dec 657, 686 NE2d 6 (1st Dist 1997); People v J.O. (In re J.O.), 269 Ill App 3d 287, 206 Ill Dec 783, 645 NE2d 1035 (1st Dist 1995).

► *Practice Guide:* A determination of probable cause is nonfinal in nature, and thus cannot bind a judge in a subsequent transfer proceeding.[7]

§ 35:07. —Minors prosecuted under criminal law

A delinquent minor is defined as any minor who, prior to his or her seventeenth birthday, has violated or attempted to violate any federal or state law, or any municipal ordinance, regardless of where the act occurred.[8] This definition does not, however, apply to a minor who is at least fifteen years old at the time he or she is charged with any of the following offenses:[9]

- first degree murder;
- aggravated criminal sexual assault;
- aggravated vehicular highjacking with a firearm;
- armed robbery committed with a firearm;
- the unlawful use of weapons while in school or on the real property comprising any school, regardless of the time of day or the time of year;[10]

---

6. People v Pico, 287 Ill App 3d 607, 222 Ill Dec 908, 678 NE2d 780 (1st Dist 1997).

7. People v W.J. (In re W.J.), 284 Ill App 3d 203, 219 Ill Dec 925, 672 NE2d 778 (1st Dist 1996).

8. 705 ILCS 405/5-105(3).

Annotation References: Duress, necessity, or conditions of confinement as justification for escape from prison. 54 ALR5th 141.
Sufficiency of random sampling of drug or contraband to establish jurisdictional amount required for conviction. 45 ALR5th 1.
Validity, construction, and application of juvenile escape statutes. 46 ALR5th 523.
Statute protecting minors in a specified age range from rape or other sexual activity as applicable to defendant minor within protected age group, 18 ALR5th 856.

Periodicals: For article, "Survey of Illinois Law: Criminal Law and Procedure," see 21 S. Ill. U.L.J. 759 (1997).

9. 705 ILCS 405/5-130(1)(a), (2)(a), (3)(a), (5)(a).

- the unauthorized manufacture or delivery of controlled substances while in or within 1,000 feet of a school or public housing property, or on any school-related conveyance, regardless of the time of day or year;[11] or

- escape or violation of bail bond.[12]

If before trial or plea an information or indictment is filed that does not charge any of the above-described offenses, the state's attorney may proceed on the lesser charge or charges, but only in juvenile court, unless before trial the minor defendant knowingly and with advice of counsel waives, in writing, his or her right to have the matter proceed in juvenile court.[13] If before trial or plea an information or indictment is filed that includes any of those charges, all of the charges arising out of the same incident must be prosecuted under the criminal code.[14] If after trial or plea the minor is convicted of first degree murder, aggravated criminal sexual assault, armed robbery committed with a firearm, or aggravated vehicular hijacking committed with a firearm, the court will have available any or all dispositions prescribed for that offense under Chapter V of the Unified Code of Corrections.[15] If the minor is convicted of a lesser or different charge, the conviction will not invalidate the verdict or the prosecution of the minor under the criminal laws of the state; however, unless the state requests a hearing for the purpose of sentencing the minor under Chapter V of the Unified Code of Corrections, the Court must proceed under the Juvenile Court Act.[16] Should the state

---

10. See 720 ILCS 5/24-1(a)(1), (4), (10).

11. See 720 ILCS 570/401.

People v. Rodriguez, 276 Ill App 3d 33, 212 Ill Dec 498, 657 NE2d 699 (2d Dist 1995).

12. 720 ILCS 5/31-6, 5/32-10.

13. 705 ILCS 405/5-130(1)(b)(i), (2)(b)(i), 3(b)(i), 5(b)(i).

14. 705 ILCS 405/5-130(1)(b)(ii), (2)(b)(ii), 3(b)(ii), 5(b)(ii).

15. 705 ILCS 405/5-130(1)(c)(i), (2)(c)(i), 3(c)(i), 5(c)(i).

16. 705 ILCS 405/5-130(1)(c)(ii), (2)(c)(ii), 3(c)(ii), 5(c)(ii).

§ 35:07   ILLINOIS JURISPRUDENCE: CRIMINAL LAW

request a hearing, it must do so by written motion within 10 days following the entry of a finding or the return of a verdict.[17] Reasonable notice of the motion must be served on the minor or his or her counsel.[18] If the state makes the motion, the court must conduct a hearing to determine if the request should be granted and in making its determination on the motion, the court must consider, among other matters:

- whether there is evidence that the offense was committed in an aggressive and premeditated manner;
- the age of the minor;
- the previous history of the minor;
- whether there are facilities particularly available to the Juvenile Court or the Department of Corrections, Juvenile Division, for the treatment and rehabilitation of the minor;
- whether the best interest of the minor and the security of the public require sentencing under Chapter V of the Unified Code of Corrections; and
- whether the minor possessed a deadly weapon when committing the offense.[19]

The rules of evidence will be the same as if at trial.[20] If after the hearing the court finds that the minor should be sentenced under Chapter V of the Unified Code of Corrections, then the court must sentence the minor accordingly, having available to it any or all dispositions so prescribed.[21]

Further, the definition of delinquent minor does not apply to any minor who at the time of an offense was at least 13 years of

See 705 ILCS 405/5-705, 5-710.

17. 705 ILCS 405/5-130(1)(c)(ii), (2)(c)(ii), 3(c)(ii), 5(c)(ii).
18. 705 ILCS 405/5-130(1)(c)(ii), (2)(c)(ii), 3(c)(ii), 5(c)(ii).
19. 705 ILCS 405/5-130(1)(c)(ii)(a)–(f), (2)(c)(ii)(a)–(f), 3(c)(ii)(a)–(f), 5(c)(ii)(a)–(f).
20. 705 ILCS 405/5-130(1)(c)(ii), (2)(c)(ii), 3(c)(ii), 5(c)(ii).
21. 705 ILCS 405/5-130(1)(c)(ii), (2)(c)(ii), 3(c)(ii), 5(c)(ii).

age and who is charged with first degree murder committed during the course of either aggravated criminal sexual assault, criminal sexual assault, or aggravated kidnapping.[22]

If before trial or plea an information or indictment is filed that does not charge first degree murder committed during the course of aggravated criminal sexual assault, criminal sexual assault, or aggravated kidnaping, the State's Attorney may proceed on any lesser charge or charges, but only in Juvenile Court.[23] The State's Attorney may proceed under the criminal laws on a lesser charge if before trial the minor defendant knowingly and with advice of counsel waives, in writing, his or her right to have the matter proceed in Juvenile Court.[24] If the information or indictment includes any of those charges, all of the charges arising out of the same incident must be prosecuted under the criminal code.[25]

If after trial or plea the minor is convicted of first degree murder committed during the course of aggravated criminal sexual assault, criminal sexual assault, or aggravated kidnaping, in sentencing the minor, the court will have available any or all dispositions prescribed for that offense under Chapter V of the Unified Code of Corrections.[26]

If the minor was not yet 15 years of age at the time of the offense and if after trial or plea the minor is convicted of an offense other than first degree murder committed during the course of either aggravated criminal sexual assault, criminal sexual assault, or aggravated kidnapping, the finding will not invalidate the verdict or the prosecution of the minor under the criminal laws.[27] The court must proceed under Sections 705 and 710 of the Juvenile Court Act, unless the State's Attorney makes a motion for a hearing as described earlier in this section.[28]

22. 705 ILCS 405/5-130(4)(a).
23. 705 ILCS 405/5-130(4)(b)(i).
24. 705 ILCS 405/5-130(4)(b)(i).
25. 705 ILCS 405/5-130(4)(b)(ii).
26. 705 ILCS 405/5-130(4)(c)(i).
27. 705 ILCS 405/5-130(4)(c)(ii).

§ 35:07   ILLINOIS JURISPRUDENCE: CRIMINAL LAW

The definition of delinquent minor does not apply to any minor who has previously been placed under the jurisdiction of the criminal court and has been convicted of a crime under an adult criminal or penal statute.[29]

The Illinois statutory provisions that require mandatory trial as an adult for certain offenses have been found not to violate equal protection.[30] For example, requiring that 15- and 16-year-old minors charged with drug offenses committed on or near public housing be tried as adults does not deny equal protection, since the classification at issue is based on the location of the charged offense, which is a permissible distinction in view of the statute's purpose to deter narcotics activity in public housing.[31]

§ 35:08. —Evidence

Evidence and adjudications in proceedings under the Juvenile Court Act are admissible as follows:

- in subsequent Juvenile Court Act proceedings concerning the same minor; or
- in criminal proceedings when the court is to determine the amount of bail, fitness of the defendant or in sentencing under the Unified Code of Corrections;[32] or
- in Juvenile Court Act or criminal proceedings in which anyone who has been adjudicated delinquent[33] is to be a

---

28. 705 ILCS 405/5-130(4)(c)(ii).

See 705 ILCS 405/5-705, 5-710.

29. 705 ILCS 405/5-130(6).

See 705 ILCS 405/5-805, 5-810.

30. People v M.A., 124 Ill 2d 135, 124 Ill Dec 511, 529 NE2d 492 (1988); People v J.S., 103 Ill 2d 395, 83 Ill Dec 156, 469 NE2d 1090 (1984); People v Beasley, 206 Ill App 3d 112, 151 Ill Dec 7, 563 NE2d 1113 (1st Dist 1990).

31. People v R.L., 158 Ill 2d 432, 199 Ill Dec 680, 634 NE2d 733 (1994), cert den 513 US 918, 130 L Ed 2d 210, 115 S Ct 296.

32. See 730 ILCS 5/1-1-1 et seq.

33. See 705 ILCS 405/5-105.

DELINQUENT MINORS § 35:10

witness including the minor or defendant if he or she testifies, and then only for purposes of impeachment and pursuant to the rules of evidence for criminal trials; or

- in civil proceedings concerning claims arising out of incidents which initially gave rise to the delinquency proceedings.[34]

§ 35:09. —Weapons

Any weapon in the possession of a minor found to be delinquent for an offense involving the use or possession of an weapon is confiscated and disposed of by the juvenile court, regardless of whether it is the minor's property or that of his or her parent or guardian.[35]

§ 35:10. Arresting or taking minor into custody

Under Illinois law, A law enforcement officer may, without a warrant:

- arrest a minor whom the officer with probable cause believes to be a delinquent minor; or
- take into custody a minor who has been adjudged a ward of the court and has escaped from any commitment ordered by the court under this Act; or
- take into custody a minor whom the officer reasonably believes has violated the conditions of probation or supervision ordered by the court[36]

Whenever a petition has been filed under Section 5-520[37] and

---

34. 705 ILCS 405/5-150(1).

Annotation References: Availability of discovery at probation revocation hearings. 52 ALR5th 559.

35. 705 ILCS 405/5-155.

See 720 ILCS 5/24-6.

36. 705 ILCS 405/5-401(1).

Forms: Warrants for apprehension of juvenile delinquent. 15 Am Jur Pl & Pr Forms (Rev), Juvenile Courts and Delinquent and Dependent Children, Forms 3–5.

37. 705 ILCS 405/5-520.

§ 35:10 ILLINOIS JURISPRUDENCE: CRIMINAL LAW

the court finds that the conduct and behavior of the minor may endanger the health, person, welfare, or property of the minor or others or that the circumstances of the minor's home environment may endanger his or her health, person, welfare or property, a warrant may be issued immediately to take the minor into custody.[38]

Except for minors accused of violation of an order of the court, any minor accused of any act under federal or State law, or a municipal or county ordinance that would not be illegal if committed by an adult, cannot be placed in a jail, municipal lockup, detention center, or secure correctional facility.[39] Juveniles accused with underage consumption and underage possession of alcohol cannot be placed in a jail, municipal lockup, detention center, or correctional facility.[40]

A minor being held in custody does not lose the protection of the Act until such time as he or she is charged with one of the offenses that subjects a minor to prosecution under criminal law rather than the Act.[41]

§ 35:11. Officers' duties

When a law enforcement officer takes a minor into custody, with or without a warrant, he or she must immediately make a reasonable attempt to contact the minor's parent or other person responsible for the minor's care or with whom the minor resides, and notify them that (1) the minor has been taken into custody and (2) the place where the minor is being held.[42] The minor must

---

See § 35:22.

38. 705 ILCS 405/5-401(2).

39. 705 ILCS 405/5-401(3).

40. 705 ILCS 405/5-401(3).

41. People v Pico, 287 Ill App 3d 607, 222 Ill Dec 908, 678 NE2d 780 (1st Dist 1997).

See § 35:07.

42. 705 ILCS 405/5-405(1), (2).

Periodicals: For article, "Recent Developments in Nontraditional

DELINQUENT MINORS § 35:11

be taken, without unnecessary delay, to the court or the place designated by the court for the reception of minors.[43]

A law enforcement officer who arrests a minor without a warrant must, if the minor is not released, immediately make a reasonable attempt to notify the parent or other person legally responsible for the minor's care, or the person with whom the minor resides (1) that the minor has been arrested and (2) where the minor is being held.[44] The law enforcement officer must, without unnecessary delay, take the minor to the nearest juvenile police officer designated for these purposes in the county of venue or must surrender the minor to a juvenile police officer in the city or village where the offense is alleged to have been committed.[45] If a minor is taken into custody for an offense which would be a misdemeanor if committed by an adult, the law enforcement officer, upon determining the minor's identity, may release the minor to the parent or other person legally responsible for the minor's care or the person with whom the minor resides.[46] If a minor is so released, the law enforcement officer must promptly notify a juvenile police officer of the circumstances of the custody and release.[47]

> ☛ *Practice Guide:* A minor being held in custody does not lose the protection of the Act until such time as he or she is charged with one of the offenses that subjects a minor to prosecution under criminal law rather than the Act.[48] Thus,

Alternatives in Juvenile Justice," see 28 Loy. U. Chi. L.J. 719 (1997).

Forms: Notice to parent of apprehension of child. 15 Am Jur Pl & Pr Forms (Rev), Juvenile Courts and Delinquent and Dependent Children, Form 1.

43. 705 ILCS 405/5-405(1).
44. 705 ILCS 405/5-405(2).
45. 705 ILCS 405/5-405(2).
46. 705 ILCS 405/5-405(2).
47. 705 ILCS 405/5-405(2).
48. People v Pico, 287 Ill App 3d 607, 222 Ill Dec 908, 678 NE2d 780 (1st Dist 1997).

§ 35:11   ILLINOIS JURISPRUDENCE: CRIMINAL LAW

the police must attempt to notify a defendant's parents or other adult guardian if he or she is to be questioned prior to being charged with such an offense.[49] However, a violation of the statute will not necessarily result in suppression of a confession; in one case the court refused to suppress the confession where at the time of the confession a youth officer was present, there was no allegation of coercion, abuse, or other circumstance to undermine the voluntary nature of defendant's statement.[50]

Upon receiving custody of the minor, the juvenile police officer may take one of the following actions:[51]

- station adjustment and release of the minor;[52]
- release the minor to his or her parents and refer the case to Juvenile Court;
- if the juvenile police officer reasonably believes that there is an urgent and immediate necessity to keep the minor in custody, the juvenile police officer must deliver the minor without unnecessary delay to the court or to the place designated by rule or order of court for the reception of minors;
- any other appropriate action with consent of the minor or a parent.

In determining whether to release a minor or to keep him or her in custody, the following factors are to be considered:

- the nature of the allegations against the minor;
- the minor's history and present situation;

See § 35:07.

49. People v Pico, 287 Ill App 3d 607, 222 Ill Dec 908, 678 NE2d 780 (1st Dist 1997).

50. People v Pico, 287 Ill App 3d 607, 222 Ill Dec 908, 678 NE2d 780 (1st Dist 1997).

51. See generally 705 ILCS 405/5-405(3).

52. See § 35:12.

- the history of the minor's family and the family's present situation;
- the educational and employment status of the minor;
- the availability of special resources or community services to aid or counsel the minor;
- the minor's past involvement with and progress in social programs;
- the attitude of the complainant and the community toward the minor; and
- the present attitude of the minor and his or her family.[53]

The records of law enforcement officers concerning all minors who are taken into custody are to be maintained separately from the general arrest records, and may not be inspected by or disclosed to the public except by court order.[54]

§ 35:12. —Station adjustment

The juvenile police officer, after receiving custody of the minor, may take an action known as a "station adjustment."[55] Station adjustment is defined as the informal handling of an alleged offender by a juvenile police officer.[56] A station adjustment occurs when the police take a minor into custody but releases him or her after deciding not to prosecute.[57] Although station adjustments are probative and relevent to transfer proceedings,[58] they in fact constitute only a verbal warning from the police.[59]

53. 705 ILCS 405/5-405(4).

54. 705 ILCS 405/5-405(5).

55. 705 ILCS 405/5-301.

   Periodicals: For article, "Recent Developments in Nontraditional Alternatives in Juvenile Justice," see 28 Loy. U. Chi. L.J. 719 (1997).

56. 705 ILCS 405/1-3(15).

57. People v M.D., 101 Ill 2d 73, 77 Ill Dec 744, 461 NE2d 367 (1984); People v D.B., 202 Ill App 3d 194, 147 Ill Dec 533, 559 NE2d 873 (1st Dist 1990).

58. See § 35:06.

§ 35:12   ILLINOIS JURISPRUDENCE: CRIMINAL LAW

In deciding whether to impose a station adjustment, either informal or formal, a juvenile police officer must consider the following factors:

- the seriousness of the alleged offense;
- prior history of delinquency of the minor;
- age of the minor;
- the culpability of the minor in committing the alleged offense;
- whether the offense was committed in an aggressive or premeditated manner; and
- whether the minor used or possessed a deadly weapon when committing the alleged offense.[60]

An informal station adjustment is a procedure by which a juvenile police officer determines that there is probable cause to believe that the minor has committed an offense.[61] A minor may receive no more than three informal station adjustments statewide for a misdemeanor offense or three for a felony within three years without prior approval from the State's Attorney's Office.[62] A minor may receive a combined total of no more than five informal station adjustments statewide during his or her minority.[63]

The juvenile police officer may impose reasonable conditions of an informal station adjustment which may include but are not limited to the following:

- curfew;

---

59. People v Clark, 119 Ill 2d 1, 115 Ill Dec 613, 518 NE2d 138 (1987), cert den 497 US 1026, 111 L Ed 2d 786, 110 S Ct 3276; People v M.D., 101 Ill 2d 73, 77 Ill Dec 744, 461 NE2d 367 (1984); People v D.B., 202 Ill App 3d 194, 147 Ill Dec 533, 559 NE2d 873 (1st Dist 1990); People v Newell, 135 Ill App 3d 417, 90 Ill Dec 327, 481 NE2d 1238 (1st Dist 1985).

60. 705 ILCS 405/5-301(A)–(F).

61. 705 ILCS 405/5-301(1)(a).

62. 705 ILCS 405/5-301(1)(b), (c).

63. 705 ILCS 405/5-301(1)(d).

DELINQUENT MINORS § 35:12

- conditions restricting entry into designated geographical areas;
- no contact with specified persons;
- school attendance;
- performing up to 25 hours of community service work;
- community mediation;
- teen court or a peer courts; or
- restitution limited to 90 days.[64]

If the minor refuses or fails to abide by the conditions of an informal station adjustment, the juvenile police officer may impose a formal station adjustment or refer the matter to the State's Attorney's Office.[65]

A formal station adjustment is a procedure by which a juvenile police officer determines that there is probable cause to believe the minor has committed an offense and an admission by the minor of involvement in the offense.[66] The minor and parent, guardian, or legal custodian must agree in writing to the formal station adjustment and must be advised of the consequences of violation of any term of the agreement.[67] The minor and parent, guardian or legal custodian must be provided a copy of the signed agreement of the formal station adjustment,[68] which must include the following:

- the offense which formed the basis of the formal station adjustment;
- acknowledgment that the terms of the formal station adjustment and the consequences for violation have been explained;

---

64. 705 ILCS 405/5-301(1)(e)(i)–(viii).
65. 705 ILCS 405/5-301(1)(f).
66. 705 ILCS 405/5-301(2)(a).
67. 705 ILCS 405/5-301(2)(b).
68. 705 ILCS 405/5-301(2)(c).

§ 35:12 ILLINOIS JURISPRUDENCE: CRIMINAL LAW

- acknowledgment that the formal station adjustments record may be expunged;[69]
- acknowledgement that the minor understands that his or her admission of involvement in the offense may be admitted into evidence in future court hearings; and
- a statement that all parties understand the terms and conditions of formal station adjustment and agree to the formal station adjustment processperforming up to 25 hours of community service work.[70]

Conditions of the formal station adjustment may include, but are not be limited to:

- the time may not exceed 120 days;
- the minor may not violate any laws;
- the juvenile police officer may require the minor to comply with additional conditions for the formal station adjustment which may include but are not limited to: attending school, abiding by a set curfew, payment of restitution, refraining from possessing a firearm or other weapon, reporting to a police officer at designated times and places, performing up to 25 hours of community service work, avoiding designated geographical areas, participating in community mediation, participating in teen court or peer court, and avoiding contact with specified persons.[71]

A formal station adjustment does not constitute an adjudication of delinquency or a criminal conviction.[72] A minor or the minor's parent, guardian, or legal custodian, or both the minor and his or her parent, guardian, or legal custodian, may refuse a formal station adjustment and have the matter referred for court action or other appropriate action.[73] If they initially consented to

69. See705 ILCS 405/5-915.

See35:04.

70. 705 ILCS 405/5-301(2)(c)(i)–(v).
71. 705 ILCS 405/5-301(2)(d)(i)–(iii).
72. 705 ILCS 405/5-301(2)(e).

formal station adjustment, they may within 30 days of the commencement of the formal station adjustment revoke their consent and have the matter referred for court action or other appropriate action.[74] This revocation must be written and personally served on the police officer or his or her supervisor.[75]

The minor's admission of involvement in the offense is admissible at further court hearings if the statement would be admissible under the rules of evidence.[76]

If the minor violates any term or condition of the formal station adjustment the juvenile police officer must provide written notice of violation to the minor and the minor's parent, guardian, or legal custodian.[77] After consultation with the minor and the minor's parent, guardian, or legal custodian, the juvenile police officer may take any of the following steps upon violation:

- warn the minor of consequences of continued violations and continue the formal station adjustment;
- extend the period of the formal station adjustment up to 180 days;
- extend the hours of community service work up to a total of 40 hours;
- terminate the formal station adjustment unsatisfactorily and take no other action; or
- terminate the formal station adjustment unsatisfactorily and refer the matter to the juvenile court.[78]

A minor may receive no more than two formal station adjustments statewide for a felony offense or three formal station adjustments statewide for a misdemeanor offense without the

---

73. 705 ILCS 405/5-301(2)(f).
74. 705 ILCS 405/5-301(2)(g).
75. 705 ILCS 405/5-301(2)(g).
76. 705 ILCS 405/5-301(2)(h).
77. 705 ILCS 405/5-301(2)(i).
78. 705 ILCS 405/5-301(2)(i).

§ 35:12   ILLINOIS JURISPRUDENCE: CRIMINAL LAW

State's Attorney's approval within a three-year period.[79] The total for formal station adjustments statewide within the period of minority may not exceed four without the State's Attorney's approval.[80]

If the minor is arrested in a jurisdiction where he or she does not reside, the formal station adjustment may be transferred to the jurisdiction of residence on written agreement of that jurisdiction to monitor the formal station adjustment.[81]

The total number of station adjustments, both formal and informal, may not exceed nine without the State's Attorney's approval for any minor arrested anywhere in Illinois.[82]

§ 35:13. —Probation adjustment

The court may authorize a probation officer to confer in a preliminary conference with a minor alleged to have committed an offense, his or her parent, guardian or legal custodian, the victim, the juvenile police officer, the State's Attorney, and other interested persons concerning the advisability of filing a petition praying that the minor be adjudged a ward of the court[83] and given a probation adjustment.[84] The probation officer should schedule a conference promptly except when the State's Attorney insists on court action or when the minor has indicated that he or she will demand a judicial hearing and will not comply with a probation adjustment.[85] No statement made during a preliminary conference concerning the offense that is the subject of the conference may be admitted into evidence at an adjudicatory

---

79. 705 ILCS 405/5-301(2)(j), (k).

80. 705 ILCS 405/5-301(2)(l).

81. 705 ILCS 405/5-301(2)(m).

82. 705 ILCS 405/5-301(2)(o).

83. 705 ILCS 405/5-520.

  Periodicals: For article, "Recent Developments in Nontraditional Alternatives in Juvenile Justice," see 28 Loy. U. Chi. L.J. 719 (1997).

84. 705 ILCS 405/5-305(1).

85. 705 ILCS 405/5-305(1).

hearing or at any criminal proceeding against the minor prior to his or her conviction.[86]

When a probation adjustment is appropriate, the probation officer must promptly formulate a written, non-judicial adjustment plan following the initial conference.[87] Non-judicial probation adjustment plans include but are not limited to the following:

- up to six months informal supervision within the family;
- up to 12 months informal supervision with a probation officer involved;
- up to six months informal supervision with release to a person other than a parent;
- referral to special educational, counseling, or other rehabilitative social or educational programs;
- referral to residential treatment programs;
- participation in a public or community service program or activity;
- any other appropriate action with the consent of the minor and a parent.[88]

In determining whether probation adjustment is appropriate, the officer must consider the same factors as in determining whether to release or keep a minor in cusbtody.[89]

§ 35:14. —Duty of officer upon arrest of juvenile

A law enforcement officer who arrests a minor with a warrant must immediately make a reasonable attempt to notify the parent or other person legally responsible for the minor's care or the person with whom the minor resides that the minor has been

---

86. 705 ILCS 405/5-305(3).
87. 705 ILCS 405/5-305(4).
88. 705 ILCS 405/5-305(5)(a)-(g).
89. 705 ILCS 405/5-305(6), 705 ILCS 405/5-420(4).
   See § 35:11.

§ 35:14 ILLINOIS JURISPRUDENCE: CRIMINAL LAW

arrested and where he or she is being held.[90] The minor must be delivered without unnecessary delay to the court or to the place designated for the reception of minors.[91]

A law enforcement officer who arrests a minor without a warrant under must, if the minor is not released, immediately make a reasonable attempt to notify the parent or other person legally responsible for the minor's care or the person with whom the minor resides that the minor has been arrested and where the minor is being held.[92] The officer mustl without unnecessary delay take the minor to the nearest juvenile police officer designated in the county of venue or must surrender the minor to a juvenile police officer in the city or village where the offense is alleged to have been committed.[93] If a minor is taken into custody for an offense which would be a misdemeanor if committed by an adult, the law enforcement officer, after determining the true identity of the minor, may release the minor to the parent or other person legally responsible for the minor's care or the person with whom the minor resides.[94] If a minor is so released, the law enforcement officer mustl promptly notify a juvenile police officer of the circumstances of the custody and release.[95]

The juvenile police officer may take one of the following actions:

- station adjustment and release of the minor;

---

90. 705 ILCS 405/5-405(1).

Annotation References: Right of bail in proceedings in juvenile courts, 53 ALR3d 848.

Practice References: Obtaining release of juvenile. 14 Am Jur Trials 619, Juvenile Court Proceedings §§ 47–49.

Forms: Petitions, detention of juvenile. 15 Am Jur Pl & Pr Forms (Rev), Juvenile Courts and Delinquent and Dependent Children, Forms 6–11.

91. 705 ILCS 405/5-405(1).

92. 705 ILCS 405/5-405(2).

93. 705 ILCS 405/5-405(2).

94. 705 ILCS 405/5-405(2).

95. 705 ILCS 405/5-405(2).

- release the minor to his or her parents and refer the case to Juvenile Court;
- if the juvenile police officer reasonably believes that there is an urgent and immediate necessity to keep the minor in custody, delivery of the minor without unnecessary delay to the court or to the place designated for the reception of minors; or
- any other appropriate action with consent of the minor or a parent.[96]

The factors to be considered in determining whether to release or keep a minor in custody shall include:

- the nature of the allegations against the minor;
- the minor's history and present situation;
- the history of the minor's family and the family's present situation; or
- the educational and employment status of the minor;
- the availability of special resource or community services to aid or counsel the minor;
- the minor's past involvement with and progress in social programs;
- the attitude of complainant and community toward the minor; and
- the present attitude of the minor and family.[97]

§ 35:15. —Shelter care

Any minor who is taken into temporary custody, and who requires care away from his or her home, but not physical restriction, is provided temporary care in a foster family home or other shelter facility designated by the court.[98] "Shelter" is defined

---

96. 705 ILCS 405/5-405(3).
97. 705 ILCS 405/5-405(4).
98. 705 ILCS 405/5-410(1).

Periodicals: For article, "Recent Developments in Nontraditional

§ 35:15   ILLINOIS JURISPRUDENCE: CRIMINAL LAW

as the temporary care of a minor in physically unrestricting facilities pending disposition or placement by the court.[99]

§ 35:16. —Detention

A minor ten years of age or older who is taken into temporary custody may be kept or detained in an authorized detention facility if there is reasonable cause to believe the minor to be delinquent and:

- secured custody is a matter of immediate and urgent necessity for the protection of the minor or the person or property of another;
- the minor is likely to flee the jurisdiction of the court; or
- the minor was taken into custody under a warrant.[1]

No minor under 12 years of age may be detained in a county jail or a municipal lockup for more than six hours.[2]

"Detention" means the temporary care of a minor alleged to be or adjudicated as a delinquent, who requires secure custody for his or her own protection, or for the protection of the community in a physically restrictive facility pending disposition by the court or the execution of a court order for placement or commitment.[3] Means of detention may include locked rooms or the secure handcuffing of the minor to a rail or other stationary object.[4]

The written authorization of the probation officer or other designated public officer (in counties with populations of 3 million or more) constitutes authority for the superintendent of any juvenile detention home to detain and keep a minor for up to 40 hours, excluding weekends and holidays.[5]

Alternatives in Juvenile Justice," see 28 Loy. U. Chi. L.J. 719 (1997).

99. 705 ILCS 405/5-105(14).

1. 705 ILCS 405/5-410(2)(a).

2. 705 ILCS 405/5-410(2)(a).

3. 705 ILCS 405/5-105(5).

4. 705 ILCS 405/5-105(5).

A probation officer or detention officer (or other public officer designated by the court in a county having 3,000,000 or more inhabitants) who does not intend to detain a minor for one of the following offenses must consult with the State's Attorney's Office prior to the release of the minor: first degree murder, second degree murder, involuntary manslaughter, criminal sexual assault, aggravated criminal sexual assault, aggravated battery with a firearm, aggravated or heinous battery involving permanent disability or disfigurement or great bodily harm, robbery, aggravated robbery, armed robbery, vehicular hijacking, aggravated vehicular hijacking, vehicular invasion, arson, aggravated arson, kidnapping, aggravated kidnapping, home invasion, burglary, or residential burglary.[6] The consultation requirement is not applicable if the probation officer or detention officer (or other public officer designated by the court in a county having 3,000,000 or more inhabitants) uses a scorable detention screening instrument developed with input by the State's Attorney to determine whether a minor should be detained.[7] It is applicable, however, where no such screening instrument is used or where the probation officer, detention officer (or other public officer designated by the court in a county having 3,000,000 or more inhabitants) deviates from the screening instrument.[8]

§ 35:17. —Confinement

As a general rule, no minor may be detained in a county jail or municipal lockup for more than 12 hours, unless the offense is a crime of violence in which case the minor may be detained up to 24 hours.[9]

> *Definition:* "Crime of violence" means any of the following crimes: murder, voluntary manslaughter, criminal

---

5. 705 ILCS 405/5-410(2)(b).
6. 705 ILCS 405/5-410(2)(b-5).
7. 705 ILCS 405/5-410(2)(b-4).
8. 705 ILCS 405/5-410(2)(b-4).
9. 705 ILCS 405/5-410(2)(c).

sexual assault, aggravated criminal sexual assault, predatory criminal sexual assault of a child, armed robbery, robbery, arson, kidnapping, aggravated battery, aggravated arson, or any other felony which involves the use or threat of physical force or violence against another individual.[10]

Violation of this principle, however, will not in itself render any evidence obtained as a result of the extended confinement inadmissible.[11] The period of detention is exclusive of any time spent transporting the minor in custody, and begins when he or she is placed in a locked room or cell or handcuffed to a stationary object in a county jail or municipal lockup.[12] Confined minors may not be permitted to come into or remain in contact with adults who are in custody in the same building.[13] Minors under 17 must be kept in separate confinement from adults, and may not at any time be kept in the same cell, room, or yard with adults confined pursuant to criminal law.[14] Any minor confined in a county jail or municipal lockup must be under periodic supervision.[15]

Upon being placed in confinement, the minor must be informed of the purpose of the detention, its probable duration, and the fact that it may not exceed 12 hours.[16] A log must be kept which shows:

- the offense upon which the detention is based;
- the reasons and circumstances underlying the decision to confine the minor; and
- the length of time the minor was actually held in detention.[17]

---

10. 20 ILCS 301/1-10; 705 ILCS 405/5-410(2)(c).
11. 705 ILCS 405/5-410(2)(c)(i).
12. 705 ILCS 405/5-410(2)(c)(i).
13. 705 ILCS 405/5-410(2)(c)(ii).
14. 705 ILCS 405/5-410(2)(c)(v).
15. 705 ILCS 405/5-410(2)(c)(ii).
16. 705 ILCS 405/5-410(2)(c)(iii).
17. 705 ILCS 405/5-410(2)(c)(iv).

If a minor age 12 or older is confined in a county jail in a county with a population below 3,000,000 inhabitants, then the minor's confinement must be implemented in such a manner that there will be no contact by sight, sound or otherwise between the minor and adult prisoners.[18] Minors age 12 or older must be kept separate from confined adults and may not at any time be kept in the same cell, room, or yard with confined adults.[19] This applies only to confinement pending an adjudicatory hearing and may not exceed 36 hours, excluding Saturdays, Sundays, and court designated holidays.[20] To accept or hold minors during this time period, county jails must comply with all monitoring standards for juvenile detention homes promulgated by the Department of Corrections and training standards approved by the Illinois Law Enforcement Training Standards Board.[21]

To accept or hold minors 12 years of age or older after 36 hours but not longer than seven days including Saturdays, Sundays, and holidays pending an adjudicatory hearing, county jails must comply with all temporary detention standards promulgated by the Department of Corrections and training standards approved by the Illinois Law Enforcement Training Standards Board.[22] To accept or hold minors 12 years of age or older any longer, county jails must comply with all programmatic and training standards for juvenile detention homes promulgated by the Department of Corrections.[23]

When a minor who is at least 15 is prosecuted for a criminal act, the court may enter an order directing the juvenile confined in the county jail.[24] A juvenile so confined must be separated from all visual, aural, or other contact with adult prisoners.[25]

18. 705 ILCS 405/5-410(2)(d)(i).
19. 705 ILCS 405/5-410(2)(d)(i).
20. 705 ILCS 405/5-410(2)(d)(i).
21. 705 ILCS 405/5-410(2)(d)(i).
22. 705 ILCS 405/5-410(2)(d)(ii).
23. 705 ILCS 405/5-410(2)(d)(iii).
24. 705 ILCS 405/5-410(2)(e).

§ 35:18. —Nonsecure custody

If the probation officer or other designated public officer in a county having 3,000,000 or more inhabitants determines that a minor may be delinquent and should be retained in custody, but does not require physical restriction, the minor may be placed in nonsecure custody for up to 40 hours pending a detention hearing.[26]

> ☞ *Definition:* "Non-secure custody" means confinement where the minor is not physically restricted by being placed in a locked cell or room, by being handcuffed to a rail or other stationary object, or by other means and it may include, but is not limited to, electronic monitoring, foster home placement, home confinement, group home placement, or physical restriction of movement or activity solely through facility staff.[27]

§ 35:19. —Home confinement

Any minor taken into temporary custody who does not require secure detention, may be detained in the home of his or her parent or guardian.[28] Such home confinement is subject to whatever conditions the court may impose.[29]

§ 35:20. Detention hearing

An allegedly delinquent minor who is taken into temporary custody must be brought before a judicial officer within 40 hours for a detention or shelter care hearing to determine whether he or she will continue to be held.[30] The 40-hour period is exclusive of

---

25. 705 ILCS 405/5-410(2)(e).
26. 705 ILCS 405/5-410(3).
27. 705 ILCS 405/5-105(11).
28. 705 ILCS 405/5-410(4).
29. 705 ILCS 405/5-410(4).
30. 705 ILCS 405/5-415(1).

Practice References: The detention hearing. 14 Am Jur Trials 619,

Saturdays, Sundays, and holidays.[31] A minor who is not brought before a judicial officer within this statutory 40-hour period must be released from custody.[32]

If the probation officer (or other designated public officer in a county having more than 3,000,000 inhabitants) determines that the minor should be retained in custody, the clerk of the court will set the matter for hearing on the calendar.[33] If court is in session, a parent, guardian, custodian, or responsible relative may request that the hearing be held immediately, or at the earliest feasible time, and the hearing will be scheduled accordingly.[34] Otherwise, the probation officer or designated public officer informs the parent, guardian, custodian, or responsible relative in writing or orally of the time and place of the hearing.[35]

After the initial 40-hour period has lapsed, the court may review the minor's custodial status at any time prior to the trial or sentencing hearing, and if new or additional information becomes available concerning the minor's conduct, the court may conduct a hearing to determine whether the minor should be placed in a detention or shelter care facility.[36] If the court finds there is probable cause that the minor is delinquent and there is immediate and urgent necessity for the protection of the minor or of the person or property of another, or that he or she is likely to flee the jurisdiction of the court, the court may order that the minor be placed in detention or shelter care.[37]

When the minor appears before the court at the hearing, all witnesses who are present are examined with regard to the

Juvenile Court Proceedings §§ 50–55.

31. 705 ILCS 405/5-415(1).
32. 705 ILCS 405/5-415(3).
33. 705 ILCS 405/5-415(2).
34. 705 ILCS 405/5-415(2).
35. 705 ILCS 405/5-415(2).
36. 705 ILCS 405/5-415(4).
37. 705 ILCS 405/5-415(4).

allegations against the minor, who must be represented at the hearing by counsel.[38] If the court finds that there is no probable cause to believe that the minor is delinquent, it dismisses the petition and releases the minor.[39] On the other hand, if the court finds that there is probable cause to believe that the minor is delinquent, the minor, along with his or her parent, guardian, custodian, or other person able to give relevant testimony, are called to be examined.[40] Following their testimony, the court may enter an order releasing the minor upon the request of a parent, guardian, or custodian who appears to take custody of the minor.[41]

If, after requesting the minor's release, his or her parent, guardian, or custodian fails to appear within 24 hours to take custody of the minor, a rehearing is set for no more than 7 days after the date of the original order, and summons is issued directing the absent party to appear.[42] At the same time, the probation department prepares a report on the minor.[43] If the parent, guardian, or custodian fails to appear at the rehearing, the judge may order the minor kept in a suitable place designated by the Department of Children and Family Services (DCFS) or a licensed child welfare agency.[44] The time a minor spends in custody after being released upon the request of a parent, guardian, or custodian, is construed as time spent in detention.[45]

Should the court find, however, that: (1) it is a matter of immediate and urgent necessity for the protection of the minor or the person or property of another, or (2) that the minor is likely to

38. 705 ILCS 405/5-501.
39. 705 ILCS 405/5-501(1).
40. 705 ILCS 405/5-501(2).
41. 705 ILCS 405/5-501(2).
42. 705 ILCS 405/5-501(6).
43. 705 ILCS 405/5-501(6).
44. 705 ILCS 405/5-501(6).
45. 705 ILCS 405/5-501(6).

flee the jurisdiction of the court, the minor may be ordered kept in a detention or shelter care facility.[46]

In making its determination that an immediate and urgent necessity exists, the court considers:

- the nature and seriousness of the alleged offense;
- the minor's record of delinquency offenses, including pending cases;
- the minor's record of willful failure to appear following the issuance of a summons or warrant; and
- the availability of noncustodial alternatives, including the presence of a parent, custodian, or responsible relative able and willing to provide supervision and care and to assure the minor's compliance with a summons.[47]

The court's order, along with its findings of fact, are entered in the record.[48] Once a minor is ordered placed in a shelter care facility, he or she is not returned to the parent, custodian, or guardian until the court finds that continued shelter care placement is no longer necessary.[49] If the shelter care facility in which the minor is placed is operated by a licensed child welfare agency, the court may appoint the appropriate agency executive as the temporary custodian of the minor.[50] In addition, the court may also enter any other orders related to the minor's temporary custody as it determines fit and proper.[51]

Only when there is reasonable cause to believe that the minor is delinquent may he or she be kept or detained in a juvenile detention home.[52] In addition, while in confinement pending an

---

46. 705 ILCS 405/5-501(2).
47. 705 ILCS 405/5-501(2).
48. 705 ILCS 405/5-501(2).
49. 705 ILCS 405/5-501(2).
50. 705 ILCS 405/5-501(2).
51. 705 ILCS 405/5-501(2).
52. 705 ILCS 405/5-501(3).

adjudicatory hearing, no minor under 12 years old must be kept separate from confined adults and may not at any time be kept in the same cell, room or yard with confined adults.[53] The prehearing confinement may not exceed 40 hours, excluding Saturdays, Sundays, and court designated holidays.[54] To accept or hold minors during this time period, county jails must comply with all monitoring standards for juvenile detention homes promulgated by the Department of Corrections and training standards approved by the Illinois Law Enforcement Training Standards Board.[55] To detain minors 12 years old or under longer than 40 hours and no longer than seven days including Saturdays, Sundays, and holidays pending an adjudicatory hearing, county jails must comply with all temporary detention standards promulgated by the Department of Corrections and training standards approved by the Illinois Law Enforcement Training Standards Board.[56] To detain minors longer than seven days, county jails must comply with all programmatic and training standards for juvenile detention homes promulgated by the Department of Corrections.[57]

Any interested party, including the state of Illinois, the temporary custodian, an agency providing services to the minor or family under the Abused and Neglected Child Reporting Act, or foster parents, may file a motion to modify or vacate a temporary custody order on the grounds that:

- it is no longer a matter of immediate and urgent necessity that the minor remain in detention or shelter care;
- there is a material change in the circumstances of the minor's natural family;

---

53. 705 ILCS 405/5-501(4)(a).
54. 705 ILCS 405/5-501(4)(a).
55. 705 ILCS 405/5-501(4)(a).
56. 705 ILCS 405/5-501(4)(b).
57. 705 ILCS 405/5-501(4)(c).

- a person is capable of assuming temporary custody of the minor; or

- services provided by DCFS or a child welfare agency or other service provider have eliminated the need for temporary custody.[58]

After a motion to vacate or modify a temporary custody order is filed, a hearing must be held within 14 days.[59] In the event that the court modifies or vacates the temporary custody order but not the finding of probable cause, it may order that appropriate services be continued or initiated on behalf of the minor and his or her family.[60]

Where a minor already has been released pursuant to statute, the procedures for the scheduling of a detention hearing no longer apply because there is no pending custody and because the need to hold a detention hearing is mooted by the minor's release.[61]

§ 35:21. Preliminary conferences; probation adjustment

The court may authorize a probation officer to confer in a preliminary conference with a minor alleged to have committed an offense, his or her parent, guardian or legal custodian, the victim, the juvenile police officer, the State's Attorney, and other interested persons concerning the advisability of filing a petition praying that the minor be adjudged a ward of the court[62] and given a probation adjustment.[63] The probation officer should schedule a conference promptly except when the State's Attorney insists on court action or when the minor has indicated that he or

---

58. 705 ILCS 405/5-501(7)(a)–(d).

59. 705 ILCS 405/5-501(7).

60. 705 ILCS 405/5-501(7).

61. People v D.T., 287 Ill App 3d 408, 222 Ill Dec 714, 678 NE2d 326 (1st Dist 1997).

62. 705 ILCS 405/5-520.

Periodicals: For article, "Recent Developments in Nontraditional Alternatives in Juvenile Justice," see 28 Loy. U. Chi. L.J. 719 (1997).

63. 705 ILCS 405/5-305(1).

she will demand a judicial hearing and will not comply with a probation adjustment.[64] No statement made during a preliminary conference concerning the offense that is the subject of the conference may be admitted into evidence at an adjudicatory hearing or at any criminal proceeding against the minor prior to his or her conviction.[65]

When a probation adjustment is appropriate, the probation officer must promptly formulate a written, non-judicial adjustment plan following the initial conference.[66] Non-judicial probation adjustment plans include but are not limited to the following:

- up to six months informal supervision within the family;
- up to 12 months informal supervision with a probation officer involved;
- up to six months informal supervision with release to a person other than a parent;
- referral to special educational, counseling, or other rehabilitative social or educational programs;
- referral to residential treatment programs;
- participation in a public or community service program or activity;
- any other appropriate action with the consent of the minor and a parent.[67]

In determining whether probation adjustment is appropriate, the officer must consider the same factors as in determining whether to release or keep a minor in custody.[68]

---

64. 705 ILCS 405/5-305(1).
65. 705 ILCS 405/5-305(3).
66. 705 ILCS 405/5-305(4).
67. 705 ILCS 405/5-305(5)(a)–(g).
68. 705 ILCS 405/5-305(6), 705 ILCS 405/5-420(4).

III. ADJUDICATORY PROCEEDINGS

Research References:

Annotation References:

ALR Digest: Juvenile Delinquents and Dependents § 9

Index and Annotations: Juvenile Courts and Delinquent Children

Practice References:

47 Am Jur 2d, Juvenile Courts and Delinquent and Dependent Children §§ 44–54

14 Am Jur Trials 619, Juvenile Court Proceedings §§ 56–73

State Legislation:

705 ILCS 405/5-101 et seq.; 720 ILCS 5/21-1.3, 550/1 et seq., 570/100 et seq; 725 ILCS 5/104-13, 114-4, 120/3(a); Supreme Court Rule 403

Forms:

15 Am Jur Pl & Pr Forms (Rev), Juvenile Courts and Delinquent and Dependent Children, Forms 51–65, 81–86

Miscellaneous References:

West's Illinois Digest 2d, Infants §§ 171–212

§ 35:22. Petition

The state's attorney may file a petition alleging delinquency in respect to a minor in the juvenile court.[69] The petition and all subsequent documents should be captioned "In the interest of [name], a minor."[70] The petition alleging delinquency must be verified, and the statements, which may be made on the basis of information and belief, must include:[71]

- sufficient facts to demonstrate jurisdiction;
- the minor's name, age, and residence;
- the names and residences of his or her parents;

---

69. 705 ILCS 405/5-520(1).

70. 705 ILCS 405/5-520(1).

71. See generally 705 ILCS 405/5-520(2), 405/5-520(3), 405/5-13(4).

Forms: Petition for determination. 15 Am Jur Pl & Pr Forms (Rev), Juvenile Courts and Delinquent and Dependent Children, Form 22.

§ 35:22 ILLINOIS JURISPRUDENCE: CRIMINAL LAW

- the names and residence of his or her legal guardian, or persons having custody or control of the minor, or the nearest known relative if no parent or guardian can be found;
- the date, if any, when detention or shelter care was ordered or a detention or shelter care hearing is to be held; and
- an allegation that it is in the best interests of both the minor and the public that he or she be adjudged a ward of the court, although no proposed disposition of the minor following adjudication of wardship need be proposed.

☛ *Practice Guide:* Jurisdiction is properly in the juvenile court where the minor, prior to his or her 17th birthday, has violated or attempted to violate any federal or state law or municipal ordinance.[72]

If any of this information is not known by the petitioner, that fact must also be stated.[73] Supplemental petitions may be filed at any time prior to dismissal of the petition or final closing and discharge.[74]

While the allegations of a petition for wardship need not meet the standards of a criminal charging instrument, the petition must apprise the accused of the precise offense charged with sufficient specificity to prepare his or her defense.[75]

§ 35:23. —Date for trial

When a petition has been filed alleging that a minor is delinquent, a trial on the issue must be held within 120 days of any party's demand.[76]

---

72. 705 ILCS 405/5-120.

    See § 35:05.

73. 705 ILCS 405/5-520(2).

74. 705 ILCS 405/5-520(5).

    See 705 ILCS 405/5-750.

75. In re J.A.J., 243 Ill App 3d 808, 184 Ill Dec 41, 612 NE2d 917 (2d Dist 1993).

☛ *Practice Guide:* No adjudicatory hearing is required where the defendant is transferred to the criminal court to be tried as an adult.[77]

The 120-day period begins to run when either party makes a formal demand for trial by making an affirmative statement in the record indicating the trial demand.[78]

However, when the state has exercised due diligence to obtain material evidence without success, and there are nonetheless reasonable grounds to believe that the evidence may be obtained at a later date, the court may continue the adjudicatory hearing for up to an additional 30 days on the state's motion.[79]

The 120-day period is tolled by:[80]

- a delay occasioned by the minor;
- a continuance allowed by the court due to the minor's physical incapacity to stand trial;[81]
- an interlocutory appeal;
- an examination for to determine the minor's fitness;[82]

---

76. 705 ILCS 405/5-601(1).

   Periodicals: For article, "Motions to Dismiss Under the Speedy Trial Act," see 85 Ill. B.J. 468 (1997).

   Practice References: The adjudicatory hearing. 14 Am Jur Trials 619, Juvenile Court Proceedings §§ 56–73.

77. People v Holcomb, 192 Ill App 3d 158, 139 Ill Dec 228, 548 NE2d 613 (1st Dist 1989).

78. People v A.F. (In re A.F.), 282 Ill App 3d 930, 218 Ill Dec 336, 668 NE2d 1168 (1st Dist 1996).

79. 705 ILCS 405/5-601(1).

80. See generally 705 ILCS 405/5-601(8).

81. See 725 ILCS 5/114-4.

   See also ch 15.

82. See 725 ILCS 5/104-13.

   See also ch 15.

- a fitness hearing;[83] or
- an adjudication of the minor's unfitness for trial.[84]

A delay occasioned by these factors temporarily suspends, for the duration of the delay, the period within which an adjudicatory hearing must be held.[85] The 120-day period resumes from the point at which the time was suspended on the day the delay ends.[86] If no adjudicatory hearing is held within the 120-day period, the court may dismiss the petition with prejudice on the motion of any party.[87]

> ☛ *Practice Guide:* The failure to hold an adjudicatory hearing within the 120-day period does not automatically warrant discharge or constitute a per se violation of the minor's rights.[88]

If a minor has multiple delinquency petitions pending against him or her in the same county, or simultaneously demands an adjudicatory hearing on more than one delinquency petition pending in the same county, the minor mustl receive a hearing or, if a hearing is waived, a finding, on at least one of the petitions prior to the expiration of the limitations period relative to any of the petitions.[89] Any remaining petitions pending against the minor will be adjudicated within 160 days from the date on which a finding is rendered on the first.[90] If the initial hearing is terminated without a finding, and there is no subsequent hearing within a reasonable time, the minor is entitled to an adjudicatory

---

83. See ch 15.

84. See ch 15.

85. 705 ILCS 405/5-601(8).

86. 705 ILCS 405/5-601(8).

87. 705 ILCS 405/5-601(3).

88. People v Holcomb, 192 Ill App 3d 158, 139 Ill Dec 228, 548 NE2d 613 (1st Dist 1989).

89. 705 ILCS 405/5-601(2).

90. 705 ILCS 405/5-601(2).

hearing on the remaining petitions within 160 days from the date of termination.[91] If either 160-day period, whether running from a finding or from termination, expires without the commencement of an adjudicatory hearing on any of the pending petitions, the remaining petitions are dismissed and barred for want of prosecution unless the delay is due to one of the factors relevant to the tolling of the normal 120-day period.[92] If no adjudicatory hearing is held within the 160-day period, the court may dismiss the petition with prejudice on the motion of any party.[93]

When a petition is filed alleging that a minor is delinquent, and the minor is in detention or shelter care, the hearing must be held within 30 judicial days after the date detention or shelter care was ordered, at the earliest possible date that adequate notice can be given to a parent, guardian, or legal custodian.[94] If, however, the petition alleges that the minor has committed an offense that involves the death of, great bodily harm to or sexual assault or aggravated criminal sexual abuse on a victim, the court may continue the adjudicatory hearing for up to 70 additional days on the state's motion.[95] The failure to comply with these time limitations results in the minor's immediate release from detention or shelter care, and the application of the normal 120-day period.[96] Nonetheless, the minor or the minor's parents or guardian may waive any of the statutory time limits.[97]

§ 35:24. —Summons and Notice

When a petition requesting an adjudicatory hearing is filed,[98] a

---

91. 705 ILCS 405/5-601(2).
92. 705 ILCS 405/5-601(2).
    See 705 ILCS 405/5-601(8).
93. 705 ILCS 405/5-601(3).
94. 705 ILCS 405/5-601(4).
    See 705 ILCS 405/5-525.
95. 705 ILCS 405/5-601(4).
96. 705 ILCS 405/5-601(4).
97. 705 ILCS 405/5-601(9).

§ 35:24   ILLINOIS JURISPRUDENCE: CRIMINAL LAW

summons, issued by the clerk of the court and including a copy of the petition, is directed to the minor's legal guardian or custodian and to each named respondent.[99]

👉 *Practice Guide:* The summons ordinarily issued to the named respondents following the filing of a petition for an adjudicatory hearing is not required to be delivered to a minor respondent who is under eight years old and for whom the court has appointed a guardian ad litem to appear on the minor's behalf, or to a parent who does not reside with the minor, does not make regular child support payments to the minor, to the minor's other parent, or to the minor's legal guardian or custodian pursuant to a support order, and has not communicated with the minor on a regular basis..[1]

👉 *Illustration:* A minor's natural parents must be named as respondents in the petition for adjudication and are entitled to a summons, and an adjudication of wardship without notice to a named parent whose address was contained in the petition is void; however, where it was doubtful that the natural father was a necessary respondent to the petition in that he did not have custody of respondent, his address was unknown, and respondent's mother stated his parental rights had been terminated, without any evidence that the mother was lying, and where respondent failed to raise the issue of the natural father's deletion from the petition in the trial court, the respondent waived the issue of lack of notice to his natural father.[2]

---

98. See § 35:22.

99. 705 ILCS 405/5-525(1)(a).

Forms: Summons and notices of hearing in juvenile court. 15 Am Jur Pl & Pr Forms (Rev), Juvenile Courts and Delinquent and Dependent Children, Forms 51–65.

1. 705 ILCS 405/5-525(a)(1).

2. People v C.T.A. (In re C.T.A.), 275 Ill App 3d 427, 211 Ill Dec 733, 655 NE2d 1116 (2d Dist 1995).

Inadequate service to the parents, who are necessary parties, violates the minor's right to due process a well as that of the parents, as notice to parents may be viewed as a right that is shared by both the minor and his or her parents.[3]

The summons must be signed by the clerk, under the seal of the court and dated on the day of its issuance.[4] It must contain a statement that the minor or respondent is entitled to have an attorney present at the hearing, and that he or she should promptly notify the clerk if he or she is financially unable to retain counsel.[5] The summons must requre each respondent to appear and answer the petition on the date set for the hearing.[6]

The summons may be served by any county sheriff, coroner or probation officer, even if the officer is the petitioner.[7] The return of the summons with the officer's endorsement is considered sufficient proof of service.[8] Service may be made by:[9]

- leaving a copy with the person summoned at least 3 days prior to the date of the hearing;
- leaving a copy with a person at least 10 years old at the summoned person's usual place of abode, provided that the person with whom a copy is left is informed of its contents and a copy is mailed to the summoned person at least 3 days prior to the scheduled appearance;
- leaving a copy with the guardian or custodian of a minor at least 3 days prior to the scheduled appearance, though if the guardian is a state agency, service may properly be had by leaving a copy with any administrative employee designated

---

3. In re C.R.H., 251 Ill App 3d 102, 190 Ill Dec 389, 621 NE2d 258 (2d Dist 1993), affd 163 Ill 2d 263, 206 Ill Dec 100, 644 NE2d 1153.

4. 705 ILCS 405/5-525(1)(c).

5. 705 ILCS 405/5-525(1)(b).

6. 705 ILCS 405/5-525(1)(c).

7. 705 ILCS 405/5-525(1)(d).

8. 705 ILCS 405/5-525(1)(d).

9. 705 ILCS 405/5-525(1)(e).

to accept service of summons on the agency's behalf;

- by certified mail marked for delivery to addressee only if service is not made on any respondent within a reasonable time, or if it appears that a respondent lives outside Illinois, in which case the regular return receipt is sufficient proof of service and the hearing will not be held until 5 days after the mailing;[10] or

- by publication in a newspaper of general circulation in the county in which the action is pending if service is not made within a reasonable time, or if a respondent is generally designated, or if service is impossible because the respondent's whereabouts are unknown.[11] An order or judgment may not be entered against any person served with process solely by publication unless published notice is given or the person appears,[12] and a copy of the publication notice must be sent to the respondent's last known address.[13] The adjudicatory hearing may not proceed until 10 days after service by publication on any custodial parent, guardian or legal custodian of an allegedly delinquent minor.[14]

If a person who has signed a written promise to appear and bring the minor to court, or who has waived or acknowledged service, fails to appear with the minor on the date set by the court, a bench warrant may be issued for that person, or the minor, or both.[15] Any appearance by a minor's legal guardian or custodian, or by a named respondent, constitutes a waiver of service of summons and a submission to the court's jurisdiction.[16] At the

10. 705 ILCS 405/5-525(2)(a).
11. 705 ILCS 405/5-525(2)(b).
12. 705 ILCS 405/5-525(2)(b).

   See 705 ILCS 405/5-525(2)(b) (statutory form of notice by publication).

13. 705 ILCS 405/5-525(2)(c).
14. 705 ILCS 405/5-525(2)(c).
15. 705 ILCS 405/5-525(1)(f).
16. 705 ILCS 405/5-525(4).

time of his or her appearance, however, the guardian, custodian, or respondent is nonetheless provided a copy of the summons and petition.[17] If it becomes necessary to change the hearing date, notice of the new date must be given by certified mail or other reasonable means, to all respondents who were served with summons either personally or by mail.[18]

It is not relevant whether custodial parent was present for motion to suppress hearing or not because the Act only requires notice for the adjudicatory hearing.[19]

§ 35:25. —Guardian ad litem

If the court finds that there may be a conflict of interest between a minor and his or her parents or other custodian, or that it is in the minor's best interest to do so, it may appoint a guardian ad litem on the minor's behalf.[20] Unless the guardian ad litem is an attorney, he or she must be represented by counsel.[21] The guardian ad litem's reasonable fees are fixed by the court and charged to the minor's parents to the extent they are able to pay.[22] If the minor's parents are unable to pay the guardian ad litem's fees, the cost is borne by the county's general fund.[23]

If, during the court proceedings, the parents, guardian, or legal custodian can prove an actual conflict of interest with the minor in that delinquency proceeding and that the parents, guardian, or legal custodian are indigent, the court must appoint a separate attorney for that parent, guardian, or legal custodian.[24]

---

17. 705 ILCS 405/5-525(4).

18. 705 ILCS 405/5-525(2)(d).

19. People v J.E. (In re J.E.), 285 Ill App 3d 965, 221 Ill Dec 249, 675 NE2d 156 (1st Dist 1996).

20. 705 ILCS 405/5-610(1).

21. 705 ILCS 405/5-610(2).

22. 705 ILCS 405/5-610(3).

23. 705 ILCS 405/5-610(3).

24. 705 ILCS 405/5-610(4).

§ 35:26. Pleas and waivers

Except in those cases in which the potential penalty is limited to a fine, a person under the age of 18 is not permitted to enter a plea of guilty or to waive trial by jury unless he or she is represented by counsel in open court.[25]

§ 35:27. Evidence

At the trial, the standard of proof and the rules of evidence applicable to criminal proceedings in Illinois govern the proceeding.[26]

Preadjudication discovery is not constitutionally mandated in juvenile proceedings, but is permissible as a matter of discretion..[27]

§ 35:28. Continuance under supervision

In the event that, prior to adjudication or after hearing the evidence, the respondent admits or stipulates to the facts underlying the petition, and if there is no objection made in open court by any party, the court may enter an order of continuance under supervision for a period not to exceed 24 months.[28] If, however, any party objects in open court to any continuance, and insists upon proceeding to findings and adjudication, the court must do so.[29] The offense charged must

---

25. Supreme Court Rule 403.
26. 705 ILCS 405/5-605(3)(a).

    See chs 17, 18 and 19.

    Annotation References: Availability of discovery at probation revocation hearings. 52 ALR5th 559.

    Forms: Evidence. 15 Am Jur Pl & Pr Forms (Rev), Juvenile Courts and Delinquent and Dependent Children, Forms 81–86.

27. In re C.J., 166 Ill 2d 264, 209 Ill Dec 775, 652 NE2d 315 (1995), cert den 516 US 993, 133 L Ed 2d 433, 116 S Ct 527.
28. 705 ILCS 405/5-615(1), 405/5-615(4).

    Periodicals: For article, "Survey of Illinois Law: Criminal Law and Procedure," see 21 S. Ill. U.L.J. 759 (1997).

not be first degree murder, a Class X felony or a forcible felony.[30]

As a condition of the continuance, the court may order the minor to do any one or more of the following:

- not violate any criminal statute of any jurisdiction;
- make a report to and appear in person before any person or agency the court may direct;
- work;
- pursue a course of study or vocational training;
- undergo medical or psychotherapeutic treatment or treatment for drug addiction or alcoholism;
- attend or reside in a facility established for the instruction or residence of probationers;
- support his or her dependents;
- pay costs;
- refrain from possessing a firearm or other dangerous weapon;
- refrain from possessing an automobile;
- permit a probation officer to visit him or her at home or elsewhere;
- reside with his or her parents or in a foster home;
- attend school;
- attend a nonresidential youth program;
- contribute to his or her own support at home or in a foster home;
- perform reasonable public or community service;
- make restitution to the victim;
- comply with court-imposed curfew requirements;
- refrain from entering a designated geographic area except on those specific terms imposed by the court;

---

29. 705 ILCS 405/5-615(2).
30. 705 ILCS 405/5-615(1).

§ 35:28   ILLINOIS JURISPRUDENCE: CRIMINAL LAW

- refrain from having any direct or indirect contact with certain specific persons or types of persons, including members of street gangs and drug users or dealers.
- refrain from ingesting any drug prohibited by the Cannabis Control Act[31] or the Illinois Controlled Substances Act,[32] unless prescribed by a physician, and submit samples of his or her blood or urine or both for tests to determine the presence of any illicit drug; or
- comply with any other conditions as may be ordered by the court[33]

☛ *Caution:* The Illinois restitution statute,[34] which governs restitution questions in the juvenile courts,[35] strictly limits the definition of a "victim" to whom restitution may be paid.[36] Thus, for example, the parent of a competent minor victim may not be recompensed for lost wages or other damages arising from his or her child's injury.[37]

☛ *Practice Guide:* Where a minor is claiming that a trial court lacks authority to order restitution as a condition of supervision, the failure to preserve the issue by specifically objecting to the imposition of restitution does not waive it for purposes of appeal.[38] However, where a minor defendant agrees to pay restitution as part of an agreement for

---

31. 720 ILCS 550/1 et seq.

See §§ 56:01 et seq.

32. 720 ILCS 570/100 et seq.

See §§ 56:08 et seq.

33. 705 ILCS 405/5-615(5).

34. 730 ILCS 5/5-5-6.

35. 705 ILCS 405/5-710(4).

36. See 725 ILCS 120/3(a).

37. In re D.R., 219 Ill App 3d 13, 161 Ill Dec 861, 579 NE2d 409 (2d Dist 1991) (disapproved as stated in People v Sams, 238 Ill App 3d 825, 178 Ill Dec 689, 605 NE2d 128).

supervision, and the court enters an order based on the defendant's invitation to do so, the issue of the court's authority to impose the condition is waived.[39]

The minor must be given a certificate which sets forth the conditions imposed by the court, and those conditions may be modified, reduced, or enlarged by the court at any time, sua sponte or on the motion of the probation officer, State's Attorney, or at the minor's own request after notice and a hearing.[40]

The continuation may be terminated at any time by the court if warranted by the minor's conduct and the ends of justice.[41] If a petition is filed charging the violation of a condition of the continuance under supervision, and if the court finds, after a hearing has been conducted, that a condition has not been fulfilled, the court may proceed to findings, adjudication, and disposition.[42] Where the alleged conduct does not constitute a criminal offense, the hearing must be held within 30 days of the filing, after which time the period of continuance is tolled.[43]

When a hearing in which a minor is alleged to be a delinquent is

---

38. In re D.R., 219 Ill App 3d 13, 161 Ill Dec 861, 579 NE2d 409 (2d Dist 1991) (disapproved as stated in People v Sams, 238 Ill App 3d 825, 178 Ill Dec 689, 605 NE2d 128); In re V.L.F., 174 Ill App 3d 930, 124 Ill Dec 492, 529 NE2d 312 (4th Dist 1988).

See also In re E., 85 Ill 2d 326, 53 Ill Dec 241, 423 NE2d 910 (1981); People v Winchell, 140 Ill App 3d 244, 94 Ill Dec 621, 488 NE2d 620 (5th Dist 1986); People v Daugherty, 104 Ill App 3d 89, 59 Ill Dec 807, 432 NE2d 391 (4th Dist 1982).

39. In re D.R., 219 Ill App 3d 13, 161 Ill Dec 861, 579 NE2d 409 (2d Dist 1991) (disapproved as stated in People v Sams, 238 Ill App 3d 825, 178 Ill Dec 689, 605 NE2d 128); People v Early, 158 Ill App 3d 232, 110 Ill Dec 670, 511 NE2d 847 (2d Dist 1987), app den 117 Ill 2d 548, 115 Ill Dec 404, 517 NE2d 1090.

40. 705 ILCS 405/5-615(6).

41. 705 ILCS 405/5-615(4).

42. 705 ILCS 405/5-615(7).

43. 705 ILCS 405/5-615(7).

continued, the court, before continuing the case, must make a finding whether or not the offense alleged to have been committed was related to or in furtherance of the activities of a gang or was motivated by the minor's membership in or allegiance to a gang, constituted aggravated assault, or is a violation of any statute that involved the unlawful use of a firearm.[44] If the court determines the question in the affirmative, it must, as part of or in addition to any other condition of the supervision, require the minor to perform community service.[45]

When a hearing in which a minor is alleged to be a delinquent for reasons that include defacement of property,[46] is continued, the court must, as a condition of the continuance under supervision, require the minor to perform community service for not less than 30 and not more than 120 hours, if community service is available in the jurisdiction.[47] The community service must include, but need not be limited to, the cleanup and repair of the damage that was caused by the alleged violation or similar damage to property located in the municipality or county in which the alleged violation occurred. This condition may be in addition to any other condition.[48]

The court must impose on a minor placed on supervision a fee of $25 for each month of supervision, unless after determining the inability of the minor placed on supervision to pay the fee, the court assesses a lesser amount.[49] The court may not impose the fee on a minor who is made a ward of the State under this Act while the minor is in placement.[50] The fee mayl be imposed only on a minor who is actively supervised by the probation and court services department.[51] A court may order the parent, guardian, or

---

44. 705 ILCS 405/5-615(9).
45. 705 ILCS 405/5-615(9).
46. See 720 ILCS 5/21-1.3.
47. 705 ILCS 405/5-615(8).
48. 705 ILCS 405/5-615(8).
49. 705 ILCS 405/5-615(10).
50. 705 ILCS 405/5-615(10).

legal custodian of the minor to pay some or all of the fee on the minor's behalf.[52]

§ 35:29. Findings and determination

After hearing the evidence, the court makes an initial finding, noted in the minutes of the proceeding, of whether or not the minor is guilty.[53] If the court finds that the minor is not guilty, it must order the petition dismissed and the minor discharged from detention or restriction.[54] If, on the other hand, the court finds that the minor is guilty, it sets a time for a sentencing hearing to determine whether it is in the best interests of the minor and the public that the minor be made a ward of the court.[55] Notice must be given to all parties-respondent prior to proceeding to a dispositional hearing.[56]

The trial court must first determine that a minor is delinquent before it can conduct a dispositional hearing, but it should not adjudicate a minor to be a ward of the court until after the dispositional hearing is held; therefore, the trial court does not err in ordering wardship of the respondent at the end of his dispositional hearing.[57]

---

51. 705 ILCS 405/5-615(10).

52. 705 ILCS 405/5-615(10)

53. 705 ILCS 405/5-620.

54. 705 ILCS 405/5-620.

55. 705 ILCS 405/5-620.

56. 705 ILCS 405/5-705(2).

See 705 ILCS 405/5-525.

See also § 35:31.

57. People v J.C. (In re J.C.), 260 Ill App 3d 872, 198 Ill Dec 68, 632 NE2d 127 (1st Dist 1994).

IV. DISPOSITION

Research References:

Annotation References:

ALR Digest: Juvenile Delinquents and Dependents § 9

Index and Annotations: Juvenile Courts and Delinquent Children

Practice References:

47 Am Jur 2d, Juvenile Courts and Delinquent and Dependent Children §§ 55–62

14 Am Jur Trials 619, Juvenile Court Proceedings §§ 74–77

State Legislation:

20 ILCS 505/5; 55 ILCS 5/3-6039; 45 ILCS 15/0.01 et seq.; 720 ILCS 5/21-1.3, 550/1 et seq., 570/100; 730 ILCS 5/3-10-2 et seq., 5/5-8A-1; 750 ILCS 30/1

Forms:

15 Am Jur Pl & Pr Forms (Rev), Juvenile Courts and Delinquent and Dependent Children, Forms 101, 107, 118, 119, 131–136, 141–157

Miscellaneous References:

West's Illinois Digest 2d, Infants §§ 221–254

§ 35:30. Social investigation report

To assist it in making its determinations, the court may order an investigation be conducted and a social investigation report prepared.[58] The report includes:

- the minor's physical and mental condition;
- the minor's family situation and background;
- the minor's economic status and personal habits;
- the minor's education and occupation;

---

58. 705 ILCS 405/5-701.

See In re J.H., 212 Ill App 3d 22, 156 Ill Dec 213, 570 NE2d 689 (3d Dist 1991); In re L.M., 189 Ill App 3d 392, 136 Ill Dec 795, 545 NE2d 319 (1st Dist 1989).

- the minor's history of delinquency or criminality, or other matters which have been brought to the attention of the juvenile court;
- special resources which might be available to assist in the minor's rehabilitation; and
- any other matters which may be helpful to the court or which the court directs to be included.[59]

The court may not order commitment to the Juvenile Division of the Department of Corrections unless it has been presented with and considered a written social investigation report prepared within the previous 60 days.[60]

Before entering an order of disposition, the court must advise all parties of the factual contents and conclusions of any reports prepared for and considered by it, and provide all parties with a fair opportunity to controvert them.[61] However, any factual contents, conclusions, documents and sources disclosed by the court may not be further disclosed without the express approval of the court pursuant to an in camera hearing.[62]

On its own motion or that of any party, the court may adjourn the hearing for a reasonable period to receive reports or other evidence.[63] In the event of an adjournment, the court makes an appropriate order for the minor's detention for a period of not more than 30 days, or on the state's motion seeking an extension of the detention period, the court may extend it up to 15 additional days, although the minor must be released if further continuances are granted.[64]

---

59. 705 ILCS 405/5-701.
60. 705 ILCS 405/5-705(1).
61. 705 ILCS 405/5-705(2).
62. 705 ILCS 405/5-705(2).
63. 705 ILCS 405/5-705(3).
64. 705 ILCS 405/5-705(3).

§ 35:31. Hearing

At the dispositional hearing, the court must determine whether or not it is in the best interests of both the minor and the public that the minor be made a ward of the court.[65] If the court decides that wardship is appropriate, then it must next determine the disposition that best serves both the minor's and the public's interests.[66] In making that determination, the court may admit and rely on all helpful evidence, including oral and written reports, regardless of its admissibility at the adjudicatory hearing, to the extent of its probative value.[67]

A record of prior continuance under supervision is admissible at the dispositional hearing, regardless of whether it was successfully completed or not.[68]

The trial judge need not enumerate all possible alternatives when making a disposition, and the judge's remarks can illustrate a consideration of alternatives.[69]

A determination of probable cause is non-final in nature and thus cannot bind a judge in a subsequent transfer proceeding.[70]

---

65. 705 ILCS 405/5-705(1).

Annotation References: Availability of discovery at probation revocation hearings. 52 ALR5th 559.
Family court jurisdiction to hear contract claims. 46 ALR5th 735.
Propriety of exclusion of press or other media representatives from civil trial. 39 ALR5th 103.
The dispositional hearing. 14 Am Jur Trials 619, Juvenile Court Proceedings §§ 74–77.

66. 705 ILCS 405/5-705(1).

67. 705 ILCS 405/5-705(1).

68. 705 ILCS 405/5-705(1).

69. In re F.N., 253 Ill App 3d 483, 191 Ill Dec 665, 624 NE2d 853 (2d Dist 1993).

70. People v W.J. (In re W.J.), 284 Ill App 3d 203, 219 Ill Dec 925, 672 NE2d 778 (1st Dist 1996).

See § 35:06.

71. See generally 705 ILCS 405/5-710(1)(a).

§ 35:32. Orders

A minor who is found to be guilty and who is adjudicated a ward of the court is subject to the following orders of disposition:[71]

- probation or conditional discharge and release to his or her parents, guardian, or legal custodian, except that a minor who is found to be delinquent for an offense that would have constituted first degree murder, a Class X felony, or a forcible felony,[72] and who is not committed to the Juvenile Division of the Department of Corrections, must be placed on probation only;[73]

- if the parent, guardian, or legal custodian is found unfit, unwilling, or unable, for other than financial reasons, to take full responsibility for the minor, he or she may be placed, with or without the imposition of probation or conditional discharge, in the custody of a suitable relative or other person, under the guardianship of a probation officer, or committed to a care or placement agency, licensed training school, or other appropriate institution,[74] and his or her parent, guardian, or legal custodian may be ordered to pay any sums necessary for the minor's needs;[75]

- admission to treatment for drug addiction;

- committment to the Department of Children and Family Services (DCFS);[76]

Periodicals: For comment, "An Illinois Physician-Assisted Suicide Act: A Merciful End to a Terminally Ill Criminal Tradition," see 28 Loy. U. Chi. L.J. 763 (1997).

For article, "Lesser-Included Offenses in Illinois: A Look at Recent Developments," see 85 Ill. B.J. 480 (1997).

72. See ch 28.

73. See § 35:33.

74. 705 ILCS 405/5-740(1).

75. 705 ILCS 405/5-710(5).

76. See 20 ILCS 505/5.

§ 35:32   ILLINOIS JURISPRUDENCE: CRIMINAL LAW

- detention in a juvenile detention home for a period not to exceed 30 days, either as the sole disposition or in conjunction with other orders, provided that the minor is at least 10 years old, and this 30-day limitation may be extended by further order of the court for a minor under age 13 committed to the Department of Children and Family Service if the court finds that the minor is a danger to himself or others.;
- partial or complete emancipation.[77]
- suspension of driver's license or driving privileges for a duration determined by the court but not beyond the minor's 18th birthday;
- probation or conditional discharge and placed in detention[78] for a period not to exceed the period of incarceration permitted by law for adults found guilty of the same offense or offenses for which the minor was adjudicated delinquent, and in any event no longer than until the minor's 21st birthday.

A delinquent minor who is at least 13 years old may be committed to the Juvenile Division of the Department of Corrections only if a term of incarceration is permitted for adults found guilty of the same offense for which the minor has been adjudicated delinquent.[79] Any time spent by the minor in custody

---

77. See 750 ILCS 30/1.
78. See 55 ILCS 5/3-6039.
79. 705 ILCS 405/5-710(1)(b).
    Forms: Orders—Commitment to correctional institutions. 15 Am Jur Pl & Pr Forms (Rev), Juvenile Courts and Delinquent and Dependent Children, Forms 101, 107, 118, 119.
80. 705 ILCS 405/5-710(1)(b).
81. 720 ILCS 570/100 et seq.
    See §§ 56:08 et seq.
82. 720 ILCS 550/1 et seq.
    See §§ 56:01 et seq.

prior to being released to a parent, guardian, or custodian is considered time spent in detention.[80]

When a minor is found to be guilty for a violation of the Illinois Controlled Substances Act[81] or the Cannabis Control Act[82] and made a ward of the court, the court may enter a disposition order requiring the minor to undergo assessment, counseling or treatment in a substance abuse program approved by the Department of Human Services.[83]

If the court orders the minor committed to the Juvenile Division of the Department of Corrections, it must prepare a statement of the basis for its decision for inclusion in the record.[84]

In addition to any order of disposition, the court may order the minor to make restitution in monetary or other form.[85] The minor's parent, guardian, or legal custodian may, however, pay some or all of the restitution on behalf of the minor.[86]

A minor found to be delinquent for reasons that include defacement of property[87] must be ordered to perform community service for not less than 30 and not more than 120 hours, if community service is available in the jurisdiction.[88] The community service must include, but need not be limited to, the cleanup and repair of the damage that was caused by the alleged violation or similar damage to property located in the municipality or county in which the alleged violation occurred.[89] The order may be in addition to any other order authorized by this section.[90]

In addition to any other order of disposition, the court must

83. 705 ILCS 405/5-710(1)(c).
84. 705 ILCS 405/5-705(4).
85. 705 ILCS 405/5-710(4).
86. 705 ILCS 405/5-710(4).
87. See 720 ILCS 5/21-1.3.
88. 705 ILCS 405/5-710(8).
89. 705 ILCS 405/5-710(8).
90. 705 ILCS 405/5-710(8).

§ 35:32　ILLINOIS JURISPRUDENCE: CRIMINAL LAW

order any minor found to be delinquent for an act which would constitute criminal sexual assault, aggravated criminal sexual abuse, or criminal sexual abuse if committed by an adult to undergo medical testing to determine whether the defendant has any sexually transmissible disease including a test for infection with human immunodeficiency virus (HIV) or any other identified cause of acquired immunodeficiency syndrome (AIDS).[91]

When a court finds a minor to be delinquent, the court must, before making a disposition, determine whether the offense committed either was related to or in furtherance of the activities of a gang or was motivated by the minor's membership in or allegiance to a gang or involved a hate crime, or a violation of any statute that involved the unlawful use of a firearm.[92] If the court determines the question in the affirmative, and the court does not commit the minor to the Department of Corrections, Juvenile Division, the court must order the minor to perform community service.[93]

A minor must be sentenced under the terms of the Juvenile Court Act where the minor is prosecuted as an adult but is not convicted of an offense designated in the automatic transfer provision.[94] The trial court may choose as it sees fit among various dispositional alternatives and need not defer to any particular disposition.[95]

§ 35:33. Probation

When an order of disposition imposes a condition of probation,

---

91. 705 ILCS 405/5-710(9).

92. 705 ILCS 405/5-710(10).

93. 705 ILCS 405/5-710(10).

94. People v De Oca, 238 Ill App 3d 362, 179 Ill Dec 500, 606 NE2d 332 (1st Dist 1992).

95. In re F.N., 253 Ill App 3d 483, 191 Ill Dec 665, 624 NE2d 853 (2d Dist 1993).

96. 705 ILCS 405/5-715(1).

Forms: Probation. 15 Am Jur Pl & Pr Forms (Rev), Juvenile Courts and Delinquent and Dependent Children, Forms 131–136.

the period may not exceed the lesser of 5 years or the minor's attaining the age of 21.[96] The period must be at least 5 years, however, where the offense for which the minor has been adjudicated delinquent constitutes first degree murder, a Class X felony or a forcible felony.[97] As a condition of probation or conditional discharge, the court may require that the minor:[98]

- not violate any criminal statute of any jurisdiction;
- make a report to and appear in person before a person or agency;
- work or pursue a course of study or vocational training;
- undergo medical or psychiatric treatment, social work services rendered by a clinical social worker, or treatment for drug addiction or alcoholism;
- attend or reside in an instructional or residential probationary facility;
- support any dependents;
- refrain from possessing a firearm, other dangerous weapon, or automobile;
- permit home or other visits by a probation officer;
- reside with his or her parents or in a foster home;
- attend school;
- attend a nonresidential youth program;
- make restitution;
- contribute to his or her own support at home or in a foster home;
- perform some reasonable public or community service;
- participate in community corrections programs;
- pay costs;

---

97. 705 ILCS 405/5-715(1).

See ch 28.

98. See generally 705 ILCS 405/5-715(2).

§ 35:33 ILLINOIS JURISPRUDENCE: CRIMINAL LAW

- refrain from entering a designated geographic area except under certain circumstances;
- refrain from having any direct or indirect contact with certain persons or types of persons, including members of street gangs and drug users or dealers;
- refrain from the use of controlled substances unless prescribed by a physician, and to submit to blood or urine tests for the presence of illicit drugs;
- refrain from acquiring a driver's license, or from the nonessential driving or operation of any motor vehicle, if the minor was adjudicated delinquent on any alcohol, cannabis, or controlled substance violation; or
- comply with any other conditions imposed by the court.

In addition, a term of home confinement may be imposed along with other conditions of probation or conditional discharge.[99] The requirements of home confinement are that the minor:

- remain within the interior premises of the place designated by the court during the hours of confinement;
- admit any person or agent designated by the court into the place of confinement at any time for the purpose of verifying the minor's compliance; and
- use an approved electronic monitoring device.[1]

The court must impose on a minor placed on probation a fee of $25 for each month on probation or conditional discharge unless after determining the inability of the minor placed on probation or conditional discharge to pay the fee, the court assesses a lesser

99. 705 ILCS 405/5-715(2)(q).

Annotation References: Jurisdiction or power of juvenile court to order parent of juvenile to make restitution for juvenile's offense, 66 ALR4th 985.

1. 730 ILCS 5/5-8A-1.

See ch 28.

2. 705 ILCS 405/5-715(5).

amount.[2]

The chief judge of each circuit must adopt a system of structured, intermediate sanctions for violation of the terms and conditions of a disposition of probation, conditional discharge, or supervision.[3]

A court may also impose multiple periods of detention, preceded by remission hearings, as a condition of juvenile probation.[4]

> *Illustration:* A juvenile who admitted and stipulated to a charge of criminal damage to property was placed on probation subject to the condition that he serve 22 days in the county youth detention center, to be served in periodic three-day detentions, each waivable in turn if the juvenile successfully abided by all other terms and conditions of his probation.[5]

The minor is given a certificate that states the conditions of his or her release on probation or conditional discharge.[6] The conditions may be reduced or enlarged by the court on its own motion, on the motion of the probation officer, or at the request of the minor after notice and a hearing.[7]

§ 35:34. —Revocation

If a petition is filed that charges the violation of a condition of

---

3. 705 ILCS 405/5-715(6).

4. In re M.D., 220 Ill App 3d 998, 163 Ill Dec 432, 581 NE2d 383 (4th Dist 1991).

5. In re M.D., 220 Ill App 3d 998, 163 Ill Dec 432, 581 NE2d 383 (4th Dist 1991).

6. 705 ILCS 405/5-715(4).

7. 705 ILCS 405/5-720(5).

See § 35:34.

8. See generally 705 ILCS 405/5-720(1).

Annotation References: Availability of discovery at probation revocation hearings. 52 ALR5th 559.

§ 35:34　　　ILLINOIS JURISPRUDENCE: CRIMINAL LAW

probation or conditional discharge, the court must proceed to:[8]

- order the minor to appear; or
- order the detention in a juvenile detention home of a minor at least 10 years old if the court finds that detention is required as a matter of immediate and urgent necessity for the protection of the minor, for the protection of the person or property of another, or that the minor is likely to flee the court's jurisdiction; and
- notify the persons named in the petition.[9]

> *Practice Guide:* A court is without authority to revoke a minor's probation when there is no timely petition filed. Further, the trial court has no authority to order the state's attorney's office to file the petition to revoke. Only the prosecutor may initiate the proceeding.[10]

The filing of a petition alleging the violation of a condition of the minor's probation or conditional discharge tolls the probation or discharge period until the final determination of the charge, including a hearing and disposition.[11] The minor may not be held in detention for more than 15 days pending a determination.[12]

At the hearing,[13] the State bears the burden of going forward with the evidence and of proving the violation by a preponderance of the evidence.[14] Evidence is presented in court and with the right of confrontation, cross-examination, and representation by counsel.[15]

---

9. See 705 ILCS 405/5-520.

　See also § 35:27.

10. In re J.K., 229 Ill App 3d 569, 171 Ill Dec 581, 594 NE2d 433 (2d Dist 1992).

11. 705 ILCS 405/5-720(1).

12. 705 ILCS 405/5-720(2).

13. 705 ILCS 405/5-720(2).

14. 705 ILCS 405/5-720(3).

15. 705 ILCS 405/5-720(3).

Following the hearing, if the court finds that the minor has violated a condition of probation or conditional discharge, it may continue the existing disposition, modify or enlarge the conditions, or revoke probation or conditional discharge and impose any other disposition initially available to it, following the procedures set forth by statute for an original sentence.[16]

Instead of filing a violation of probation or of conditional discharge, the probation officer, with the concurrence of his or her supervisor, may serve on the minor a notice of intermediate sanctions.[17] The notice mustl contain the technical violation or violations involved, the date or dates of the violation or violations, and the intermediate sanctions to be imposed.[18] On receipt of the notice, the minor must immediately accept or reject the intermediate sanctions.[19] If the sanctions are accepted, they must be imposed immediately; if they are rejected or the minor does not respond to the notice, a violation of probation or of conditional discharge must immediately befiled with the court.[20] The State's Attorney and the sentencing court must be notified of the notice of sanctions.[21] Upon successful completion of the intermediate sanctions, a court may not revoke probation or conditional discharge or impose additional sanctions for the same violation.[22] A notice of intermediate sanctions may not be issued for any violation of probation or conditional discharge which

---

16. 705 ILCS 405/5-720(4), 405/5-720(6).

   See 705 ILCS 405/5-705, 405/5-710.

17. 705 ILCS 405/5-720(7).

18. 705 ILCS 405/5-720(7).

19. 705 ILCS 405/5-720(7).

20. 705 ILCS 405/5-720(7).

21. 705 ILCS 405/5-720(7).

22. 705 ILCS 405/5-720(7).

23. 705 ILCS 405/5-720(3).

24. In re J.E., 228 Ill App 3d 315, 169 Ill Dec 429, 591 NE2d 933 (Cal App 2nd Dist 1992).

could warrant an additional, separate felony charge.[23]

Where an order imposing probation on a juvenile is void because the trial court lacked the statutory authority to enter the order, any subsequent order revoking probation is likewise void.[24]

§ 35:35. Protective supervision

If a minor is released to the custody of his or her parents, guardian, or legal custodian under an order of disposition, or if the order continues an existing custodial relationship, the court may place the person who has custody of the minor under the supervision of the probation office.[25] No such supervision may be ordered, however, where the custodian is a representative of a public or private agency or a governmental department.[26] The terms of the protective supervision may be modified or terminated by the court at any time in order to best serve the interests of the minor and the public.[27]

§ 35:36. —Enforcement

Orders of protective supervision may be enforced by a citation to show cause for contempt of court due to any violation, and, if required to protect the minor's welfare, by the issuance of a warrant to take the alleged violator into custody and to bring him or her before the court.[28]

§ 35:37. Placement with legal custodian

If the court finds that (1) the parents, guardian or legal custodian of a minor who is adjudicated a ward of the court are unfit, unwilling, or unable for other than financial reasons to care for, protect, train, or discipline the minor; and (2) that services aimed at preserving or reunifying the family have been

---

25. 705 ILCS 405/5-725.

See In re J.H., 212 Ill App 3d 22, 156 Ill Dec 213, 570 NE2d 689 (3d Dist 1991).

26. 705 ILCS 405/5-725.
27. 705 ILCS 405/5-725.
28. 705 ILCS 405/5-735(1).

unsuccessful; and (3) that it is in the best interest of the minor to be removed from his or her parents, guardian, or custodian, the court may:

- place the minor in the custody of a suitable relative or other person;
- place the minor under the guardianship of a probation officer;
- commit the minor to an agency for care or placement other than one under the authority of the Department of Corrections or the Department of Children and Family Services (DCFS);
- commit the minor to a licensed training school or industrial school; or
- commit the minor to an appropriate institution designed for the care of delinquent children other than one under the authority of the Department of Corrections or the DCFS.[29]

Parental rights are terminable only when clear, convincing evidence establishes a parent's unfitness.[30] In determining whether a parent is unfit, the trial court should not consider the best interests of the child.[31]

☞ *Practice Guide:* The Illinois Appellate Court has held that a parent's failure to acknowledge that sexual abuse has occurred, and to take steps to prevent a child's exposure to

---

29. 705 ILCS 405/5-740(1).

Periodicals: For article, "Recent Developments in Nontraditional Alternatives in Juvenile Justice," see 28 Loy. U. Chi. L.J. 719 (1997).

30. In re Paul, 101 Ill 2d 352, 461 NE2d 983 (1984); In re Clarence T.B., 215 Ill App 3d 85, 158 Ill Dec 765, 574 NE2d 878 (2d Dist 1991).

31. In re Clarence T.B., 215 Ill App 3d 85, 158 Ill Dec 765, 574 NE2d 878 (2d Dist 1991); In re Henry, 175 Ill App 3d 778, 125 Ill Dec 413, 530 NE2d 571 (2d Dist 1988).

32. In re Clarence T.B., 215 Ill App 3d 85, 158 Ill Dec 765, 574 NE2d 878 (2d Dist 1991); In re A.C.B., 153 Ill App 3d 704, 106 Ill Dec 653, 506 NE2d 360 (4th Dist 1987).

§ 35:37   ILLINOIS JURISPRUDENCE: CRIMINAL LAW

abuse, is sufficient to support a finding of unfitness by clear and convincing evidence.[32]

When making a placement, the court is encouraged by statute to select a person or private agency of the same religious faith as the minor.[33] In addition, in weighing alternate placement options, the court is to ascertain and consider the minor's views and preferences where appropriate.[34] The clerk of the court issues a certified copy of the court's order to the legal custodian or guardian, which serves as proof of his or her authority.[35] No other process is necessary as authority for the keeping of the minor.[36]

When a minor is placed with a suitable relative or other person, he or she is appointed the legal custodian or guardian of the minor's person.[37] A legal custodian or guardian of the minor's person has the right and responsibility to be concerned with the minor's general welfare and to make important decisions in matters having a permanent effect on the life and development of the minor, including:

- the authority to consent to marriage;
- the authority to consent to enlistment in the armed forces;
- the authority to consent to major medical, psychiatric, or surgical treatment;
- the authority and duty of reasonable visitation;
- the rights and responsibilities of legal custody;
- the power, if conferred by the court, to consent to the minor's adoption.[38] The custodian or guardian also has the duty to

---

33. 705 ILCS 405/5-740(2).
34. 705 ILCS 405/5-740(2).
35. 705 ILCS 405/5-740(5).
36. 705 ILCS 405/5-740(5).
37. 705 ILCS 405/5-740(3).
38. 705 ILCS 405/5-740(3).
    See 705 ILCS 405/1-3(8).
    See also § 35:44.

protect, train, and sdiscipline the minor, and to provide food, shelter, education, and ordinary medical care, except as these are limited by residual parental rights and responsibilities and the rights and responsibilities of the guardian of the person, if any.[39]

In addition, a probation officer or an agency whose representative is appointed custodian or guardian of the minor's person may place the minor in any licensed or approved child care facility.[40] However, no minor may be placed in a child care facility other than one that is in compliance with the Children and Family Service Act.[41] Any out-of-state child care facility in which the minor is placed must be in compliance with the Interstate Compact on the Placement of Children.[42]

Custody or guardianship, once granted, continues until the court orders otherwise, or until the minor reaches the age of 21.[43] No legal custodian or guardian may be removed without his or her consent until he or she is given notice and an opportunity to be heard by the court.[44]

§ 35:38. —Court review

The court may require any legal custodian or guardian to periodically provide a full and accurate report of its actions on behalf of the minor, either by a verified affidavit or under oath in

---

39. 705 ILCS 405/5-740(3).

See 705 ILCS 405/1-3(9).

See also § 35:44.

40. 705 ILCS 405/5-740(3).

41. 705 ILCS 405/5-740(3).

See 20 ILCS 505/5 et seq.

42. 705 ILCS 405/5-740(4).

See 45 ILCS 15/0.01 et seq.

43. 705 ILCS 405/5-740(6).

44. 705 ILCS 405/5-745(3).

45. 705 ILCS 405/5-745(1).

open court.[45] Based on the contents of the report presented to it, the court may remove the custodian or guardian and appoint another, or restore the minor to the custody of his or her parents or former guardian or custodian.[46]

In addition, a guardian or custodian must file an updated case plan with the court every six months, and an agency having guardianship must file a supplemental petition for court review every 18 months.[47] The petition must state facts relevant to the child's present physical, mental, and emotional health, as well as facts pertaining to his or her custodial or foster care.[48] The petition is set for hearing, and notice provided by certified mail to the person or agency having physical custody of the child, the minor, and other interested parties, unless a written waiver of notice is filed with the petition.[49] A ward of the court may enforce his or her rights against any public agency by a mandamus action.[50]

The minor, or any other interested person, may apply to the court for a change of custody and the appointment of a new custodian or guardian or the restoration of the minor to the custody of his or her parents or former custodian or guardian.[51] Unless the court orders otherwise, when a minor is 18 years old and his or her guardian or custodian petitions the court for a termination order, the guardianship or custody automatically terminates 30 days after the petition is received.[52]

§ 35:39. Commitment of minor

When any delinquent is adjudicated a ward of the court, the

46. 705 ILCS 405/5-745(1).
47. 705 ILCS 405/5-745(2).
48. 705 ILCS 405/5-745(2).
49. 705 ILCS 405/5-745(2).
50. 705 ILCS 405/5-745(2).
    See § 35:41.
51. 705 ILCS 405/5-745(3).
52. 705 ILCS 405/5-745(3).

court may commit him or her to the Juvenile Division of the Department of Corrections if it finds that: (1) his or her parents, guardian, or legal custodian is unfit, unwilling, or unable for nonfinancial reasons to care for, protect, train, or discipline the minor, and that the minor's and the public's best interests would not be served by the appointment of a custodian or guardian; or (2) that commitment is necessary to ensure the public's protection from the consequences of the delinquent's criminal activity.[53]

When a minor at least 13 years of age is adjudged delinquent for the offense of first degree murder, the court must declare the minor a ward of the court and order the minor committed to the Department of Corrections, Juvenile Division, until the minor's 21st birthday, without the possibility of parole, furlough, or non-emergency authorized absence for a period of five years from the date the minor was committed to the Department, except that the time that a minor spent in custody for the offense before being committed to the Department is considered as time credited towards the five-year period.[54] This subsection does not preclude the state's attorney from prosecuting a minor as an adult.[55] In determining whether a minor should be committed to the Juvenile Division of the Department of Corrections, a trial judge may properly consider the protection of the public and inadequate parental or guardian supervision[56].

The commitment of a delinquent is for an indeterminate term that terminates automatically on his or her 21st birthday, unless the delinquent is discharged earlier from parole or custodianship is otherwise terminated.[57]

---

53. 705 ILCS 405/5-750(1).

See In re T.M., 210 Ill App 3d 651, 155 Ill Dec 348, 569 NE2d 529 (2d Dist 1991).

54. 705 ILCS 405/5-750(2).

55. 705 ILCS 405/5-750(2).

56. In re A.D., 228 Ill App 3d 272, 169 Ill Dec 445, 591 NE2d 949 (Cal App 3rd Dist 1992).

57. 705 ILCS 405/5-750(3).

When a minor is committed to the Department of Corrections, the Assistant Director of Corrections, Juvenile Division, is appointed legal custodian, and the minor is conveyed immediately to the appropriate reception station or other place designated by the Department.[58] A certified copy of the commitment order, issued to the Assistant Director by the clerk of the court, constitutes proof of his or her authority,[59] which terminates automatically by petition upon the minor's lawful discharge.[60] The clerk also forwards to the Juvenile Division the disposition order, all reports, the court's statement of the basis for the order, and all additional matters as directed by the court.[61]

A person who is committed to the Juvenile Division is initially examined with regard to his or her medical, psychological, social, educational and vocational condition and history, including any use of alcohol and other drugs, the circumstances of the offense for which he or she is committed, and any other information required by the Department of Corrections.[62] Based on this examination, the Department may:

- require the delinquent to participate in rehabilitative vocational, physical, educational and corrective training and activities;
- place the delinquent in any Juvenile Division institution or facility;
- order replacement or referral to the Probation and Pardon Board as often as desirable;

---

58. 705 ILCS 405/5-750(4).

Annotation References: Authority of court to order juvenile delinquent incarcerated in adult penal institution, 95 ALR3d 568.

59. 705 ILCS 405/5-750(4).

60. 705 ILCS 405/5-750(6).

61. 705 ILCS 405/5-750(5).

62. 730 ILCS 5/3-10-2(a).

63. 730 ILCS 5/3-10-2(b).

- enter into agreements with other state departments, courts having probation officers, and with private agencies or institutions for separate care or treatment of the delinquent.[63]

Periodic reexaminations are made at least annually to determine whether or not the existing orders should be modified or continued,[64] and a record of treatment decisions, including any modifications and their underlying bases, is included in the committed person's master record file.[65] The parent, guardian, or nearest relative of the committed person must be notified by certified mail of the person's physical location and any change.[66]

While committed to the Juvenile Division, the delinquent is subject to its disciplinary rules, which allow restrictions on visitation, work, education or program assignments, the use of toilets, washbowls and showers, but bar corporal punishment and restrictions on diet, medical or sanitary facilities, clothing, bedding, mail, and reductions in the frequency of use of toilets, washbowls, and showers.[67] No person committed to the Juvenile Division may be isolated for disciplinary reasons for more than 7 consecutive days, or for more than 15 out of any 30 days except in cases of violence or attempted violence against person or property.[68] Generally, disciplinary actions are governed by statutory principles, and are subject to review by a formal grievance procedure.[69]

§ 35:40. —Transfer to Department of Mental Health and Developmental Disabilities

A delinquent committed to the Juvenile Division may be

64. 730 ILCS 5/3-10-2(c).
65. 730 ILCS 5/3-10-2(d).
66. 730 ILCS 5/3-10-2(e).
67. 730 ILCS 5/3-10-8(a)(1) and (2).
68. 730 ILCS 5/3-10-8(a)(3).
69. 730 ILCS 5/3-10-8.
   See 730 ILCS 5/3-8-8.
70. 730 ILCS 5/3-10-5(a).

transferred, if necessary, to the Department of Human Services with or without his or her consent for up to 6 months while still under the authority of the Department of Corrections.[70] If the delinquent consents, the transfer may occur without the procedural steps described below.[71] The parent, guardian, or nearest relative, along with the attorney of record, must be advised of their right to object to the transfer.[72] If an objection is made, or if the delinquent withholds his or her consent, the Assistant Director of the Juvenile Division files a petition in the circuit court seeking his or her commitment.[73] A certificate from a physician, licensed clinical social worker, psychologist, or psychiatrist that the transfer is necessary must be attached to the petition, and copies furnished to the person, his or her parents, guardian or nearest relative, the committing court, and the state's attorneys of the county from which the transfer is made.[74] Following a hearing, if the person is found to be in need of commitment for treatment or habilitation, the court may commit him or her to the Department of Human Services.[75]

When a person no longer meets the standard for admission of a minor to a mental health facility, or is suitable for administrative admission to a developmental disability facility, the Department of Human Services returns the individual to the Juvenile Division, and, if a parole hearing has not been held within the last 6 months, one is held within 45 days of the transfer.[76]

71. 730 ILCS 5/3-10-5(a).
72. 730 ILCS 5/3-10-5(b).
73. 730 ILCS 5/3-10-5(e).
74. 730 ILCS 5/3-10-5(e).
75. 730 ILCS 5/3-10-5(f).
76. 730 ILCS 5/3-10-6.

See also 730 ILCS 5/3-10-7, 730 ILCS 5/3-10-11 (transfers from Department of Children and Family Services).

77. 705 ILCS 405/1-1 et seq.
78. 705 ILCS 405/5-755(1).

§ 35:41. Wardship of court—Duration

As a general rule, all proceedings under the Juvenile Court Act[77] automatically terminate when the minor attains the age of 21.[78] At any time when the court finds that the best interests of the minor and the public no longer require the wardship, it may order the wardship terminated and all proceedings respecting the minor finally closed and discharged.[79] At the same time, the court may terminate any guardianship or custodianship.[80]

An exception to the automatic termination at age 21 are extended jurisdiction juvenile prosecutions, which occur when the State's Attorney files a petition, at any time prior to commencement of the minor's trial, to designate the proceeding as an extended jurisdiction juvenile prosecution and the petition alleges the commission by a minor 13 years of age or older of any offense which would be a felony if committed by an adult.[81] If the assigned juvenile judge determines that there is probable cause to believe that the allegations in the petition and motion are true, there is a rebuttable presumption that the proceeding will be designated as an extended jurisdiction juvenile proceeding.[82] Among the dispositions in an extended jurisdiction juvenile prosecution is an adult criminal sentence.[83]

§ 35:42. Habitual juvenile offenders

Any minor who is adjudicated a delinquent for a third time after having been twice adjudicated a delinquent for offenses which would have been classified as felonies had he or she been prosecuted as an adult, is adjudged an habitual juvenile offender if the following conditions are met:

- the third offense occurred after adjudication on the second; and

---

79. 705 ILCS 405/5-755(2).
80. 705 ILCS 405/5-755(2).
81. 705 ILCS 405/5-810(1).
82. 705 ILCS 405/5-810(1).
83. 705 ILCS 405/5-810(4).

§ 35:42   ILLINOIS JURISPRUDENCE: CRIMINAL LAW

- the second was for an offense that occurred after adjudication on the first; and
- the third offense was based on commission or attempted commission of first or second degree murder, involuntary manslaughter, criminal sexual assault, aggravated criminal sexual assault, aggravated or heinous battery involving the permanent disability or disfigurement of or great bodily harm to the victim, burglary of a home, home invasion, robbery or armed robbery, or aggravated arson.[84]

The State must serve written notice to the minor of its intent to prosecute him or her as an habitual juvenile offender within five days of filing the delinquency petition that alleges the third offense.[85] Alternatively, the state may elect to seek prosecution of the minor as an adult.[86]

The petition on which the notice is based must contain the information and averments generally required of delinquency petitions,[87] although the petition may not allege any prior adjudication.[88]

Unless the minor demands otherwise, in open court and on the advice of counsel, the trial is by jury.[89] The delinquency proceeding in the habitual juvenile offender context is generally identical to any other,[90] except that no evidence or other disclosure of prior adjudications may be presented to the court or jury unless otherwise permitted by issues properly raised or for

84. 705 ILCS 405/5-815(a).
85. 705 ILCS 405/5-815(b).
86. 705 ILCS 405/5-815(a).
87. See § 35:22.
88. 705 ILCS 405/5-815(c).
89. 705 ILCS 405/5-815(d).
90. See §§ 35:22 to 35:29.
91. 705 ILCS 405/5-815(e).
92. 705 ILCS 405/5-815(e).

purposes of impeaching the minor's own testimony.[91]

After an admission of the facts in the petition, or an adjudication of delinquency, the State's Attorney may file with the court a verified written statement concerning any prior adjudication.[92] The minor is then informed of the allegations and of his or her right to a hearing and counsel.[93]

If, after a hearing on the subject, the court finds that the prerequisites for adjudication as an habitual juvenile offender have been proven, the minor is adjudicated an habitual juvenile offender and committed to the Juvenile Division of the Department of Corrections until his or her 21st birthday.[94] While the commitment is made without possibility of parole, furlough, or nonemergency authorized absence, the minor is nonetheless entitled to earn one day of good conduct credit for each day served as a reduction against the determinate period of confinement.[95]

§ 35:42.50. Violent juvenile offenders

A minor who was previously adjudicated a delinquent minor for an offense which, had the minor been prosecuted as an adult, would have been a Class 2 or greater felony involving the use or threat of physical force or violence against an individual or a Class 2 or greater felony for which an element of the offense is possession or use of a firearm, and who is adjudicated a delinquent minor for a second time for any of those offenses is considerd a "violent juvenile offender" if: (1) the second adjudication is for an offense occurring after adjudication on the first; and (2) the second offense occurred on or after January 1, 1995.[96]

The state must serve on the minor written notice of its intention

---

93. 705 ILCS 405/5-815(e).

94. 705 ILCS 405/5-815(f).

95. 705 ILCS 405/5-815(f).

96. 705 ILCS 405/5-820(a).

97. 705 ILCS 405/5-820(b).

to prosecute the minor as a violent juvenile offender within five judicial days of the filing of any delinquency petition which would mandate the minor's disposition as a violent juvenile offender.[97] Only the state's attorney may file a notice to seek prosecution as a violent juvenile offender.[98] The petition on which the violent juvenile offender notice is based must contain the information and averments required for all other juvenile delinquency petitions and it must be served in the same manner as other petitions under the Juvenile Court Act.[99] No prior adjudication may be alleged in the petition.[1]

Trial on the petition must be by jury unless the minor demands, in open court and with advice of counsel, a trial by the court without a jury.[2] The provisions of the Act concerning delinquency proceedings generally are applicable to violent juvenile offender proceedings.[3]

No evidence or other disclosure of prior adjudication may be presented to the court or jury during the adjudicatory hearing unless otherwise permitted by the issues properly raised in that hearing.[4] After an admission of the facts in the petition, or an adjudication of delinquency, the State's Attorney may file with the court a verified written statement concerning any prior adjudication.[5] The minor is then informed of the allegations and of his or her right to a hearing and counsel.[6]

If the court finds that the prerequisites for violent juvenile

98. 705 ILCS 405/5-820(c).

99. 705 ILCS 405/5-820(c).

705 ILCS 405/1-1 et seq.

1. 705 ILCS 405/5-820(c).

2. 705 ILCS 405/5-820(d).

3. 705 ILCS 405/5-820(d).

705 ILCS 405/1-1 et seq.

4. 705 ILCS 405/5-820(e).

5. 705 ILCS 405/5-820(e).

6. 705 ILCS 405/5-820(e).

offender status have been proven, it must commit the minor to the Department of Corrections, Juvenile Division, until his or her 21st birthday, without possibility of parole, furlough, or non-emergency authorized absence.[7] However, the minor willl be entitled to earn one day of good conduct credit for each day served as reductions against the period of his or her confinement.[8]

§ 35:43. Appeals

Appeals from final judgments in delinquent minor proceedings are generally governed by the rules applicable to criminal cases.[9] Upon the filing of a notice of appeal in a proceeding in which a minor has been found delinquent, or in which probation or conditional discharge has been revoked, the court must determine whether or not the minor is represented by counsel on appeal.[10] If not, and if the court determines that the minor is indigent and desires counsel on appeal, the court appoints counsel.[11]

An appeal may be taken to the Appellate Court from an adjudication of wardship if an order of disposition has not been entered within 90 days of the adjudication.[12] An appeal may also be taken to the Appellate Court from an order empowering a guardian of the person of a minor to consent to his or her adoption.[13]

---

7. 705 ILCS 405/5-820(f).

8. 705 ILCS 405/5-820(f).

9. Supreme Court Rule 660(a).

   Forms: Review. 15 Am Jur Pl & Pr Forms (Rev), Juvenile Courts and Delinquent and Dependent Children, Forms 141–157.

10. Supreme Court Rule 607(a).

11. Supreme Court Rule 607(a).

12. Supreme Court Rule 662(a).

13. Supreme Court Rule 663.

PART SIX

PARTICULAR CRIMES AND OFFENSES

CHAPTER 36

ABANDONMENT

by

Carol J. Browder, J.D.

and

Robert L. Margolis, Esq.

Scope of Chapter:

This chapter discusses the offense of child abandonment under the Abandoned Child Prevention Act. Discussed are the acts or omissions constituting abandonment as well as the penalty imposed for the offense.

Treated Elsewhere:

Charging instruments, see Chapter 9.

Criminal prosecution, see Chapter 12.

Defenses, see Chapter 3.

Evidentiary matters, see Chapters 17–19, 21.

Sentencing, see Chapter 28.

Venue, see Chapter 13.

Research References:

Text References:

Decker, Illinois Criminal Law 2d ed § 9.49A

Annotation References:
ALR Digest: Infants § 10

Index and Annotations: Abandonment of Person; Custody and Support of Children

Practice References:
23 Am Jur 2d, Desertion and Nonsupport §§ 1–5, 51–115

State Legislation:
720 ILCS 5/12-21.5

Miscellaneous References:
West's Illinois Digest 2d, Parent and Child § 17

Auto-Cite®: Cases and annotations referred to in this chapter can be further researched through the Auto-Cite® computer-assisted research service. Use Auto-Cite® to check citations for form, parallel references, prior and later history, and annotation references.

§ 36:01.   Generally
§ 36:02.   Act or omissions constituting abandonment

§ 36:01. Generally

When a father, mother, guardian, or any person having physical custody or control of a child under the age of 13 years, without regard for the mental or physical health, safety, or welfare of the child, knowingly leaves that child without supervision by a responsbile person over the age of 14 for a period of 24 hours or more, he or she commits the offense of child abandonment, a Class 4 felony.[1] A second offense and conviction

---

1. 720 ILCS 5/12-21.5(a).

Sentence of imprisonment, see 730 ILCS 5/5-8-1.

Text References: Decker, Illinois Criminal Law 2d ed § 9.49A.

Annotation References:
Who has custody or control of child within terms of penal statute punishing cruelty or neglect by one having custody or control, 75 ALR3d 934.

Periodicals: For article, "1997 Illinois Supreme Court Criminal Survey: Fitness Hearings, Proportionate Punishment, and More," see 86 Ill. B.J. 202 (1998).

after a prior conviction is a Class 3 felony.[2]

In determining whether the child was left without regard for his or her mental or physical health, safety, or welfare, the following factors may be considered:[3]

- the age of the child;
- the number of children left at the location;
- special needs of the child, including whether the child is physically or mentally handicapped, or otherwise in need of ongoing prescribed medical treatment such as periodic doses of insulin or other medications;
- the duration of time in which the child was left without supervision;
- the condition and location of the place where the child was left without supervision;
- the time of day or night when the child was left without supervision;
- the weather conditions, including whether the child was left in a location with adequate protection from the natural elements such as adequate heat or light;
- the location of the parent, guardian, or other person having physical custody or control of the child at the time the child was left without supervision, and the distance the child was from that person supervision;
- whether the child's movement was restricted, or the child was otherwise locked within a room or other structure;

For article, "Lesser-Included Offenses in Illinois: A Look at Recent Developments," see 85 Ill. B.J. 480 (1997).

For article, "Survey of Illinois Law: Criminal Law and Procedure," see 21 S. Ill. U.L.J. 759 (1997).

See also ch 28.

2. 720 ILCS 5/12-21.5(a).

Sentence of imprisonment, see 730 ILCS 5/5-8-1.

3. See generally 705 ILCS 5/12-21.5(b).

- whether the child was given a phone number of a person or location to call in the event of an emergency and whether the child was capable of making an emergency call;
- whether there was food and other provision left for the child;
- whether any of the conduct is attributable to economic hardship or illness and the parent, guardian or other person having physical custody or control of the child made a good faith effort to provide for the health and safety of the child;
- the age and physical and mental capabilities of the person or persons who provided supervision for the child;
- whether the child was left under the supervision of another person; and
- any other factor that would endanger the health or safety of that particular child.

§ 36:02. Act or omissions constituting abandonment

As interpreted in the context of the prior statute, abandonment requires conduct which evinces a settled purpose to forego all parental duties and relinquish all parental claims to a child.[4]

> *Practice Guide:* The practitioner should note that the statute which became effective on September 9, 1993, indicates that "abandonment" involves less than foregoing all parental duties but only the leaving of a child under the age of 13 without supervision by a person over the age of 14 for a period of 24 hours or more without regard for the mental or physical heatlh, safety or welfare of the child.[5]

---

4. In re Bartha, 107 Ill App 2d 214, 245 NE2d 779 (2d Dist 1969).
5. See 720 ILCS 5/12-21.5.

CHAPTER 37

ABDUCTION, KIDNAPPING, AND RELATED OFFENSES

by

Carol J. Browder, J.D.

and

Robert L. Margolis, Esq.

Scope of Chapter:
This chapter covers the offenses of kidnapping and child abduction as well as the lesser offenses of unlawful restraint, forcible detention and harboring a runaway.

Treated Elsewhere:
Charging instruments, see Chapter 9.
Conspiracy, see Chapter 50.
Criminal prosecution, see Chapter 12.
Defenses, see Chapter 3.
Evidentiary matters, see Chapters 17–19, 21.
Homicide, see Chapter 60.
Sentencing, see Chapter 28.
Venue, see Chapter 13.

Research References:
  Text References:
  Decker, Illinois Criminal Law 2d ed §§ 7.01 et seq
  Annotation References:
  ALR Digest: Kidnapping § 1–3
  Index and Annotations: Abduction and Kidnapping; Parental Kidnapping Prevention Act
  Practice References:
  1 Am Jur 2d, Abduction and Kidnapping § 1 et seq.

§ 37:01   ILLINOIS JURISPRUDENCE: CRIMINAL LAW

State Legislation:
225 ILCS 10/2–21; 325 ILCS 5/1 et seq.; 705 ILCS 405/3–5; 720 ILCS 5/1–6(i), (o), 5/10–1 et seq., 5/33A–1, 5/36–1 et seq.; 735 ILCS 5/13–202.1; 750 ILCS 30/1 et seq.

Miscellaneous References:
West's Illinois Digest 2d, Kidnapping § 1 et seq.

Auto-Cite®: Cases and annotations referred to in this chapter can be further researched through the Auto-Cite® computer-assisted research service. Use Auto-Cite® to check citations for form, parallel references, prior and later history, and annotation references.

§ 37:01.   Kidnapping
§ 37:02.   Aggravated kidnapping
§ 37:03.   Civil aspects
§ 37:04.   Unlawful restraint
§ 37:05.   Forcible detention
§ 37:06.   Child abduction
§ 37:07.   —Affirmative defenses
§ 37:08.   —Aggravating factors
§ 37:09.   —Aiding and abetting child abduction
§ 37:10.   Harboring a runaway
§ 37:11.   Venue

§ 37:01. Kidnapping

The Criminal Code provides that kidnapping occurs when one of three events occurs:

- a person knowingly and secretly confines another against his or her will,

- by force or threat of imminent force carries another from one place with intent secretly to confine him or her against that individual's will, or

- by deceit or enticement induces another to go from one place to another with intent secretly to confine that individual against his or her will.[1]

---

1. 720 ILCS 5/10-1.

    Annotation References: Seizure or detention for purpose of committing rape, robbery, or other offense as constituting separate crime of kidnapping, 39 ALR5th 283.
    Validity, construction, and application of "hold to service" provision of

ABDUCTION, KIDNAPPING, AND RELATED OFFENSES § 37:01

> ☛ *Practice Guide:* The secret confinement element of kidnapping may be shown by proof of the secrecy of either the confinement or the place of confinement.[2] And confinement, though usually meaning enclosure within something such as a car or house, is not strictly limited to those types of places.[3] Thus, in one case, the secret confinement element was established when the victim was taken to a secluded bridge and bound.[4]

In addition, confinement of a child under the age of 13 years constitutes kidnapping and is against the child's will if the confinement is without the consent of the child's parent or legal guardian.[5]

Kidnapping is a Class 2 felony.[6]

To determine whether asportation or detention rises to the level of kidnapping as a separate offense, the court must consider the duration of the asportation or detention, whether the asportation or detention occurred during the commission of a separate offense, whether the asportation or detention that occurred is inherent in the separate offense, and whether the asportation or

---

kidnapping statute, 28 ALR5th 754.
Coercion, compulsion, or duress as defense to charge of kidnapping, 69 ALR4th 1005.
Necessity and sufficiency of showing, in kidnapping prosecution, that detention was with intent to "secretly" confine victim, 98 ALR3d 733.
Seizure of prison official by inmates as kidnapping, 59 ALR3d 1306.
Seizure or detention for purpose of committing rape, robbery, or similar offense as constituting separate crime of kidnapping, 43 ALR3d 699.

2. People v Pasch, 152 Ill 2d 133, 178 Ill Dec 38, 604 NE2d 294 (1992); People v Enoch, 122 Ill 2d 176, 119 Ill Dec 265, 522 NE2d 1124 (1988); People v Riley, 219 Ill App 3d 482, 162 Ill Dec 194, 579 NE2d 1008 (1st Dist 1991).

3. People v Jackson, 281 Ill App 3d 759, 217 Ill Dec 185, 666 NE2d 854 (1st Dist 1996).

4. People v Jackson, 281 Ill App 3d 759, 217 Ill Dec 185, 666 NE2d 854 (1st Dist 1996).

5. 720 ILCS 5/10-1.

6. 720 ILCS 5/10-1.

detention created a significant danger to the victim independent of that posed by the separate offense.[7] Four factors to be considered in determining when an act of detention or asportation rises to the level of kidnapping as a separate offense are: (1) the deviation of the detention or asportation, (2) whether the detention or asportation occurred during the commission of a separate offense, (3) whether the detention or asportation which occurred is inherent in the separate offense, and (4) whether the asportation or detention created a significant danger to the victim independent of that posed by the separate offense.[8]

> ☛ *Illustration:* Thus, in one case, the defendant's kidnapping convictions in connection with criminal sexual assault conviction were proper where the victim was forced off the street and then into a garage, as the victim's asportation from the street to the garage was not inherent in the sexual assault and posed a significant danger to her separate from that posed by the sexual assault.[9] In another, asportation occurred where defendant forced the victim, at knifepoint, to walk with him approximately 1½ blocks to his apartment.[10]

§ 37:02. Aggravated kidnapping

A person is guilty of the offense of aggravated kidnapping when he or she commits one of the following acts:

- kidnaps for the purpose of obtaining ransom from the person kidnapped or from any other person,[11]

---

7. People v Jackson, 281 Ill App 3d 759, 217 Ill Dec 185, 666 NE2d 854 (1st Dist 1996).

8. People v Lamkey, 240 Ill App 3d 435, 181 Ill Dec 333, 608 NE2d 406 (1st Dist 1992); People v Casiano, 212 Ill App 3d 680, 156 Ill Dec 762, 571 NE2d 742 (1st Dist 1991).

9. People v Sherrod, 220 Ill App 3d 429, 163 Ill Dec 102, 581 NE2d 53 (1st Dist 1991).

10. People v Casiano, 212 Ill App 3d 680, 156 Ill Dec 762, 571 NE2d 742 (1st Dist 1991).

ABDUCTION, KIDNAPPING, AND RELATED OFFENSES § 37:02

- takes as his or her victim a child under the age of 13 years, or an institutionalized severely or profoundly mentally retarded person,[12]
- inflicts great bodily harm or commits another felony upon the victim,[13]
- wears a hood, robe or mask or conceals his or her identity,[14] or
- commits the offense of kidnapping while armed with a dangerous weapon.[15]

"Armed with a dangerous weapon" means carrying a handgun, sawed-off shotgun, sawed-off rifle, any other firearm small enough to be concealed upon the person, semiautomatic firearm, machine gun, rifle, shotgun, spring gun, other firearm, stun gun or taser, knife with a blade of at least 3 inches in length, dagger, dirk, switchblade knife, stiletto, axe, hatchet, or other deadly or dangerous weapon or instrument of like character, bludgeon, black-jack, slungshot, sand-bag, sand-club, metal knuckles, billy, or other dangerous weapon of like character.[16]

Aggravated kidnapping for ransom is a Class X felony.[17] If a

---

11. 720 ILCS 5/10-2.

    Annotation References: Failure of police to preserve potentially exculpatory evidence as violating criminal defendant's rights under state constitution. 40 ALR5th 113.

    Periodicals: For article, "Survey of Illinois Law: Criminal Law and Procedure," see 21 S. Ill. U.L.J. 759 (1997).

12. 720 ILCS 5/10-2(a)(2).

13. 720 ILCS 5/10-2(a)(3).

    Annotation References: What is "harm" within provisions of statutes increasing penalty for kidnapping where victim suffers harm, 11 ALR3d 1053.

14. 720 ILCS 5/10-2(a)(4).

15. 720 ILCS 5/10-2(a)(5).

16. 720 ILCS 5/33A-1.

17. 720 ILCS 5/10-2(b).

§ 37:02   ILLINOIS JURISPRUDENCE: CRIMINAL LAW

person is convicted of a second or subsequent offense of aggravated kidnapping, he or she must be sentenced to life imprisonment, unless the second or subsequent offense was not committed after the conviction on the first offense.[18] As used in this context, "ransom" includes money, benefit or other valuable thing or concession.[19]

The penalties for aggravated kidnapping and armed violence are unconstitutionally disproportionate; the elements of each offense are identical but aggravated kidnapping is a Class 1 felony while armed violence is a Class X felony.[20] Thus, an armed violence charge,[21] predicated on unlawful restraining violates the Illinois Constitution.[22]

The "secret confinement" element contemplated by the aggravated kidnapping statute may be shown by proof of the secrecy of confinement or the place of confinement; "secret" has been variously defined as concealed, hidden, not made public, kept from the knowledge or notice of persons liable to be affected by the act.[23]

§ 37:03. Civil aspects

Any vessel, vehicle or aircraft used with the knowledge and consent of the owner in the commission of or in the attempt to commit aggravated kidnapping may be subject to seizure and forfeiture.[24] Similarly, any building used in the commission of a

---

18. 720 ILCS 5/10-2(b).

19. 720 ILCS 5/10-2(a).

20. People v Christy, 139 Ill 2d 172, 151 Ill Dec 315, 564 NE2d 770 (1990).

Text References: Decker, Illinois Criminal Law 2d ed §§ 9.56–9.61.

21. 720 ILCS 5/33A-2.

22. People v Murphy, 284 Ill App 3d 1019, 200 Ill Dec 9, 635 NE2d 1102 (2d Dist 1994).

23. People v Franzen, 251 Ill App 3d 813, 190 Ill Dec 847, 622 NE2d 877 (2d Dist 1993).

24. 720 ILCS 5/36-1.

Annotation References: Running of limitations against action for civil

kidnapping or aggravated kidnapping may be deemed a public nuisance and subject to abatement proceedings.[25] The spouse of the owner of a vehicle seized for a violation of this statute may make a showing that the seized vehicle is the only source of transportation, and if it is determined that the financial hardship to the family as a result of the seizure outweighs the benefit to the State from the seizure, the vehicle may be forfeited to the spouse or family member and the title to the vehicle transferred to that person if he or she is properly licensed and requires the use of the vehicle for employment or family transportation purposes.[26]

> ☛ *Caution:* The practitioner should be aware that the statute governing the abatement of a nuisance was held to be unconstitutional by the Illinois supreme court.[27]

Actions for damages may be brought against individuals convicted of kidnapping and aggravated kidnapping.[28] In addition, whenever a verdict or judgment in excess of $500 is rendered against the Department of Corrections or any past or present employee or official in favor of any individual for damages incurred while that person was committed to the Department of Corrections, the department within 14 days of rendering of the verdict or judgment must notify the state's attorney of the county from which the person was committed.[29] The state's attorney must in turn, within 14 days, send the same

damages for sexual abuse of child. 9 ALR5th 321.

Periodicals: Jochner, From fiction to fact: the Supreme court's re-evaluation of civil asset forfeiture laws 82 Ill BJ 560 (1994).

25. 720 ILCS 5/37-1 et seq.

Abatement proceedings, see ch 57.

26. 720 ILCS 5/36-1.

27. 720 ILCS 5/37-4.

People v Sequoia Books, Inc., 127 Ill 2d 271, 130 Ill Dec 235, 537 NE2d 302 (1989), cert den 493 US 1042, 107 L Ed 2d 831, 110 S Ct 835.

28. 735 ILCS 5/13-202.1(a).

29. 735 ILCS 5/13-202.1(d).

notice to the victim or victims of the crime for which the offender was committed, along with the information that the victim or victims may contact the state's attorney for advice concerning their rights to sue for damages under the law.[30] If so requested, the state's attorney's office must provide such advice, but in no instance may the state's attorney institute a civil action for damages on behalf of the victim or victims.[31] Civil actions may not be brought against the Department of Corrections, the state's attorney, a county, or any past or present employee or agent for any alleged violation by any of these entities of the preceding notification requirements.[32]

§ 37:04. Unlawful restraint

A person commits the offense of unlawful restraint when he or she knowingly detains another without legal authority.[33] The offense of aggravated unlawful restraint occurs when a person knowingly detains another, without legal authority, while using a deadly weapon.[34] Unlawful restraint is Class 4 felony;[35] aggravated unlawful restraint is a Class 3 felony.[36]

Actual or physical force is not a necessary element of unlawful restraint as long as an individual's freedom of locomotion is impaired.[37] The gist of unlawful restraint is the detention of a person by some conduct which prevents him or her from moving from one place to another, which detention must be willful, against the victim's consent, and prevent movement from one

30. 735 ILCS 5/13-202.1(d).

31. 735 ILCS 5/13-202.1(d).

32. 735 ILCS 5/13-202.1(d).

33. 720 ILCS 5/10-3(a).

Text References: Decker, Illinois Criminal Law 2d ed §§ 7.20–7.22.

34. 720 ILCS 5/10-3.1(a).

35. 720 ILCS 5/10-3(b).

36. 720 ILCS 5/10-3.1(b).

37. People v Bowen, 241 Ill App 3d 608, 182 Ill Dec 43, 609 NE2d 346 (4th Dist 1993), cert den 510 US 946, 126 L Ed 2d 336, 114 S Ct 387.

place to another.[38]

Motive is not an element of the offense of aggravated unlawful restraint.[39] Thus, evidence that the defendant held the victim while using a pistol or other dangerous weapon is enough for conviction without regard to motive.[40]

A lawful detention pursuant to a provision of the Mental Health Code[41] cannot be the basis of a false imprisonment claim.[42] However, such a detention may be followed by a unlawful detention that is actionable as false imprisonment.[43]

§ 37:05. Forcible detention

Forcible detention is committed when two components are present. A person must hold an individual hostage without lawful authority for the purpose of obtaining performance of demands by a third person.[44] This must be coupled with one of the following acts:

- the person holding the hostage is armed with a dangerous weapon[45] or
- the hostage is known to the person holding him or her to be a peace officer or correctional employee engaged in the performance of his or her official duties.[46] This offense is a Class 2 felony.[47]

---

38. People v Bowen, 241 Ill App 3d 608, 182 Ill Dec 43, 609 NE2d 346 (4th Dist 1993), cert den 510 US 946, 126 L Ed 2d 336, 114 S Ct 387.

39. People v Watkins, 238 Ill App 3d 253, 179 Ill Dec 422, 606 NE2d 254 (1st Dist 1992).

40. People v Watkins, 238 Ill App 3d 253, 179 Ill Dec 422, 606 NE2d 254 (1st Dist 1992).

41. 405 ILCS 5/101 et seq.

42. Sassali v DeFauw, 297 Ill App 3d 50, 231 Ill Dec 646, 696 N.E.2d 1217 (2d Dist 1998).

43. Sassali v. DeFauw, 696 N.E.2d 1217 (1998).

44. 720 ILCS 5/10-4(a).

45. 720 ILCS 5/10-4(a)(1).

☞ *Definition:* "Armed with a dangerous weapon" means carrying a handgun, sawed-off shotgun, sawed-off rifle, any other firearm small enough to be concealed upon the person, semiautomatic firearm, machine gun, rifle, shotgun, spring gun, other firearm, stun gun or taser, knife with a blade of at least 3 inches in length, dagger, dirk, switchblade knife, stiletto, axe, hatchet, or other deadly or dangerous weapon or instrument of like character, bludgeon, black-jack, slungshot, sand-bag, sand-club, metal knuckles, billy, or other dangerous weapon of like character.[48]

§ 37:06. Child abduction

The Criminal Code provides that a person commits child abduction when he or she commits one of the following acts:

- intentionally violates any terms of a valid court order granting sole or joint custody, care or possession to another, by concealing or detaining the child or removing the child from the jurisdiction of the court;[49]

- intentionally violates a court order prohibiting the person from concealing or detaining the child or removing the child from the jurisdiction of the court;[50]

- intentionally conccals, dctains or removes the child without the consent of the mother or lawful custodian of the child if the person is a putative father and either the paternity of the child has not been legally established or the paternity of the child has been legally established but no orders relating to custody have been entered;[51] however, regardless of the presumption that when parties have never been married to

---

46. 720 ILCS 5/10-4(a)(2).
47. 720 ILCS 5/10-4(b).
48. 720 ILCS 5/33A-1.
49. 720 ILCS 5/10-5(b)(1).
50. 720 ILCS 5/10-5(b)(2).
51. 720 ILCS 5/10-5(b)(3).

each other the mother has legal custody of a child unless a valid court order states otherwise, a mother commits child abduction when she intentionally conceals or removes a child whom she has abandoned or relinquished custody of from an unadjudicated father who has provided sole ongoing care and custody of the child in her absence;[52]

- intentionally conceals or removes the child from a parent after filing a petition or being served with process in an action affecting marriage or paternity but prior to the issuance of a temporary or final order determining custody;[53]
- at the expiration of visitation rights outside Illinois, intentionally fails or refuses to return or impedes the return of the child to the lawful custodian in this state;[54]
- being a parent of the child, and where the parents of the child are or have been married and there has been no court order of custody, conceals the child for 15 days and fails to make reasonable attempts within the 15-day period to notify the other parent as to the specific whereabouts of the child, including a means by which to contact such child, or to arrange reasonable visitation or contact with the child[55] (though it is not an act of child abduction for a person fleeing domestic violence to take the child with him or her to housing provided by a domestic violence program);[56]

---

52. 720 ILCS 5/10-3(b)(3).

Creation of presumption, see 720 ILCS 5/10-5(a)(3).

53. 720 ILCS 5/10-5(b)(4).

Text References: Decker, Illinois Criminal Law 2d ed § 7.24.

Annotation References: Liability of legal or natural parent, or one who aids and abets, for damages resulting from abduction of own child, 49 ALR4th 7.

Kidnapping or related offense by taking or removing of child by or under authority of parent or one in loco parentis, 20 ALR4th 823.

54. 720 ILCS 5/10-5(b)(5).

55. 720 ILCS 5/10-5(b)(6).

56. 720 ILCS 5/10-5(b)(6).

§ 37:06   ILLINOIS JURISPRUDENCE: CRIMINAL LAW

- being a parent of the child and where the parents of the child are or have been married and there has been no court order of custody, conceals, detains, or removes the child with physical force or threat of physical force;[57]
- conceals, detains, or removes the child for payment or promise of payment at the instruction of a person who has no legal right to custody;[58]
- retains in Illinois for 30 days a child removed from another state without the consent of the lawful custodian or in violation of a valid court order of custody;[59] or
- intentionally lures or attempts to lure a child under the age of 16 into a motor vehicle, building, house trailer, or dwelling place without the consent of the parent or lawful custodian of the child for other than a lawful purpose.[60]

☛ *Definition:* While the term "parent" is not defined by the kidnapping statute, it should be given its plain and ordinary meaning of father or mother related by blood.[61]

☛ *Practice Guide:* A defendant may be convicted of child abduction when he takes a child at a time when the defendant has neither established paternity nor has been presumed by

---

57. 720 ILCS 5/10-5(b)(7).

58. 720 ILCS 5/10-5(b)(8).

59. 720 ILCS 5/10-5(b)(9).

Annotation References: Recognition and enforcement of out-of-state custody decree under § 13 of the Uniform Child Custody Jurisdiction Act (UCCJA) or the Parental Kidnapping Prevention Act (PKPA), 28 USCS § 1738A(a). 40 ALR5th 227.
Pending proceeding in another state as ground for declining jurisdiction under § 6(a) of the Uniform Child Custody Jurisdiction Act (UCCJA) or the Parental Kidnapping Prevention Act (PKPA), 28 USCS § 1738A(g). 20 ALR5th 700.

60. 720 ILCS 5/10-5(b)(10).

61. People v Algarin, 200 Ill App 3d 740, 146 Ill Dec 494, 558 NE2d 457 (1st Dist 1990).

ABDUCTION, KIDNAPPING, AND RELATED OFFENSES § 37:06

law to be the father of the child.[62] A finding of paternity which comes after taking the child cannot provide a defense to the child abduction charge.[63]

The luring or attempted luring of a child under the age of 16 into a motor vehicle, building, house trailer, or dwelling place without the consent of the child's parent or lawful custodian is prima facie evidence of "other than a lawful purpose".[64] A child-abduction offense is complete when one intentionally attempts to lure a child into a car.[65]

> *Definition:* The phrase "other than a lawful purpose" means any purpose which is unlawful and cannot reasonably be said to involve violations of administrative regulations or city ordinances.[66] Thus, in one case, the defendant's conviction for child abduction was reversed where the State failed to prove the two elements of "unlawful intent" and "attempted entry," notwithstanding the State's contention that the evidence proved beyond a reasonable doubt the defendant was following a young girl in his vehicle and intentionally attempted to lure her into the vehicle for an unlawful purpose, since the only real evidence going to the elements of the offense was the girl's testimony the defendant waved three times for her to come toward him as he sat in his vehicle talking to some other girls who were standing outside the vehicle, and without other affirmative conduct evidencing an intent to lure the girl into the vehicle, the defendant's innocuous gestures could not sustain his conviction.[67]

Every law enforcement officer investigating an alleged incident

---

62. People v Shephard, 171 Ill App 3d 977, 121 Ill Dec 795, 525 NE2d 1102 (1st Dist 1988).

63. People v Shephard, 171 Ill App 3d 977, 121 Ill Dec 795, 525 NE2d 1102 (1st Dist 1988).

64. 720 ILCS 5/10-5(b).

65. People v Branham, 217 Ill App 3d 650, 160 Ill Dec 478, 577 NE2d 803 (5th Dist 1991).

66. People v Williams, 133 Ill 2d 449, 141 Ill Dec 444, 551 NE2d 631 (1990).

§ 37:06   ILLINOIS JURISPRUDENCE: CRIMINAL LAW

of child abduction must make a written police report of any bona fide allegation and the disposition of the investigation.[68] Whenever law enforcement officer has reason to believe a child abduction has occurred, that officer must provide the lawful custodian a summary of his or her rights including the procedures and available relief.[69]

If, during the course of an investigation, the child is found in the physical custody of the defendant or another, the law enforcement officer must return the child to the parent or lawful custodian from whom the child was concealed, detained or removed, unless there is good cause for the law enforcement officer or the Department of Children and Family Services to retain temporary protective custody of the child pursuant to statute.[70]

The court may order an abducted child to be returned to the parent or lawful custodian from whom the child was concealed, detained or removed.[71] This provision is not intended to be used as a tool for effecting a change in custody based solely on removing the children to another state but rather as a means of reestablishing the status quo by giving the court the power to return the children to their lawful custodian, and the outcome of the civil custody proceeding in the foreign jurisdiction will govern the custody issue.[72] In addition to any sentence imposed, the court may assess against any person convicted of child abduction any reasonable expense incurred in searching for or returning the child.[73]

---

67. People v Wenger, 258 Ill App 3d 561, 197 Ill Dec 274, 631 NE2d 277 (1st Dist 1994).

68. 720 ILCS 5/10-5(g).

69. 720 ILCS 5/10-5(h).

70. 720 ILCS 5/10-5(i).

Abused and Neglected Child Reporting Act, see 325 ILCS 5/1 et seq.

71. 720 ILCS 5/10-5(e).

72. People v Olsewski, 257 Ill App 3d 1018, 196 Ill Dec 434, 630 NE2d 131 (2d Dist 1994).

A person convicted of child abduction is guilty of a Class 4 felony.[74]

It also is a crime to interfere with the visitation rights of another by detaining or concealing a child with the intent to deprive another of his or her rights to visitation.[75] Unlawful visitation interference is a petty offense for the first two convictions and a Class A misdemeanor for each subsequent conviction..[76]

§ 37:07. —Affirmative defenses

The following constitute affirmative defenses to an accusation of child abduction:

- the person accused of abduction had custody of the child pursuant to a court order granting legal custody or visitation rights which existed at the time of the alleged violation;[77]
- the accused had physical custody of the child pursuant to a court order granting legal custody or visitation rights and failed to return the child as a result of circumstances beyond his or her control, and the person notified and disclosed to the other parent or legal custodian the specific whereabouts of the child and a means by which the child could be contacted or made a reasonable attempt to notify the other parent or lawful custodian of the child of the circumstances and made such disclosure within 24 hours after the visitation

---

73. 720 ILCS 5/10-5(e).
74. 720 ILCS 5/10-5(d).
75. 720 ILCS 5/10–5.5(b).
76. 720 ILCS 5/10–5.5(b).
77. 720 ILCS 5/10-5(c)(1).

Annotation References: Recognition and enforcement of out-of-state custody decree under § 13 of the Uniform Child Custody Jurisdiction Act (UCCJA) or the Parental Kidnapping Prevention Act (PKPA), 28 USCS § 1738A(a). 40 ALR5th 227.

Pending proceeding in another state as ground for declining jurisdiction under § 6(a) of the Uniform Child Custody Jurisdiction Act (UCCJA) or the Parental Kidnapping Prevention Act (PKPA), 28 USCS § 1738A(g). 20 ALR5th 700.

§ 37:07   ILLINOIS JURISPRUDENCE: CRIMINAL LAW

period had expired and returned the child as soon as possible;[78]

- the accused was fleeing an incidence or pattern of domestic violence;[79] or
- the accused lured or attempted to lure a child under the age of 16 into a motor vehicle, building, house trailer, or dwelling place for a lawful purpose.[80]

☛ *Illustration:* In one case, where the defendant mother was awarded sole legal custody of the two minor children in dissolution proceedings prior to moving them to a foreign jurisdiction, the existence of the unasserted affirmative defense in the child abduction statute that the defendant was the legal custodian at the time of the violation necessitated reversal of the defendant's child abduction conviction on appeal, in the absence of any evidence rebutting the defense.[81]

☛ *Illustration:* In another, the evidence was insufficient to support defendant's affirmative defense that when he took the child he was fleeing an incident of domestic violence where the record established that the allegedly abusive babysitter had been fired when the abuse was discovered and spanking and pinching by another babysitter was not found by the court to be domestic violence.[82]

It is an affirmative defense to the crime of unlawful visitation interference[83] that the defendant committed the act to protect the

---

78. 720 ILCS 5/10-5(c)(2).

79. 720 ILCS 5/10-5(c)(3).

80. 720 ILCS 5/10-5(c)(4).

81. People v Olsewski, 257 Ill App 3d 1018, 196 Ill Dec 434, 630 NE2d 131 (2d Dist 1994).

82. People v Welacha, 186 Ill App 3d 860, 134 Ill Dec 581, 542 NE2d 927 (1st Dist 1989).

83. See § 37:06.

child from imminent physical harm, provided the defendant's belief that physical harm was imminent was a reasonable belief and the defendant's conduct was a reasonable response to the perceived harm.[84] It also is an affirmative defense that the act was committed with the mutual consent of all parties with a right to custody and visitation of the child or that the act was otherwise authorized by law.[85]

§ 37:08. —Aggravating factors

A court may impose a more severe sentence on an individual convicted of child abduction if, upon sentencing, the court finds evidence of any of the following aggravating factors:

- the defendant abused and neglected the child following the concealment, detention or removal of the child;[86]
- the defendant inflicted or threatened to inflict physical harm on a parent or lawful custodian of the child or on the child with intent to cause the parent or lawful custodian to discontinue criminal prosecution of the defendant;[87]
- the defendant demanded payment in exchange for return of the child or demanded that he or she be relieved of the financial or legal obligation to support the child in exchange for return of the child;[88]

---

84. 720 ILCS 5/10–5.5(g)(1).

85. 720 ILCS 5/10–5.5(g)(1), (2).

86. 720 ILCS 5/10-5(d)(1).

Annotation References: Recognition and enforcement of out-of-state custody decree under § 13 of the Uniform Child Custody Jurisdiction Act (UCCJA) or the Parental Kidnapping Prevention Act (PKPA), 28 USCS § 1738A(a). 40 ALR5th 227.

Pending proceeding in another state as ground for declining jurisdiction under § 6(a) of the Uniform Child Custody Jurisdiction Act (UCCJA) or the Parental Kidnapping Prevention Act (PKPA), 28 USCS § 1738A(g). 20 ALR5th 700.

87. 720 ILCS 5/10-5(d)(2).

88. 720 ILCS 5/10-5(d)(3).

- the defendant has previously been convicted of child abduction;[89]
- the defendant committed the abduction while armed with a deadly weapon or the taking of the child resulted in serious bodily injury to another;[90] or
- the defendant committed the abduction while in a school, in a playground, or any conveyance used for the transporting of students to or from school or a school-related activity, or on school property or on a public way within 1000 feet of school property.[91]

§ 37:09. —Aiding and abetting child abduction

A person is guilty of aiding and abetting a child abduction when before or during the commission of a child abduction and with the intent to promote or facilitate the offense, he or she intentionally aides or abets another in the planning or commission of child abduction, unless, before the commission of the offense, the individual makes proper effort to prevent the commission of the offense.[92] Further, an individual is guilty of aiding and abetting when he or she knowingly destroys, alters, conceals or disguises physical evidence or furnishes false information with the intent to prevent the apprehension of a person known to have committed child abduction, or with the intent to obstruct or prevent efforts to locate the child victim of a child abduction.[93]

Aiding and abetting child abduction is a Class 4 felony.[94]

§ 37:10. Harboring a runaway

An individual who knowingly gives shelter to an unemancipated minor[95] for more than 48 hours without the consent of the

---

89. 720 ILCS 5/10-5(d)(4).
90. 720 ILCS 5/10-5(d)(5).
91. 720 ILCS 5/10-5(d)(6).
92. 720 ILCS 5/10-7(a)(i).
93. 720 ILCS 5/10-8(a)(ii).
94. 720 ILCS 5/10-8(b).

minor's parent or guardian and without notifying the local law enforcement authorities of the minor's name and the fact that the minor is being provided shelter commits the offense of harboring a runaway.[96] The statutory mandates against harboring a runaway do not apply to agencies or associations providing crisis intervention services[97] or an operator of a youth emergency shelter.[98]

The offense of harboring a runaway is a Class A misdemeanor.[99]

§ 37:11. Venue

A trial for a charge of kidnapping may be held in any county in which the kidnapping victim has traveled or has been confined during the course of the offense.[1] A person who commits the offense of child abduction may be tried in any county in which the victim has traveled, been detained, concealed or removed to during the course of the offense.[2] Notwithstanding this, absent a showing of good cause, the preferred place of trial is in the county of residence of the child's lawful custodian.[3]

---

95. Emancipation of Mature Minors Act, see 750 ILCS 30/1 et seq.

96. 720 ILCS 5/10-6(a).

97. See Juvenile Court Act of 1987, 705 ILCS 405/3-5.

98. See Child Care Act of 1969, 225 ILCS 10/2.21.

99. 720 ILCS 5/10-6.

1. 720 ILCS 5/1-6(i).

2. 720 ILCS 5/1-6(o).

3. 720 ILCS 5/1-6(o).

CHAPTER 38

ABORTION

by

Carol J. Browder, J.D.

Diane C. Busch, J.D.

and

Robert L. Margolis, Esq.

Scope of Chapter:

This chapter covers the criminal aspects of abortion under the Abortion Law of 1975. The discussion includes when an abortion can be performed, preservation of life and health of the fetus, required reporting, and associated penalties. In addition, parental consent and notice under the Parental Notice of Abortion Act of 1995 is covered. This discussion includes the procedure for waiver of parental notice, exceptions to the statutory provisions and penalties.

Treated Elsewhere:

Charging instruments, see Chapter 9.

Criminal prosecution, see Chapter 12.

Defenses, see Chapter 3.

Evidentiary matters, see Chapters 17–19, 21.

Sentencing, see Chapter 28.

Venue, see Chapter 13.

Research References:

Annotation References:

ALR Digest: Abortion § 1–8

Index and Annotations: Abortion

§ 38:01   ILLINOIS JURISPRUDENCE: CRIMINAL LAW

Practice References:

1 Am Jur 2d, Abortion § 1 et seq.; 61 Am Jur 2d, Physicians, Surgeons and Other Healers § 84

State Legislation:

210 ILCS 5/7, 85/7; 225 ILCS 60/22, 65/10–45, 65/15–50, 95/21; 720 ILCS 510/1 et seq., 513/1 et seq., 515/1 et seq., 520/1 et seq.; 745 ILCS 30/0.01 et seq., 70/1 et seq.; 750 ILCS 70/1 et seq.

Forms:

19A Am Jur Pl & Pr Forms (Rev), Physicians, Surgeons and Other Healers, Form 14

Miscellaneous References:

West's Illinois Digest 2d, Abortion and Birth Control § 1 et seq.

Auto-Cite®: Cases and annotations referred to in this chapter can be further researched through the Auto-Cite® computer-assisted research service. Use Auto-Cite® to check citations for form, parallel references, prior and later history, and annotation references.

§ 38:01.   In general
§ 38:02.   Constitutional considerations
§ 38:03.   Medical judgment
§ 38:04.   Viability of fetus
§ 38:05.   Preservation of life and health of fetus
§ 38:06.   Other statutory considerations
§ 38:07.   Penalties for violation
§ 38:08.   Abortion referral fee
§ 38:09.   Liability for conscientious objections
§ 38:09.50. Partial-Birth Abortion Ban Act
§ 38:10.   Parental consent and notification
§ 38:11.   —Penalty for unauthorized waiver
§ 38:12.   —Exceptions
§ 38:13.   —Penalties

§ 38:01. In general

It is the longstanding policy of Illinois that an unborn child is a human being from the time of conception and is, therefore, a legal person for purposes of the right to life and is entitled to this right from conception under the laws and state constitution.[1] Further,

---

1. 720 ILCS 510/1.

Annotation References: Validity, under Federal Constitution, of abortion

the state's policy to protect the right to life of the unborn child from conception by prohibiting abortion unless necessary to preserve the life of the mother is impermissible only because of the decisions of the United States Supreme Court.[2] Therefore, if those decisions are ever reversed or modified, or the United States Constitution is amended to allow protection of the unborn, then the former policy to prohibit abortions, unless necessary for the preservation of the mother's life, will be reinstated.[3]

§ 38:02. Constitutional considerations

Issues relating to the validity of abortion legislation initially appear to have been settled by the United States Supreme Court in its landmark decision in Roe v. Wade.[4] Although a pregnant women has no absolute constitutional right to an abortion on demand,[5] and her right to terminate a pregnancy may be limited by the legitimate interest of states in ensuring that abortions are safely performed,[6] it has been held that a women's right to privacy encompasses the decision to terminate her pregnancy.[7]

Under Roe v. Wade, during the first trimester of pregnancy, the state may not interfere with or regulate an attending physician's decision, reached in consultation with his or her patient, that the patient's pregnancy should be terminated.[8] Also, no state may regulate the abortion procedure during the second trimester of pregnancy, except to the extent that the regulation is limited and related to the preservation and protection of maternal health.[9] However, from and after the point the fetus becomes viable, a

laws, 28 L Ed 2d 1053.

2. 720 ILCS 510/1.
3. 720 ILCS 510/1.
4. Roe v Wade, 410 US 113, 35 L Ed 2d 147, 93 S Ct 705 (1973).
5. Doe v Bolton, 410 US 179, 35 L Ed 2d 201, 93 S Ct 739 (1973).
6. Roe v Wade, 410 US 113, 35 L Ed 2d 147, 93 S Ct 705 (1973).
7. Roe v Wade, 410 US 113, 35 L Ed 2d 147, 93 S Ct 705 (1973).
8. Roe v Wade, 410 US 113, 35 L Ed 2d 147, 93 S Ct 705 (1973).
9. Roe v Wade, 410 US 113, 35 L Ed 2d 147, 93 S Ct 705 (1973).

§ 38:02   ILLINOIS JURISPRUDENCE: CRIMINAL LAW

state may prohibit abortions altogether as long as the law includes exceptions for pregnancies that endanger a woman's life or health.[10] During the entire term of pregnancy, a state may legitimately require that all abortions be performed by licensed physicians.[11] Yet, the availability of abortions may not be unduly restricted.[12] Therefore, a state may not require that during the first trimester, abortions be performed in hospitals, nor may it require that they be performed only in hospitals accredited by the Joint Commission on Accredidation of Hospitals.[13] Generally, state law may not impose rigid requirements pertaining to medical approval of abortions[14] or consent by the fathers of the fetuses[15] or parents of pregnant minors.[16] Though, in Rust v. Sullivan,[17] the Supreme Court held that regulations interpreting Title X which mandated that federal funds appropriated to family planning projects could not be used in programs where abortion is a method of family planning and that family planning projects receiving these funds may not provide counseling concerning the use of abortion or referral for abortion as a method of family planning were held to be constitutional.

Other constitutional concerns include: literature discussing the

10. Planned Parenthood v Casey, 505 US 833, 120 L Ed 2d 674, 112 S Ct 2791 (1992).

11. Roe v Wade, 410 US 113, 35 L Ed 2d 147, 93 S Ct 705 (1973).

12. Doe v Bolton, 410 US 179, 35 L Ed 2d 201, 93 S Ct 739 (1973).

13. Doe v Bolton, 410 US 179, 35 L Ed 2d 201, 93 S Ct 739 (1973).

14. Doe v Bolton, 410 US 179, 35 L Ed 2d 201, 93 S Ct 739 (1973).

15. Planned Parenthood v Casey, 505 US 833, 120 L Ed 2d 674, 112 S Ct 2791 (1992).

Annotation References: Woman's right to have abortion without consent of, or against objections of, child's father, 62 ALR3d 1097.

16. See § 38:10.

Annotation References: Right of minor to have abortion performed without parental consent, 42 ALR3d 1406.

17. 500 US 173, 114 L Ed 2d 233, 111 S Ct 1759, 91 CDOS 3713, 91 Daily Journal DAR 6006 (1991).

alternative of abortion;[18] the use of public facilities or funds for the performance of abortions;[19] and informed consent laws that require that a woman receive certain information prior to the abortion.[20]

> *Illustration:* For example, the Supreme Court held a state statute making it a misdemeanor, by sale or circulation of any publication, to encourage or prompt the procuring of an abortion, unconstitutionally infringes upon the First Amendment Rights of Free Speech and Press of a newspaper editor who is prosecuted under that statute for publishing an advertisement of an out-of-state organization which offers services relating to obtaining legal abortions in the state where the organization is located.[21]

§ 38:03. Medical judgment

An abortion may only be performed by a physician after he or she has determined that the abortion is necessary, or he or she has received a written statement or oral communication by another physician certifying that the abortion is necessary.[22] The physician must exercise his or her best clinical judgment in determining the necessity of the abortion.[23] Any person who intentionally or knowingly performs an abortion contrary to these requirements commits a Class 2 felony.[24]

---

18. Bigelow v Virginia, 421 US 809, 44 L Ed 2d 600, 95 S Ct 2222, 1 Media L R 1919 (1975).

19. Webster v Reproductive Health Services, 492 US 490, 106 L Ed 2d 410, 109 S Ct 3040 (1989).

20. Planned Parenthood v Casey, 505 US 833, 120 L Ed 2d 674, 112 S Ct 2791 (1992).

21. Bigelow v Virginia, 421 US 809, 44 L Ed 2d 600, 95 S Ct 2222, 1 Media L R 1919 (1975).

22. 720 ILCS 510/3.1.

23. 720 ILCS 510/3.1.

24. 720 ILCS 510/3.1.

☞ *Caution:* A previous version of this statutory provision has been held unconstitutional because it unnecessarily interfered with both the confidentiality of a woman's abortion decision and the physician-patient consultation.[25]

§ 38:04. Viability of fetus

When a fetus is viable, an abortion cannot be performed unless, in the medical judgment of the attending or referring physician based on the particular facts of the case before him or her, it is necessary to preserve the life or health of the mother.[26] The intentional, knowing, or reckless failure to conform to these requirements is a Class 2 felony.[27] When the fetus is viable, the physician must certify in writing, on a form prescribed by law,[28] the medical indications which, in the physician's medical judgment, warrant performance of the abortion.[29]

☞ *Caution:* Previous versions of this statutory provision have been held to be unconstitutional as they were not narrowly drawn to meet legitimate state interests and because they had no rational connection to needs of either the patient or the fetus.[30]

§ 38:05. Preservation of life and health of fetus

A physician who intentionally performs an abortion when there is a reasonable likelihood of sustained survival of the fetus outside the womb, with or without artificial support, must utilize that method of abortion which, in his or her medical judgment, is most likely to preserve the life and health of the fetus.[31] Any physician

---

25. Charles v Carey, 579 F Supp 464 (ND Ill 1983), affd in part and revd in part 749 F2d 452 (CA7 Ill).

26. 720 ILCS 510/5(1).

27. 720 ILCS 510/5(1).

28. See § 38:06.

29. 720 ILCS 510/5(2).

30. See Wynn v Scott, 449 F Supp 1302 (ND Ill 1978), affd 599 F2d 193 (CA7 Ill).

who intentionally, knowingly, or recklessly violates this provision commits a Class 3 felony.[32] The physician must certify in writing, on a prescribed form,[33] the available methods considered and the reasons for choosing the method employed.[34]

An abortion cannot be performed or induced when the fetus is viable unless there is a physician in attendance, other than the physician performing or inducing the abortion, to take control of and provide immediate care for any child born alive as a result of the abortion.[35] This requirement does not apply when, in the medical judgment of the physician performing or inducing the abortion, there exists a medical emergency.[36] In the case of an emergency, the physician must describe the basis of this judgment on a prescribed form.[37] Any physician who intentionally performs or induces such an abortion and who intentionally, knowingly, or recklessly fails to arrange for the attendance of a second physician commits a Class 3 felony.[38]

Subsequent to the abortion, if a child is born alive, the second physician required to be in attendance must exercise the same degree of professional skill, care, and diligence to preserve the life and health of the child as would be required of a physician providing immediate medical care to a child born alive in the course of a pregnancy termination which was not an abortion.[39] Any physician who intentionally, knowingly, or recklessly violates

---

31. 720 ILCS 510/6(1)(a).
32. 720 ILCS 510/6(1)(c).

   Annotation References: Homicide based on killing of unborn child, 40 ALR3d 444.

33. See § 38:06.
34. 720 ILCS 510/6(1)(b).
35. 720 ILCS 510/6(2)(a).
36. 720 ILCS 510/6(2)(a).
37. 720 ILCS 510/6(2)(a).
38. 720 ILCS 510/6(2)(a).
39. 720 ILCS 510/6(2)(b).

this provision commits a Class 3 felony.[40]

Any physician who intentionally performs an abortion when, in that physician's medical judgment based on the particular facts of the case before him or her, there is a reasonable possibility of sustained survival of the fetus outside the womb, with or without artificial support, must use that method of abortion most likely to preserve the life and health of the fetus.[41] However, there is no requirement that a physician employ a method of abortion which, in the medical judgment of the physician performing the abortion, would increase the medical risk to the mother.[42] The physician must certify in writing, on a prescribed form, the available methods considered and the reasons for choosing the method employed.[43] An intentional, knowing, or reckless violation of this provision by any physician constitutes a Class 3 felony.[44]

When the fetus is viable and there is reasonable medical certainty that the particular method of abortion to be employed will cause organic pain to the fetus, and that use of an anesthetic or analgesic would abolish or alleviate the organic pain to the fetus, the physician who is to perform the abortion, or his or her physician's agent, or the referring physician, or his or her agent, must inform the woman upon whom the abortion is to be performed whether an anesthetic or analgesic is available.[45] Any person who performs an abortion with knowledge that any such reasonable medical certainty exists and that such an anesthetic or analgesic is available, and intentionally fails to inform the woman or to ascertain that the woman has been so informed, commits a Class B misdemeanor.[46] These requirements do not apply when, in the medical judgment of the physician who is to perform the

---

40. 720 ILCS 510/6(2)(b).
41. 720 ILCS 510/6(4)(a).
42. 720 ILCS 510/6(5).
43. 720 ILCS 510/6(4)(b).
44. 720 ILCS 510/6(4)(c).
45. 720 ILCS 510/6(6).
46. 720 ILCS 510/6(6).

abortion or of the referring physician, based on the particular facts of the case, there exists a medical emergency or the administration of such an anesthetic or analgesic would decrease the possibility of sustained survival of the fetus apart from the body of the mother, with or without artificial support.[47] A further exception exists when the physician who is to perform the abortion administers an anesthetic or an analgesic to the woman or the fetus and the physician knows there exists reasonable medical certainty that the use will abolish organic pain caused to the fetus during the course of the abortion.[48]

An abortion may not be intentionally performed with the knowledge that the pregnant woman is seeking the abortion solely on account of the sex of the fetus.[49] However, the performance of an abortion on account of the sex of the fetus because of a genetic disorder linked to that sex is not proscribed.[50] It should be noted that the statute prohibiting abortion on account of the sex of the fetus currently contains no distinction between viability and nonviability of the fetus.[51] However, should it be held to be invalid to the period of pregnancy prior to viability, the statute contains a provision which states that such invalidity will not affect the statute's application to the period of pregnancy subsequent to viability.[52]

> ☛ *Caution:* Part of the statute referenced above and previous versions of the same statute have been held to be unconstitutional.[53] In particular, the portion of the statute concerning the experimentation on a fetus was held

---

47. 720 ILCS 510/6(6).
48. 720 ILCS 510/6(6).
49. 720 ILCS 510/6(8).
50. 720 ILCS 510/6(8).
51. 720 ILCS 510/6(8).
52. 720 ILCS 510/6(8).
53. See Lifchez v Hartigan, 735 F Supp 1361 (ND Ill 1990), affd without op 914 F2d 260 (CA7 Ill), reported in full 1990 US App LEXIS 15796 (CA7), cert

unconstitutional.[54] Also, a previous version of the secion requiring physicians to inform women of the possibility of organic pain to the fetus was held unconstitutional.[55]

§ 38:06. Other statutory considerations

There are also statutory provisions that require the filing of specified reports[56] and the analysis of fetal tissue.[57]

☛ *Caution:* The provision of the Illinois statute stating that no person shall sell or experiment upon a fetus produced by fertilization of human ovum by human sperm was held to be unconstitutional on the basis that it impermissibly restricted a woman's fundamental right of privacy.[58]

§ 38:07. Penalties for violation

An intentional violation of any provision of the Abortion Law of 1975[59] constitutes a Class A misdemeanor unless a specific penalty is otherwise provided.[60] Any person who intentionally

---

den 498 US 1069, 112 L Ed 2d 850, 111 S Ct 787; Charles v Carey, 579 F Supp 464 (ND Ill 1983), affd in part and revd in part 749 F2d 452 (CA7 Ill).

54. 520 ILCS 510/6(7).

Lifchez v Hartigan, 735 F Supp 1361 (ND Ill 1990), affd without op 914 F2d 260 (CA7 Ill), reported in full 1990 US App LEXIS 15796 (CA7), cert den 498 US 1069, 112 L Ed 2d 850, 111 S Ct 787.

55. Charles v Carey, 579 F Supp 464 (ND Ill 1983), affd in part and revd in part 749 F2d 452 (CA7 Ill).

56. 720 ILCS 510/10, 510/10.1.

57. 720 ILCS 510/12.

58. 720 ILCS 510/6(7).

Lifchez v Hartigan, 735 F Supp 1361 (ND Ill 1990), affd without op 914 F2d 260 (CA7 Ill), reported in full 1990 US App LEXIS 15796 (CA7), cert den 498 US 1069, 112 L Ed 2d 850, 111 S Ct 787.

59. 720 ILCS 510/1 et seq.

60. 720 ILCS 510/11(1).

Annotation References: Rights as to notice and hearing in proceeding to revoke or suspend license to practice medicine. 10 ALR5th 1.

falsifies any required writing also commits a Class A misdemeanor.[61]

Under the Medical Practice Act of 1987,[62] the Nursing and Advanced Practice Nursing Act,[63] and the Physician Assistance Practice Act of 1987,[64] an intentional, knowing, reckless, or negligent violation constitutes unprofessional conduct which causes public harm.[65] Further, intentional, knowing, reckless, and negligent violations constitute grounds for refusal, denial, revocation, suspension, or withdrawal of licenses, certificates, or permits pursuant to statute.[66]

Any hospital or licensed facility which, or any physician who, intentionally, knowingly, or recklessly fails to submit a complete report to the Department of Public Health in accordance with statutory provisions[67] commits a Class B misdemeanor.[68] Further, any person who intentionally, knowingly, recklessly, or negligently fails to maintain the confidentiality of any required report[69]

Periodicals: For article, "The Physician Fee-Splitting Ban and the Role of Medico-Ethical History in Statutory Construction," see 85 Ill. B.J. 374 (1997).

For note, "Governing Physician-Associated Risk Disclosure by Adopting the ADA "Direct Threat' Approach: Doctors, Pack Up Your Stethoscopes and Get Out Your Checkbooks," see 1997 U. Ill. L. Rev. 1199.

61. 720 ILCS 510/11(1).

62. 225 ILCS 60/22.

63. 225 ILCS 65/10-45 and 15-50.

64. 225 ILCS 95/21.

65. 720 ILCS 510/11(1).

66. 720 ILCS 510/11(1).

See also 225 ILCS 85/30; 210 ILCS 85/7, 210 ILCS 5/7.

Forms: Petition to revoke license—Performance of illegal abortion by physician. 19A Am Jur Pl & Pr Forms (Rev), Physicians, Surgeons and Other Healers, Form 14.

67. 720 ILCS 510/10.

68. 720 ILCS 510/11(2).

69. See 720 ILCS 510/10.1 or 720 ILCS 510/12.

§ 38:07   ILLINOIS JURISPRUDENCE: CRIMINAL LAW

commits a Class B misdemeanor.[70]

Unless by prescription of a physician, the sale of any drug, medicine, instrument or other substance which the seller knows to be an abortifacient and which is in fact an abortifacient, is guilty of a Class B misdemeanor.[71] Any person who prescribes or administers any instrument, medicine, drug, or other substance or device which that individual knows to be an abortifacient, and which is in fact an abortifacient, and intentionally, knowingly, or recklessly fails to inform the person for whom it is prescribed or upon whom it is administered that it is an abortifacient commits a Class C misdemeanor.[72]

The intentional, knowing, or reckless, performance on a woman of what is represented to that woman to be an abortion when the individual performing the procedure knows or should know that the woman is not pregnant commits a Class 2 felony.[73] The offender will also be answerable in civil damages equal to three times the amount of proved damages.[74]

> ☞ *Caution:* Previous versions of the statute on which this section is based have been found to be unconstitutional.[75] In particular, the Seventh Circuit struck down a provision making the nonprescription sale of abortifacients and prescription and administration of abortifacients without informing the recipient a misdemeanor.[76] In addition, the provision imposing a criminal penalty for any person intentionally, knowingly, or recklessly performing an "abortion procedure" upon a non-pregnant woman was struck

---

70. 720 ILCS 510/11(2).
71. 720 ILCS 510/11(3).
72. 720 ILCS 510/11(3).
73. 720 ILCS 510/11(4).
74. 720 ILCS 510/11(4).
75. See Charles v Carey, 579 F Supp 464 (ND Ill 1983), affd in part and revd in part 749 F2d 452 (CA7 Ill).
76. See Charles v Daley, 749 F2d 452 (CA7 Ill 1984).

down as unconstitutionally vague.[77]

§ 38:08. Abortion referral fee

The payment or receipt of a referral fee, the transfer of anything of value between the doctor who performs an abortion or an operator or employee of a clinic at which an abortion is performed and the person who advised the woman receiving the abortion to use the services of that doctor or clinic,[78] in connection with the performance of an abortion constitutes a Class 4 felony.[79]

§ 38:09. Liability for conscientious objections

No physician, hospital, ambulatory surgical center, or an employee of any of these entities, is required against his, her, or its conscience, declared in writing, to perform, permit, or participate in any abortion.[80] The failure or refusal to do so cannot be the basis for any civil, criminal, administrative or disciplinary action, proceeding, penalty or punishment.[81] If any request for an abortion is denied, the patient must be promptly notified.[82]

§ 38:09.50. Partial-Birth Abortion Ban Act

In 1998, the Illinois legislature passed the Partial-Birth Abortion Ban Act, which imposed criminal and civil penalties

---

77. See Charles v Daley, 749 F2d 452 (CA7 Ill 1984).

78. 720 ILCS 510/11.1(b).

  Periodicals: For article, "The Physician Fee-Splitting Ban and the Role of Medico-Ethical History in Statutory Construction," see 85 Ill. B.J. 374 (1997).

79. 720 ILCS 510/11.1(a).

80. 720 ILCS 510/13.

  See also the Abortion Performance Refusal Act, 745 ILCS 30/0.01 et seq., and the Right of Conscience Act, 745 ILCS 70/1 et seq., whch provide generally that a person refusing to perform an abortion may not be liable in damages to any person or discriminated against because of his or her beliefs.

81. 720 ILCS 510/13.

82. 720 ILCS 510/13.

on persons who performed so-called "partial-birth abortions."[83] The Act defined "partial-birth abortions" as abortions in which the person performing the procedure partially vaginally delivers a living human fetus or infant before killing the fetus or infant and completing the delivery.[84] Exceptions were provided for such abortions necessary to save the life of a mother because her life is endangered by a physical disorder, physical illness, or physical injury, including life-endangering conditions caused by or arising from the pregnancy itself, provided that no other medical procedure would suffice for that purpose.[85] The day before that bill was to become effective, the Northern District of Illinois granted preliminary and permanent injunctive relief enjoining the bill's enactment on the grounds that it was unconstitutionally vague and burdensome on the rights of women.[86]

§ 38:10. Parental consent and notification

In 1995, the Illinois legislature repealed the Abortion Parental Consent Act[87] and the Parental Notice of Abortion Act of 1983,[88] both of which had been held unconstitutional.[89]

These Acts were replaced with the Parental Notice of Abortion Act of 1995.[90] The 1995 Act provides the non-criminal penalty of

83. 720 ILCS 513/1 et seq.

84. 720 ILCS 513/5.

85. 720 ILCS 513/10.

86. Hope Clinic v Ryan, 995 F Supp 847 (ND Ill 1998).

87. Former 720 ILCS 515/1 et seq.

88. Former 720 ILCS 520/1 et seq.

89. See Wynn v Carey, 599 F2d 193 (CA7 Ill 1979) (Abortion Parental Consent Act); Wynn v Carey, 582 F2d 1375 (CA7 Ill 1978) (same); Zbaraz v Hartigan, 763 F2d 1532 (CA7 Ill 1985) (Parental Notice of Abortion Act of 1983).

90. 750 ILCS 70/1 et seq.

Annotation References: Right of minor to have abortion performed without parental consent, 42 ALR3d 1406.

Periodicals: O'Connor, Illinois adolescents' rights to confidential health

ABORTION § 38:13

subjecting a physician who wilfully fails to provide notice to a minor's parents to referral to the Illinois State Medical Disciplinary Board for action.[91]

☞ *Comment:* It should be noted that the United States Supreme Court has upheld the validity of several state parental consent statutes.[92]

§ 38:11. —Penalty for unauthorized waiver

The only criminal penalty provided in the Parental Notice of Abortion Act of 1995 is that any unauthorized person who signs any waiver of notice for a minor or incompetent person seeking an abortion is guilty of a Class 3 misdemeanor.[93]

§ 38:12. —Exceptions

Because, with the exception of unauthorized persons signing waivers,[94] the Parental Notice of Abortion Act provides civil penalties only, exceptions to liability for physicians are beyond the scope of this treatise.

§ 38:13. —Penalties

The only criminal penalty provided in the Parental Notice of Abortion Act of 1995 is that any unauthorized person who signs any waiver of notice for a minor or incompetent person seeking an abortion is guilty of a Class 3 misdemeanor.[95] Physicians who

---

care,82 Ill BJ 24 (1994).

91. 750 ILCS 70/40.

92. Planned Parenthood v Casey, 505 US 833, 120 L Ed 2d 674, 112 S Ct 2791 (1992).

93. 750 ILCS 70/40(b).

Annotation References: Requisites and conditions of judicial consent to minor's abortion, 23 ALR4th 1061.

94. See § 38:11.

95. 750 ILCS 70/40(b).

fail to provide the requisite notice under the statute are referred to the Illinois State Medical Disciplinary Board for action.[96]

---

96. 750 ILCS 70/40(a).

CHAPTER 39

ABUSE OF PROCESS

by

Carol J. Browder, J.D.

and

Robert L. Margolis, Esq.

§ 39:01. Generally

§ 39:01. Generally

Abuse of process is generally considered to be a tort[1] and a cause of action created by common law, and, therefore, is not covered here.

---

1. Zielinski v Schmalbeck, 269 Ill App 3d 572, 207 Ill Dec 89, 646 NE2d 655 (4th Dist 1995); Holiday Magic, Inc. v Scott, 4 Ill App 3d 962, 282 NE2d 452 (1st Dist 1972).

CHAPTER 40

ANIMALS

by

Carol J. Browder, J.D.

and

Robert L. Margolis, Esq.

Scope of Chapter:
   This chapter discusses specific crimes relating to animals including their care, their use in entertainment and damage done to animal research and production facilities. Associated penalties are also discussed.

Treated Elsewhere:
   Charging instruments, see Chapter 9.
   Criminal prosecution, see Chapter 12.
   Defenses, see Chapter 3.
   Evidentiary matters, see Chapters 17–19, 21.
   Sentencing, see Chapter 28.
   Venue, see Chapter 13.

Research References:
   Annotation References:
      ALR Digest: Animals § 32, 33, 41–43
      Index and Annotations: Animals
   Practice References:
      4 Am Jur 2d, Animals §§ 20–45
   State Legislation:
      510 ILCS 5/1 et seq., 70/3, 70/4.01, 70/16, 720 ILCS 5/12-4.8
   Miscellaneous References:
      West's Illinois Digest 2d, Animals §§ 35, 36, 38–42, 45, 57

§ 40:01   ILLINOIS JURISPRUDENCE: CRIMINAL LAW

Auto-Cite®: Cases and annotations referred to in this chapter can be further researched through the Auto-Cite® computer-assisted research service. Use Auto-Cite® to check citations for form, parallel references, prior and later history, and annotation references.

§ 40:01.   Human care of animals
§ 40:02.   Animals for use in entertainment
§ 40:03.   Domestic animals running at large
§ 40:04.   Animal research and production facilities protection
§ 40:05.   —Penalties
§ 40:06.   —Private rights of action
§ 40:07.   —Investigation of alleged violations
§ 40:08.   Dangerous animals

§ 40:01. Human care of animals

For each animal owned, an owner must provide the following:

- sufficient quantity of good quality, wholesome food and water;[1]
- adequate shelter and protection from the weather;[2]
- veterinary care when needed to prevent suffering;[3] and
- humane care and treatment.[4]

An owner who fails to provide these things for his or her animal, if that animal is a dog, commits a Class C misdemeanor.[5]

No person or owner may beat, cruelly treat, torment, starve, overwork or otherwise abuse any animal.[6] Further, no owner may abandon any animal where it may become a public charge or may suffer injury, hunger or exposure.[7] A person convicted of violating

---

1. 510 ILCS 70/3(a).
2. 510 ILCS 70/3(b).
3. 510 ILCS 70/3(c).
4. 510 ILCS 70/3(d).
5. 510 ILCS 70/16(c)(9).
6. 510 ILCS 70/3.01.

Annotation References: Applicability of state animal cruelty statute to medical or scientific experimentation employing animals, 42 ALR4th 860.

these provisions, where the animal involved is a dog, is guilty of a Class C misdemeanor.[8] A second conviction for violation of these provisions is a Class B misdemeanor and a third or subsequent conviction constitutes a Class A misdemeanor.[9]

> *Illustration:* In one case the court held the ten—day incarceration imposed on the defendant for a first offense of cruelty to an animal was substantially less than the maximum sentence the trial court could have imposed and under the terms of the sentence defendant could avoid incarceration entirely by complying with the other terms of the sentence; therefore the sentence was not excessive.[10]

§ 40:02. Animals for use in entertainment

The ownership, capture, breeding, training, or leasing of any animal which is intended for use in a show, exhibition, program, or other activity featuring or otherwise involving a fight between the animal and any other animal or the intentional killing of an animal for the purpose of sport, wagering, or entertainment is prohibited.[11] Further, no person can promote, conduct, advertise, collect money for or in any other manner assist or aid in the presentation for purposes of sport, wagering or entertainment, any such show, exhibition, program, or other activity.[12] In addition, the sale or offer for sale, shipment, transport, or other movement, or delivery or receipt of any animal which has been captured, bred, or trained, or will be used to fight another animal or be intentionally killed, for purposes of sport, wagering, or entertainment is prohibited.[13] A person convicted of violating any

---

7. 510 ILCS 70/3.01.

8. 510 ILCS 70/16(c)(6).

9. 510 ILCS 70/16(c)(6).

10. People v Thornton, 286 Ill App 3d 624, 222 Ill Dec 60, 676 NE2d 1024 (2d Dist 1997).

11. 510 ILCS 70/4.01(a).

12. 510 ILCS 70/4.01(b).

13. 510 ILCS 70/4.01(c).

§ 40:02   ILLINOIS JURISPRUDENCE: CRIMINAL LAW

of these provisions involving animals other than dogs is guilty of a Class A misdemeanor.[14] Where the animals are dogs, the violationis a Class 4 felony.[15]

The manufacture for sale, shipment, transportation or delivery of any device or equipment intended for use in any show, exhibition, program, or other activity featuring or otherwise involving a fight between two or more animals with the intentional killing of an animal for purposes of sport, wagering or entertainment is prohibited.[16] Also prohibited is the ownership, possession, sale or offer for sale, shipment, transportation or movement of any equipment or device which is intended for use in connection with any such show, exhibition, program, or activity for purposes of sport, wagering or entertainment.[17] Further, no person may make available any site, structure, or facility, whether enclosed or not for these purposes.[18] A violation of these provisions involving animals other than dogs constitutes a Class B misdemeanor.[19] Where the animals are dogs, the violation is a Class A misdemeanor if the defendant knew or should have known that the device, equipment, or structure was to be used to violate the statute involving only dogs.[20] If the defendant did not now or should not reasonably have been expected to know the only animals involved would be dogs, the violation is a Class B misdemeanor.[21]

The patronization of these shows, exhibitions, and programs, is also prohibited.[22] Violation of this provision whether or not the

14. 510 ILCS 70/16(b)(2).
15. 510 ILCS 70/16(c)(2).
16. 510 ILCS 70/4.01(d).
17. 510 ILCS 70/4.01(e).
18. 510 ILCS 70/4.01(f).
19. 510 ILCS 70/16(b)(4).
20. 510 ILCS 70/16(c)(3).
21. 510 ILCS 70/16(c)(3).
22. 510 ILCS 70/4.01(g).

animals are constitutes a Class C misdemeanor.[23]

A live animal may not be tied or attached or fastened to any powered machine or device for the purpose of causing the animal to be pursued by dogs where the dogs are intended to used in a dog fight.[24] A person convicted of violating this prohibition is guilty of a Class A misdemeanor.[25]

§ 40:03. Domestic animals running at large

A person who knowingly and willfully brings or causes to be brought into Illinois sheep or other domestic animals infected with contagious disease, or who knowingly and willfully suffers or permits sheep or other domestic animals infected with contagious disease to run at large, is guilty of a petty offense, and is liable in a civil action for all damages occasioned by that conduct.[26]

Further, any person or owner of livestock who allows the livesotck to run at large is guilty of a Class C misdemeanor.[27] If the person violating this statute is a corporation or partnership, any officer, director, manager, or managerial agent who causes the corporation or partnership to commit the violation is guilty of a Class C misdemeanor.[28]

§ 40:04. Animal research and production facilities protection

In Illinois, the following acts associated with animal facilities are prohibited:

- releasing, stealing, or otherwise intentionally causing the death, injury, or loss of any animal at or from an animal

---

23. 510 ILCS 70/16(b)(5), (c)(4).
24. 510 ILCS 70/4.01(h).
25. 510 ILCS 70/16(b)(2).
26. 720 ILCS 5/12-4.8.

    Annotation References: Construction and application of ordinances relating to unrestrained dogs, cats, and other domesticated animals, 1 ALR4th 994.

27. 510 ILCS 55/1, 55/3.1.
28. 510 ILCS 55/3.1.

§ 40:04   ILLINOIS JURISPRUDENCE: CRIMINAL LAW

facility and not authorized by the facility;[29]

- damaging, vandalizing, or stealing any property in or on an animal facility;[30]
- obtaining access to a facility by false pretenses for the purpose of performing acts not authorized by the facility;[31]
- entering into a facility with an intent to destroy, alter, duplicate, or obtain unauthorized possession of records, data, materials, equipment, or animals;[32]
- by means of theft, or deception knowingly obtaining control or exerting control over records, data, material, equipment, or animals of any facility for the purpose of depriving the rightful owner or facility of the records, material, data, equipment, or animals or for the purpose of concealing, abandoning, or destroying the records, material, data, equipment, or animals;[33] or
- entering or remaining on a facility with the intent to commit a prohibited act.[34]

☛ *Definition:* "Animal facility" means any facility engaging in legal scientific research or agricultural production of or involving the use of animals.[35]

§ 40:05. —Penalties

The penalty imposed for violation of the provisions protecting animal facility property depends on the dollar value of the loss, theft, or damage done to the facility.[36]

---

29. 720 ILCS 215/4(1).
30. 720 ILCS 215/4(2).
31. 720 ILCS 215/4(3).
32. 720 ILCS 215/4(4).
33. 720 ILCS 215/4(5).
34. 720 ILCS 215/4(6).
35. 720 ILCS 215/3(c).
36. 720 ILCS 215/5.

Penalties range from a Class 4 felony to a Class 1 felony.[37] For loss, theft or damage up to $300, the violation is a Class 4 felony; between $300 and $10,000 is a Class 3 felony; between $10,000 and $100,000 is a Class 2 felony; and exceeding $100,000 is a Class 1 felony.[38]

Any person who, with the intent to commit a violation of the provisions protecting animal facilities, agrees with another to the commission of the violation and commits an act in furtherance of this agreement is guilty of the same level felony as the primary violator.[39] The penalty imposed in this situation is also dependent on the dollar value of the loss, theft, or damage done to the facility.[40]

The court must conduct a hearing to determine the reasonable cost of replacing materials, data, equipment, animals and records that may have been damaged, destroyed, lost or cannot be returned.[41] Further, the reasonable cost of repeating any experimentation that may have been interrupted or invalidated will also be determined.[42] Any individuals convicted of violating the provisions protecting animal facilities will be ordered jointly and severally to make restitution to the owner, operator, or both, of the animal facility in the full amount of the reasonable cost determined at the hearing.[43]

§ 40:06. —Private rights of action

Animal facilities are not precluded from seeking appropriate relief under any other provision of law or remedy including the issuance of a permanent injunction against any person who violates the statutory provisions protecting animal facilities.[44] The

37. 720 ILCS 215/5(a)(1)–(a)(4).
38. 720 ILCS 215/5(a)(1)–(a)(4).
39. 720 ILCS 215/5(b).
40. 720 ILCS 215/5(b).
41. 720 ILCS 215/5(c)(1).
42. 720 ILCS 215/5(c)(1).
43. 720 ILCS 215/5(c)(2).

animal facility owner or operator may petition the court to permanently enjoin the person from violating the statutory provisions and the court must provide this release.[45]

§ 40:07. —Investigation of alleged violations

The director of the Illinois Department of Agriculture or the director's authorized representative has the authority to investigate any alleged violation of the statutory provisions protecting animal facilities, along with any other law enforcement agency, and may take any action within his or her authority necessary for the enforcement of these provisions.[46] The State's attorneys, state police and other law enforcement officials must provide any assistance required in the conduct of an investigation and prosecution.[47] Before the director reports a violation for prosecution, he or she may give the owner or operator of the animal facility and the alleged violator an opportunity to present his or her views at an administrative hearing.[48]

§ 40:08. Dangerous animals

Vicious dogs — defined by statute as those dogs who when unprovoked will bite or attack humans or have the propensity to do so — must be kept within a fence or structure at least six-feet high, which is suitable to keep out young children and confine the dog.[49] Any person who fails to keep a vicious dog properly confined is guilty of a Class A misdemeanor, unless the violation is intentional, in which case the violation is a Class 4 felony.[50]

---

44. 720 ILCS 215/6.
45. 720 ILCS 215/6.
46. 720 ILCS 215/7.
47. 720 ILCS 215/7.
48. 720 ILCS 215/7.
49. 510 ILCS 5/15(a)(1), (a)(2).
50. 510 ILCS 5/26(b).

CHAPTER 41

ARSON

by

Carol J. Browder, J.D.

and

Robert L. Margolis, Esq.

Scope of Chapter:

This chapter covers the specific crime of arson as well as aggravated arson, possession of explosives and seizure and forfeiture.

Treated Elsewhere:

Charging instruments, see Chapter 9.

Criminal prosecution, see Chapter 12.

Defenses, see Chapter 3.

Evidentiary matters, see Chapters 17–19, 21.

Sentencing, see Chapter 28.

Venue, see Chapter 13.

Research References:

Text References:

Decker, Illinois Criminal Law 2d ed §§ 1.17, 13.19–13.29

Annotation References:

ALR Digest: Arson § 1 et seq.; Explosions and Explosives § 8, 9

Index and Annotations: Arson; Explosions and Explosives; Fires

Practice References:

5 Am Jur 2d, Arson and Related Offenses § 1 et seq.; 31A Am Jur 2d, Explosions and Explosives §§ 214–251; 35 Am Jur 2d, Fires §§ 5, 6

§ 41:01 ILLINOIS JURISPRUDENCE: CRIMINAL LAW

2 Am Jur Trials 171, Investigating Particular Crimes §§ 2–8; 19 Am Jur Trials 685, Preparation and Trial of Arson Case § 1 et seq.

State Legislation:

720 ILCS 5/20-1, et seq; 5/36-1, et seq.; 570/406.1

Miscellaneous References:

West's Illinois Digest 2d, Arson § 1 et seq.; Explosives § 5

Auto-Cite®: Cases and annotations referred to in this chapter can be further researched through the Auto-Cite® computer-assisted research service. Use Auto-Cite® to check citations for form, parallel references, prior and later history, and annotation references.

§ 41:01. Generally
§ 41:02. Aggravated arson
§ 41:03. Possession of explosives or explosive or incendiary devices
§ 41:04. Seizure and forfeiture

§ 41:01. Generally

A person commits arson when, by means of fire or explosive, he or she knowingly:

- damages any real property, or any personal property having a value of $150 dollars or more, of another without that individual's consent;[1] or

- with intent to defraud an insurer, damages any property or any personal property having a value of $150 or more.[2]

☞ *Definition:* "Property of another" means the building or other property, whether real or personal, in which a person other than the offender has an interest which the offender has no authority to defeat or impair, even though the offender

---

1. 720 ILCS 5/20-1(a).

   Text References: Decker, Illinois Criminal Law 2d ed §§ 13.19, 13.21–13.25.

2. 720 ILCS 5/20-1(b).

   Text References: Decker, Illinois Criminal Law 2d ed § 13.26.

   Annotation References: Burning of building by mortgagor as burning property of another so as to constitute arson, 76 ALR2d 524.

may also have an interest in the building or property.[3] In one case, a conviction was upheld where although it was true the aggravated arson indictment naming the Department of Housing and Urban Development as the owner of the fire-damaged property did not name any entity as owner which had the requisite property interest at the time of the fire, because HUD had only an interest contingent on passage of title to the agency on completion of foreclosure proceedings initiated prior to the fire by the mortgage company; the defendant could adequately prepare her defense and was protected from double jeopardy by testimony at trial from persons or about persons having the requisite interest, in that an agency official named two owners of the property in addition to the defendant owner and three tenants who had leasehold interests in the property at the time of the fire testified regarding the defendant's threats to burn the apartment building and other incriminating evidence.[4]

The corpus delicti for arson consists of two elements: the burning of a building which is caused by an individual's criminal act.[5] While it is not necessary to establish motive in an arson case, motive can be established by evidence pertaining to defendant's financial condition and the possible effect of insurance thereon.[6] The State is not required to prove the nature of the object used to set the fire.[7] The arson statute does not require a "burning"; it is

3. 720 ILCS 5/20-1.

Text References: Decker, Illinois Criminal Law 2d ed § 13.25.

4. People v Smith, 258 Ill App 3d 633, 196 Ill Dec 53, 629 NE2d 598 (1st Dist 1994).

5. People v Carter, 200 Ill App 3d 760, 146 Ill Dec 526, 558 NE2d 489 (1st Dist 1990).

6. People v Musitief, 201 Ill App 3d 872, 147 Ill Dec 347, 559 NE2d 520 (2d Dist 1990).

Annotation References: Liability for spread of fire intentionally set for legitimate purpose. 25 ALR5th 391.

7. People v Hanes, 204 Ill App 3d 35, 149 Ill Dec 379, 561 NE2d 1075 (3d Dist 1990).

sufficient that defendant, by means of fire, knowingly damaged the building.[8] The elements of the crime of arson may be shown by circumstantial evidence.[9]

> *Illustration:* For example, in one case the evidence was sufficient to sustain a conviction even though the parties' experts disagreed as to whether the fire was started intentionally where the restaurant destroyed was not the defendant's property and the defendant was the last person to leave the restaurant on the night of the fire.[10]

A person who commits the crime of arson is guilty of a Class 2 felony.[11]

> *Comment:* In August of 1998, the legislature passed a law proscribing "residential arson," by making it a Class 1 felony to, in the course of committing an arson, knowingly damage, partially or totally, any building or structure that is the dwelling place of another.[12]

§ 41:02. Aggravated arson

A person commits aggravated arson, a Class X felony,[13] when

---

8. People v Lockwood, 240 Ill App 3d 137, 181 Ill Dec 59, 608 NE2d 132 (1st Dist 1992).

9. People v Smith, 253 Ill App 3d 443, 191 Ill Dec 648, 624 NE2d 836 (2d Dist 1993).

10. People v Smith, 253 Ill App 3d 443, 191 Ill Dec 648, 624 NE2d 836 (2d Dist 1993).

11. 720 ILCS 5/20-1(c).

Annotation References: What constitutes "burning" to justify charge of arson, 28 ALR4th 482.
Admissibility, in prosecution for criminal burning of property, or for maintaining fire hazard, of evidence of other fires, 87 ALR2d 891.

Practice References: Arson. 2 Am Jur Trials 171, Investigating Particular Crimes §§ 2–8.
19 Am Jur Trials 685, Preparation and Trial of Arson Case § 1 et seq.

12. 720 ILCS 5/20-1.2.

13. 720 ILCS 5/20-1.1(b).

in the course of committing arson he or she knowingly damages, partially or totally, any building or structure, including any adjacent building or structure, and:

- he or she knows or reasonably should know that one or more persons are present in the building or structure[14] or

- any person suffers great bodily harm, or permanent disability or disfigurement as a result of the fire or explosion;[15] or

- a firefighter or police officer who is present at the scene acting in the line of duty, is injured as a result of the fire or explosion.[16]

☛ *Caution:* The prior provision that the arsonist may be liable if he or she knew or reasonably should have known that one or more persons were present in the building or structure was held unconstitutional by the Illinois Supreme Court.[17] However, the current version of the statute, by incorporating the elements of arson, including the mental state of knowledge, has cured the infirmity.[18]

The damage element of aggravated arson is satisfied by proof of even partial damages to the structure.[19]

☛ *Illustration:* Thus, in one case it was held that the defendant was properly convicted of aggravated arson even though the only damage inflicted on the property was a scorching and blackening of the door, where the defendant

Text References: Decker, Illinois Criminal Law 2d ed §13.27.

14. 720 ILCS 5/20-1.1(a)(1).

15. 720 ILCS 5/20-1.1(a)(2).

16. 720 ILCS 5/20-1.1(a)(3).

17. People v Johnson, 114 Ill 2d 69, 101 Ill Dec 882, 499 NE2d 470 (1986).

18. People v Thomas, 137 Ill 2d 500, 148 Ill Dec 752, 561 NE2d 57 (1990); People v Williams, 228 Ill App 3d 163, 170 Ill Dec 78, 592 NE2d 514 (1st Dist 1992).

19. People v Lockwood, 240 Ill App 3d 137, 181 Ill Dec 59, 608 NE2d 132 (1st Dist 1992).

had set the fire early in the morning and the court held the defendant should not benefit from an alert tenant's vigilence in notifying police of the fire before it could spread.[20]

The elements of aggravated arson may be shown by circumstantial evidence. Issues such a motive, opportunity, or knowledge can be inferred from the surrounding facts of each case.[21]

Although a sentencing court is precluded from considering an element inherent in the crime in imposing punishment on a defendant, consideration of the jeopardy firefighters are placed in when fighting fires as a factor in aggravation is appropriate where the danger posed is not an element of the offense of aggravated arson even though an injury suffered by a firefighter may be an element, and the trial court may consider information other than statutory elements of the offense.[22] If the building collapses and injuries to a fireman are fatal, those are aggravating factors that may be considered in sentencing defendant in a conviction for aggravated arson.[23] It also is proper to consider as an aggravating factor that the defendant received compensation for committing the offense, but it is not proper to consider that as an employee the defendant had a duty not to destroy his employer's property.[24]

Defendant's guilt of the offense of aggravated arson does not depend on the happenstance of whether the decedent expired before or after defendant struck the match; whether the victim dies shortly before or shortly after the fire was ignited is not

20. People v Lockwood, 240 Ill App 3d 137, 181 Ill Dec 59, 608 NE2d 132 (1st Dist 1992).

21. People v Burrett, 216 Ill App 3d 185, 159 Ill Dec 624, 576 NE2d 293 (1st Dist 1991).

22. People v Smith, 258 Ill App 3d 633, 196 Ill Dec 53, 629 NE2d 598 (1st Dist 1994).

23. People v Myers, 292 Ill App 3d 757, 226 Ill Dec 733, 686 NE2d 363 (3d Dist 1997).

24. People v Myers, 292 Ill App 3d 757, 226 Ill Dec 733, 686 NE2d 363 (3d Dist 1997).

material to the fulfillment of the purpose of the statute.[25]

§ 41:03. Possession of explosives or explosive or incendiary devices

The possession, manufacture or transportation of any explosive compound, timing or detonating device for use with any explosive compound or incendiary device is prohibited where an individual either intends to use the explosive or device to commit any offense or knows that another intends to use the explosive or device to commit a felony.[26] Possession of explosives or an explosive or incendiary device in violation of this prohibition is a Class 2 felony.[27]

§ 41:04. Seizure and forfeiture

Any vessel, vehicle or aircraft used with the knowledge and consent of the owner in the commission of, or in an attempt to commit arson or possession of explosives or explosive or incendiary devices, may be seized and delivered to the sheriff of the county of seizure.[28] The state's attorney in the county in which the seizure occurred, must then bring an action for forfeiture in

---

25. People v Thomas, 137 Ill 2d 500, 148 Ill Dec 751, 561 NE2d 57 (1990), cert den 498 US 1127, 112 L Ed 2d 1196, 111 S Ct 1092.

26. 720 ILCS 5/20-2(a).

   Annotation References: Possession of bomb, Molotov cocktail, or similar device as criminal offense, 42 ALR3d 1230.

27. 720 ILCS 5/20-2(b).

28. 720 ILCS 5/36-1.

   Procedure for seizure, see ch 56.

   Text References: Decker, Illinois Criminal Law 2d ed § 1.17.

   Annotation References: Delay in setting hearing date or in holding hearing as affecting forfeitability under Uniform Controlled Substances Act or similar statute. 6 ALR5th 711.
   Forfeitability of property under Uniform Controlled Substances Act or similar statute where amount of controlled substance seized is small. 6 ALR5th 652.

   Periodicals: Jochner, From fiction to fact: the Supreme court's re-evaluation of civil asset forfeiture laws, 82 Ill BJ 560 (1994).

§ 41:04   ILLINOIS JURISPRUDENCE: CRIMINAL LAW

the circuit court within whose jurisdiction the seizure and confiscation took place.[29]

The spouse of the owner of a vehicle seized for a violation of this statute may make a showing that the seized vehicle is the only source of transportation, and if it is determined that the financial hardship to the family as a result of the seizure outweighs the benefit to the State from the seizure, the vehicle may be forfeited to the spouse or family member and the title to the vehicle transferred to that person if he or she is properly licensed and requires the use of the vehicle for employment or family transportation purposes.[30]

Any building used in the commission of the prohibited acts of possession of explosives or an explosive or incendiary device or used in the commission of an inchoate offense relative to these acts is a public nuisance.[31]

A person convicted of knowingly maintaining a public nuisance commits a Class A misdemeanor[32] with each subsequent offense being a Class 4 felony.[33]

The sentencing provisions of the forfeiture statute[34] and the statute making it a crime to permit or make a building available for use for the purpose of unlawfully manufacturing or delivering a controlled substance[35] are similar in that both prohibit the use of buildings for the commission of criminal offenses; however, the provisions are not identical, and the availability of different penalties for offenses that are similar or related, but not identical,

---

29. 720 ILCS 5/36-2(a).

Procedure for forfeiture, see ch 56.

30. 720 ILCS 5/36-1.

31. 720 ILCS 5/37-1.

Posession of explosives or explosive or incendiary device, see § 41:03.

32. 720 ILCS 5/37-1(b).

33. 720 ILCS 5/37-1(b).

34. 720 ILCS 5/37-1.

35. 720 ILCS 570/406.1.

does not violate the constitution.[36]

Any building used in the commission of this offense with the intentional, knowing, reckless or negligent permission of the owner or the agent of the owner managing the building will, together with the underlying real estate, all fixtures and other property used to commit the offense, be subject to a lien and may be sold to pay any unsatisfied judgment that may be recovered and any unsatisfied fine that may be levied and to pay any person not maintaining the nuisance his or her damages as a consequence of the nuisance; provided, that the lien created does not affect the rights of any purchaser, mortgagee, judgment creditor or other lienholder arising prior to the filing of a notice of the lien.[37]

---

36. People v Parker, 277 Ill App 3d 585, 214 Ill Dec 347, 660 NE2d 1296 (4th Dist 1996).

37. 720 ILCS 5/37-2.

CHAPTER 42

ASSAULT AND BATTERY

by

Carol J. Browder, J.D.

and

Robert L. Margolis, Esq.

Scope of Chapter:
    This chapter covers the specific crimes of assault and battery. Also included in the discussion are aggravated assault and battery, and heinous battery. Associated penalties are also covered.

Treated Elsewhere:
    Changing instruments, see Chapter 9.
    Criminal prosecution, see Chapter 12.
    Defenses, see Chapter 3.
    Evidentiary matters, see Chapters 17–19, 21.
    Sentencing, see Chapter 28.
    Venue, see Chapter 13.

Research References:
  Text References:
    Decker, Illinois Criminal Law 2d ed § 9.01 et seq.
  Annotation References:
    ALR Digest: Assault and Battery § 23 et seq.
    Index and Annotations: Assault and Battery
  Practice References:
    Bailey & Rothblatt, Handling Misdemeanor Cases §§ 209–232 (1976)
    6 Am Jur 2d, Assault and Battery §§ 8–108

§ 42:01   ILLINOIS JURISPRUDENCE: CRIMINAL LAW

State Legislation:
720 ILCS 5/12–1 et seq, 5/33A-1 et seq., 570/401(a), (c)

Miscellaneous References:
West's Illinois Digest 2d, Assault and Battery § 47 et seq.

Auto-Cite®: Cases and annotations referred to in this chapter can be further researched through the Auto-Cite® computer-assisted research service. Use Auto-Cite® to check citations for form, parallel references, prior and later history, and annotation references.

§ 42:01.   Assault
§ 42:02.   Aggravated assault
§ 42:03.   Battery
§ 42:04.   —Unborn child
§ 42:05.   —Aggravated battery
§ 42:06.   ——With firearm
§ 42:07.   ——Of child
§ 42:08.   ——Of unborn child
§ 42:09.   ——Of senior citizen
§ 42:10.   —Heinous
§ 42:11.   —Food, drugs and cosmetics

§ 42:01. Assault

A person commits an assault when, without lawful authority, he or she engages in conduct which places another in reasonable apprehension of receiving a battery.[1] Assault is a Class C misdemeanor.[2] In addition to any other sentence that may be imposed, the court must order any person convicted of assault to

---

1. 720 ILCS 5/12-1(a).

    Text References: Decker, Illinois Criminal Law 2d ed §§ 9.02–9.08.

    Annotation References: Validity, construction, and effect of assault and battery exclusion in liability insurance policy at issue. 44 ALR5th 91.
    Consent as defense to charge of criminal assault and battery, 58 ALR3d 662.

    See § 42:03 (battery).

2. 720 ILCS 5/12-1(b).

    See also ch 28.

    Practice References: Bailey & Rothblatt, Handling Misdemeanor Cases §§ 209–232, Assault (1976).

ASSAULT AND BATTERY § 42:01

perform between 30 and 120 hours of community service.[3]

The victim's apprehension must be reasonable under the circumstances.[4] Words alone are not usually enough to constitute assault.[5] Because the apprehension must be reasonable, a victim's emotional response to the defendant's words will be examined, but the response must be reasonable for it to result in a conviction.[6]

> ☛ *Illustration:* Thus, in one case the conviction was reversed where the victim's feeling of being petrified that the defendant was going to harm her when the defendant rode a bicycle towards the victim and stated "come here you" was not a sufficient apprehension of receiving a battery needed for an assault conviction, as it lacked objective reasonableness.[7]

A person who has authority to touch the victim cannot be convicted of assault.[8]

> ☛ *Illustration:* Thus, in one case, an officer who was justified in conducting a strip search, had proper authority to imply that he would carry out the search himself if the person being searched had failed to comply with his instructions, so the search did not constitute an assault.[9]

---

3. 720 ILCS 5/12-1(c).

4. People v Floyd, 278 Ill App 3d 568, 215 Ill Dec 324, 663 NE2d 74 (1st Dist 1996).

Text References: Decker, Illinois Criminal Law 2d ed § 9.06.

5. People v Floyd, 278 Ill App 3d 568, 215 Ill Dec 324, 663 NE2d 74 (1st Dist 1996).

Text References: Decker, Illinois Criminal Law 2d ed § 9.05.

6. People v Floyd, 278 Ill App 3d 568, 215 Ill Dec 324, 663 NE2d 74 (1st Dist 1996).

7. People v Floyd, 278 Ill App 3d 568, 215 Ill Dec 324, 663 NE2d 74 (1st Dist 1996).

8. Kraushaar v Flanigan, 45 F3d 1040 (CA7 Ill 1995).

§ 42:02. Aggravated assault

An aggravated assault is committed when, during the commission of an assault, an individual:

- uses a deadly weapon or any device manufactured and designed to be substantially similar in appearance to a firearm, other than by discharging a firearm in the direction of another person, peace officer, correctional officer, or fireman, or in the direction of a vehicle occupied by another person, a peace officer, a person summoned by the peace officer, a correction officer, or fireman while the officer or fireman are engaged in official duties, or to prevent the officer or fireman from performing those duties, or in retaliation for doing so;[10]

9. Kraushaar v Flanigan, 45 F3d 1040 (CA7 Ill 1995).
10. 720 ILCS 5/12-2(a)(1).

Text References: Decker, Illinois Criminal Law 2d ed §§ 9.09–9.12.

Annotation References: Failure of police to preserve potentially exculpatory evidence as violating criminal defendant's rights under state constitution. 40 ALR5th 113.
Propriety of using prior conviction for drug dealing to impeach witness in criminal trial. 37 ALR5th 319.
Kicking as aggravated assault, or assault with dangerous or deadly weapon, 19 ALR5th 823.
Kicking as aggravated assault, or assault with dangerous or deadly weapon. 19 ALR5th 823.
Stationary object or attached fixture as deadly or dangerous weapon for purposes of statute aggravating offenses such as assault, robbery, or homicide, 8 ALR5th 775.
Sufficiency of bodily injury to support charge of aggravated assault. 5 ALR5th 243
Parts of the human body, other than feet, as deadly or dangerous weapons for purposes of statutes aggravating offenses such as assault and battery, 8 ALR4th 1268.
Walking cane as deadly or dangerous weapon for purpose of statutes aggravating offenses such as assault and battery, 8 ALR4th 842.
Dog as deadly or dangerous weapon for purposes of statutes aggravating offenses such as assault and battery, 7 ALR4th 607.
Pocket or clasp knife as deadly or dangerous weapon for purposes of statute aggravating offenses such as assault, robbery, or homicide, 100 ALR3d 287.

ASSAULT AND BATTERY § 42:02

- is hooded, robed or masked in such a manner as to conceal the individual's identity or any device manufactured and designed to be substantially similar in appearance to a firearm;[11]
- knows the individual assaulted to be a teacher or other person employed in any school and the teacher or other employee is on the grounds of a school or grounds adjacent to the school, or is any part of a building used for school purposes;[12]
- knows the individual assaulted to be a supervisor, director, instructor or other person employed in any park district and that individual is on the grounds of the park or grounds adjacent to the park or is in any part of a building used for park purposes;[13]
- knows the individual assaulted to be a caseworker, investigator, or other person employed by the State Department of Public Aid, a County Department of Public Aid, or the Department of Human Services and that individual is on the grounds of a public aid office or grounds adjacent to the officer, or is in any part of a building used for public aid purposes, or on the grounds of a home of a public aid applicant, recipient or any other person being interviewed or investigated in the employee's discharge of his or her duties, or on grounds adjacent to the home, or is in

---

Automobile as dangerous or deadly weapon within meaning of assault or battery statute, 89 ALR3d 1026.

Robbery by means of toy or simulated gun or pistol, 81 ALR3d 1006.

Kicking as aggravated assault, or assault with dangerous or deadly weapon, 33 ALR3d 922.

Intent to do physical harm as essential element of crime of assault with deadly or dangerous weapon, 92 ALR2d 635.

Periodicals: For article, "Lesser-Included Offenses in Illinois: A Look at Recent Developments," see 85 Ill. B.J. 480 (1997).

11. 720 ILCS 5/12-2(a)(2).
12. 720 ILCS 5/12-2(a)(3).
13. 720 ILCS 5/12-2(a)(4).

§ 42:02 ILLINOIS JURISPRUDENCE: CRIMINAL LAW

any part of a building in which the applicant, recipient, or other person resides or is located;[14]

- knows the individual assaulted to be a peace officer, person summoned and directed by the peace officer, a fireman, correctional officer, or a correctional employee, while that person is engaged in the execution of any of his or her official duties, or to prevent that person from performing official duties, or in retaliation for doing so and the assault is by other than discharging a firearm in that person's general direction;[15]

- knows the individual assaulted to be an emergency medical technician engaged in the execution of any of his or her official duties;[16]

- knows the individual assaulted to be the driver, operator, employee or passenger of any transportation facility or system engaged in the business of transportation of the public for hire and the individual assaulted is then performing in that capacity or then using public transportation as a passenger or using any area of any description designated by the transportation facility or system as a vehicle boarding, departure, or transfer location;[17]

- or the individual assaulted is on or about a public way, public property, or public place of accommodation or amusement;[18]

- knows the individual assaulted to be an employee of Illinois, a municipal corporation in the state or a political subdivision

---

14. 720 ILCS 5/12-2(a)(5).

15. 720 ILCS 5/12-2(a)(6), (14), (15).

   Annotation References: Right to resist excessive force used in accomplishing lawful arrest, 77 ALR3d 281.
   Modern status of rules as to right to forcefully resist illegal arrest, 44 ALR3d 1078.

16. 720 ILCS 5/12-2(a)(7).

17. 720 ILCS 5/12-2(a)(8).

18. 720 ILCS 5/12-2(a)(9).

of the state, engaged in the performance of his or her authorized duty;[19]

- knowingly or without legal justification, commits an assault on a physically handicapped person;[20]
- knowingly and without legal justification, commits an assault on a person 60 years of age or older;[21] or
- discharges a firearm.[22]

The first five of the above categories of aggravated assault, plus the seventh through twelfth, constitute a Class A misdemeanor.[23] The sixth category is a Class A Misdemeanor with respect to a peace officer or fireman if a firearm is not used or a Class 4 felony if a firearm is used.[24] With respect to a correctional officer or correctional employee, it is a Class 4 felony in all cases.[25]

A person commits the additional offense of armed violence when, while armed with a dangerous weapon, he or she commits a felony.[26] The penalty imposed for this violation depends upon the type of weapon used during the offense with penalties ranging from Class X to Class 2 felonies.[27] The commission of a robbery

19. 720 ILCS 5/12-2(a)(10).
20. 720 ILCS 5/12-2(a)(11).
21. 720 ILCS 5/12-2(a)(12).

   Annotation References: Criminal assault or battery statutes making attack on elderly person a special or aggravated offense, 73 ALR4th 1123.

22. 720 ILCS 5/12-2(a)(13).
23. 720 ILCS 5/12-2(b).

   Sentencing, see ch 28.

24. 720 ILCS 5/12-2(b).

   Sentencing, see ch 28.

25. 720 ILCS 5/12-2(b).

   Sentencing, see ch 28.

26. 720 ILCS 5/33A-2.
27. 720 ILCS 5/33A-3.

§ 42:02   ILLINOIS JURISPRUDENCE: CRIMINAL LAW

while armed with a handgun also constitutes armed violence, an offense punishable by a mandatory minimum term of 15 years' imprisonment, which when predicated on robbery committed with a category I weapon, violated the proportionate penalties clause.[28]

> *Practice Tip:* Aggravated discharge of a firearm is not a lesser included offense of aggravated assault because it does not require the victim to be aware of the defendant's presence.[29]

> *Definition:* A Category I weapon, which carries a minimum sentence of 15 years imprisonment, is a handgun, sawed-off shotgun, sawed-off rifle, any other firearm small enough to be concealed upon the person, semiautomatic firearm, or machine gun.[30] A Category II weapon, which carries a minimum sentence of 10 years, is any other rifle, shotgun, spring gun, other firearm, stun gun or taser, knife with a blade of at least 3 inches in length, dagger, dirk, switchblade knife, stiletto, axe, hatchet, or other deadly or dangerous weapon or instrument of like character.[31] A Category III weapon, a violation with which is a Class 2 felony, is a bludgeon, black-jack, slungshot, sand-bag, sand-club, metal knuckles, billy, or other dangerous weapon of like character.[32]

Where an offense was committed in any school, or any conveyance owned, leased, or contracted by a school to transport

---

28. People v Lewis, 175 Ill 2d 412, 222 Ill Dec 296, 677 NE2d 830 (1996).

29. People v James, 246 Ill App 3d 939, 186 Ill Dec 876, 617 NE2d 115 (1st Dist 1993).

Text References: Decker, Illinois Criminal Law 2d ed § 9.12.

30. 720 ILCS 5/33A-1(b), 5/33A-3(a).

31. 720 ILCS 5/33A-1(b), 5/33A-3(b).

See 720 ILCS 5/24-1(a)(10) (defining taser).

32. 720 ILCS 5/33A-1(c), 5/33A-3(b).

students to or from school or a school related activity, on the real property comprising any school or public park, and where the offense was related to the activities of an organized gang, the offense is a Class X felony for which the defendant must be sentenced to a term of imprisonment of not less than 10 years and not more than 20 years.[33]

§ 42:03. Battery

A person commits battery if he or she intentionally or knowingly without legal justification and by any means causes bodily harm to an individual or makes physical contact of an insulting or provoking nature with the individual.[34] Battery is a Class A misdemeanor.[35]

There need not be direct evidence of injury to sustain a conviction of battery based on bodily harm. Basically, evidence of contact between defendant and the victim, combined with the jury's common knowledge, is sufficient to establish that defendant's conduct has caused bodily harm.[36] For purposes of the battery statute, bodily harm consists of some sort of physical

---

33. 720 ILCS 5/33A-3(a).

34. 720 ILCS 5/12-3(a).

See ch 55, Domestic Violence.

Text References: Decker, Illinois Criminal Law 2d ed §§ 9.13–9.19.

Annotation References: Secondary smoke as battery. 46 ALR5th 813.
Validity, construction, and effect of assault and battery exclusion in liability insurance policy at issue. 44 ALR5th 91.

Periodicals: For article, "Lesser-Included Offenses in Illinois: A Look at Recent Developments," see 85 Ill. B.J. 480 (1997).

35. 720 ILCS 5/12-3(b).

Practice References: Bailey & Rothblatt, Handling Misdemeanor Cases §§ 216–220, Battery (1976).

36. People v Norfleet, 259 Ill App 3d 381, 197 Ill Dec 107, 630 NE2d 1231 (1st Dist 1994); People v Gaither, 221 Ill App 3d 629, 164 Ill Dec 172, 582 NE2d 735 (5th Dist 1991).

Text References: Decker, Illinois Criminal Law 2d ed § 9.16.

§ 42:03 ILLINOIS JURISPRUDENCE: CRIMINAL LAW

pain or damage to the body, like lacerations, bruises or abrasions, whether temporary or permanent.[37] The victim's testimony is sufficient to support a battery conviction and visible evidence of bodily harm is not necessary to obtain a conviction.[38]

The touching which constitutes a battery may be by the defendant or by a substance put in force by the defendant.[39]

☛ *Illustration:* The throwing of urine or water onto a prison correctional officer and nurse amounted to physical contact of an insulting or provoking nature.[40]

Battery is a specific intent crime which is not reduced by mitigating factors.[41] Because it is a specific intent crime, intoxication, voluntary or involuntary, is a complete defense, negating the necessary intent.[42]

The absence of legal justification is not an element of the offense of battery, but justification is an affirmative defense to be raised by the defendant.[43] Defendant is entitled to have a jury consider his or her claim of the justifiable use of force where that defense has some foundation in the evidence. This is true even

---

37. People v Rodarte, 190 Ill App 3d 992, 138 Ill Dec 635, 547 NE2d 1256 (1st Dist 1989).

Text References: Decker, Illinois Criminal Law 2d ed §§ 9.19.

38. Simmons v Pryor, 26 F3d 650 (CA7 Ill 1994).

39. Pechan v DynaPro, Inc., 251 Ill App 3d 1072, 190 Ill Dec 698, 622 NE2d 108 (1993).

Text References: Decker, Illinois Criminal Law 2d ed § 9.17.

40. People v Walker, 291 Ill App 3d 597, 225 Ill Dec 633, 683 NE2d 1296 (4th Dist 1997).

41. People v Renehan, 226 Ill App 3d 453, 168 Ill Dec 466, 589 NE2d 866 (1st Dist 1992).

Text References: Decker, Illinois Criminal Law 2d ed § 9.18.

42. Talarico v Dunlap, 281 Ill App 3d 662, 217 Ill Dec 481, 667 NE2d 570 (1st Dist 1996), aff'd 177 Ill 2d 185, 226 Ill Dec 222, 685 NE2d 325.

43. Simmons v Pryor, 26 F3d 650 (CA7 Ill 1994).

where the evidence concerning that theory is very slight, inconsistent, or of doubtful credibility.[44] When a theory of self-defense is raised in a battery case, evidence of the peaceful or violent character of either the accused or the victim may be relevant as circumstantial evidence to show which party was the initial aggressor. Evidence of specific instances of conduct probative of the violent character of either party may be admissible.[45]

§ 42:04. —Unborn child

If a person intentionally or knowingly without legal justification and by any means causes bodily harm to an unborn child, that individual has committed the offense of battery of an unborn child.[46] In this context, "unborn child" means any individual from fertilization until birth.[47] The term "person" does not include the pregnant woman whose unborn child is harmed.[48] Battery of an unborn child is a Class A misdemeanor.[49]

These provisions do not apply to acts which cause bodily harm to an unborn child if those acts were committed during an abortion to which the pregnant woman has consented.[50] Further, these prohibitions do not apply to acts which were committed pursuant to usual and customary standards of medical practice during diagnostic testing or therapeutic treatment.[51]

---

44. People v Dailey, 188 Ill App 3d 683, 135 Ill Dec 953, 544 NE2d 449 (4th Dist 1989).

45. People v Carreon, 225 Ill App 3d 133, 167 Ill Dec 263, 587 NE2d 532 (1st Dist 1992); People v Ware, 180 Ill App 3d 921, 129 Ill Dec 663, 536 NE2d 713 (1st Dist 1988).

46. 720 ILCS 5/12-3.1(a).

Text References: Decker, Illinois Criminal Law 2d ed § 9.27.

47. 720 ILCS 5/12-3.1(b).

48. 720 ILCS 5/12-3.1(b).

49. 720 ILCS 5/12-3.1(c).

50. 720 ILCS 5/12-3.1(d).

Illinois Abortion Law of 1975, see 720 ILCS 510/2.

§ 42:05. —Aggravated battery

A person commits aggravated battery if, during the course of committing a battery, the individual also commits one of the following acts:

- intentionally or knowingly causes great bodily harm, or permanent disability or disfigurement;[52]
- uses a deadly weapon other than by the discharge of a firearm;[53]
- is hooded, robed or masked, in a manner that conceals his or her identity;[54]
- knows the individual harmed to be a teacher or other person employed in any school and that teacher or other employee is on the grounds of a school or grounds adjacent to the school, or is in any part of a building used for school purposes;[55]
- knows the individual harmed to be a supervisor, director, instructor or other person employed in any park district and that employee is on the grounds of the park or grounds adjacent to the park, or is in any part of a building used for park purposes;[56]
- knows the individual harmed to be a caseworker, investigator, or other person employed by the State Department of Public Aid, a County Department of Public Aid, or the Department of Human Services and that employee is on the grounds of a public aid office or

---

51. 720 ILCS 5/12-3.1(d).

52. 720 ILCS 5/12-4(a).

Text References: Decker, Illinois Criminal Law 2d ed §§ 9.20–9.24.

53. 720 ILCS 5/12-4(b)(1).

54. 720 ILCS 5/12-4(b)(2).

55. 720 ILCS 5/12-4(b)(3).

Duty of school superintendent to report incidents of battery committed against educational employees, see 105 ILCS 5/10-21.7.

56. 720 ILCS 5/12-4(b)(4).

§ 42:05

grounds adjacent to the office, or is in any part of a building used for public aid purposes, or on the grounds of a home of a public aid applicant, recipient or any other person being interviewed or investigated in the employee's discharge of his or her duties, or on adjacent grounds, or is any part of a building in which the applicant, recipient, or other such person resides or is located;[57]

- knows the individual harmed to be a peace officer, or a person summoned and directed by him or her, a correctional institution employee, or a fireman, while the officer, employee, or fireman is engaged in the execution of any of his or her official duties including arrest or attempted arrest or to prevent him or her from performing official duties, or in retaliation for doing so and he offense is committed other than by discharging a firearm;[58]

- knows the individual harmed to be an emergency medical technician, paramedic, ambulance driver or other medical assistant or first aid personnel employed by a municipality or other governmental unit and is engaged in the execution of any of his or her official duties or to prevent that person from performing those duties, or in retaliation for doing so;[59]

- is, or the person battered is, on or about a public way, public property or public place of accommodation or amusement;[60]

- knows the individual harmed to be the driver, operator, employee or passenger of any transportation facility or system engaged in the business of transportation of the public for hire and the individual assaulted is then performing in that capacity or then using public transportation as a passenger or using any area of any description designated by the transportation facility or system as a vehicle boarding, departure, or transfer location;[61]

---

57. 720 ILCS 5/12-4(b)(5).
58. 720 ILCS 5/12-4(b)(6).
59. 720 ILCS 5/12-4(b)(7).
60. 720 ILCS 5/12-4(b)(8).

§ 42:05   ILLINOIS JURISPRUDENCE: CRIMINAL LAW

- knowingly and without legal justification and by any means causes bodily harm to an individual of 60 years of age or older;[62]
- knows the individual harmed is pregnant;[63]
- knows the individual harmed to be a judge whom the person intended to harm as a result of the judge's performance of his or her official duties as a judge;[64]
- knows the individual harmed to be an employee of the Illinois Department of Children and Family Services engaged in the performance of his or her authorized duties as an employee;[65]
- knows the individual harmed to be a person who is physically handicapped;[66] or
- knowingly and without legal justification and by any means causes bodily harm to a merchant who detains the person for an alleged commission of retail theft.[67]

☛ *Definition:* A "physically handicapped person" is a person who suffers from a permanent and disabling physical characteristic, resulting from disease, injury, functional disorder, or congenital condition[68].

---

61. 720 ILCS 5/12-4(b)(9).
62. 720 ILCS 5/12-4(b)(10).

Annotation References: Criminal assault or battery statutes making attack on elderly person a special or aggravated offense, 73 ALR4th 1123.

63. 720 ILCS 5/12-4(b)(11).
64. 720 ILCS 5/12-4(b)(12).
65. 720 ILCS 5/12-4(b)(13).
66. 720 ILCS 5/12-4(b)(14).
67. 720 ILCS 5/12-4(b)(15).
68. 720 ILCS 5/12–4(b).

§ 42:05

☞ *Definition:* A "merchant" is an owner or operator of any retail mercantile establishment or any agent, employee, lessee, consignee, officer, director, franchisee or independent contractor of the owner or operator.[69].

☞ *Definition:* "Deadly weapon" is not defined by statute; therefore whether a particular weapon is deadly depends on the facts and circumstances of each case.[70]

A person also commits aggravated battery when he or she administers to an individual or causes that individual to take, without his or her consent or by threat or deception, and for other than medical purposes, any intoxicating, poisonous, stupefying, narcotic, anesthetic, or controlled substance.[71] A person who knowingly gives another person any food that contains any substance or object that is intended to cause physical injury if eaten commits aggravated battery.[72]

"Simple battery" requires physical pain or damage to the body, such as lacerations, bruises or abrasions, either temporary or permanent, whereas "aggravated battery" requires more serious injury and is determined by the actual injuries received.[73] A defendant charged with knowingly causing great bodily harm must be consciously aware that his or her conduct, while in commission of a battery, will cause great bodily harm, in other words, the result of his conduct is in issue.[74] This knowledge

---

69. 720 ILCS 5/16A–2.4.

70. People v T.G. (In re T.G.), 285 Ill App 3d 838, 221 Ill Dec 126, 674 NE2d 919 (1st Dist 1996).

71. 720 ILCS 5/12-4(c).

Text References: Decker, Illinois Criminal Law 2d ed § 9.32.

72. 720 ILCS 5/12-4(d).

73. People v T.G. (In re T.G.), 285 Ill App 3d 838, 221 Ill Dec 126, 674 NE2d 919 (1st Dist 1996).

74. People v Lopez, 245 Ill App 3d 41, 185 Ill Dec 195, 614 NE2d 329 (1st Dist 1993), aff'd 166 Ill 2d 441, 171 Ill Dec 854, 594 NE2d 1374; People v Lovelace, 251 Ill App 3d 607, 190 Ill Dec 829, 622 NE2d 859 (2d Dist 1993).

§ 42:05

element does not require showing that the defendant knew precisely what injuries he or she would cause, but rather, it only requires knowing that the defendant knew some sort of physical pain or damage to the body would be caused.[75] In the context of aggravated battery, great bodily harm has been held not susceptible of precise legal definition. It requires an injury of a greater or more serious character than ordinary battery. The determination of whether great bodily harm as occurred centers on the injuries the victim received and does not depend on whether the victim received medical attention. The question of whether a victim's injuries constitute great bodily harm is one to be dedicated by the trier of fact.[76] "Great bodily harm" includes, but is not limited to, temporary or permanent lacerations, bruises, or abrasions.[77]

Consent is not a defense to a battery based on injurious touching.[78] However, legal justification is a defense.[79]

When ascertaining whether or not defendant's actions were reckless or intentional, courts look to the manner in which

Periodicals: For note, "The Void Left in Illinois Homicide Law after People v. Lopez: The Elimination of Attempted Second Degree Murder," see 46 De Paul L. Rev. 227 (1997).
For article, "Lesser-Included Offenses in Illinois: A Look at Recent Developments," see 85 Ill. B.J. 480 (1997).

75. People v Lovelace, 251 Ill App 3d 607, 190 Ill Dec 829, 622 NE2d 859 (2d Dist 1993).

76. People v Psichalinos, 229 Ill App 3d 1058, 171 Ill Dec 854, 594 NE2d 1374 (2d Dist 1992); People v Figures, 216 Ill App 3d 398, 160 Ill Dec 135, 576 NE2d 1089 (1st Dist 1991).

Annotation References: Sufficiency of bodily injury to support charge of aggravated assault. 5 ALR5th 243

77. People v Doran, 256 Ill App 3d 131, 194 Ill Dec 763, 628 NE2d 260 (1st Dist 1993).

78. People v Reckers, 251 Ill App 3d 790, 191 Ill Dec 221, 623 NE2d 811 (4th Dist 1993).

79. People v Reyes, 265 Ill App 3d 985, 202 Ill Dec 782, 638 NE2d 650 (1st Dist 1993).

ASSAULT AND BATTERY § 42:06

defendant used the weapon, and the severity of the victim's injuries.[80]

Aggravated battery constitutes a Class 3 felony.[81]

§ 42:06. ——With firearm

If a person, while committing a battery, knowingly causes any injury to another as set forth below by means of the discharging of a firearm, that individual commits aggravated battery with a firearm:[82]

- causes injury to any other person;[83]
- causes injury to a person he or she knows to be a peace officer, a community policing volunteer, a correctional institution employee or a fireman while the officer, volunteer, employee or fireman is engaged in the execution of any of his or her official duties, or to prevent that person from performing those duties, or in retaliation for doing so;[84]
- causes injury to a person he or she knows to be an emergency medical technician-ambulance, emergency medical technician-intermediate, emergency medical technician-paramedic, ambulance driver, or other medical assistance or first aid personnel, employed by a municipality or other governmental unit, while that personl is engaged in the

---

80. People v Solis, 216 Ill App 3d 11, 159 Ill Dec 451, 576 NE2d 120 (1st Dist 1991).

81. 720 ILCS 5/12-4(e).

82. 720 ILCS 5/12-4.2(a).

   Text References: Decker, Illinois Criminal Law 2d ed §§ 9.24.

   Annotation References: Fact that gun was unloaded as affecting criminal responsibility, 68 ALR4th 507.

   Periodicals: For note, "The Void Left in Illinois Homicide Law after People v. Lopez: The Elimination of Attempted Second Degree Murder," see 46 De Paul L. Rev. 227 (1997).

83. 720 ILCS 5/12-4.2(a)(1).

84. 720 ILCS 5/12-4.2(a)(2).

execution of any of his or her official duties, or to prevent that person from performing those duties, or in retaliation for doing so.[85]

Aggravated battery with a firearm is a Class X felony.[86] The second and third categories of aggravated battery with a firearm described above carry with them a sentence of imprisonment of no less than 15 years and no more than 60 years.[87]

> *Illustration:* In one case, where the victim testified the defendant intentionally hit him in the face with his gun, that conduct satisfied the definition of aggravated battery with a deadly weapon.[88]

The statute creating the offense of aggravated battery with a firearm has been held constitutional despite the contention that it violated due process by providing a greater penalty than the more serious offenses of inflicting great bodily harm while committing a simple battery or committing a battery with another deadly weapon; the court held the legislature could properly take into consideration the fact that the risk of death from firearms exceeds the frequency and risk of death from other weapons, firearms are not considered equally as dangerous as other weapons, and aggravated battery with a firearm is distinguished from aggravated battery by requiring the additional element of knowingly causing injury to another.[89]

§ 42:07. ——Of child

The offense of aggravated battery of a child occurs when any person 18 years or older intentionally or knowingly and without

---

85. 720 ILCS 5/12-4.2(a)(3).

86. 720 ILCS 5/12-4.2(b).

87. 720 ILCS 5/12-4.2(b).

88. People v Hall, 291 Ill App 3d 411, 225 Ill Dec 611, 683 NE2d 1274 (1st Dist 1997).

89. People v Lee, 167 Ill 2d 140, 212 Ill Dec 231, 656 NE2d 1065 (1995); People v Roberts, 265 Ill App 3d 400, 202 Ill Dec 713, 638 NE2d 359 (1st Dist 1994).

ASSAULT AND BATTERY § 42:07

legal justification and by any means, causes great bodily harm or permanent disability or disfigurement to any child under the age of 13 years or any institutionalized severely or profoundly mentally retarded person.[90] Aggravated battery of a child is a Class X felony.[91]

Infliction of great bodily harm, which requires an injury of greater or more serious character than ordinary battery, is an essential element of the offense of aggravated battery of a child.[92] The determination of whether "great bodily harm" occurred centers on the injuries the victim received, and does not depend upon whether the victim received medical attention.[93]

The defendant's acts need not be the sole and immediate cause of the minor's injury for a conviction for aggravated battery of a child.[94]

> *Illustration:* Thus, in one case, the defendant was convicted of aggravated battery of a child where occupants of a car opened fire on the defendant, where the defendant then ran 10 to 12 feet to the child victim, picked him up, and held the child's body in front of his face and chest, thereby

---

90. 720 ILCS 5/12-4.3.

Text References: Decker, Illinois Criminal Law 2d ed §§ 9.25.

Annotation References: Validity and construction of penal statute prohibiting child abuse, 1 ALR4th 38.

91. 720 ILCS 5/12-4.3.

Periodicals: For article, "Survey of Illinois Law: Criminal Law and Procedure," see 21 S. Ill. U.L.J. 759 (1997).
For comment, "The Sixth Amendment: Protecting Defendants' Rights at the Expense of Child Victims," see 30 J. Marshall L. Rev. 767 (1997).

92. People v Psichalinos, 229 Ill App 3d 1058, 171 Ill Dec 854, 594 NE2d 1374 (2d Dist 1992).

93. People v Psichalinos, 229 Ill App 3d 1058, 171 Ill Dec 854, 594 NE2d 1374 (2d Dist 1992).

94. People v Hall, 273 Ill App 3d 838, 210 Ill Dec 290, 652 NE2d 1266 (1st Dist 1995).

§ 42:07   ILLINOIS JURISPRUDENCE: CRIMINAL LAW

shielding himself from the fired bullets, causing the child to be shot in the head and leg, because the defendant was both the actual and "legal" cause of the child's injuries and because the jury was authorized by the evidence to conclude the defendant must have been aware that, by putting the child between himself and the shooter, into the line of fire, the child was practically certain to get shot.[95]

A person is said to act "knowingly" in the context of an offense defined in terms of a particular result, such as aggravated battery of a child, when he or she is consciously aware that his or her conduct is practically certain to cause the result.[96] In determining whether an adult intentionally or knowingly injured a child by shaking the child, the trial court may consider the great disparity in size and strength between the defendant and the victim, as well as the nature of the injuries caused, because a defendant is presumed to intend the probable consequences of his or her actions.[97] The defendant need not admit knowledge for the trier of fact to conclude that he or she had the requisite mental state.[98]

Any person who distributes to or encourages the ingestion of a drug by a person under the age of 18 with the intent that the minor ingest the drug for the purpose of a quick weight gain or loss in connection with participation in athletics is guilty of the offense of drug induced infliction of aggravated battery of a child athlete.[99] This does not apply to care under usual and customary standards of medical practice by a physician licensed to practice medicine in all its branches nor to the sale of drugs or products by

95. People v Hall, 273 Ill App 3d 838, 210 Ill Dec 290, 652 NE2d 1266 (1st Dist 1995).

96. People v Hall, 273 Ill App 3d 838, 210 Ill Dec 290, 652 NE2d 1266 (1st Dist 1995).

97. People v Ripley, 291 Ill App 3d 565, 226 Ill Dec 259, 685 NE2d 362 (3d Dist 1997); People v Rader, 272 Ill App 3d 796, 209 Ill Dec 330, 651 NE2d 258 (4th Dist 1995).

98. People v Rader, 272 Ill App 3d 796, 209 Ill Dec 330, 651 NE2d 258 (4th Dist 1995).

99. 720 ILCS 5/12-4.9(a).

ASSAULT AND BATTERY § 42:10

a retail merchant.[1] Drug induced infliction of aggravated battery of a child athlete is a Class A misdemeanor.[2] A second or subsequent violation is a Class 4 felony.[3]

§ 42:08. ——Of unborn child

A person who, in committing battery of an unborn child, intentionally or knowingly causes great bodily harm, or permanent disability or disfigurement commits aggravated battery of an unborn child.[4] Aggravated battery of an unborn child is a Class 2 felony.[5]

§ 42:09. ——Of senior citizen

When an individual causes great bodily harm or permanent disability or disfigurement to an individual of 60 years of age or older during the commission of battery, that person has committed the offense of aggravated battery of a senior citizen.[6] Aggravated battery of a senior citizen is a Class 2 felony.[7]

§ 42:10. —Heinous

A person who, while committing a battery, knowingly causes

1. 720 ILCS 5/12-4.9(a).
2. 720 ILCS 5/12-4.9(b).
3. 720 ILCS 5/12-4.9(b).
4. 720 ILCS 5/12-4.4(a).

   Text References: Decker, Illinois Criminal Law 2d ed § 9.28.

5. 720 ILCS 5/12-4.4(b).
6. 720 ILCS 5/12-4.6(a).

   Text References: Decker, Illinois Criminal Law 2d ed § 9.30.

   Annotation References: Criminal assault or battery statutes making attack on elderly person a special or aggravated offense, 73 ALR4th 1123.

   Periodicals: For comment, "An Illinois Physician-Assisted Suicide Act: A Merciful End to a Terminally Ill Criminal Tradition," see 28 Loy. U. Chi. L.J. 763 (1997).

7. 720 ILCS 5/12-4.6(b).

§ 42:10   ILLINOIS JURISPRUDENCE: CRIMINAL LAW

severe and permanent disability or disfigurement by means of a caustic or flammable substance commits heinous battery.[8] Heinous battery is a Class X felony.[9]

> *Illustration:* Boiling water is considered a "caustic substance."[10] Thus, when an infant burned by scalding bath water while in the defendant's care suffered severe and permanent disfigurement, as necessary for a heinous battery conviction (burns covered 10 percent of the infant's body including his buttocks, thighs, and tip and base of penis, the wounds were so severe that the infant had to be transferred to a second hospital to receive specialized treatment, and a burn reconstruction specialist testified that although the wounds had healed, the infant had suffered permanent scarring), a conviction was upheld.[11] The evidence supported the jury's finding that the defendant's actions were knowingly committed where a burn specialist testified that it was highly unlikely that an infant would have fallen into a tub and stayed in the position necessary for the type of burns he sustained and that a child of that age would not have been able to sit in the tub and reach up and turn on the tap himself and where no contrary medical expert evidence was presented.[12]

---

8. 720 ILCS 5/12-4.1(a).

Text References: Decker, Illinois Criminal Law 2d ed § 9.25.

Periodicals: For comment, "An Illinois Physician-Assisted Suicide Act: A Merciful End to a Terminally Ill Criminal Tradition," see 28 Loy. U. Chi. L.J. 763 (1997).

9. 720 ILCS 5/12-4.1(b).

10. People v Hicks, 101 Ill2d 366, 78 Ill Dec 354, 462 NE2d 473 (1984); People v Cooper, 283 Ill App 3d 86, 218 Ill Dec 494, 669 NE2d 637 (1st Dist 1996).

11. People v Cooper, 283 Ill App 3d 86, 218 Ill Dec 494, 669 NE2d 637 (1st Dist 1996).

12. People v Cooper, 283 Ill App 3d 86, 218 Ill Dec 494, 669 NE2d 637 (1st Dist 1996).

A defendant convicted of heinous battery may not also be sentenced for aggravated battery of a child based on the same incident where the aggravated battery conviction was a lesser offense of heinous battery.[13]

§ 42:11. —Food, drugs and cosmetics

Knowingly putting any substance capable of causing death or great bodily harm into any food, drug or cosmetic offered for sale or consumption constitutes the offense of tampering with food, drugs or cosmetics.[14] This offense is a Class 2 felony.[15]

The unlawful delivery of a controlled substance to another resulting in any person experiencing great bodily harm or permanent disability as a result of the injection, inhalation or ingestion of any amount of that controlled substance constitutes the offense of drug induced infliction of great bodily harm[16] which is a Class 1 felony.[17]

---

13. People v Cooper, 283 Ill App 3d 86, 218 Ill Dec 494, 669 NE2d 637 (1st Dist 1996).

14. 720 ILCS 5/12-4.5(a).

   Text References: Decker, Illinois Criminal Law 2d ed § 9.31.

   Periodicals: For comment, "An Illinois Physician-Assisted Suicide Act: A Merciful End to a Terminally Ill Criminal Tradition," see 28 Loy. U. Chi. L.J. 763 (1997).

15. 720 ILCS 5/12-4.5(b).

16. 720 ILCS 5/12-4.7(a).

   See 720 ILCS 570/401(a), (c).

   Text References: Decker, Illinois Criminal Law 2d ed §§ 9.32.

17. 720 ILCS 5/12-4.7(b).

CHAPTER 43

AUTOMOBILES AND OTHER VEHICLES

by

Carol J. Browder, J.D.

and

Robert L. Margolis, Esq.

Scope of Chapter:
    This chapter covers specific offenses related to automobiles and other vehicles. Included in the discussion are driving under the influence, vehicle registration, automobile theft, and reckless homicide. The associated penalties are also covered.

Treated Elsewhere:
    Charging instruments, see Chapter 9.
    Criminal prosecutions, see Chapter 12.
    Defenses, see Chapter 3.
    Evidentiary matters, see Chapters 17–19, 21.
    Sentencing, see Chapter 28.
    Venue, see Chapter 13.

Research References:
  Text References:
    Decker, Illinois Criminal Law 2d ed §§ 2.12, 9.46A, 9.49, 11.12, 12.15A, 12.15B, 16.02 et seq., 16.12 et seq.
  Annotation References:
    ALR Digest: Automobiles and Highway Traffic §§ 15–49.5; Receiving Stolen Property § 1
    Index and Annotations: Automobiles and Highway Traffic; Blood Test; Breath Tests; Chemical Sobriety Test; Driving While Intoxicated; Hit and Run; Vehicular Homicide

Practice References:

Bailey & Rothblatt, Handling Misdemeanor Cases §§ 388–511, 740–756 (1976)

Nichols Drinking/Driving Lit § 1 et seq.

7 Am Jur 2d, Automobiles and Highway Traffic §§ 90–95, 112–149, 296–393

17 Am Jur POF2d 1, Defense to Charge of Driving Under the Influence of Alcohol § 1 et seq.; 4 Am Jur POF3d 229, Proof and Disproof of Alcohol-Induced Driving Impairment Through Breath Alcohol Testing § 1 et seq.; 4 Am Jur POF3d 438, Unreliability of the Horizontal Gaze Nystagmus Test; 9 Am Jur POF3d 459, Proof and Disproof of Alcohol-Induced Driving Impairment Through Evidence of Observable Intoxication and Coordination Testing § 1 et seq.

2 Am Jur Trials 171, Investigating Particular Crimes §§ 16–18, 58, 59; 13 Am Jur Trials 295, Vehicular Homicide § 1 et seq.; 19 Am Jur Trials 123, Defense on Charge of Driving While Intoxicated § 1 et seq.

State Legislation:

620 ILCS 5/43d; 625 ILCS 5/2-118, 5/3-701 et seq., 5/4-103 et seq., 5/6-203.1, 5/6-205, 5/6-208, 5/6-507, 5/8-101 et seq., 5/9-101 et seq., 5/11-401, 5/11-501 et seq.; 720 ILCS 5/9-3, 5/11-204.1, 5/12-2.5, 5/12-5, 5/18-3, 550/1 et seq., 570/100 et seq., 690/0.01 et seq.

Forms:

3A Am Jur Pl & Pr Forms (Rev), Automobiles and Highway Traffic, Forms 41–56

Miscellaneous References:

West's Illinois Digest 2d, Automobiles §§ 55, 106, 107, 144–144.3, 315–361

Auto-Cite®: Cases and annotations referred to in this chapter can be further researched through the Auto-Cite® computer-assisted research service. Use Auto-Cite® to check citations for form, parallel references, prior and later history, and annotation references.

§ 43:01.   Registration
§ 43:02.   Driving under influence
§ 43:03.   Suspension of driving licenses and privileges
§ 43:03.50. —Restoration of driving privilege
§ 43:04.   Anti-theft laws—Felonious utilization of vehicles and their parts
§ 43:05.   —Vehicle theft conspiracy

§ 43:06. Vehicular hijacking
§ 43:07. Aggravated vehicular hijacking
§ 43:08. Vehicular endangerment
§ 43:09. Aircraft—Intoxicated persons

§ 43:01. Registration

Motor vehicles cannot be operated, nor can an owner knowingly permit operation, on any highway unless there is attached to and displayed on the vehicle as required by law, proper evidence of Illinois registration.[1] The current and valid Illinois registration sticker or stickers and plate or plates, and Illinois temporary registration permit, or a driveaway decal or in-transit permit issued by the Secretary of State is or are required for vehicles in this state.[2] A vehicle eligible for reciprocity requires a current and valid reciprocal foreign registration plate or plates or a temporary registration issued for the vehicle by the reciprocal state.[3] In addition, when required by the Secretary of State, a current and valid Illinois Reciprocity Permit or Prorate Decal is required.[4]

It is a Class A misdemeanor[5] to operate or permit operation of a vehicle when the registration has been cancelled, suspended or revoked.[6] The same holds true for a vehicle properly registered in

1. 625 ILCS 5/3-701.

   Annotation References: Automobiles: necessity or emergency as defense in prosecution for driving without operator's license or while license is suspended, 61 ALR3d 1041.
   Validity and construction of statute making it a criminal offense for the operator of a motor vehicle not to carry or display his operator's license or the vehicle registration certificate, 6 ALR3d 506.

2. 625 ILCS 5/3-701(1).

   Annotation References: Search and seizure: lawfulness of demand for driver's license, vehicle registration, or proof of insurance pursuant to police stop to assist motorist, 19 ALR5th 884.

3. 625 ILCS 5/3-701(2).

4. 625 ILCS 5/3-701(2).

5. 625 ILCS 5/3-702(c).

6. 625 ILCS 5/3-702(a)(1).

another reciprocal state, the foreign registration of which, or the Illinois Reciprocity Permit or decal of which has been cancelled, suspended or revoked.[7] Further, no person can use, nor can an owner use and knowingly permit the use of any Illinois registration plate, plates or registration sticker, or any Illinois Reciprocity Permit or Prorate Decal which has been cancelled, suspended or revoked.[8] Such use constitutes a Class A misdemeanor.[9] If the registration of a motor vehicle has been suspended for noninsurance or failure to purchase a vehicle tax sticker, the individual convicted is guilty of a business offense and the person must pay a fine between $500 and $1000.[10]

The general use of a vehicle registration or certificate of title is also highly regulated. An individual may not lend to another person any certificate of title, registration card, registration plate, registration sticker, special plate or permit or any other evidences of proper registration if the person who desires to borrow the item would not be entitled to its use.[11] Further, a person may not display on a vehicle any of these items not issued for that vehicle.[12] Registration plates and stickers may not be duplicated, altered, or attempts made at their reproduction.[13] The fraudulent use of evidences of registration or certificates of title issued erroneously by the Secretary of State is prohibited.[14] Further, the manufacture, advertisement, distribution or sale of any certificate of title, registration card, registration plate, registration sticker, special plate or permit or other evidences of proper registration is

---

7. 625 ILCS 5/3-702(a)(2).

8. 625 ILCS 5/3-702(b).

9. 625 ILCS 5/3-701(c).

10. 625 ILCS 5/3-702(c)(1), (2).

See 625 ILCS 5/3-708.

11. 625 ILCS 5/3-703.

12. 625 ILCS 5/3-703.

13. 625 ILCS 5/3-703.

14. 625 ILCS 5/3-703.

prohibited.[15] The Secretary of State may seek a restraining order against anyone who advertises fraudulent registration materials.[16]

Any violation of these provisions constitutes a Class C misdemeanor.[17]

§ 43:02. Driving under influence

An individual may not drive or be in actual physical control of any vehicle within Illinois while:

- the alcohol concentration in that person's blood or breath is 0.08 or more based on the statutory definition of blood and breath units;[18]
- under the influence of alcohol;[19]
- under the influence of any intoxicating compound or combination of intoxicating compounds to a degree that

---

15. 625 ILCS 5/3-703.

16. 625 ILCS 5/3-703.

17. 625 ILCS 5/3-703.

18. 625 ILCS 5/11-501(a)(1).

   Text References: Decker, Illinois Criminal Law 2d ed § 2.12.

   Annotation References: Validity, construction, and application of statutes directly proscribing driving with blood-alcohol level in excess of established percentage, 54 ALR4th 149.
   Construction and application of statutes creating presumption or other inference of intoxication from specified percentages of alcohol present in system, 16 ALR3d 748.

   Periodicals: For article, "Survey of Illinois Law: Criminal Law and Procedure," see 21 S. Ill. U.L.J. 759 (1997).
   For article, "The Supreme Court Turns Back the Clock on Civil Forfeiture in Bennis," see 85 Ill. B.J. 314 (1997).

   Practice References: 4 Am Jur POF3d 229, Proof and Disproof of Alcohol-Induced Driving Impairment Through Breath Alcohol Testing § 1 et seq.

19. 625 ILCS 5/11-501(a)(2).

   Practice References: 9 Am Jur POF3d 459, Proof and Disproof of Alcohol-Induced Driving Impairment Through Evidence of Observable Intoxication and Coordination Testing § 1 et seq.

§ 43:02   ILLINOIS JURISPRUDENCE: CRIMINAL LAW

renders the person incapable of driving safely;[20]

- under the influence of any other drug or combination of drugs to a degree which renders the person incapable of safely driving;[21]
- under the combined influence of alcohol and any other drug or drugs which renders the person incapable of safely driving;[22] or
- there is any amount of a drug, substance or compound in the person's blood or urine resulting from the unlawful use or consumption of cannabis or controlled substance.[23]

☞ *Definition:* Alcohol concentration means either grams of alcohol per 100 milliliters of blood or grams of alcohol per 210 liters of breath.[24]

The offense has two elements: (1) a defendant must be driving a

---

20. 625 ILCS 5/11-501(a)(3).

21. 625 ILCS 5/11-501(a)(4).

Annotation References: Cough medicine as "intoxicating liquor" under DUI statute, 65 ALR4th 1238.
Automobiles: Driving under the influence, or when addicted to the use, of drugs as criminal offense, 17 ALR3d 815.

22. 625 ILCS 5/11-501(a)(5).

23. 625 ILCS 5/11-501(a)(6).

Cannabis Control Act, see 720 ILCS 550/1 et seq.

Controlled Substances Act, see 720 ILCS 570/100 et seq.

Text References: Decker, Illinois Criminal Law 2d ed § 16.02 et seq.; 16.12 et seq.

Annotation References: Permissibility under Fourth Amendment of detention of motorist by police, following lawful stop for traffic offense, to investigate matters not related to offense, 118 ALR Fed 567.
Driving while intoxicated: subsequent consent to sobriety test as affecting initial refusal, 28 ALR5th 459.

Practice References: Driving under the influence: Tactical considerations in sobriety checkpoint cases, 59 Am Jur Trials 79.

24. 625 ILCS 5/11-501.2.

AUTOMOBILES AND OTHER VEHICLES § 43:02

vehicle, and (2) defendant must be intoxicated while driving.[25]

A person need not drive to be in actual physical control of a vehicle, nor is the person's intent to put the car in motion relevant to the determination of actual physical control.[26] The issue of actual physical control is determined on a case by case basis giving consideration to factors such as whether the motorist is positioned in the driver's seat of the vehicle, has possession of the ignition key and has the physical capability of starting the engine and moving the vehicle.[27]

> *Illustration:* In one case, where the officer testified that defendant was pushing his car by hand along the roadway, which meant the car had to be in neutral, and the defendant's car could not be in neutral unless the keys were in the ignition, the ignition key was in the defendant's front pocket and he admitted shutting off the ignition, the trial court could rationally conclude the defendant was in actual physical control of the vehicle.[28]

While section (a)(2) requires that there be sufficient alcohol in the person's blood to render him or her incapable of driving safely[29] subdivision (a)(4) does not require that the person have enough alcohol in his or her system to be incapable of driving safely, or that the person have sufficient drugs in his or her system so as to be incapable of driving safely, only that there be some alcohol present and some other drug or drugs present and that the combined influence of the two render the person incapable of

---

25. People v Rhoden, 253 Ill App 3d 805, 192 Ill Dec 785, 625 NE2d 940 (4th Dist 1993).

26. City of Naperville v Watson, 175 Ill 2d 399, 222 Ill Dec 421, 677 NE2d 955 (1997); People v Scapes, 247 Ill App 3d 848, 187 Ill Dec 645, 617 NE2d 1366 (4th Dist 1993).

27. City of Naperville v Watson, 175 Ill 2d 399, 222 Ill Dec 421, 677 NE2d 955 (1997).

28. People v Eyen, 291 Ill App 3d 38, 225 Ill Dec 249, 683 NE2d 193 (2d Dist 1997).

29. 625 ILCS 5/11-501(a)(2).

§ 43:02 ILLINOIS JURISPRUDENCE: CRIMINAL LAW

driving safely.[30] Making it a criminal act to drive a vehicle while any amount of cannabis or a controlled substance is present in the blood or urine is a reasonable exercise of the police power, since, unlike alcohol, there is no set standard by which the level of these drugs in the body can be correlated with the extent to which driving ability may be impaired.[31] Similarly, absolute liability for driving under the influence of alcohol is a reasonable exercise of police power and does not violate due process.[32]

Even though an officer must have probable cause to believe a driver is chemically impaired to arrest the driver for driving under the influence of alcohol, at that point the officer may request any or all of the tests to determine whether the driver is in fact chemically impaired; there is no requirement that an officer have individualized suspicion of drugs and/or alcohol before requesting multiple chemical tests.[33]

A violation of any of these provisions or a similar provision of a local ordinance constitutes a Class A misdemeanor.[34] A second

30. People v Vanzandt, 287 Ill App 3d 836, 223 Ill Dec 186, 679 NE2d 130 (5th Dist 1997).

625 ILCS 5/11-501(a)(4).

31. People v Fate, 159 Ill 2d 267, 201 Ill Dec 117, 636 NE2d 549 (1994).

32. People v Avery, 277 Ill App 3d 824, 214 Ill Dec 507, 661 NE2d 361 (1st Dist 1995).

33. People v Kirk, 291 Ill App 3d 610, 225 Ill Dec 752, 684 NE2d 437 (4th Dist 1997).

34. 625 ILCS 5/11-501(c).

Practice References: Bailey & Rothblatt, Handling Misdemeanor Cases §§ 328–511 (1976).
Nichols Drinking/Driving Lit § 1 et seq.
17 Am Jur POF2d 1, Defense to Charge of Driving Under the Influence of Alcohol § 1 et seq.
19 Am Jur Trials 123, Defense on Charge of Driving While Intoxicated § 1 et seq.

Annotation References: What constitutes driving, operating, or being in control of motor vehicle for purposes of driving while intoxicated statutes, 93 ALR3d 7.
Applicability, to operation of motor vehicle on private property, of

conviction committed within five years of a previous violation requires mandatory sentencing of a minimum of 48 consecutive hours of imprisonment or assigned assignment to a minimum of 100 hours of community service as determined by the court.[35] The imprisonment or assignment cannot be subject to suspension nor can the person be eligible for probation in order to reduce the sentence or assignment.[36] Every person who violates these provisions or a similar provision of a local ordinance while transporting a person aged 16 or younger is subject to a mandatory minimum fine of $500 and a mandatory 5 days of community service in a program benefiting children.[37] Every person convicted a second time for violating this section or a similar provision of a local ordinance while transporting a person aged 16 or younger within 5 years of a previous violation of the section or a similar provision of a local ordinance is subject to a mandatory minimum fine of $500 and 10 days of mandatory community service.[38]

If a person violates one of the above provisions while his or her driving privileges are revoked or suspended for driving while intoxicated is guilty of a Class 4 felony.[39] A person who violates this Section a third time during a period in which his or her driving privileges are revoked or suspended for driving while intoxicated is guilty of a Class 3 felony.[40] A fourth or subsequent violation is a Class 3 felony.[41]

Every person convicted of violating these provisions or a

legislation making drunken driving a criminal offense, 29 ALR3d 938.
Right to trial by jury in criminal prosecution for driving while intoxicated or similar offense, 16 ALR3d 1373.

35. 625 ILCS 5/11-501(c).
36. 625 ILCS 5/11-501(c).
37. 625 ILCS 5/11-501(c).
38. 625 ILCS 5/11-501(c).
39. 625 ILCS 5/11-501(c-1)(1).
40. 625 ILCS 5/11-501(c-1)(2).
41. 625 ILCS 5/11-501(c-1)(3).

§ 43:02   ILLINOIS JURISPRUDENCE: CRIMINAL LAW

similar provision of a local ordinance who had a child under age 16 in the vehicle at the time of the offense must have his or her punishment under this Act enhanced by two days of imprisonment for a first offense, ten days of imprisonment for a second offense, 30 days of imprisonment for a third offense, and 90 days of imprisonment for a fourth or subsequent offense, in addition to the fine and community service required and the possible imprisonment required for aggravated driving under the influence.[42] The imprisonment or assignment under this subsection is not subject to suspension nor is the person eligible for probation to reduce the sentence or assignment.[43]

A person convicted of committing a violation of one of the previous provisions will be guilty of aggravated driving under the influence of alcohol, other drug or drugs, or intoxicating compound or compounds, or any combination thereof, a Class 4 felony,[44] if:

- the person committed a violation for the third or subsequent time;[45]
- the person committed a violation while driving a school bus with children on board;[46]
- the person in committing a violation was involved in a motor vehicle accident which resulted in great bodily harm or permanent disability or disfigurement to another, when the violation was the proximate cause of the injuries; or[47]
- the person committed his or her second violation and has been previously convicted of reckless homicide under the influence of alcohol, other drug or drugs, or intoxicating compound or compounds,[48] or was involved in an accident

---

42. 625 ILCS 5/11-501(c-3).

43. 625 ILCS 5/11-501(c-3).

44. 625 ILCS 5/11-501(d).

45. 625 ILCS 5/11-501(d)(1).

46. 625 ILCS 5/11-501(d)(2).

47. 625 ILCS 5/11-501(d)(3).

resulting in great bodily harm or permanent disability of another the person committed a violation while driving a school bus with children on board.[49]

Every person sentenced for aggravated DUI who receives a term of probation or conditional discharge must serve a minimum term of 30 days community service as a condition of the probation or conditional discharge.[50] This mandatory minimum term of community service may not be suspended and nor subject to reduction by the court.[51]

Because the underlying cause of both misdemeanor and aggravated DUI is driving while under the influence and the two, therefore are based on the same act, charges should be brought in one proceeding.[52] Where driving under the influence is used to enhance defendant's reckless homicide convictions, driving under the influence of alcohol serves as a lesser included offense of reckless homicide; therefore under double jeopardy principles, the defendant may not be convicted and sentenced on the lesser included offense.[53] However, in cases where the elements of the DUI charge and the violation of the statute proscribing the failure to take a breathalizer test are different,[54] because each proceeding is premised on different allegations and requires different proofs by the state, the double jeopardy clause is not violated.[55] Further,

48. 720 ILCS 5/9-3.

49. 625 ILCS 5/11-501(d)(2).

50. 625 ILCS 5/11-501(h).

51. 625 ILCS 5/11-501(h).

52. People v Quigley, 183 Ill 2d 1, 231 Ill Dec 950, 697 NE2d 735 (1998); People v Green, 294 Ill App 3d 139, 228 Ill Dec 513, 689 NE2d 385 (1st Dist 1997).

53. People v Beck, 295 Ill App 3d 1050, 230 Ill Dec 419, 693 NE2d 897 (2d Dist 1998).

54. 625 ILCS 5/11-501.1(d).

55. People v Parmenter, 283 Ill App 3d 688, 219 Ill Dec 283, 670 NE2d 1171 (3d Dist 1996); People v Lopeman, 279 Ill App 3d 1058, 216 Ill Dec 623, 665 NE2d 881 (3d Dist 1996).

§ 43:02   ILLINOIS JURISPRUDENCE: CRIMINAL LAW

because summary suspension of a driver's license is fairly characterized as a remedial civil sanction rather than as a punishment, a suspension does not constitute punishment for double jeopardy purposes.[56]

Two counts of aggravated driving may arise where the driver causes separate injuries to two different people.[57]

For a conviction for misdemeanor DUI to be enhanced to a felony under section (d)(3),[58] the State must prove beyond a reasonable doubt that the DUI was the proximate cause of great bodily harm or permanent disability or disfigurement to another in its case in chief and such aggravating factor is not to be merely noted by the trial court at the sentencing stage as the court would mention the sentencing factors considered under the Unified Code of Corrections as reasons for imposing an extended-term sentence.[59]

> *Illustration:* In one case, an aggravated driving while under the influence charge was improperly dismissed on the defendant's pretrial motion when the state alleged a prior DUI violation resulting in supervision as one of the two required enhancing offenses; thus, a DUI charge for which a defendant successfully completed a term of supervision may serve to enhance a subsequent charge of the same offense.[60]
>
> *Illustration:* In another, the trial court properly enhanced a DUI offense to aggravated DUI based on the defendant's prior DUI offense culminating in court supervision and prior

---

56. People v Eck, 279 Ill App 3d 541, 216 Ill Dec 219, 664 NE2d 1147 (5th Dist 1996); People v Fasbinder, 278 Ill App 3d 855, 215 Ill Dec 538, 663 NE2d 1052 (4th Dist 1996).

57. People v Lavallier, 298 Ill App 3d 648, 232 Ill Dec 613, 698 NE2d 704 (5th Dist 1998), app gr 181 Ill 2d 581, 235 Ill Dec 945, 706 NE2d 500.

58. 625 ILCS 5/11-501(d)(3).

59. People v Martin, 266 Ill App 3d 369, 203 Ill Dec 718, 640 NE2d 638 (4th Dist 1994).

60. People v Sheehan, 168 Ill 2d 298, 213 Ill Dec 692, 659 NE2d 1339 (1995).

DUI conviction, where the term "committed" a violation of DUI in the statutory enhancement provision was construed to encompass a disposition of court supervision, since even though the charges are dismissed without a finding of guilt on the successful completion of supervision and the statute provides for the sealing or expungement of the order under certain circumstances, the legislature's use of the word "committed" evidenced its intent to expand the enhancing factor beyond convictions, thereby allowing the court to recognize unexpunged orders of supervision as enhancing factors for those who commit two subsequent DUI offenses.[61]

After a finding of guilt and prior to any final sentencing, or an order for supervision, for an offense based on an arrest for violation of the above provisions or a similar provision of a local ordinance, individuals are required to undergo professional evaluation to determine if any alcohol or other drug abuse problem exists and the extent of the problem.[62] The driving privileges of any person convicted for violating the above provisions will be revoked by the secretary of state.[63]

When a police officer conducts a valid traffic stop based on evidence obtained through his or her observations, the subsequent use of his or her power as an officer to acquire further evidence not available to a private citizen does not invalidate an arrest; so the use of emergency lights, field sobriety tests and breathalyzer tests used to effect arrest and obtain evidence of DUI are proper.[64]

The strict liability imposed on persons arrested for driving under the influence affects only those motorists who have controlled substances in their systems as the result of the unlawful

---

61. People v Tinkham, 266 Ill App 3d 391, 203 Ill Dec 358, 639 NE2d 917 (4th Dist 1994).

62. 625 ILCS 5/11-501(e).

63. 625 ILCS 5/11-501(g).

64. People v Plummer, 287 Ill App 3d 250, 223 Ill Dec 71, 678 NE2d 1079 (4th Dist 1997).

§ 43:02   ILLINOIS JURISPRUDENCE: CRIMINAL LAW

use of those substances, not those who ingested controlled substances inadvertently or unknowingly.[65]

§ 43:03. Suspension of driving licenses and privileges

Both a driver's license and the privilege of driving may be suspended under certain circumstances. Any person who drives or is in actual physical control of a motor vehicle on any public highway in Illinois is deemed to have given consent to a chemical test or tests of blood, breath, or urine for the purpose of determining the content of alcohol, or other drugs in the person's blood if arrested for driving under the influence.[66] Consent is

---

65. People v Gassman, 251 Ill App 3d 681, 190 Ill Dec 815, 622 NE2d 845 (2d Dist 1993).

66. 625 ILCS 5/11-501.1(a).

Driving under the influence, see 625 ILCS 5/11-501.

See § 43:02.

Annotation References: Admissibility, in motor vehicle license suspension proceedings, of evidence obtained by unlawful search and seizure, 23 ALR5th 108.
Search and seizure: lawfulness of demand for driver's license, vehicle registration, or proof of insurance pursuant to police stop to assist motorist, 19 ALR5th 884.
Validity and application of statute or regulation authorizing revocation or suspension of driver's license for reason unrelated to use of, or ability to operate, motor vehicle, 18 ALR5th 542.
Validity, construction, application, and effect of statute requiring conditions, in addition to expiration of time, for reinstatement of suspended or revoked driver's license. 2 ALR5th 725.
Drunk driving: motorist's right to private sobriety test, 45 ALR4th 11.
Admissibility in criminal case of evidence that accused refused to take test of intoxication, 26 ALR4th 1112.
Destruction of ampoule used in alcohol breath test as warranting suppression of result of test, 19 ALR4th 509.
Admissibility in criminal case of blood-alcohol test where blood was taken despite defendant's objection or refusal to submit to test, 14 ALR4th 690.
Request for prior administration of additional test as constituting refusal to submit to chemical sobriety test under implied consent law, 98 ALR3d 572.
Request before submitting to chemical sobriety test to communicate with counsel as refusal to take test, 97 ALR3d 852.

evidenced by the issuance of a Uniform Traffic Ticket for any DUI offense or a similar provision of a local ordinance.[67] The test or tests must be administered at the direction of the arresting officer and the law enforcement agency employing the officer must designate whether a blood, breath, or urine test should be administered.[68]

> *Practice Guide:* The provision that law enforcement agencies "shall designate" chemical tests is not mandatory. Therefore, a defendant may not raise the issue of noncompliance with the designation requirement at a rescission hearing.[69]

A "public highway," as defined by the implied-consent statute, includes publicly maintained property that is open to use by the public for vehicular travel.[70]

A person need not drive to be in actual physical control of a vehicle, nor is the person's intent to put the car in motion relevant to the determination of actual physical control.[71] The issue of actual physical control is determined on a case by case basis giving consideration to factors such as whether the motorist is

---

Necessity and sufficiency of proof that tests of blood alcohol concentration were conducted in conformance with prescribed methods, 96 ALR3d 745.

Driving while intoxicated: duty of law enforcement officer to offer suspect chemical sobriety test under implied consent law, 95 ALR3d 710.

Admissibility in criminal case of blood alcohol test where blood was taken from unconscious driver, 72 ALR3d 325.

Periodicals: For article, "A Practical Guide to the DUI Summary Suspension Laws," see 85 Ill. B.J. 381 (1997).

For article, "Representing Revoked or Suspended Drivers Before the Secretary of State," see 84 Ill. B.J. 556 (1997).

67. 625 ILCS 5/11-501.1(a).

68. 625 ILCS 5/11-501.1(a).

69. People v Tomlinson, 295 Ill App 3d 193, 230 Ill Dec 41, 692 NE2d 1207 (4th Dist 1998).

70. People v Culbertson, 258 Ill App 3d 294, 196 Ill Dec 554, 630 NE2d 489 (2d Dist 1994).

§ 43:03   ILLINOIS JURISPRUDENCE: CRIMINAL LAW

positioned in the driver's seat of the vehicle, has possession of the ignition key and has the physical capability of starting the engine and moving the vehicle.[72]

Even though an officer must have probable cause to believe a driver is chemically impaired to arrest him or her for driving under the influence of alcohol, at that point the officer may request any or all of the tests to determine whether the driver is in fact chemically impaired; there is no requirement that an officer have individualized suspicion of drugs and/or alcohol before requesting multiple chemical tests.[73]

The implied-consent statute requires only that the summary suspension warnings be given in order for motorists suspected of drunken driving to have been properly waived. The statute does not require that a motorist understand the consequences of refusing to take a blood-alcohol test before the state may summarily suspend his or her driver' license for failure to take the test.[74]

A person requested to submit to a test must be warned by the law enforcement officer requesting it that a refusal to submit to the test will result in the statutory summary suspension of the

---

71. City of Naperville v Watson, 175 Ill 2d 399, 222 Ill Dec 421, 677 NE2d 955 (1997); People v Scapes, 247 Ill App 3d 848, 187 Ill Dec 645, 617 NE2d 1366 (4th Dist 1993).

72. Court finds defendant had physical control over vehicle despite defense that defendant may have intended only to use the vehicle for shelter while achieving sobriety. City of Naperville v Watson, 175 Ill 2d 399, 222 Ill Dec 421, 677 NE2d 955 (1997).

Where officer testified defendant was pushing his car by hand along the roadway, which meant the car had to be in neutral and defendant's car could not be in neutral unless keys were in ignition, ignition key was in defendant's front pocket and he admitted shutting off the ignition, the trial court could rationally conclude defendant was in actual physical control of vehicle. People v Eyen, 291 Ill App 3d 38, 225 Ill Dec 249, 683 NE2d 193 (2d Dist 1997).

73. People v Kirk, 291 Ill App 3d 610, 225 Ill Dec 752, 684 NE2d 437 (4th Dist 1997).

74. People v Wegielnik, 152 Ill 2d 418, 178 Ill Dec 693, 605 NE2d 487 (1992).

§ 43:03 AUTOMOBILES AND OTHER VEHICLES

person's privilege to operate a motor vehicle.[75] Further, the person must be warned that if he or she submits to the test and the alcohol concentration is 0.08 or greater, or any amount of a drug substance or compound resulting from the unlawful consumption of cannabis or a controlled substance is detected in his or her blood or urine, a statutory summary suspension of driving privileges will be imposed.[76]

> ☞*Illustration:* The warning is not easily excused. In one case, where the defendant suspected of driving under the influence was uncooperative and physically combative, and where the officer decided it was futile to attempt to read the "Warning to Motorist," including the required warning about refusal to submit to breath testing and its consequences, the trial court was held to have erred in ruling that the required warnings were excused by the defendant's combativeness. The defendant was conscious and present, so the officer needed to make an effort and the court could not sanction the officer making the subjective determination that compliance with the statutory mandate would be futile; however, had the officer attempted to warn the defendant of the consequences of refusal, the court indicated it would have upheld the trial court's finding of a constructive refusal.[77]

---

75. 625 ILCS 5/11-501.1(c).

76. 625 ILCS 5/11-501.1(c).

Cannabis Control Act, see 720 ILCS 550/1 et seq.

Controlled Substances Act, see 720 ILCS 570/100 et seq.

Text References: Decker, Illinois Criminal Law 2d ed § 16.02 et seq.; 16.12 et seq.

Annotation References: Permissibility under Fourth Amendment of detention of motorist by police, following lawful stop for traffic offense, to investigate matters not related to offense, 118 ALR Fed 567.

Driving while intoxicated: subsequent consent to sobriety test as affecting initial refusal, 28 ALR5th 459.

Miscellaneous References: Driving under the influence: Tactical considerations in sobriety checkpoint cases, 59 Am Jur Trials 79.

§ 43:03   ILLINOIS JURISPRUDENCE: CRIMINAL LAW

A person under the age of 21 who is requested to submit to a sobriety test must, in addition to the warnings provided for in the statute, be further warned by the law enforcement officer requesting the test that if the person submits to the test or tests and the alcohol concentration is greater than 0.00 and less than 0.08, a suspension of the person's privilege to operate a motor vehicle will be imposed.[78] The results of this test are admissible in a civil or criminal action.[79]

If the person refuses testing or submits to a test which discloses an alcohol concentration of 0.08 or more, or any amount of a drug, substance, or compound in the person's blood or urine resulting from the unlawful use or consumption of cannabis or other controlled substance, the law enforcement officer must immediately submit a sworn report to the circuit court and to the Secretary of State certifying that the test was requested pursuant to statute and that the person refused to submit to the test, or submitted to testing which disclosed an alcohol concentration of 0.08 or more.[80] The defendant's noncommittal answer in response to a request to take a test may be considered a refusal to take the test, and in such a case, the later consent to take a breathalyzer

---

77. City of Highland Park v Didenko, 274 Ill App 3d 24, 210 Ill Dec 916, 653 NE2d 1378 (2d Dist 1995).

78. 625 ILCS 5/11-501.1(c).

79. 625 ILCS 5/11-501.1(c).

80. 625 ILCS 5/11-501.1(d).

Cannabis Control Act, see 720 ILCS 550/1 et seq.

Controlled Substances Act, see 720 ILCS 570/100 et seq.

Text References: Decker, Illinois Criminal Law 2d ed § 16.02 et seq.; 16.12 et seq.

Annotation References: Sufficiency of showing of physical inability to take tests for driving while intoxicated to justify refusal, 68 ALR4th 776.

Periodicals: Locallo, Using Blood Tests in DUI and Reckless Homicide Prosccutions, 77 Ill BJ 874, December 1989.

Forms: Judicial review of operator's license suspension. 3A Am Jur Pl & Pr Forms (Rev), Automobiles and Highway Traffic, Forms 41–56.

test will not change the outcome of the case.[81] Absent a showing that the machine is not in proper working order or that defendant is not physically able to take the test, the failure to provide the breathalyzer machine with an adequate air sample is a sufficient basis for a determination that defendant refused to take the test.[82]

On receipt of the sworn report, the Secretary of State must enter the statutory summary suspension.[83]

The law enforcement officer submitting the sworn report must serve immediate notice of the statutory summary suspension on the person.[84] In cases where the blood alcohol concentration of 0.08 or greater or any amount of a drug, substance, or compound resulting from the unlawful use or consumption of cannabis as covered by the Cannabis Control Act,[85] a controlled substance listed in the Illinois Controlled Substances Act,[86] or an intoxicating compound listed in the Use of Intoxicating Compounds Act[87] is established by a subsequent analysis of blood or urine collected at the time of arrest, the arresting officer or arresting agency must give notice and the statutory summary suspension will begin onthe 46th day following the giving of notice.[88] The officer must confiscate any Illinois driver's license or permit on the person at the time of arrest.[89] If the person has a

---

81. People v Shaffer, 261 Ill App 3d 304, 199 Ill Dec 431, 634 NE2d 31 (3d Dist 1994).

82. People v Bank, 251 Ill App 3d 187, 190 Ill Dec 601, 621 NE2d 1054 (5th Dist 1993).

83. 625 ILCS 5/11-501.1(e).

Period of statutory summary alcohol or other drug-related suspension, see 625 ILCS 5/6-208.1.

84. 625 ILCS 5/11-501.1(c).

85. 720 ILCS 550/1 et seq.

86. 720 ILCS 550/1 et seq.

87. 720 ILCS 690/0.01.

88. 625 ILCS 5/11-501.1(f), (g).

89. 625 ILCS 5/11-501.1(f).

valid driver's license or permit, the officer must issue the person a receipt, in a form prescribed by the Secretary of State, that will allow that person to drive during the period of statutory suspension.[90] The officer must immediately forward the driver's license or permit to the circuit court of venue along with the sworn report described above.[91]

On receipt of the sworn report from the law enforcement officer, the Secretary of State must confirm the statutory summary suspension by mailing a notice of the effective date of the suspension to the person and the court of venue.[92] However, should the sworn report be defective by not containing sufficient information or be completed in error, the confirmation of the statutory summary suspension may not be mailed to the person or entered to the record, instead the sworn report must be forwarded to the court of venue with a copy returned to the issuing agency identifying any defect.[93]

> *Illustration:* In one case, where the defendant's driver's license was suspended because he refused to take a breathalyzer test at the time he was arrested for driving under the influence of alcohol, the trial court was held to have erred in rescinding the defendant's statutory summary suspension, since it appeared the trial court based its decision on the belief that the arresting officer's report needed to set forth adequate grounds for the defendant's arrest, but the summary suspension statute merely directs the officer to submit a sworn report certifying that the driver was asked to take the test and that he refused, and because there was no statutory requirement that the report contain a dissertation of facts supporting defendant's arrest, the trial court could not have properly relied on the statute as the basis for finding that the sworn report was inadequate.[94]

---

90. 625 ILCS 5/11-501.1(f).
91. 625 ILCS 5/11-501.1(f).
92. 625 ILCS 5/11-501.1(h).
93. 625 ILCS 5/11-501.1(h).

The results of a defendant's breath test for alcohol may be admitted if the State establishes that the tests were performed according to the uniform standard adopted by the Illinois Department of Public Health; the operator administering the tests was certified by the Department of Public Health; the machine used was a model approved by the Department of Public Health, was tested regularly for accuracy, and was working properly; the defendant was observed for the requisite 20 minutes prior to the test and, during the period, did not smoke, regurgitate, or drink; and the results appearing on the "printout" sheet can be identified as the tests given to the defendant.[95]

An Illinois law enforcement officer who is investigating the person for any DUI offense may travel into an adjoining state, where the person has been transported for medical care, to complete an investigation and to request that the person submit to the test or tests set forth in this section.[96] The requirements of this section that the person be arrested are inapplicable, but the officer must issue the person a uniform traffic ticket for an offense prior to requesting that the person submit to the test or tests, which will not constitute an arrest, but serves the purpose of notifying the person that he or she is subject to the provisions of statute proscribing driving while intoxicated and of the officer's belief of the existence of probable cause to arrest.[97] Upon returning to this state, the officer will file the uniform traffic ticket with the circuit clerk of the county where the offense was committed, and must seek the issuance of an arrest warrant or a summons for the person.[98]

The mandatory revocation of a license or permit will take place

---

94. People v Sarver, 262 Ill App 3d 513, 201 Ill Dec 599, 636 NE2d 1031 (3d Dist 1994).

95. People v Witt, 258 Ill App 3d 124, 196 Ill Dec 459, 630 NE2d 156 (2d Dist 1994).

96. 625 ILCS 5/11-501.1(a).

97. 625 ILCS 5/11-501.1(a).

98. 625 ILCS 5/11-501.1(a).

§ 43:03   ILLINOIS JURISPRUDENCE: CRIMINAL LAW

upon receipt of a report of a driver's conviction of any of the following offenses:

- reckless homicide resulting from the operation of a motor vehicle;[99]
- operating or being in physical control of a vehicle while under the influence of alcohol, other drug, intoxicating compound or compounds, or any combination thereof;[1]
- any felony under the laws of Illinois or the federal government in the commission of which a motor vehicle was used;[2]
- leaving the scene of a traffic accident involving death or personal injury;[3]
- perjury or the making of a false affidavit or statement under oath to the Secretary of State or under any other law relating to the ownership or operation of motor vehicles;[4]
- three charges of reckless driving[5] committed within a period of 12 months;[6]

---

99. 625 ILCS 5/6-205(a)1.

Annotation References: Homicide by automobile as murder, 21 ALR3d 116.
What amounts to negligence within meaning of statutes penalizing negligent homicide by operation of motor vehicle, 20 ALR3d 473.

Practice References: 13 Am Jur Trials 295, Vehicular Homicide § 1 et seq.

1. 625 ILCS 5/6-205(a)2.

2. 625 ILCS 5/6-205(a)3.

3. 625 ILCS 5/6-205(a)4.

Annotation References: Sufficiency of showing of driver's involvement in motor vehicle accident to support prosecution for failure to stop, furnish identification, or render aid, 82 ALR4th 232.
Necessity and sufficiency of showing in a criminal prosecution under a "hit-and-run" statute accused's knowledge of accident, injury, or damage, 23 ALR3d 497.

4. 625 ILCS 5/6-205(a)5.

5. 625 ILCS 5/11-503.

AUTOMOBILES AND OTHER VEHICLES § 43:03

- automobile theft;[7]
- drag racing;[8]
- operating a medical transport vehicle without providing the Secretary of State with proof of financial responsibility;[9]
- engaging in the business or holding him or herself out as being engaged in the business of renting out motor vehicles without providing the Secretary of State with proof of financial responsibility;[10]
- reckless conduct arising from the use of a motor vehicle.[11]
- aggravated fleeing or attempting to allude a police officer;[12] or
- driving a commercial motor vehicle on the highway while the driver's driving privilege, license or permit is suspended, revoked, cancelled, or subject to disqualification or subject to an "out-of-service" order.[13]

Annotation References: Statute prohibiting reckless driving: certainty and definiteness, 52 ALR4th 1161.

Practice References: Bailey & Rothblatt, Handling Misdemeanor Cases §§ 740–756 (1976).

6. 625 ILCS 5/6-205(a)6.

7. 625 ILCS 5/6-205(a)7.

8. 625 ILCS 5/6-205(a)8.

Drag racing, see 625 ILCS 5/11-504.

9. 625 ILCS 5/8-101 et seq., 5/9-101 et seq.

10. 625 ILCS 5/9-101 et seq.

11. 625 ILCS 5/6-205(a)10.

Reckless conduct, see 720 ILCS 5/12-5.

12. 625 ILCS 5/6-205(a)11.

Aggravated fleeing or attempting to allude police officer, see 625 ILCS 5/11-204.1.

13. 625 ILCS 5/6-205(a)12.

Commercial driver's license requirement, see 625 ILCS 5/6-507(b).

§ 43:03　ILLINOIS JURISPRUDENCE: CRIMINAL LAW

The Secretary of State is also authorized to suspend the driving privileges of individuals arrested in another state for driving under the influence of alcohol or drugs who have refused to submit to a chemical test under the provisions of implied consent.[14]

The so-called zero-tolerance law applies to persons under 21 years of age.[15] A person under 21 who drives or is in actual physical control of a motor vehicle on the public highways of Illinois is deemed to have given consent to a chemical test or tests of blood, breath, or urine for the purpose of determining the alcohol content of his or her blood if arrested, if a police officer has probable cause to believe that the driver has consumed any amount of an alcoholic beverage based on evidence of the driver's physical condition or other first-hand knowledge of the police officer.[16] The test or tests are to be administered at the direction of the arresting officer.[17] A person requested to submit to a test must be warned by the law enforcement officer requesting the test that a refusal to submit to the test, or submission to the test resulting in an alcohol concentration of more than 0.00 may result in the loss of that person's privilege to operate a motor vehicle.[18] If the person refuses testing or submits to a test that discloses an alcohol concentration or more than 0.00, the law enforcement officer must immediately submit a sworn report the Secretary of State.[19] Upon receipt of the report, the Secretary of State must enter the driver's license sanction on the individual's driving record.[20] The

Annotation References: Automobiles: necessity or emergency as defense in prosecution for driving without operator's license or while license is suspended, 61 ALR3d 1041.

14. 625 ILCS 5/6-203.1(a).
15. 625 ILCS 5/11-501.8.
16. 625 ILCS 5/11-501.8(a).
17. 625 ILCS 5/11-501.8(a).
18. 625 ILCS 5/11-501.8(c).
19. 625 ILCS 5/11-501.8(d).
20. 625 ILCS 5/11-501.8(d).

law enforcement officer submitting the report must serve immediate notice of the sanction on the person and the sanction is effective on the 46th day following the date notice was given.[21] The results of any chemical testing performed on a person under 21 are not admissible in any civil or criminal proceedings, except that the results may be considered at a suspension hearing.[22]

☛ *Practice Commentary:* The zero-tolerance provision does not provide for issuance of a judicial driving permit.[23]

Because summary suspension of a driver's license is fairly characterized as a remedial civil sanction rather than as a punishment, a suspension does not constitute punishment for double jeopardy purposes.[24] Similarly, in cases where the elements of the DUI charge and the violation of the summary supension statute are different, because each proceeding is premised on different allegations and requires different proofs by the state, the double jeopardy clause is not violated.[25]

In a procedure in which a driver seeks to have the suspension of his or her license rescinded,[26] the driver is first required to make a prima facie case that the determination of alcohol concentration in the blood is inaccurate; if that proof is made, the burden then shifts to the State to lay a foundation for the admission of the test results and to prove those results.[27] Laying the required

21. 625 ILCS 5/11-501.8(d).

22. 625 ILCS 5/11-501.8(f).

For hearings, see 625 ILCS 5/2-118, 5/2-118.1.

23. People v Schmidt, 286 Ill App 3d 322, 221 Ill Dec 671, 676 NE2d 11 (3d Dist 1997).

24. People v Eck, 279 Ill App 3d 541, 216 Ill Dec 219, 664 NE2d 1147 (5th Dist 1996); People v Fasbinder, 278 Ill App 3d 855, 215 Ill Dec 538, 663 NE2d 1052 (4th Dist 1996).

25. People v Parmenter, 283 Ill App 3d 688, 219 Ill Dec 283, 670 NE2d 1171 (3d Dist 1996); People v Lopeman, 279 Ill App 3d 1058, 216 Ill Dec 623, 665 NE2d 881 (3d Dist 1996).

26. See 625 ILCS 5/2-118, 5/2-118.1.

foundation requires presenting evidence that the tests were performed according to the uniform standard adopted by the Illinois Department of Public Health, evidence that the operator administering the tests was properly certified, evidence that the machine used was properly approved, tested for accuracy and was working properly, evidence that the motorist was observed for the requisite 20 minutes prior to the test and during that time did not smoke, regurgitate, or drink, and evidence that the results appearing on the printout sheet can be identified as the tests given to the motorist.[28] A hearing to rescind a summary suspension is civil in nature, and the civil standard of proof of preponderance of the evidence controls.[29] The Illinois scheme does not offend the due process clause of the U.S. Constitution because the hearing to determine if suspension should be rescinded comes after rather than before the revocation of driving privileges.[30]

Absolute liability for driving under the influence of alcohol is a reasonable exercise of police power and does not violate due process.[31]

§ 43:03.50. —Restoration of driving privilege

Generally, the period of license, permit, or privilege to drive suspension may not exceed one year.[32] Any person whose license,

---

27. People v Orth, 124 Ill 2d 326, 125 Ill Dec 182, 530 NE2d 210 (1988); People v Culpepper, 254 Ill App 3d 215, 192 Ill Dec 713, 625 NE2d 868 (4th Dist 1993).

28. People v Culpepper, 254 Ill App 3d 215, 192 Ill Dec 713, 625 NE2d 868 (4th Dist 1993).

29. People v Sanders, 176 Ill App 3d 467, 125 Ill Dec 882, 531 NE2d 61 (4th Dist 1988).

30. Burgess v Ryan, 996 F2d 180 (CA7 Ill 1993), cert den 510 US 1092, 127 L Ed 2d 216, 114 S Ct 923.

31. People v Avery, 277 Ill App 3d 824, 214 Ill Dec 507, 661 NE2d 361 (1st Dist 1995).

32. 625 ILCS 5/6-208(a).

Periodicals: Freese, Sherman, The road to reinstatement after a DUI

permit, or privilege to drive has been revoked may apply for a new license if the revocation was for a cause which has been removed[33] or

- after expiration of one year from the effective date of the revocation;[34]
- in the case of an accident, involuntary death, or personal injury[35] after expiration of three years;[36]
- in the case of reckless homicide[37] after the expiration of two years;[38]
- in the case of a second violation of any of the above statutes within a 20-year period, after the expiration of five years;[39]
- in the case of a third violation of any of the above statutes within a 20-year period, after the expiration of ten years;[40]

Privileges will not be restored until the applicant pays the required fee to the Secretary of State[41] and the Secretary determines after a hearing that the grant of the privilege of dricing willnot endanger the public safety or welfare.[42] In

conviction82 Ill BJ 198 (1994).

33. 625 ILCS 5/6-208(b).
34. 625 ILCS 5/6-208(b)(1).
35. 625 ILCS 5/11-401.
36. 625 ILCS 5/6-208(b)(1).
37. 720 ILCS 5/9-3.
38. 625 ILCS 5/6-208(b)(1).
39. 625 ILCS 5/6-208(b)(2).
40. 625 ILCS 5/6-208(b)(3).
41. 625 ILCS 5/6-208(b)(3).
42. 625 ILCS 5/6-208(b)(3).

Grams v Ryan, 263 Ill App 3d 390, 200 Ill Dec 793, 635 NE2d 1376 (4th Dist 1994) (privileges may be reinstated if there is a showing the person does not have a current problem with alcohol, he or she is a low or minimal risk to repeat the past abusive behavior and operate a motor vehicle while under the influence of alcohol, the person had complied with all other standards as

determining whether a person's driving privileges will be reinstated, the hearing officer may consider the frequency, type and severity of the person's traffic violations, the person's efforts at rehabilitation or reform of past driving practices, his or her demeanor at the hearing, his or her credibility, the credibility and weight of any documentary evidence, and the person's total driving record.[43]

Persons who have had their privilege to drive summarily suspended[44] are eligible to have their driving privileges restored as follows:

- six months from the effective date of a summary suspension for failure to take a blood or alcohol test, or three years for a repeat offender;[45]

- three months from the effective date of a summary suspension for a person who submitted to the test and had an alcohol concentration of 0.08 or more or any amount of cannabis or controlled substance in his or her blood or urine, and one year for a repeat offender.[46]

Privileges are to be restored at these times unless the person is otherwise disqualified.[47]

For persons under the age of 21, a person whose privilege to drive has been suspended under the summary suspension statute, is not eligible for restoration of the privilege until:

---

specified in the regulations adopted by the Secretary of State, and the reinstatement of driving privileges will not endanger the public safety and welfare).

43. Grams v Ryan, 263 Ill App 3d 390, 200 Ill Dec 793, 635 NE2d 1376 (4th Dist 1994).

44. See § 43:03.

45. 625 ILCS 5/6-208.1(a)(1), (3).

46. 625 ILCS 5/6-208.1(a)(2), (4).

47. 625 ILCS 5/6-208.1(b).

- six months from the effective date of a summary suspension for failure to take a blood or alcohol test, or two years for a repeat offender;[48]
- three months from the effective date of a summary suspension for a person who submitted to the test and had an alcohol concentration of 0.00 or more in his or her blood or urine, and one year for a repeat offender.[49]

Following a suspension of the privilege to drive, full driving privileges must be restored unless the person is otherwise disqualified.[50] The Secretary of the State may also, as a condition of the reissuance of a driver's license or permit to an individual under age 18 years whose driving privileges have been suspended, require the applicant to participate in a driver remedial education course and be retested.[51]

§ 43:04. Anti-theft laws—Felonious utilization of vehicles and their parts

When a person not entitled to the possession of a vehicle or a central part of the vehicle receives, possesses, conceals, sells, disposes, or transfers it, knowing it to have been stolen or converted, that person has committed a Class 2 felony.[52] It will be inferred that a person exercising exclusive unexplained possession over a stolen or converted vehicle or an essential part of a stolen

---

48. 625 ILCS 5/6-208.2(a)(1), (3).

49. 625 ILCS 5/6-208.2(a)(2), (4).

50. 625 ILCS 5/6-208.2(b).

51. 625 ILCS 5/6-208.2(c).

52. 625 ILCS 5/4-103(a)(1), 5/4-103(b).

> **Text References:** Decker, Illinois Criminal Law 2d ed § 11.12.
>
> **Annotation References:** Participation in larceny or theft as precluding conviction for receiving or concealing the stolen property. 29 ALR5th 59.
> Possession of stolen property as continuing offense, 24 ALR5th 132.
>
> **Practice References:** Automobile thefts. 2 Am Jur Trials 171, Investigating Particular Crimes §§ 16–78.

§ 43:04   ILLINOIS JURISPRUDENCE: CRIMINAL LAW

or converted vehicle has knowledge that the vehicle or its part is stolen or converted, regardless of whether the date on which the vehicle or part was stolen is recent or remote.[53]

To prove defendant guilty of possession of a stolen motor vehicle, the State must prove beyond a reasonable doubt, that defendant possessed a motor vehicle, that the vehicle was stolen and that defendant knew the vehicle was stolen.[54] A defendant's knowledge may be established by proof of circumstances that would cause a reasonable person to believe property had been stolen.[55] Evidence of flight may be considered to infer defendant's knowledge that the vehicle was stolen.[56] In addition, the condition of the vehicle is one of the most significant factors courts consider in determining whether defendant had knowledge of the vehicle's theft.[57] That the vehicle in question was stolen is essential to the charge of the unlawful possession of a stolen vehicle and this element may not be proved by inadmissible hearsay.[58] There is an inference that a person exercising exclusive and unexplained possession of a stolen vehicle has knowledge that the vehicle is stolen.[59] The question of knowledge is a question of fact to be resolved by the trier of fact.[60] It is not necessary to prove

53. 625 ILCS 5/4-103(a)(1).

Annotation References: What amounts to "exclusive" possession of stolen goods to support inference of burglary or other felonious taking, 51 ALR3d 727.

54. People v Whitfield, 214 Ill App 3d 446, 158 Ill Dec 82, 573 NE2d 1267 (1st Dist 1991).

55. People v Whitfield, 214 Ill App 3d 446, 158 Ill Dec 82, 573 NE2d 1267 (1st Dist 1991).

56. People v Smith, 226 Ill App 3d 433, 168 Ill Dec 495, 589 NE2d 895 (1st Dist 1992); People v Whitfield, 214 Ill App 3d 446, 158 Ill Dec 82, 573 NE2d 1267 (1st Dist 1991).

57. Knowledge properly inferred where the steering column was peeled and the key in the ignition would not start the vehicle. People v Abdullah, 220 Ill App 3d 687, 163 Ill Dec 116, 581 NE2d 67 (1st Dist 1991).

58. People v Cordero, 244 Ill App 3d 390, 184 Ill Dec 364, 613 NE2d 391 (2d Dist 1993).

ownership of a stolen vehicle; however, there must be proof that someone other defendant had a superior interest in the car identified in the indictment.[61] In lieu of proof of ownership, chain of custody evidence, linking the recovered car to the car named in the indictment may form the basis of a proper inference identification.[62] The inference of knowledge arising from exclusive possession of recently stolen property may be rebutted by defendant's explanation; however, defendant must offer a reasonable story or be judged by its improbabilities.[63]

The statute governing felonious offenses relating to motor vehicles is intended to prohibit all persons, not just organized motor vehicle thieves, from possessing stolen motor vehicles.[64]

Knowingly removing, altering, defacing, destroying, forging, or falsifying a manufacturer's identification number of a vehicle or an engine number of a motor vehicle or any part of the vehicle which has an identification number constitutes a Class 2 felony.[65]

---

59. People v Smith, 226 Ill App 3d 433, 168 Ill Dec 495, 589 NE2d 895 (1st Dist 1992).

Element of knowledge could be inferred from the testimony of two witnesses that the defendant either attempted to sell or sold them "repossessed" luxury cars lacking valid title and identification numbers, which was corroborated by the defendant's accomplice in a scheme to market stolen cars, concocted when they were prison cellmates, and the trial court as the trier of fact could determine the defendant was less credible than the prosecution witnesses and the accomplice, even though the accomplice had a lengthy criminal record involving automobile-related offenses. People v Kaye, 264 Ill App 3d 369, 201 Ill Dec 450, 636 NE2d 882 (1st Dist 1994), reh den (Jul 22, 1994).

60. People v Smith, 226 Ill App 3d 433, 168 Ill Dec 495, 589 NE2d 895 (1st Dist 1992).

61. People v Smith, 226 Ill App 3d 433, 168 Ill Dec 495, 589 NE2d 895 (1st Dist 1992).

62. People v Smith, 226 Ill App 3d 433, 168 Ill Dec 495, 589 NE2d 895 (1st Dist 1992).

63. People v Ferguson, 204 Ill App 3d 146, 149 Ill Dec 422, 561 NE2d 1118 (1st Dist 1990).

64. People v Bryant, 128 Ill 2d 448, 132 Ill Dec 415, 539 NE2d 1221 (1989).

§ 43:04   ILLINOIS JURISPRUDENCE: CRIMINAL LAW

Further, to buy, receive, possess, sell or dispose of a vehicle or any essential part of it with knowledge that the identification number of the vehicle or the part has been removed or falsified is a Class 2 felony.[66]

> *Practice Commentary:* To uphold the constitutionality of the statute regarding possession of a vehicle with knowledge that the vehicle identification number has been removed, on the basis of due process, the knowledge element must be read to mean "criminal knowledge," since otherwise a person who innocently possessed a vehicle missing a VIN plate who had no criminal purpose would be subject to a felony conviction and any attempt to report the difficulty with the VIN plate would constitute admission to a felony.[67]

Concealing or misrepresenting the identity of a vehicle or any part thereof is a Class 2 felony.[68] In addition, knowingly possessing, buying, selling, exchanging, giving away, or offering to buy, sell, exchange or give away, any manufacturer's identification number plate, mylar sticker, federal certificate label, State police reassignment plate, Secretary of State assigned plate, rosette rivet, or facsimile thereof which has not yet been attached to or has been removed from the original or assigned vehicle is a Class 2 felony.[69] Finally, it is a Class 2 felony for any person to knowingly make a false report of the theft or conversion of a vehicle to any Illinois police officer.[70]

---

65. 625 ILCS 5/4-103(a)(2).

Annotation References: Validity and construction of statute making it a criminal offense to "tamper" with motor vehicle or contents, or to obscure registration plates, 57 ALR3d 606.

66. 625 ILCS 5/4-103(a)(4).

67. People v DePalma, 256 Ill App 3d 206, 194 Ill Dec 594, 627 NE2d 1236 (2d Dist 1994).

68. 625 ILCS 5/4-103(a)(3).

69. 625 ILCS 5/4-103(a)(5).

70. 625 ILCS 5/4-103(a)(6).

Repetition of these acts within a specified period of time may constitute aggravated offenses, which are Class 1 felonies.[71]

For a passenger in a stolen vehicle to be found guilty of possession of a stolen vehicle, the element of possession must be proved by evidence that the passenger exercised sufficient control over the vehicle or participated in the theft of the vehicle or a part thereof.[72]

Possession of a stolen motor vehicle is a lesser included offense of the offenses of robbery, armed robbery, vehicular hijacking, and aggravated hijacking.[73]

§ 43:05. —Vehicle theft conspiracy

A person commits vehicle theft conspiracy when, with the intent to commit a violation of statutory prohibitions against felonious offenses relating to motor vehicles,[74] that person agrees with another to the commission of such an offense.[75] No person may be convicted of vehicle theft conspiracy unless an overt act in furtherance of the agreement is alleged and proved to have been committed by that person or by a coconspirator, and further, that the accused is part of a common plan or scheme to engage in the unlawful activity.[76]

---

71. See 625 ILCS 5/4-103.2.

72. People v Anderson, 294 Ill App 3d 1039, 229 Ill Dec 357, 691 NE2d 830 (1st Dist 1998), app gr 178 Ill 2d 583, 232 Ill Dec 848, 699 NE2d 1033.

73. Double jeopardy clause barred prosecution of defendant on charges of robbery and vehicular hijacking where defendant had pleaded guilty to possession of a stolen motor vehicle in another county, and the charges arose out of the same incident. People v Eggerman, 292 Ill App 3d 644, 226 Ill Dec 493, 685 NE2d 948 (1st Dist 1997).

74. 625 ILCS 5/4-103.

See § 43:04.

75. 625 ILCS 5/4-103.1.

Annotation References: Participation in larceny or theft as precluding conviction for receiving or concealing the stolen property. 29 ALR5th 59.

76. 625 ILCS 5/4-103.1.

§ 43:05   ILLINOIS JURISPRUDENCE: CRIMINAL LAW

It is not a defense to vehicle theft conspiracy that the person(s) with whom the accused is alleged to have conspired:

- has not been prosecuted or convicted;[77]
- has been convicted of a different offense;[78]
- is not amenable to justice;[79]
- has been acquitted;[80] or
- lacks the capacity to commit an offense.[81]

Vehicle theft conspiracy constitutes a Class 2 felony if the intent is to violate statutory provisions prohibiting felonious offenses related to motor vehicles.[82] The intent to violate statutory provisions prohibiting aggravated felonious offenses relating to motor vehicles constitutes a Class 1 felony.[83]

A person commits the offense of organizer of a vehicle theft conspiracy if he or she intentionally violates the statutory provisions prohibiting aggravated felonious offenses relating to motor vehicles[84] with the agreement of three or more other individuals, and that person is known by the other coconspirators as the organizer, supervisor, financier or otherwise leader of the conspiracy.[85] Organizer of a vehicle theft conspiracy is a Class X felony.[86]

---

77. 625 ILCS 5/4-103.1(b)(1).
78. 625 ILCS 5/4-103.1(b)(2).
79. 625 ILCS 5/4-103.1(b)(3).
80. 625 ILCS 5/4-103.1(b)(4).
81. 625 ILCS 5/4-103.1(b)(5).
82. 625 ILCS 5/4-103.1(c).

   See 625 ILCS 5/4-103.

   See § 43:04.

83. 625 ILCS 5/4-103.1(c). See 625 ILCS 5/4-103.

   See § 43:04.

84. 625 ILCS 5/4-103.2.
85. 625 ILCS 5/4-103.3.

§ 43:06. Vehicular hijacking

A person commits vehicular hijacking when he or she takes a motor vehicle from the person or the immediate presence of another by the use of force or by threatening the imminent use of force.[87] Vehicular hijacking is a Class 1 felony.[88]

In a prosecution for vehicular hijacking, venue is proper in the county where the defendant exerted control over the stolen vehicle.[89]

Possession of a stolen motor vehicle is a lesser included offense of the offenses of robbery, armed robbery, vehicular hijacking, and aggravated hijacking.[90]

Vehicular hijacking is a general intent crime, and proof of defendants specific intent to commit the offense is not necessary.[91]

☞ *Illustration:* In one case, where the defendant's conduct in beating the victim, throwing bottles at him, and then taking his van amounted to a series of continuous acts that forced the victim to leave the area so the defendant could take the victim's car, there was sufficient connection between the taking of the property and the use of force to constitute vehicular hijacking.[92]

---

86. 625 ILCS 5/4-103.3(e).

87. 720 ILCS 5/18-3(a).

Text References: Decker, Illinois Criminal Law, §§ 12:15A, 12:15B.

88. 720 ILCS 5/18-3(c).

89. People v Eggerman, 292 Ill App 3d 644, 226 Ill Dec 493, 685 NE2d 948 (1st Dist 1997).

90. People v Eggerman, 292 Ill App 3d 644, 226 Ill Dec 493, 685 NE2d 948 (1st Dist 1997).

91. People v Aguilar, 286 Ill App 3d 493, 221 Ill Dec 803, 676 NE2d 324 (1st Dist 1997).

92. People v Aguilar, 286 Ill App 3d 493, 221 Ill Dec 803, 676 NE2d 324 (1st Dist 1997).

§ 43:07. Aggravated vehicular hijacking

A person commits aggravated vehicular hijacking when he or she violates the statute prohibiting vehicular hijacking[93] and the person from whose immediate presence the motor vehicle is taken is either a physically handicapped person or a person 60 years of age or over; or a person under 16 years of age is a passenger in the motor vehicle at the time of the offense; or the defendant carries or is otherwise armed with a dangerous weapon.[94] Aggravated vehicular hijacking is a Class X felony.[95]

In a prosecution for aggravated vehicular hijacking, venue is proper in the county where the defendant exerted control over the stolen vehicle.[96]

Possession of a stolen motor vehicle is a lesser included offense of the offenses of robbery, armed robbery, vehicular hijacking, and aggravated hijacking.[97]

§ 43:08. Vehicular endangerment

Any person who, with intent to strike a motor vehicle, causes by any means an object to fall from an overpass in the direction of a moving motor vehicle traveling on any highway in Illinois, if that object strikes a motor vehicle, is guilty of vehicular endangerment.[98] Vehicular endangerment is a Class 2 felony, except when

---

93. 720 ILCS 5/18-3.

Text References: Decker, Ilinois Criminal Law, §§ 12:15A, 12:15B.

See § 43:06.

94. 720 ILCS 5/18-4(a)(1)-(3).

95. 720 ILCS 5/18-4(b).

96. People v Eggerman, 292 Ill App 3d 644, 226 Ill Dec 493, 685 NE2d 948 (1st Dist 1997).

97. People v Eggerman, 292 Ill App 3d 644, 226 Ill Dec 493, 685 NE2d 948 (1st Dist 1997).

98. 720 ILCS 5/12-2.5(a).

Text References: Decker, Ilinois Criminal Law, §§ 9.46A, 9.49.

Periodicals: For article, "Lesser-Included Offenses in Illinois: A Look at

death results. If death results, vehicular endangerment is a Class 1 felony.[99]

§ 43:09. Aircraft—Intoxicated persons

No person may do any of the following:

- operate or attempt to operate any aircraft in Illinois while under the influence of intoxicating liquor or any narcotic drug or other controlled substance;[1]

- knowingly permit any individual who is under the influence of intoxicating liquor or any narcotic drug or other controlled substance to operate any aircraft owned by the person or in his or her custody or control;[2]

- perform any act in connection with the maintenance or operation of any aircraft when under the influence of intoxicating liquor or any narcotic drug or other controlled substance, except medication prescribed by a physician which will not render the person incapable of performing his or her duties safely;[3] or

- (i) consume alcohol within eight hours prior to operating or acting as a crew member of any aircraft within Illinois; (ii) act as a crew member of any aircraft within Illinois while under the influence of alcohol; (iii) operate or act as a crew member of any aircraft within Illinois when the alcohol concentration in the person's blood and breath is 0.04 or more; or (iv) operate or act as a crew member of any aircraft within Illinois when there is any amount of a drug, substance, or compound in the person's blood or urine resulting from the unlawful use or consumption of cannabis or a controlled substance.has been acquitted.[4]

Recent Developments," see 85 Ill. B.J. 480 (1997).

99. 720 ILCS 5/12-2.5(b).

1. 620 ILCS 5/43d(a)(1).

2. 620 ILCS 5/43d(a)(2).

3. 620 ILCS 5/43d(a)(3).

Any person who violates this statute is guilty of a Class A misdemeanor.[5]

---

4. 620 ILCS 5/43d(a)(4).

5. 620 ILCS 5/43d(b).

CHAPTER 44

BLACKMAIL

by

Carol J. Browder, J.D.

and

Robert L. Margolis, Esq.

§ 44:01.   In general

§ 44:01. In general

In Illinois, prohibitions against blackmail are covered under the statutory provisions governing intimidation. These provisions are discussed in full in Chapter 61.

CHAPTER 45

BREACH OF PEACE

by

Carol J. Browder, J.D.

and

Robert L. Margolis, Esq.

Scope of Chapter:

This chapter covers the offense of breach of the peace. Included are the general procedures used in bringing a complaint and carrying through with the proceeding as well as the associated penalties.

Treated Elsewhere:

Charging instruments, see Chapter 9.

Criminal prosecution, see Chapter 12.

Defenses, see Chapter 3.

Evidentiary matters, see Chapters 17–19, 21.

Sentencing, see Chapter 28.

Venue, see Chapter 13.

Research References:

Annotation References:

ALR Digest: Breach of Peace § 1 et seq.

Index and Annotations: Breach of Peace and Disorderly Conduct

Practice References:

12 Am Jur 2d, Breach of Peace and Disorderly Conduct §§ 1–17, 41–51

State Legislation:

725 ILCS 5/110A-5 et seq.

§ 45:01 ILLINOIS JURISPRUDENCE: CRIMINAL LAW

Miscellaneous References:

West's Illinois Digest 2d, Breach of the Peace § 1 et seq.

Auto-Cite®: Cases and annotations referred to in this chapter can be further researched through the Auto-Cite® computer-assisted research service. Use Auto-Cite® to check citations for form, parallel references, prior and later history, and annotation references.

§ 45:01.   Generally
§ 45:02.   Complaint
§ 45:03.   Warrant
§ 45:04.   Examination
§ 45:05.   When complaint is not sustained
§ 45:06.   Recognizance
§ 45:07.   Filing of recognizance—Prosecutions
§ 45:08.   Costs
§ 45:09.   Breach of peace in presence of court
§ 45:10.   Remittance of part of penalty
§ 45:11.   Surrender of principal by sureties
§ 45:12.   Amendments
§ 45:13.   Minors—Improper supervision

§ 45:01. Generally

All courts are conservators of the peace and must enforce all laws made for the preservation of the peace.[1] Courts may require persons to give security to keep the peace, or for their good behavior, or both.[2]

§ 45:02. Complaint

When a complaint is made to a judge that a person has threatened or is about to commit an offense against the person or property of another, the court must examine on oath the complaint, and any other witness who may be produced, reduce the complaint to writing, and cause it to be subscribed and sworn

---

1. 725 ILCS 5/110A-5.

   Annotation References: Insulting words addressed directly to police officer as breach of peace or disorderly conduct, 14 ALR4th 1252.
   Participation of student in demonstration on or near campus as warranting imposition of criminal liability for breach of peace, disorderly conduct, trespass, unlawful assembly, or similar offense, 32 ALR3d 551.

2. 725 ILCS 5/110A-5.

BREACH OF PEACE § 45:05

to by the complainant.[3]

A complaint may be issued electronically or electromagnetically by use of a facsimile transmission machine.[4] A complaint of this nature has the same validity as a written complaint.[5]

§ 45:03. Warrant

If the court is satisfied that there is a danger that an offense will be committed, the court must issue a warrant requiring the proper officer to whom it is directed to immediately apprehend the person complained of and bring that person before the court.[6] The warrant may be issued electronically or electromagnetically by use of a facsimile transmission machine.[7] Such a warrant has the same validity as a written warrant.[8]

§ 45:04. Examination

When the person complained of is brought before the court, if the charge is controverted, the testimony produced on behalf of the plaintiff and the defendant will be heard.[9]

§ 45:05. When complaint is not sustained

If it appears that there is no just reason to fear the commission of the offense, the defendant will be discharged.[10] If the court is of the opinion that the prosecution was commenced maliciously without probable cause, the court may enter judgment against the complainant for the cost of the prosecution.[11]

The elements of a malicious prosecution action are:

3. 725 ILCS 5/110A-10.
4. 725 ILCS 110A-10.
5. 725 ILCS 5/110A-10.
6. 725 ILCS 5/110A-15.
7. 725 ILCS 5/110A-15.
8. 725 ILCS 5/110A-15.
9. 725 ILCS 5/110A-20.
10. 725 ILCS 5/110A-25.
11. 725 ILCS 5/110A-25.

1) the commencement or continuation of a legal proceeding by the defendants;

2) the termination of the proceeding;

3) the absence of probable cause for such proceeding;

4) the presence of malice; and

5) damages resulting to the plaintiff.[12]

> ☛ *Illustration:* In one case, a malicious prosecution not sufficiently alleged where there was no allegation in the complaint that officer in any way pressured or coerced the state's attorney to file charges against the defendant, complaint did not specify what information in officer's affidavit to state's attorney was false and allegations of malice and lack of probable cause were mere conclusions.[13]

§ 45:06. Recognizance

If there is just reason to fear the commission of an offense, the defendant will be required to give a recognizance with sufficient security in a sum as the court directs for a period of time, not to exceed 12 months.[14] The defendant is not bound over unless he or she also is charged with some other offense for which he or she ought to be held to answer at that court.[15]

If the defendant complies with the order requiring recognizance, he or she will be discharged.[16] However, if he or she refuses or neglects to recognize, the court must commit the individual to jail during the period for which he or she was required to give security, or until he or she gives the recognizance.[17] Under those

---

12. Kincaid v Ames Dep't Stores, 670 NE2d 1103 (Ill App 1st Dist 1996).

13. Davis v Temple, 284 Ill App 3d 983, 220 Ill Dec 593, 673 NE2d 737 (5th Dist 1996).

14. 725 ILCS 5/110A-30.

15. 725 ILCS 5/110A-30.

16. 725 ILCS 5/110A-35.

17. 725 ILCS 5/110A-35, 5/110A-45.

circumstances, the warrant must state the cause of the commitment, with the sum and time for which the security was required.[18]

§ 45:07. Filing of recognizance—Prosecutions

Every recognizance taken is to be filed of record by the clerk and, on a breach of the condition, will be prosecuted by the State's Attorney.[19] In proceeding on a recognizance it is not necessary to show a conviction of the defendant of an offense against the person or property of another.[20]

§ 45:08. Costs

When a person is required to give security to keep the peace, or for his or her good behavior, the court may order that the cost of the prosecution, or any part of the costs, are to be paid by that individual who will stand committed until the costs are paid or he or she is otherwise legally discharged.[21]

§ 45:09. Breach of peace in presence of court

A person who, in the presence of the court, commits or threatens to commit an offense against the person or property of another, may be ordered, without process, to enter into recognizance to keep the peace for a period not exceeding 12 months, and, in case of refusal, be committed as in other cases.[22]

§ 45:10. Remittance of part of penalty

When, on an action brought on a recognizance, the penalty is adjudged to be forfeited, the court may, on the petition of any defendant, remit any portion of it as the circumstances of the case render just and reasonable.[23]

---

18. 725 ILCS 5/110A-35.
19. 725 ILCS 5/110A-50.
20. 725 ILCS 5/110A-55.
21. 725 ILCS 5/110A-40.
22. 725 ILCS 5/110A-60.
23. 725 ILCS 5/110A-65.

§ 45:11. Surrender of principal by sureties

The sureties of any person bound to keep the peace may, at any time, surrender their principal, the defendant, to the sheriff of the county in which he or she is bound, under the same rules and regulations governing the surrender of the principal in other criminal cases.[24] The defendant may again be discharged on giving new recognizance, with sufficient sureties, for the remainder of the period that security is required.[25]

§ 45:12. Amendments

No proceeding to prevent a breach of the peace will be dismissed on account of any informality or insufficiency in the complaint or any process or proceeding.[26] The complaint may be amended by order of the court to conform to the facts in the case.[27]

§ 45:13. Minors—Improper supervision

Any parent, legal guardian or other person commits improper supervision of a child when he or she knowingly permits a child in his or her custody or control under the age of 18 years to commit an act tending to break the peace.[28] A person convicted of improper supervision for the first or second time is guilty of a petty offense.[29] A person convicted of third or subsequent time is guilty of a Class B misdemeanor.[30]

> ☛ *Illustration:* Commensurate with the parental obligation to supervise a child's activities outside the home is a duty on the part of the State not to place one of its charges with an

---

24. 725 ILCS 5/110A-70.
25. 725 ILCS 5/110A-75.
26. 725 ILCS 5/110A-80.
27. 725 ILCS 5/110A-80.
28. 720 ILCS 640/1.
29. 720 ILCS 640/2.
30. 720 ILCS 640/2.

adult that it knows cannot exercise that responsibility. When a Department of Child and Family Services caseworker places a child in a home knowing that the child's caretaker cannot provide reasonable supervision, and the failure to provide that degree of supervision and care results in injury to the child outside of the home, it might be appropriate, depending on the facts culminating in the injury, for the caseworker to be held liable for a deprivation of liberty.[31]

---

31. Camp v Gregory, 67 F3d 1286, 32 FR Serv 3d 627 (CA7 Ill 1995), cert den 517 US 1244, 135 L Ed 2d 190, 116 S Ct 2498.

CHAPTER 46

BRIBERY

by

Carol J. Browder, J.D.

Scope of Chapter:
> This chapter discusses the specific offense of bribery as it relates to public officers and employees, bribery in contests, and jurors and witnesses.

Treated Elsewhere:
> Charging instruments, see Chapter 9.
>
> Criminal prosecution, see Chapter 12.
>
> Defenses, see Chapter 3.
>
> Evidentiary matters, see Chapters 17–19, 21.
>
> Sentencing, see Chapter 28.
>
> Venue, see Chapter 13.

Research References:
> **Text References:**
>> Decker, Illinois Criminal Law 2d ed §§ 14.25, 14.26, 14.36 et seq., 15.28 et seq.
>
> **Annotation References:**
>> ALR Digest: Bribery § 1 et seq.
>>
>> Index and Annotations: Bribery
>
> **Practice References:**
>> 12 Am Jur 2d, Bribery § 1 et seq; 26 Am Jur 2d, Embracery §§ 1 et seq; 58 Am Jur 2d, Obstructing Justice § 63
>>
>> 37 Am Jur Trials 273, Handling the Defense in a Bribery Prosecution § 1 et seq.
>
> **State Legislation:**
>> 720 ILCS 5/33-1, Ill Rev Stat ch 38, pars 29-1, 29-2, 29-3, 29A-1, 29A-2, 29A-3, 32-4, 33-1, 33-2

§ 46:01   ILLINOIS JURISPRUDENCE: CRIMINAL LAW

Forms:
22 Am Jur Pl & Pr Forms (Rev), Sheriffs, Police and Constables, Form 9

Miscellaneous References:
West's Illinois Digest 2d, Bribery § 1 et seq.

Auto-Cite®: Cases and annotations referred to in this chapter can be further researched through the Auto-Cite® computer-assisted research service. Use Auto-Cite® to check citations for form, parallel references, prior and later history, and annotation references.

§ 46:01.   Public officer or employee
§ 46:02.   —Failure to report bribe
§ 46:03.   In contests—Offering bribe
§ 46:04.   —Accepting bribe
§ 46:05.   —Failure to report offer of bribe
§ 46:06.   Commercial bribery—offering bribe
§ 46:07.   —Accepting
§ 46:08.   Jurors and witnesses

§ 46:01. Public officer or employee

A person commits bribery when:

- with intent to influence the performance of any act related to the employment or function of any public officer, public employee, juror or witness, he or she promises or tenders to that person any property or personal advantage which he or she is not authorized by law to accept;[1]

- with intent to influence the performance of any act related to the employment or function of any public officer, public employee, juror or witness, he or she promises or tenders to one whom he or she believes to be a public officer, public employee, juror or witness, any property or personal advantage which a public officer, public employee, juror or witness would not be authorized by law to accept;[2]

---

1. 720 ILCS 5/33-1(a).

Chicago Day School v Wade, 297 Ill App 3d 465, 231 Ill Dec 835, 647 NE2d 389 (1st Dist 1998).

Text References: Decker, Illinois Criminal Law 2d ed §§ 14.36, 14.37.

- with intent to cause any person to influence the performance of any act related to the employment or function of any public officer, public employee, juror or witness, he or she promises or tenders to that person any property or personal advantage which he or she is not authorized by law to accept;[3]

- he or she receives, retains, or agrees to accept any property or personal advantage which he or she is not authorized by law to accept knowing that the property or personal advantage was promised or tendered with intent to cause the person to influence the performance of any act related to the employment or function of any public officer, public employee, juror or witness;[4] or

- he or she solicits, receives, retains or agrees to accept any property or personal advantage pursuant to an understanding that he or she will improperly influence or attempt to influence the performance of any act related to the employment or function of any public officer, public employee, juror or witness.[5]

☛ *Illustration:* The act of offering or promising the tender of a prohibited commodity or act is sufficient to constitute the completed offense of bribery.[6]

Bribery is a Class 2 felony.[7]

---

2. 720 ILCS 5/33-1.

Text References: Decker, Illinois Criminal Law 2d ed §§ 14.36, 14.38.

3. 720 ILCS 5/33-1.

Text References: Decker, Illinois Criminal Law 2d ed §§ 14.36, 14.38.

4. 720 ILCS 5/33-1(d).

Text References: Decker, Illinois Criminal Law 2d ed §§ 14.36, 14.39.

5. 720 ILCS 5/33-1.

Text References: Decker, Illinois Criminal Law 2d ed §§ 14.36, 14.41.

6. People v Trowers, 215 Ill App 3d 862, 159 Ill Dec 418, 576 NE2d 87 (1st Dist 1991).

§ 46:02. —Failure to report bribe

Any public officer, public employee or juror who fails to immediately report to the local state's attorney, or in the case of a state employee to the department of any state police, an offer made to him or her in violation of the statutory prohibitions against bribery[8] commits a Class A misdemeanor.[9] In the case of a state employee, making a report to the department of the state police discharges the employee from any further duty.[10] The report msut be made to the state's attorney in he county in which the offer of the bribe took place.[11] Upon receipt of the report, the department of state police must immediately transmit a copy of it to the appropriate state's attorney.[12]

---

7. 720 ILCS 5/33-1(f).

Annotation References: Validity of state statute prohibiting award of government contract to person or business entity previously convicted of bribery or attempting to bribe state public employee, 7 ALR4th 1202.
Criminal offense of bribery as affected by lack of authority of state public officer or employee, 73 ALR3d 374.
Furnishing public official with meals, lodging, or travel, or receipt of such benefits, as bribery, 67 ALR3d 1231.
Criminal liability of corporation for bribery or conspiracy to bribe public official, 52 ALR3d 1274.
Entrapment to commit bribery or offer to bribe, 69 ALR2d 1397.
Solicitation or receipt of funds by public officer or employee for political campaign expense or similar purposes as bribery, 55 ALR2d 1137.

Practice References: 37 Am Jur Trials 273, Handling the Defense in a Bribery Prosecution § 1 et seq.

Forms: Complaint—solicitation and acceptance of bribes. 22 Am Jur Pl & Pr Forms (Rev), Sheriffs, Police and Constables, Form 9.

8. 720 ILCS 5/33-1.

Text References: Decker, Illinois Criminal Law 2d ed § 14.42.

9. 720 ILCS 5/33-2.
10. 720 ILCS 5/33-2.
11. People v Choura, 84 Ill App 3d 228, 34 Ill Dec 740, 405 NE2d 493 (1980).
12. 720 ILCS 5/33-2.

§ 46:03. In contests—Offering bribe

Any person who, with intent to influence any person participating in, officiating or connected with any professional or amateur athletic contest, sporting event or exhibition, gives, offers or promises any money, bribe or other thing of value or advantage to induce the participant, official or other person not to use his or her best efforts in connection with the contest, event or exhibition commits a Class 4 felony.[13]

When a person who, with the intent to influence the decision of any individual, offers or promises any money, bribe or other thing of value or advantage to induce the individual to attend, refrain from attending or continuing to attend a particular public or private institution of secondary education or higher education for the purpose of participating or not participating in interscholastic athletic competition for that institution, that individual commits a Class A misdemeanor.[14] This prohibition does not apply to the following:

- offering or awarding any type of scholarship, grant or other bona fide financial aid or employment to an individual;[15]
- offering of any type of financial assistance by the individual's family;[16] or
- offering any item of de minimis value by the institution's authorities if the item is of the nature of an item that is commonly provided to any or all students or prospective students.[17]

---

[13] 720 ILCS 5/29-1(a).

Text References: Decker, Illinois Criminal Law 2d ed §§ 15.28 et seq.

Annotation References: Bribery in athletic contests, 49 ALR2d 1234.

[14] 720 ILCS 5/29-1(b).

Text References: Decker, Illinois Criminal Law 2d ed § 15.29.

[15] 720 ILCS 5/29-1(b)(1).

[16] 720 ILCS 5/29-1(b)(2).

[17] 720 ILCS 5/29-1(b)(3).

Any person who gives any money, goods or other thing of value to an individual enrolled in an institution of higher education who participates in interscholastic competition and represents or attempts to represent the individual in future employment negotiations with any profession sports team commits a Class A misdemeanor.[18]

§ 46:04. —Accepting bribe

Any person participating in, officiating or connected with any professional or amateur athletic contest, sporting event or exhibition who accepts or agrees to accept any money, bribe or other thing of value or advantage with the intent, understanding or agreement that he or she will not use his or her best efforts in connection with the contest, event or exhibition commits a Class 4 felony.[19]

§ 46:05. —Failure to report offer of bribe

If a person participating, officiating or connected with any professional or amateur athletic contest, sporting event or exhibition fails to immediately report to his or her employer, the promoter of the contest, event or exhibition, a peace officer or the local state's attorney any offer or promise made to him or her in violation of the prohibitions against contest bribes,[20] he or she commits a Class A misdemeanor.[21]

§ 46:06. Commercial bribery—offering bribe

A person commits commercial bribery when he or she confers, or offers or agrees to confer, any benefit on an employee, agent or fiduciary without the consent of the latter's employer or principal, with intent to influence the individual's conduct in relation to the

---

18. 720 ILCS 5/29-1(c).

19. 720 ILCS 5/29-2.

   Text References: Decker, Illinois Criminal Law 2d ed § 15.30.

20. 720 ILCS 5/29-1.

   Text References: Decker, Illinois Criminal Law 2d ed § 15.31.

21. 720 ILCS 5/29-3.

employer's or principal's affairs.[22]

☛ *Practice Guide:* Commercial bribery is a business offense for which a fine not exceeding $5000 will be imposed.[23]

§ 46:07. —Accepting

An employee, agent or fiduciary commits commercial bribe receiving when, without consent of his or her employer or principal, the individual solicits, accepts or agrees to accept any benefit from another person on an agreement or understanding that the benefit will influence his or her conduct in relation to the employer's or principal's affairs.[24] Commercial bribe receiving is a business offense for which a fine not exceeding $5000 will be imposed.[25]

§ 46:08. Jurors and witnesses

When a person communicates directly or indirectly with intent to influence any person whom he or she believes has been summoned as a juror, regarding any matter which is or may be brought before the juror and the communication is otherwise then as authorized by law, that individual commits a Class 4 felony.[26]

A person who, with intent to deter any party or witness from testifying freely, fully and truthfully as to any matter pending in court, or before a grand jury, administrative agency or any other state or local government or unit, forcibly detains that party or

---

22. 720 ILCS 5/29A-1.

    Text References: Decker, Illinois Criminal Law 2d ed § 15.32.

    Annotation References: Validity and construction of statutes punishing commercial bribery, 1 ALR3d 1350.

23. 720 ILCS 5/29A-3.

24. 720 ILCS 5/29A-2.

    Text References: Decker, Illinois Criminal Law 2d ed § 15.32.

25. 720 ILCS 5/29A-3.

26. 720 ILCS 5/32-4(a).

    Text References: Decker, Illinois Criminal Law 2d ed § 14.25.

§ 46:08   ILLINOIS JURISPRUDENCE: CRIMINAL LAW

witness, or communicates, directly or indirectly, to the party or witness any knowingly false information or threat of injury or damage to the property or person of the party or witness or to the property or person of any individual, or offers, delivers, or threatens to withhold money or another thing of value to any individual, commits a Class 3 felony.[27]

A person who identified in the criminal discovery process as a person who may be called as a witness in a criminal proceeding may not accept or receive, directly or indirectly, any payment or benefit in consideration for providing information obtained as a result of witnessing an event or occurrence or having personal knowledge of certain facts in relation to the criminal proceeding.[28] A violation is a Class B misdemeanor for which the court may impose a fine not to exceed three times the amount of compensation requested, accepted, or received.[29] The prohibition on payments for information does not apply to lawful compensation paid to expert witnesses, investigators, employees, or agents by a prosecutor, law enforcement agency, or an attorney employed to represent a person in a criminal matter; lawful compensation or benefits provided to an informant by a prosecutor or law enforcement agency, or under a local anti-crime program; lawful compensation provided by a private individual to another private individual as a reward for information leading to the arrest and conviction of specified offenders; or lawful compensation paid to a publisher, editor, reporter, writer, or other person connected with or employed by a newspaper, magazine, television or radio station or any other publishing or media outlet for disclosing information obtained from another person relating to an offense.[30]

---

27.   720 ILCS 5/32-4(b).

Text References: Decker, Illinois Criminal Law 2d ed § 14.26.

28.   720 ILCS 5/32-4c(a).
29.   720 ILCS 5/32-4c(b).
30.   720 ILCS 5/32-4c(d).

CHAPTER 47

BURGLARY

by

Thomas Curry, J. D.

and

Robert L. Margolis, Esq.

Scope of Chapter:
   This chapter discusses the crime of burglary and related offenses including residential burglary and possession of burglary tools.

Treated Elsewhere:
   Charging instruments, see Chapter 9.
   Criminal prosecution, see Chapter 12.
   Defenses, see Chapter 3.
   Evidentiary matters, see Chapters 17–19, 21.
   Sentencing, see Chapter 28.
   Theft, see Chapter 70.
   Trespass, see Chapter 71.
   Venue, see Chapter 13.

Research References:
   Text References:
      Decker, Illinois Criminal Law 2d ed §§ 9.54, 9.55, 13.02 et seq., 13.13 et seq.
   Annotation References:
      ALR Digest: Burglary § 1 et seq.
      Index and Annotations: Breaking and Entering; Burglary
   Practice References:
      13 Am Jur 2d, Burglary § 1 et seq.

§ 47:01   ILLINOIS JURISPRUDENCE: CRIMINAL LAW

2 Am Jur Trials 171, Investigating Particular Crimes §§ 9–14

State Legislation:

625 ILCS 5/1-100 et seq., 5/4-102; 720 ILCS 5/12-11, 5/19-1, 19-2, 19-3, 36-1, 36-2; 730 ILCS 5/5-1-1 et seq., 5/5-5-3

Miscellaneous References:

West's Illinois Digest 2d, Burglary § 1 et seq.

Auto-Cite®: Cases and annotations referred to in this chapter can be further researched through the Auto-Cite® computer-assisted research service. Use Auto-Cite® to check citations for form, parallel references, prior and later history, and annotation references.

§ 47:01.   Burglary
§ 47:02.   Residential burglary
§ 47:03.   Possession of burglary tools
§ 47:04.   Home invasion
§ 47:05.   Seizure and forfeiture

§ 47:01. Burglary

A person commits burglary when, without authority, he or she knowingly enters or remains within a building, housetrailer, watercraft, aircraft, motor vehicle as defined in the Illinois Vehicle Code,[1] railroad car, or any part thereof, with intent to commit therein felony or theft.[2] The offense of burglary is separate from

---

1. 625 ILCS 5/1-100 et seq..

Text References: Decker, Illinois Criminal Law 2d ed §§ 13.02 et seq.

Annotation References: Use of fraud or trick as "constructive breaking" for purpose of burglary or breaking and entering offense, 17 ALR5th 125.
  Minor's entry into home of parent as sufficient to sustain burglary charge, 17 ALR5th 111.
  Burglary, breaking, or entering of motor vehicle, 72 ALR4th 710.

Periodicals: For article, "Lesser-Included Offenses in Illinois: A Look at Recent Developments," see 85 Ill. B.J. 480 (1997).

2. 720 ILCS 5/19-1(a).

Annotation References: What is "building" or "house" within burglary or breaking and entering statute, 68 ALR4th 425.
  Maintainability of burglary charge, where entry into building is made with consent, 58 ALR4th 335.
  Breaking and entering of inner door of building as burglary, 43 ALR3d

§ 47:01

the offense of residential burglary since residential burglary can be committed only in dwelling places, while simple burglary cannot occur in a dwelling place.[3] It also differs from the misdemeanor offenses relating to motor vehicles which are set out in the Vehicle Code.[4]

> ☛ *Practice Guide:* There is no statutory prohibition against charging defendant with a burglary, as opposed to residential burglary, simply because the building entered happened to be a dwelling place. Since burglary and residential burglary are distinct and different crimes, the prosecutor has the authority to charge defendant with either one.[5]

The offense of burglary is a Class 2 felony.[6]

To be convicted of burglary, the defendant need only enter with the necessary intent to commit a belony or theft and need not actually assert control over the owner's property to complete the burglary.[7] While the law in Illinois no longer requires a common

---

1147.

Practice References: Burglary. 2 Am Jur Trials 171, Investigating Particular Crimes §§ 9–14.

3. 720 ILCS 5/19-3.

People v Childress, 158 Ill 2d 275, 198 Ill Dec 794, 633 NE2d 635 (1994), cert den 513 US 881, 130 L Ed 2d 143, 115 S Ct 215.

See § 47:02.

Text References: Decker, Illinois Criminal Law 2d ed §§ 13.13 et seq.

4. 720 ILCS 5/19-1(a).

See 625 ILCS 5/4-102.

5. People v Edgeston, 243 Ill App 3d 1, 183 Ill Dec 196, 611 NE2d 49 (2d Dist 1993), cert den 510 US 1168, 127 L Ed 2d 547, 114 S Ct 1199.

6. 720 ILCS 5/19-1(b).

7. People v Flores, 269 Ill App 3d 196, 206 Ill Dec 798, 645 NE2d 1050 (1st Dist 1995).

See also People v Hamilton, 179 Ill 2d 319, 228 Ill Dec 189, 688 NE2d 1166 (1997), where an indictment that alleged that the defendant entered the

§ 47:01   ILLINOIS JURISPRUDENCE: CRIMINAL LAW

law breaking as an essential element of the crime of burglary, the statute requires an entry which is both without authority and with intent to commit a felony or theft.[8]

The crime of burglary can be proved by circumstantial evidence, and such evidence is generally sufficient to support a conviction if it is inconsistent with any reasonable hypothesis of innocence, but the trier of fact need not search out all possible explanations consistent with innocence and raise them to a level of reasonable doubt.[9] When the trier of fact in a burglary case decides whether the evidence was sufficient to infer defendant's intent to commit theft, relevant circumstances it should consider include the time. place, and manner of entry into the premises, defendant's activity within the premises and any alternative explanations which may explain his or her presence.[10] Absent inconsistent circumstances, an inference of an intent to commit theft which will sustain a conviction of burglary arises when there is evidence of unlawful breaking and entry into a building where a theft could occur.[11] While the exclusive and unexplained

---

dwelling place with the intent to commit a theft, implied that the defendant intended to obtain authorized control over and deprive another of property.

Text References: Decker, Illinois Criminal Law 2d ed §§ 13.05 et seq.

8. People v Wilson, 155 Ill 2d 374, 185 Ill Dec 542, 614 NE2d 1227 (1993).

9. People v Cole, 256 Ill App 3d 1, 195 Ill Dec 249, 628 NE2d 713 (1st Dist 1993).

See also People v Szydloski, 283 Ill App 3d 274, 218 Ill Dec 569, 669 NE2d 712 (3d Dist 1996), where evidence that at the time the defendant entered a grocery store he possessed a bag that was subsequently used to conceal and remove stolen merchandise was sufficient to establish that the defendant possessed the intent to commit theft at the time he entered the store as required to support a burglary conviction.

People v Grayson, 165 Ill App 3d 1038, 117 Ill Dec 550, 520 NE2d 901 (1st Dist 1988).

10. People v Hopkins, 229 Ill App 3d 665, 171 Ill Dec 208, 593 NE2d 1028 (4th Dist 1992).

11. People v Mackins, 222 Ill App 3d 1063, 165 Ill Dec 454, 584 NE2d 888 (2d Dist 1991).

possession of recently stolen property is insufficient, standing alone, to prove burglary beyond a reasonable doubt, it may be used with other corroborating evidence of guilt to support a conviction.[12]

An intent to commit a theft prior to entry of the building to be burgled, is required to uphold a burglary conviction.[13] A criminal intent formulated after lawful entry will not satisfy the statute.[14] Authority to enter a building open to the public extends only to those who enter with a purpose consistent with the reason that the building is open.[15] A building open to the public can be the subject of a burglary; examples include a laundromat, museum, supermarket, car wash, and a discount store.[16] When the burglary involves a public building, the element of entry without authority need not be established apart from the element of entry with intent to commit a theft.[17] Vacant residential rental property to

12. People v Skinner, 220 Ill App 3d 479, 163 Ill Dec 301, 581 NE2d 252 (1st Dist 1991).

Text References: Decker, Illinois Criminal Law 2d ed §§ 13.10.

13. People v Powell, 224 Ill App 3d 127, 166 Ill Dec 631, 586 NE2d 589 (1st Dist 1991).

14. People v Powell, 224 Ill App 3d 127, 166 Ill Dec 631, 586 NE2d 589 (1st Dist 1991).

15. People v Powell, 224 Ill App 3d 127, 166 Ill Dec 631, 586 NE2d 589 (1st Dist 1991); People v Drake, 172 Ill App 3d 1026, 123 Ill Dec 56, 527 NE2d 519 (4th Dist 1988).

Text References: Decker, Illinois Criminal Law 2d ed §§ 13.06.

16. People v Durham, 252 Ill App 3d 88, 191 Ill Dec 420, 623 NE2d 1010 (3d Dist 1993); People v Ybarra, 272 Ill App 3d 1008, 209 Ill Dec 490, 651 NE2d 668 (1st Dist 1995).

17. People v Bailey, 188 Ill App 3d 278, 135 Ill Dec 591, 543 NE2d 1338 (5th Dist 1989).

Evidence established that the defendant without authority remained within the church with the intent to commit theft and, thus, was sufficient to support a burglary conviction where, after being instructed to stay at the church door, the defendant and his companion went into another part of the church, found a storage area, and took vacuums that were located there; thus, evidence

which a new tenant is planning within a reasonable period of time to move and establish a residence is a dwelling within the meaning of the statute.[18]

Joint possession with others of recently stolen property can be considered exclusive for purposes of inferring defendant's guilt in a burglary.[19] The essential elements of the offense could be satisfied when defendant simply aided or abetted another in the commission of the offense.[20]

It is not essential to a burglary conviction that the State prove the actual commission of the felony intended at the time of entry; just as a burglary conviction will stand if the evidence establishes that defendant intended to commit a theft but his or her efforts were aborted once inside, it will stand as well upon satisfactory proof that defendant intended to commit one felony and succeeded in committing another.[21]

§ 47:02. Residential burglary

To commit the offense of residential burglary, a person must knowingly and without authority enter the dwelling place of another with the intent to commit a felony or theft[22] within that

---

established that the defendant no longer had authority to remain in the church when he decided not to remain at the door as instructed, deciding instead to go into another part of the church and steal vacuum cleaners. People v Glover, 276 Ill App 3d 934, 213 Ill Dec 448, 659 NE2d 78 (2d Dist 1995).

18. People v Pearson, 183 Ill App 3d 72, 131 Ill Dec 646, 538 NE2d 1202 (5th Dist 1989).

19. People v Johnson, 175 Ill App 3d 908, 125 Ill Dec 469, 530 NE2d 627 (4th Dist 1988).

20. Fact that there was not direct evidence to show that the defendant participated in the actual break-in of a railroad car or formed the intention to rob the railroad car was irrelevant to the issue of whether defendant was legally accountable for the burglary. People v Jointer, 180 Ill App 3d 364, 129 Ill Dec 274, 535 NE2d 1039 (1st Dist 1989).

21. People v Monigan, 204 Ill App 3d 686, 149 Ill Dec 662, 561 NE2d 1358 (3d Dist 1990).

22. See ch 70.

BURGLARY § 47:02

dwelling place.[23]

The offense of burglary is separate from the offense of residential burglary since residential burglary can be committed only in dwelling places, while simple burglary cannot occur in a dwelling place.[24]

Because of the perceived seriousness of violating a home and endangering its occupants, the offense of residential burglary is a Class 1 felony.[25] A person convicted of residential burglary cannot be sentenced to a period of probation or a term of periodic imprisonment or conditional discharge.[26] The court must sentence the offender to not less than the minimum term of imprisonment set forth in the Unified Code of Corrections.[27] The court may also order a fine or restitution or both in conjunction with the term of imprisonment.[28] The trial court lacks authority to impose

23. 720 ILCS 5/19-3(a).

Text References: Decker, Illinois Criminal Law 2d ed §§ 13.13 et seq.

Annotation References: Minor's entry into home of parent as sufficient to sustain burglary charge, 17 ALR5th 111.
What is "building" or "house" within burglary or breaking and entering statute, 68 ALR4th 425.
Maintainability of burglary charge, where entry into building is made with consent, 58 ALR4th 335.
Occupant's absence from residential structure as affecting nature of offense as burglary or breaking and entering, 20 ALR4th 349.
Entry through partly opened door or window as burglary, 70 ALR3d 881.

Periodicals: For article, "Lesser-Included Offenses in Illinois: A Look at Recent Developments," see 85 Ill. B.J. 480 (1997).

24. 720 ILCS 5/19-3.

People v Childress, 158 Ill 2d 275, 198 Ill Dec 794, 633 NE2d 635 (1994), cert den 513 US 881, 130 L Ed 2d 143, 115 S Ct 215.

See § 47:02.

Text References: Decker, Illinois Criminal Law 2d ed §§ 13.13 et seq.

25. 720 ILCS 5/19-3(b).

26. 730 ILCS 5/5-5-3(c)(2)(G).

27. 730 ILCS 5/1-1-1 et seq..

§ 47:02   ILLINOIS JURISPRUDENCE: CRIMINAL LAW

probation in combination with imprisonment, consecutively or otherwise.[29]

The elements of the crime of residential burglary are entry into a building without authority, or remaining after authority to enter has been withdrawn, with the intent to commit a felony or theft.[30]

An attached garage of a single-family home was a "dwelling" within the statute proscribing residential burglary where the inside door of the garage leads directly into the residence's laundry room.[31]

The residential burglary statute applies to burglaries of structures intended for use as residences, regardless of whether the structure was being actively used as a residence at the time of the burglary.[32]

Burglary may be proved by circumstantial evidence such as fingerprints and the Illinois Supreme Court has held that where there is no question about the chain of custody and the prints involved are fresh, the fingerprints were more probably left at the time of the offense rather than at some other time.[33]

Defendant's intent to commit a theft or felony is an essential

---

28. 730 ILCS 5/5-5-3(c)(2).

29. People v Hale, 289 Ill App 3d 273, 225 Ill Dec 20, 682 NE2d 764 (3d Dist 1997).

30. People v. Campbell, 146 Ill. 2d 363, 166 Ill. Dec. 932, 586 N.E.2d 1261 (1992).

31. People v Borgen, 282 Ill App 3d 116, 218 Ill Dec 71, 668 NE2d 234 (2d Dist 1996).

Since the attached garage the defendant unlawfully entered led directly into a room of the victims' house, it would be considered a part of the victims' dwelling for purposes of the residential burglary statute and the State was not required to prove that anyone was actually "living" in the garage in order to sustain the defendant's conviction for residential burglary. People v Cunningham, 265 Ill App 3d 3, 202 Ill Dec 511, 637 NE2d 1247 (2d Dist 1994).

32. People v Moore, 206 Ill App 3d 769, 151 Ill Dec 883, 565 NE2d 154 (1st Dist 1990).

Text References: Decker, Illinois Criminal Law 2d ed § 13.15.

element of residential burglary.[34] In the absence of inconsistent circumstances, the fact finder may infer the requisite intent to commit theft from proof of an unlawful breaking and entry into a building containing personal property that could be the subject of larceny.[35] However, the specific intent to commit a theft or felony cannot be proved merely by the entry itself.[36] Such an inference of intent is permissible only when the circumstantial evidence of the facts surrounding the occurrence, including the time, place, and manner of entry into the premises, defendant's activity within the premises, and any lack of alternative explanations for his and her presence, justifies this conclusion.[37]

If the evidence is sufficient for the finder of fact to determine that an owner or occupant genuinely possessed the subjective intent to reside on the premises in question within a reasonable

33. People v Dotson, 263 Ill App 3d 571, 200 Ill Dec 220, 635 NE2d 559 (1st Dist 1994).

See also People v Washington, 297 Ill App 3d 790, 232 Ill Dec 311, 697 NE2d 1241 (4th Dist 1998), where it was held that given the victim's identification of the accused and his fingerprint on the bottom of the VCR moved during the burglary, a rational jury could have found beyond a reasonable doubt that defendant entered the victim's home without her permission and with intent to commit a theft therein.

34. People v Storms, 225 Ill App 3d 558, 167 Ill Dec 845, 588 NE2d 486 (2d Dist 1992), revd, remanded 155 Ill 2d 498, 187 Ill Dec 467, 617 NE2d 1188.

35. People v Storms, 225 Ill App 3d 558, 167 Ill Dec 845, 588 NE2d 486 (2d Dist 1992), revd, remanded 155 Ill 2d 498, 187 Ill Dec 467, 617 NE2d 1188.

Text References: Decker, Illinois Criminal Law 2d ed §§ 13.15.

36. People v Storms, 225 Ill App 3d 558, 167 Ill Dec 845, 588 NE2d 486 (2d Dist 1992), revd, remanded 155 Ill 2d 498, 187 Ill Dec 467, 617 NE2d 1188.

37. People v Storms, 225 Ill App 3d 558, 167 Ill Dec 845, 588 NE2d 486 (2d Dist 1992), revd, remanded 155 Ill 2d 498, 187 Ill Dec 467, 617 NE2d 1188.

See also People v Hamilton, 179 Ill 2d 319, 228 Ill Dec 189, 688 NE2d 1166 (1997), where the court held that theft was sufficiently identified as a lesser included offense of the charged offense of residential burglary where the indictment alleged that the defendant entered the dwelling place with the intent to commit a theft, inferring the defendant intended to obtain authorized control over and deprive another of property.

§ 47:02   ILLINOIS JURISPRUDENCE: CRIMINAL LAW

period of time, the premises is a dwelling for purposes of the residential burglary statute.[38]

> ☛ *Illustration:* In one case, the courtheld the premises qualified as a dwelling under the statute where the dwelling at issue was a camp with five rooms, heat, air conditioning and telephone services throughout the year even though the burglary took place in winter when the owner did not stay at the camp on a regular basis.[39]

§ 47:03. Possession of burglary tools

In order to further discourage the offense of burglary, the Criminal Code makes it an offense to possess burglary tools.[40] The term "tools" includes any key, instrument, device, or any explosive, suitable for use in breaking into a building, house trailer, watercraft, aircraft, motor vehicle as defined in the Vehicle Code,[41] railroad car, or any depository designed for the

---

38. A defendants' convictions for residential burglary were reduced to burglary where the building they entered, which had been unoccupied for over seven years and in which no one intended to reside within a reasonable time, was not a dwelling within the meaning of the statute. People v. Bonner, 221 Ill App 3d 887, 164 Ill Dec 502, 583 NE2d 56 (1st Dist 1991).

Premises met the statutory definition of dwelling although the house had been unoccupied for approximately one year where the owner-occupier, who was in a nursing home due to health problems, testified that he hoped to return to the premises as soon as his health permitted and clearly possessed the intent to return. People v Walker, 212 Ill App 3d 410, 156 Ill Dec 546, 570 NE2d 1268 (5th Dist 1991)

39. People v Smith, 209 Ill App 3d 1091, 154 Ill Dec 417, 568 NE2d 417 (4th Dist 1991) (criticized by People v Cunningham, 265 Ill App 3d 3, 202 Ill Dec 511, 637 NE2d 1247 (2d Dist)) and (criticized in People v Borgen, 282 Ill App 3d 116, 218 Ill Dec 71, 668 NE2d 234 (2d Dist)).

40. 720 ILCS 5/19-2(a).

Text References: Decker, Illinois Criminal Law 2d ed § 13.12.

Annotation References: Validity, construction and application of statutes relating to burglars' tools, 33 ALR3d 798.

41. 625 ILCS 5/1-100 et seq.

BURGLARY § 47:04

safekeeping of property, or any part thereof.[42] A person commits the offense of possession of burglary tools when he or she possesses such a device with intent to enter any of those designated places and with intent to commit within any of those places a felony or theft.[43]

The offense of possession of burglary tools is a Class 4 felony.[44]

Defendant's intent is the controlling factor in a possession of burglary tools charge when the tools in question could be used for innocent purpose as well as illegal purposes.[45] Tools originally designed and intended for an innocent purpose may nonetheless be considered burglary tools where they are suitable for use in a burglary and are intended for such use.[46]

§ 47:04. Home invasion

Home invasion involves the entry into the dwelling place of another by a person who is without authority and who is not a peace officer acting in the line of duty.[47] The person entering the dwelling place of another must know or have reason to know that one or more persons is present or the person must knowingly enter the dwelling place of another and remain in that dwelling place until he or she knows or has reason to know that one or more persons is present.[48] To commit the offense of home invasion, the person entering the dwelling place of another must be armed with a dangerous weapon and use force or threaten the imminent use of force upon any person or persons within the

---

42. 720 ILCS 5/19-2(a).

43. 720 ILCS 5/19-2(a).

44. 720 ILCS 5/19-2(b).

45. People v Whitfield, 214 Ill App 3d 446, 158 Ill Dec 82, 573 NE2d 1267 (1st Dist 1991).

46. People v Waln, 169 Ill App 3d 264, 120 Ill Dec 407, 523 NE2d 1318 (1st Dist 1991).

47. 720 ILCS 5/12-11(a).

Text References: Decker, Illinois Criminal Law 2d ed §§ 9.54, 9.55.

48. 720 ILCS 5/12-11(a).

§ 47:04   ILLINOIS JURISPRUDENCE: CRIMINAL LAW

dwelling place whether or not injury occurs or the person must intentionally cause injury to any person or persons within the dwelling place.[49]

When one is charged with home invasion based on knowingly entering the dwelling place of another and remaining in that dwelling place until the accused knows or has reason to know that one or more persons is present, it is an affirmative defense that the accused either immediately left the premises or surrendered to the person or persons lawfully present in the dwelling without either attempting to cause or causing serious bodily injury to any person present in the dwelling.[50]

For purposes of this Section, "dwelling place of another" includes a dwelling place where the defendant maintains a tenancy interest but from which the defendant has been barred by a divorce decree, judgment of dissolution of marriage, order of protection, or other court order.[51] Domestic battery is not a lesser included offense of home invasion.[52]

Home invasion is classified as a Class X felony.[53]

The gravamen of the offense of home invasion is unauthorized entry.[54] The determination of whether an entry is unauthorized

---

49. 720 ILCS 5/12-11(a)(1), 5/12-11(2).

50. 720 ILCS 5/12-11(b).

51. 720 ILCS 5/12-11(d).

52. Any evidence that the ex-wife allowed the defendant into her home on previous occasions did not make more or less probable the issue of whether she allowed defendant in her home on the night in question and the evidence clearly showed on the night in question she explicitly refused the defendant entry. People v Priest, 297 Ill App 3d 797, 232 Ill Dec 385, 698 NE2d 223 (4th Dist 1998).

   Periodicals: For article, "Lesser-Included Offenses in Illinois: A Look at Recent Developments," see 85 Ill. B.J. 480 (1997).

53. 720 ILCS 5/12-11(c).

54. People v Peeples, 155 Ill 2d 422, 186 Ill Dec 341, 616 NE2d 294 (1993), cert den 510 US 1016, 126 L Ed 2d 578, 114 S Ct 613.

   Text References: Decker, Illinois Criminal Law 2d ed §§ 9.54, 9.55.

depends on whether defendant possessed the intent to perform a criminal act therein at the time entry was granted.[55] If the defendant gains access to the victim's residence through trickery and deceit and with the intent to commit criminal acts, his or her entry is unauthorized and the consent given vitiated because the true purpose for the entry exceeded the limited authorization granted.[56] Conversely, where defendant enters with an innocent intent, his or her entry is authorized, and criminal actions thereafter engaged in by defendant do not change the status of the entry.[57]

Intent to harm may be proven by evidence that persons within the home were threatened.[58]

> *Illustration:* Defendant was proved guilty of the offense of home invasion where he slashed a screen and knocked in the front door of a dwelling and entered the foyer with a raised knife. The fact that the person he sought to harm was not present did not absolve him of responsibility for violation of the home invasion statute, as others were present and, under the facts presented, were clearly threatened.[59]

To cause an injury within the meaning of the home invasion statute, one must cause bodily harm, thus committing a battery.[60] The intentional causation of even a slight physical injury is sufficient to support a home invasion conviction.[61]

---

55. People v Bush, 157 Ill 2d 248, 191 Ill Dec 475, 623 NE2d 1361 (1993).

56. People v Bush, 157 Ill 2d 248, 191 Ill Dec 475, 623 NE2d 1361 (1993).

57. People v Bush, 157 Ill 2d 248, 191 Ill Dec 475, 623 NE2d 1361 (1993).

58. People v Ader, 176 Ill App 3d 613, 126 Ill Dec 112, 531 NE2d 407 (2d Dist 1988).

59. People v Ader, 176 Ill App 3d 613, 126 Ill Dec 112, 531 NE2d 407 (2d Dist 1988).

60. People v Kolls, 179 Ill App 3d 652, 128 Ill Dec 491, 534 NE2d 673 (2d Dist 1989).

61. People v Ehrich, 165 Ill App 3d 1060, 116 Ill Dec 922, 519 NE2d 1137 (4th Dist 1988).

In a prosecution for home invasion, knowledge may be proven by circumstantial evidence so long as the State presents sufficient evidence form which an inference of knowledge can be made.[62]

The "limited authority" doctrine holds that even if the defendant has consent to enter, the consent is limited to the purpose for which the defendant is granted entry.[63] Exceeding the scope of that authority by threatening or injuring an occupant may render the perpetrator guilty of home invasion. In order to prove defendant guilty of home invasion, the State must prove beyond a reasonable doubt that defendant entered the residence without authority.[64]

Where the basis of a home invasion count was the intentional infliction of injury by means of digital sexual penetration, the same element alleged for aggravated criminal sexual assault, the home invasion was an included offense of aggravated criminal assault because every element necessary to prove home invasion was included in the charged offense of aggravated criminal sexual assault.[65]

§ 47:05. Seizure and forfeiture

The Criminal Code authorizes the seizure of any vessel, vehicle or aircraft used with the knowledge and consent of the owner in the commission of, or in the attempt to commit the offenses of burglary, residential burglary or possession of burglary tools.[66]

---

62. People v Ramey, 240 Ill App 3d 456, 181 Ill Dec 439, 608 NE2d 512 (1st Dist 1992).

63. People v Donnelly, 226 Ill App 3d 771, 168 Ill Dec 575, 589 NE2d 975 (4th Dist 1992).

64. People v Donnelly, 226 Ill App 3d 771, 168 Ill Dec 575, 589 NE2d 975 (4th Dist 1992).

65. People v Conerty, 296 Ill App 3d 459, 231 Ill Dec 125, 695 NE2d 898 (4th Dist 1998).

66. 720 ILCS 5/36-1.

Annotation References: Forfeitability of property under Uniform Controlled Substances Act or similar statute where amount of controlled substance seized is small. 6 ALR5th 652.

The state's attorney in the county in which the seizure occurs may bring an action for forfeiture in the circuit court within whose jurisdiction the seizure and confiscation took place.[67] However, the state's attorney may exercise his or her discretion and cause the forfeiture to be remitted if he or she finds that the forfeiture was incurred without willful negligence or without any intention on the part of the owner of the property, or any person whose right, title or interest is of record, to violate the law or that the existence of mitigating circumstances justify remission of the forfeiture.[68] If the property is sold at public auction, any amount remaining after payment of all liens and deduction of reasonable charges and expenses incurred in the storing and selling of the property is paid into the general fund of the county where the property was seized.[69]

> ☞ *Illustration:* In one case, the evidence established that the defendant's car was used to get to and from the site of the burglaries and the car trunk was used to exchange and secrete the stolen property; therefore, the car was an integral part of the burglary offense and was properly forfeited.[70]

The spouse of the owner of a vehicle siezed under the forfeiture statute may make a showing that the seized vehicle is the only source of transportation, and if it is determined that the financial hardship to the family as a result of the seizure outweighs the benefit to the State from the seizure, the vehicle may be forfeited to the spouse or family member and the title to the vehicle will be transferred to the spouse or family member who is properly

Periodicals: Jochner, "From fiction to fact: the Supreme court's re-evaluation of civil asset forfeiture laws," 82 Ill BJ 560 (1994).

67. 720 ILCS 5/36-2(a).
68. 720 ILCS 5/36-2(a).
69. 720 ILCS 5/36-2(c).
70. People ex rel. Waller v 1996 Saturn, 298 Ill App 3d 464, 232 Ill Dec 776, 699 NE2d 223 (2d Dist 1998).

licensed and who requires the use of the vehicle for employment or family transportation purposes.[71]

---

71. 720 ILCS 5/36-1.

CHAPTER 48

CIVIL RIGHTS

by

Diane C. Busch, J.D.

and

Robert L. Margolis, Esq.

Scope of Chapter:

This chapter covers civil rights violations to the extent that a criminal remedy exists. For example, discriminatory practices in the sale or lease of residential real estate is discussed in some detail. The chapter also covers the rights and privileges lost by defendants upon incarceration and the restoration of those rights upon release. In addition, victims and witnesses have a statutory "bill of rights" which is discussed briefly.

Treated Elsewhere:

Charging instruments, see Chapter 9.

Criminal prosecution, see Chapter 12.

Defenses, see Chapter 3.

Ethnic intimidation, see Chapter 61.

Evidentiary matters, see Chapters 17–19, 21.

Sentencing, see Chapter 28.

Venue, see Chapter 13.

Research References:

Annotation References:

ALR Digest: Civil Rights § 16, 33, 34, 78, 79; Elections § 9; Labor § 87–93; Officers § 15.5

Index and Annotations: Civil Rights; Conviction; Criminal Law; Elections and Voting; Picketing; Public Officers and Employees; Prisons and Prisoners; Victims

§ 48:01 ILLINOIS JURISPRUDENCE: CRIMINAL LAW

Practice References:

7A Am Jur 2d, Automobiles and Highway Traffic § 115 et seq.; 15 Am Jur 2d, Civil Rights §§ 251, 262; 21A Am Jur 2d, Criminal Law §§ 1022 et seq.; 25 Am Jur 2d, Elections §§ 94, 177; 48A Am Jur 2d, Labor and Labor Relations §§ 2051 et seq.; 63A Am Jur 2d, Public Officers and Employees §§ 48–50

State Legislation:

720 ILCS 5/21.1-2, 5/21.1-3, 120/6, 590/1 et seq.; 725 ILCS 120/1 et seq.; 30 ILCS 5/5-5-5; 735 ILCS 5/2-2001; 775 ILCS 30/1 et seq.

Miscellaneous References:

West's Illinois Digest 2d, Automobiles § 144.3; Civil Rights § 131; Convicts § 1; Elections § 90; Labor Relations § 300; Officers and Public Employees § 31

Auto-Cite®: Cases and annotations referred to in this chapter can be further researched through the Auto-Cite® computer-assisted research service. Use Auto-Cite® to check citations for form, parallel references, prior and later history, and annotation references.

§ 48:01. Violations and offenses generally
§ 48:02. Loss and restoration of rights
§ 48:03. Rights of victims and witnesses
§ 48:04. —Disabled persons

§ 48:01. Violations and offenses generally

Although violations of civil rights are generally remedied in civil courts, there are criminal statutes prohibiting and punishing discrimination in the sale of real estate.[1] Under that statute, it is unlawful for any person or corporation to knowingly:

- solicit for sale, lease, listing, or purchase any residential real estate within Illinois, on the grounds of loss of value due to the present or prospective presence in the vicinity of the property involved of any person or persons of a particular race, color, religion, national origin, ancestry, creed, handicap, or sex;[2]

---

1. 720 ILCS 590/0.01 et seq.

Text References: Decker, Illinois Criminal Law 2d ed § 1:18.

2. 720 ILCS 590/1(a).

- distribute or cause to be distributed, written material or statements intended to induce any owner of residential real estate in Illinois to sell or lease his or her property due to any present or prospective changes in the race, color, religion, national origin, ancestry, creed, handicap, or sex, of residents in the vicinity of the property;[3] or
- intentionally create alarm among residents of the community, transmitted in any manner, with an intent to induce any owner of residential real estate in Illinois to sell or lease his or her property due to the present or prospective presence of any person or persons of any particular race, color, religion, national origin, ancestry, creed, handicap, or sex.[4]

Illinois law makes it a criminal offense for any person or corporation to solicit an owner of residential real estate to sell or list that property at any time after that person or corporation has notice that the owner does not desire to sell the property.[5] Notice is properly given by the owner personally or by a third party in the owner's name in the form of an individual notice or a list.[6] That notice must clearly state whether each owner seeks to avoid both solicitation for listing and sale, or only for listing, or only for sale, as well as the period of time that solicitation is to be avoided.[7] The notice must be dated and must either be signed by each owner or it must be accompanied by an affidavit stating that all the names on the notice are genuine as to the identity of the persons listed and that those persons have requested not to be solicited as indicated.[8] That notice must be served personally or

Annotation References: Validity and construction of anti-blockbusting regulations, designed to prevent brokers from inducing sales of realty because of actual or rumored entry of racial group into neighborhood, 34 ALR3d 1432.

3. 720 ILCS 590/1(b).
4. 720 ILCS 590/1(c).
5. 720 ILCS 590/1(d).
6. 720 ILCS 590/1(d)(1).
7. 720 ILCS 590/1(d)(2).

§ 48:01   ILLINOIS JURISPRUDENCE: CRIMINAL LAW

by certified or registered mail, return receipt requested.[9]

> ☞ *Caution:* By leaving "solicit," the central term, undefined, subsection (d) forces real estate brokers to guess at its meaning, necessarily "chills" speech and, thus, has been found to violate the First Amendment of the U.S. Constitution.[10]

A person who violates the Discrimination in Sale of Real Estate Act is guilty of a Class A misdemeanor.[11] However, a person who has been previously convicted for a violation of the Act is guilty of a Class 4 felony.[12]

It is also a criminal offense to picket a person's residence or dwelling, unless that residence or dwelling is used as a place of business.[13] However, a person may peacefully picket his or her own residence or dwelling, nor is it a violation to peacefully picket a place of employment involved in a labor dispute or the place where a meeting or assembly is held if those premises are commonly used to discuss subjects of general public interest.[14] A person who unlawfully pickets a residence is guilty of a Class B misdemeanor.[15]

---

8. 720 ILCS 590/1(d)(2).

9. 720 ILCS 590/1(3).

10. Pearson v Edgar, 965 F Supp 1104 (ND Ill 1997), affd in part and vacated in part 153 F3d 397 (CA7 Ill).

11. 720 ILCS 590/2(a).

12. 720 ILCS 590/2(b).

13. 720 ILCS 5/21-1.2.

> **Annotation References:** Peaceful picketing of private residence, 42 ALR3d 1353.

14. 720 ILCS 5/21-1.2.

> **Annotation References:** Legality of peaceful labor picketing on private property, 10 ALR3d 846.

15. 720 ILCS 5/21.1-3.

§ 48:02. Loss and restoration of rights

As a general proposition, a defendant does not lose his or her civil rights as a result of conviction and disposition.[16] However, by statute, a defendant's rights may be affected as follows:

- a person convicted of a felony is ineligible to hold an office created by the Illinois Constitution until he or she has served the prescribed sentence;[17]

- a person sentenced to imprisonment loses the right to vote until released;[18] and

- upon, or at any time after, the completion of a sentence of imprisonment or discharge from probation, conditional discharge, or periodic imprisonment, all license rights and privileges granted by Illinois which were revoked or suspended as a result of conviction must be restored unless the authority controlling those license rights finds, after investigation and a hearing, that restoration of those rights is not in the public interest.[19]

☞ *Practice Guide:* This provision does not apply to the suspension or revocation of a license to operate a motor vehicle.[20]

---

16. 730 ILCS 5/5-5-5(a).

17. 730 ILCS 5/5-5-5(b).

Annotation References: Elections: effect of conviction under federal law, or law of another state or country, on right to vote or hold public office, 39 ALR3d 303.

What constitutes conviction within statutory or constitutional provision making conviction of crime ground of disqualification for, removal from, or vacancy in, public office, 71 ALR2d 593.

18. 730 ILCS 5/5-5-5(c).

Annotation References: What constitutes "conviction" within constitutional or statutory provision disfranchising one convicted of crime, 36 ALR2d 1238.

19. 730 ILCS 5/5-5-5(d).

20. 730 ILCS 5/5-5-5(d).

§ 48:02

Although a convicted felon does regain some civil rights upon release from prison, the right to possess a firearm is not one of them.[21]

Once a person has been discharged from incarceration, parol, or probation, the court that committed him or her may enter an order to certify that the sentence has been completed, if the court believes that it would assist in that person's rehabilitation and would be consistent with public welfare.[22] The order may be entered upon the motion of the defendant, the State, or on the court's own motion.[23] At the time that the order is entered, the court must issue to the person a certificate stating that his or her behavior after conviction has warranted the issuance of the order.[24]

§ 48:03. Rights of victims and witnesses

Victims and witnesses of violent crimes possess specific statutory rights.[25] These rights are set forth in detail in the Bill of Rights for Victims and Witnesses of Violent Crime Act.[26] This Act is intended to implement, preserve and protect the rights guaranteed to crime victims by the Illinois Constitution to ensure that crime victims are treated with fairness and respect for their dignity and privacy throughout the criminal justice system and to increase the effectiveness of the criminal justice system by affording certain basic rights and considerations to the witnesses of violent crime who are essential to prosecution.[27] Article I

---

21. Melvin v United States, 78 F3d 327 (CA7 Ill 1996), cert den 519 US 963, 136 L Ed 2d 301, 117 S Ct 384.

22. 730 ILCS 5/5-5-5(e).

23. 730 ILCS 5/5-5-5(e).

24. 730 ILCS 5/5-5-5(f).

25. 725 ILCS 120/1 et seq.

26. 725 ILCS 120/1 et seq.

Annotation References: Measure and elements of restitution to which victim is entitled under state criminal statute, 15 ALR5th 391.

27. 725 ILCS 120/2.

Section 8.1 of the Illinois Constitution, the Crime Victim's Bill of Rights, provides that crime victims, as defined by law, have the following rights as provided by law:[28]

- the right to be treated with fairness and respect for their dignity and privacy throughout the criminal justice process;
- the right to notification of court proceedings;
- the right to communicate with the prosecution;
- the right to make a statement to the court at sentencing;
- the right to information about the conviction, sentence, imprisonment, and release of the accused;
- the right to timely disposition of the case following the arrest of the accused;
- the right to be reasonably protected from the accused throughout the criminal justice process;
- the right to be present at the trial and all other court proceedings on the same basis as the accused, unless the victim is to testify and the court determines that the victim's testimony would be materially affected if the victim hears other testimony at the trial;
- the right to have present at all court proceedings, subject to the rules of evidence, an advocate or other support person of the victim's choice; and
- the right to restitution.

There are procedures in place to implement the rights of crime victims.[29] Among other things, law enforcement, prosecutors, judges and corrections must provide information at specified proceedings; provisions are set forth as to the procedures to be followed and extent of the information provided by the State's Attorney; and the rights of crime victims with regard to the parole process.[30]

28. Ill. Const. Art. 1, § 8.1.
29. 725 ILCS 120/4.5.
30. 725 ILCS 120/4.5.

§ 48:03   ILLINOIS JURISPRUDENCE: CRIMINAL LAW

A victim of crime has a cause of action against a defendant who has been convicted of a crime, or found not guilty by reason of insanity or guilty but mentally ill of a crime, to recover damages suffered by the victim of the crime.[31]

The passage of the Rights of Crime Victims and Witnesses Act and the existence of the victim's rights amendment require the court to give formal consideration to the interests of the victims of violent crimes, weighing the memory of the deceased victims and the well being of their innocent survivors in considering whether a conviction should be abated ab initio and when such a balancing of rights is considered in the context of violent crime, abatement of convictions is precluded.[32]

Witnesses have the following rights:[33]

- to be notified by the state's attorney of all court proceedings at which the witness's presence is required in a reasonable amount of time prior to the proceeding, and to be notified of the cancellation of any scheduled court proceeding in sufficient time to prevent an unnecessary appearance in court, where possible;
- to be provided with appropriate employer intercession services by the state's attorney's office or the victim advocate personnel to ensure that employers of witnesses will cooperate with the criminal justice system to minimize an employee's loss of pay and other benefits resulting from court appearances;
- to be provided, whenever possible, a secure waiting area during court proceedings that does not require witnesses to be in close proximity to defendants and their families and friends; and

---

31. 735 ILCS 5/2-2001.

32. People v Robinson, 298 Ill App 3d 866, 232 Ill Dec 901, 699 NE2d 1086 (1st Dist 1998), app gr 181 Ill 2d 585, 235 Ill Dec 947, 706 NE2d 502.

33. 725 ILCS 120/5(a).

- to be provided with notice by the Office of the State's Attorney, where necessary, of the right to have a translator present whenever the witness's presence is required.

In any case where a defendant has been convicted of a violent crime or a juvenile has been adjudicated a delinquent for a violent crime, e,xcept those in which both parties have agreed to the imposition of a specific sentence, if a victim of the crime is present in the courtroom during thesentencing or the disposition hearing, the victim may address the court regarding the impact of the defendant's conduct on the victim.[34] If the victim chooses to exercise this right, the impact statement must have been prepared in writing in conjunction with the state's attorney prior to the initial hearing or sentencing, before it can be presented orally or in writing at the sentencing hearing.[35] The court mustl consider any statements made by the victim, along with all other appropriate factors in determining the sentence of the defendant or disposition of such juvenile.[36]

§ 48:04. —Disabled persons

It is the policy of Illinois to encourage and enable the blind, the visually handicapped and the otherwise physically disabled to participate fully in the social and economic life of Illinois and to engage in remunerative employment.[37] The blind, the visually handicapped, the hearing impaired and the otherwise physically disabled have the same rights as the able-bodied to the full and free use of the streets, highways, sidewalks, walkways, public buildings, public facilities and other public places.[38] These individuals are entitled to full and equal accommodations, advantages, facilities and privileges of all common carriers, airplanes, motor vehicles, railroad trains, motor buses, street

---

34. 725 ILCS 120/6(a).

35. 725 ILCS 120/6(a).

36. 725 ILCS 120/6(a).

37. 775 ILCS 30/2.

38. 775 ILCS 30/3.

cars, boats or any other public conveyances or modes of transportation, hotels, lodging places, places of public accommodation, amusement or resort, and other places to which the general public is invited, subject only to the conditions and limitations established by law and applicable alike to all persons.[39] Any person or persons, firm or corporation, or their agent who denies or interferes with admittance to or enjoyment of the public facilities enumerated in the Act or otherwise interferes with the rights of a disabled person is guilty of a Class A misdemeanor.[40]

---

39. 775 ILCS 30/3.
40. 775 ILCS 30/4.

CHAPTER 49

COMPUTER CRIMES

by

Diane C. Busch, J.D.

and

Robert L. Margolis, Esq.

Scope of Chapter:
    This chapter discusses the statutes governing computer crimes. Computer tampering and computer fraud are covered in depth and the definitions and penalties applicable to each offense are set forth. In addition, separate sections have been included which provide the statutory requirements governing the forfeiture of computer equipment when an offense has been committed. The procedural aspects of forfeiture are also discussed.

Treated Elsewhere:
    Charging instruments, see Chapter 9.
    Criminal prosecution, see Chapter 12.
    Defenses, see Chapter 3.
    Evidentiary matters, see Chapters 17–19, 21.
    Sentencing, see Chapter 28.
    Venue, see Chapter 13.

Research References:
  Text References:
    Decker, Illinois Criminal Law 2d ed §§ 11.42 et seq.
  Annotation References:
    ALR Digest: Computers and Data Bases § 13–15
    Index and Annotations: Computers; Larceny or Theft

§ 49:01

Practice References:
26 Am Jur 2d, Embezzlement § 13; 50 Am Jur 2d, Larceny § 77
33 Am Jur Trials 1, Defense of Computer Crime Cases § 1 et seq.

State Legislation:
720 ILCS 5/16D-1 et seq.

Auto-Cite®: Cases and annotations referred to in this chapter can be further researched through the Auto-Cite® computer-assisted research service. Use Auto-Cite® to check citations for form, parallel references, prior and later history, and annotation references.

§ 49:01.   Generally
§ 49:02.   Computer tampering
§ 49:03.   Computer fraud
§ 49:04.   Forfeiture
§ 49:05.   —Proceedings

§ 49:01. Generally

The Computer Crime Prevention Law makes it a criminal offense to access a computer without the appropriate authorization.[1] The statutory computer crimes include computer tampering, aggravated computer tampering, and computer fraud.[2] The statute also contains forfeiture provisions.[3] It should also be noted that, by statute, there is a rebuttable presumption that a computer was accessed without the authorization of its owner or in excess of the authority granted if a person accesses or causes to be accessed a computer, and that access requires a confidential or proprietary code which has not been issued to or authorized for use by that person.[4]

---

1. 720 ILCS 5/16D-1 et seq.

   Text References: Decker, Illinois Criminal Law 2d ed §§ 11.42 et seq.

   Practice References: 33 Am Jur Trials 1, Defense of Computer Crime Cases § 1 et seq.

2. 720 ILCS 5/16D-3 to 5/16D-5.
3. 720 ILCS 5/16D-6.
4. 720 ILCS 5/16D-7.

☞ *Caution:* Counsel should be aware that the statute explicitly defines various terms. Consequently, although there is no case law construing the Act, the construction of the statute may be dramatically affected by the application of the statutory definitions.[5]

The statute also authorizes a victim of computer tampering to obtain relief in a civil action.[6]

☞ *Practice Guide:* If the victim of computer tampering maintains a civil action pursuant to the Computer Crime Prevention Law, the court is permitted to award reasonable attorneys fees and other expenses of litigation to the prevailing party.[7]

§ 49:02. Computer tampering

A person commits computer tampering when he or she knowingly and without the authorization of a computer's owner, or in excess of the authority granted to him or her does any of the following:

- accesses or causes to be accessed any part of a computer, or a program or data,[8] which is a Class B misdemeanor.[9]
- accesses or causes to be accessed any part of a computer, or a program or data, and obtains data or services,[10] which is a

---

5. 720 ILCS 5/16D-2.
6. 720 ILCS 5/16D-3(c).
7. 720 ILCS 5/16D-3(c).
8. 720 ILCS 5/16D-3(a)(1).

Text References: Decker, Illinois Criminal Law 2d ed § 11.43.

Annotation References: Criminal liability for theft of, interference with, or unauthorized use of, computer programs, files, or systems, 51 ALR4th 971.
Computer programs as property subject to theft, 18 ALR3d 1121.

9. 720 ILCS 5/16D-3(b)(1).
10. 720 ILCS 5/16D-3(a)(2).

§ 49:02 ILLINOIS JURISPRUDENCE: CRIMINAL LAW

Class A misdemeanor, or a Class 4 felony if it is a subsequent offense.[11]

- accesses or causes to be accessed any part of a computer, or a program or data, and damages or destroys the computer or changes, deletes, or removes a computer program or data,[12] which is a Class 4 felony, or a Class 3 felony for a subsequent offense.[13]

- inserts or attempts to insert a program into a computer or computer program knowing, or having reason to believe, that the program contains information or commands that will or may: (1) damage or destroy that computer, or any other computer accessing or being accessed by that computer; (2) change, delete, or remove a computer program or data from that computer, or any computer program or data in any other computer accessing or being accessed by that computer; or (3) cause loss to the users of that computer or the users of a computer which accesses or is accessed by the program.[14] A person who commits computer tampering in this manner is guilty of a Class 4 felony, or for a subsequent offense, a Class 3 felony.[15]

A person commits aggravated computer tampering if he or she knowingly and without authorization of a computer's owner, or in excess of the authority granted to him or her, accesses or causes to be accessed any part of a computer, or a program or data, and damages or destroys the computer or changes, erases, or removes a computer program or data and:

- he or she knowingly causes disruption of or interference with vital services or operations of the State or a local government or public entity, which is a Class 3 felony; or

---

11. 720 ILCS 5/16D-3(b)(2).
12. 720 ILCS 5/16D-3(a)(3).
13. 720 ILCS 5/16D-3(b)(3).
14. 720 ILCS 5/16D-3(a)(4).
15. 720 ILCS 5/16D-3(b)(3).

COMPUTER CRIMES § 49:03

- he or she knowingly creates a strong probability of death or great bodily harm to one or more individuals, which is a Class 2 felony.[16]

§ 49:03. Computer fraud

The offense of computer fraud is committed when a person knowingly:

- accesses or causes to be accessed any part of a computer, or a program or data, for the purpose of devising or executing any scheme or artifice to defraud, or as part of a deception,[17] which is a Class 4 felony.[18]

- obtains the use of, damages, or destroys any part of a computer, or changes, erases, or removes any program or data contained in that computer, in connection with any scheme, artifice to defraud, or as part of a deception,[19] which is a Class 3 felony.[20]

- accesses or causes to be accessed any part of a computer, or a program or data, and obtains money or control over any money, property, or the services of another in connection with any scheme, artifice to defraud, or as part of a deception,[21] If the value of the money, property, or services is $1,000 or less, the person is guilty of a Class 4 felony; if the value of the money, property, or services is more than $1,000 but less than $50,000, he or she is guilty of a Class 3 felony; or if the money, property, or services has a value of $50,000 or more, he or she is guilty of a Class 2 felony.[22]

---

16. 720 ILCS 5/16D-4.

Text References: Decker, Illinois Criminal Law 2d ed § 11.44.

17. 720 ILCS 5/16D-5(a)(1).

Text References: Decker, Illinois Criminal Law 2d ed § 11.45.

18. 720 ILCS 5/16D-5(b)(1).
19. 720 ILCS 5/16D-5(a)(2).
20. 720 ILCS 5/16D-5(b)(2).
21. 720 ILCS 5/16D-5(a)(3).

§ 49:04. Forfeiture

Any person who commits computer fraud must forfeit any monies, profits or proceeds, and any interests or properties which the sentencing court determines that he or she has acquired or maintained, directly or indirectly, in whole or in part, as a result of the commission of that offense.[23] The offender must also forfeit any interest in, security, claim against, or contractual right of any kind which provides him or her with a source of influence over any enterprise which he or she has established, operated, controlled, conducted or participated in conducting, where his or her relationship or connection is traceable to any item or benefit which he or she has obtained or acquired through the offense of computer fraud.[24] Further, any person who commits a felony under the Computer Crime Prevention Law or any other statute and the instrumentality used to commit the offense or used in connection with or to further a scheme or design to commit the offense, is a computer owned by the defendant or if the defendant is a minor, owned by his or her parents or legal guardian, the computer is subject to forfeiture.[25] However, the computer, or any part of it, accessed in the commission of the offense, is not subject to forfeiture if it is owned or leased by the victim or an innocent third party at the time that the crime was committed or if the rights of creditors, lienholders, or any person having a security interest in the computer would be adversely affected.[26]

§ 49:05. —Proceedings

Forfeiture proceedings are instituted by petition filed by the prosecuting attorney, whether it is the Attorney General or a

---

22. 720 ILCS 5/16D-5(b)(3)(i)–(iii).

23. 720 ILCS 5/16D-6(1).

   Periodicals: Jochner, "From fiction to fact: the Supreme court's re-evaluation of civil asset forfeiture laws," 82 Ill BJ 560 (1994).

24. 720 ILCS 5/16D-6(1).

25. 720 ILCS 5/16D-6(2).

26. 720 ILCS 5/16D-6(2).

State's attorney.[27] The petition is filed with the sentencing court at any time following sentencing.[28] The sentencing court must then conduct a hearing to determine whether any property or property interest is subject to forfeiture under the Computer Crime Prevention Law.[29] At the forfeiture hearing the prosecutor has the burden of establishing, by a preponderance of the evidence, that the property or property interests are subject to forfeiture.[30] In any forfeiture action, the circuit courts have jurisdiction to enter any restraining orders, injunctions or prohibitions, or to take any other action in connection with any real, personal, or mixed property or other interest subject to forfeiture as they consider proper.[31]

In any forfeiture action where a restraining order, injunction or prohibition, or any other action is sought in connection with any property or interest subject to forfeiture, the circuit court presiding over the trial of the defendant charged with computer fraud must first determine whether there is probable cause to believe that he or she has committed the offense and whether the property or interest is subject to forfeiture under the Computer Crime Prevention Law.[32] Therefore, the court must conduct a hearing, without a jury, and the State must establish:

- probable cause that the defendant has committed the offense of computer fraud; and
- probable cause that any property or interest may be subject to forfeiture under the Computer Crime Prevention Law.[33]

The hearing may be conducted simultaneously with a preliminary hearing if the prosecution is commenced by

---

27. 720 ILCS 5/16D-6(1)(a).
28. 720 ILCS 5/16D-6(1)(a).
29. 720 ILCS 5/16D-6(1)(a).
30. 720 ILCS 5/16D-6(1)(a).
31. 720 ILCS 5/16D-6(1)(b).
32. 720 ILCS 5/16D-6(1)(c).
33. 720 ILCS 5/16D-6(1)(c).

§ 49:05   ILLINOIS JURISPRUDENCE: CRIMINAL LAW

information or complaint.[34] Alternatively, the hearing may be conducted by motion of the State at any stage in the proceedings.[35] For purposes of the forfeiture section of the Computer Crime Prevention Law, sufficient evidence to support a finding of probable cause arises at a preliminary hearing following the filing of an information charging the offense of computer fraud or the return of an indictment by a grand jury charging that offense.[36]

Once the court makes a finding of probable cause, it must enter the restraining order, injunction or prohibition, or take other action in connection with any property or other interest subject to forfeiture as necessary to insure that that property is not removed from the jurisdiction of the court, concealed, destroyed, or otherwise disposed of prior to a forfeiture hearing.[37] The prosecuting agency must then file a certified copy of that restraining order, injunction, or other prohibition with a recorder of deeds or registrar of title in each county where any of that property may be located.[38] However, no injunction, restraining order, or other prohibition may affect the rights of any bona fide purchaser, mortgagee, judgment creditor, or other lienholder arising prior to the date of the filing of the certified copy of the order.[39]

The court may, at any time and upon verified petition by the defendant, conduct a hearing to release all or any portions of any property or interest which the court previously determined to be subject to forfeiture or subject to any restraining order, injunction, prohibition or other action.[40] Under those circumstances, the court may release that property to the defendant for

---

34. 720 ILCS 5/16D-6(1)(c).
35. 720 ILCS 5/16D-6(1)(c).
36. 720 ILCS 5/16D-6(1)(c).
37. 720 ILCS 5/16D-6(1)(c).
38. 720 ILCS 5/16D-6(1)(c).
39. 720 ILCS 5/16D-6(1)(c).
40. 720 ILCS 5/16D-6(1)(c).

good cause shown and the matter is vested to the sound discretion of the court.[41]

Once a person is convicted of computer fraud, the court must authorize the Attorney General to seize and sell all property or other interest declared forfeited unless that property is required by law to be destroyed or is harmful to the public.[42] Following the entry of an order of forfeiture, the Attorney General must publish notice of that order and of his or her intent to dispose of the property.[43] Within the 30 days following publication, any person may petition the court to adjudicate the validity of his or her alleged interest in the property.[44] When the court enters its order of forfeiture, it may also order the Attorney General to segregate funds from the proceeds of that sale sufficient to satisfy:

- any order of restitution, as the court deems appropriate;
- any legal right, title, or interest which the court deems superior to any right, title, or interest of the defendant at the time that the acts giving rise to forfeiture were committed; or
- any bona fide purchaser for value of the right, title, or interest in the property who was without reasonable notice that the property was subject to forfeiture.[45]

The forfeiture provisions of the Computer Crime Prevention Law also set forth how the Attorney General may distribute those funds, the proportions of distributions to various governmental agencies, and the use to which those funds may be put.[46]

---

41. 720 ILCS 5/16D-6(1)(c).
42. 720 ILCS 5/16D-6(1)(d).
43. 720 ILCS 5/16D-6(1)(d).
44. 720 ILCS 5/16D-6(1)(d).
45. 720 ILCS 5/16D-6(1)(d).
46. 720 ILCS 5/16D-6(1)(1).

CHAPTER 50

CONSPIRACY

by

Diane C. Busch, J.D.

and

Robert L. Margolis, Esq.

Scope of Chapter:

The discussion in this chapter focuses on the statutory provisions governing the offense of conspiracy generally. The sentence for conspiracy is also covered in a separate section. This chapter does not discuss in detail specific types of conspiracies which are covered under the statutory schemes governing the underlying offenses, such as criminal drug conspiracies which are governed by provisions of the many controlled substances acts. A discussion of a particular type of conspiracy may be found in the chapter covering the specific underlying offense.

Treated Elsewhere:

Charging instruments, see Chapter 9.

Criminal prosecution, see Chapter 12.

Defenses, see Chapter 3.

Drug conspiracies, see Chapter 56.

Evidentiary matters, see Chapters 17–19, 21.

Sentencing, see Chapter 28.

Venue, see Chapter 13.

Research References:

  Text References:

    Decker, Illinois Criminal Law Ch 4

    Wharton's Criminal Evidence §§ 608–610 (14th ed. 1986)

  Annotation References:

    ALR Digest: Conspiracy § 17 et seq.

§ 50:01

Index and Annotations: Conspiracy

Practice References:

16 Am Jur 2d, Conspiracy §§ 1–48

8 Am Jur POF2d 231, Withdrawal From or Abandonment of Criminal Enterprise § 1 et seq.

20 Am Jur Trials 351, Handling the Defense in a Conspiracy Prosecution § 1 et seq.

State Legislation:

405 ILCS 5/6-102; 720 ILCS 5/8-2, 5/11-15 et seq., 5/24-1, 5/28-1, 5/28-3, 5/28-4, 550/9, 570/401 et seq.

Miscellaneous References:

West's Illinois Digest 2d, Conspiracy § 23 et seq.

Auto-Cite®: Cases and annotations referred to in this chapter can be further researched through the Auto-Cite® computer-assisted research service. Use Auto-Cite® to check citations for form, parallel references, prior and later history, and annotation references.

§ 50:01.   Generally
§ 50:02.   Sentence

§ 50:01. Generally

A person commits conspiracy when he or she agrees with another person to the commission of an offense, with the intent that that offense be committed.[1] However, a person may not be convicted of conspiracy unless an act in furtherance of the agreement is alleged and proved to have been committed by him

---

1. 720 ILCS 5/8-2(a).

Text References: Decker, Illinois Criminal Law 2d ed Ch 4.

Annotation References: Criminal conspiracy between spouses, 74 ALR3d 838.

When does statute of limitations begin to run against civil action or criminal prosecution for conspiracy, 62 ALR2d 1369.

Periodicals: For article, "Survey of Illinois Law: Criminal Law and Procedure," see 21 S. Ill. U.L.J. 759 (1997).

Practice References: 8 Am Jur POF2d 231, Withdrawal from or Abandonment of Criminal Enterprise § 1 et seq.

20 Am Jur Trials 351, Handling the Defense in a Conspiracy Prosecution § 1 et seq.

CONSPIRACY § 50:01

or her or by a coconspirator.[2]

An indictment for conspiracy must allege an agreement by the defendants to perform an illegal act and an act in furtherance of the agreement by one of the defendants.[3] It need not allege all the elements of the substantive offense which is the object of the conspiracy.[4] Furthermore, because the gist of conspiracy is the agreement to commit a crime, it is unnecessary to allege the means by which the act of conspiracy was to be accomplished.[5]

Conspiracy constitutes a continuing offense where overt acts are performed in furtherance of it.[6] Although the unlawful combination alone constitutes the offense of conspiracy and no act in furtherance of the unlawful design is necessary to complete the offense, every such act is regarded, in law, as a renewal or continuance of the unlawful agreement.[7] A conspiracy, once formed, is presumed to exist whenever and wherever one of the conspirators does some act in furtherance of its purpose.[8] Since the overt act is a renewal of the conspiracy, the offense is continuous so long as overt acts in furtherance of its purpose are

---

2. 720 ILCS 5/8-2(a).

Text References: Decker, Illinois Criminal Law § 4.10.
Wharton's Criminal Evidence §§ 608–610 (14th ed. 1986).

Annotation References: Comment Note.—Impossibility of consummation of substantive crime as defense in criminal prosecution for conspiracy or attempt to commit crime, 37 ALR3d 375.

3. People v Buffman, 260 Ill App 3d 505, 201 Ill Dec 351, 636 NE2d 783 (1st Dist 1994).

4. People v Buffman, 260 Ill App 3d 505, 201 Ill Dec 351, 636 NE2d 783 (1st Dist 1994).

5. People v Buffman, 260 Ill App 3d 505, 201 Ill Dec 351, 636 NE2d 783 (1st Dist 1994).

6. People v Cooper, 239 Ill App 3d 336, 179 Ill Dec 873, 606 NE2d 705 (5th Dist 1992).

7. People v Cooper, 239 Ill App 3d 336, 179 Ill Dec 873, 606 NE2d 705 (5th Dist 1992).

8. People v Cooper, 239 Ill App 3d 336, 179 Ill Dec 873, 606 NE2d 705 (5th Dist 1992).

§ 50:01   ILLINOIS JURISPRUDENCE: CRIMINAL LAW

done.[9]

A conspiracy conviction requires an agreement based on the bilateral theory of conspiracy rather than the unilateral theory.[10] An agreement based on the bilateral theory is one between defendant and at least one other person where both parties actually intend to agree.[11] Under the bilateral theory, a purported agreement between defendant and a governmental agent only feigning agreement will not support a conspiracy conviction because there is no actual agreement and actual agreement is a necessary element of conspiracy.[12]

The State does not have to prove that the conspirators actually met and entered into a specific agreement. Instead, the agreement can be by words, acts, or understanding.[13] Through circumstantial evidence, conspiracy can be proven by showing a common criminal purpose[14]. Even so, the State must prove that the accused had the specific intent to commit conspiracy.[15]

The requisite mens rea element of a consipiracy charge is satisfied with proof of an agreement to comit an offense with an intent that the offense be committed.[16]

It is not a defense to a conspiracy charge that the person or

---

9. People v Cooper, 239 Ill App 3d 336, 179 Ill Dec 873, 606 NE2d 705 (5th Dist 1992).

10. People v Breton, 237 Ill App 3d 355, 177 Ill Dec 916, 603 NE2d 1290 (2d Dist 1992).

Text References: Decker, Illinois Criminal Law §§ 4.04, 4.05.

11. People v Breton, 237 Ill App 3d 355, 177 Ill Dec 916, 603 NE2d 1290 (2d Dist 1992).

12. People v Breton, 237 Ill App 3d 355, 177 Ill Dec 916, 603 NE2d 1290 (2d Dist 1992).

13. People v Adams, 238 Ill App 3d 733, 179 Ill Dec 747, 606 NE2d 579 (1992).

14. People v Adams, 238 Ill App 3d 733, 179 Ill Dec 747, 606 NE2d 579 (1992).

15. People v Adams, 238 Ill App 3d 733, 179 Ill Dec 747, 606 NE2d 579 (1992).

CONSPIRACY § 50:01

persons with whom the accused is alleged to have conspired has not been prosecuted or convicted; has been convicted of a different crime; is not amenable to justice; has been acquitted; or lacked the capacity to commit an offense.[17]

> ☛ *Practice Guide:* Counsel should be aware that there are statutes punishing particular types of conspiracies. For example, a person who conspires to unlawfully cause any person to be involuntarily admitted to a mental health facility is guilty of a Class A misdemeanor.[18] Similarly, there are specific grades of felony attached to criminal drug conspiracies.[19] In addition, any person who engages in a streetgang criminal drug conspiracy is guilty of a Class X felony for which the offender must be sentenced to a term of imprisonment.[20]

If a prosecution is based on the testimony of a coconsipirator, there must be independent corrobrating evidence.[21]

> ☛ *Illustration:* Thus, in one case, a rational trier of fact could readily have found defendant guilty beyond a reasonable doubt of murder and conspiracy to commit murder, notwithstanding that the prosecution's case was based almost entirely on the testimony of a codefendant; the codefendant provided a complete account of the conspiracy, including her

---

16. People v Melgoza, 231 Ill App 3d 510, 172 Ill Dec 591, 595 NE2d 1261 (1st Dist 1992).

17. 720 ILCS 5/8-2(b).

Annotation References: Prosecution or conviction of one conspirator as affected by disposition of case against coconspirators, 19 ALR4th 192.

18. 405 ILCS 5/6-102.

19. 720 ILCS 550/9, 570/405.

20. 720 ILCS 570/405.2.

Periodicals: Bauman, Conspiring drug kingpins: twice in jeopardy? 61 U Chi L Rev 197 (1994).

21. People v Smith, 177 Ill 2d 53, 226 Ill Dec 425, 685 NE2d 880 (1997).

own role, and the State was able to provide independent corroboration of many aspects of the codefendant's testimony.[22]

Since the crime of conspiracy is complete with the agreement and an overt act, no subsequent action can exonerate the conspirator of that crime.[23]

Conspiracy and the substantive offense are separate and distinct crimes.[24]

As generally stated, "Wharton's Rule" prohibits the prosecution for conspiracy to commit a particular crime where the commission of that crime requires the participation of more than one person.[25] Wharton's rule does not prohibit prosecution of consipracy simply because the substantive crime involves the participation of two or more actors, but prohibits it when the cooperative conduct inherent in the substantive offiense is indistinguishable from the element of agreement in the alleged conspiracy.[26]

☛ *Illustration:* Thus, the crimes of dueling, bigamy, adultery, and incest are paradigm examples of Wharton's Rule offenses.[27]

§ 50:02. Sentence

A person convicted of conspiracy may be fined or imprisoned or both.[28] The sentence cannot exceed the maximum provided for

---

22. People v Smith, 177 Ill 2d 53, 226 Ill Dec 425, 685 NE2d 880 (1997).

23. People v Adams, 176 Ill App 3d 197, 125 Ill Dec 746, 530 NE2d 1155 (1st Dist 1988).

24. People v Zubik, 225 Ill App 3d 950, 167 Ill Dec 796, 588 NE2d 437 (3d Dist 1992).

25. People v Laws, 155 Ill 2d 208, 184 Ill Dec 430, 613 NE2d 747 (1993).

Text References: Decker, Illinois Criminal Law § 4.13.

26. People v Laws, 155 Ill 2d 208, 184 Ill Dec 430, 613 NE2d 747 (1993).

27. People v Laws, 155 Ill 2d 208, 184 Ill Dec 430, 613 NE2d 747 (1993).

28. 720 ILCS 5/8-2(c).

the offense which is the underlying object of the conspiracy.[29] However, a person may be sentenced for a Class 3 felony if the underlying offense is:

- soliciting for a prostitute;[30]
- pandering;[31]
- keeping a place of prostitution;[32]
- pimping;[33]
- one of those specified for unlawful use of weapons;[34]
- gambling;[35]
- keeping a gambling place;[36]
- registration of federal gambling stamps;[37]
- the manufacture, distribution, advertisement, or possession of a look-alike substance;[38]
- distribution and manufacture of a controlled substance;[39] or
- an inchoate offense related to any of the above principle offenses.[40]

Periodicals: For article, "Survey of Illinois Law: Criminal Law and Procedure," see 21 S. Ill. U.L.J. 759 (1997).

29. 720 ILCS 5/8-2(c).
30. 720 ILCS 5/11-15.
31. 720 ILCS 5/11-16.
32. 720 ILCS 5/11-17.
33. 720 ILCS 5/11-19.
34. 720 ILCS 5/24-1(a)(1), 5/24-1(a)(7).
35. 720 ILCS 5/28-1.
36. 720 ILCS 5/28-3.
37. 720 ILCS 5/28-4.
38. 720 ILCS 570/404.
39. 720 ILCS 570/406.
40. 720 ILCS 5/8-2(c).

§ 50:02   ILLINOIS JURISPRUDENCE: CRIMINAL LAW

A person may not be sentenced in excess of a Class 2 felony for the offenses of conspiracy to commit:

- treason;
- first degree murder; or
- aggravated kidnapping.[41]

A person may not be sentenced in excess of a Class 4 felony for conspiracy to commit any offense other than those specified above and other than:[42]

- manufacture and delivery of a controlled substance;[43]
- possession of a controlled substance;[44] or
- manufacture, delivery, or sales of a controlled substance.[45]

---

41. 720 ILCS 5/8-2(c).
42. 720 ILCS 5/8-2(c).
43. 720 ILCS 570/401.
44. 720 ILCS 570/402.
45. 720 ILCS 570/407.

CHAPTER 51

CONTRIBUTING TO THE CRIMINAL DELINQUENCY OF A JUVENILE

by

Lisa K. Fox, J.D.

and

Robert L. Margolis, Esq.

Scope of Chapter:
This chapter defines the crime of contributing to the delinquency of a juvenile, the requisite ages of the offenders and the resulting penalties.

Treated Elsewhere:
Charging instruments, see Chapter 9.
Criminal prosecution, see Chapter 12.
Defenses, see Chapter 3.
Evidentiary matters, see Chapters 17–19, 21.
Juveniles, see Chapter 35.
Sentencing, see Chapter 28.
Venue, see Chapter 13.

Research References:
Annotation References:
ALR Digest: Juvenile Delinquents and Dependents § 10
Index and Annotations: Juvenile Courts and Delinquent Children

Practice References:
47 Am Jur 2d, Juvenile Courts and Delinquent and Dependent Children § 63 et seq.

State Legislation:

720 ILCS 5/33D-1

Forms:

15 Am Jur Pl & Pr Forms (Rev), Juvenile Courts and Delinquent and Dependent Children, Form 161

Miscellaneous References:

West's Illinois Digest 2d, Infants § 20

Auto-Cite®: Cases and annotations referred to in this chapter can be further researched through the Auto-Cite® computer-assisted research service. Use Auto-Cite® to check citations for form, parallel references, prior and later history, and annotation references.

§ 51:01.   Definition
§ 51:02.   Sentence

§ 51:01. Definition

The offense of contributing to the delinquency of a juvenile is defined as a person who is 21 years old or older intentionally compelling, soliciting or directing any other person under the age of 17 to commit a felony.[1]

§ 51:02. Sentence

Contributing to the delinquency of a juvenile is a felony under the law.[2] Which class of felony the adult who contributed to the delinquency will be charged with is determined by the felony which the juvenile was compelled to commit.[3] The adult will be charged with a felony one grade higher than that which the

---

1. 720 ILCS 5/33D-1(a).

    Annotation References: Giving, selling, or prescribing dangerous drugs as contributing to the delinquency of a minor, 36 ALR3d 1292.

    Mens rea or guilty intent as necessary element of offense of contributing to delinquency or dependency of minor, 31 ALR3d 848.

    Criminal liability for contributing to delinquency of minor as affected by the fact that minor has not become a delinquent, 18 ALR3d 824.

    Forms: Affidavit, contribution to delinquency of minor. 15 Am Jur Pl & Pr Forms (Rev), Juvenile Courts and Delinquent and Dependent Children, Form 161.

2. 720 ILCS 5/33D-1(b).

3. 720 ILCS 5/33D-1(b).

juvenile committed, except where the offense committed by the juvenile is first degree murder or a Class X felony.[4] In the event the juvenile commits either first degree murder or a Class X felony, the adult will receive the penalty imposed for first degree murder or the Class X felony committed, respectively.[5]

---

4. 720 ILCS 5/33D-1(b).

5. 720 ILCS 5/33D-1(b).

CHAPTER 52

DECEPTIVE PRACTICES AND FALSE PERSONATION

by

Lisa K. Fox, J.D.

and

Robert L. Margolis, Esq.

Scope of Chapter:
    This chapter defines the offenses falling under the deceptive practices umbrella, including, but not limited to, the offenses of deceptive practices, fraud, forgery and false personation.

Treated Elsewhere:
    Charging instruments, see Chapter 9.
    Criminal prosecution, see Chapter 12.
    Defenses, see Chapter 3.
    Drug offenses, see Chapter 57.
    Evidentiary matters, see Chapters 17–19, 21.
    Sentencing, see Chapter 28.
    Venue, see Chapter 13.

Research References:
  Text References:
    Decker, Illinois Criminal Law §§ 11.48 et seq., 14.28 et seq.
  Annotation References:
    ALR Digest: Banks and Banking § 228–230; False Pretenses and Allied Offenses § 1 et seq.; Forgery § 1 et seq.; Fraud and Deceit § 8, 9–16, 24; Larceny § 7; Public Assistance § 30–35
    Index and Annotations: Bad Checks; Banks and Banking; Checks and Drafts; False Pretenses; Forgery; Fraud and Deceit; Impersonation; Odometers

§ 52:01   ILLINOIS JURISPRUDENCE: CRIMINAL LAW

Practice References:

10 Am Jur 2d, Banks §§ 221–269; 32 Am Jur 2d, False Personation § 1 et seq.; 32 Am Jur 2d, False Pretenses § 1 et seq.; 37 Am Jur 2d, Forgery § 1 et seq.; 37 Am Jur 2d, Fraud and Deceit § 1 et seq.; 50 Am Jur 2d, Larceny § 7; 79 Am Jur 2d, Welfare Laws §§ 111–113

5 Am Jur Proof of Facts 363, Fraud

2 Am Jur Trials 171, Investigating Particular Crimes §§ 23–31

Federal Legislation:

18 USCS § 471 et seq.

State Legislation:

5 ILCS 175/1 et seq; 205 ILCS 705/1 et seq.; 720 ILCS 5/17-1 et seq., 5/32-5 et seq.

Miscellaneous References:

West's Illinois Digest 2d, Banks and Banking §§ 60–62; False Personation § 1 et seq.; False Pretenses § 1 et seq.; Forgery § 1 et seq.; Fraud §§ 68, 69; Larceny § 14

Auto-Cite®: Cases and annotations referred to in this chapter can be further researched through the Auto-Cite® computer-assisted research service. Use Auto-Cite® to check citations for form, parallel references, prior and later history, and annotation references.

§ 52:01.   Counterfeiting
§ 52:02.   Deceptive practices—Generally
§ 52:03.   —Deception on financial institutions
§ 52:04.   —Check fraud
§ 52:05.   —Possession of identification card
§ 52:06.   False personation
§ 52:07.   Forgery
§ 52:08.   Fraud
§ 52:09.   —Women, infants and children benefits fraud

§ 52:01. Counterfeiting

Counterfeiting is not specifically provided for under the Illinois statutes, rather the crime of counterfeiting in Illinois is dealt with under federal law.[1]

---

1. 18 § 471 et seq.

Annotation References: Modern status of rule that crime of false pretenses cannot be predicated upon present intention not to comply

§ 52:02. Deceptive practices—Generally

The offense of deceptive practices occurs where a person, acting with the intent to defraud:

- causes another person, through the use of deception or threat, to execute a document which disposes of property or a document which creates a financial obligation;[2] or

- while in the position of officer, manager, or other position which participates in the administration of a financial institution, knowingly receives or permits the receipt of a deposit or other investment, with the knowledge that the institution is insolvent;[3] or

- makes or directs someone else to make a false or deceptive statement in an effort to sell property or services;[4] or

- attempts to buy property or gain control over it, labor or services or attempts to satisfy a tax obligation, by issuing or delivering a check or other payment order on a real or fictitious depository, with the knowledge that the depository will not pay the orde, and it is prima facie evidence of the offender's intent to defraud if there are insufficient funds to cover the check or order when issued, delivered or presented

---

with promise or statement as to future act, 19 ALR4th 959.

Embezzlement, larceny, false pretenses, or allied criminal fraud by a partner, 82 ALR3d 822.

When statute of limitations begins to run against criminal prosecution for embezzlement, fraud, false pretenses, or similar crimes, 77 ALR3d 689.

Criminal liability of corporation for extortion, false pretenses, or similar offenses, 49 ALR3d 820.

Admissibility, in prosecution for obtaining money or property by fraud or false pretenses, of evidence of subsequent payments made by accused to victim, 10 ALR3d 572.

Attempts to commit offenses of larceny by trick, confidence game, false pretenses and the like, 6 ALR3d 241.

2. 720 ILCS 5/17-1(B)(a).

3. 720 ILCS 5/17-1(B)(b).

Annotation References: Bank officer's or employee's misapplication of funds as state criminal offense, 34 ALR4th 547.

4. 720 ILCS 5/17-1(B)(c).

§ 52:02   ILLINOIS JURISPRUDENCE: CRIMINAL LAW

on two separate occasions at least seven days apart;[5]

- issues or delivers a check or other payment order on a real or fictitious depository for an amount greater than $150 to satisfy payment for property, labor or services or to satisfy the entire outstanding amount of a credit obligation for property, labor or services with the knowledge that the depository will not pay and subsequently, does not provide funds to the depository within seven days of receiving notice from the depository or payee of the dishonor of the order.[6]

☞ *Definition:* "Intent to defraud" is defined as acting wilfully and with the specific intent to deceive or cheat another out of something financial or with the specific intent to gain financially for himself or herself. It need not be shown that the victim was actually defrauded or deceived.[7]

☞ *Definition:* "Financial institution" is defined as any bank, savings and loan association, credit union, or other depository of money, or medium of savings and collective investment.[8]

To sustain a conviction for theft by deception, the State must prove the owner was induced to part with money, the transfer of the money was based on deception, the defendant intended to permanently deprive the owner of the money and the defendant acted with specific intent to defraud the owner, and for purposes

---

5. 720 ILCS 5/17-1(B)(d).

   Annotation References: Constitutionality of "bad check" statute, 16 ALR4th 631.
   Application of "bad check" statute with respect to postdated checks, 52 ALR3d 464.
   Reasonable expectation of payment as affecting offense under "worthless check" statutes, 9 ALR3d 719.
   Construction and effect of "bad check" statute with respect to check in payment of pre-existing debt, 59 ALR2d 1159.

6. 720 ILCS 5/17-1(B)(e).

7. 720 ILCS 5/17-1(A)(iii).

8. 720 ILCS 5/17-1(A)(i).

DECEPTIVE PRACTICES AND FALSE PERSONATION § 52:02

of theft by deception, the term "owner" encompasses a person who has "authorized control" over the money, even where that person possesses the money for the benefit of a third party.[9]

> *Illustration:* In one case, where an escrow agreement was established in connection with a house the defendant was building and the defendant obtained money from the escrow agent by presenting falsified lien waivers, the defendant was properly convicted of theft by deception, notwithstanding his contention that the State failed to prove he intended to defraud the escrow agent or deprive the agent of the use and benefit of the money. The fact that the defendant's actions were contrary to the terms of the escrow agreement implied the defendant knew his actions were not entirely above board, so a reasonable trier of fact could have found the defendant acted with the intent to defraud, and the clear evidence that the defendant did not intend to return the funds to the escrow agent warranted the conclusion that he intended to deprive the agent of the funds permanently, despite the agent's right to possess the funds until proper documentation was presented.[10]

A conviction for deceptive practices requires that the defendant had the specific intent to defraud at the time he or she tendered the dishonored check or instrument, and the requisite intent is defined as acting willfully and with the specific intent to deceive or cheat, for the purpose of causing financial loss to another, or to bring some financial gain to oneself, and it is not necessary to establish that any person was actually defrauded or deceived.[11]

Conviction for any of the foregoing acts of deception results in

---

9. People v Moran, 260 Ill App 3d 154, 198 Ill Dec 504, 632 NE2d 1115 (2d Dist 1994); People v Butcher, 257 Ill App 3d 1051, 196 Ill Dec 501, 630 NE2d 198 (2d Dist 1994); People v Lighthall, 175 Ill App 3d 700, 125 Ill Dec 163, 530 NE2d 81 (2d Dist 1988).

Text References: Decker, Illinois Criminal Law § 11.48.

10. People v Moran, 260 Ill App 3d 154, 198 Ill Dec 504, 632 NE2d 1115 (2d Dist 1994).

§ 52:02 ILLINOIS JURISPRUDENCE: CRIMINAL LAW

a Class A misdemeanor.[12] However, if a person is convicted of intending to gain control over property or pay for property, labor or services or a tax obligation with a check or other payment order which that person knows will not be honored by the depository the check or order is drawn on, and the property value for a single transaction or for multiple transactions within a 90-day period exceeds $150 that person is guilty of a Class 4 felony.[13] In the case of multiple transactions within a 90 days period which exceed $150 in total, the charging instrument will allege the transactions as a single charge.[14] Further, a second or subsequent conviction for fraudulently attempting to gain control or pay for property, labor or services or a tax obligation results in a Class 4 felony.[15]

> ☛ *Illustration:* In one case, the indictment was sufficient to charge the defendant with deceptive practices where it charged that when defendant deposited a $21,500 check on a closed account she (1) knew the check would not be honored, (2) intended to defraud the bank, and (3) intended to obtain control over the bank's property.[16]

11. People v Butcher, 257 Ill App 3d 1051, 196 Ill Dec 501, 630 NE2d 198 (2d Dist 1994).

12. 720 ILCS 5/17-1(B).

   See also ch 28.

13. 720 ILCS 5/17-1(B).

   Annotation References: Chronological or procedural sequence of former convictions as affecting enhancement of penalty under habitual offender statutes. 7 ALR5th 263.

   See also ch 28.

14. 720 ILCS 5/17-1(B).

   See also ch 28.

15. 720 ILCS 5/17-1(B).

   See also ch 28.

16. People v Boyd, 292 Ill App 3d 94, 226 Ill Dec 295, 685 NE2d 398 (2d Dist 1997).

DECEPTIVE PRACTICES AND FALSE PERSONATION § 52:03

A defendant charged with deceptive practices based on a bad check is properly charged with a misdemeanor if the check was for $150 or less and a felony if it was for greater than $150.[17]

§ 52:03. —Deception on financial institutions

A person who, with the intent to defraud, makes or causes to be made a false statement which the offender intends for the institution to rely on while attempting to set up an account with a bank or other financial institution is guilty of a Class A misdemeanor.[18]

> *Definition:* "Financial institution" is defined as any bank, savings and loan association, credit union, or other depository of money, or medium of savings and collective investment.[19]

For the purpose of this provision, a false statement may consist of any false information regarding the person's identity, address, or employment or the identity, address or employment of any person, firm or corporation.[20]

> *Illustration:* In one case, the indictment was sufficient to charge the defendant with deceptive practices where it charged that when defendant deposited a $21,500 check on a closed account she (1) knew the check would not be honored, (2) intended to defraud the bank, and (3) intended to obtain control over the bank's property.[21]

---

17. People v Boyd, 292 Ill App 3d 94, 226 Ill Dec 295, 685 NE2d 398 (2d Dist 1997).

18. 720 ILCS 5/17-1(C)(1).

Text References: Decker, Illinois Criminal Law § 11.51.

Annotation References: Chronological or procedural sequence of former convictions as affecting enhancement of penalty under habitual offender statutes. 7 ALR5th 263.

See also ch 28.

19. 720 ILCS 5/17-1(A)(i).

20. 720 ILCS 5/17-1(C)(1).

§ 52:03   ILLINOIS JURISPRUDENCE: CRIMINAL LAW

In the event the property fraudulently obtained from a single transaction or from multiple transactions within a 90-day period values in total more than $150, the offender is guilty of a Class 4 felony.[22]

§ 52:04. —Check fraud

Possession of stolen or fraudulently obtained checks occurs where a person, with the intent to defraud, possesses a check or other order to pay, whether on a real or fictitious account, without the consent of the account holder or the issuing institution.[23]

> *Definition:* "Account holder" is defined as anyone who possesses a checking or savings account at a financial institution.[24]
>
> "Financial institution" is defined as any bank, savings and loan association, credit union, or other depository of money, or medium of savings and collective investment.[25]

A person guilty of possessing stolen or fraudulently obtained checks is guilty of a Class A misdemeanor.[26] However, if a person commits the offense of possessing stolen or fraudulently obtained checks with three or more checks at the same time or consecutively within a 12 month period, that person is guilty of a Class 4 felony.[27]

---

21. State properly alleged elements of a felony; by depositing $21,500 on a closed account into another bank account, the defendant gained control over the funds, notwithstanding that she did not actually withdraw money. People v Boyd, 292 Ill App 3d 94, 226 Ill Dec 295, 685 NE2d 398 (2d Dist 1997).

22. 720 ILCS 5/17-1(C).

23. 720 ILCS 5/17-1(C)(2).

24. 720 ILCS 5/17-1(A)(ii).

25. 720 ILCS 5/17-1(A)(i).

26. 720 ILCS 5/17-1(C)(2).

> **Text References:** Decker, Illinois Criminal Law § 11.51.
>
> See also ch 28.

In the event the property fraudulently obtained from a single transaction or from multiple transactions within a 90 day period values in total more than $150, the offender is guilty of a Class 4 felony.[28]

☛ *Illustration:* In one case, the indictment was sufficient to charge the defendant with deceptive practices where it charged that when defendant deposited a $21,500 check on a closed account she (1) knew the check would not be honored, (2) intended to defraud the bank, and (3) intended to obtain control over the bank's property.[29]

§ 52:05. —Possession of identification card

Anyone who possesses a check imprinter, signature imprinter or "certified" stamp with the intent to defraud and without the consent of the account holder or financial institution is guilty of a Class A misdemeanor.[30]

☛ *Definition:* "Intent to defraud" is defined as acting wilfully, and with the specific intent to deceive or cheat another out of something financial or with the specific intent

---

27. 720 ILCS 5/17-1(C)(2).

See also ch 28.

28. 720 ILCS 5/17-1(C).

Text References: Decker, Illinois Criminal Law § 11.51.

Annotation References: Chronological or procedural sequence of former convictions as affecting enhancement of penalty under habitual offender statutes. 7 ALR5th 263.

See also ch 28.

29. State properly alleged elements of a felony; by depositing $21,500 on a closed account into another bank account, the defendant gained control over the funds, notwithstanding that she did not actually withdraw money. People v Boyd, 292 Ill App 3d 94, 226 Ill Dec 295, 685 NE2d 398 (2d Dist 1997).

30. 720 ILCS 5/17-1(C)(3).

Text References: Decker, Illinois Criminal Law § 11.51.

See also ch 28.

§ 52:05   ILLINOIS JURISPRUDENCE: CRIMINAL LAW

to gain financially himself or herself. It need not be shown that the victim was actually defrauded or deceived.[31]

☞ *Definition:* "Account holder" is defined as anyone who possesses a checking or savings account at a financial institution.[32]

"Financial institution" is defined as any bank, savings and loan association, credit union, or other depository of money, or medium of savings and collective investment.[33]

However, violating this provision within a 12-month period by possessing three or more of the previously described check fraud implements at the same time or consecutively is a Class 4 felony.[34]

In addition, anyone who possesses a check guarantee card or key card or identification card for cash for an automated teller with the intent to defraud and without the consent of the account holder or the issuing institution, is guilty of a Class A misdemeanor, except where that person violates this provision by having three or more cards belonging to different people at the same time or consecutively within a 12-month period, in which case the offender is guilty of a Class 4 felony.[35]

In the event the property fraudulently obtained from a single transaction or from multiple transactions within a 90-day period values in total more than $150, the offender is guilty of a Class 4 felony.[36]

---

31. 720 ILCS 5/17-1(A)(iii).

32. 720 ILCS 5/17-1(A)(ii).

33. 720 ILCS 5/17-1(A)(i).

34. 720 ILCS 5/17-1(C)(3).

See also ch 28.

35. 720 ILCS 5/17-1(C)(4).

Annotation References: Chronological or procedural sequence of former convictions as affecting enhancement of penalty under habitual offender statutes. 7 ALR5th 263.

See also ch 28.

§ 52:06. False personation

False personation occurs where a person falsely represents himself or herself to be someone he or she is not.[37] A person commits the offense of false personation when that person:

- falsely represents himself or herself to be a member of any police, fraternal or veteran's organization;
- falsely represents himself or herself to be a representative of any charitable organization;
- displays or uses a decal, badge or insignia of any police organization without the consent of that organization;[38]
- falsely represents himself or herself to be a veteran in seeking employment or public office, and in this subsection, "veteran" means a person who has served in the Armed Services or Reserved Forces of the United States;[39] or
- uses the words "Chicago police," "Chicago Police Department," "Chicago Patrolman," "Chicago Sergeant," "Chicago Lieutenant," "Chicago Peace Officer" or other such words in the title of any organization, magazine, or other publication without the express consent of the Chicago Police Board.[40]

A person found guilty of any of the foregoing acts is guilty of a Class C misdemeanor,[41] with the exception of impersonating a veteran, which is a Class A misdemeanor.[42]

---

36. 720 ILCS 5/17-1(C).
37. 720 ILCS 5/17-2, 5/32-5 et seq.

    Periodicals: Kehoe, "Jury instructions for fraud cases,"80 Ill BJ 20.

38. 720 ILCS 5/17-2(a).
39. 720 ILCS 5/17-2(a-5).
40. 720 ILCS 5/17-2(b).
41. 720 ILCS 5/17-2(d).

    Text References: Decker, Illinois Criminal Law § 11.52.

    See also ch 28.

§ 52:06   ILLINOIS JURISPRUDENCE: CRIMINAL LAW

Persons soliciting advertising for firefighters', law enforcement and police officers' magazines, journals or other publications must have a current certificate of qualification.[43] The certificate is obtained by presenting proof to the Attorney General that the person requesting the certificate does in fact legitimately represent either the firefighters, law enforcement or police officers.[44] The Attorney General has the power to promulgate rules to govern the issuance of the certificates of qualification to solicit advertisements for the previously described publications.[45] Not having the required certificate is a Class A misdemeanor.[46] After the first conviction, a second or subsequent conviction is a Class 4 felony.[47]

False personation can also occur in other situations.[48] Falsely representing oneself as a licensed attorney, public officer or public employee is a Class B misdemeanor.[49]

> ☛ *Illustration:* In a prosecution for false personation of attorney, judicial, or governmental officials, the state must prove beyond a reasonable doubt that the defendant knew his or her representation was false when made, and in one case, the trial court erred in refusing defendant's request that

---

42. 720 ILCS 5/17-2(d).

See also ch 28.

43. 720 ILCS 5/17-2(c).

44. 720 ILCS 5/17-2(c).

45. 720 ILCS 5/17-2(c).

46. 720 ILCS 5/17-2(d).

See also ch 28.

47. 720 ILCS 5/17-2(d).

See also ch 28.

48. 720 ILCS 5/32-5 et seq.

49. 720 ILCS 5/32-5.

Text References: Decker, Illinois Criminal Law § 14.28.

See also ch 28.

DECEPTIVE PRACTICES AND FALSE PERSONATION § 52:06

the word "knowledge" be inserted into the instruction setting forth the elements of this offense.[50]

In addition, a person who knowingly falsely represents himself or herself as a peace officer is guilty of a Class 4 felony.[51] Further, if a person knowingly falsely represents himself or herself as a peace officer during the commission or attempted commission of a felony, that person is guilty of a Class 3 felony.[52]

> *Practice Guide:* The plain and ordinary meaning of the section unambiguously holds an individual liable for false impersonation of a peace officer of a real or fictitious jurisdiction.[53]

Falsely representing oneself as a parent, legal guardian, or other relative of a minor child to any public official, public employee, or elementary or secondary school employer or administrator commits a Class A misdemeanor.[54]

A person who performs an act which that person is not authorized under the law to perform is also guilty of false personation.[55] For example, a person who knowingly:

- conducts a marriage ceremony; or

---

50. People v Abdul-Mutakabbir, 295 Ill App 3d 558, 229 Ill Dec 767, 692 NE2d 756 (1st Dist 1998).

51. 720 ILCS 5/32-5.1.

See also ch 28.

52. 720 ILCS 5/32-5.2.

Text References: Decker, Illinois Criminal Law § 14.30.

See also ch 28.

53. People v Ellis, 296 Ill App 3d 862, 231 Ill Dec 272, 696 NE2d 1 (1st Dist 1998).

54. 720 ILCS 5/32-5.3.

See also ch 28.

55. 720 ILCS 5/32-6.

Text References: Decker, Illinois Criminal Law § 14.31.

§ 52:06   ILLINOIS JURISPRUDENCE: CRIMINAL LAW

- acknowledges the execution of a document which the law allows to be recorded; or
- becomes a surety for another person in a criminal or civil proceeding

when not authorized by law to do so, is guilty of a Class 4 felony.[56]

§ 52:07. Forgery

Forgery, which is a Class 3 felony,[57] occurs when a person, with the intent to defraud, knowingly:

- executes or changes a document for the purpose of defrauding another in such a way that it appears to have been executed by someone else, or at some other time, or with different provisions, or by someone who did not have the authority to execute or change the document;[58] or
- issues or delivers the altered document with the knowledge that it was altered; or
- possesses the altered document, knowing it to have been altered, with the intent to issue or deliver it; or

---

56. 720 ILCS 5/32-6.

See also ch 28.

57. 720 ILCS 5/17-3(d).

See also ch 28.

Text References: Decker, Illinois Criminal Law § 11.53.

58.

  Annotation References: Falsifying of money order as forgery, 65 ALR3d 1307.
  Procuring signature by fraud or forgery, 11 ALR3d 1074.
  Alteration of figures indicating amount of check, bill, or note, without change in written words, as forgery, 64 ALR2d 1029.
  Admissibility, in forgery prosecution, of other acts of forgery, 34 ALR2d 777.

  Practice References: 2 Am Jur Trials 171, Investigating Particular Crimes §§ 23–31, Forgery.

- unlawfully uses the digital signature, as defined in the Financial Institutions Digital Signature Act, of another or unlawfully uses the signature device of another to create an electronic signature of that other person, as those terms are defined in the Electronic Commerce Security Act.[59]

☛ *Definition:* "Intent to defraud" is defined as the intention to cause another to assume, create, transfer, alter or terminate any right, obligation or power over any person or property. "Document" includes, but is not limited to, any document, representation, or image produced manually, electronically, or by computer.[60]

☛ *Practice Guide:* A document capable of defrauding another includes, but is not limited to, a document by which any right, obligation, or power over a person or property may be created, transferred, altered or terminated. A document includes any record or electronic record as those terms are defined in the Electronic Commerce Security Act.[61]

For an information charging the defendant with forgery-by-delivery to withstand a motion to dismiss, it must allege that the document was apparently capable of defrauding another, that one person made or altered the document so that it was purported to have been made by another, and that the defendant, knowing the document to be so altered delivered the document with the intent to defraud.[62]

---

59. 720 ILCS 5/17-3(a).

See 205 ILCS 705/1 et seq. (Financial Institutins Digital Signature Act); 5 ILCS 175/1 et seq. (Electronic Commerce Security Act).

60. 720 ILCS 5/17-3(b).

61. 720 ILCS 5/17-3(c).

See 5 ILCS 175/1 et seq.

62. People v Smith, 259 Ill App 3d 492, 197 Ill Dec 516, 631 NE2d 738 (4th Dist 1994).

§ 52:07　　ILLINOIS JURISPRUDENCE: CRIMINAL LAW

> ☛ *Illustration:* In one case, although the charging instrument failed to identify the actual victim of the alleged forgery, the information was not deemed fatally defective and the issues instruction on forgery the defendant cited in support of her argument misstated the law in that regard, since the essence of the offense of forgery is the defendant's intent to defraud in the making of the false document rather than any intent directed toward an individual, and the State is not required to prove that a person was defrauded; there any use of language in the charging instrument identifying a victim is mere surplusage.[63]

Intent to defraud may be inferred from the facts and circumstances surrounding the transaction, and if the forged document is delivered, then this intent will be presumed.[64]

It is no longer necessary in a forgery prosecution to attach to the charging instrument a copy of the document in question or set it out in haec verba, but it is permissible to give a description of the document.[65]

Whether a document is apparently capable of defrauding is an element of forgery and is a question for the fact finder.[66] The test of whether a forged instrument is apparently capable of defrauding another is whether a reasonable or ordinary person might be deceived into accepting the document as genuine.[67] An

---

63. People v Smith, 259 Ill App 3d 492, 197 Ill Dec 516, 631 NE2d 738 (4th Dist 1994).

64. People v Carr, 225 Ill App 3d 170, 167 Ill Dec 274, 587 NE2d 543 (1st Dist 1992); People v Whitley, 219 Ill App 3d 917, 162 Ill Dec 459, 579 NE2d 1273 (5th Dist 1991); People v Kunce, 196 Ill App 3d 388, 143 Ill Dec 92, 553 NE2d 799 (3d Dist 1990).

65. People v Rennels, 227 Ill App 3d 263, 169 Ill Dec 250, 591 NE2d 130 (5th Dist 1992).

66. People v Mattingly, 180 Ill App 3d 573, 129 Ill Dec 573, 536 NE2d 257 (4th Dist 1989).

67. People v Turner, 179 Ill App 3d 510, 128 Ill Dec 159, 534 NE2d 179 (2d Dist 1989).

instrument need not be in due legal form or so skillfully prepared that it requires an expert to detect the forgery to be found capable of defrauding another.[68]

In a forgery prosecution, if a handwriting analysis by a bona fide expert would reveal that defendant did not write the note in question, then the trial court commits reversible error in denying defendant the funds for such an analysis.[69]

§ 52:08. Fraud

In Illinois, the offense of fraud is broken down into several specific offenses.[70] The crimes that have their basis in fraud are specific intent crimes, including: deceptive altering or sale of coins,[71] deceptive collections practices,[72] state benefits fraud,[73] promotion of pyramid sales schemes,[74] health care benefits

68. People v Turner, 179 Ill App 3d 510, 128 Ill Dec 159, 534 NE2d 179 (2d Dist 1989).

69. People v Dickerson, 239 Ill App 3d 951, 179 Ill Dec 930, 606 NE2d 762 (4th Dist 1992).

70. 720 ILCS 5/17-4 et seq.

71. 720 ILCS 5/17-4.

Text References: Decker, Illinois Criminal Law § 11.54.

72. 720 ILCS 5/17-5.

Text References: Decker, Illinois Criminal Law § 11.55.

73. 720 ILCS 5/17-6.

Text References: Decker, Illinois Criminal Law § 11.56.

Annotation References: Criminal liability under state laws in connection with application for, or receipt of, public welfare payments, 22 ALR4th 534.
Criminal prosecution or disciplinary action against medical practitioner for fraud in connection with claims under Medicaid, Medicare, or similar welfare program for providing medical services, 50 ALR3d 549.

74. 720 ILCS 5/17-7.

Text References: Decker, Illinois Criminal Law § 11.57.

Annotation References: Validity of pyramid distribution plan, 54 ALR3d 217.

§ 52:08 ILLINOIS JURISPRUDENCE: CRIMINAL LAW

fraud,[75] public aid wire fraud,[76] public aid mail fraud[77] odometer fraud,[78] hour meter fraud,[79] fraudulent advertisement of a corporate name,[80] fraudulent land sales,[81] party to a fraudulent land conveyance,[82] acknowledgment of fraudulent conveyance,[83] fraudulent production of infant,[84] fraudulent issuance of stock,[85] fraudulent signing of stock by an officer,[86] use of words "Pawners' Society" in name,[87] obstrcting gas, wter, and electric current meters,[88] obstructing service meters,[89] and providing false information on an application for employemnt with certain public or private agencies.[90]

---

75. 720 ILCS 5/17-8.

   Text References: Decker, Illinois Criminal Law § 11.58.

76. 720 ILCS 5/17-9.

   Text References: Decker, Illinois Criminal Law § 11.59.

77. 720 ILCS 5/17-10.

   Text References: Decker, Illinois Criminal Law § 11.60.

78. 720 ILCS 5/17-11.

   Text References: Decker, Illinois Criminal Law § 11.61.

   Practice References: 5 Am Jur Proof of Facts 363, Fraud.

   Annotation References: Construction and application of statute making it unlawful to tamper with motor vehicle odometer, 76 ALR3d 981.

79. 720 ILCS 5/17-11.1.
80. 720 ILCS 5/17-12.
81. 720 ILCS 5/17-13.
82. 720 ILCS 5/17-14.
83. 720 ILCS 5/17-15.
84. 720 ILCS 5/17-16.
85. 720 ILCS 5/17-17.
86. 720 ILCS 5/17-18.
87. 720 ILCS 5/17-19.
88. 720 ILCS 5/17-20.
89. 720 ILCS 5/17-21.

☛ *Illustration:* In a prosecution for state benefits fraud, misrepresentation regarding income is not an essential element, and knowing misstatements about one's employment status or financial status are sufficient to support a conviction.[91]

Along with wrongful intent, the elements of fraud include making a false representation of a material fact, knowing or believing it to be false and doing it for the purpose of inducing the other party to act.[92] Whether specific intent to defraud exists is a question of fact which may be established by circumstantial evidence.[93] Proof of this element, however, cannot be based merely on supposition, guess or conjecture.[94] A defendant's failure to perform on a contract is not proof of a specific intent to defraud.[95]

§ 52:09. —Women, infants and children benefits fraud

A person who knowingly (i) uses, acquires, possesses, or transfers Illinois Department of Public Health or Department of Human Services Special Supplemental Food Program for Women, Infants and Children (WIC) food instruments or authorizations to participate in WIC in any manner not authorized by law or the rules of the Illinois Department of Public Health or (ii) alters, uses, acquires, possesses, or transfers altered WIC food instruments or authorizations to participate in

---

90. 720 ILCS 5/17-22.

91. People v Brown, 295 Ill App 3d 128, 229 Ill Dec 406, 691 NE2d 879 (3d Dist 1998).

92. People v Yarbrough, 128 Ill 2d 460, 132 Ill Dec 422, 539 NE2d 1228 (1989).

93. People v Reich, 241 Ill App 3d 666, 182 Ill Dec 700, 610 NE2d 124 (3d Dist 1993).

94. People v Reich, 241 Ill App 3d 666, 182 Ill Dec 700, 610 NE2d 124 (3d Dist 1993).

95. People v Reich, 241 Ill App 3d 666, 182 Ill Dec 700, 610 NE2d 124 (3d Dist 1993).

§ 52:09   ILLINOIS JURISPRUDENCE: CRIMINAL LAW

WIC is guilty of fraud.[96] In addition, any person who possesses for an unlawful purpose another person's identification document issued by the Department of Public Health or the Department of Human Services is guilty of a Class 4 felony.[97] For purposes of this section, "identification document" includes, but is not limited to, an authorization to participate in WIC or a card or other document that identifies a person as being entitled to benefits in WIC.[98]

The penalties for fraud with respect to WIC benefits are as follows:[99]

- if the total amount of money involved in the violatoin, including the monetary value of the WIC food instruments and the value of commodioties, is less than $150, the violationois a Class A misdemeanor;
- the total amount of money involved in the violation, including the monetary value of the WIC food instruments and the value of commodities, is $150 or more but less that $1000, the violation is a Class 4 felony;
- the total amount of money involved in the violation, including the monetary value of the WIC food instruments and the value of commodities, is $1000 or more but less that $5000, the violation is a Class 3 felony;
- the total amount of money involved in the violation, including the monetary value of the WIC food instruments and the value of commodities, is $5000 or more but less that $10, 000, the violation is a Class 2 felony;
- the total amount of money involved in the violation, including the monetary value of the WIC food instruments and the value of commodities, is $10, 000 or more, the violation is a Class 1 felony and the defendant will be

---

96. 720 ILCS 5/17B-5.
97. 720 ILCS 5/17B-15.
98. 720 ILCS 5/17B-15.
99. 720 ILCS 5/17B-20(a).

permanently ineligible to participate in WIC.

A person who commits a felony violation forfeits any moneys, profits, or proceeds the person acquired, in whole or in part, as a result of committing the violation and any property or interest in property that the sentencing court determines the person acquired as a result of committing the violation or the person maintained or used to facilitate the commission of the violation.[1] The person must forfeit any interest in, securities of claim against, or contractual right of any kind that affords the person a source of influence over any enterprise that the person has established, operated, controlled, conducted, or participated in conducting, if it is traceable to any benefit the person has obtained as a result of the felony violation.[2]

---

1. 720 ILCS 5/17B-25.
2. 720 ILCS 5/17B-25.

CHAPTER 53

DISORDERLY CONDUCT

by

Lisa K. Fox, J.D.

and

Robert L. Margolis, Esq.

Scope of Chapter:
This chapter discusses the elements and classes of offense for the situations constituting disorderly conduct. Beyond the offense of disorderly conduct, this chapter also covers the related offenses of interference with emergency communications and unsolicited use of a facsimile machine, their respective elements and classes.

Treated Elsewhere:
Charging instruments, see Chapter 9.
Criminal prosecution, see Chapter 12.
Defenses, see Chapter 3.
Evidentiary matters, see Chapters 17–19, 21.
Sentencing, see Chapter 28.
Venue, see Chapter 13.

Research References:
  Text References:
   Bailey & Rothblatt, Handling Misdemeanor Cases §§ 306–322 (1976)
   Decker, Illinois Criminal Law §§ 15.21 et seq.
  Annotation References:
   ALR Digest: Breach of Peace § 1 et seq.; Disorderly Persons § 1 et seq.; Fire Department § 4 et seq.
   Index and Annotations: Breach of Peace and Disorderly Conduct; Fire Department and Fire Fighters

§ 53:01   ILLINOIS JURISPRUDENCE: CRIMINAL LAW

Practice References:
12 Am Jur 2d, Breach of Peace and Disorderly Conduct §§ 1–17, 28–40

State Legislation:
210 ILCS 45/1-101 et seq.; 225 ILCS 425/1 et seq.; 320 ILCS 15/1 et seq.; 325 ILCS 5/4; 720 ILCS 5/26-1, 26-2, 26-3

Miscellaneous References:
West's Illinois Digest 2d, Breach of the Peace §§ 1–14; Disorderly Conduct § 1 et seq.

Auto-Cite®: Cases and annotations referred to in this chapter can be further researched through the Auto-Cite® computer-assisted research service. Use Auto-Cite® to check citations for form, parallel references, prior and later history, and annotation references.

§ 53:01.   Elements—Generally
§ 53:02.   Interference with emergency communication
§ 53:03.   Unsolicited use of a facsimile machine

§ 53:01. Elements—Generally

Disorderly conduct may occur in any one of twelve situations.[1]

It is a Class C misdemeanor where the perpetrator knowingly and unreasonably alarms or disturbs another person in such a way that a breach of peace results.[2] A Class A misdemeanor

---

1. 720 ILCS 5/26-1.

   Text References: Decker, Illinois Criminal Law § 15.21.

   Periodicals: For article, "Lesser-Included Offenses in Illinois: A Look at Recent Developments," see 85 Ill. B.J. 480 (1997).
   For article, "Recent Decisions: The Hate Crimes Act: Broadening the Scope of Culpability," see 85 Ill. B.J. 564 (1997).

2. 720 ILCS 5/26-1(a)(1), 5/26-1(b).

   See also ch 28.

   Text References: Decker, Illinois Criminal Law §§ 15.21 et seq.

   Annotation References: Insulting words addressed directly to police officer as breach of peace or disorderly conduct, 14 ALR4th 1252.
   Vagueness as invalidating statutes or ordinances dealing with disorderly persons or conduct, 12 ALR3d 1448.

   Practice References: Bailey & Rothblatt, Handling Misdemeanor Cases

results when a perpetrator knowingly makes a false report to the Department of Children and Family Services (DCFS) regarding an abused or neglected child;[3] transmits or causes to be transmitted a false report to any public safety agency without the reasonable grounds necessary to believe that transmitting the report is necessary for the safety and welfare of the public; or calls 911 with the purpose of making a false alarm or complaint and reporting information when, at the time the call is made, the person knows there is no reasonable ground for making the call and further knows the call could result in the emergency response of any public safety agency.[4] However, a subsequent or second charge with respect to any of these Class A misdemeanor offenses is a Class 4 felony.[5]

A Class B misdemeanor charge is the proper charge in three situations: where a perpetrator looks into the dwelling of another for a lewd or unlawful purpose,[6] where a perpetrator makes a false report to the Department of Public Health regarding nursing home care,[7] or where a perpetrator makes a false report of abuse and violence.[8]

§§ 306–322 (1976).

3. 720 ILCS 5/26-1(a)(7), 5/26-1(b).

See 325 ILCS 5/4.

See also ch 28.

4. 720 ILCS 5/26-1(a)(11), (12), 5/26-1(b).

See also ch 28.

5. 720 ILCS 5/26-1(b).

See also ch 28.

6. 720 ILCS 5/26-1(a)(5), 5/26-1(b).

See also ch 28.

7. 720 ILCS 5/26-1(a)(8), 5/26-1(b).

See 210 ILCS 45/1-101 et seq.

See also ch 28.

8. 720 ILCS 5/26-1(a)(10), 5/26-1(b).

There are four instances in which disorderly conduct charges will result in Class 4 felonies.[9] The first is where a person transmits a false fire alarm to a fire department, knowing at the time of the transmission that there is no reasonable grounds for believing that a fire exists.[10] Another situation is where a person falsely transmits to another that a bomb or other explosive device is concealed in such a place that its explosion would endanger human life, knowing at the time of the transmission that there is no reasonable grounds for believing that a bomb or other explosive is in fact concealed.[11] It also is a Class 4 Felony to transmit to any peace officer, public officer or public employee a false report to the effect that an offense will be committed, is being committed, or has been committed, knowing at the time of the transmission that there is no reasonable ground for believing the report.[12] The final Class 4 Felony is to transmit to any police or fire department, or any privately owned and operated ambulance service, a false request for an ambulance, emergency medical technician-ambulance or emergency medical technician-paramedic knowing at the time there is no reasonable ground for believing that the assistance requested is required.[13]

See 320 ILCS 15/1 et seq.

See also ch 28.

9. 720 ILCS 5/26-1(b).

10. 720 ILCS 5/26-1(a)(2).

   Annotation References: Misuse of telephone as minor criminal offense, 97 ALR2d 503.

11. 720 ILCS 5/26-1(a)(3).

   See also ch 28.

   Annotation References: Criminal offense of bomb hoax or making false report as to planting of explosive, 93 ALR2d 304.

12. 720 ILCS 5/26-1(a)(4).

   See also ch 28.

13. 720 ILCS 5/26-1(a)(4).

   See also ch 28.

DISORDERLY CONDUCT § 53:01

The last situation which can result in a disorderly conduct charge is punishable by fine.[14] If a perpetrator knowingly harasses, annoys or intimidates an alleged debtor over the phone in an effort to collect an alleged debt while acting as a collection agency or as an agent of a collection agency, that person is subject to a fine not to exceed $3000.[15]

☞ *Illustration:* In one case, the defendant was properly convicted of disorderly conduct based on an incident in which he urinated while standing approximately 30 feet from a person who was seated in the outdoor eating area of a restaurant, since the statutory definitions of neither public indecency nor obscenity applied under the circumstances, but urination in public, as in the defendant's case, could be done in such an unreasonable manner as to alarm or disturb another and to provoke a breach of peace.[16]

☞ *Illustration:* In another, the petitions and stipulations sufficiently set forth charges of disorderly conduct against respondents by alleging that they displayed certain patently offensive depictions of violence toward African-Americans that disturbed an individual and provoked a breach of the peace.[17]

☞ *Illustration:* In another, defendant knowingly committed an act in an unreasonable manner so as to alarm or disturb another, where two had history of disagreements, defendant

---

14. 720 ILCS 5/26-1(a)(6), 5/26-1(b).

See also ch 28.

15. 720 ILCS 5/26-1(a)(6), 5/26-1(b).

See 225 ILCS 425/1 et seq.

See also ch 28.

16. People v Duncan, 259 Ill App 3d 308, 197 Ill Dec 581, 631 NE2d 803 (4th Dist 1994).

17. People v B.C. (In re B.C.), 176 Ill 2d 536, 223 Ill Dec 919, 680 NE2d 1355 (1997).

§ 53:01　　ILLINOIS JURISPRUDENCE: CRIMINAL LAW

stopped his car in the roadway, thus blocking complainant's passage, and essentially trapping her in her car while he approached her and she testified she was alarmed and disturbed by his actions.[18]

Arguing can be disorderly conduct depending on the circumstances and the argument's tendency to create public disorder.[19] Sexual remarks that an adult might just find annoying may become alarming and disruptive when directed at minors and, thus, may fall within the disorderly conduct statute.[20].

§ 53:02. Interference with emergency communication

Interference with emergency communication is itself an offense, separate from the offense of disorderly conduct, but related to it in kind.[21] A person is guilty of the crime of interfering with emergency communication if that person knowingly, intentionally and without lawful justification interrupts, impedes or in any other way interferes with communication over a band radio, the purpose of which is to inform or inquire about an emergency.[22]

> *Definition:* An emergency, for the purposes of this section is a situation where a person is or is reasonably believed to be by the person transmitting the message in imminent danger of bodily harm or property is in imminent danger of damage or destruction.[23]

---

18. People v Davis, 291 Ill App 3d 552, 225 Ill Dec 597, 683 NE2d 1260 (3d Dist 1997).

19. Biddle v Martin, 992 F2d 673 (CA7 Ill 1993).

20. Where defendant's disruptive conduct consisted of inappropriate or vulgar sexual remarks which included threat to destroy victim's reputation, evidence was sufficient to support a conviction. People v Allen, 288 Ill App 3d 502, 223 Ill Dec 845, 680 NE2d 795 (4th Dist 1997).

21. 720 ILCS 5/26-1, 5/26-2.

See also § 53:01.

Text References: Decker, Illinois Criminal Law § 15.22.

22. 720 ILCS 5/26-2(a).

23. 720 ILCS 5/26-2(b).

Generally, interfering with emergency communication is a Class B misdemeanor, but where serious bodily injury or property damage valued greater than $1000 results, it is a Class A misdemeanor.[24]

§ 53:03. Unsolicited use of a facsimile machine

Any person, public or private corporation, unit of government, partnership or unincorporated association who uses a facsimile machine to send unsolicited material for advertising or fundraising to another person, public or private corporation, unit of government, partnership or unincorporated association is guilty of unsolicited use of a facsimile machine.[25] However, an exception is made for a person sending unsolicited material who reasonably believes that he or she has the recipient's consent on a continuing or case by case basis.[26]

> ☞ *Definition:* A facsimile machine, for the purposes of this offense, is defined as a machine which may send or receive facsimiles of documents through the use of the telephone lines.[27]

The sentence for someone making unlawful use of a facsimile machine is that which is appropriate for someone guilty of a petty offense, that being that the offender will be charged a fine in an amount not greater than $500.[28]

---

24. 720 ILCS 5/26-2(c).

See also ch 28.

25. 720 ILCS 5/26-3.

Text References: Decker, Illinois Criminal Law § 15.23.

26. 720 ILCS 5/26-3(b).

27. 720 ILCS 5/26-3(a)(1).

28. 720 ILCS 5/26-3(c).

CHAPTER 54

DISSEMINATING CONVICTION INFORMATION

by

Lisa K. Fox, J.D.

and

Robert L. Margolis, Esq.

Scope of Chapter:
This chapter discusses what information is made available to the public, how it may be obtained and what the penalties are for disseminating false or inaccurate conviction information.

Treated Elsewhere:
Charging instruments, see Chapter 9.
Criminal prosecution, see Chapter 12.
Defenses, see Chapter 3.
Evidentiary matters, see Chapters 17–19, 21.
Sentencing, see Chapter 28.
Venue, see Chapter 13.

Research References:
  Annotation References:
  ALR Digest: Criminal Law § 224; Records and Recording Laws § 9
  Index and Annotations: Conviction; Records and Recording
  Practice References:
  21A Am Jur 2d, Criminal Law §§ 1020, 1021; 66 Am Jur 2d, Records and Recording Laws §§ 12–30
  State Legislation:
  20 ILCS 2635/1 et seq; 705 ILCS 405/1-1 et seq.; 730 ILCS 5/5-3-4, 110/12. 185/0.01

§ 54:01　　　ILLINOIS JURISPRUDENCE: CRIMINAL LAW

Auto-Cite®: Cases and annotations referred to in this chapter can be further researched through the Auto-Cite® computer-assisted research service. Use Auto-Cite® to check citations for form, parallel references, prior and later history, and annotation references.

§ 54:01.　Generally
§ 54:02.　Dissemination of information
§ 54:03.　Restrictions
§ 54:04.　Procedure
§ 54:05.　Remedies

§ 54:01. Generally

In promulgating the Illinois Uniform Conviction Information Act,[1] the Illinois Legislature ensured public availability of factually correct conviction information and established the means by which the public may obtain that information.[2] The act also defines the means by which a person may seek redress in the event that inaccurate information is being disseminated about them.[3]

The Act applies only to information which is collected and maintained by the Department of State Police pursuant to statutory mandate and does not apply to statistical information.[4] Statistical information is that data which is impossible to verify in terms of accuracy because it does not identify an individual by name.[5]

---

1. 20 ILCS 2635/1.

　Annotation References: Validity, construction, and application of statutory provisions relating to public access to police records, 82 ALR3d 19.

　Periodicals: For comment, "The Sixth Amendment: Protecting Defendants' Rights at the Expense of Child Victims," see 30 J. Marshall L. Rev. 767 (1997).

2. 20 ILCS 2635/1 et seq.

See also §§ 54:04, 54:05.

3. 20 ILCS 2635/1.

See also §§ 54:04, 54:05.

4. 20 ILCS 2635/4(A), 2635/4(B).

To the extent that the Act conflicts with specified provisions regarding conviction information in the Juvenile Court Act,[6] the Unified Code of Corrections,[7] the Probation Officers Act,[8] the Criminal Identification and Investigation Act[9] or the Pretrial Services Act,[10] the specified provisions of those acts govern, unless otherwise indicated.[11]

§ 54:02. Dissemination of information

The Department of State Police (Department) has the duty of maintaining accurate conviction information.[12] This duty includes correcting any errors found through audit, individual review or challenge procedures and updating the records as necessary.[13] In fact, the Department is required to notify a requester if within 30 days of a response to a request a subsequent disposition or modification to the conviction record occurs, unless a longer time period is allowed by law.[14]

Criminal justice agencies have priority in obtaining information regarding convictions.[15]

☞ *Definition:* A criminal justice agency is an agency empowered to administer criminal laws and which allots a significant portion of its budget to that purpose or an agency

---

5. 20 ILCS 2635/3(O).
6. 705 ILCS 405/1-1 et seq.
   See also ch 35.
7. 730 ILCS 5/5-3-4.
8. 730 ILCS 110/12.
9. 20 ILCS 2630/2.1.
10. 725 ILCS 185/0.01 et seq.
11. 20 ILCS 2635/4(B).
12. 20 ILCS 2635/12.
13. 20 ILCS 2635/12.
14. 20 ILCS 2635/12.
15. 20 ILCS 2635/6(A).

§ 54:02   ILLINOIS JURISPRUDENCE: CRIMINAL LAW

which is publicly funded primarily to administer criminal laws and which has been designated by the Department of State Police as a criminal justice agency.[16]

☛ *Definition:* "Request" means the submission to the Department, in the form and manner required, the necessary data elements or fingerprints, or both, to allow the Department to initiate a search of its criminal history record information files.[17]

After accommodating the requests of criminal justice agencies, the Department may furnish requested information to noncriminal justice agencies.[18]

☛ *Definition:* A noncriminal justice agency is a state, federal or local agency which is not designated as a criminal justice agency. It does not include private individuals, corporations or nongovernmental agencies or organizations.[19]

If requests for information from both criminal and noncriminal agencies are satisfied, then public requests will be handled.[20] The requests are handled as expediently as possible, but in any case will be responded to within two weeks of submission of the request, subject to the priority requests from the criminal and noncriminal agencies.[21]

Subsequent dissemination by a requester is permitted for 30 days following the receipt of the conviction information furnished to the requester by the Department, except in the case of exigency or where further dissemination is permitted by law.[22] In the event a requester wants to further disseminate the information beyond

16. 20 ILCS 2635/3(H).
17. 20 ILCS 2635/3(M-5).
18. 20 ILCS 2635/6(A).
19. 20 ILCS 2635/3(M).
20. 20 ILCS 2635/6(A).
21. 20 ILCS 2635/6(B).
22. 20 ILCS 2635/13.

the 30 days immediately following the receipt of the information, the requester must initiate a new request to the Department for current information.[23] As with the initial grant of information, a formal review need not be made in the case of exigency or where not required by law.[24]

§ 54:03. Restrictions

To obtain conviction information, a request must be submitted to the Department of State Police (Department), and maintain on file for at least two years a release signed by the individual to whom the information request pertains.[25] The Department must funish the requester with a copy of its response.[26] Each requester must provide the individual who is the subject of the request with a copy of the Departments' response.[27] The individual who is the subject of the inquiry has seven working days to notify the requester of any inaccuracy in the response.[28]

If the requester is not notified by either the named individual or the Department that the information in the response is inaccurate, regardless of the purpose of the request, the requester is not liable for damages resulting from the use of the inaccurate information if:

- the requester acted in good faith belief that the information was accurate and complete;
- the requester complied with the requirements of obtaining the information; and
- the information identifying the individual about whom the requester wanted information was accurate.[29]

---

23. 20 ILCS 2635/13.
24. 20 ILCS 2635/13.
25. 20 ILCS 2635/7(A)(1).
26. 20 ILCS 2635/7(A)(1).
27. 20 ILCS 2635/7(A)(2).
28. 20 ILCS 2635/7(A)(2).
29. 20 ILCS 2635/7(A)(3), 2635/7(B).

In the event of inaccuracy, the named individual may seek redress under the provisions of the Criminal Identification and Investigation Act.[30] Proceedings challenging a record furnished by the Department take priority over other individual record reviews and challenges filed with the Department.[31]

The Department will not furnish information to anyone if that person has not complied with the requirements of the Illinois Uniform Conviction Information Act.[32] The requester may appeal the Department's refusal to furnish the requested information.[33] To appeal, the requester must submit a written application to the Director of the Department.[34] The Director will then hold a hearing to evaluate whether disseminating the requested information would be in violation of the act or in violation of any other state or federal law regarding conviction information, .[35] If so, the Department will be prohibited from disseminating that information to the requester under the terms and for the time period set by the Director.[36]

§ 54:04. Procedure

The request response from the Department of State Police (Department) will either:

- give the information requested with an explanation as to codes or abbreviations;
- state the reason information cannot be transmitted; or
- explain any deficiencies in the request.[37]

---

30. 20 ILCS 2635/7(A)(4).

    See also 20 ILCS 2630/7.

31. 20 ILCS 2635/7(A)(4).
32. 20 ILCS 2635/1.
33. 20 ILCS 2635/17.
34. 20 ILCS 2635/17.
35. 20 ILCS 2635/17.
36. 20 ILCS 2635/17.
37. 20 ILCS 2635/9(A).

Prior to providing the requested information, however, the Department will update the information and check it for completeness, except:

- in the case of exigency;
- where a criminal justice agency is requesting the information;
- where the information requested is less than 30 days old; or
- where the information is intentionally fabricated based on a written authorization from the Director of the Department in an effort to protect undercover operations.[38]

Where conviction information is requested by anyone other than a criminal justice agency, the Department will keep a record for three years of:

- to whom the information disseminated pertained;
- who requested the information;
- the date of the request;
- the name and address of the private individual, corporation, organization, employer, employment agency, labor organization or noncriminal justice agency requesting the information; and
- the date the information was sent.[39]

☛ *Definition:* A criminal justice agency is an agency empowered to administer criminal laws and which allots a significant portion of its budget to that purpose or an agency which is publicly funded primarily to administer criminal laws and which has been designated by the Department of State Police as a criminal justice agency.[40]

☛ *Definition:* A noncriminal justice agency is a state, federal or local agency which is not designated as a criminal justice

---

38. 20 ILCS 2635/9(B).
39. 20 ILCS 2635/9(B).
40. 20 ILCS 2635/3(H).

agency. It does not include private individuals, corporations or nongovernmental agencies or organizations.[41]

§ 54:05. Remedies

Either the State's Attorney or the Attorney General may bring suit in the circuit court to prevent violations of the statutory provisions governing the dissemination of conviction information.[42] Also, the Department of State Police (Department) may request that the Attorney General bring a suit.[43]

If the violation is caused by a state agency or unit of local government, the aggrieved party has the right to seek legal or equitable remedies in a civil action.[44] The rights of the aggrieved party extend to allow that person to bring suit to compel the Department to correct or disclose information in its records, once administrative remedies have been exhausted.[45] The statute specifies what an aggrieved party is entitled to in terms of civil compensatory damages, costs and attorney's fees.[46]

In terms of criminal penalties, a person is guilty of a Class A misdemeanor where that person intentionally and knowingly:

- requests, obtains, or seeks to obtain conviction information under false pretenses;
- disseminates inaccurate or incomplete conviction information;
- fails to disseminate or make public conviction information where required to by law;
- fails to update or correct a conviction record where necessary for the purpose of causing harm to the person who was the subject of the inquiry; or

---

41. 20 ILCS 2635/3(M).
42. 20 ILCS 2635/14(A).
43. 20 ILCS 2635/14(A).
44. 20 ILCS 2635/14(B).
45. 20 ILCS 2635/14(B).
46. 20 ILCS 2635/16, 2635/18.

- violates any other statutory provision regarding conviction information.[47]

---

47. 20 ILCS 2635/18.

ILLINOIS JURISPRUDENCE

SUPPLEMENT

Issued December 2000

4

CRIMINAL LAW AND PROCEDURE

§§ 30:01-54:05

By the Editorial Staff of the Publisher

LEXIS Publishing™

LEXIS®-NEXIS® · MARTINDALE-HUBBELL®
MATTHEW BENDER® · MICHIE™· SHEPARD'S®

Cite by title and section, e.g.
Illinois Jur, Criminal Law and Procedure § 30:01

This cumulative supplement pamphlet includes material derived from the following sources:

Illinois Reporter
Illinois Appellate Reporter
Northeastern Reporter
Illinois Decisions
Supreme Court Reporter
Federal Reporter
Federal Supplement
Federal Rules Decisions
Bankruptcy Reports
Chicago Kent Law Review
DePaul Business Law Journal
DePaul Law Review
Illinois Bar Journal
John Marshall Journal of Practice and Procedure
John Marshall Law Review
Loyola University of Chicago Law Journal
Northern Illinois University Law Review
Northwestern University Law Review
Southern Illinois University Law Journal
University Chicago Law Review
University Illinois Law Forum
University Illinois Law Review
American Law Reports

© 2000 Matthew Bender & Company, Inc.,

one of the LEXIS Publishing™ Companies.

All rights reserved.

ISBN 0-327-00072-4 (set)

LEXIS, NEXIS, *Shepard's* and Martindale-Hubbell are registered trademarks, LEXIS Publishing and MICHIE are trademarks, and *lexis.com* is a service mark of Reed Elsevier Properties Inc., used under license. Matthew Bender is a registered trademark of Matthew Bender Properties Inc.

6347414

Editorial Offices
2 Park Avenue, New York, NY 10016-5675 (212) 448-2000
201 Mission St., San Francisco, CA 94105-1831 (415) 908-3200
701 East Water Street, Charlottesville, VA 22902-7585 (804)972-7600

www.lexis.com

CRIMINAL LAW AND PROCEDURE

CHAPTER 30

APPELLATE REVIEW

§ 30:07. Interlocutory appeals

Case authorities:

The defendant intelligently and knowingly waived his right to a speedy trial when he moved for a continuance; moreover, where he did not request a continuance to a certain date, all of the time between the motion for continuance and the next trial setting was attributable to him. People v Majors, 308 Ill App 3d 1021, 242 Ill Dec 474, 721 NE2d 753 (4th Dist 1999).

§ 30:10. Right of defendant

Statutes, rules, etc.:

The 1999 amendment of 730 ILCS 5/5-6-3.1 by P.A. 91-127, effective January1, 2000, inserted subdivision (c)(17), which provides that the court may in addition to other reasonable conditions relating to the nature of the offense or the rehabilitation of the defendant as determined for each defendant in the proper discretion of the court require that the person to refrain from operating any motor vehicle not equipped with an ignition interlock device as defined in Section 1-129.1 of the Illinois Vehicle Code. Under this condition the court may allow a defendant who is not self-employed to operate a vehicle owned by the defendant's employer that is not equipped with an ignition interlock device in the course and scope of the defendant's employment

The 1998 amendment of 730 ILCS 5/5-6-3.1 by P.A. 90-784, effective January1, 1999, added subsection (m), which provides that the court shall require a defendant placed on supervision for a violation of Section 3-707 of the Illinois Vehicle Code [625 ILCS 5/3-707] or a similar provision of a local ordinance, as a condition of supervision, to give proof of his or her financial responsibility as defined in Section 7-315 of the Illinois Vehicle Code [625 ILCS 5/7-315]. The proof shall be maintained by the defendant in a manner satisfactory to the Secretary of State for a minimum period of one year after the date the proof is first filed. The Secretary of State shall suspend the driver's license of any person determined by the Secretary to be in violation of this subsection

§ 30:68. Matters not shown by record

Case authorities:

The defendant intelligently and knowingly waived his right to a speedy trial when he moved for a continuance; moreover, where he did not request a continuance to a certain date, all of the time between the motion for continuance and the next trial setting was attributable to him. People v Majors, 308 Ill App 3d 1021, 242 Ill Dec 474, 721 NE2d 753 (4th Dist 1999).

§ 30:69. Pretrial matters

Case authorities:

The defendant intelligently and knowingly waived his right to a speedy trial when he moved for a continuance; moreover, where he did not request a continuance to a certain date, all of the time between the motion for continuance and the next trial setting was attributable to him. People v Majors, 308 Ill App 3d 1021, 242 Ill Dec 474, 721 NE2d 753 (4th Dist 1999).

CHAPTER 32
PARDON AND PAROLE

§ 32:06. Hearings

Case authorities:

The legislature intended the Board to have complete discretion in determining whether to grant parole when the denial of parole is not mandated by the statute. Heidelberg v Illinois Prisoner Review Bd., 163 F3d 1025 (CA7 Ill 1998), cert den 145 L Ed 2d 298, 120 S Ct 382 (US).

§ 32:10. Release and supervision

Statutes, rules, etc.:

The 1999 amendment of 730 ILCS 5/3-14-1 by P.A. 91-506, effective August 13, 1999, inserted the next-to-last sentence in subsection (c), providing that if a person convicted of a felony who is in the custody of the Department of Corrections or on parole or mandatory supervised release informs the Department that he or she has resided, resides, or will reside at an address that is a housing facility owned, managed, operated, or leased by a public housing agency, the department must send written notification of that information to the public housing agency that owns, manages, operates, or leases the housing facility.

§ 32:13. —Revocation proceedings

Case authorities:

A probation revocation hearing is in the nature of a civil proceeding arising in the wake of a previous conviction and sentence of probation, and the violation of previously imposed conditions of probation, not the commission of the culpable offense, must be proved, accordingly, the state's burden of proof is preponderance of the evidence. People v. Williams, 303 Ill. App. 3d 264, 236 Ill. Dec. 602, 707 N.E.2d 729 (4th Dist. 1999).

Compelling defendant to testify as a witness for the state did not deprive him of any due process safeguards due him in a probation violation hearing. People v. Bell, 296 Ill. App. 3d 146, 230 Ill. Dec. 704, 694 N.E.2d 673 (4th Dist. 1998).

Calling defendant as a witness at a probation revocation hearing did not violate the Fifth Amendment of the United States Constitution. People v. Bell, 296 Ill. App. 3d 146, 230 Ill. Dec. 704, 694 N.E.2d 673 (4th Dist. 1998).

§ 32:14. —Eligibility after revocation

Case authorities:

The decision to award meritorious good conduct credit to qualifying prisoners is discretionary and, therefore, is not subject to a writ of mandamus. Helm v Washington, 308 Ill App 3d 255, 241 Ill Dec 871, 720 NE2d 326 (3d Dist 1999).

Good conduct credit cannot be revoked on the basis of a frivolous pleading in a proceeding for a writ of mandamus. Helm v Washington, 308 Ill App 3d 255, 241 Ill Dec 871, 720 NE2d 326 (3d Dist 1999).

A prison inmate serving consecutive sentences for a Class X felony conviction and some other, non-Class X felony is not eligible for enhanced good-time credit against that portion of his sentence attributable to the non-Class X conviction. People v Duke, 305 Ill App 3d 169, 238 Ill Dec 381, 711 NE2d 484 (4th Dist 1999).

§ 32:15. Discharge from parole

Case authorities:

The trial court did not abuse its discretion when it sentenced the defendant to 10 years imprisonment for a drug offense, notwithstanding the defendant's contention that the sentence should be reduced because he showed rehabilitative potential; the defendant's recidivism while on bond in the case weighed against a sentence at the lower end of the 4 to 15 year range for the offense. People v Hunzicker, 308 Ill App 3d 961, 242 Ill Dec 486, 721 NE2d 765 (3d Dist 1999).

CHAPTER 33
EXPUNGEMENT

§ 33:01. Arrest records

Statutes, rules, etc.:

The 1999 amendment of 20 ILCS 2630/5 by P.A. 91-295, effective January 1, 2000, amended the version of this section before amendment by P.A. 90-590, effective until January 1, 2000, by inserting "(as those provisions existed before their deletion by Public Act 89-313)" in the fourth sentence of the second paragraph of subsection (a); and, in subsection (c) substituted "State's Attorney" for "States Attorney"; the 1999 amendment by P.A. 91-295 effective January 1, 2000, amending the version of this section after amendment by P.A. 90-590, effective January 1, 2000, inserted "(as those provisions existed before their deletion by Public Act 89-313)"; added subsection (c-5); and added "Except as otherwise provided in subsection (c-5) of this Section" at the beginning of the first sentence of subsection (g).

The 1999 amendment of 20 ILCS 2630/5 by P.A. 91-357, effective July 29, 1999, made identical amendments to two versions of this section, the version before amendment by P.A. 90-590, effective until January 1, 2000, and the version after amendment by P.A. 90-590, effective January 1, 2000, as follows: in the fourth sentence of the second paragraph of subsection (a) substituted "Section 12-4.3(b)(1)" for "Section 12-4.3b(1)" and added the parenthetical clause; and made stylistic changes.

Case authorities:

The language of subsection (d)(2) of 625 ILCS 5/11-501 precludes the imposition of an extended-term sentence. People v Mathews, 304 Ill App 3d 514, 238 Ill Dec 332, 711 NE2d 435 (5th Dist 1999).

Defendant could be charged as felon in possession of firearm prior to his discharge from probation and subsequent restoration of his civil rights, because defendant was considered convicted of a felony during the period of probation.U.S. v. Lloyd, 184 F.3d 695, 1999 U.S.App. LEXIS 16541 (7th Cir. 1999).

CHAPTER 34
COSTS AND FEES

§ 34:02. Defense counsel's fees

Statutes, rules, etc.:

The 1999 amendment of 725 ILCS 5/113-3, effective January 1, 2000, substituted "2,000,000" for "1,000,000" in subsections (b) and (e); and added subsection (f), which provides that the provisions of this section relating to appointment of counsel, compensation of counsel, and payment of expenses in capital cases apply except when the compensation and expenses are being provided under the Capital Crimes Litigation Act.

Case authorities:

The trial court erred in ordering defendant to reimburse the county $300 for appointed counsel's fees, where the trial court set the fees without holding a hearing on defendant's ability to pay and prior to services being rendered. People v. Exum, 307 Ill. App. 3d 1000, 241 Ill. Dec. 481, 719 N.E.2d 342 (4th Dist. 1999).

The proceedings with regard to reimbursement by the defendant of the cost of his private appointed counsel did not comply with due process standards where, although the defendant was technically on notice that the prosecutor would seek a public defender reimbursement because such a motion was on file, he had no notice that the matter would be taken up during the sentencing hearing and, in fact, the matter was not mentioned at the sentencing hearing until the prosecutor, during his sentencing recommendation, referred to the pending motion. People v. Spotts, 305 Ill. App. 3d 702, 239 Ill. Dec. 341, 713 N.E.2d 1191 (2d Dist. 1999).

Defendant is entitled to a hearing into his financial circumstances before the trial court may properly order him to reimburse the county for the services of a public defender. People v. Jenkins, 303 Ill. App. 3d 854, 237 Ill. Dec. 279, 709 N.E.2d 265 (4th Dist. 1999).

CHAPTER 35
DELINQUENT MINORS

§ 35:02. Rights of parties

Case authorities:

The respondents failed to indicate how they were prejudiced by their trial counsel's failure to obtain verbatim transcripts so as to prove a claim of ineffective assistance of counsel, therefore, it could not be said respondents were deprived of the hearing and appeal guarantees provided under the Act. People v. A.W. (In re W.L.W.), 299 Ill. App. 3d 881, 234 Ill. Dec. 266, 702 N.E.2d 606 (2d Dist. 1998).

When a minor is the ward of a court and under its protection, the juvenile court has the authority to vacate any dispositional order upon a finding that a change in circumstances has occurred warranting such an action. In re DS, 307 Ill App 3d 362, 307 Ill App 362, 717 NE 2d 497, 240 Ill Dec 404 (Ill App Ct 5th Dist 1999).

Periodicals:

For note, "Guardians Ad Litem: The Guardian Angels of Our Children in Domestic Violence Courts," see 30 Loy. U. Chi. L.J. 281 (1999).

§ 35:03. Confidentiality of records

Statutes, rules, etc.:

The 1999 amendment of 705 ILCS 405/1-7 by P.A. 91-368, effective January 1, 2000, substituted "permitted or required under Section 5-805" for "permitted under Section 5-4 or required under Section 5-4" in subsections (A)(3)(a) through (A)(3)(c) and (C); in subsection (B)(1) substituted "Section 5-805" for "Section 5-4"; and in the middle of subsection (G) inserted "or fire department" following "correctional institution" and made related changes.

Case authorities:

The trial court erred in releasing the respondent's juvenile court records to the owner of an apartment complex, which was engaged in a civil action arising from the respondent's murder of a five year old child in a vacant apartment at the complex. People v. J.R. (In re J.R.), 307 Ill. App. 3d 175, 240 Ill. Dec. 375, 717 N.E.2d 468 (1st Dist. 1999).

Once school officials received a report of a student's inebriation through a reciprocal reporting agreement with the police department, even though police violated the student's right to confidentiality under 705 ILCS 405/1-7 by releasing the report, school officials were not precluded from commencing a disciplinary action based on the report. Jordan by Edwards v O'Fallon Twp. High Sch. Dist. No. 203 Bd. of Educ., 302 Ill App 3d 1070, 706 NE 2d 137, 235 Ill. Dec. 877 (Ill App Ct 5th Dist 1999).

Under a reciprocal reporting agreement between a school and a police department, a police report on a student's inebriation was improperly provided to school officials since this report did not pertain to specific offenses referred to in 705 ILCS 405/1-7(A)(8) and the police officers were compelled to guard its confidentiality. Jordan by Edwards v O'Fallon Twp. High Sch. Dist. No. 203 Bd. of Educ., 302 Ill App 3d 1070, 706 NE 2d 137, 235 Ill. Dec. 877 (Ill App Ct 5th Dist 1999).

§ 35:06. Limitations on criminal prosecutions; transfer from Juvenile Courts

Statutes, rules, etc.:

The 1999 amendment of 705 ILCS 405/5-805 by P.A. 91-15, effective January 1, 2000, added subdivision (1)(d); and inserted "(Public Act 90-590)" following "Reform Provisions of 1998" in subdivision (2)(a).

§ 35:07. —Minors prosecuted under criminal law

Statutes, rules, etc.:

The 1999 amendment of 705 ILCS 405/5-130 by P.A. 91-15, effective January 1, 2000, in subsection (1)(a) inserted the language beginning "aggravated battery" and concluding "that the offense was committed," in the first sentence, and added the definitions of "school" and "school related activity" as well as the introductory sentence preceding these definitions.

The 1999 amendment of 705 ILCS 405/5-130 by P.A. 91-673, effective December 22, 1999, in subsection 2(a) substituted "operated or managed" for "operated and managed" and inserted "or leased by a public housing agency as part of a scattered site or mixed-income development" three times following "public housing agency."

§ 35:32

§ 35:32. Orders

Statutes, rules, etc.:

The 1999 amendment of 705 ILCS 405/5-710 by P.A. 91-98, effective January1, 2000, added subdivision (1)(a)(ix) and made a related change.

§ 35:37. Placement with legal custodian

Case authorities:

The court acted properly in conducting a permanency hearing to determine the appropriateness of foster placement and was not deprived of jurisdiction by failure of foster parents to pursue service appeal of transfer notice which had been previously withdrawn once parties had agreed to proceed to the permanency hearing. In re M.V., 303 Ill. App. 3d 190, 236 Ill. Dec. 522, 707 N.E.2d 649 (1st Dist. 1999).

§ 35:39. Commitment of minor

Case authorities:

The failure to provide juvenile with a jury trial did not deprive him of equal protection of the law as guaranteed by the Fourteenth Amendment of the United States Constitution and Article I, section 2 of the Illinois Constitution. People v. G.O. (In re G.O.), 191 Ill.2d 37, 245 Ill.Dec. 269, 727 N.E.2d 1003 (2000).

§ 35:40. —Transfer to Department of Mental Health and Developmental Disabilities

Case authorities:

The 1995 amendment to 730 ILCS 5/3-10-11 did not amount to an ex post facto law because it did not increase the length of the minor's confinement; rather, it simply altered the location of their confinement. People v. J.R. (In re J.R.), 302 Ill. App. 3d 87, 235 Ill. Dec. 236, 704 N.E.2d 809 (1st Dist. 1998).

The 1995 amendment does not serve a punitive purpose. People v. J.R. (In re J.R.), 302 Ill. App. 3d 87, 235 Ill. Dec. 236, 704 N.E.2d 809 (1st Dist. 1998).

The 1995 amendment to 730 ILCS 5/3-10-11 is more properly viewed as a security classification provision, integral to the juvenile detention system, than as an increase in punishment violative of the ex post facto clause. People v. J.R. (In re J.R.), 302 Ill. App. 3d 87, 235 Ill. Dec. 236, 704 N.E.2d 809 (1st Dist. 1998).

§ 35:42. Habitual juvenile offenders

Statutes, rules, etc.:

The 1998 amendment of 705 ILCS 405/5-815 by P.A. 90-590, effective January 1, 1999, renumbered this section which previously had been 705 ILCS405/5-35.

CHAPTER 37
ABDUCTION, KIDNAPPING, AND RELATED OFFENSES

§ 37:01. Kidnapping

Statutes, rules, etc.:

The 1999 amendment of 720 ILCS 5/10-2 by P.A. 91-404, effective January 1, 2000, added language relating to use of a firearm during the offense of kidnapping as aggravated kidnapping, and the sentence for such

Case authorities:

Evidence was sufficient to show that defendant intended to secretly confine the victims where he approached two girls, nine and ten years old, in his car, offered them candy, told them he would take them wherever they wanted to go if they got in the car and, after being rebuffed, continued to prowl the neighborhood fleeing only when approached by the mother of one of the girls. People v. Williams, 295 Ill. App. 3d 663, 230 Ill. Dec. 369, 693 N.E.2d 498 (3d Dist. 1998).

§ 37:02. Aggravated kidnapping

Statutes, rules, etc.:

The 1999 amendment of 720 ILCS 5/33A-1 by P.A. 91-404, effective January 1, 2000, amended the section heading; added subsections (a)(1) through (a)(3); inserted subsections (b)(1) through (b)(3); and inserted the subsection (c),(c)(1), (c)(2) and (c)(3) designations, providing, among other things, that the legislature finds and declares the following: (1) the use of a dangerous weapon in the commission of a felony offense poses a much greater threat to the public health, safety, and general welfare, than when a weapon is not used in the commission of the offense. (2) Further, the use of a firearm greatly facilitates the commission of a criminal offense because of the more lethal nature of a firearm and the greater perceived threat produced in those confronted by a person wielding a firearm. Unlike other dangerous weapons such as knives and clubs, the use of a firearm in the commission of a criminal felony offense significantly escalates the threat and the potential for bodily harm, and the greater range of the firearm increases the potential for harm to more persons. Not only are the victims and bystanders at greater risk when a firearm is used, but also the law enforcement officers whose duty is to confront and apprehend the armed suspect. (3) Current law does contain offenses involving the use or discharge of a gun toward or against a person, such as aggravated battery with a firearm, aggravated discharge of a firearm, and reckless discharge of a firearm; however, the general assembly has legislated greater penalties for the commission of a felony while in possession of a firearm because it deems such acts as more serious. (b)(1) In order to deter the use of firearms in the commission of a felony offense, the general assembly deems it appropriate for a greater penalty to be imposed when a firearm is used or discharged in the commission of an offense than the penalty imposed for using other types of weapons and for the penalty to increase on more serious offenses. (2) With the additional elements of the discharge of a firearm and great bodily harm inflicted by a firearm being added to armed violence and other serious felony offenses, it is the intent of the general assembly to punish those elements more severely during commission of a felony offense than when those elements stand alone as the act of the offender.

The 1999 amendment of 720 ILCS 5/33A-3 by P.A. 91-404, effective January 1, 2000, inserted subsections (b-5) and (b-10) regarding classification and terms of imprisonment for violations of particular statutes with a firearm; and added subsections (c-5) and (d), relating to armed violence.

Case authorities:

Circumstantial evidence was sufficient to establish that the defendant secretly confined a 10 year old boy before killing him where the boy was last seen leaving a boat ramp at about the same time as the defendant and traveling in the same direction as the defendant, the boy was supposed to be riding home but never made it there, his body was found a week later in a shallow grave in another county, two hairs matching the boy's were found in the defendant's car, and the boy's blood was found in the defendant's car's trunk. People v Buss, 187 Ill 2d 144, 240 Ill Dec 520, 718 NE2d 1 (1999).

The elements of the armed violence counts were not identical to the elements of the aggravated criminal sexual abuse counts or the aggravated kidnapping counts, therefore the differences between the sentences did not violate the proportionate penalties clause. People v. Koppa, 184 Ill. 2d 159, 234 Ill. Dec. 479, 703 N.E.2d 91 (1998).

§ 37:02   CRIMINAL LAW AND PROCEDURE

A predicated felony of aggravated kidnapping was enhanced from kidnapping by the aggravated factor of concealment of identity and the weapon factor enhanced aggravated kidnapping to armed violence; therefore there was no improper double enhancement. People v. Koppa, 184 Ill. 2d 159, 234 Ill. Dec. 479, 703 N.E.2d 91 (1998).

The elements of the armed violence counts were not identical to the elements of the aggravated criminal sexual abuse counts or the aggravated kidnapping counts, therefore differences between sentences did not violate the proportionate penalties clause. People v. Koppa, 184 Ill. 2d 159, 234 Ill. Dec. 479, 703 N.E.2d 91 (1998).

Evidence was sufficient to show that defendant intended to secretly confine the victims where he approached two girls, nine and ten years old, in his car, offered them candy, told them he would take them wherever they wanted to go if they got in the car and, after being rebuffed, continued to prowl the neighborhood fleeing only when approached by the mother of one of the girls. People v. Williams, 295 Ill. App. 3d 663, 230 Ill. Dec. 369, 693 N.E.2d 498 (3d Dist. 1998).

Armed violence predicated on the commission of aggravated battery (public way) consists of three principal statutory elements while aggravated battery consists of only two, therefore, the armed violence offenses charged were not identical to the aggravated battery charge and no dismissal based on proportionate penalties was required. People v Espinoza, 184 Ill. 2d 252, 234 Ill. Dec. 372, 702 N.E.2d 1275 (1998).

CHAPTER 38
ABORTION

§ 38:09. Liability for conscientious objections

Case authorities:

Nothing in the Partial-Birth Abortion Act requires parental consent to a partial-birth abortion. Hope Clinic v Ryan, 195 F3d 857 (CA7 Ill 1999).

The Partial-Birth Abortion Ban Act can be applied in a constitutional manner, and whether that occurs depends on the state court which alone can settle questions about its construction. Hope Clinic v Ryan, 195 F3d 857 (CA7 Ill 1999).

CHAPTER 40
ANIMALS

§ 40:02. Animals for use in entertainment

Statutes, rules, etc.:

The 1999 amendment of 510 ILCS 70/16 by P.A. 91-291, effective January 1, 2000, added the last sentence of subsection (e) which provides that any second or subsequent violation of Section 3.02 is a class 4 felony; added the subsection (f) designation; and added subsection (g), which provides that the Department may enjoin a person from a continuing violation of the Humane Care for Animals Act.

CHAPTER 41

ARSON

§ 41:01. Generally

Case authorities:

Where the trial court entered a general finding of guilt as to criminal damage to property, the general finding had the effect of finding the defendant guilty of any of the several acts enumerated in the criminal damage to property statute considered to be lesser included offenses of the aggravated arson charge to which the proof was applicable. People v. Kyles, 303 Ill. App. 3d 338, 236 Ill. Dec. 805, 708 N.E.2d 391 (1st Dist. 1998).

While the information did not charge that the defendant acted without the property owner's consent, as required by subdivisions (1)(a) and (1)(c) of 720 ILCS 5/21-1, that element was implied from the fact that the building and property were state-owned and being used for state purposes. People v. Kyles, 303 Ill. App. 3d 338, 236 Ill. Dec. 805, 708 N.E.2d 391 (1st Dist. 1998).

The evidence did not support a conviction under subdivision (1)(c) of 720 ILCS 5/21-1 since it showed only that the mattress, bedding and paper piled together in the defendant's jail cell, were set afire. People v. Kyles, 303 Ill. App. 3d 338, 236 Ill. Dec. 805, 708 N.E.2d 391 (1st Dist. 1998).

The defendant could not be found guilty of violating subdivision (1)(b) of 720 ILCS 5/21-1 because there was no evidence presented at trial that the defendant acted recklessly when he ignited the mattress in his jail cell, only that he intentionally and knowingly ignited the fire. People v. Kyles, 303 Ill. App. 3d 338, 236 Ill. Dec. 805, 708 N.E.2d 391 (1st Dist. 1998).

CHAPTER 42
ASSAULT AND BATTERY

§ 42:01. Assault

Statutes, rules, etc.:

The 1999 amendment of 720 ILCS 5/12-3.2, effective January 1, 2000, added subsection (c), which provides that for any conviction for domestic battery, if a person under 18 years of age who is the child of the offender or of the victim was present and witnessed the domestic battery of the victim, the defendant is liable for the cost of any counseling required for the child at the discretion of the court in accordance with subsection (b) of section 5-5-6 of the Unified Code of Corrections

The 1999 amendment of 720 ILCS 5/12-3.2, effective October 1, 1999, inserted the second sentence in subsection (b), which provides that domestic battery is a Class 4 felony if the defendant has any prior conviction under this Code for aggravated battery (Section 12-4), stalking (Section 12-7.3), aggravated stalking (Section 12-7.4), unlawful restraint (Section 10-3), or aggravated unlawful restraint (Section 10-3.1), when any of these offenses have been committed against a family or household member as defined in Section 112a-3 of the Code of Criminal Procedure of 1963

Case authorities:

Under the 1996 version of 720 ILCS 5/12-3.2, the use of the word "violation," instead of "conviction," showed that the legislature did not intend that a second conviction of domestic battery was required to enhance a defendant's charge. People v Jones, 306 Ill App 3d 793, 239 Ill Dec 811, 715 NE2d 256 (2d Dist 1999).

§ 42:02. Aggravated assault

Statutes, rules, etc.:

The 1999 amendment of 720 ILCS 5/12-2 by P.A. 91-672, effective January 1, 2000, added subsection (a-5) which states: "A person commits an aggravated assault when he or she knowingly and without lawful justification shines or flashes a laser gunsight or other laser device that is attached or affixed to a firearm, or used in concert with a firearm, so that the laser beam strikes near or in the immediate vicinity of any person."; and in subsection (b) inserted "and as defined in subsection (a-5) of this Section"preceding "is a Class 4 felony."

The 1998 amendment of 720 ILCS 5/12-2 by P.A. 90-651, effective January 1, 1999, incorporated the amendments by P.A. 90-406; and in subdivision (a)(6), substituted "a community policing volunteer" for "a person summoned and directed by him", and inserted "community policing volunteer" twice thereafter.

§ 42:05. —Aggravated battery

Statutes, rules, etc.:

The 1999 amendment of 720 ILCS 5/12-4 by P.A. 91-488, effective January 1, 2000, inserted subsection (d-5), which provides that an inmate of a penal institution who causes or attempts to cause a correctional employee of the penal institution to come into contact with blood, seminal fluid, urine, or feces, by throwing, tossing, or expelling that fluid or material commits aggravated battery. For purposes of this subsection (d-5), "correctional employee" means a person who is employed by a penal institution

The 1999 amendment of 720 ILCS 5/12-4 by P.A. 91-619, effective January 1, 2000, inserted "or hospital emergency room personnel" after "first aid personnel" throughout subsection (b)(7), and made related changes.

The 1999 amendment of 105 ILCS 5/10-21.7 by P.A. 91-491, effective August 13, 1999, added subsection (a) and designated the second paragraph as subsection (b); and in subsection (b), in the first sentence inserted "or other appropriate administrative officer for a private school" and substituted "immediately" for "no later than 24 hours", and added the last sentence.

The 1998 amendment of 720 ILCS 5/12-4 by P.A. 90-651, effective January 1, 1999, incorporated the amendments by P.A. 90-115; and in subdivision (b)(6), substituted "a community policing volunteer" for "a person summoned and directed by a peace officer", and inserted "volunteer"twice thereafter.

Case authorities:

Evidence was sufficient to show great bodily harm where the victim received a gunshot wound, notwithstanding the fact that she did not immediately feel pain, she was not hospitalized, and her only medical treatment was a gauze pad which she wore for one day, where the bullet went through her leg, she later felt significant pain, and she retained a scar from the incident. People v. Edwards, 304 Ill. App. 3d 250, 237 Ill. Dec. 877, 710 N.E.2d 507 (2d Dist. 1999).

ASSAULT AND BATTERY § 42:06

The indictment did not actually charge the defendant with armed violence based on aggravated battery with a deadly weapon where the indictment nowhere referred to subdivision (b)(1) of 720 ILCS 5/12-4 and the phrase "armed with a dangerous weapon" merely tracked the armed violence statute itself. People v. Dean, 303 Ill. App. 3d 758, 237 Ill. Dec. 298, 709 N.E.2d 284 (2d Dist. 1999).

The offense of aggravated battery is a lesser included offense of aggravated battery of a senior citizen. People v. Lee, 303 Ill. App. 3d 356, 236 Ill. Dec. 871, 708 N.E.2d 457 (1st Dist. 1999).

While the defendant presented evidence of possible brutality at the hands of correctional officers, that evidence did not vitiate the testimony at trial that the defendant committed aggravated battery upon two correctional officers during a jail cell altercation. People v. Kyles, 303 Ill. App. 3d 338, 236 Ill. Dec. 805, 708 N.E.2d 391 (1st Dist. 1998).

There was sufficient evidence to establish defendant's convictions for aggravated battery based on the accountability theory where the course of events that culminated in the wounding of the two children began when the car entered the territory over which defendant and his gang claimed suzerainty and were present and defendant fired on the car believing it carried rival gang members. People v. Jones, 302 Ill. App. 3d 892, 236 Ill. Dec. 347, 707 N.E.2d 192 (1st Dist. 1998).

Where the defendant was charged with aggravated battery based on great bodily harm, and armed violence with a category III weapon based on aggravated battery causing great bodily harm and murder, the aggravated battery charge was a lesser included offense of the armed violence charge and was vacated since the elements of the aggravated battery served as a predicate felony for armed violence. People v. Moore, 301 Ill. App. 3d 728, 234 Ill. Dec. 922, 704 N.E.2d 80 (3d Dist. 1998).

Given the substantial factors in aggravation, including the defendant's prior failed attempt at rehabilitation through probation, and the lack of mitigating factors, a mid range sentence of five years for aggravated battery of a police officer was well within the discretion of the trial court. People v Jones, 299 Ill App 3d 739, 234 Ill Dec 330, 702 NE2d 984 (3d Dist 1998).

Because the outcome of the case depended upon the jury's credibility determinations, and because the introduction of inadmissible evidence of defendant's prior unrelated battery arrests undermined his credibility, there was reasonable probability this error affected the outcome of the trial so a new trial was warranted. People v. Valentine, 299 Ill. App. 3d 1, 233 Ill. Dec. 172, 700 N.E.2d 700 (1st Dist. 1998).

Even if one assumes that defense counsel's actions were well intentioned trial tactics, the admission of prior arrests for battery in aggravated battery trial was unduly prejudicial. People v. Valentine, 299 Ill. App. 3d 1, 233 Ill. Dec. 172, 700 N.E.2d 700 (1st Dist. 1998).

A fifteen-year sentence for aggravated battery was vacated as beyond the permissible range for a Class 3 felony. People v. Curry, 296 Ill. App. 3d 559, 230 Ill. Dec. 661, 694 N.E.2d 630 (1st Dist. 1998).

The defendant's offenses of aggravated battery and unlawful possession of a weapon by a person in the custody of the Department of Corrections were separate and distinct for purposes of imposing an extended term sentence for the conviction of aggravated battery. People v. Keene, 296 Ill. App. 3d 183, 230 Ill. Dec. 522, 693 N.E.2d 1273 (4th Dist. 1998).

Armed violence predicated on the commission of aggravated battery (public way) consists of three principal statutory elements while aggravated battery consists of only two, therefore, armed violence offenses charged were not identical to the aggravated battery charge and no dismissal based on proportionate penalties was required. People v Espinoza, 184 Ill 2d 252, 234 Ill Dec 372, 702 NE 2d 1275 (1998).

§ 42:06. ——With firearm

Statutes, rules, etc.:

The 1999 amendment of 720 ILCS 5/12-4.2 by P.A. 91-434, effective January 1, 2000, added item (4) in subsection (a) and made related changes.

The 1998 amendment of 720 ILCS 5/12-4.2 by P.A. 90-651, effective January 1, 1999, in subsection (a), substituted "a community policing volunteer" for "a person summoned by a peace officer", and inserted "volunteer"- three times thereafter.

Case authorities:

It was plain error for the trial court to admit a gun found in the defendant's nightstand as no proper evidentiary foundation was laid. People v. Jackson, 299 Ill. App. 3d 323, 234 Ill. Dec. 250, 702 N.E.2d 590 (5th Dist. 1998).

The court declined to find the legislature's determination that a greater penalty should be imposed for armed violence with a category I weapon than for aggravated battery with a firearm was so disproportionate as to shock the moral sense of the community. People v. Shields, 298 Ill. App. 3d 943, 233 Ill. Dec. 67, 700 N.E.2d 168 (1st Dist. 1998).

Eyewitness testimony was more than sufficient to uphold defendant's conviction even though there was no physical evidence to corroborate the eyewitness identifications.

§ 42:06 CRIMINAL LAW AND PROCEDURE

People v. Negron, 297 Ill. App. 3d 519, 231 Ill. Dec. 775, 697 N.E.2d 329 (1st Dist. 1998).

Jury verdicts of not guilty of aggravated battery with a firearm and guilty of second degree murder were not legally inconsistent. People v. Luckett, 295 Ill. App. 3d 342, 230 Ill. Dec. 179, 692 N.E.2d 1345 (3d Dist. 1998).

§ 42:07. ———Of child
Statutes, rules, etc.:

The 1999 amendment of 720 ILCS 5/12-4.3 by P.A. 91-404, effective January 1, 2000, added the subsection (b) designation; and added subsections (b)(1), (b)(2), and (b)(3).

Case authorities:

Evidence was sufficient to support a conviction for aggravated battery of a four month old child where (1) the child sustained fatal injuries when she was alone with the defendant, (2) her injuries were consistent with shaken baby syndrome and shaken baby impact syndrome, (3) her injuries were inconsistent with a fall from five feet onto a carpeted floor, and (4) shaking and failed CPR attempts could not have caused the extensive retinal hemorrhaging detected in her eye tissue. People v. Lind, 307 Ill. App. 3d 727, 240 Ill. Dec. 835, 718 N.E.2d 316 (4th Dist. 1999).

§ 42:09. ———Of senior citizen
Case authorities:

The offense of aggravated battery is a lesser included offense of aggravated battery of a senior citizen. People v. Lee, 303 Ill. App. 3d 356, 236 Ill. Dec. 871, 708 N.E.2d 457 (1st Dist. 1999).

CHAPTER 43
AUTOMOBILES AND OTHER VEHICLES

§ 43:02. Driving under influence

Statutes, rules, etc.:

The 1999 amendment of 720 ILCS 5/9-3 by P.A. 91-122, effective January 1, 2000, inserted "except as otherwise provided in subsection (e-5)" in the first sentence of subsection (e); and inserted subsection (e-5), which provides that in cases involving reckless homicide in which the defendant was determined to have been under the influence of alcohol or any other drug or drugs as an element of the offense, or in cases in which the defendant is proven beyond a reasonable doubt to have been under the influence of alcohol or any other drug or drugs, if the defendant kills 2 or more individuals as part of a single course of conduct, the penalty is a Class 2 felony, for which a person, if sentenced to a term of imprisonment, shall be sentenced to a term of not less than 6 years and not more than 28 years

The 1998 amendment of 625 ILCS 5/11-501.2 by P.A. 90-779, effective January 1, 1999, in subsection (a) substituted "or drugs, or intoxicating compound or compounds, or any combination" and "or combination"; in subdivision (c)1. substituted "drug or drugs, or intoxicating compound or compounds, or any combination thereof" for "drugs, or combination of both"; and in subdivision (c)2. substituted "other drug or drugs, or intoxicating compound or compounds, or any combination thereof" for "any other drug or combination of both".

The 1998 amendment of 625 ILCS 5/11-501 by P.A. 90-611, effective January 1, 1999, incorporated the amendments by P.A. 90-43 and P.A. 90-400; and in subsection (i), in the first sentence, substituted "may use" for "shall establish a pilot program to test the effectiveness of", substituted "when granting driving relief to" for "upon", and inserted "or a similar provision of a local ordinance"; and in the second sentence, deleted "population and" preceding "procedures."

The 1998 amendment of 625 ILCS 5/11-501 by P.A. 90-738, effective January 1, 1999, rewrote subsection (c-1).

The 1998 amendment of 625 ILCS 5/11-501 by P.A. 90-779, effective January 1, 1999, in the section heading substituted "or drugs, intoxicating compound or compounds or any combination thereof" for ", or combination of both"; added present subdivision (a)(3) and redesignated former subdivisions (a)(3) through (5) as present subdivisions (a)(4) through (6); in subdivision (a)(5) substituted ", other drug or drugs, or intoxicating compound or compounds" for "and any other drug or drugs"; in subdivision (a)(6) added "breath" and ", or an intoxicating compound listed in the Use of Intoxicating Compounds Act"; in subsection (b) substituted "other drug or drugs, or intoxicating compound or compounds, or any combination thereof" for "or other drugs, or any combination of both"; in the introductory paragraph of subdivision (d)(1) substituted ", other drug or drugs, or intoxicating compound or compounds, or any combination thereof" for "or drugs or a combination of both"; in subdivision (d)(1)(D) substituted ", other drug or drugs, or intoxicating compound or compounds" for "or any other drug or drugs"; in subdivision (d)(2) substituted ", other drug or drugs, or intoxicating compound or compounds, or any combination thereof" for "or drugs or a combination of both"; and in subsection (e) substituted ",drug, or intoxicating compound" for "or other drug."

The 1999 amendment of 625 ILCS 5/11-501 by P.A. 91-126, effective July 16,1999, added subsection (j).

Case authorities:

Subsection (d)(1)(C) of 625 ILCS 5/11-501 is intended only to enhance the misdemeanor offense of driving under the influence of alcohol to a felony if that offense resulted in an accident causing great bodily harm or permanent disability or disfigurement to another, regardless of the number of individuals injured; the occurrence of injuries to more than one person other than the offender does not transform a single act of driving under the influence of alcohol into a separate felony for each additional person injured. People v. Lavallier, 187 Ill. 2d 464, 241 Ill. Dec. 529, 719 N.E.2d 658 (1999).

A deputy was authorized to travel to an adjoining state where the defendant was receiving medical services to obtain the defendant's blood sample. People v. Every, 184 Ill. 2d 281, 234 Ill. Dec. 797, 703 N.E.2d 897 (1998).

Once a motorist has established a prima facie case at a rescission hearing and the burden has shifted to the state on the issue of the reliability of a blood test result, the state must lay a foundation for introducing into evidence

§ 43:02 CRIMINAL LAW AND PROCEDURE

the blood test results by complying with the admissibility requirements under subsection (a)(1) of 625 ILCS 5/11-501.2 and thereby demonstrate that the chemical analysis of the blood was performed according to standards promulgated by the Department of Public Health. People v. Massie, 305 Ill. App. 3d 550, 238 Ill. Dec. 864, 713 N.E.2d 110 (1st Dist. 1999).

Where the chemical test used is a physician-ordered blood test, the evidentiary foundation requirements of subsection (a)(1) of 625 ILCS 5/11-501.2 apply in a civil rescission hearing. People v. Massie, 305 Ill. App. 3d 550, 238 Ill. Dec. 864, 713 N.E.2d 110 (1st Dist. 1999).

625 ILCS 5/11-501.8 (the zero tolerance statute) does not provide for the issuance of a JDP to a 17-year-old defendant who has a BAC greater than 0.00. People v. Delcorse, 305 Ill. App. 3d 76, 238 Ill. Dec. 556, 711 N.E.2d 1217 (2d Dist. 1999).

Defendant's conviction for aggravated DUI had to be vacated as a lesser included offense of reckless homicide also charged where both convictions were based on the same acts. People v. Latto, 304 Ill. App. 3d 791, 237 Ill. Dec. 649, 710 N.E.2d 72 (1st Dist. 1999).

Where two officer's at the scene smelled a strong odor of alcohol emanating from the defendant and witnessed the defendant in an excited state, even though a nurse and a paramedic did not notice an odor of alcohol and the defendant successfully completed sobriety tests four hours after the accident, the evidence of the defendant's physical condition was sufficient to support a finding of guilt on the charge of aggravated DUI. People v. Latto, 304 Ill. App. 3d 791, 237 Ill. Dec. 649, 710 N.E.2d 72 (1st Dist. 1999).

Defendant's conviction for aggravated DUI had to be vacated as a lesser included offense of reckless homicide also charged where both convictions were based on the same acts. People v. Latto, 304 Ill. App. 3d 791, 237 Ill. Dec. 649, 710 N.E.2d 72 (1st Dist. 1999).

The language of subsection (d)(2) of 625 ILCS 5/11-501 precludes the imposition of an extended-term sentence. People v Mathews, 304 Ill App 3d 514, 238 Ill Dec 332, 711 NE2d 435 (5th Dist 1999).

Where officer testified that upon asking defendant for his driver's license and insurance card, he smelled a strong odor of alcohol emanating from the car, the defendant's eyes were bloodshot and glossy and his speech was slurred, such observations at the time of the traffic stop were necessary to put the DUI investigation into a proper context and exclusion of the evidence was an abuse of discretion. Village of Plainfield v. Anderson, 304 Ill. App. 3d 338, 237 Ill. Dec. 507, 709 N.E.2d 976 (3d Dist. 1999).

Based on officer's observation that there was a strong odor of alcohol emanating from the car, defendant's eyes were bloodshot and glossy and his speech was slurred, a limited detention to ascertain whether the defendant was under the influence of alcohol was reasonable. Village of Plainfield v. Anderson, 304 Ill. App. 3d 338, 237 Ill. Dec. 507, 709 N.E.2d 976 (3d Dist. 1999).

A rational jury could have found the defendant guilty beyond a reasonable doubt where the defendant was driving a vehicle, the defendant made statements he was on Tylenol 3 with codeine, the officer testified to the defendant's erratic driving and his lack of balance and his inability to pass the field sobriety test. People v. Shelton, 303 Ill. App. 3d 915, 237 Ill. Dec. 12, 708 N.E.2d 815 (5th Dist. 1999).

Officer's experience in transporting people who had overdosed on drugs and limited training indicating that narcotic users are a little more confused than those under the influence of alcohol did not provide a sufficient foundation to qualify the officer to render an opinion that the defendant's off balance, moody, agitated, and talkative behavior indicated that he was under the influence of drugs and the defendant was denied a fair trial. People v. Shelton, 303 Ill. App. 3d 915, 237 Ill. Dec. 12, 708 N.E.2d 815 (5th Dist. 1999)

Subdivision (c)(2) of 625 ILCS 5/11-501.2 authorizes involuntary blood tests. People v. Ruppel, 303 Ill. App. 3d 885, 237 Ill. Dec. 21, 708 N.E.2d 824 (4th Dist. 1999).

Blood test was authorized under subdivision (c)(2) of 625 ILCS 5/11-501.2 where the police officer had probable cause to believe the defendant was DUI at the time of the accident and the defendant's driving caused personal injury. People v. Ruppel, 303 Ill. App. 3d 885, 237 Ill. Dec. 21, 708 N.E.2d 824 (4th Dist. 1999).

Where a breathalyzer machine tests a certified controlled reference sample and the result is .09, .10, or .11, the machine may be considered accurate within 0.01% as required by the relevant regulation and may be properly certified. People v. Morris, 301 Ill. App. 3d 603, 234 Ill. Dec. 823, 703 N.E.2d 923 (5th Dist. 1998).

The police had reasonable grounds to believe defendant was driving under the influence of alcohol: 1) defendant fell against vehicle when exiting, 2) had a runny nose and watery, glassy and bloodshot eyes, 3) strong odor of alcohol and 4) failed field sobriety test. People v. Fortney, 297 Ill. App. 3d 79, 231 Ill. Dec. 720, 697 N.E.2d 1 (2d Dist. 1998).

Defendant failed to present a prima facie case where her case was based on an inaccurate breathalyzer test and on her own testimony which was equivocal, where the trial court did

AUTOMOBILES AND OTHER VEHICLES § 43:03

not find defendant's testimony credible. People v. Fortney, 297 Ill. App. 3d 79, 231 Ill. Dec. 720, 697 N.E.2d 1 (2d Dist. 1998).

Officer was authorized under subdivision (c)(2) of 625 ILCS 5/11-501.2 to order the blood test, providing he had probable cause to believe the plaintiff was under the influence of alcohol, even if the plaintiff did not consent. Ruppel v. Ramseyer, 33 F. Supp. 2d 720 (C.D. Ill. 1999).

Plaintiff could not hold the defendants, who were hospital employees, liable for forcing her to submit to an unwanted medical procedure where they were ordered by a law enforcement officer to withdraw blood from plaintiff after the plaintiff was involved in an accident and was arrested for DUI. Ruppel v. Ramseyer, 33 F. Supp. 2d 720 (C.D. Ill. 1999).

§ 43:03. Suspension of driving licenses and privileges

Statutes, rules, etc.:

The 1998 amendment of 625 ILCS 5/6-205, effective January 1, 1999, added subsection (h), which provides that the Secretary of State may use ignition interlock device requirements when granting driving relief to individuals who have been arrested for a second or subsequent offense under Section 11-501 of this Code [625 ILCS 5/11-501] or a similar provision of a local ordinance. The Secretary shall establish by rule and regulation the procedures for use of the interlock system..

The 1998 amendment of 625 ILCS 5/6-205, effective January 1, 1999, in subdivision (a)2., inserted "or drugs, intoxicating compound or compounds" and substituted "or any combination thereof" for "or combination of both".

The 1998 amendment of 625 ILCS 5/6-208 by P.A. 90-738, effective January 1, 1999, in subsection (b)1. substituted "subparagraphs 2, 3, and 4," for "subparagraphs 2 and 3,", in subsection (b)3. inserted "except as provided in subparagraph 4," and added subsection (b)4.

The 1999 amendment of 625 ILCS 5/6-208 by P.A. 91-357, effective July 29, 1999, inserted the item designations (i) and (ii) in subsection (b); inserted "as provided in the following subparagraphs" in subsection (b)(ii); inserted "the person may make application for a license" in subsection (b)(ii)(1); inserted the subsection designations (b)(ii)(2)(A) through (D); and made stylistic changes.

The 1998 amendment of 625 ILCS 5/6-208.1 by P.A. 90-738, effective January 1, 1999, in subsection (a)3. substituted "Three years" for "Two years" at the beginning; and in subsection (g) substituted "may issue a restricted driving permit if at least 2 years have elapsed since the effective date of the statutory summary suspension" for "shall not issue a restricted driving permit."

The 1998 amendment of 625 ILCS 5/6-208.1 by P.A. 90-779, effective January 1, 1999, added ", or intoxicating compound" and made minor stylistic changes throughout the section; in subdivision (a)2., added "intoxicating" and "breath"; and in subdivisions (a)2. and (a)4. added "or an intoxicating compound listed in the Use of Intoxicating Compounds Act."

The 1999 amendment of 625 ILCS 5/6-208.1 by P.A. 91-357, effective July 29, 1999, incorporated the amendments by P.A. 90-738 and P.A. 90-779.

The 1998 amendment of 625 ILCS 5/6-205 by P.A. 90-590, effective January 1, 1999, incorporated the amendment by P.A. 90-369; and substituted "Section 5-901" for "Section 1-8" in subdivision (b)1.

The 1998 amendment of 625 ILCS 5/6-205 by P.A. 90-779, effective January 1, 1999, in subdivision (a)2., inserted "or drugs, intoxicating compound or compounds" and substituted "or any combination thereof" for "or combination of both."

The 1998 amendment of 625 ILCS 5/6-303 by P.A. 90-738, effective January 1, 1999, in subsection (d) deleted the last sentence which read: "For any prosecution under this Section, a certified copy of the driving abstract of the defendant shall be admitted as proof of any prior conviction." and added it as subsection (f).

The 1999 amendment of 625 ILCS 5/11-501.8 by P.A. 91-357, effective July 29, 1999, substituted "and" for "or" at the end of subsections (e)(4) and (e)(6).

Case authorities:

Summary suspension does not automatically terminate at the provisional reinstatement date but continues until the holder of the suspended license pays the reinstatement fees. People v. Martinez, 184 Ill. 2d 547, 235 Ill. Dec. 452, 705 N.E.2d 65 (1998).

Defendant's failure to pay her reinstatement fees did not extend her period of suspension; therefore, the defendant may have been driving without a valid driver's license but defendant was not driving while her license was suspended as the suspension period had passed. People v. Martinez, 184 Ill. 2d 547, 235 Ill. Dec. 452, 705 N.E.2d 65 (1998).

If the legislature had intended that the failure to pay reinstatement fees should effectively extend the period of suspension, the legislature could have so stated. People v. Martinez, 184 Ill. 2d 547, 235 Ill. Dec. 452, 705 N.E.2d 65 (1998).

Subdivision (a)(3) of 625 ILCS 5/6-208.1 and subsection (g) do not violate the substantive due process rights as the two year

§ 43:03 CRIMINAL LAW AND PROCEDURE

suspension with no hardship relief provides arrested drivers with an incentive to submit to testing which is rationally related to the goal of promoting highway safety. People v. Fisher, 184 Ill. 2d 441, 235 Ill. Dec. 454, 705 N.E.2d 67 (1998).

The possibility of a 14 day delay between the effective date of the suspension and the date of the hearing does not render the statutory summary suspension scheme unconstitutional. People v. Fisher, 184 Ill. 2d 441, 235 Ill. Dec. 454, 705 N.E.2d 67 (1998).

The civil penalties for a refusal to submit to a chemical test are not admissible as evidence of guilt in a prosecution for driving while intoxicated. City of Rockford v Elliott, 308 Ill App 3d 735, 242 Ill Dec 436, 721 NE2d 715 (2d Dist 1999).

The defendant failed to establish a prima facie case entitling him to a rescission of the statutory summary suspension of his driver's license since, among other evidence (1) an officer observed the defendant's car parked along a road at 3 A.M., (2) the defendant appeared unconscious in the driver's seat, and the officer could not tell if he was dead or alive, (3) at the officer's request, the defendant rolled down the window, at which time the officer detected a strong smell of alcohol, and (4) the officer arrested the defendant after determining that he was intoxicated. People v. Carlson, 307 Ill. App. 3d 77, 240 Ill. Dec. 302, 716 N.E.2d 1249 (3d Dist. 1999).

The state may prove that a defendant's license was revoked from facts other than a driving abstract; thus, the defendant's admission that he was guilty of the elements of the offense, which was inherent in his defense of necessity, was sufficient to show that his license had been revoked. People v Carter, 306 Ill App 3d 867, 240 Ill Dec 139, 715 NE2d 1196 (4th Dist 1999), app gr 186 Ill 2d 573, 243 Ill Dec 563, 723 NE2d 1164.

The language of subsection (d)(2) of 625 ILCS 5/11-501 precludes the imposition of an extended-term sentence. People v Mathews, 304 Ill App 3d 514, 238 Ill Dec 332, 711 NE2d 435 (5th Dist 1999).

The trial court's order rescinding defendant's statutory summary suspension was against the manifest weight of the evidence; his blood alcohol concentration was found to be .11, his driving was erratic, he failed several field sobriety tests, he had glassy eyes, he had slurred speech and a strong odor of alcohol. People v. Thill, 297 Ill. App. 3d 7, 231 Ill. Dec. 604, 696 N.E.2d 1175 (2d Dist. 1998).

An all-terrain vehicle was a motor vehicle as contemplated by this subsection of 625 ILCS 5/6-303 for purposes of determining whether the defendant could be convicted of driving a motor vehicle while his license was suspended.

People v. Martinez, 184 Ill. 2d 547, 235 Ill. Dec. 452, 705 N.E.2d 65 (1998).

A summary suspension does not terminate until the license holder pays the reinstatement fee. People v Martinez,184 Ill. 2d 547, 235 Ill. Dec. 452, 705 N.E.2d 65 (1998).

§ 43:04. Anti-theft laws—Felonious utilization of vehicles and their parts

Statutes, rules, etc.:

The 1999 amendment of 625 ILCS 5/4-103 by P.A. 91-450, effective January 1, 2000, added the language providing that is a violation for a person to knowingly make a false report of the theft or conversion of a vehicle to any employee of a law enforcement agency of this state designated by the law enforcement agency to take, receive, process, or record reports of vehicle theft or conversion take, receive, process, or record reports of vehicle theft or conversion

Case authorities:

The prosecution of the defendant for a Class 2 felony for falsely reporting a vehicle theft did not violate the due process clause where the defendant falsely reported that her former husband had stolen her car and later told the police that her report was false. People v. Fuller, 187 Ill. 2d 1, 239 Ill. Dec. 582, 714 N.E.2d 501 (1999).

The imposition of a penalty of a Class 2 felony for falsely reporting a vehicle theft was not disproportionate where the defendant falsely reported that her former husband had stolen her car and later told the police that her report was false. People v. Fuller, 187 Ill. 2d 1, 239 Ill. Dec. 582, 714 N.E.2d 501 (1999).

The trial court did not abuse its discretion when it sentenced the defendant to 10 years imprisonment for a drug offense, notwithstanding the defendant's contention that the sentence should be reduced because he showed rehabilitative potential; the defendant's recidivism while on bond in the case weighed against a sentence at the lower end of the 4 to 15 year range for the offense. People v Hunzicker, 308 Ill App 3d 961, 242 Ill Dec 486, 721 NE2d 765 (3d Dist 1999).

Evidence was sufficient to infer the defendant's knowledge that a truck in his possession was stolen where an officer testified that when he saw the truck, the defendant was the only person in it, the defendant had the key to the truck, the truck was parked outside his apartment building when it was seized, and the defendant offered no evidence indicating that he did not have exclusive possession or explaining why he had possession of a stolen

AUTOMOBILES AND OTHER VEHICLES § 43:07

truck. People v Steading, 308 Ill App 3d 934, 242 Ill Dec 510, 721 NE2d 789 (2d Dist 1999).

Trial court did not abuse its discretion in sentencing defendant to greater than minimum sentence of three years under 730 ILCS 5/5-8-1 for conviction of unlawful possession of a stolen vehicle as this was not defendant's first conviction nor even his first felony. People v. Williams, 303 Ill. App. 3d 264, 236 Ill. Dec. 602, 707 N.E.2d 729 (4th Dist. 1999).

§ 43:05. —Vehicle theft conspiracy

Case authorities:

Evidence was sufficient to infer the defendant's knowledge that a truck in his possession was stolen where an officer testified that when he saw the truck, the defendant was the only person in it, the defendant had the key to the truck, the truck was parked outside his apartment building when it was seized, and the defendant offered no evidence indicating that he did not have exclusive possession or explaining why he had possession of a stolen truck. People v Steading, 308 Ill App 3d 934, 242 Ill Dec 510, 721 NE2d 789 (2d Dist 1999).

§ 43:07. Aggravated vehicular hijacking

Statutes, rules, etc.:

The 1999 amendment of 720 ILCS 5/18-4 by P.A. 91-404, effective January 1, 2000, added "other than a firearm" following "dangerous weapon" in subsection (a)(3); added subsections (a)(4) through (a)(6); and in subsection (b) added the third, fourth, and fifth sentences.

CHAPTER 47
BURGLARY

§ 47:01. Burglary

Statutes, rules, etc.:

The 1999 amendment of 720 ILCS 5/19-1 by P.A. 91-360, effective July 29,1999, added the last sentence of subsection (b).

Case authorities:

Because the defendant's testimony at trial made up his entire defense making his credibility a central issue, the trial court did not abuse its discretion in holding that evidence of defendant's prior convictions of burglary should be admitted for impeachment purposes. People v Atkinson, 186 Ill 2d 450, 239 Ill Dec 1, 713 NE2d 532 (1999).

The offenses of home invasion and residential burglary were carved from the same physical act of the defendant entering the dwelling, therefore, the conviction for residential burglary was vacated. People v McLaurin, 184 Ill 2d 58, 234 Ill Dec 399, 703 NE2d 11 (1998).

The trial court erred when it took judicial notice that 120 stolen T-shirts had a value of at least $300 since clothing varies greatly in price, dependent upon the quality and maker of the item, and this disparity was such that it could not be said that one could properly infer the value of the T-shirts without any evidence regarding their quality, design, or price. People v. Burks, 304 Ill. App. 3d 861, 238 Ill. Dec. 62, 710 N.E.2d 859 (1st Dist. 1999).

Where evidence showed that the defendant did in fact have the intent to commit a felony when he entered the apartment to beat the resident, there was sufficient evidence to support defendant's conviction. People v. Ranstrom, 304 Ill. App. 3d 664, 237 Ill. Dec. 638, 710 N.E.2d 61 (1st Dist. 1999).

Evidence was sufficient to support a conviction for burglary, even though the evidence would also have supported a conviction for residential burglary, where the defendant entered an apartment building which was not a dwelling place as such, with the intent to commit a theft or felony in that building. People v. Maskell, 304 Ill. App. 3d 77, 237 Ill. Dec. 819, 710 N.E.2d 449 (2d Dist. 1999).

Where the guilty but mentally ill instruction given was later found unconstitutional, this did not warrant reversal of the case, since the defendant was found guilty on both counts of burglary and therefore the jury did not reach a compromise verdict, there was no evidence of jury confusion and the defendant, rather than the State, proffered the instruction. People v. Wanke, 303 Ill. App. 3d 772, 237 Ill. Dec. 30, 708 N.E.2d 833 (2d Dist. 1999) reversed on other grounds 311 Ill App 3d 801, 244 Ill Dec 546, 726 NE 2d 142 (2000).

The evidence showed the building where defendant entered to steal tools, CDs and CD player was not inhabitable at the time as it was under remodeling and it was therefore not a dwelling under the residential burglary statute; therefore the defendant was properly convicted of burglary. People v. Willard, 303 Ill. App. 3d 231, 236 Ill. Dec. 679, 707 N.E.2d 1249 (3d Dist. 1999).

There was no good reason for the jury to know the police officer received a burglary in progress call as there was no issue concerning the officer's reason or motive for going to the scene, therefore the admission of the call was error. People v. Warlick, 302 Ill. App. 3d 595, 236 Ill. Dec. 369, 707 N.E.2d 214 (1st Dist. 1998).

The legislature intended to afford the protection of the burglary statute to vehicles that were created to be self propelled, regardless of whether they are in operation at the time of the offense. People v. Crump, 296 Ill. App. 3d 758, 231 Ill. Dec. 163, 695 N.E.2d 1282 (1st Dist. 1998).

Even though the plaintiff claimed the state's eyewitness never saw him in the house and that he thought he was helping a friend move a relative's belongings, the court properly concluded a rational trier of fact could have found plaintiff guilty based on eyewitness's testimony. United States ex rel. Jones v. Tally, 48 F. Supp. 2d 773 (N.D. Ill. 1999).

§ 47:02. Residential burglary

Case authorities:

The offenses of home invasion and residential burglary were carved from the same physical act of the defendant entering the dwelling, therefore, the conviction for residential burglary was vacated. People v McLaurin, 184 Ill 2d 58, 234 Ill Dec 399, 703 NE2d 11 (1998).

Even though the plaintiff claimed the state's eyewitness never saw him in the house and that he thought he was helping a friend move a relative's belongings, the court properly concluded a rational trier of fact could have found plaintiff guilty based on eyewitness's testimony.

BURGLARY

United States ex rel. Jones v. Tally, 48 F. Supp. 2d 773 (N.D. Ill. 1999).

§ 47:04. Home invasion

Statutes, rules, etc.:

The 1999 amendment of 720 ILCS 5/12-11, effective January 1, 2000, added subsections (a)(3) through (a)(5) relating to use of a firearm during the commission of home invasion; and in subsection (c), added the second, third, and fourth sentences relating to classification and sentence for home invasion

Case authorities:

The defendant entered the "dwelling of another" and, therefore, was properly convicted for home invasion where he entered his former marital residence, notwithstanding that his name was still on the title to the residence, as the residence had been awarded to his wife in their dissolution proceeding. People v. Oakley, 187 Ill. 2d 472, 241 Ill. Dec. 525, 719 N.E.2d 654 (1999).

Evidence was sufficient to establish that the defendant entered the dwelling place of another, notwithstanding that the dwelling was his former marital residence and that his name was on the title and mortgage for the residence, where the judgment dissolving his marriage gave his wife permanent exclusive possession of, and all the equity in the residence and gave the defendant responsibility for the debts related to the residence and where the wife was in the process of having the defendant's name removed from the title and mortgage. People v Oakley, 187 Ill 2d 472, 241 Ill Dec 525, 719 NE2d 654 (1999).

CHAPTER 48
CIVIL RIGHTS

§ 48:01. Violations and offenses generally

Case authorities:

Because it was not shown how the provision of subsection (d) of 720 ILCS 590/1 advances the state's interest in protecting against blockbusting and protecting residential privacy, the provision does not pass the test for restrictions on commercial speech and violates the First Amendment of the U.S. Constitution. Pearson v. Edgar, 153 F.3d 397 (7th Cir. Ill. 1998).

§ 48:03. Rights of victims and witnesses

Statutes, rules, etc.:

The 1999 amendment of 725 ILCS 120/4.5 by P.A. 91-237, effective January 1, 2000, added subsection (e), which provides that the officials named in this section may satisfy some or all of their obligations to provide notices and other information through participation in a statewide victim and witness notification system established by the attorney general under section 8.5 of the Rights Of Crime Victims And Witnesses Act.

Case authorities:

When a defendant dies while his direct appeal is pending before the appellate court, all of the proceedings abate ab initio; the Crime Victim's Rights Amendment has neither application nor reference to the abatement of criminal prosecutions. People v Robinson, 187 Ill 2d 461, 241 Ill Dec 533, 719 NE2d 662 (1999).

CHAPTER 49
COMPUTER CRIMES

§ 49:01. Generally
Statutes, rules, etc.:

The 1999 amendment of 720 ILCS 5/16D-2, effective January 1, 2000, added subdivision (a-5), providing a definition of "computer network"; added subdivision (b-5), providing a definition of "computer services"; and added subdivision (c-5), providing a definition for "electronic mail service provider".

CHAPTER 50
CONSPIRACY

§ 50:01. Generally

Case authorities:

Accountability cannot be used to make the requisite showing that the defendant obtained more than $500 from the conspiracy. People v. Pendleton, 307 Ill. App. 3d 966, 241 Ill. Dec. 459, 719 N.E.2d 320 (3d Dist. 1999).

The state failed to establish an essential element of the calculated criminal drug conspiracy charge because it did not prove beyond a reasonable doubt that he received more than $500 from the drug sale where the state established only that an undercover officer gave $1,000 to one of the defendant's two co-conspirators. People v. Pendleton, 307 Ill. App. 3d 966, 241 Ill. Dec. 459, 719 N.E.2d 320 (3d Dist. 1999).

CHAPTER 51

CONTRIBUTING TO THE CRIMINAL DELINQUENCY OF A JUVENILE

§ 51:01. Definition

Statutes, rules, etc.:

The 1999 amendment of 720 ILCS 5/33D-1 by P.A. 91-337, effective January 1, 2000, in subsection (a), substituted "an offense that is either a felony or misdemeanor" for "a felony", substituted "the offense" for "such felony"; in subsection (b), inserted "if the offense committed is a felony" and added the last sentence, which provides that contributing to the criminal delinquency of a juvenile is a misdemeanor one grade higher than the offense committed, if the offense committed is a misdemeanor, except when the offense committed is a Class A misdemeanor. If the offense committed is a Class A misdemeanor, the penalty for contributing to the criminal delinquency of a juvenile is a Class 4 felony.

CHAPTER 52
DECEPTIVE PRACTICES AND FALSE PERSONATION

§ 52:06. False personation

Statutes, rules, etc.:

The 1999 amendment of 720 ILCS 5/17-2 by P.A. 91-301, effective July 29, 1999 rewrote this section entitled "Impersonating Veteran, Member of Police, Fraternal or Veterans' Organization, or Representative of Charitable Organization – Use of Words "Chicago Police" etc. – Sentence."

The 1999 amendment of 720 ILCS 5/17-2 by P.A. 91-302, effective July 29, 1999, added subsection (b-5), which provides no person shall use the words "Cook County Sheriff's Police" or "Cook County Sheriff"or any other words to the same effect in the title of any organization, magazine, or other publication without the express approval of the office of the Cook County Sheriff's Merit Board. The references to names and titles in this section may not be construed as authorizing use of the names and titles of other organizations or public safety personnel organizations otherwise prohibited by this section or the Solicitation for Charity Act.

§ 52:07. Forgery

Statutes, rules, etc.:

The 1998 amendment of 720 ILCS 5/17-3 by P.A. 90-759, effective July 1, 1999, added subsection (a)(4) and made minor stylistic changes; and in subsection (c) added the last sentence.

§ 52:09. —Women, infants and children benefits fraud

Statutes, rules, etc.:

The 1999 amendment of 720 ILCS 5/17B-5 by P.A. 91-155, effective July 16, 1999, reenacted this section with no additional changes.

The 1999 amendment of 720 ILCS 5/17B-15 by P.A. 91-155, effective July 16,1999, re-enacted this section with no additional changes.

The 1999 amendment of 720 ILCS 5/17B-20 by P.A. 91-155, effective July 16,1999, re-enacted this section with no additional changes.

The 1999 amendment of 720 ILCS 5/17B-25 by P.A. 91-155, effective July 16,1999, re-enacted this section with no additional changes.

CHAPTER 53
DISORDERLY CONDUCT

§ 53:01. Elements—Generally

Statutes, rules, etc.:

The 1999 amendment of 720 ILCS 5/26-1 by P.A. 91-115, effective January 1, 2000, in subdivision (b)(1) inserted "(a)(5)" in the second sentence and deleted "(a)(5)" following "A violation of subsection" in the third sentence; and added the last sentence in subsection (b).

The 1999 amendment of 720 ILCS 5/26-1 by P.A. 91-121, effective July 15, 1999, in subdivision (a)(3) twice inserted "or a container holding poison gas, a deadly biological or chemical contaminant, or radioactive substance" and inserted "or release"; and in subdivision (b)(1) deleted "(a)(3)"following "(a)(2)" and added the second sentence.

Case authorities:

An information which alleged that the defendant transmitted a report of the offense of domestic battery, while knowing that there was no reasonable ground for such report, was legally insufficient because it failed to set forth the offense with sufficient specificity, insofar as it did not describe with particularity the time, date, or location of the alleged domestic battery and the acts comprising the battery, and did not identify the alleged batterer or the victim or otherwise specify the statement that was falsely reported. People v Swanson, 308 Ill App 3d 708, 242 Ill Dec 351, 721 NE2d 630 (2d Dist 1999).

Probable cause existed to arrest a bystander who followed and argued with officers during the course of an arrest. Humphrey v. Staszak, 148 F.3d 719 (7th Cir. Ill. 1998).

§ 53:02. Interference with emergency communication

Case authorities:

An information which alleged that the defendant transmitted a report of the offense of domestic battery, while knowing that there was no reasonable ground for such report, was legally insufficient because it failed to set forth the offense with sufficient specificity, insofar as it did not describe with particularity the time, date, or location of the alleged domestic battery and the acts comprising the battery, and did not identify the alleged batterer or the victim or otherwise specify the statement that was falsely reported. People v Swanson, 308 Ill App 3d 708, 242 Ill Dec 351, 721 NE2d 630 (2d Dist 1999).

CHAPTER 54
DISSEMINATING CONVICTION INFORMATION

§ 54:04. Procedure

Statutes, rules, etc.:

The 1999 amendment of 20 ILCS 2635/9 by P.A. 91-357, effective July 29, 1999, substituted "subsection (B)" for "subsections (B)and (C)" in subsection (A).